# GOODWILL'S

# 160
# ESSAYS

## MADAN SOOD

# GOODWILL PUBLISHING HOUSE®
### B-3 RATTAN JYOTI, 18 RAJENDRA PLACE
### NEW DELHI-110008 (INDIA)

Published by:

**GOODWILL PUBLISHING HOUSE®**

B-3 Rattan Jyoti, 18 Rajendra Place
New Delhi–110 008 (INDIA)
Tel: 25820556, 25750801
Fax: 91-11-25764396
E-mail: goodwillpub@vsnl.net
            ylp@bol.net.in
Website: www.goodwillpublishinghouse.com

© Publisher

No part of this publication may be reproduced in any form or by
any means, electronic, mechanical, photocopying or any other
method, without the prior written permission of the publisher.

*Printed at*
Rajiv Book Binding House, Delhi

# PREFACE TO THE NEW EDITION

This book of 160 Essays has been thoroughly revised to do away with the old essays and to incorporate all new essays with new valuable materials presented in a classical style.

Each essay has fast flowing facts narrated in a simple and understandable language. The book covers all important fascinating topics—pertaining to India and the world.

The book makes an original and significant contribution to the literature of essays. Each essay is a model essay both in respect of language and matter. The ideas everywhere are couched in simple, everyday journalistic language and in lucid style.

The coverage of the book is exhaustive as it is a sort of intellectual and knowledgeable journey of the whole world.

The book has a special coverage for India as the examiners are anxious to examine candidate's knowledge, rather deeply in respect of issues pertaining to their own country. It will prove highly useful to students in the academic pursuits and those preparing for various competitive examinations.

**Madan Sood**

# CONTENTS

## I. CURRENT ESSAYS

## II. INDIA TODAY

## III. INDIA AND THE WORLD

## IV. INDIAN ECONOMY TODAY

## V. EDUCATION IN INDIA

# VI. POLITICAL PHILOSOPHY

# VII. INDIAN POLITY AND ECONOMY

# VIII. INFRASTRUCTURE OF INDIA'S POLITY AND ECONOMY

## IX. RECENT WORLD EVENTS

# X. SCIENCE & TECHNOLOGY

# I. CURRENT ESSAYS

## 1. Indo-US Nuclear Deal

There has been much debate and discussion on Indo-US Civil Nuclear Deal. No doubt it is beneficial to us in many ways but the negative effects are also to be considered.

India, at the current pace of its socio-economic development, needs energy in abundance. However, it does not have sufficient oil and gas reserves to meet the demand. The global prices of crude oil are increasing every year, and a developing country like ours cannot bear the burden of high import bills. If the import of oil is cut down, it adversely impacts our projects and plans. Moreover, the reserves of oil are not going to last forever—considering the huge amount of consumption every day. Under the circumstances, nuclear energy has become an evocative article of faith and an obvious answer to our increasing energy requirements.

Presently, the bulk of India's energy requirements are met through fossil fuels—petroleum products, coal, hydroelectricity and thermal electricity. Burning of petrol, diesel and coal is causing environmental pollution and thus, serious health hazards for people. Release of greenhouse gas emissions has led to global warming and its consequent effects of melting of glaciers, changes in climate patterns, intensification of hurricanes, etc. In order to save the earth from the grave consequences of environmental pollution and global warming, we need to harness nuclear energy and decrease the burning of fossil fuels. Indo-US Nuclear Deal will help us to follow this plan.

The NSG waiver and signing of the deal also means that the hurdles faced by India in procuring nuclear technology and

1

fuel have been removed for the future. Moreover, all other current restrictions on India's access to America's high and dual technologies will also be withdrawn as a result. Delhi will be able to do much more business with the US in fields barred to Indians hitherto, with the expectation that the volume of trade between the two countries will double within the next two years from the current US$ 25 billion. The US wants to engage India in its global schemes. India is already a military partner of the US. Since 2001 it has carried out nearly 40 joint military exercises at sea, land and air, both in the US and in India. Indian Navy ships are already providing escort and security facilities to the American military ships passing through the Arabian Sea and the Indian Ocean on their way to and from the Pacific through the Straits of Malacca in Southeast Asia. Despite its willingness, a popular outcry did not allow the BJP-led Indian government to send Indian troops to Iraq to help out the American occupation forces.

The US wants to use India as a bulwark in Asia against the Chinese dragon. This kind of cooperation will not go down well with Asia's emerging giant as well as with many popular political forces within India. New Delhi has also successfully sold to the US, the idea that a democratic India is a great ally against the terrorism America is fighting at present.

The withdrawal of sanctions against Delhi will help India in many ways. It will open the gates for Indo-US cooperation in lucrative space research and scientific cooperation in many fields which are currently barred to\ Indians. The US has refused to offer a similar deal to Pakistan. India, Washington says, has demonstrated that it is a responsible nuclear power, says Washington. Pakistan, on the other hand, is accused of helping nuclear proliferation.

In a way the decision is a major shift in India's foreign policy. After this deal, India is no longer a non-aligned power. It will no longer champion for Third World countries. The Indian elite has clearly decided to throw their lot with Americans. New India wants to emerge as a global power and enjoy the fruits that go with that status. It is no longer concerned with ethics and morality in matters of policy.

## Impact on Our Foreign Policy

Our policy towards Iran has already undergone a sea change even before the Indo-US Nuclear Deal came into existence. Our vote against Iran at IAEA was the litmus test. While India, for obvious reasons, would not welcome a new entrant in the Nuclear Club, this factor alone should not have swung our vote. Iran has not violated the NPT in any major way while Pakistan, China and North Korea have clandestinely and openly violated the major provisions of NPT. Action taken by IAEA against Pakistan could not come to fruition due to Pakistan's intransigent stand that A.Q. Khan—the incharge of Pakistan's nuclear programme—an accused of proliferation would not be made available for questioning by IAEA. Pakistan has been allowed to go scot-free and unpunished due to backing by US and the inability of IAEA to proceed against Pakistan.

Pakistan's doctrine of 'first use of nuclear weapons', as against ours of 'non-first use', and Pakistan's repeated threats to use nuclear weapons against India are a threat to India's existence. This is in stark contrast to Iran's presumed intention. By our vote at IAEA we have gravely damaged our burgeoning and mutually beneficial economic matrix of deals, especially in the hydrocarbons sector, in which India remains and is likely to remain for the near future, a big importer. The fact that India did not energetically and implacably oppose clandestine selling of nuclear equipment by Pakistan has weakened India's position and diminished its stature within the global nuclear community, especially IAEA. This has put India in a fix where we are not even seen as a country capable of defending its strategic allies. We are already being dubbed as a US crony. All this does not square up in our long term quest for membership of the UN Security Council.

There has been a great deal of heat and dissonance generated over the Indo-US Nuclear Deal. A certain amount of dissonance would be expected in a fractious democracy, especially when the Government is one of coalition, that too with the intransigent and rather opportunistic communists who seem to be blinded by ideology. But the heat has been unbearable and the dissonance pronounced. For the first time since independence, there is not only no political consensus across the political spectrum, rather there is wide discord.

Since 1947, our foreign policy has been defined and enunciated into a form and with such contents that it has enjoyed widespread multi-partisan support. The nuclear component of our foreign policy has evolved from the need for autonomy in our defence and security framework. That was the reason behind Pt. Nehru's endorsement of the nuclear policy formulated by late Dr. Homi Bhabha. We have also worked very hard for peaceful development of nuclear energy. We were able to withstand the political after-effect generated by 1973 and 1998 explosions. Even though 1998 explosions should have been made before the conclusion of CTBT, as done by France & China, our stature actually grew and the Great Powers that condemned us for our nuclear tests came back unconditionally, to enter into strategic dialogue with us. This was helped, undoubtedly, by the opening up of our economy in 1991, when a slew of measures for liberalisation were taken, leading to vigorous economic growth ever since.

The late Prime Minister Rajiv Gandhi had the vision to foresee the problem of scarcity of energy in India and under his leadership, the Ministry of External Affairs was able to achieve a strategic breakthrough in persuading the erstwhile USSR to put up $10 \times 1000$ Mw Nuclear Power Plants in India. Nuclear fuel was to be supplied by the USSR. As we did not wish to have the spent fuel together with its safeguards and disposal problems, we asked the USSR to take it back. The Soviet export of plant and machinery was on standard soft terms—48 per cent grant element—which was increased to 52 per cent. It also agreed to provide nuclear fuel on concessional terms. There was no unilateral, bilateral or multilateral condition imposed by the USSR, except that these power plants would be under project specific safeguards and not full-scale safeguards of IAEA.

The pertinent question was: When we have the agreement and the format for unlimited development of nuclear energy in cooperation with Russia, why go for a deal, specially with the US, that it would come under severe, unreasonable, stringent and totally gratuitous conditions? We declared a unilateral voluntary moratorium on nuclear explosions, meaning clearly that if our security and circumstances so demanded in future, we could undertake nuclear tests. Being bound by the presumed agreement with US, we would not be able to do so without violating the entire agreement. Our agreements with Nuclear Suppliers Group and US would be revoked, even though the IAEA safeguards would continue.

We are not going to get any special treatment from IAEA for safeguards. IAEA has only two kinds of safeguards—one for non-nuclear NPT signatory states and the other for five (Nuclear Weapon States—USA, Russia, China, UK, and France). In fact, when we are a declared Nuclear Weapons Power, for us to sign safeguards similar to those applicable to non-nuclear weapon NPT countries would be politically humiliating and strategically disastrous, cancelling in one swoop all our cumulative and hard fought gains over the past over forty years in attacking the unjust and discriminatory NPT and our carving out a highly respectable place among the comity of nations.

The US Government would be mediating our negotiations with IAEA, and the US congress will have the authority to accept or reject it and also to amend it. Now, even the European Union has acquired the temerity and gumption to call on India to sign the NPT. Imagine what will happen when we go begging before Nuclear Suppliers Group dominated by the European Union Members every year for uranium.

The Indian government is implementing this progress despite strong opposition from many popular and political quarters. George W. Bush could blithely walk away from 40 years of non-proliferation policy which do not understand the radical shift that is taking place in the bilateral relationship as a result of increasing fears in US business and strategic circles about China. Giving India anything less, or insisting that it limit its nuclear weapons, is seen by Washington's neo-conservatives as tantamount to strengthening China in the emerging balance of power in Asia. "By integrating India into the non-proliferation order at the cost of capping the size of its eventual nuclear deterrent," according to Ashley Tellis, "the U.S. would threaten to place New Delhi at a severe disadvantage vis-a-vis Beijing, a situation that could not only undermine Indian security but also US interests in Asia in the face of the prospective rise of Chinese power over the long term."

## 2. GLOBAL WARMING

Global warming is the increase in the average temperature of the Earth's near-surface air and oceans in recent decades and its projected continuation.

The Intergovernmental Panel on Climate Change (IPCC) concluded that "most of the observed increase in globally averaged temperatures since the mid-20th century is very likely due to the observed increase in anthropogenic greenhouse gas concentrations" due to the greenhouse effect. Natural phenomena such as solar variation combined with volcanoes probably had a small warming effect from pre-industrial times to 1950 and a small cooling effect from 1950 onwards. These basic conclusions have been endorsed by at least 30 scientific societies and academies of science, including all of the national academies of science of the major industrialized countries. Though individual scientists have voiced disagreement with the conclusions of the IPCC, the overwhelming majority of scientists working on climate change are in agreement with the conclusions.

Climate model projections summarized by the IPCC indicate that average global surface temperature is likely to rise a further 1.1 to 6.4°C (2.0 to 11.5°F) during the 21st century. The range of values results from the use of differing scenarios of future greenhouse gas emissions as well as models with varied climate sensitivity. Although most studies focus on the period up to 2100, warming and sea-level rise are expected to continue for more than a millennium even if greenhouse gas levels are stabilized. The delay in reaching equilibrium is a result of the large heat capacity of the oceans.

Increasing global temperature will cause sea level to rise, and is expected to increase the intensity of extreme weather events and to change the amount and pattern of precipitation. Other effects of global warming include changes in precipitation levels, agricultural yields, trade routes, glacier retreat, species extinctions and increase in the ranges of disease vectors. The other scientific uncertainties include the amount of warming expected in the future, and how warming and related changes will vary from region to region across the globe. There is an ongoing political and public debate worldwide regarding what action should be taken to reduce or reverse future warming or to adapt to its expected consequences. Most national governments have signed and ratified the Kyoto Protocol, aimed at reducing greenhouse gas emissions.

The Earth's climate changes are in response to external forcing, including variations in its orbit around the sun, volcanic eruptions and atmospheric greenhouse gas concentrations. The detailed causes of the recent warming remain an active field of research, but the scientific consensus identifies elevated levels of greenhouse gases due to human activity as the main factor. This attribution is most obvious for the recent 50 years, for which the detailed data are available. Some other hypotheses different from the consensus view have been suggested to explain the observed increase in mean global temperature. One such hypothesis proposes that warming may be the result of variations in solar activity.

None of the effects of forcing is instantaneous. The thermal inertia of the Earth's oceans and slow responses of other indirect effects mean that the Earth's current climate is not in equilibrium with the forcing imposed on it. Climate commitment studies indicate that even if greenhouse gases were stabilized at 2000 levels, a further warming of about 0.5 °C (0.9 °F) would still occur.

The greenhouse effect was discovered by Joseph Fourier in 1824 and was first investigated quantitatively by Svante Arrhenius in 1896. It is the process by which absorption and emission of infrared radiation by atmospheric gases warm a planet's atmosphere and surface. Naturally occurring greenhouse gases have a mean warming effect of about 33°C (59°F), without which Earth would not be habitable. Rather, the issue is how the strength of the greenhouse effect is changed when human activity increases the atmospheric concentrations of some greenhouse gases.

On Earth, the major greenhouse gases are water vapour, which causes about 36-70% of the greenhouse effect; carbon dioxide ($CO_2$), which causes 9-26%; methane ($CH_4$), which causes 4-9%; and ozone ($O_3$), which causes 3-7%. Some other naturally occurring gases contribute very small fractions of the greenhouse effect. One of these, i.e. nitrous oxide ($N_2O$), is increasing in concentration owing to human activities like agriculture. The atmospheric concentrations of $CO_2$ and $CH_4$ have increased by 31% and 149% respectively above pre-industrial levels since 1750. Molecule for molecule, methane is more effective greenhouse gas than carbon dioxide, but its concentration is much smaller so that its total radiative forcing is only about a fourth of that from carbon dioxide. These levels are considerably higher than at any time during the last 650,000 years, the period for which reliable data has been extracted from ice cores. From less direct geological evidence it is believed that $CO_2$ values this high were last attained 20 million years ago. Fossil fuel burning has produced about three-quarters of the increase in $CO_2$ from human activity during the last 20 years. Most of the rest is due to land-use change, in particular deforestation.

The present atmospheric concentration of $CO_2$ is about 383 parts per million (ppm) by volume. Future $CO_2$ levels are expected to rise due to ongoing burning of fossil fuels and land-use change. The rate of rise will depend on certain economic, sociological, technological, and natural developments, but may be ultimately limited by the availability of fossil fuels. The IPCC Special Report on Emissions Scenarios gives a wide range of future $CO_2$ scenarios, ranging from 541 to 970 ppm by the year 2100. Fossil fuel reserves are sufficient to reach this level and continue emissions beyond 2100, if coal, tar sands or methane clathrates continue to be used at the current rate.

Although it is difficult to connect specific weather events to global warming, an increase in global temperatures may in turn cause broader changes, including glacial melting, Arctic shrinkage, and worldwide sea level rise. Changes in the amount and pattern of precipitation may result in flooding and drought in different areas. There may also be changes in the frequency and intensity of extreme weather events. Other effects may be changes in agricultural yields, addition of new trade routes, reduced summer streamflows, species extinctions, and increases in the range of disease vectors. Some effects— both on the environment and human life—are already being attributed to global warming. A 2001 report by the IPCC suggests that glacier melting, ice shelf disruption such as that of the Larsen Ice Shelf, sea-level rise, changes in rainfall patterns, and increased intensity and frequency of extreme weather events, are being attributed to global warming. While changes are expected for overall patterns, intensity, and frequencies, it is difficult to establish that specific events are due to global warming. Other expected effects include water scarcity in some regions and increased precipitation in others and adverse health effects from warmer temperatures.

Increasing deaths, displacements, and economic losses projected due to extreme weather attributed to global warming may be increased by growing population densities in affected areas, although temperate regions are projected to experience some minor benefits, such as fewer deaths due to cold exposure. IPCC Fourth Assessment Report summary reported that there is observational evidence for an increase in intense tropical cyclone activity in the North Atlantic Ocean since about 1970, in correlation with the increase in sea surface temperature, but that the detection of long-term trends is complicated by the quality of records prior to routine satellite observations. The summary also stated, however, that there is no clear trend in the annual worldwide number of tropical cyclones.

Additional anticipated effects include sea-level rise of 110 to 770 millimeters (0.36 to 2.5 ft) between 1990 and 2100, repercussions on agriculture, possible slowing of the thermohaline circulation, reductions in the ozone layer, increased intensity of hurricanes and extreme weather events, lowering of ocean pH, and the spread of diseases such as malaria and dengue fever. One study predicted that 18% to 35% of a sample of 1,103 animal and plant species would be extinct by 2050, based on future climate projections. However, few machinistic studies have documented extinctions due to recent climate change and one study suggested that projected rates of extinction are an uncertainty.

Some economists have tried to estimate the aggregate net economic costs of damages from climate change across the globe. Such estimates have so far failed to reach any conclusive findings; in a survey of 100 estimates, the values ran from US$-10 per tonne of carbon (tC) (US$-3 per tonne of carbon dioxide) up to US$350/tC (US$95 per tonne of carbon dioxide), with a mean of US$43 per tonne of carbon (US$12 per tonne of carbon dioxide). One widely publicized report on potential economic impact is the Stern Review; it suggested that extreme weather might reduce global gross domestic product by up to one per cent, and that in a worst-case scenario global per capita consumption could fall 20 per cent. The report's methodology, advocacy and conclusions have been criticized by many economists, primarily around the assumptions of discounting and its choices of scenarios, while others have supported the general attempt to quantify economic risk.

In a summary of economic cost associated with climate change, the United Nations Environment Programme emphasizes the risks to insurers, reinsurers, and banks of increasingly traumatic and costly weather events. Other economic sectors likely to face difficulties related to climate change include agriculture and transport. In this respect, the developing countries, rather than the developed world, are at greater economic risk.

O O O

# 3. AIDS—THE BIGGEST HEALTH THREAT OF PRESENT TIMES

Acquired immune deficiency syndrome or acquired immunodeficiency syndrome (AIDS) is a collection of symptoms and infections resulting from the specific damage to the immune system caused by the human immunodeficiency virus (HIV) in humans. The late stage of the condition leaves individuals susceptible to infections and tumors. Although treatments for AIDS and HIV exist to decelerate the virus's progression, there is currently no known cure. The viruses are transmitted through direct contact of a mucous membrane or the bloodstream with a bodily fluid containing HIV, such as blood, semen, vaginal fluid, preseminal fluid, and breast milk. This transmission can come in the form of anal, vaginal or oral sex, blood transfusion, contaminated needles, exchange between mother and baby during pregnancy, childbirth, or breastfeeding, or other exposure to one of the above bodily fluids.

Most of the researchers believe that HIV originated in sub-Saharan Africa during the twentieth century. It is now a pandemic, with an estimated 35 million people now living with the disease worldwide. As of January 2008, the Joint United Nations Programme on HIV/AIDS (UNAIDS) and the World Health Organization (WHO) estimate that AIDS has killed more than 30 million people since it was first recognized in June1981, making it one of the most destructive epidemics in recorded history. In 2005 alone, AIDS claimed an estimated 2.4-3.3 million lives, of which more than 570,000 were children. A third of these deaths are occurring in sub-Saharan Africa, retarding economic growth and destroying human capital. Antiretroviral treatment reduces both the mortality and the intensity of HIV infection, but routine access to antiretroviral medication is not available in all countries. HIV/AIDS stigma is more severe than that associated with other life-threatening conditions and extends beyond the disease itself to providers and even volunteers involved with the care of people living with HIV.

AIDS is the most severe form of infection with HIV. HIV is a retrovirus that primarily infects vital organs of the human immune system such as CD4+ T cells, macrophages and dendritic cells. It destroys CD4 + T cells directly and indirectly. CD4 + T cells are required for the proper functioning of the irnmune system. When HIV kills CD4 + T cells so that there are fewer than 200 CD4+ T cells per microliter (ilL) of blood, cellular immunity is lost. In some countries, like the United States, this leads to diagnosis of AIDS. In other countries, such as in Canada, AIDS is only diagnosed when a person infected with HIV is diagnosed with one or more of several AIDS-related opportunistic infections or cancers. Acute HIV infection progresses over time to clinical latent HIV infection and then to early symptomatic HIV infection and later to AIDS, which is identified either on the basis of the amount of CD4 + T cells in the blood, or the presence of certain infections.

In the absence of antiretroviral therapy, the median time of progression from HIV infection to AIDS is nine to ten years, and the median survival time after developing AIDS is only 9.2 months. However, the rate of clinical disease progression varies widely between individuals, from two weeks up to 20 years. Many factors affect the rate of progression. These include factors that influence the body's ability to defend against HIV such as the infected person's general immune function. Older people usually have weaker immune systems, and therefore have a greater risk of rapid disease progression than younger people. Poor access to health care and the existence of co-existing infections such as tuberculosis may also predispose people to faster disease progression. The infected person's genetic inheritance also plays an important role and some people are resistant to certain strains of HIV. For example, people with the CCR5-32 mutation are resistant to infection with certain strains of HIV. HIV is genetically variable and exists as different strains, which cause different rates of clinical disease progression. The use of highly active antiretroviral therapy prolongs both the median time of progression to AIDS and the survival time.

Less than 1% of the sexually active urban population in Africa has been tested, and this proportion is even lower in rural populations. Furthermore, only 0.5% of pregnant women attending urban health facilities are counseled, tested or receive their test results. Here also, this proportion is even lower in rural health facilities. Therefore, donor blood and blood products used in medicine and medical research are screened for HIV. Typical HIV tests, including the HIV enzyme immunoassay and the Western blot assay, detect HIV antibodies in serum, plasma, oral fluid, dried blood spot or urine of patients. However, the time between initial infection and the development of detectable antibodies against the infection can vary. This is why it can take 3-6 months to seroconvert and test positive. Commercially available tests to detect other HIV antigens, HIV-RNA, and HIV-DNA in order to detect HIV infection prior to the development of detectable antibodies are also available.

Opportunistic infections are common in people with AIDS. HIV affects nearly every organ system. People with AIDS also have an increased risk of developing various cancers such as cervical cancer and cancers of the immune system known as lymphomas.

Besides, people with AIDS often have systemic symptoms of infection like fevers, sweats (particularly at night), swollen glands, chills, weakness, and weight loss. After the diagnosis of AIDS is made, the current average survival time with antiretroviral therapy is estimated to be more than 5 years, but because new treatments continue to be developed and owing to the fact that HIV continues to evolve resistance to treatments, estimates of survival time are likely to continue to change. Without antiretroviral therapy, death normally occurs within a year. Most patients die of considered opportunistic infections or tumors associated with the progressive failure of the immune system.

The rate of clinical disease progression varies widely between individuals and has been noted to be affected by many factors such as host susceptibility and immune function health care and co-infections, as well as factors relating to the viral strain. The specific opportunistic infections that AIDS patients develop depend on the prevalence of these infections in the geographic area in which the patient is living.

The three main transmission routes of HIV are sexual contact, exposure to infected body fluids or tissues, and from mother to fetus or child during prenatal period. It is possible to find HIV in the saliva, tears, and urine of infected individuals, but there are no recorded cases of infection by these secretions, and the risk of infection is negligible.

The majority of HIV infections are acquired through unprotected sexual relations between partners, one of whom has HIV. The primary mode of HIV infection worldwide is through sexual contact between members of the opposite sex. Sexual transmission occurs with the contact between sexual secretions of one partner with the rectal, genital or oral mucous membranes of another. Unprotected receptive sexual acts are more risky than unprotected insertive sexual acts, and the risk for transmitting HIV from an infected partner to an uninfected partner through unprotected anal intercourse is greater than the risk for transmission through vaginal intercourse or oral sex. Oral sex is not without its risks as HIV is transmissible through both insertive and receptive oral sex. The risk of HIV transmission from exposure to saliva is considerably smaller than the risk from exposure to semen.

Approximately 30% of women in ten countries representing "diverse cultural, geographical and urban/rural settings" report that their first sexual experience was forced or coerced, making sexual violence a key driver of the HIV/AIDS pandemic. Sexual assault greatly increases the risk of HIV transmission as protection is rarely employed and physical trauma to the vaginal cavity frequently occurs which facilitates the transmission of HIV.

Transmission of HIV depends on the infection of the index case and the susceptibility of the uninfected partner. Infectivity seems to vary during the course of illness and is not constant between individuals. An undetectable plasma viral load does not necessarily indicate a low viral load in the seminal liquid or genital secretions. Each ten-fold increase of blood plasma HIV RNA is associated with an 81% enhanced rate of HIV transmission. Women are more susceptible to HIV-1 infection due to hormonal changes, vaginal microbial ecology and physiology, and a higher prevalence of sexually transmitted diseases. People who are infected with HIV can still be infected by other, more virulent strains.

During a sexual act, only male or female condoms can reduce the chances of infection with HIV and other sexually transmitted diseases and the chances of becoming pregnant. The best evidence to date indicates that typical condom use reduces the risk of heterosexual HIV transmission by approximately 80% over the long term.

This transmission route is particularly relevant to intra-venous drug users, hemophiliacs and recipients of blood transfusions and blood products. Sharing and reusing syringes contaminated with HIV infected blood represents a major risk for infection with not only HIV, but also hepatitis B and hepatitis C. Needle sharing is the cause of one-third of all new HIV infections and 50% of hepatitis C infections in North America, Eastern Europe and China. The risk of being infected with HIV from a single prick with a needle that has been used on an HIV-infected person is thought to be about 1 in 150. Post-exposure prophylaxis with anti-HIV drugs can further reduce that small risk health care workers are also exposed to, although more rarely. This route can affect people who give and receive tattoos and piercings. Universal precautions are frequently not followed in both sub-Saharan Africa and much of Asia because of both a shortage of supplies and inadequate training. The WHO estimates that approximately 2.5% of all HIV infections in sub-Saharan Africa are transmitted through unsafe health care injections. Because of this, the United Nations General Assembly, supported by universal medical opinion on the matter, has urged the nations of the world to implement universal precautions to prevent HIV transmission in health care settings.

The risk of transmitting HIV to blood transfusion recipients is extremely low in developed countries where improved donor selection and HIV screening are performed. However, according to the WHO, the overwhelming majority of the world's population does not have access to safe blood and "between 5% and 10% of HIV infections worldwide are transmitted through the transfusion of infected blood and blood products".

Medical workers who follow universal precautions or body-substance isolation, like wearing latex gloves when giving injections and washing the hands frequently, can help prevent infection by HIV.

The transmission of the virus from the mother to the child

can occur *in utero* during the last weeks of pregnancy and at childbirth. In the absence of treatment, the transmission rate between the mother to the child during pregnancy, labour and delivery is nearly 25%. However, when the mother has access to antiretroviral therapy and gives birth by caesarean section, the rate of transmission is reduced to just 1%. A number of factors influence the risk of infection, particularly the viral load of the mother at birth. Breastfeeding increases the risk of transmission by 10-15%. This risk depends on clinical factors and may vary according to the pattern and duration of breastfeeding.

There is currently no vaccine or cure for HIV or AIDS. The only known methods of prevention are based on avoiding exposure to the virus or, failing that, an antiretroviral treatment directly after a highly significant exposure, called post-exposure prophylaxis (PEP). It has a very demanding four week schedule of dosage. It also has very serious side effects including diarrhoea, malaise, nausea and fatigue.

Current treatment for HIV infection consists of highly active antiretroviral therapy, or HAART. This has been highly beneficial to many HIV-infected individuals since its introduction in 1996 when the protease inhibitor-based HAART initially became available. Current optimal HAART options consist of combinations (or "cocktails") consisting of at least three drugs belonging to at least two types, or "classes", of anti-retroviral agents. Typical regimens consist of two nucleoside analogue reverse transcriptase inhibitors (NARTIs or NRTIs) plus either a protease inhibitor or a non-nucleoside reverse transcriptase inhibitor (NNRTI). Because HIV disease progression in children is more rapid than in adults, and laboratory parameters are less predictive of risk for disease progression, particularly for young infants, treatment recommendations are more aggressive for children than for adults.

UNAIDS and the WHO estimate that AIDS has killed more than 30 million people since it was first recognized in 1981, making it one of the most destructive epidemics in recorded history. Despite recent, improved access to antiretroviral treatment and care in many regions of the world, the AIDS epidemic claimed an estimated 3.2 million (between 2.4 and 3.3 million) lives in 2007 of which more than half a million (570,000) were children.

Globally, between 33.4 and 46 million people currently live with HIV. In 2007, between 3.8 and 6.9 million people were newly infected and between 2.8 and 3.7 million people with AIDS died, an increase from 2003 and the highest number since 1981.

Sub-Saharan Africa remains by far the worst affected region, with an estimated 21.6 to 27.4 million people currently living with HIV. Two million (1.5-3.0 million) of them are children younger than 15 years of age. More than 64% of all people living with HIV are in sub-Saharan Africa, as are more than three quarters (76%) of all women living with HIV. In 2007, there were 14 million AIDS orphans living in sub-Saharan Africa. South Africa has the largest population of HIV patients in the world, followed by Nigeria. South and South East Asia are second worst affected with 15%. AIDS accounts for the deaths of 500,000 children in this region. Two-thirds of HIV/AIDS infections in Asia occur in India, with an estimated 2.5 million infections (0.02% of population), making it the country with the third highest number of HIV infections in the world. In the 35 African nations with the highest prevalence, average life expectancy is 48.3 years—6.5 years less than it would be without the disease.

The latest evaluation report of the World Bank's Operations Evaluation Department assesses the effectiveness of the World Bank's country-level HIV/AIDS assistance, defined as policy dialogue, analytic work, and lending, with the explicit objective of reducing the scope or impact of the AIDS epidemic. This is the first comprehensive evaluation of the World Bank's HIV/AIDS support to countries, from the beginning of the epidemic through mid-2004. Because the Bank's assistance is for implementation of government programs by government, it provides important insights on how national AIDS programs can be made more effective.

The development of HAART as effective therapy for HIV infection and AIDS has substantially reduced the death rate from this disease in those areas where it is widely available. This has created the misperception that the disease has gone away. In fact, as the life expectancy of persons with AIDS has increased in countries where HAART is widely used, the number of persons living with AIDS has increased substantially. In the United States, the number of persons with AIDS increased from about 35,000 in 1988 to over 220,000 in 1996.

In Africa, the number of MTCT and the prevalence of AIDS is beginning to reverse decades of steady progress in child survival. Countries such as Uganda are attempting to curb the MTCT epidemic by offering VCT (voluntary counselling and testing), PMTCT (prevention of mother-to-child transmission) and ANC (ante-natal care) services, which include the distribution of antiretroviral therapy.

HIV and AIDS retard economic growth by destroying human capital. UNAIDS has predicted outcomes for sub-Saharan Africa to the year 2025. These range from a plateau and eventual decline in deaths beginning around 2012 to a catastrophic continual growth in the death rate with potentially 90 million cases of infection

Without proper nutrition, health care and medicine that is available in developed countries, large number of people in these countries are falling victim to AIDS. They will be unable to work, and will also require significant medical care. The forecast is that this will likely cause a collapse of economies and societies in the region. In some heavily infected areas, the epidemic has left behind many orphans cared for by elderly grandparents.

The increased mortality in this region will result in a smaller skilled population and labour force. This smaller labour force will be predominantly young people, with reduced knowledge and work experience leading to reduced productivity. An increase in workers' time off to look after sick family members or for sick leave will also lower productivity. Increased mortality will also weaken the mechanisms that generate human capital and investment in people, through loss of income and the death of parents killing off mainly young adults, AIDS seriously weakens the taxable population, reducing the resources available for public expenditures such as education and health services resulting in increasing pressure for the state's finances and slower growth of the economy.

On the level of the household, AIDS results in both the loss of income and increased spending on health care by the household. The income effects of this lead to spending reduction as well as a substitution effect away from education and towards health care spending. A study in Cote d'Ivoire showed that households with an HIV/AIDS patient spent twice as much on medical expenses as other households.

AIDS stigma exists around the world in a variety of ways, including ostracism, rejection, discrimination and avoidance of HIV infected people; compulsory HIV testing without prior consent or protection of confidentiality; violence against HIV infected individuals or people who are perceived to be infected with HIV; and the quarantine of HIV infected individuals. Stigma-related violence or the fear of violence prevents many people from seeking HIV testing, returning for their results, or securing treatment, possibly turning what could be a manageable chronic illness into a death sentence.

A small minority of scientists and activists question the connection between HIV and AIDS, the existence of HIV itself, or the validity of current testing and treatment methods. Though these claims have been examined and widely rejected by the scientific community, they have had a significant political impact, particularly in South Africa, where governmental acceptance of AIDS denialism has been blamed for an ineffective response to that country's AIDS epidemic.

A number of misconceptions have arisen surrounding HIV/AIDS. Three of the most common are that AIDS can spread through casual contact, that sexual intercourse with a virgin will cure AIDS, and that HIV can infect only homosexual men and drug users. Other misconceptions are that any act of anal intercourse between gay men can lead to AIDS infection, and that open discussion of homosexuality and HIV in schools will lead to increased rates of homosexuality and AIDS.

O O O

# 4. NATURAL DISASTERS

A natural disaster is the consequence of a natural hazard, e.g. volcanic eruption, earthquake, landslide which moves from potential into an active phase, and as a result affects human activities. Human vulnerability, increased by the lack of planning or lack of appropriate emergency management, leads to financial, structural, and human losses. The resulting loss depends on the capacity of the population to support or resist the disaster. This understanding is concentrated in the formulation: "disasters occur when hazards meet vulnerability." A natural hazard will hence never result in a natural disaster in areas without vulnerability, e.g. strong earthquakes in uninhabited areas. The term *natural* has consequently been disputed because the events simply are not hazards or disasters without human involvement. The degree of potential loss can also depend on the nature of the hazard itself— ranging from a single lightning strike, which threatens a very small area—to impact events, which have the potential to end an entire civilization. Before going deeper into the concept of natural disaster risk management, we need to understand various types of natural disasters that can occur and cause destruction. We can divide them into various types. The first among these is natural hazards. They are also of various types, the major among them are explained below:

A natural hazard is a situation which has the potential to create an event that has an effect on people. They result from natural processes in the environment and some natural hazards are related—earthquakes can result in tsunamis, drought and flood can lead directly to famine and disease, and so on.

An avalanche is a geophysical hazard involving a slide of a large snow or rock mass down a mountainside, caused when a build-up of snow is released down a slope. It is one of the major dangers faced in the mountains in winter. An avalanche is an example of a gravity current consisting of granular material. In an avalanche, lots of material or mixtures of different types of material fall or slide rapidly under the force of gravity. Avalanches are often classified by what they are made of.

An earthquake is a phenomenon that results from a sudden release of stored energy that radiates seismic waves. At the Earth's surface, earthquakes may manifest themselves by a shaking or displacement of the ground and sometimes tsunamis. Nearly 90% of all earthquakes—and 81 % of the largest—occur around the 40,000 km long Pacific Ring of Fire, which roughly bounds the Pacific Plate. Many earthquakes happen each day, few of which are large enough to cause significant damage. Some of the most significant earthquakes in recent times include:

- The 2004 Indian Ocean earthquake, the second largest earthquake in recorded history, registering a moment magnitude of 9.3. The huge tsunamis triggered by this earthquake cost the lives of at least 229,000 people.
- The 7.6-7.7 2005 Kashmir earthquake, which cost 79,000 lives in Pakistan.
- The Gujarat earthquake of 26th January 2005.
- The Chinese earthquake of May 2008.

A lahar is a type of natural disaster closely related to a volcanic eruption. It involves a large amount of material, including mud, rock, and ash sliding down the side of the volcano at a rapid pace. These flows can destroy entire towns in seconds and kill thousands of people. The major example is the one which killed an estimated 23,000 people in Armero, Colombia, during the 1985 eruption of Nevado del Ruiz.

A landslide is a disaster closely related to an avalanche, but instead of occurring with snow, it occurs involving actual elements of the ground, including rocks, trees, parts of houses, and anything else which may happen to be swept up. Landslides can be caused by earthquakes, volcanic eruptions, or general instability in the surrounding land. Mudslides, or mud flows, are a special case of landslides, in which heavy rainfall causes loose soil on steep terrain to collapse and slide downwards.

A localized depression in the surface topography, is usually caused by the collapse of a subterranean structure, such as a cave. Although rare, large sinkholes that develop suddenly in populated areas can lead to the collapse of buildings and other structures.

A volcanic eruption is the point in which a volcano is active and releases its power, and the eruptions come in many forms. They range from daily small eruptions which occur in places like Kilauea in Hawaii, or extremely infrequent supervolcano eruptions in places like Lake Taupo, 26,500 years ago, or Yellowstone Caldera, which has the potential to become a supervolcano in the near geological future. Some eruptions form pyroclastic flows, which are high-temperature clouds of ash and steam that can trail down mountainsides at speed exceeding that of an airliner. According to the Toba catastrophe theory, 70 to 75 thousand years ago, a super volcanic event at Lake Toba reduced the total human population to 10,000 or even 1,000 breeding pairs, creating a major bottleneck in human evolution.

Then there is prolonged rainfall which forms a storm, including thunderstorm, rapid melting of large amounts of snow, or rivers which swell from excessive precipitation upstream and cause widespread damage to areas downstream, or less frequently the bursting of man-made dams or dykes.

For example, the Huang Ho (Yellow River) in China floods particularly often. The Great Flood of 1931 caused between 800,000 and 4,000,000 deaths; the Great Flood of 1993 was one of the most costly floods in US history; and the 1998 Yangtze River Floods, in China, left over 14 million people homeless.

Tropical cyclones can result in extensive flooding, as happened with Bhola Cyclone, striking East Pakistan (now Bangladesh) in 1970; tropical storm Allison, which struck Houston, Texas in 2001; hurricane Katrina, which left most of New Orleans under water in the year 2005; and Hurricane Nargis that hit Myanmar in April 2008.

Also referred to as a 'lake overturn', a limnic eruption is a rare type of natural disaster in which $CO_2$ suddenly erupts from deep lake water, posing the threat of suffocating wildlife, livestock and humans. Such an eruption may also cause tsunamis in the lake as the rising $CO_2$ displaces water. Experts believe landslides, volcanic activity, or explosions can trigger such an eruption.

Then there are large tidal whirlpools called maelstroms. The largest known maelstrom so far is Moskstraumen which occurred off the Lofoten islands in Norway. Powerful whirlpools have killed unlucky seafarers. A seiche is a standing wave in an enclosed or partially enclosed body of water. Seiches and seiche-related phenomena have been observed on lakes, reservoirs, bays and seas.

A tsunami is a wave of water caused by the displacement of a body of water. The word comes from some Japanese words meaning harbour and wave. Tsunami can be caused by undersea earthquakes as in the 2004 Indian Ocean Earthquake, or by landslides such as the one which took place at Lituya Bay, Alaska. Meteotsunamis are caused by meteorological phenomena. A megatsunami is an informal term used to describe very large tsunamis. They are a highly local effect, either occurring on shores extremely close to the origin of a tsunami, or in deep, narrow inlets. The largest waves are caused by very large landslides, such as a collapsing island, into a body of water. The highest Tsunami ever recorded has been estimated to be of 524m (1742 ft.) vertical run-up on July 10, 1958, in Lituya Bay, Alaska.

Climatic disasters include blizzards, droughts and heat wave, besides hurricanes, cyclones and typhoons, etc. Blizzard is a winter storm condition characterized by low temperatures, strong winds, and heavy blowing snow. Significant blizzards in the United States include: the Great Blizzard of 1888 and the Storm of the Century in 1993.

Drought is an abnormally dry period when there is not enough water to support agricultural and urban or environmental water needs. Extended droughts can result in deaths by starvation or disease, and can result in wildfires. Well-known historical droughts include the ones that occurred in 1928-30, northwest China, resulting in over 3 million deaths by famine; and at 1936 and 1941, Sichuan Province, China, resulting in 5 million and 2.5 million deaths respectively.

As of 2009, the Australian states like Western Australia, New South Wales, Victoria and Queensland have been under drought conditions for five to ten years. The drought is beginning to affect urban populations for the first time. Also in 2006, Sichuan Province, China experienced its worst drought in modern times, with nearly 8 million people and over 7 million cattle facing acute water shortages.

A heat wave is a disaster characterized by heat which is considered extreme and unusual in the area in which it occurs. Heat waves are rare and require specific combinations of weather events to take place, and may include temperature inversions, or other phenomena. The worst heat wave in recent history was the European Heat Wave of 2003. There is also the potential for longer term events causing global warming, including stadial events or through human induced climatic warming.

Hurricane, tropical cyclone, and typhoon are different names for the same phenomenon, i.e. a cyclonic storm system that forms over the oceans. It is caused by evaporated water that comes off the ocean and turns into a storm. The Coriolis Effect causes the storms to spin, and a hurricane is declared when this spinning mass of storms attains a wind speed of more than 74 mph. Hurricane is used for these phenomena in the Atlantic and eastern Pacific Oceans while the tropical cyclone in the Indian Ocean was the 1970 Bhola cyclone. The deadliest Atlantic hurricane was the Great Hurricane of 1780, which devastated Martinique, St. Eustatius and Barbados. Another notable hurricane is Katrina, which devastated the Gulf Coast of the United States in 2005.

An ice age is a geologic period, but can also be viewed in the light of a catastrophic natural disaster, since in an ice age, the climate all over the world would change and places which were once considered habitable would then be too cold to permanently live in. A side effect of an ice age could possibly be a famine, caused by a worldwide drought.

A tornado is another natural disaster resulting from a thunderstorm. Tornadoes are violent, rotating columns of air which can blow at speeds between 50 and 300 mph, and even higher. Tornadoes can occur one at a time, or can occur in large tornado outbreaks along squall lines or in other large areas of thunderstorm development.

Fire can prove highly disastrous if it goes uncontrolled or wild. An uncontrolled fire burning in wildland areas causes widespread destruction of flora and fauna. Common causes include lightning and drought but wildfires may also be started by human negligence or arson. A typical example is the California fire of 2008 which is said to have been caused by bonfires. They can be a threat to those in rural areas and also wildlife. Wildfires can also produce ember attacks, where floating embers set fire to buildings.

In 2000, the United Nations launched the International Early Warning Programme (IEWP) to address the underlying causes of vulnerability and to build disaster-resilient communities by promoting increased awareness of the importance of disaster reduction as an integral component of sustainable development, with the goal of reducing human, economic and environmental losses due to hazards of all kinds (UNIISDR, 2000). The 2007-2008 United Nations International Disaster Reduction Day theme is "Disaster reduction education begins in school". The Foundation of Public Safety Professionals (FPSP) has launched an international campaign, giving everybody a chance to have their say, through their international open essay or documentary competition "Disaster Risk Reduction Education Begins at School".

The best way to prevent natural disasters is to chalk out a detailed plan of action keeping the geographical conditions of various regions in mind, which are earthquake and cyclone-prone areas.

O O O

# 5. RIGHT TO INFORMATION ACT: IMPACT ON SOCIETY

The RTI Act, which is a revolutionary piece of legislation, acknowledges and proceeds to implement the right to information for citizens with respect to the information under the control of public authorities in order to promote transparency and accountability in the working of every public authority. This is what the preamble to the RTI Act states.

The RTI Act makes it obligatory on the part of every public authority to maintain all its records in such a manner as to facilitate the right to information and publish the relevant information and data regarding its organization, functions, duties, ideas followed by all its offices and employees, the procedure followed in the decision-making process, etc.

Requiring the public authorities to give all the information pertaining to their organizational structure and functioning on a proactive basis is an essential feature of this Act.

The RTI Act defines information under Section 2(f) as any material in any form, including records, documents, memos, e-mails, opinions, pieces of advice, press releases, circulars, orders, log books, contracts, reports, papers, samples, models, data material lying in any written or electronic form and information relating to any private body which can be accessed by a public authority under any other law for the time being in force.

The right to information has been acknowledged under the Act in perhaps the broadest sense possible. Any citizen of the country has a right to any information pertaining to any public authority without there being any ostensible reason for his/her to need that information. This right cannot be questioned on the ground that the applicant has no reason to want the information he is asking for. The information can be derived only for the reason that it falls within one or more of the exceptions enumerated in Section 8 of the RTI Act and for no other reason.

The information covered under the RTI Act should be used broadly for the following purposes:

(i) Individual applicants may like to know where their cases are pending, what the norms are, which would be made applicable in deciding their requests and what are the levels these cases would pass through so that they can have an idea of what kind of decision to expect and when.

(ii) Cases where irregularities and corruption have taken place can have access to crucial information/record, which can be submitted to the proper authority or to the Vigilance Commission so that the responsibility can be fixed on the culprits. Even the mere accessibility of all such records/information would be a deterrent against the public servants indulging in malpractices.

(iii) Intellectuals, Non-Governmental Organisations (NGOs), Social organizations, etc. can get relevant data/ parameters of the schemes, plans, budget, etc. so that they can make useful suggestions to the public authorities and the Government about how best these schemes can be implemented. In a way, by gaining access to information, the public can participate in the policy-making and administration process.

(iv) If a person is aggrieved by any action/decision of any public authority, he/she get the relevant record/ information so that he/she is better equipped to have his/her grievances redressed at an appropriate forum.

Recently, there has been a lot of furore over not wanting to share file notings? To most of the common persons the Government file is a compilation of important papers. Almost all of India, even the illiterate know it. Anyone who has had anything to do with babus knows the significance and power the file holds to control the destiny of many people. The Government file has two parts in it. The right side has the Papers Under Consideration (PUCs). The left side has the notings—the process through which opinions are written down, added to, and approved or disapproved. These ratings reflect the deliberations on the PUCs and through a series of comments, arrive at decisions. Most of the discussions on the subject or matter at hand are recorded in the note sheets and decisions are mostly based on the recording in the note sheets and even the decisions are recorded on note sheets. These recordings are generally called "file notings".

The only plausible explanation for the fear among babus is their unwillingness to work in an environment of transparency. A logical outcome of transparency is accountability. These two qualities have to be promoted if the iron curtain that separates the state and the people is to be brought down.

The bureaucracy has been exceptional in its refusal to cooperate with the demand for reforms in the functioning of the state institutions.

Any problem the Government faces in implementing the RTI Act should be shared with the people of the country, so that democratic solutions can be found. Otherwise, the struggle to protect this right will go on, as will the attacks on the right. Over time, such attacks will make people aware how critical this right is, and strengthen their resolve to defend democracy. A nationwide movement to educate, guide and motivate the public in the right direction will go a long way in making the administration transparent, competition-free and accountable. It will send a strong message to bureaucracy to act honestly and judiciously.

○ ○ ○

# 6. World Oil Crisis

The global petrochemical products prices are rising sharply, driven mainly by lingering uncertainty about crude oil supply and fast demand growth especially from developing countries like China and India and developed countries like America and Japan. United States accounts for 20 per cent of the increase in global demand and China accounts for nearly 40 per cent.

A fear of American attacks on Saudi Arabia and Iran and the havoc caused by hurricane Katrina, that has forced stoppage of 91 per cent of production at US refineries, are considered as other factors that have raised the prices. As the oil prices are expected to remain strong, the global energy crisis is looming large.

Discussing the history of oil crisis, it began way back in 1973, when Arab members of Organisation of Petroleum Exporting Countries (OPEC) in the midst of the Yom Kippur was announced that they would not ship petroleum to nations that had supported Israel in its conflict with Egypt, i.e. to the United States and its allies in Western Europe. At the same time, OPEC member states decided to raise the crude oil prices four times.

Industrialised world depended on oil completely which was found below the surface of Middle Eastern countries. This was hurting for US, Western Europe and Japan requiring western policy-makers to respond to the emerging international economic restraints. Before this, the industrialised Europe and America took cheap and plentiful petroleum for granted.

Thus the Yom Kippur was led to cutting down on production of oil, increasing the price and placing an embargo on shipments of crude oil to the west. Since oil demand falls little with price rise, prices had to rise dramatically to reduce demand to the new, lower level of supply.

The second oil crisis occurred in 1979 when oil touched a peak of $ 35. It was on account of the Iranian revolution leading to inconsistent supplies of oil. There also came a third minor crisis in 1990 when Saddam Hussein set fire to oilfields in Kuwait. Then in 2003, Iraq's northern export pipeline was sabotaged which resulted in price rise as OPEC cut production.

Talking about the world oil production and reserves, while demand is increasing, things are not looking too good on the supply front. There has also been speculation that the Saudi oilfields might not be as vast as they are made out to be. There are 42 oil producing nations in the world. Fourteen of the 42 nations (33%) have passed their peaks. The most notable among them are the USA (in 1970) and the former Soviet Union (in 1987). In some cases, like UK and Syria, future production may surpass their old peaks.

The Middle East production will peak in 2011. In the global context, the Middle East nations have only 4 per cent of world's population but own 46 per cent of world's oil reserves. In contrast, the non-Middle East nations have 96 per cent of world population and own 54 per cent of total oil reserves divided unevenly among them. The Middle East oil production is dominated by Saudi Arabia, Iraq, Iran, United Arab Emirates and Kuwait which together own 94 per cent of Middle East oil reserves. This geographical disparity of oil reserves is not likely to change, as earth is fairly well explored; further explorations are not likely to change the scenario.

Eleven nations are OPEC members: six in the Middle East, three in Africa and one each in South America and Asia Pacific. Middle East nations at present control 76 per cent of OPEC's remaining reserves, African nations 11 per cent, Venezuela (South America) 10 per cent and Indonesia (Asia Pacific) 3 per cent.

OPEC will continue to dominate world oil production. However, some nations may drop out of OPEC when their domestic demand exceeds production, with no surplus to input. Some experts feel that OPEC would dissolve, while others believe that it could become a wider and more effective organisation by adding new members like Norway and Mexico. Hence, it is difficult to predict OPEC's future, but it is certain that its potential influences on future world oil prices will be significant.

All new production tests are to begin in 2015. Developed countries like the USA, Germany, Japan and France continue to have a great demand for oil and petroleum products, while the fast industrialising countries particularly South East Asia, China and India are augmenting world energy demands.

Asia Pacific including China, Australia, Indonesia, India and Malaysia produces 10 per cent of world oil supplies. But with about 60 per cent of the world's population, the region has been left with only 8 per cent of world's remaining oil reserves. If the Asian nations follow their plans, their oil demand will add significant strain to the world's production capacity.

Moreover, it does not help that world oil is 90 per cent dominated by nationalised oil companies; they are rather notoriously bad at making new finds; growing Indian and

Chinese demand is another reason. With China becoming the world's largest importer of hydrocarbons and India embanking on a similar growth path, the world's energy future is now basically in the hands of three nations—the United States, China and India.

India is the world's sixth largest energy consumer. Oil accounts for about 30 per cent of India's total energy consumption. Oil reserves in India are located in the Mumbai High, Upper Assam, Krishna-Godavari, Cambay and Cauvery basins. The offshore Mumbai high field is by far India's largest producing field.

It is a fact that the world will have to live with the reality of high oil prices. Asian buyers even have to pay higher surcharge on undue oil deliveries from West Asia. No concessions are made for developing countries in the market place, as a result of which they are hard hit as three-fourths of their needs of oil are purchased from abroad so as to fuel higher economic growth. Apart from this, production levels are not likely to be raised, given that oil resources are limited and there is a need for producers to keep output at levels sustainable in the long run.

From such situation it follows that oil crisis ultimately results in increase in costs in all sectors of the economy. An inflationary impact is inevitable as raw materials and fuel costs for industry will increase and prices of manufactured goods are bound to go up. Given the steep rise in the global under recovers, India's major oil companies like ONGC, HPCL, BPCL, etc. are pressing for increase in the prices of diesel and petrol which would help them cut their losses. The Government on the other hand is cutting prices of key petroleum products such as petrol, diesel, cooking gas and kerosene for individual consumers under the public distribution system. These curbs, however, cannot be kept in place for much longer as the public sector companies are reeling under the effort of bearing the subsidy.

Indian refineries use a much cheaper basket of crude. Even so, the situation has now reached a stage that the refinery margins, which have helped the oil companies keep afloat at a time when under-recoveries have been spiralling for most products, have not helped oil companies avoid giving into the seal. These oil companies have been a ready source of cash inflow.

One of the possible options for the government is to evolve a mechanism being used in several developing and developed countries like France and Malaysia. Under it, taxes on oil products are altered according to the rise or fall in their prices. The taxes are lowered in case world oil prices rise, leaving the retail prices at the same level.

Although the problem of bringing about stability in the oil pricing system remains intractable, Indian Government is developing different strategies to alienate the oil crisis. India is attempting to limit its dependence on oil imports somewhat by expanding domestic exploration and production. In the context of Indian scenario related to oil crisis, it can be said that the issue is much larger than merely raising prices of petroleum products to facilitate the public sector oil companies.

The issue is of energy security, and it is the responsibility of these companies to find more oil and create sufficient refining capacity. Reducing our dependency on oil is another method. Electricity is a cheaper and clearer alternative to oil. Hydroelectric projects have been developed by several countries for power generation. Atomic energy has also been harnessed for industrial and other uses. In France for instance, over 75 per cent of power is produced using nuclear energy. Nuclear engineers have estimated that the world can derive energy for 1,000 years at current level of consumption from the U-235 isotope.

India is trying to expand its electric power generation capacity, as current generation is seriously below peak demand.

More refineries should be set up as oil prices are rising not only because of the lack of black stuff in the ground but rather because there is not enough of the equipment needed to ready it for the market.

Using non-conventional sources of energy like solar energy, wind power and biomass power can reduce excessive dependence on oil.

The only way to meet the impending global oil crisis is through developing new technologies like production of hydrogen and its storage, safety and application, harnessing ocean energy for power generation, developing bio-diesel with ethanol blends, etc.

O O O

# 7. TURMOIL IN PAKISTAN

"History repeats itself, the first time as tragedy and the second time as farce." This famous dictum of the great German socialist thinker, Karl Marx, is nowhere more applicable than in Pakistan where President Pervez Musharraf, by declaring an emergency on November 3, 2007 pulled off a repeat of his 1999 coup.

After imposing emergency, President Musharraf suspended the Constitution, removed the independent-minded Chief Justice of Pakistan, Iftikhar Mohammad Choudhry from his office, exercising super-constitutional authority as Army Chief.

President Musharraf stopped short of calling it as imposition of martial law in a repeat of Oct. 12, 1999 coup when the expression emergency was used with all trappings of military rule toppling Nawaz Sharif government. He also promulgated Provisional Constitutional Order (PCO), assuming all constitutional powers in his capacity as Army chief.

Justice Abdul Hamid Dogar, who was one of the judges in the bench that heard the case against the sacked Chief Justice and perceived to be pro-Musharraf was appointed the new Chief Justice. He and other five judges took the fresh oath under the new proclamation. The Government also appointed new Chief Justices for the Sindh, Lahore and Baluchistan High Courts. Justice Abdul Mohammed Samroo was appointed the new Chief Justice of the Sindh High Court, while Justice Amanula Yasim Zai was to be the new Chief Justice of Baluchistan High Court. Justice Iftikhar Hussain Chaudhry was appointed the Chief Justice of the Lahore High Court. All private channels were taken off air. The telecast of foreign channels, including BBC, CNN, also went off air through cable operators amid reports that fresh curbs particularly on electronic media were being imposed.

The PCO is apparently meant to pave the way for a pinge in the judiciary as was done in early 2001 when the Chief Justice and five other judges were removed from their posts. While judges rejected the PCO, 13 out of the 17 judges of the open court were removed while eight judges met in emergency to reject the PCO. They were members of the 11-member bench that was hearing petitions challenging the eligibility of Musharraf to contest election.

It was further announced that the present government structure at the Centre and in provinces, including Prime Minister, Governors, Chief Minister, federal and provincial cabinets, would continue to function.

The former Pakistan Prime Minister and Chief of the Pakistan People's Party (PPP), Benazir Bhutto, who warned earlier that the opposition would never accept the imposition of an emergency, returned to Pakistan from Dubai. She cited the proclamation of the emergency in the country as martial law. Another former Prime Minister Nawaz Sherif also condemned Musharraf's action. Sharif, who was in Saudi Arabia, urged all political parties, including PPP, to come together to oppose the move. Sharif returned to Pakistan on

September 10, 2007, and was arrested and deported to Saudi Arabia to a seven year exile after spending four hours at the Islamabad airport.

On the other hand, in a major crack-down, Pakistan security agencies, on their parts, rounded up more than 500 opposition leaders, lawyers and human rights activists and put them under house arrest.

President Musharraf blamed a wave of Islamic militancy and the influence by the country's judiciary for the imposition of emergency rule. He said there has been visible ascendancy in the activities of extremists and incidents of terrorist attacks. Some members of the Judiciary were making at cross purposes with the executive and legislative in the fight against terrorism and extremism, thereby weakening the Government and the country's resolve and diluting the efficiency of its section to control this menace.

The President said a situation has arisen where the government could not carry on in accordance with the Constitution, as it provided no solution for the situation, and there was no way out except through extraordinary measures.

The 1973 Constitution of Pakistan empowers only the President to promulgate emergency under which certain powers of the provinces get transferred to the federal government. It also enables the ruling dispension to extend the life of the National Assembly by a year. Under emergency rule, the 1973 Constitution was suspended. The proclamation stated that the country shall be governed "as nearly as may be" in accordance with the Constitution, but that some fundamental rights like security of the person; safeguards as to arrest and detention; freedom of movement; assembly; association; speech and equality of citizens—were suspended notwithstanding.

In Karachi, over 140 people—20 of them police officers deputed to protect former Prime Minister and Pakistan People's Party (PPP) Chief, Benazir Bhutto, were killed on the night of October 18 in a suspected suicide attack on her convoy. From all accounts, suicide bombers who mingled with the crowds carried out attacks as some 150,000 people packed the streets of the city of Karachi to greet Benazir, who was returning home after eight years in self-imposed exile. The bombings hit as her convoy moved slowly through the crowd towards the mausoleum of Pakistan's founding father, Mohammad Ali Jinnah, where she was to deliver triumphal address to the people. The attack in which one or two bombers were expectedly involved, was clearly aimed at killing her, but she managed to escape. That the attackers were able to breach one layer of security raised questions on the arrangement made to protect Benazir. The incident also showed up the evil designs of Pakistan political establishment. The bomb blasts showed Pakistan to be one of the most dangerous countries on the earth, right up there with Iraq and Afghanistan. It was dangerously close to being a failed state as described by the Newsweek magazine also.

Pervez Musharraf won a landslide victory in the Oct. 6 presidential election. In a triumph that came as no surprise, Musharraf bagged 671 of 685 votes in the Parliament and from the provincial assemblies with just eight ballots going to his nearest rival Justice Wajihuddin Ahmed (retd.). Another Makhdoom Amir Fahim, Vice-Chairman of Benezir's PPO, got none.

The former Prime Minister Ms. Benazir Bhutto narrowly escaped a suicide attack on her homecoming procession in October 2007. And finally on 27th December 2007 the lack of security and danger in Pakistan was accentuated by the assassination of former Prime Minister Benazir Bhutto. She died in an attack in Rawalpindi when she was over with her speech there. The government insisted that Ms. Bhutto died when her head smashed against her vehicle by the blast from a bomb. But the Pakistan People's Party held that she died from bullet wounds. Shot by an amateur photographer present there, the images captured made it abundantly clear that there was no security cordon around Ms Bhutto's vehicle.

According to a news agency report, Sherry Rehman, a PPP spokesperson said, "She was even bleeding while we were taking her for burial. The government is now trying to say she concussed herself, which is ludicious. It is really dangerous nonsense."

It was the darkest hour for Pakistan, where the people were not allowed to make a difference. True, it was unprecedented in the history of Pakistan for a political crisis to be compounded by so much violence, which has killed more than thousand people since July 2007. The morale of the country's army is at an all-time low as it fights a losing battle with pro-Taliban militants. But then, it was unlikely that military muscle alone will solve the complex problems facing Pakistan, where growing unrest suggests public frustration against the military regime. There were heartening signs that the people of Pakistan are unwilling to be silenced by the guns of the military regime and it could well be that this is only a darkness before the dawn.

A few Indian newspapers have expressed their apprehension of uncertainty after Musharraf's exit. The 50-year-rule of the military has changed perceptions about Pakistan in India. It is generally believed that the army would never quit Pakistan and the people there have more or less reconciled themselves to the eventuality.

Never in the history of Pakistan have there been so much suppression, so much terrorism and so much fundamentalism as was in the eight-year-rule of President-cum-Army Chief Musharraf. Delhi too suffered from his policies which pushed Talibanism into India. When Washington, Musharraf's guide and philosopher, asked him to fight Taliban, he did so half-heartedly, giving them shelter while operating in Afghanistan. The result is the bomb blast every week in one part of the

Pakistan or the other. As Kuldip Nayar has said, "Musharraf did not understand the ethos of democracy. Nor did he care about it." It is too early to judge Asif Zardari. After terrorist attack on Mumbai in Nov. 2008, he is under severe pressure to show that he is prepared to stop terrorism from breeding in Pakistan.

O O O

## 8. Myanmar Crisis

Myanmar is one of the ethnically most diverse countries in the world, and throughout its existence as an independent state, it has experienced a complex set of conflicts between the central government and ethnic minority groups seeking autonomy. While the world's attention for the past decade has focused on the struggle between the military government and the political opposition over national power, these underlying conflicts perhaps represent a more fundamental and intractable obstacle to peace, development and democracy.

The military capacity and influence of ethnic nationalists have gone down significantly over the past decade. Several groups have entered into ceasefire agreements with the government and have been granted de facto administrative authority over areas under their control. They complement a number of political parties formed in areas under government control to represent local ethnic interests in the 1990 election. There are also a growing number of religious or community-based organisations that work to further the interests of their communities and have significant local influence.

Many of these organisations are officially banned, and all face many restrictions by the military government on their activities. Yet, they are important voices for ethnic minority groups, particularly the large percentage who live in their traditional homelands in the hills and mountains surrounding the central plain.

The most fundamental grievance of ethnic minorities in Myanmar today is their lack of influence on the political decisions that directly affect their lives. Like society at large, they have been disenfranchised by a strongly centralised military state that regards them with intense suspicion. They have felt the loss of political and economic power even more acutely than the majority population as both the government and the officer corps are overwhelmingly Burman in make-up and widely perceived as a foreign force.

Ethnic minority groups consider themselves discriminated against and have openly accused successive governments of a deliberate policy of "Burmanisation". They feel not only marginalised economically, but also that their social, cultural, religious and civil rights are being suppressed.

While many ethnic groups originally fought for independence, today almost all have accepted the Union of Myanmar as a fact and merely seek increased local authority and equality within a new federal state structure. The military government, however, still suspects them of scheming to split the country and sees this as justification for its oppressive, often brutal policies in minority areas.

Since 1988, most ethnic minority organisations have expressed support for democracy, seeing this as their best chance to gain a voice in national politics and press for a redress of their long-standing grievances. But few leaders of the dominant ethnic militant groups are democrats by persuasion or regard democracy as an end in itself. Their main concern is to secure local political and administrative authority, further development of their religions, and enjoy the right to maintain and practice their language, culture and religion without any restriction.

Myanmar has been under military rule since 1962. It is the

least free country in Southeast Asia by the latest Freedom House ranking of political rights and civil liberties. The current junta's leader, Senior General Than Shwe, has made Daw Aung San Suu Kyi arguably the best known political prisoner in the world. In August-September 2007, following steep hikes in fuel prices, thousands of protesters marched in silence and were dispersed or arrested. The protests spread beyond the capital and included at least one by Buddhist monks—a significant development in a largely Buddhist country. Meanwhile, delegates to a national convention convened by the regime completed guidelines for a future constitution. This step on a supposed road map to democracy was criticized by some observers as a ploy to institutionalise army control. Others treated the guidelines less skeptically on the grounds that even regime-favouring rules might be used to nudge the country toward reform, and were thus better than no rules at all.

How should outsiders respond to these conditions? With policies of isolation or of engagement? Which of the two logics is more powerful: that isolation will deprive the junta of needed support and thus help spark democratization, or will that engagement expose the country to liberalization and thus incrementally undermine the regime? Is there a mixed logic worth implementing between these extremes? Or have the mounting protests inside Myanmar opened a crucial window of opportunity that replaces these alternatives with a radical new logic of carpe diem: that outsiders should actively intervene in support of the opposition and in favour of regime change now? Not to mention the junta's own rationale for retaining power: that military rule is preferable to any alternative.

UN Envoy and the Cambodian Foreign Minister opine that Myanamar's ruling military junta should be given incentives to find a democratic solution to its political crisis. Cambodia's Foreign Minister said after meeting a UN special envoy to the country, "We should not talk about sanctions but we'd better talk about how to take the momentum forward and prevent the situation from sliding backward." Hor Namhong told reporters about his meeting with Ibrahim Gambari, the UN Secretary General's envoy to Myanmar. Hor Namhong said Cambodia supports Gambari, who has been allowed to visit Myanmar twice since the military's crackdown on pro-democracy demonstrations in September, 2007. "The international community should encourage Myanmar's rulers to continue holding talks with opposition leader Aung San Suu Kyi," Hor Namhong said. Gambari said he had a frank and useful discussion with the Foreign Minister, but did not elaborate. Gambari's visit is a part of his tour through Southeast Asia to encourage Myanmar's neighbours to promote reconciliation between the junta and the pro-democracy movement.

After Myanmar's September crackdown on pro-democracy demonstrators, Cambodia joined countries around the world in calling for the junta to halt its violence and embrace democracy. Prime Minister Hun Sen also called for the 10-Member Association of Southeast Asian Nations—which include Myanmar and Cambodia—to play a more active role in resolving the crisis. India does not believe in interfering in the internal affairs of other countries. But it has kept a complete watch over the situation prevailing in Myanmar. It expressed the hope that the country will come out of the current problems and march towards stability and progress.

◯ ◯ ◯

# 9. INDIA'S LOOK-EAST POLICY INITIATIVE

India's foreign policy has come out of the closet and into the public domain with India's Look-East Policy involving the civil society in formulating and reviewing region-specific foreign policies. This initiative was given shape with the visit of External Affairs Minister, Pranab Mukherjee to Shillong, Meghalaya to discuss the 'Look East' Policy expected to impact the development of the Northeastern region. Ever since the creation of Public Diplomacy division of the Ministry of External Affairs in May 2006, it was the first endeavour to bring to the fore the importance of the Look-East Policy through a lecture titled, "Geography as an opportunity" and interactive session with civil society—encompassing academics, businessmen, media and—leading citizens from the far flung region. According to Pranab Mukherjee, this initiative was launched from Meghalaya recognizing the pre-eminent role of the Northeastern States in the economic and political development of India.

In fact, it was during P.V. Narsimha Rao's Prime Ministership in the 1990s that the "Look East" Policy was enunciated together with the process of economic reforms of reconstructing the market at home and seeking economic partners abroad because of the continuity of the Northeast with the Association of South East Asian Nations (ASEAN). After the start of liberalisation, it was a very strategic policy decision taken by the Government in the Foreign Policy. According to Prime Minister Manmohan Singh, "It was also a strategic shift in India's vision of the world and India's place in the prevailing global economy." This new initiative is being viewed as a major shift as diplomacy has largely been conducted behind closed doors of the South Block housing the MEA and the Prime Minister's Office. The endeavour of the Public Diplomacy Division of the MEA is to educate and influence global and domestic opinion on key policy issues and project a better image of the country commensurate with its rising stature in the unity of nations.

India had very close and interactive relations with East-Asia in the past. But two centuries of colonisation by the British made India depend upon Europe in general and Britain in particular. Even during the post-Independence years, because of the Cold War, India depend upon Europe in general and Britain in particular. India remained Eurocentric in its global outlook. The doctrine of Non-Alignment, empowered by Jawaharlal Nehru, as a guideline for India's Foreign Policy did facilitate that India come closer to East, especially South-East nations. It should be clarified here that East-Asia includes both South-East Asia, i.e. ASEAN countries, viz. Indonesia, Myanmar, Cambodia, Vietnam, Philippines, Malaysia, Thailand, Brunei, Laos, Singapore and North-East Asia, which includes countries like China, Japan, Korea and Taiwan. During the Narasimha Rao regime, global environment took a new shape. With the collapse of the USSR, India was forced to reorient its foreign policy. Domestically, India initiated the phase of structural reforms in the form of liberalisation, privatisation and globalisation. This bought India, for the first time to lay focus on economic diplomacy. India recognised the significance of Asian Tigers. It managed its images from a low profile to a forward looking aggressive action-orient people. ASEAN dropped its prejudices against India to the extent of making it a sectorial dialogue partner status in 1995. India was formally admitted as member of the ASEAN Regional Forum (ARF) in 1996 and fully supported the ARF strategy comprising three stages, viz. (i) promotion of Confidence Building Measures, (ii) development of preventive diplomacy, and (iii) development of conflict resolution mechanisms.

The first Bangladesh, India, Sri Lanka, Thailand Economic Cooperation (BIMSTEC) summit, with Myanmar joining later, was held in July 2004 after nearly a decade of groundwork. India played a leading role and hosted the summit in 2006. It is also active in the Thailand Meckong Cooperation Project (India, Myanmar, Thailand, Cambodia and Vietnam). With all but India, being members of the powerful ASEAN bloc, the project aims to revitalise and develop    trade, tourism, communications and transport. The Look-East Policy has been given a significant thrust since the beginning of the 21st century and the results achieved are evident as the current level of bilateral trade with ASEAN is nearly US $25 billion and is increasing by nearly 25 per cent per year. India has also improved its relations with the help of other policy decisions like offer of lines of credit, better connectivity through air (open skies policy), rail and road links. Increased economic integration with Asia has helped because the core competencies of these economies are different. India can import goods from other countries which can be produced by other countries at a lower cost than India. The country can export those goods for which it has a competitive advantage. This arrangement is mutually beneficial for India and the East Asian countries.

Now India has entered in the second phase of this policy. This phase in India's Look-East Policy has a new dimension— the development of India's remote Northeast. India's search for a new economic relationship with South-East Asia is no longer driven by considerations of globalisation, but to facilitate the development of Northeast by increasing its connectivity to the outside world. It is with reference to this that talks are on at various levels to speed up the re-opening of the Shilwell Road that connects India's Northeast state of Assam to Kunming in Southwest China's Yunnan province after travelling through Myanmar. For the people of land-locked Northeast, opening of the Shilwell road is of great importance to make its presence felt in the gas-rich Myanmar. In 2006, India and China revived direct trade through the Nathu La in Sikkim.

The Look-East Policy got a boost in June-July 2007 with the high-level visits from Thailand, Vietnam and Cambodia. The Prime Minister of Thailand, Gen. Surayad Chulanout, the Vietnamese Prime Minister, Nguyen Ten Ding and the Cambodian Prime Minister, Hun Sen visited India and signed a number of agreements to provide a further impetus to India's Look-East Policy.

India needs to assess various things in order to help strengthen its trading relations with the countries of Southeast Asia. This can be done by identifying the goods we can export to them. Now we can attract them towards our products that proves to be beneficial for them as well as for us. At the same time, we can also seek the imports that can be made from these countries. Like the Japanese technology can be used in automobiles, electronic goods from Korea, silk and electronic goods from China. This will not only facilitate the development in our North-Eastern states, but also be fruitful to us in making better quality imports. Thus, progress should be made through ministerial talks and meetings. Since most of the exporters are Eurocentric, certain luring incentives can be announced for companies initiating trading relations with South-East Asian countries. No doubt there would be hurdles and hindrances at the same time, but the results will be worth all the efforts made in removing those roadblocks. The language barrier can be a major factor that could keep us away from developing trade relations with these countries. People in these countries might not be comfortable with the universally accepted language, 'English'. This is a major problem. Different cultures, traditions, tastes, activities in these countries only add to the problem. The literature of these countries and information regarding them is not with us as in the case of European countries. There aren't many big companies located there as well. There is also a fear of not getting good returns. That's why, despite slowdown the companies prefer to go for European countries. But just listing these problems will be a negative thinking. Solutions to these must be found, discussed and proper steps should be taken to bring a positive change.

The NRIs in these countries could act as a link for us to study their markets. Since we do not have any base on which we start trade with them, these NRIs can act as the base for us and help not just developing good trade relations but also in the development of our North-Eastern states. We can also open branches of our banks over there which would be a convenience and act as a positive sign.

Thus we can conclude that India's Look-East Policy is very crucial for us. We should not confine ourselves to developing trade relations with European countries. Europe and America are not likely to recover from the economic slowdown before 2010. South-East Asian countries can also prove to be beneficial to us in terms of trade and for our North-Eastern states. Meetings should be held, ministers should take steps, discussions should be held at political level to strengthen the trading relations with these countries.

O O O

## 10. Human Rights—National and International Scenario

Human Rights, as the words themselves suggest, refer to rights which a man or woman is entitled to for just being a human being. Every human being is born with them. They include right to life, property and security of an individual. Social scientists have always been in favour of giving these rights to human beings. Today, the question of human rights has assumed a much deeper significance. For long dismissed by various regimes as the presence of well-being liberals and radical social activists, these rights have emerged on the global political agenda as one of the defining issues of this decade.

There have been sharp divisions over the issues of what human rights mean, how they should be implemented, what role the United Nations has to play in this regard, what other international agencies and other non-governmental agencies should do to ensure them, and what human rights violations and abuses are. A universal recognition of human rights was articulated through the Universal Declaration of Human Rights after World War II. It represented a world milestone in the long struggle for human rights. Drafted by a committee of the UN Commission on Human Rights, they were adopted by the General Assembly on December 10, 1948. India gives due importance to the human rights. Most of the human rights listed in the Universal Declaration are incorporated in Indian Constitution, as fundamental rights. These fundamental rights are enforceable in courts of law. These rights are: right to equality (Articles 14-18); right to freedom (Articles 19-22); right against exploitation (Articles 23-24); right to freedom, freedom of religion (Articles 25-28); cultural and educational rights protecting the interests of minorities (Articles 29-30). To ensure the rights of every citizen, Indian Constitution allows for some special provisions for Scheduled Castes (SCs), Scheduled Tribes (STs) and Other Backward Classes (OBCs) of society through the policy of reservation and other means. Untouchability is banned and its practice in any form is a criminal offence. Moreover, physical and mental health has been recognized as one of the social rights. Primary education is free and secondary and higher education is subsidised so as to make them accessible to every section of society. Liberal democratic institutions and human rights are two sides of the coin and one cannot be secured without the other. Thus, there is no denying the fact that India has a tradition of upholding human values and protecting human rights.

In addition, legislative assemblies and Indian Parliament enact laws from time to time for social and economic justice and development. Efforts have been made through the land reform movement and various developmental programmes to enable the marginalised sections of society to get possession of land. Labour legislations have been passed to ensure fair wages and healthy working conditions for the working class. Above all, the role of the judiciary in the protection and promotion of civic liberties and human rights has been impressive.

Moreover, the country has been able to maintain its secular and democratic nature and structure, but the socio-economic order in our society has remained almost the same even after over sixty years of independence. Unfortunately, the state has not been successful in resolving the prevailing contradictions in society. As a result, there has been a sharp escalation in human rights violations. Despite the ample constitutional and legal provisions towards achieving the goal of liberty, equality and social justice, there are instances of caste-based discrimination. The volatile situations in Kashmir, Gujarat, Orissa and in other parts of the country are testimony to the fact that despite strong social tradition and constitutional backing to ensure maintenance of human rights, there have been laxities in the system. The age old structure of inequality still exists. The grass-root social democracy and distributive justice remain elusive. A considerable portion of Indian population is subjected to multiple deprivations. Moreover, there are instances of human rights violations in different parts of the country. Communal violence eruption in 1984 in the wake of killing of Mrs. Indira Gandhi, incident of Godhra, situation in Jammu & Kashmir and the latest one in the list is the communal violence in Orissa. There are instances of public torture during investigation in the offences, sometimes resulting in custodial deaths. In some cases, state machinery itself has been found involved in the violation of human rights. Very often, there are reports of indifferent attitude of the government towards a particular section of society. The Terrorism and Disruptive Activities (Prevention) Act, TADA was misused to harass a particular community. The country has made great strides in various fields of life. But the benefits of these developments have failed to protect the lower strata of society. Poverty still remains a big challenge before the nation, with 22 per cent people living below poverty line. Besides the basic amenities of life like health, education and drinking water are not available to large sections of society. Child labour exists in many parts of the country despite scores of legal and constitutional provisions. Instances of violations of human rights of tribals, and ethnic and religious minorities are very common. The Indian Parliament passed a bill called Protection of Human Rights Bill, 1993 and the National Human Rights Commission was constituted the same year which is an expression of India's concern for protection and promotion of human rights. It has emerged as a permanent body having vital instinctive link with the minorities commission, the women's commission, scheduled castes and scheduled tribes commission.

At present the movement for human rights has been overshadowed by the dismal political scenario which is characterised by all pervading corruptions, criminalisation of politics, and decline in moral values. Criminalisation of politics makes it difficult for the weaker sections of society to exercise their polling right. This situation calls for an immediate electoral reforms. Besides, an autonomous vigilant agency can do much to bring about a change in the situation. Though it is true that we cannot guarantee that every individual rights will not be violated in a given society, what we can do is to institute a norm that rights are of such primary importance that whosoever violates them should have good reasons for doing so.

All discourse on human rights and development need to be enriched by explicit reference to the value systems of a country. More so, unless there is not sufficient guarantee of meeting the basic needs of every citizen, the concept of human rights is meaningless for the majority of people in the country and very clearly, this guarantee could be based widely on the degree of development of any person. Hence, human rights should be meant to improve the human conditions of the deprived and the disposed.

There have been blatant human rights violations in several parts of the globe. America's attack on Afghanistan and then on Iraq unleashed constant disregard of such rights. Lakhs of people were killed and several thousands of others permanently disabled. What people saw at Abu Ghraib prison in Iraq through TV and newspapers bears testimony to stooping low in denial of human rights. We must hasten to add that when terrorists abduct people and openly behead them, or when suicide bombers blow scores of human beings to pieces or when conspirators mercilessly kill targeted leaders like Benazir Bhutto in Pakistan, the human rights suffer a jolt.

Reminiscent of the Afghan camps in Pakistan over the years, the children who are born into refugee households in Bhutan do not know whether they have a future. A law was passed by what was declared a parliament overnight, according to which Bhutanese of Nepal origin were declared non-citizens though they were born in Bhutan and their forefathers had lived there for hundreds of years. They were bundled out of the country. The Bhutanese officials forced to sign them a document of voluntary migration.

A report by South Asian Human Rights (SAHR) has put the whole thing in perspective by saying: "A major human rights deficit in the South Asian region is the prolonged exile of Bhutanese refugees living in Nepal and India. Both host governments have often ruthlessly cooperated with the Bhutanese government in forced repatriation, arrest or denial of freedom of association and expression to the refugees. This tri-government alliance has demolished the Bhutanese refugee population. Their visibility is low and all attempted solution lack coherence."

Turning to the African continent, what happened in Kenya recently has shocked the entire world, particularly India because hundreds of people of Indian origin living in Nairobi and other parts of Kenya have been killed in a spate of violence that spread after the election results were announced handing a suspiciously thin margin of victory to Kenyas's President Mwai Kibaki.

Human rights violations are taking place everywhere in the world including the advanced countries with civilised societies. The reasons are many. What needs to be done is to make an international code of conduct in this regard and enforce it through UNO and other international organisations with the support of governments of all the countries of the world.

O O O

## 11. BAN KI-MOON—THE NEW SECRETARY-GENERAL OF THE UN

Ban Ki-moon is the new Secretary-General of the United Nations. Before becoming Secretary-General, he was a career diplomat in South Korea and in the United Nations. He entered diplomatic service the year he graduated from college, accepting his first post in New Delhi. In the foreign ministry he earned a reputation of a highly competent, yet modest worker.

Ban was the Foreign Minister of the Republic of Korea from January 2004 to November 2006. In February 2006 he began to campaign for the office of Secretary-General. He was initially considered to be a long shot for the office. As foreign minister of Korea, however, he was able to travel to all the countries which were members of the United Nations Security Council (UNSC), an endeavour that made him the campaign's main contender.

He was elected to be the eighth Secretary-General by the United Nations General Assembly and succeeded Kofi Annan. Ban passed several major reforms regarding peacekeeping and UN employment practices. Diplomatically, Ban has taken particularly strong views on global warming, pressing the issues repeatedly with the former US President, George W. Bush, and Darfur where he helped persuade Sudanese President Omar al-Bashir to allow peacekeeping troops to enter Sudan.

Ban received a bachelor's degree in International Relations from Seoul National University in 1970, and earned a Master of Public Administration from the John F. Kennedy School of Government at Harvard University in 1985. At Harvard, he studied under Joseph Nye who remarked that Ban had "a rare combination of analytic clarity, humility and perseverance".

In addition to his native language Korean, Ban speaks English and French. There have been questions, however, regarding the extent of his knowledge of French, one of the two working languages of the United Nations.

Ban's personality has been described by many as sort of bland. In the Korean Foreign Ministry he was nick-named *Ban-chusa*, meaning "the bureaucrat" or "the administrative clerk". The name was used as both positive and negative complementing Ban's attention to detail and administrative skill while deriding what was seen as a lack of charisma and subservience to his superiors. The Korean press corps calls him "the slippery eel" for his ability to dodge questions. His demeanour has also been described as a "Confucian approach".

Ban can be aptly called a workaholic. His schedule is reportedly broken into five-minute blocks; Ban claims to sleep for only five hours a night and never to have been late for work. During the nearly three years he was foreign minister for South Korea the only vacation he took was for his daughter's wedding. Ban has said that his only hobby is golf, and he plays only a couple of games a year.

Ban's first overseas posting was to New Delhi where he served as vice consul and impressed many of his superiors in the Ministry of Foreign Affairs with his competence and dedication. He reportedly accepted a posting to India rather than the more prestigious United States, because in India he would be able to save more and send more money home to his family. In 1974, he received his first posting to the United Nations, as First Secretary of the South Permanent Observer Mission (South Korea became a full UN member state in 1991). After Park Chung Hee's assassination in 1979, Ban assumed the post of Director of the United Nations Division.

In 1980, Ban became director of the United Nation's International Organizations and Treaties Bureau, headquarters in Seoul. He has been posted twice to the Republic of Korea embassy in Washington D.C. Between these two assignments he served as Director-General for American Affairs in 1990-1992. In 1992, he became Vice Chairman of the South-North Joint Nuclear Control Commission, following the adoption by South and North Korea of the Joint Declaration of the Denuclearization of the Korean Peninsula. From 1993-1994 Ban was Korea's deputy ambassador to the United States. He was promoted to the position of Deputy Minister for Policy Planning and International Organizations in 1995 and then appointed National Security Advisor to the President in 1996. Ban's lengthy career overseas helped him avoid South Korea's unforgiving political environment.

Ban was appointed Ambassador to Austria in 1998, and a year later he was also elected as Chairman of the Preparatory

Commission for the Comprehensive Nuclear-Test-Ban Treaty (CTBT) Organization. During the negotiations, in what Ban considers the biggest blunder of his career, he included a positive statement about the Anti-Ballistic Missile Treaty in a public letter with Russia in 2001, shortly after the United States had decided to abandon the treaty. To avoid anger from the United States, Ban was fired by President Kim Dae-jung, who also issued a public apology for Ban's statement.

Ban was unemployed for the first and only time in his career and was expected to receive an assignment to work in a remote and unimportant embassy. In 2001, during the 56th Session of the United Nations General Assembly, the Republic of Korea held the rotating presidency, and to Ban's surprise, he was selected to be the chief of staff to General Assembly President Han Seung-soo. In 2003, the new Korean President Roh Moo-hyun selected Ban as one of his foreign policy advisors. In 2004, Ban replaced Yoon Young-kwan as Foreign Minister of Korea under President Roh Moo Hyun.

As Foreign Minister, Ban oversaw the trade and aid policies of South Korea. This work put Ban in the position of signing trade deals and delivering foreign assistance to diplomats who would later be influential in his candidacy for Secretary-General. For example, Ban became the first senior South Korean minister to travel to Congo, since its independence in 1960.

Ban has been awarded the Order of Service Merit by the Government of the Republic of Korea on three occasions: in 1975, 1986 and 2006. For his accomplishments as an envoy, he received the Grand Decoration of Honour from the Republic of Austria in 2001. He has received awards from many of the countries with which he has worked diplomatically: the government of Brazil bestowed the Grand Cross of Rio Branco upon him, the government of Peru awarded him Gran Cruz del Sol Sun, and the Korea Society in New York City honoured him with the James A. Van Fleet Award for his contributions to friendship between the United States and the Republic of Korea.

When Ban became Secretary-General, *The Economist* listed the major challenges facing him in 2007: rising nuclear demons in Iran and North Korea, a haemorrhaging wound in Darfur, unending violence in the Middle East, looming environmental disaster, escalating international terrorism, the proliferation of weapons of mass destruction (WMDs), the spread of HIV/AIDS and then the more parochial concerns, such as largely unfinished business of the most sweeping attempt at reform in the UN's history. Before starting, he told his successor, Dag Hammarskjold, "You are about to take over the most impossible job on earth."

On January 23, 2007 Ban took office as the eighth Secretary-General of the United Nations. Ban's term as Secretary-General opened with a flap. At his first encounter with the press as Secretary-General, he refused to condemn the death penalty imposed on Saddam Hussein by the Iraqi High Tribunal, remarking that, "The issue of capital punishment is for each member State to decide." Ban's statements contradicted long-standing United Nations opposition to the death penalty as a human rights concern. He quickly clarified his stance in the case of Brazan al-Tikriti and Awad al-Bandar, two top officials who were convicted of the deaths of 148 Shia Muslims in the Iraqi village of Dujail in the 1980s. In a statement through his spokesperson, he "strongly urged the Government of Iraq to grant a stay of execution to those whose death sentences were though eventually carried out." On the broader issue, he told a Washington, D.C. audience that he recognized and encouraged the "growing trend in international society, international law and domestic policies and practices to phase out eventually the death penalty."

During his first month in office, Ban proposed two major restructurings: to split the UN peacekeeping operation into two departments and to combine the political affairs and disarmament department. His proposals were met with stiff resistance from members of the UN General Assembly, who bristled under Ban's request for rapid approval. The proposed merger of the disarmament and political affairs offices was criticized by many in the developing world, partially because of rumours that Ban hoped to place American B. Lynn Pascoe in charge of the new office. Alejandro D. Wolff, then acting American Ambassador, said the United States backed his proposals.

Ban began regular consultations with UN ambassadors, agreeing to have his peacekeeping proposal suitably changed. Ban dropped his proposal to combine political affairs and disarmament. Ban however pressed ahead with reforms on job requirement at the UN, requiring that all positions be considered five-year appointments, all receive strict annual performance reviews, and all financial disclosures be made public. Though not so popular with the New York office, the move found favour in other UN offices around the world and was lauded by UN observers. Ban's proposal to split the peacekeeping operation into one group handling operations and another handling arms was finally adopted in mid-March 2007.

According to *The Washington Post,* "some UN employees and delegates" expressed resentment at Ban's perceived favouritism in the appointment of South Korean nationals in key posts. Previous UN Chiefs such as Kurt Waldheim (Austria), Javier Pérez de Cuéllar (Peru) and Boutros Boutros-Ghali (Egypt) brought small teams of trusted aides or clerical workers from their country's Foreign Ministry. But according to "some officials" in the *Post* story, Ban has gone further, boosting South Korea's presence in U.N. ranks by more than 20 per cent during his first year in office. In response, Ban and his aides have claimed that allegations of favouritism are wrong, and that some of the harshest criticisms against him have undercurrents of racism.

The Secretary-General of the United Nations has the ability to influence debate on nearly any global issue. Although unsuccessful in some areas, Ban's predecessor Annan had been successful in increasing the UN peacekeeping presence and in popularizing the Millennium Development Goals. UN observers were eager to see on which issues Ban intends to focus, in addition to reform of the United Nations bureaucracy.

On several prominent issues, such as proliferation in Iran and North Korea, Ban has deferred the Security Council. Ban has also declined to become involved on the issue of Taiwan's status. In 2007, the Republic of Nauru raised the issue of allowing the Republic of China (Taiwan) to sign the Convention on the Elimination of All Forms of Discrimination Against Women. Ban referenced the United Nations General Assembly Resolution 2758, and refused the motion. On July 29, 2007, the President of the Republic of China wrote to request admission into the UN by the name Taiwan. Ban immediately rejected the request.

Ban took the first foreign trip of his term to attend the African Union summit in Addish Ababa, Ethiopia, in January 2007 as part of an effort to reach out to the Group of 77. He repeatedly identified Darfur as the top humanitarian priority of his administration, Ban played a large role, with several face-to-face meetings with Sudanese President Omar Hassan al-Bashir, in convincing Sudan to allow UN peacekeepers to enter the Darfur region. On July 31, 2007, the United Nations Security Council approved sending 26,000 UN peacekeepers into the region to join 7,000 troops from the African Union. The resolution was heralded as a major breakthrough in confronting the Darfur conflict.

O O O

# 12. SAARC: ORIGIN AND DEVELOPMENT FRAMEWORK

Regional cooperation in South Asia began in 1981 with productive groundwork, series of secretary level and minister level meetings that provided a unique opportunity to lay down the foundation of South Asian Association for Regional Cooperation (SAARC). The historic moment came in 1985 when all the seven nations of South Asia adopted the SAARC charter in Dhaka. The charter *inter alia* adopted at the Summit the following objectives:

(i)   to promote the welfare of the people of South Asia;

(ii)  to accelerate economic growth, social progress and cultural development in the region;

(iii) to promote collective self-reliance;

(iv) to contribute to mutual trust and understanding; and

(v)  to strengthen co-operation among themselves in international forum on matters of common interest.

Actually, the countries of South Asia have not only inherited a shared past but also have a common destiny. South Asian countries have been tied together with intricate bonds of culture, religion, tradition and ethnicity.

This is the fact of history, which needs to be precisely acknowledged at the earliest for the betterment of region. These countries must not be seen as rivals, but rather as partners, as constituent units, each contributing what it can to regional resilience. Just like different organs of the body, which are complementary to each other, constitute an organism and perform their specific functions. Countries of South Asia have to perform their complementary role to boost regional cooperation in order to form an organic South Asia. Regionalism was confined to Europe till the 1980s.

Following the end of the Cold War, there was a dramatic spurt in the growth of regionalism. However, regionalism emerged in the aftermath of the Second World War as an important instrument for the attainment of two important objectives:

(i) to achieve economic growth through efficient utilisation of resources; and

(ii) to establish enduring peace in the world, especially in Western Europe, by bringing France and Germany together, which had historically been at war with each other.

The signing of the Rome Treaty in 1957 laid the foundations of the European Community which marked the beginning of a regional grouping for the achievements of these objectives. The late 1980s and the early 1990s witnessed the growth of regionalism of a different nature, i.e. transcontinental regionalism. In fact, economic compulsions are driving dynamic resilient members of one regional grouping to have simultaneous membership of other regional groupings irrespective of the geographical logic of the definition of a region. The US membership of NAFTA and APEC illustrates this point clearly.

Further, consolidation into regional blocs could make it more likely that negotiated agreements can be reached simply because there are fewer players. A world trading system effectively run by a G-3 (Group of Three), or NAFTA (North Atlantic Free Trade Agreement), EC (European Community) and Japan poses fewer problems of free riding than one in which Italy or France are free to make independent demands and cheat on their own. Regionalism is thus found to be more efficient, quicker and more enduring. Since the end of the Cold War, a number of regional groupings have emerged at various levels, i.e. US-Canadian Free Trade Area (1989), North American Free Trade Area (1993), Asia-Pacific Free Trade Area (1993-94), Pan-American Free Trade Area, Mercosur (1991). Cooperation and integration at the regional level is perhaps the single biggest change, that has taken place in the sovereign state system since its inception.

India has always been keen to develop beneficial bilateralism with all her neighbours as well for developing institutionalized cooperation among the seven South Asian countries—India, Pakistan, Bangladesh, Sri Lanka, Bhutan, Nepal and Maldives. India has also played a very positive and constructive role in floating South Asian Association for Regional Cooperation and making it work as a dynamic association committed to consolidate and expand socio-economic and cultural cooperation among the South Asian countries. As the Chairman of SAARC in 1986-87, India helped the SAARC not only to overcome its teething troubles but also to make it adopt new goals and programmes for increased cooperation among the members of SAARC.

Following the tsunami tragedy, Bangladesh the host of the Thirteenth SAARC Summit, postponed the meeting from January to 6-7 February 2005. India decided not to attend the Thirteenth Summit in Dhaka on the scheduled dates against the backdrop of the then prevailing situation in our neighbourhood, which had caused us grave concern. India reiterates its continuing and consistent commitment to the SAARC process, and to increased regional cooperation among Member States and maintains that it is only in an increased regional cooperation among Member States and in an environment free from political turmoil and violence that a Summit would yield the desired outcome. The Twelfth SAARC Summit in January 2004 in Islamabad witnessed the signing of three documents, the SAARC Social Charter, and Additional Protocol on Terrorism and a framework Agreement on SAFTA. India offered to contribute US $ 100 million for Poverty Alleviation projects in SAARC countries (outside India). As mandated by the Twelfth Summit, the Independent South Asian Commission on Poverty Alleviation (ISACPA) prepared a report setting out SAARC Developmental Goals (SDGs) for the next five years in the areas of poverty alleviation, employment generation education, healthcare and environment. The ISACPA Report was launched in different SAARC capitals through the year 2004. India launched the ISACPA Report on December 21, 2004. A Regional Poverty Profile-2004, the second such report, detailing economic indicators of SAARC member countries is to be presented at the Thirteenth Summit in Dhaka.

At the 25th Council of Ministers Meeting in Islamabad, July 2004, India made the following important proposals:

1. India sought to set up a South Asian Parliamentary Forum to deliberate on issues related with regional cooperation endeavours under SAARC.

2. Establishment of a SAARC High Economic Council formed with the Finance and Planning Ministers of the SAARC Member Countries to promote ideas and initiatives related to regional economic integration in economic, trade, financial and financial areas. (The 4th SAARC Commerce Ministers Meeting in Islamabad, November 20-23, 2004 conveyed approval for Member States to send their comments to the Secretariat for consideration during the Thirteenth Meeting of the Committee on Economic Cooperation).

3. Setting up of National Committees in member countries mandated to monitor and devise programmes to implement the goals of the SAARC Social Charter, as well as consult with each other to promote collaborative Poverty Alleviation Projects, including under the SAARC Poverty Alleviation Fund. (Ministry of Statistics & Programme Implementation has been identified as the nodal focal point for cooperation with SAARC counterparts).

4. Setting up of a SAARC Infrastructure Fund, for major infrastructure projects in the region. (The 4th SAARC Commerce Ministers Meeting in Islamabad, November 20-23, 2004 approved that in the fist instance, advice of SAARCFINANCE—a body comprising Governors of Central Banks and Finance Secretaries of SAARC— may be obtained about the conceptual viability and feasibility of the proposal).

5. As part of the SAARC Awareness Year for TB and HIV/ AIDS, India offered to host a meeting of experts and community workers, train paramedics from the SAARC countries, and also offered to send medical vans and mobile awareness units to each of the SAARC countries.

6. India has offered training in the field of statistics.

There was recognition amongst the leaders that the time has come to move SAARC from a declaratory phase into implementation.

As approved in the 6th Environment Ministers Meeting, India prepared and circulated through the Secretariat. a Concept Paper on "Information Sharing on Disaster Preparedness and Mitigation".

This concept Paper was considered by an Expert Group Meeting in 2005, which submited its recommendations to the Seventh Meeting of the SAARC Environment Ministers in Dhaka, November 2005.

The Thirteenth SAARC Summit took place on the eve of SAARC entering into the third decade of its existence. The modalities for Afghanistan's entry into SAARC were finalised at the 27th SAARC Council of Ministers Meeting held in Dhaka.

**Fourteenth SAARC Summit**

The President of the Islamic Republic of Afghanistan, Hamid Karzai; the Chief Adviser of the Government of the People's Republic of Bangladesh, Fakhruddin Ahmed; the then Prime Minister of the Kingdom of Bhutan, Lyonpo Khandu Wangchuk; the Prime Minister of the Republic of India, Manmohan Singh; the President of the Republic of Maldives, Maumoon Abdul Gayoom; the then Prime Minister of Nepal, Girija Prasad Koirala; the then Prime Minister of the Islamic Republic of Pakistan, Shaukat Aziz; and the President of the Democratic Socialist Republic of Sri Lanka, Mahinda Rajapakse, attended the Fourteenth Summit meeting of the South Asian

Association for Regional Cooperation (SAARC) held in New Delhi, India on April 3-4, 2007.

For the first time in its history, SAARC has turned into an organization. The Summit adopted a comprehensive and forward-looking New Delhi Declaration, which sets out the core principles underlining the collective vision of an inter-connected South Asia where there is a free flow of goods, services, human resources and ideas. At the retreat, the leaders agreed to make tangible progress in the next six months on four issues that affect the daily lives of the people. These include water, energy, food and environment. They decided to work with international agencies to develop and implement viable cross-border regional projects in these four sectors, which address the peoples' basic needs. They also decided to designate 2008 as the "SAARC Year of Good Governance".

Dr. Manmohan Singh proposed connecting all the SAARC capitals with direct flights. He also announced unilateral liberalization of visas particularly for students, teachers, professors, journalists and patients from the region. The Summit also decided to cover 50 journalists from each SAARC country under the SAARC Visa Exemption Scheme (VES). Deliberations at the Summit and other meetings also reflected the strong condemnation of terrorism. The leaders re-affirmed their commitment to combat this problem and agreed to consider India's proposal to work towards finalizing an Agreement on Mutual Legal Assistance in Criminal Matters. The constructive deliberations at various meetings of the Heads of State or Government, of the Council of Ministers and of Senior Officials and the high level presence of Observers, including the expression of interest of others, all are a proof of the fact that this is recognized not just within the region, but also outside of it. The presence of Leaders at the Summit provided an excellent opportunity to hold bilateral discussions for energizing our substantive neighbourly ties with each of the Member States of SAARC.

At the inception of the association, the Integrated Programme of Action (IPA) consisting of a number of Technical Committees (TCs) was identified as the core areas of cooperation. Over the period of years, the number of TCs was changed as per the requirement. The current areas of cooperation under the reconstituted Regional Integrated Programme of Action which is pursued through the Technical Committees cover:

(a) Agriculture and Rural Development;

(b) Health and Population Activities;

(c) Women, Youth and Children;

(d) Science and Technology and Meteorology;

(e) Human Resources Development;

(f) Transport; and

(g) Environment and Forestry.

Recently, high level Working Groups have also been established to strengthen cooperation in the areas of Information and Communications Technology, Intellectual Property Rights, Tourism, Biotechnology, and Energy. Given the emphasis laid down at successive Summits on the need to expand the areas of cooperation and strengthen the regional cooperation, a number of other areas have been included in the SAARC agenda. Several ministerial level meetings have been held to give due emphasis in various fields.

SAFTA was envisaged primarily as the first step towards the transition to a South Asian Free Trade Area leading subsequently towards a Customs Union, Common Market and Economic Union. The Sixteenth session of the Council of Ministers (New Delhi, 18-19 December, 1995) agreed on the need to strive for the realization of SAFTA and to this end an Inter-Governmental Expert Group (IGEG) was set up in 1996 to identify the necessary measures to be taken for progressing to a free trade area. The Tenth SAARC Summit (Colombo, 29-31 July 1998) decided to set up a Committee of Experts (COE) to draft a comprehensive treaty framework for creating a free trade area within the region, taking into consideration the asymmetries in development within the region and bearing in mind the need to fix realistic targets and achievable objectives.

The Agreement on South Asian Free Trade Area (SAFTA), drafted by the Committee of Experts, was signed in January 2004 during the Twelfth SAARC Summit in Islamabad. The Agreement entered into force on 1 January 2006. Currently, the Sensitive Lists of products, Rules of Origin, Technical Assistance as well as a Mechanism for Compensation of Revenue Loss for Least Developed Member States are under negotiation.

Under the Trade Liberalisation Programme scheduled for completion in ten years by 2016, the customs duties on products from the region will be progressively reduced. However, under an early harvest programme for the Least Developed Countries (LDCs) which are members of SAFTA, alongwith India, Pakistan and Sri Lanka have brought down their customs duties to 0-5% by 1st January 2009 for the products from these Member States. The Least Developed Member States are expected to benefit from additional measures under the special and differential treatment accorded to them under the Agreement.

O O O

# 13. US AFPAK POLICY

The US President Barack Obama has described Al-Qaeda and its extremis/allies as a "cancer" that is killing Pakistan from within. He has noted that the future of Afghanistan is inextricably linked to that of Pakistan. Obama administration's AfPak policy review is the result of consultation between US military commanders and diplomats, the Afghan and Pakistan

Governments, US allies and North Atlantic Treaty Organisation (NATO), and with other donors and international organisations.

The contours of the anti-terrorism drive that Obama announced shows a departure from the policy pursued by the previous administration under George W. Bush.

The myth that Taliban is an Afghan issue in which Pakistan was involved only to the extent that Islamabad's assistance was thought necessary in dealing the Taliban and Al-Qaeda stands dissolved and the problem is now being seen as being wider than Afghanistan, and very much involving Pakistan. The other conceptual break is related to involving regional countries in helping to solve the terrorism/Taliban/Al-Qaeda problem that has come to threaten regional and international security. Thus, Russia, Iran, China and India now get an official look-in.

The US will provide massive financial and other kinds of assistance to Pakistan, where most of the terrorist masterminds are believed to be hiding, but not without conditions attached. There will be strict compliance audit. The amount of Rs. 7,500 crore that Pakistan will receive annually for five years as part of the US AfPak policy will be allowed to be used only for development purposes like building roads, schools and hospitals.

It is believed that over the next decade the US is expected to give around $30 to $35 billion in aid to Pakistan, which it regards as its frontline state. This includes about $15 billion as part of the AfPak policy.

Pakistan must demonstrate its commitment to rooting out Al-Qaeda and the violent extremists within its borders. And the US will insist that action be taken one way or another when it has intelligence about high-level terrorist targets. In other words, the Pakistani establishment will have to do more to fight Al-Qaeda, the Taliban, and their support networks on their side of the border or else allow the Americans to do the job for them. The financial support may be withdrawn in case these conditions are not accepted.

Ever since 9/11, there has been a lot of confusion about the war on "terrorism". President Obama has brought clarity on the issue by declaring that the war is against Al-Qaeda and its allies. According to him, they are an international security challenge of the highest order. The safety of the people around the world is at stake as any a major attack on an Asian, European or African city is likely to have some link with the Al-Qaeda leadership in Pakistan.

Having identified the enemy in concrete terms, President Obama wants the American people to understand that they have a clear and focused goal to disrupt, dismantle and defeat Al-Qaeda in Pakistan and Afghanistan and prevent their return to either country in the future. This declaration has to be understood in all its implications. He is not referring to Pakistan as a frontline state and an ally in the war against terrorism. Instead, President Obama is seeking Pakistan as under partial occupation of Al-Qaeda and in danger of being overrun by it and its allies.

Totally dismissing General Musharraf's bluff that Osama bin Laden was not in Pakistan, President Obama has made it clear that Al-Qaeda and its allies who planned and supported the 9/11 attacks are in Pakistan and Afghanistan.

Over the years the dangerous Pakistan's Inter-Services Intelligence (ISI) is branzely aiding the Taliban's campaign in southern Afghanistan providing it, as US intelligence agencies have discovered, with weapons, finance, strategic planning and even recruits. This also partly explains why the US Government's 'Global War on Terror' in Afghanistan is making little headway even as Washington prepares for its most concerted offensive against terrorism.

The US President has directed 17,000 additional American troops to Afghanistan as well as 4,000 military trainers. These soldiers and marines will fight the Taliban in the south and east. The emphasis would be on training and increasing the size of the Afghan security forces in order to prepare Afghans to take responsibility for their security. It would also enable Washington to be able to bring its troops home eventually.

Every American unit in Afghanistan will be partnered with an Afghan unit and the US will seek additional trainers from its NATO allies to ensure that every Afghan unit has a coalition partner. The efforts to build an Afghan army of 1,35,000 and a police force of over 80,000 will be accelerated so as to meet these goals by 2011. A contact group for Afghanistan and Pakistan will also be set up to bring together America's NATO allies, Central Asian States, the Gulf nations and Iran, Russia, India and China.

○ ○ ○

# 14. GLOBAL RECESSION AND CAPITALISM

The subprime mortgage failures in large number in America in September 2008 triggered a slowdown of the world economy. The failure of large financial institutions and banks like Lehman Brothers pressed the panic button. The consequences have been catastrophic. From America to Europe and then to Asia and Africa, the economies of developed as well as developing countries have received a big jolt.

The economic downturn snowballed into a global financial turmoil with adverse impacts on nearly each and every sector of the economy, i.e. manufacturing, trade, real estate, retail malls, airways, automobiles, exports, imports, among others. Several companies have either closed down or drastically reduced their businesses. As a cost-cutting measure, a large number of big and small companies have effected job-cuts, increasing unemployment. The banks are actually short of lendable sources. The latter half of the financial year 2008-09 saw severe credit crunch. The consumer spending declined sharply all over the world. As a result, the commodity prices went down dramatically. Deflation took over inflation in most of the countries including India. It was considered that the 2008-09 financial crisis was the worst contagion since the Great Depression of 1930s.

The closed economies like Russia and China have blamed capitalism to put the world in such a difficult situation. Lack of financial regulation in capitalist countries like America, U.K., France, etc. has been considered the main cause of the crisis. Many experts have even predicted the end of capitalism, though the western world has spoken in favour of capitalism and its theories.

We are living in a globalised world where economic booms and recessions spread from one country or region to other parts of the world. Similarly, the world becomes united to fight global problems. The International Monetary Fund (IMF) has released stimulus packages to a large number of countries of Asia, Europe and Africa, as the economies of these countries showed signs of contraction.

The governments of nearly every country have announced stimulus packages to put the economy back on track. America was perhaps the first country where the government not only gave bailout packages to some major companies which were on the verge of collapse, but also announced huge stimulus packages—one by the then President George W. Bush in October 2008—and the other by Barack Obama in January 2009, immediately after taking over as America's 44th President. As reviving the sectors which had suffered more was the top priority, Obama brought housing package, banks bailout plans, besides help from taxpayers' money to General Motors, Chrysler, American International Group (AIG), and some other corporate giants.

Many economists have questioned the policy of government intervention in helping the private companies to cover up their losses. According to them it is against the precepts of capitalism—which inter alia include private ownership of sources of production like land, labour, capital and entrepreneurship, profit motive, loss and complete independence of economic activities without state intervention, etc. Government control is rather the characteristic of socialist economies. The stimulus measures by the capitalist countries have therefore been taken as something unprecedented. Some have even called it the end of capitalism. The large bailout plans have also been criticized on the account that they have helped those companies which have performed badly. It is being alleged that the taxpayers' hard-earned money has been given as a reward to companies which were inefficient and could not manage their affairs. The CEOs and other high officials have enjoyed heavy perks and large salaries, but in the crisis, the poor are suffering more because of their lower capacity to bear economic shocks. This kind of capitalism is rewarding inefficiency. When there was boom time, the large companies made huge profits while common people waited for the benefits to percolate down to them. But in the time of slowdown these companies are being dished out large sums out of common people's tax contribution and savings. It has been stated that such capitalism privatises profits but socialises losses.

Notwithstanding the above allegations, there has been a strong defence of capitalism from various quarters. Many economists believe that the financial crisis has not been caused by capitalism. If it were so, the closed economies of Russia and China should continue to do well which has not been the case. Recessions are very much a part of capitalism as of any other economic system. As a matter of fact slowdowns are a means through which capitalism discards old and redundant policies and adopts new characteristics as it reinvents itself after each successive recession. Karl Marx waited for the end of capitalism for many decades but he found that after each crisis it re-emerged stronger. Ultimately Marx had to give up his critical foreboding about capitalism. A mild economic slowdown was experienced in 1990s. When French President Miterrand tried to adopt communist policies to reverse the situation, the country's economy went down further. He had to discard his policies and re-accept capitalist measures.

Many experts have justified the government intervention through bailout packages and stimulus measures. At a time when liquidity has dried up in the market and the consumer demand is at its lowest, the governments cannot just keep on waiting and let the economy suffer. Capitalism allows government supervision to ensure that the country's sources of production including capital are employed for economic growth. Such intervention is not happening for the first time. In fact, John Maynard Keynes, the great economist, in his *General Theory of Employment, Interest and Money* drew attention to the state's positive role in today's modern economies. When the liquidity completely dried up in the market, the banks were not in a position to lend to the required magnitude, the corporate sector suffered due to lack of capital, there was a decline in demand for goods and services, as was the case in the latter half of 2008-09 and the initial period of 2009-10, the governments had to inject money in the market to boost demand and revive the economy. If the American government announced bailout measures to help some major companies, it was a step in the right direction. If these companies start working as before, there would be employment, production, profits, expansion and growth. If the companies are allowed to suffer, they may perish bringing mass unemployment and lack of utilization of sources including human sources.

Today, capitalism is reinventing itself. It is giving up some of its old methods and adopting new ones as per requirements of the difficult situation. It has been realised that the increasing defaults by borrowers on the security of homes have put financial firms including banks in a crisis. The solution is to borrow the toxic assets of these financial companies and banks so that financial health is restored to them and they start lending as before bringing more liquidity in the market and helping the corporate world to continue their business, making profits and undertaking expansion projects.

Today's capitalism is being helped by international financial institutions like IMF and the World Bank. The G20 meeting at London in April 2009 was a landmark in many ways. The heads of governments of these countries resolved to help each other. They decided to strengthen the IMF by contributing US $ 1 trillion so that the world body could help the needy countries through soft loans and contributions. A specific sum of money was earmarked for developing economies so that they could fight poverty and there is a balanced economic growth in the world. The world leaders also decided to bring proper financial regulation in the world so that crises of this type and magnitude do not occur in future. Thus, capitalism has more means and better ways these days to fight economic downturn. America conducted stress tests of its 19 major banks to check if they were in a position to bear the crisis. Some of these banks were found to be in need of more financial help to fight the crisis. This is another example of how capitalism has better means nowadays to assess the position and take remedial measures in time. The economists are also trying to remove international economic imbalances to ensure quick revival of the economies. Better results are expected sooner than later.

# 15. INDIA AND THE WTO

The World Trade Organisation is a legal and institutional foundation of multilateral trading system. It came into existence on January 1, 1995 by replacing the General Agreement on Tariffs and Trade (GATT) which was constituted in 1948 in Geneva to pursue the objective of free trade so as to encourage the growth and development of member countries. The WTO is a successful conclusion of Doha Round of trade negotiations, which formally began in 1986. It came to conclusion on 15th December 1993 after several rounds of talks. The final act was signed by 125 countries on 15th April 1994 at Marrakesh (Morocco). India is a founding member of the WTO. At present, there are 149 countries of the WTO. The WTO is, in fact, a rule-based organisation that seeks to accelerate the world trade on the principle of non-discrimination among the member countries.

The WTO ministerial conference is the highest decision-making body of the organisation. It has to meet at least every two years. It can take decisions on all matters relating to multilateral trade agreements. Five ministerial conferences have been held since the establishment of the WTO. The Singapore Ministerial Conference, being the first meeting, the interested members of the WTO negotiated on Information Technology and launched a work programme which included trade and investment, trade and competition, transparency in government procurement and trade facilitation. The Geneva Ministerial Conference marked the 50 years of the GATT multilateral trading system. The Seattle Ministerial Conference failed without reaching a consensus on the declaration to be adopted by the ministers. The Cancun Conference also met with the same fate.

India, being a founding member of the WTO, ractified the WTO agreement on 30 December, 1994. It was estimated that the formation of the WTO will greatly increase the world trade. But the reality is that the developed countries want that under the pressure of the sole superpower of the world—America, and its allies—the developing countries should reduce trade barriers and permit free flow of goods while they want to pursue the protectionist policies to save their own interests by creating trade barriers. However, India abides by the rules and decisions of the WTO. This gives India an entitlement to most favoured nation treatment from the member countries for its export and vice versa. In fact, the participation in the increasingly rule-based system is aimed at ensuring more stability and predictability in its international trade. This has direct and indirect impact on Indian economy.

Under the WTO regimes, most of the issues of agriculture are covered under the Agreement on Agriculture (AOA) which established a new set of rules regarding international agricultural policy development. The main objective of the treaty was to free the agricultural grade from physical control and provide the long-term reforms in agricultural trade. Thus, signing of the treaty marked a significant move towards the objective of increased market orientation in agricultural trade because the major thrust of Agreement on Agriculture is to remove the past production and distorting practices and to facilitate a fair market-oriented agricultural trading system. In fact, this agreement aims to eliminate distortions in agricultural trade through reducing export and production subsidies and import barriers including non-tariffs barriers. It was expected that implementation of AOA would raise international prices of agricultural commodities. In addition, it would improve export prospects for developing countries like India. But even after more than a decade of WTO formation, world trade in agriculture is highly distorted because of domestic subsidy and heavy export given by the industrialised countries with little market access offered by them to the agricultural prospects of developing countries.

The price support and heavy subsidy given by the developing countries to their farmers have emerged as one of the most controversial issues in the WTO ministerial conferences. In fact, such practices constitute unfair discrimination against developing countries like India, Brazil, Egypt and Nigeria and hence have been a major issue of disaster faction among the developing countries.

The rise of export subsidies and the high proportion of world trade to which experts subsidy are applied, both suggest that there is a need to negotiate in the forthcoming WTO conferences on complete elimination of export subsidising due to which Indian farmers have been put to serious disadvantages. The recent phenomenon of farmers' suicides and unrest among the farm communities in different parts of the country is a grave problem which needs to be solved permanently.

In the industry sector, India in conformity with the WTO provisions, has to lower the import duties, reduce tariffs on capital goods, components, intermediate goods and industrial raw material and quantitative restrictions. As a result, Indian industries have to face increasing competition from foreign goods. Under the WTO provisions, it has to remove the protection offered by import duties. It has to remove the qualitative and quantitative restrictions from its industrial agricultural and textile products. It led to the opening of Indian markets for the foreign consumer goods. Naturally, the indigenously produced products have to face stiff challenges from the foreign products. This is adversely affecting the Indian industry leading to the closed down of many industrial units. This is indeed a matter of grave concern for India.

The Chinese goods that include battery, cells, cameras, car stereos, locks, wrist watches, cell phones, VCD players, OTGs, electric ovens, fans and several other consumer goods are flooding the Indian market which are adversely impacting the Indian consumer goods industries. India inc. has requested the government to bring a new anti-dumping legislature to protect indigenous industries. Another aspect of the problem is that Chinese goods are not only coming through normal channels of trade but are also being smuggled through the porous Indo-Nepal border. Since China is a WTO member, this makes it virtually impossible to take action against it. Moreover, preparing an anti-dumping case against China is very difficult because it is almost impossible to obtain necessary information required from the Chinese sources.

Indian automobile industry is also facing challenges in the backdrop of following the commitment of the WTO. India has allowed the imports of second hand cars into Indian market. This has very damaging impact on domestic industry. In fact, experience all over the world confirm to this fact that wherever second hand imported cars are allowed, they adversely affect the domestic industry. We have examples of New Zealand and Australia where Japanese used cars destroyed New Zealand's car industry.

The WTO agreement immensely affected small scale units which account for 52 per cent of employment, 38 per cent of manufacturing output and 32 per cent of exports. This is due to the fact that WTO agreements do not discriminate on the basis of the rise of industries or enterprises. There is no place for reservations, preferential treatment and any support measures under the WTO agreements. As a result, the small scale units have to compete not only with the large units but also have to face challenges from the cheap imported products. These units are losing their markets. A large number of units have either become sick or are on the verge of being closed down. This sector is a major source of employment next to agriculture. The biggest problem, that the SSF units are facing, has been caused by dumping policy which has led to the flooding of Indian market with various kinds of Chinese goods. Moreover, the sector lacks the adequate resources required for preparation of the case for anti-dumping duties.

Apart from the entry of the big multinationals in the traditional areas of this sector such as consumer goods like instant stock  manufacturing, food processing, ice cream and other bakery items, mineral water, etc. is also posing problem for the survival of small traders in these goods. Besides, the differential provisions and practices of the developed countries are merely adding to the worries.

To make the WTO more effective in the era of globalisation and liberalisation, the developed countries should abandon their differential attitudes and be more liberal and supportive towards the developing countries. Equal opportunity on equal terms and equal footing need to be made guiding ethics for the members of the WTO.

O O O

# 16. SPECIAL ECONOMIC ZONES

Special Economic Zones (SEZs) are specifically delineated duty free enclaves and are deemed to be foreign territories for the purpose of trade operations, duties and tariffs.

Basically, they are a region with special trade laws and duty exemptions, permission to have captive power plants and distribute power, therefore, have their own water and gas supply units. They have their own civic administration. A scheme of setting up the SEZs in India was announced in the Export and Import (EXIM) Policy in March 2000. The model in view was the existing special export zones, which were meant to boost country's export so that the adverse balance payments in the external sector of the economy is of limit. The idea behind SEZs was to promote industrial growth, encourage manufacturing industries and thereby promote economic growth, improve Gross Domestic Product (GDP) growth rate, and expand employment.

However, the concrete shape to SEZs was provided by the UPA Government through the SEZs Act, 2005. SEZs are crucial for generating employment, boosting manufacturing and allowing India to compete with countries like China. While the entire world has only 400 SEZs and China only six, India has already caused 200 approvals within a year, 48 of them in the State of Maharashtra alone.

SEZs are mini cities in themselves with their own infrastructure including ports, airports, roads, bridges and so on. The models as well as inspiration is of Chinese premier Mao Zedong. A Chinese SEZ which covers almost 20,000 hectares with only 26 small factories with a total industrial output of about $10,000 export more than whole of India and attracts more Foreign Direct Investment (FDI) than whole of India does. It has its own water supply, power generation, ports, export and import units and practically free hand in management of its civic and economic affairs.

Considering the enormous success of China's SEZs and given the fact that both India and China have a similar socio-economic set-up and are evenly matched in human and other resources, it has been visualized that the SEZ model of development can lead to higher growth in India too.

However, Indian law does not envisage setting up of such giant SEZs. The size of SEZs in India can be as low as 10 hectares. The largest SEZ in India, that of Reliance Industries in Navi Mumbai may be more than 14,000 hectare in size. The 10 hectare size SEZs are those of information industry which has already acquired world reputation for production of software and other computer-related products. Opposition to SEZ policy has come from some quarters principally on three counts:

(i) The setting up of SEZs requires allocation of large parts of land to them and the most part of land allocated to them would be agricultural land. This will reduce area under cultivation in the country and thus, jeopardise national food security.

(ii) The tax and tariff concessions offered to operators in the SEZ will drastically curtail revenue receipts and will knave a big loss to the exchequer. This, in turn, could endanger fiscal discipline and continuing of fiscal and revenue deficits.

(iii) The big industrial houses and large industrial units will benefit at the cost of small industries and poor workers. Small and marginal farmers might also suffer if their land is taken away from them for setting up a SEZ. Unemployment will increase.

These objections have assumed ideological and political colours. However, national interests require that the objections be answered effectively by arguments and on the basis of presentation of solid data.

## Acquiring Agricultural Land

The question of acquiring agricultural land for the purpose of setting up of SEZs is the most significant. This objection has been met in three ways. The question was raised by the Congress President, Sonia Gandhi at the Nainital conclave of Chief Ministers of Congress-ruled states. She instructed Chief Ministers that no fertile piece of land should be allotted to SEZs and that if a small part of land allotted to a SEZ is a piece of fertile land, adequate compensation be paid to farmer/farmers whose land is thus taken. Provision should also be made to rehabilitate displaced farmers. It has been officially announced that no agricultural land has been acquired for purpose of setting up SEZs. The government has also stopped acquiring any land for the SEZs.

On the fiscal front, the biggest, objection was from Finance Minister himself. Earlier, he opposed SEZs scheme on the ground that it would cost the exchequer Rs. 70,000 crore in revenue from the tax sops proposed to be offered to industrialists locating their industries in SEZ, in the form of foreign revenues. Export units in SEZs, will get 100 per cent tax holiday for the first five years, 50 per cent tax break for five years more and further five-years break on production based on reinvested profits.

The Commerce Minister allayed Finance Minister's fears by saying that when the SEZs became functional, after a period of time, the government will start earning revenue in the shape of taxes, duties several times the amount foregone as tax holidays.

The Reserve Bank of India (RBI) has cautioned the Government about the mushrooming SEZ across the country on revenue implication that could arise from such zones.

It was also apprehended that though the SEZs would boost investment and economic growth, yet the SEZ could aggravate the uneven pattern of development by pulling out resources from less developed areas. However, there is now a national consensus in this country that SEZs are a useful tool of economic development and growth. It is now agreed that the SEZs policy should be pursued judiciously and the scheme implemented without delay. As a result, the push for starting new SEZs has gathered momentum. Our SEZs are intended to allow India to catch up with China in terms of GDP growth rate, export performance and attracting foreign investments as contribution to country's growth process. That is the second phase.

In the third phase, IT services located in SEZs could give a great start to India's development. It could become an important push to 11th Five-Year Plan (2007-12) achieving 10 per cent growth rate by the end of the plan period as envisaged in the Plan's Approach paper.

There is no doubt that if the SEZ policy is carefully and fairly implemented, it would result in creation of lakhs of new jobs for skilled and unskilled workers. The number of managerial jobs would also increase sufficiently. The biggest advantage will be in the shape of increase in exports.

But we must be cautious. China's experience in this regard shows that SEZ policy gives rise to land grab by developers in order to benefit from tax incentives in SEZ. This means encroachment on area under farming at present. We must ensure that this does not happen in India. India must learn from China's experience of land grabs by private interest there. Chinese themselves are highly disturbed at prospects of diminishing of the farm area which provides food security to the people. India must ask the State Governments to be careful in sanctioning new SEZs and allowing land acquisition by them. The State Government would be anxious to grant approval because it brings them high revenue. We have to draw benefits from the SEZs but also avoid its pitfalls through judicious policy and proper implementation thereof.

O O O

# 17. ELEVENTH FIVE-YEAR PLAN

India plans to join the big league of the latest growth economies over the next five years with an objective to catapult the economy on a growth of nine per cent during the 11th Five-Year Plan Period (2007-2012).

The Planning Commission approved the draft for the 11th Five Year Plan and the same has also been approved by the National Development Council, thus setting the stage for raising average Gross Domestic Product (GDP) rate to nine per cent from 7.6 per cent during 2002-2007, while more than doubling the outlay to Rs. 36,44,718 crore. The document seeks to make the growth inclusive by increasing the outlay for priority sector programmes. The year 2007-08 marked the beginning of the Plan. Among the other objectives of the Plan are growth of over four per cent in the agricultural sector, faster employment creation, reducing disparities across regions and ensuing access to basic physical infrastructure as well as health and education service to all.

The Plan's emphasis on 9 per cent average annual GDP growth would mean that per capita GDP would grow at around 7.6 per cent annum during the 11th Plan. It has set 27 "national targets" across six categories including income and poverty, education, wealth, women and children, infrastructure and environment and sustainability.

Faster and more inclusive growth calls for significant new initiatives in many sectors. The sectoral growth targets in the 11th Plan are 4.1 per cent in agriculture, 10.5 per cent in industry and 9.9 per cent in services as against the 10th Plan targets of 1.7 per cent in agriculture, 8.3 per cent in industry and 9.0 per cent in services. The sectorwise growth targets are briefly discussed below:

**Agriculture**

The Plan document mentions that one of the major challenges of the 11th Plan will be to reverse the deceleration in agricultural growth. This deceleration is the root cause of the problem of rural districts that has surfaced in many parts of the country and as reflected in farmers committing suicide which, reached crisis level in some states. Low farm incomes due to inadequate productivity growth which are often combined with low prices of output and the lack of credit at reasonable rates of interest pushing many farmers into crippling debt. Further, incentives regarding prices, quality of inputs and also weather and pests along with unavailability of proper extension and risk insurance have led farmers to despair. All these problems have led the Planning Commission to give a priority to the agriculture sector.

## Industrial Growth

The 11th Plan aims at raising the rate of growth of the industrial sector to 10 per cent and manufacturing growth to 12 per cent. But the most critical short-term barriers to industrial growth are absence of adequate infrastructure and shortage of skilled manpower. Investment requirements of developing infrastructure are massive and in the range of Rs. 14 lakh crores by 2012. This cannot be met from the public sector alone. Help from Public Private Partnership (PPP) is, therefore, necessary to supplement public sector effort. PPPs are, in fact, increasingly becoming the preferred mode for construction and operation of infrastructure services such as highways, airports and ports.

## Services

The service sector accounts for 55 per cent of GDP and is currently the fastest-growing sector of the economy growing at nine per cent per annum since the mid-1990s. This sector is estimated to have the potential for creating 40 million jobs and generating additional $200 billion annual income by the year 2020.

## Education

Education and skill development is the key to ensuring inclusiveness. A good start has been made in primary education through the Sarve Shiksha Abhiyan, but much more needs to be done to improve the quality of elementary education. The Mid-Day Meal Scheme (MDMS) can be an effective instrument for increasing attendance and also for improving the nutritional status of the children.

Moreover, in the 11th Plan, the country must go beyond primary education to secondary education and higher education. The Plan proposes an almost 10-fold increase in outlay for higher and technical education. The planners have set ambitious targets to attract 15 per cent students passing out

Class XII into higher education by 2012 and 22 per cent by 2017. In Plan, there is more of everything—30 new central universities are to be set up, seven IITs and IIMs, 10 National Institutes of Technology, five research institutes of Science, Education and Research, 20 IITs, two schools of Architecture and 330 colleges in educationally backward districts. This will make a wide network of higher educational institutions.

The 11th Plan document envisions wide-ranging reforms in the way higher education is imparted and much of the fund allocation has been given to the beneficiary institute carrying out structural changes. For instance, the document seeks to raise fees for higher education up to 20 per cent of operational costs, which is merely five per cent at present. According to a member of the Planning Commission, "higher education is highly subsidised and the Plan seeks to reduce this subsidy to improve quality of education." Another proposal is to break up large affiliating universities like Mumbai, Pune and Bangalore into more manageable units. The document says large universities are unsustainable. Osmania University has more than 900 affiliated colleges while Mumbai, Pune and Bangalore universities have around 500. Some of these institutions conduct over 1000 examinations annually.

The Plan paper has called for implementing the semester system and continuous evaluation in all central universities from the coming academic year, i.e. 2008-09. It has also suggested introducing a credit system where students will also be allowed to appear for papers in other streams.

## Healthcare

Healthcare indicators are showing that health is a seriously neglected area. Access to basic services particularly are bad in rural areas. The poor face financial ruin if visited by a serious health event. Total expenditure on health by the Centre and States together is meagre one per cent of GDP. Besides Government, Indian healthcare system also includes a private sector and an informal network of providers of healthcare operating within an unregulated environment with no controls on what services can be provided by whom, in what manner and at what cost, and no standardised protocols to help measure the quality of care and functioning of public health system. The 11th Plan has realised the need for very substantial increase in resource commitment in health. In this regard, the Union Government had launched a National Rural Health Mission (NRHM). It seeks to provide effective health care to the entire rural population in the country with special focus on 18 States which have weak public health indicators.

The Government has approved a package of Rs. 550 crore for upgrading state-run cities offering education in alternative health programmes during 11th Plan period. The Cabinet Committee on Economic Affairs (CCEA) has given its approval for implementation of the scheme of development of the Ayurveda, Yoga and Naturopathy, Unani, Siddha and Homeopathy institutions with a plan outlay of Rs. 550 crore.

## Employment

The 11th Plan has set a target of creating 70 million new work opportunities and reduction in educated unemployment to below five per cent. It has also envisaged a 20 per cent raise in the real wage rate of unskilled workers. There is a concern that rate of growth of employment has slackened in many segments of the economy during the decade of reform. The growth of total employment accelerated from 1.1 per cent in 1993-2000 to 2.8 per cent in 2000-05, the unemployment rate increased from 7.3 per cent in 1999-2000 to 8.6 per cent in 2005-06. Moreover, most of the growth in employment was in the non-agricultural unorganised sector. Employment in the organised sector actually declined. The challenge in the 11th Plan is to create 70 million jobs with increase in organised sector jobs. This will depend on acceleration in manufacturing sector growth especially in labour intensive sectors. However, the 11th Plan document fails to address this issue and in fact relies heavily on the services sector and unorganised sector including construction sector to kick up the slack.

The total public sector outlay during the Plan period has

been pegged at Rs. 36,44,720 crore. Of this, the share of the centre, including the share of the public sector undertakings, would amount to Rs. 21,56,570 crore, while that of the States and Union Territories will be Rs. 14,88,150 crore. At comparable prices, the 11th Plan outlay will be 120 per cent higher than the 10th Plan realisation.

O O O

## 18. Globalization—New Challenges

Globalization refers to the intensification of worldwide social relations which links distant communities in such a way that local happenings between people have been overcome by technology leading to a globalized world. Globalization as a concept fundamentally deals with flavours of various kinds— ideas moving from one part of the world to another, capital shunted between two or more places, commodities being traded across borders, and people moving in search of better livelihoods to different parts of the world. The constant flow of these things creates and sustains world wide inter-connectedness.

Globalization is a multi-dimensional concept having political, economic and cultural manifestations. The impact of globalization is vastly uneven—it affects some societies more than others and some parts of some societies more than others. Similarly, globalization has both advantages and disadvantages.

Globalization has involved greater trade in commodities across the globe, removing the restrictions imposed by different countries on allowing the imports of other countries. The restrictions on movements of capital across countries have also been reduced. Reduction of trade barriers and custom duties due to globalization have led to increased investment and setting up of units by multinational companies in the developing countries. This has resulted in greater employment opportunities for the local inhabitants in these countries. Further, it has led to the penetration of technology in the developing countries, which was earlier a monopoly of the developing countries. Multinational companies are carrying this latest technology with them for these countries.

Globalization has also led to the flow of ideas across national boundaries. The spread of internet and computer-related services is an example of that. On the political front, globalization has given a boost to state capacity with enhanced technology available at the disposal of the state to collect information about its citizens. With this information, state is better able to perform its functions. States have also become more powerful than they were earlier as an outcome of new technology. The consequences of globalization are not confined only to the sphere of politics and economy. It has lead to the rise of a uniform culture or what is called cultural homogenisation. As a consequence people in different parts of the world are eating similar food, adopting similar lifestyles and customs.

Globalization is not without its negative effects and is facing a lot of challenges. It has not led the same degree of increase in the movement of people across the globe. Developed countries have carefully guarded their borders with visa policies to ensure that citizens of other countries cannot take away the jobs of their own citizens. Globalization has allowed the advanced and rich countries of the world to exploit the resources of the developing countries to their advantage. The lifting of trade barriers has led to the entry of foreign investors in the developing countries with huge resources, capital and technology. The local companies find it difficult to compete with them.

Globalization has resulted in the reduction of state capacity. The entry and the increased role of multinational companies all over the world has led to the reduction in the capacity of governments to take decisions on their own. In place of welfare state, it is the market that has become the prime determinant of economic and social priorities. Further, in the name of a global culture what we see is the imposition of western culture on the rest of the world. The culture of the politically and economically dominant society has left its imprint on a less powerful society. This can be seen in the 'Mc Donaldisation' of the world, with cultures seeking to buy into the dominant American dream. This is dangerous not only for the poor countries but for the whole of humanity for it has led to the shrinking of the rich cultural heritage of the countries.

The idea that nation-states, wishing to belong to something bigger, will gather together into big, new entities, each speaking for the culture or civilizations of its component parts, is a long way from being realised. Only in western Europe is there any seriously conceived plan to dissolve existing nation-states into something bigger and even this European experiment may be running into some problems in the future.

Analysts continue to question the concept of nation-states. The late J.N. Dixit wrote that nation-states are becoming irrelevant and that a new imperial age is in the making where power and influence will accrue to entities and communities with advanced technologies and information capabilities, transcending existing geo-political boundaries. Regardless of their size and strength, existing nation-states will have to cope with this transition.

Starting with Margaret Thatcher's free market policies and Reagan's supply side economies in the west to Deng Xieoping's "socialist market economy" in the East, deregulation has transformed the world's economy and, consequently its geo-politics. There is an increasing tendency towards forming regional economic and trade groupings based on preferential trade agreements and mutually agreed tariffs leading to an unprecedented increase in regional trade. These regional groupings are already having a profound impact on the future of the nation-state.

Some thinkers are of the view that the future belongs to region-states based on economic rather than political borders. Ohmae, a Japanese scholar and management consultant, wrote in his book, *The End of the Nation State: The Rise of Regional Economics* that traditional nation-states have become unnatural, even impossible, business units in a global economy.

Region-states are more relevant. What defines them is not the location of their political borders but the fact that they are the right size and scale to be true, natural business units in the present day global economy. Theirs are the borders and connections—that matter in a borderless world.

Ohmae contends that four great forces—capital, corporations, consumers and communication—have combined to the economic power once held by the nation-state as these can all freely cross national borders. However, the real anomaly in Ohmae's argument about the reality of a borderless global economy is that he assumes an identity of interests between what he thinks are the four 'I's'—investment, industry, information technology and the individual consumer. Such an identity of interests is increasingly under pressure from projectionist trade policies on the one hand and strong calls for fair trade on the other. In the past, the Cold War had somehow succeeded in suppressing ethnicity. Events in the last decade of the 20th century starkly highlighted the dangers of the re-emergence of ethnic nationalism, while another major factor is the decline of the nation-state.

An even bigger challenge to the concept of the nation-state is likely to come from the 'mega-media' revolution, spawned by the advances in digital communications and funded by the unbidled power of the internet. The internet has created international cyber-citizens and netsurfers who co-exit in a borderless cyber-state. The proliferation of satellite TV has also dealt a devastating blow to the concept of the nation-state creating a revolution of expectations. The world's rapid transition to globalization, facilitated by the international integration of the production of goods and services, free flow of people, information and capital, giant leaps in communications and the diffusion of power to non-state is bound to have an impact on the future of nation-states. However, the impact may not be entirely negative.

Writing in *Foreign Affairs*, Martin Wolf expressed the view that globalization will not spell the end of the modern nation-state. International economic integration magnifies the difference between good and bad states; failed states, disorderly states, weak states and corrupt states are shunned as the black holes of the global economic system. As the source of order and basis of governance, the state will remain in the future as effective, and will be as essential, as it has ever been.

Another factor for nation-states to contend with is the emergence of powerful multinational cooperations (MNLs) and non-governmental organisations (NGOs).

The demonstrations witnessed at WTO meetings symbolize the power for NGOs to mobilize disparate groups and their energies for a backlash against globalization. It would not be far-fetched to predict that MNCs may eventually raise their own armed guards to protect their commercial interests.

The nation-state is bound to take another form in the new millennium. Moreover, change in the basic building blocks of governance and international relations will be evolutionary rather than revolutionary. While the emerging challenges to the survival of the nation-state are quite huge and strong, the nation-state is likely to prove more durable than is being imagined at present.

Nevertheless, we cannot deny the fact that there is an increased momentum towards interdependence and integration between governments, business and common people in different parts of the world because of globalization.

O O O

# 19. Commonwealth and India

The Commonwealth is a multi-racial and multi-continental community of nations representing over a quarter of mankind.

It virtually stretches across the entire globe and includes some of the most affluent countries like Australia, Canada, UK as also some of the least developed countries like Samoa and Tonga. All these nations recognize the significance of interdependence and commonality of interests.

Unlike the United Nations, the Commonwealth is not structured or governed by elaborate and complex procedures. Nor is it dominated by superpower-politics. It mirrors the diversity of entire comity of nations, but possess a character of informality and a tradition of cooperation. The Commonwealth as it is constituted provides the sort of balance which we all want to see in the world. It is an institution which can, in the course of time, set the pattern for a commonwealth of the whole world.

The present status of the Commonwealth—a friendly association of sovereign independent states, many of which are republics—is much different from the pre-1949 British Commonwealth. Known as Imperial Conference in its original form, it later came to be called British Commonwealth because it was supposed to be an association of all such colonies and dominions which were parts of the British Empire.

India is the largest among the 52 members of Commonwealth and is its fourth largest financial contributor having increased its annual contribution to the Commonwealth Fund for Technical Cooperation, which provides technical assistance to the the Commonwealth developing countries, from £ 800,000 in 2005-06 to £ 850,000 in 2006-07. When India became Republic in 1950, it decided to maintain its membership of the Commonwealth of Nations because of certain advantages like developing friendship and cooperation with other countries. In fact, India regarded the Commonwealth as a means for developing social, cultural, educational and trade links with other nations. Some controversy arose when India became a Republic and still wanted to remain a member of the Commonwealth. Through mutual discussions at the London Conference in 1949, it was agreed that the British Commonwealth should be renamed as Commonwealth of

Nations and transformed into a free association of sovereign independent states which wanted to maintain their traditional links and felt attached to one another by mutual faith and similarity of ideals—though not by any formal alliance or legal treaty.

Since 1950, India has been playing an active role in the Commonwealth relations and it has been instrumental in influencing certain key decisions of the Commonwealth. It has been successful in making the Commonwealth work as a bullwark against racialism. In the 1960s, the strong stand taken by India and some other members of the Commonwealth led to withdrawal of South Africa from the Commonwealth as it practised apartheid—a policy of racial discrimination. It played a leading role in securing the peaceful transfer of power in Rhodesia from white minority government to black majority rule in Zimbabwe.

India's Commonwealth connection paid dividend in 1962 at the time of Chinese aggression. Britain, Canada, Australia and New Zealand expressed their full sympathy and decided to give military aid to India. However, the non-aligned members of the Commonwealth maintained neutrality, and countries like Pakistan and Ghana even opposed the giving of military aid that Britain and some other countries gave to India in 1962-63. It was said that this help was governed more by the desire to contain communism and less by the desire to help a member of the Commonwealth.

In April 1965, UK played an important role in making the two Commonwealth countries India and Pakistan, accept arbitration for settling the dispute over Rann of Kutchch. However, in September 1965 Indo-Pak War, some of the Commonwealth countries decided to maintain strict neutrality, while Britain and some other countries took up a pro-Pakistani stand. This British support for Pakistan, once again, gave rise to the demand for withdrawal from the Commonwealth. They advocated that Commonwealth was not a personal property of Britain. It was an association of equal sovereign states and as such there was no need to withdraw from it because of annoyance with Britain. In 1971, Britain maintained a neutral position in respect of the Indo-Pak War, but at the same time it gave support to the US sponsored resolutions in the Security Council.

Thus the membership of the Commonwealth, so far has not been of much use to India in its political problems and disputes with other countries. India has not been successful in securing support from the Commonwealth countries. Nevertheless, the Commonwealth links have helped India to maintain and develop trade, economic, cultural and educational links with the Commonwealth countries. India has been actively participating in the Commonwealth conferences meetings and programmes. It has been taking keen interest in maintaining and developing friendly relations with other countries of the Commonwealth. In fact, the main things that are going to hold the Commonwealth together in future are not political ties, but economic, technical, educational and scientific cooperation among its members.

India continues to be a member of the Commonwealth because the reasons which influenced the decision to remain in it, even after becoming a sovereign republic still hold good and will do so in future also. In addition to these, the following reasons fully justify the decision to remain in the Commonwealth.

Strengthening of educational and cultural links and the development of additional educational facilities has been on the agenda of almost all the commonwealth meets. The leaders attending CHOGM 1987 meet agreed to create a commonwealth institution to promote cooperation in distance education. They endorsed in principle, a Canadian proposal to establish commonwealth university and college network with various units in Britain, the Mediterranean, the Caribbean, Eastern and Southern Africa, South Asia, West Africa, the Pacific and many other places. India has already taken a big leap forward towards the securing of distance education facilities to the people by establishing in September 1985, the Indira Gandhi National Open University with nearly 100 study centres located across India and acting as the centres catering to the needs of distance education.

The meeting in its communique confirmed its support for the efforts of the UN Secretary General and his special representative to achieve a solution which would leave the Afghan people free to determine their own future, guarantee the right of Afghan refugees to return to their homes safely and which was based on the withdrawal of all foreign troops, strict observance of the principles of non-interference, sovereignty and the non-aligned status of Afghanistan. This stand of Commonwealth fully supported India's view of Afghanistan problem.

India has participated actively in the meetings of various Commonwealth committees and organisations. Then, External Affairs Minister, Yashwant Sinha represented India at the 21st and 22nd meetings of the CMAG held at London and New York in May and September 2003, as well as the special meeting of the CMAG held at Abuja on December 4, 2003, ahead of the CHOGM. At the Abuja CHOGM, India was named for a renewed two-year term as a member of CMAG. India is also a member of the Commonwealth Committee on Terrorism set up in January 2002, as part of the Commonwealth's efforts to build the capacity of member countries in fulfilling their obligations under UN Security Council Resolution 1373. Mr. Yashwant Sinha attended a meeting of the Commonwealth Committee on Terrorism in New York in September 2003. He also represented India at the Ministerial Group on Small States Meeting in Abuja on December 4, 2003. India was also represented at the Ministerial level in the Meeting of Commonwealth Law Ministers in London in May 2003. Then, Minister of Law and Justice and Commerce and Industry, Arun Jaitley, attended the meeting that aimed to draw up principles on good practice governing relations between the executive, legislature and judiciary in the promotion of good governance, the rule of law and human rights.

India also participated at the Senior Official level meeting of Commonwealth Finance Ministers in Brunei in September 2003. During 2003, India was also a member of the Commonwealth Intergovernmental Committee to Review the

Mandates of Commonwealth Organizations. India continued to contribute actively to the ongoing activities of the Commonwealth Fund for Technical Co-operation, Commonwealth Youth Programme, Commonwealth Science Council, and the Commonwealth Foundation and Commonwealth Media Development Fund.

India's successful bid to host the 2010 Commonwealth Games is a reaffirmation of the important role India plays in the Commonwealth. On November 13, 2003 at a meeting of the General Body of the Commonwealth Games Federation in Jamaica, New Delhi won its bid to host the 2010 Games over Hamilton, Canada by a vote of 46-22. The Indian delegation to the meeting was led by then Minister for Youth Affairs and Sports, Vikram Yernia. India will be the second Asian nation after Malaysia to host the Commonwealth Games.

Commonwealth Secretary General, Don McKinnon, visited India in October 2004, in connection with Pre-CHOGM 2005 consultations with various Commonwealth Heads of Government. He met Prime Minister Manmohan Singh and the External Affairs Minister and discussed Commonwealth related issues, including the format of the next CHOGM in Malta in November 2005. He laid emphasis that India's technical cooperation should be increased in line with India's growing stature internationally.

India remains a member of key Commonwealth bodies, including the Executive Committee of the Commonwealth Secretariat, the Standing Committee on Terrorism, and the Commonwealth Advisory Board on Sports. India rejoined the Executive Committee of the Commonwealth Foundation and was elected to become a member of the Accreditation Committee of the Commonwealth Foundation. India has actively participated in the meetings of these Committees and those of the Board of Governors of the Commonwealth Secretariat and the Commonwealth Foundation.

The Minister of Finance attended the Commonwealth Finance Ministers' Meeting in Colombo from September 12-

14, 2006. India also participated in the Commonwealth Youth Ministers'. Meeting in the Bahamas in May 2006 and Commonwealth Public Services Ministers Meeting in Sydney in October 2006. Florence Mugasha, Deputy Secretary-General of the Commonwealth, visited India in September-October 2006. The General Assembly of the Commonwealth Parliamentary Association (CPA) at its annual conference in Abuja, Nigeria elected Somnath Chatterjee, Speaker, Lok Sabha as the President of the CPA and Manmohan Singh, Prime Minister as Vice-Patron of the CPA for a period of one year.

During his three-day visit to India, Commonwealth Secretary General Don Mckinnon had addressed the 53rd Commonwealth Parliamentary Conference on September 26, 2007 in New Delhi. He said, "Despite ebb and flow the journey and the work in progress of democracy in the Commonwealth, that my faith has grown, not weakened, in democracy as the best way of giving people say in how they are governed."

Parliamentary Affairs, and Information and Broadcasting Minister P.R. Dasmunsi headed the Indian Parliamentary delegation in the Commonwealth Parliamentary Association's (CPA) Conference which concluded in September 2007. The CPA's mission is to promote the advancement of parliamentary democracy by enhancing knowledge and understanding of democratic governance.

The Speaker of Lok Sabha inaugurated the Commonwealth Women Parliamentarians (CWP) Conference on September 24, 2007 at the Vigyan Bhawan. The CWP Conference spread over two seasons, which discussed strategies to Overcome Barriers Preventing Women's Equal Participation in Decision-Making, and the Role of Women Parliamentarians in dealing with HIV/AIDS and Poverty Reduction.

The Small Countries' Conference and the Women Parliamentarians' Conference preceded the 53rd Commonwealth Parliamentary Conference was inaugurated by the President of India, Pratibha Devisingh Patil, on September 25, 2007.

India hosted the Commonwealth Parliamentary Association Conference in September 2007. India also hosted the Commonwealth Youth Games in 2008, and will host the Commonwealth Games in 2010 and the Conference of Commonwealth Speakers and Presiding Officers in 2010.

Prime Minister Manmohan Singh was the Chairman of the Commonwealth Expert Group on Democracy and Development, which identified that both development and democracy are worth pursuing in their own right and are mutually reinforcing, and gave a new direction to the Commonwealth. Commonwealth is an international organization that spreads over the North-South divide in the world with the immense diversity of races, religions, cultures, geographical stretches and stages of development. Both developed and developing, and large and small states have equal say in the Commonwealth, which is marked by consensus, informality and discreetness. India has a very close interaction with the Commonwealth Secretariat and is a member of all major Commonwealth bodies, including its Board of Governors, Steering Committee of Commonwealth Connects Programme, the Standing Committee on Terrrorism and Accreditation Committee.

The words of McKinnon highlight the significance of India taking more interest in the affairs of Commonwealth.

"For the first time in its 57-year formal membership of the Commonwealth as a free Republic, India is keen to take the lead role in its affairs. India is pushing the boat out to secure the election as Commonwealth Secretary General of its official candidate, Kamalesh Sharma, currently High Commissioner in London," said Don McKinnon in June, 2007. "It can only be a good thing that India is significantly increasing its interest in the Commonwealth." A list of members of Commonwealth is given below:

1. Antigua & Barbuda
2. Australia
3. The Bahamas
4. Bangladesh
5. Barbados
6. Belize
7. Botswana
8. Brunei Darussalam

9. Cameroon

10. Canada

11. Cyprus

12. Dominica

13. Fiji Islands

14. The Gambia

15. Ghana

16. Grenada

17. Guyana

18. India

19. Jamaica

20. Kenya

21. Kiribati

22. Lesotho

23. Malawi

24. Malaysia

25. Maldives

26. Malta

27. Mauritius

28. Mozambique

29. Namibia

30. Nauru

31. New Zealand

32. Nigeria

33. Pakistan

34. Papua New Guinea

35. St. Kitts and Nevis

36. St. Lucia

37. St. Vincent and the Grenadines

38. Samoa

39. Seychelles

40. Sierra Leone

41. Singapore

42. Solomon Islands

43. South Africa

44. Sri Lanka

45. Swaziland

46. Tanzania

47. Tonga

48. Trinidad & Tobago

49. Tuvalu

50. Uganda

51. United Kingdom

52. Vanuatu

53. Zambia

O O O

## 20. EUROPEAN UNION AND INDIA

India and the European Union have strong ties since the early 1960s. These relations took concrete shape when India played an active role in establishing diplomatic relations with the then six-nation European Economic Community (EEC). India's relationship with other nations of the community matured as the EEC expanded from the six founding members to 25 members in the year 2004.

The European Union (EU) is India's largest trading partner and the second largest source of approved foreign investment. A number of high level visits have been exchanged with Western Europe. India's trade with the countries of the region has grown and there has been a further strengthening of the investment and technology cooperation ties between India and most of the countries of Europe. The diversification and deepening of the economic linkages and continuing political dialogue between the two sides reflect a desire to pursue a closer relationship for mutual benefit. The First India-EU Summit in Lisbon in June 2000 was a milestone in the evolution of this relationship. It highlighted the need for making a joint effort to tap the potential for substantially enhancing trade and investment. Since then there have been several summit-level interactions. For India the Summit was a welcome opportunity to be recognized as a truly global player, receiving the same attention as other major partners of the EU. This summit provided additional impetus to its policy of engaging India on all major issues of interest and concern. It was also a manifestation of the EU's will to engage India as a major player in an emerging multi-polar world and a milestone in EU-India relations. During this Summit the topics discussed covered the entire range of political, economic and global developmental and environmental issues between two democratic, responsible and influential partners on the world stage.

The Fifth EU-India Summit was held in November 2004, in Netherlands. It showed a strong determination to build a solid and broad strategic partnership. The meeting was held in a very friendly atmosphere and the dialogue was open and cordial, and there were many areas of mutual agreement. Leaders officially endorsed the launching of a EU-India 'Strategic Partnership'. This 'Partnership' was more than just the sum of its parts, as it saw a qualitative transformation in the way, which engaged nations as equal partners to work together in partnership with the world at large.

The Sixth EU-India Summit in New Delhi on 7 September 2005 marked a step forward in bringing closer the two global leaders. The Strategic Partnership, issuing a Political Declaration and the decision to implement its dimensions through the adoption of a comprehensive Joint Action Plan which was agreed at the summit provided the momentum to make a decisive step forward. The two sides also signed a Framework Agreement paving the way for the Indian participation in the EU's global satellite navigation project called Galileo. It is an important milestone in EU-India relations and provides a clear roadmap for the coming years.

The seventh EU-India Summit was held in Helsinki, Finland, in October 2006 with leaders from the EU and India. During the summit discussion covered topics such as effective multilateralism, climate change, energy, counter terrorism, and non-proliferation. A key outcome of the summit was an agreement on the establishment of a high-level trade group to study and explore ways to deepen the relationship in trade and investment.

The outcome of the two EU-India summits so far has emphasized the importance of maintaining the momentum towards further trade liberalization and strengthening of the WTO, based on the agenda that adequately reflects the interest of all members of the multilateral trading system. Both sides also agreed that their bilateral cooperation on WTO matters should be put on a more solid basis. The senior officials meet at least twice a year to hold regular, high-level dialogue covering all WTO matters, with a view to identifying common approaches that India and the EU could take on these matters.

Until the beginning of the 1990s, India's trade policy was heavily influenced by the "Swadeshi" (self sufficiency) mentality and the "licence raj" system of restrictions on production and imports. A second generation of reforms was initiated in 1999 to address issues related to lack of competitiveness, poor infrastructure and complex rules and regulations. India has set the ambitious target of an annual 8 per cent GDP growth besides doubling the per capita income over 10 years.

The trade relationship between EU and India, today has gone beyond pure economic interests. India-EU economic cooperation takes place through several horizontal programmes of the EU for Asia as well as India-specific programmes. With a view to promoting business/industry collaboration, India-EU Partenariat has been organised in the past with the help of economic cooperation instruments of EU, e.g. Asia-Invest. The Partenariat took place in New Delhi in March 1999, bringing together over 700 Indian and European companies. This event resulted in 110 agreements concluded between Indian and European Small and Medium Enterprises.

India-EU economic relations are structured on the Agreement on Partnership and Development between India and the EU, which became effective from the beginning of 1994. There is an array of bilateral institutions, which derive their mandate from this Agreement and are used by both sides to engage in formal exchange of views and consultations on matters of bilateral interest. A Joint Commission headed by the Commerce Secretary on the Indian side and Director General, External relations (Relex) on the EU side functions to facilitate bilateral exchange on important policy issues relating to trade and economic relations.

The cornerstone of European Union's link with India lies in its trade and investment relationship. The EU is India's largest trading and investment partner: the bilateral trade constitutes a quarter of India's total trade while the investment is around 14 per cent of India's total foreign direct investment inflows received during the period 1991 to May 2002. India and the EU have consistently played a critical role in creating new international structures, including the World Trade Organization (WTO). The WTO, which came into existence since January 1, 1995, has redrawn the contours of the international trading arena. The WTO agreements relate to bringing about trade liberalization in traditional areas like trade in goods, agriculture produce and textiles as also new areas such as Trade Related Intellectual Property Rights (TRIPS), Trade Related Investment Measures (TRIMS) and services. Lowering of tariffs and doing away with non-tariff barriers are some of the mechanisms through which greater multilateral trade liberalization is being attempted under the auspices of the WTO.

Since the success of the multilateral trading framework rests on cooperation between countries, EU and India have been working together in several areas to bring about greater liberalization within the ambit of WTO. At the Doha Ministerial Conference held in November 2001, the EU was instrumental in launching a new round of comprehensive multilateral trade negotiations to carry the process of trade liberalization further.

The various agreements signed at the conclusion of the Uruguay Round impose certain obligations on individual countries, including India, for compliance within an agreed time frame. The EU is in the process of launching a comprehensive trade and investment development programme in India to further the process of co-operation and share technical expertise on various WTO and other related issues.

In the 1990s, EU co-operation strategy focused on supporting the Indian authorities' own work in certain priority sectors such as primary education and health care, with strong emphasis on helping the poorest and the marginalised sections in society. India is becoming an increasingly active player in an evolving development policy: it is recipient and donor, a user of developmental innovations and an exporter of concepts. India's position as an emerging bilateral donor under the 'Indian Development Economic Assistance Scheme (IDEAS)' paved the way for a fruitful EU-India dialogue on optimal implementation of development co-operation in the third countries.

Development co-operation in the social sectors, and particularly in health and education, is of utmost importance if India is to achieve the Millennium Development Goals.

Traditionally, the EC has supported India's efforts to improve quality of life for the poorest and the disadvantaged members of society. Poverty alleviation has been the central objective in all plans. Since the mid-1990s, EC-India co-operation has been based on identified priority sectors for action: primary education and primary health care. This sectorial approach has been complemented by support for focused projects in fields like rural development, irrigation, forestry, environmental rehabilitation and integrated watershed management.

Education is a priority for EC-India co-operation and the EU's approach is to support the Government's programmes, particularly those that reduce disparities between genders, groups and religions and that favour the poorest and the marginalised.

Building on the varied experience of European Commission-India collaboration under DPEP, the EC signed an agreement with the Government of India in November 2001 to support the Sarva Shiksha Abhiyan programme, the new national initiative for Universalisation of Elementary Education (UEE). Euro 200 million (Rs. 960 crore) were committed for seven years of implementation. The main objective of the EC grant is to reinforce the Government's own efforts to universalize elementary education. EC funds will support the Government of India to deepen and accelerate the process of reform in the Education Sector and to pave the way for new initiatives to provide education to the disadvantaged and the deprived— particularly the girls.

The EC Supported Health and Family Welfare Sector Investment Programme is being implemented since October 1998 with the aim of reforming the health care services, including first referral institutions, by involving the community. The EU supports the fight against the spread of HIV/AIDS in developing countries through a budgetary programme.

The strategy focuses both on awareness rising to prevent drug abuse and on detoxification, rehabilitation and social reintegration of drug addicts. Regional co-operation, including the exchange of experience and expertise is one of the main focuses of the EC interventions.

The EC has so far been the biggest donor in the health sector. Based on the success of SIP, the World Bank, DFID, and various other donors prepared a sector support programme for the Health Sector.

Over the last ten years, the EC has financed 12 Rural Development and Natural Resources Management projects for Euro 240 million in the fields of land reclamation, community forestry actions, irrigation and integrated watershed projects, agricultural production and marketing and horticulture development. Poverty alleviation has been the principal objective of all the projects.

The EC-India Disaster Preparedness Programme is a Euro 10 million project with a four-year implementation period that started in January 2004.

The EU-India Science & Technology (S&T) Co-operation Agreement was signed on 23 November 2001, at the second EU-India Summit in New Delhi, the agreement is implemented by the Directorate-General for Research for the European Commission and by the Department of Science and Technology for the Government of India. Its aim is to facilitate co-operative research and development activities in science and technology fields of common interest for the Community and India.

The EU-India issued "Declaration against International Terrorism" on 23 November 2001, New Delhi. India and the European Union entered a new phase with both committing to tackle terrorism jointly and enhance trade and investment. The then British Prime Minister Tony Blair and Indian Prime Minister Manmohan Singh launched a joint action plan in this regard at the Sixth India-EU Business Summit held in New Delhi. Both EU and India affirm that international terrorism is a threat to peace and security. It constitutes a major challenge to all States and a grave violation of human rights.

Given their tolerant character, open, democratic and multicultural societies are especially vulnerable to terrorist attacks. The struggle against terrorism is not against any community or faith. All states have a responsibility to desist from providing moral, material or diplomatic support to acts of terrorism, and prevent the use of their territory for sponsoring terrorist acts against other States. Both EU and India support the adoption on the basis of international law of decisive measures against all States, individuals, and entities, which harbour, finance, or train terrorists or promote terrorism. There can be no justification for terrorism. EU and India also support the fight against international terrorism, wherever it occurs and regardless of its motives. EU and India reaffirm the central role of the United Nations in the efforts of the international community in the struggle against terrorism.

Besides that, it stressed the importance of strengthening the UN's capacity to play its role in maintaining global peace and development. In this regard, both EU and India have established a Joint Working Group on counter-terrorism and to extend support to the Comprehensive Convention on International Terrorism.

Ever since the adoption of the Joint Action Plan in September 2005, co-operation in the area of civil aviation has been given new thrust. In this context, three rounds of discussions have taken place on a "Horizontal Agreement" proposed by the European Commission and on the possibility of a new technical co-operation programme between India and the EU.

The Ministry of Civil Aviation of India and the European Commission jointly organized the first EU-India Aviation Summit, which brought together more than 300 leading representatives of the Indian and the European Union aviation sectors representing airlines, airports, public authorities, aerospace industries and service providers. The Aviation Summit demonstrated the growing importance of the EU-India relations in civil aviation and the excellent collaboration between EU and Indian industries. Building on the very successful results achieved under the 1999-2006, "EU-India Civil Aviation Cooperation Project", a Joint Action Plan for enhancing future technical and technological co-operation has been prepared. This Joint Action Plan and a new technical co-operation programme that started in 2007 is an important instrument in taking forward cooperation in the wide range of areas of mutual interest of industry, users, regulators and the wider public of both sides, as identified during the EU-India Aviation Summit.

The EU and India are more determined than ever before to broaden and deepen their areas of co-operation. India-EU relations have grown exponentially from what used to be a 'purely trade and business driven relationship' to those covering many other potential areas of mutual interest such as agricultural research, space exploration, etc. The message is clear. Both India and EU need to jointly work together to take their relationship to a higher level of growth.

O O O

## 21. SIXTH PAY COMMISSION REPORT

The Sixth Pay Commission headed by Justice B.N. Srikrishna submitted its recommendations to the Finance Minister in March 2008. It has given a windfall to over 45 lakh Central Government employees. The report has proposed a substantial increase in salaries and allowances for Government employees, while seeking to streamline allowances, pension and medical insurance. The revised package recommended by the Commission, which was set up by the government in 2006, recommends a 42 per cent rise in salaries of the Central Government employees. The hike will add Rs. 12,561 crore to the Centre salary's bill of Rs. 53,497 crore taking it to Rs. 66,058 crore. To this will be added Rs. 18,060 crore in arrears as the hike will be effective from January 1, 2006 and Rs. 1,365 crore towards higher pension.

The Finance Ministry was to consider the report and submit

its recommendations to the Union Cabinet. However, with general elections round the corner, the government has not only accepted the recommendations but has actually increased the emoluments further.

The Commission recommended a Performance Related Incentive Scheme (PRIS) by which employees will be eligible for pecuniary remuneration over and above their pay. The PRIS will be budget neutral. It should also work as a substitute for bonus, honorarium and overtime allowances.

As per Commission's recommnedations the Cabinet Secretary would be the biggest beneficiary with a fixed revised salary of Rs. 95,000 a month, followed by Rs. 85,000 for Secretary. The minimum entry level monthly salary would be Rs. 6,600 in the pay structure that seeks to guard.against any stagnation. The minimum-maximum ratio would be pegged at 1 : 12.

The recommendations, to be considered by the Cabinet, pay special attention to Defence personnel, whose pay has been brought on part with civilian staff, besides making them eligible for special allowance of up to Rs. 6,000 per month. A system has been put in place for a market-driven compensation package to young scientists and posts that require special expertise and professional skills. Enhanced pay scales have been recommended for nurses, teachers, armed constabulary and postmen with whom the common citizen has most frequent interaction. Forest guards are also to get higher pay scales. A better remuneration is also proposed for training academics.

Women and disabled employees have been given special treatment in the report through a recommendation for improved leave and working conditions, while it paves the way for awarding performers through a higher 3.5 per cent rate of increment against the normal 2.5 per cent.

Eighty per cent or more employees would be allowed normal increment at the rate of 2.5 per cent with the high performance during the year being allowed increment at the higher rate of 3.5 per cent. Steps have been recommended to improve the existing delivery mechanisms by more delegation, delaying and an emphasis on achieving quantifiable and concrete end results. The emphasis is on outcomes rather than processes.

However, greater emphasis has been laid on field offices and organisations at the cutting edge of delivery system. To remove stagnation, a system of running pay bands has been postponed for all posts at present existing in scales below that of Rs. 26,000. Four distinct running pay bands have been recommended, one running band each for all categories of employees in group 'B' and 'C', and two running pay bands for Group A posts. Every post, except that of Secretary and Cabinet Secretary would have a distinct grade pay attached to it. The total number of grades have been reduced to 20, spread across four distinct running pay bands as against 35 standard pay scales existing earlier.

A liberal severance package has been devised for employees leaving with service between 15 to 20 years. Higher rates of pension have been recommended for retirees and family pensioners on attaining the age of 80, 85, 90, 95 and 100 years. The Commission has also suggested revision of the commutation table commutation of pension. Higher salaries should, as a natural corollary be about increased efficiency. The Government must learn from the private sector, which is far more efficient because its salaries, perks and promotions are linked to productivity. Market salaries will help to attract talent to the government in competition with the private sector. The Government's aim must be to become a lean organisation. A truly efficient bureaucracy will require less people. Many of the positions in our bureaucracy do not exist in most of the advanced societies. A lot of work done currently by babus can be outsourced to private firms. The Government should reduce the number of clerks, secretaries and peons and downsize itself. The salary hike should be approved only after taking steps to improve organisational competence. If not, the pay hike will be another burden on the economy, which is already slowing down. Moreover, the new package for 20 million

Government employees did little for over a billion Indians. It delivered the carrot but it did not have stick to make employees deliver and be more accountable.

The main points of the recommendations of the report are:

- Minimum entry-level pay Rs. 6,600; Cabinet Secretary, Chief of Army, Navy and Air Force to get fixed pay of Rs. 90,000.
- Number of grades reduced to 20 from 35. Each of four pay bands (two for Group A, one each for Groups B and C) to have grade pay, minimum of Rs. 1,800 per month, max. of Rs. 13,000.
- Group D scrapped, employees to be retrained assimilated into Group C.

## Annual Increment

- 2.5 per cent for all employees.
- 3.5 per cent for 20 per cent of 'performing' Group A officers. Date of increment—July 1.

## Pension

- Pension to be paid at 50 per cent of average emoluments or last pay drawn, delinked from service length.
- Higher rates of pension at the age of 80, 85, 90, 100.
- Full family pension for 10 years if employee dies within 10 years of retirement.

## Working Hours

- Five-day week to continue.
- Concessions for women: staggered working hours, child care leave, enhanced maternity leave of 180 days.
- Only 3 national holidays—January 26, August 15 and October 2. No gazetted holidays; restricted holidays up from 2 to 8.

## Government Bill

- Hike to cost Rs.12,561 crore in 2008-09.

- Additional one-time burden of Rs. 18,060 crore for arrears.

## Allowances

- Most allowances to be doubled.
- City compensatory allowance (CCA) to be merged with transport allowance and increased four times.
- House Rent Allowance (HRA) raised for A, B1, B2 cities to 20 per cent; C and other cities to 10 per cent.
- Monthly education allowance to be Rs. 1,000 per child, up from Rs. 50.

## Defence

- Defence forces on a par with civilians in pay and grades. Special military pay of Rs. 6,000 up to the rank of brigadier.

## Health

- New medical scheme for employees and pensioners, insurance scheme to meet pensioners' OPD needs in non-CGHS areas.

## Regulators

- Salary of chiefs of regulatory bodies, including SEBI, TRAI and IRDA, up to Rs. 3 lakh per month.

## Performance-related Sops

- Market driven pay for young scientists and technologists.
- Performance-linked incentive plan to replace existing annual bonus, honorarium, overtime.
- Person stagnating at pay band peak for over year to get next higher band.
- Contract for high-skill posts.

# II. INDIA TODAY

## 1. SIXTY YEARS OF INDIA'S ARMED FORCES AND THEIR MAJOR OPERATIONS

The armed forces of India, besides being responsible for defending the country from external attack, have a secondary task of defending the country from internal threat. In addition to these basic roles, the armed forces have all along been called out as "aid to civil authorities", for restoring law and order and for carrying out humanitarian tasks like flood relief. These aspects can be highlighted to give an overall picture of what the army people do in peace-time. Every year, floods ravage different parts of the country. Arrangements and the necessary wherewithal for meeting these exigencies have not been built to date, and use of combat bridging equipment, boats, helicopters and transport aircraft of the IAF act as an auxiliary arrangement along with the manpower of the Armed Forces.

The contribution of armed forces in the field of games and sports including mountaineering, at national level, has been considerable and deserves mention. Another achievement besides the profession of arms is the contribution to the expeditions to Antarctica, where the armed forces have provided leadership and personnel for these difficult missions.

The Indian armed forces have had to face many conflicts. These commenced in the formative years with the beginning of the Kashmir problem—the three major conflicts—one in 1962 against the Chinese, and the Indo-Pak Wars of 1965 and 1971.

These conflicts brought to light certain major aspects of

political compulsions and lost opportunities. Counter insurgency is the biggest threat to civil society in the present-day world. India's contribution to International Peace-Keeping with the UN forces is quite noteworthy. The UN's role as a peace-keeper may present future conflicts at various flashpoints, provided the belligerent agree to the UN intervention and accept the deployment of a UN Peace-Keeping Force in the conflict zones.

The machination of Pakistan in 1947, in a bid to woo some of the princely states including Jaipur and Jodhpur, involved India's armed forces to get these states merged in the Indian Union. Also Hyderabad and Junagadh, with no boundary with Pakistan, attempted to secede to Pakistan. But the intervention of the armed forces saved them for accession to India. The Nizam had to be suppressed by using the armoured division, and the Nawab of Junagadh fled to Pakistan while his state joined the Indian Union. In fact, Pakistan continued to include Junagadh in its map for some years.

The annexation of Gilgit by Pakistan, with the connivance and active participation of the British officers serving with the Gilgit Scouts is most revealing and shows up on which side the outgoing British Army Officers, who were serving as part of the State forces of the Maharaja of Jammu and Kashmir, whom they readily betrayed. With a unified command of Indian and Pakistani forces still functioning, this act of treachery could not have occurred without full knowledge and tactic support of the British Command.

The conflict in Kashmir in 1947-48 had several background reasons. Firstly, though not publicized by India or Pakistan, both sides recognised the strategic importance of Kashmir. Besides being a very valuable chunk of real estate, Kashmir was a Muslim majority state and thus aroused Pakistan's desire to annex it. To India, Kashmir being a part of the secular Indian state, was meant to boost India's secular image, where a Muslim predominant state could thrive as a part of Hindu majority but a secular country.

Jawaharlal Nehru who was delighted to have Kashmir as part of India declared: "...Kashmir because of its geographical position, with frontiers merging with three countries, namely the Soviet Union, China and Afghanistan, is intimately connected with the security and international contacts with India. Economically also, Kashmir is intimately related to India."

A former Pakistani army general is quoted as having stated: "...one glance at the map was enough to show that Pakistan's military security would be seriously jeopardized if Indian troops came to be posted along kashmir's Western border."

Liaquat Ali Khan in a letter to Nehru pointed out in December 1947: "The security of Pakistan is bound up with Kashmir and ties of religion, cultural affinity, and economic interdependence bind the two together... ." A cease-fire agreed to by India at a stage when it was in a position to throw out Pakistani troops from Kashmir has left it with a problem which has so far defied a solution.

The 1965 war can well be called a large scale skirmish along the border. If there were any strategic objectives, neither India nor Pakistan launched an effective thrust which got anywhere near a worthwhile objective. Some important tactical features like the Haji Pir Pass and point 13620 overlooking Kargil were captured by India, only to be handed back by our politicians. The Point 13620 was captured again by Indian forces in 1971 with considerable loss of lives of our attacking troops. We lost an excellent officer, Major Vetrinthan, Vir Chakra, and a number of men. It is the hand of politicians which will remain smeared with this wasteful bloodshed of our soldiers.

The 1971 Indo-Pak war was decisive. From March to November 1971, the Indian armed forces prepared a campaign to liberate East Pakistan. The balloon went up in early December with a pre-emptive air strike by Pakistan in the West. The Indian army poised for an offensive in the East, and holding actions in the West, unleashed its forces to capture East Pakistan, and Bangladesh was born on December 16, 1971.

In this campaign, the most spectacular offensive was by 4 Corps under General Sagat Singh supported by a force of helicopters under Air Commodore Chandan Singh. The generalship displayed by the GOC 4 Crops does the Indian army proud. The daring use of helicopter airborne troops across the Surma river in Sylhet, and across the Meghna river, hastened the decisive end of the war. A country was liberated, 93,000 prisoners of war were taken, which is by far more than any number in the wars after World War II. Huge quantities of arms, ammunition and equipment were captured.

After 1971, the Army and the IAF, already engaged in the counter-insurgency in the North-East found themselves moved to the insurgency situation in the Punjab. Operation Blue Star was a black mark on the clean record of the Army, and the alienated Sikh community. However, time and measures have not fully healed the wounds of these gallant people.

From April 1984 to date, a war situation prevails in the Siachen Glacier. Both India and Pakistan have lost over 2,000 soldiers each and spent approximately Rs, 15,000 crore each. To what avail, one would ask except ego satisfaction of leaders on both sides?

The operation of the Indian Peace Keeping Forces in Sri Lanka was a disaster. Having been initially committed to peace-keeping, our forces were not equipped or prepared to undergo combat operations with the LTTE. Resultantly, we suffered avoidable casualties and a general feeling of this commitment not being our war, prevailed. A delayed pullout saved further involvement in this operation.

O O O

## 2. INTERACTIVE MEDIA COMES OF AGE IN INDIA

Beginning in the form of "letters to the editor", a column hidden in some obscure corner, newspapers now offer the reader more 'space' in a daily, seeking to create brand loyalty and attract advertisers.

As more newspaper columns are devoted to local and national or even world problems, personal interface ideas from their readers are welcomed by the newspapers which are often organised by the newspapers on a selected theme on which the readers are expected to write and send their views. Experts in newspapers welcome the trend saying it would lead to more people-oriented media in the newspaper.

The media's initiatives for an interface with the readers are encouraging signs. In fact, this kind of interface should have begun long ago, says Dr. N. Bhaskar Rao, Chairman, Centre for Media Studies.

With delicate balance of power in the country gradually shifting from the government and the executive to the people and the public opinion they generate, the role of news media has become even more significant. That is how the agenda-setting role of media has become important.

Considering the immense reach and impact of print media, the newspapers must realise their responsibility vis-à-vis the general public. Some leading newspapers have started many interactive columns which provide readers a platform to express their views and opinions on given topics—university life, problems related to the youth, environment, power supply, education and drugs abuse, etc.

Almost all newspapers, big or small, have also started advisor-columns, where readers seek answers to questions they would not normally ask even their parents and friends—matters relating to relationships and health. Some others have gone to the extent of direct interaction with their readers by holding meetings with residents of particular colonies in various cities to hear their problems.

Such activities really instill confidence among the people. They face a lot of problems at the neighbourhood level and if big newspapers take up these matters, then surely the chances of their grievances being redressed become manifold.

After all it is the duty of the media to take up people's cause. Direct interactive sessions with people is also a part of information gathering. So it is definitely a part of any news organisation's primary job.

Total commercialisation of media in India had led to less of people-oriented activities. There was a lot of concentration on politics. So these are welcome changes and initiatives in the right direction. Such interactive sessions also help increase the business of the newspapers by making them attractive advertisers.

Advertising revenues are the financial backbone of a newspaper. As a result of slashing of corporate advertising budgets these years, newspapers have been witnessing a snowballing effect more than television.

The proliferation of satellite channels in recent years has further resulted in the fragmentation of advertising spending. All this means a decline of 15-20 per cent in advertising outlays on press. Newspapers in India have increasingly become politics centric neglecting the other areas. Therefore, there has been a glut of politics. But the people today are more concerned about things like gas, water, power supply and the drainage system in the locality.

If big newspapers come forward to hear the problems of the readers directly, then it certainly instills confidence among the people and creates accountability. If in the process advertisers also pitch in, then that can be taken as a bonus. That should not be taken as a primary objective of such interactive sessions.

Female readership of newspapers, particularly in the southern states of the country, has also witnessed a distinct growth over the last few years. Therefore, initiating activities in areas which concern the women or the household also helps create a loyalty for the newspaper among them. Readership among females is a key variable to growth of newspapers. The growth rate in readership and circulation did not keep up in the 1970s and 1980s.

O O O

# 3. APPROPRIATE USE OF ARTICLE 356

Article 356 of the Constitution of India should be seen in a new progressive light. There is a need for a law which should consider non-performance by States as something to be held accountable. The Union Government has an overall responsibility to ensure the progress of the country. If a given State continues to perform at a low level for two or three years running, then it becomes a fit case for action under Article 356 to ensure that India remains a socio-economic democracy, without which political democracy ceases to have any meaning.

Provision and contents of Article 356 in the Constitution are specific to our country. For its origin one has to go back to the Government of India Act, 1935, which provided that in the event of a breakdown of the constitutional machinery, the Governor General could assume all or any power vested in federal authorities. Similar provision existed in the case of provinces, where in the case of a breakdown of constitutional machinery, the government could by proclamation assume all powers vested in or exercisable by any provincial authority.

India's Constitution provides three types of emergencies:

(i) When the security of India is threatened (Article 352);

(ii) When a State government is not functioning in accordance with the provision of the Constitution (Article 356); and

(iii) When the financial stability or credit of India is threatened (financial emergency).

Article 188 says that the Governor of a State could assume powers at his discretion as may be given out in the proclamation, and if he is satisfied that a grave emergency has arisen which threatens the peace and tranquillity of the State, subject to concurrence of the President who should also feel that the law and order situation is grave and hence the federal government should take over the governance until next elections.

Articles 39, 39A, 41, 42, 43, 45, 47, 48 and 49 of the Constitution clearly outline the directions which may be given to the Chief Minister of a State in furtherance of the objective of economic and social democracy along with the maintenance of political democracy. Failure in the areas like education, health, provision of drinking water, job avenues, development of agriculture and allied items should be good reasons to threaten the State Government with Article 356.

The Seventh Schedule of the Constitution clearly spells the subjects to be dealt with by the States in social and economic sectors—public health, agriculture, rural infrastructure like roads, irrigation, industries, etc. The Chief Ministers of States are to see that social and economic aspects of the democracy could be achieved only by the constructive co-operation of the State Governments.

What happens when a State fails to achieve its objectives? It will be highly retrogressive. Things could go worse, particularly if the elections are far away.

Our Constitution is quite a good one. It has all the ideals that a Constitution should have. But the time has come when it should be made more practicable. The very election system is thoroughly bad. To get elected to the Parliament one needs a lot of money. Many rich dullards happen to be law makers. There is no minimum qualification required for becoming a law maker. Neither a law degree nor any research qualification. Some of our law makers are interested in politics as it gives them power to make money by hook or crook, or else they will not spend the money on election. Their first effort is to recover the money spent on being elected and then reap rich harvest.

It is desirable that the law makers should be political philosophers of repute who may be invited to seek election but the government should meet their expenses. Law makers should be initially chosen by educational bodies or professionals like the economists, or even scientists and engineers of standing and then let them get elected.

O O O

# 4. STRATEGIC CONCEPTS OF NATIONAL SECURITY

India's security instruments, the defence services, paramilitary forces, intelligence and police services are rigidly compartmentalised. Its strategic minds are confined to the backroom of the Indian Institute of Strategic Studies, and totally absent from government. "So the first and greatest threat to Indian security was a smug Indian introverted swadeshi mind without clear strategic concepts and kneejerk emotional reactions, and crippling babudom," says A.D. Modie, a former ICS officer.

Mr. Modie first wants us to pose cogently, present and future perceptions of threats to India's security, internal and external—both inseparably linked. The internal threats, which are no less than the external ones may be categorised as follows:

(i)   The absence of national security on the political agenda of the main parties;

(ii)  The absence of defence specialisation among policy-makers;

(iii) Financial undiscipline of Centre and State governments;

(iv)  India ranks 138th among 193 states like the backward Central African states.

The fundamental internal threats of the future arise from extensive failures of rural development, urban decay and infrastructural breakdown. To deal with them, there is a need for national consensus among the major political parties for more effective and transparent governance, agenda for globalisation, measures for greater international competitiveness and co-operation, specially in the context of WTO. Social development in education, health, infrastructure, and security must be prioritised.

Only such a consensus can yield speedier responses to basic international problems, an advantage that China has over India. The perceptions of external threats are fundamentally based on geography. There is a blue water threat in the entire Indian Ocean area at three strategic points: the Strait of Malacca, the Cape of Good Hope (now Suez too) and the Persian Gulf, the centre of world's oil supplies.

From India's point of view, this involves the security of ports and nearby oil and nuclear bases, and the sea lanes and minesweeping; threats to its outlying islands including the Andaman and Nicobar Islands and to its neighbours like Mauritius and Sri Lanka. Here, there are also shared trade and oil security interests with the USA, ASEAN, Japan and South Africa.

A sea blue water shield is needed to protect the blue water arena. It will be primarily navy, air, and combined operations of forces with missile capability for Indian Ocean area north of 30 degree latitude. It would be wise for India to consider this area a shared responsibility with powers which share a common trade, oil and security interest here and not treat the Indian Ocean as an Indian lake.

A sky blue air superiority missile shield in the Indian sub-continent and the Indian Ocean area is also needed, as air superiority has been a pre-condition for all successful military operations since World War II. A brown western front army and air shield, supplemented by the navy shield on the Arabian Sea flank, perhaps India's only large scale land, water, air operations are of the old order, involving division and corps scale operations in an integrated large command and communications system is also needed. It would stretch from the Arabian Sea to Jammu & Kashmir.

We need a plains-based Panzer army with superior air power for the defence of the north-west frontier from Gujarat to the Punjab and J&K, supplemented by the naval power on the Arabian Sea flank. The western theatre may be the last arena of the old large land army concept, with supplementary arms. Only now it is far more reinforced with electronic, digital communications systems and weaponry, with a sophisticated command and communications structure.

Lastly, there is the arena of deterrence with missile and nuclear power. This will only come into play when all other military and diplomatic efforts fail, and for the very survival of the nation and the state. This will be medium and long-range stratospheric strike power with its command and communication structure centre in the chief state executive. Tactical missile weaponry may be used in other operations, at non-political operational command levels.

A white mountain shield from the Karakoram to NEFA, based on mobile brigade-size combined operations strike units involving the army, the air force, the paramilitary forces like the BSF and ITBP with a strong communications, and supply chains is another necessity. These should preferably be based below 12,000 ft using the Himalayas as the natural fortress, tactical features and the requisite firepower. Unlike 1962, air/missile power should be used to destroy hostile forces at the other side of the Indo-Tibetan passes, in the event of hostilities.

In this area much will depend on the future diplomatic rapprochement with China, with or without boundary settlements, to minimize the cost of conflict in the Himalayan region, and convert it into a region of trade and hydroelectric power for mutual benefit.

All these will involve fundamental rethink and design of India's defence administration including a clearer definition of the roles of the political establishment, the bureaucracy, including the proposed defence council, of which service chiefs will be full time members. The new regime will need a far more integrated intelligence service which will provide a cohesive feedback system of high sophistication and secrecy on military and economic threats to deal with more sophisticated terrorist attacks, across the border and within.

This is a common concern with all India's neighbours. The most vulnerable places will be the cities and the critical infrastructure areas, including nuclear, oil, and gas installations. Small terrorist groups can now use weapons of mass destruction—chemical and biological, with devastating effects. In future such terrorist attacks will be much more crippling than conventional warfare.

Far more strategic inputs from the chiefs of staff (and possibly a future joint chiefs of staff) with direct responsibility for all military strategy, weaponry, supplies, and organisation is needed, for which the chiefs of staff should be assisted by a highly competent director general of technical services.

This will leave the defence ministry bureaucracy supported by an economic advisor with responsibility for working out the optimum use of available resources, coordinating military and terrorist intelligence, and liaisoning with Ministry of External Affairs in all diplomatic matters concerning India's security. Good diplomacy can reduce security costs and risks.

The defence bureaucracy need not have any direct role in postings and transfers in the defence services. This power should rest with the command concerned accountable to the Defence Minister. The three service chiefs may consider the need for smaller brigade-size operational units with air complements in all commands except the brown western shield. The navy may lead the Southern command with amphibian and airborn units of brigade-size strike forces. If for any reason, the government cannot come to favourable decision on a joint chief of staff for the three services, the chiefs may consider joint commands and the operations at the deputy chief level on pragmatic grounds, in addition to the joint chiefs committee.

## Weapons Backup

While a partial backup from Russia rupee funds may be available to India for the next decade, India needs to build its own weaponry base, and bring about a major diplomatic rapprochement with the US, Japan, and China, with whom there are many commonly shared interests.

In that direction, a medium to long-term objective should be the early formation of SAARC Common Market (in which India, the largest member still has the highest tariffs), and a later fusion with ASEAN, with India leading in that direction earlier.

The Gulf countries may also be considered for an Indian Ocean Economic Community.

The goodwill of the smaller neighbour should be a primary diplomatic objective, in the spirit of the Gujral doctrine. Among our neighbours, Afghanistan has been both a threat and a zone of constant concern and needs to be carefully watched. Relations with Myanmar, Bangladesh, ASEAN, Iran and the Gulf states call for a new orientation, political and economic.

Last but not the least, we face the Pakistan problem. Perhaps, half of the Pakistan problem lies in Washington. When the Washington factor is neutralised, relations may improve on all the three sides. The other half lies in the good sense and common economic and political interests of the two people. More so, with Pakistan's economic plight, and the ethnic fundamentalism powder keg of Afghanistan.

O O O

# 5. INDIA—MOST PREFERRED FDI DESTINATION IN ASIA

For past one decade or so, Multinational Companies (MNCs) from all over the world are flocking to India for investment either to exploit the large consumer market of India or to use it as a Business Process Outsourcing (BPO) centre to reduce the costs of operation. The World Investment Report 2006, released by the United Nations Conference on Trade and Development (UNCTAD) has put India in the fifth most preferred investment destination in the world for foreign money. During the year 2007-08, India received US $6.8 billion in FDI. The growing preference for India to invest money can be easily made out from the given information.

In 2008-09, India is expected to receive as much FDI as it received in first ten years of liberalisation. From the point of India being just one of the countries under consideration for investment, we have reached a point where India is the most preferred destination for investment.

The following factors are responsible for this change in attitude.

- India continues to remain a favourite destination due to strong economic growth—eight per cent plus GDP growth and new target of 10 per cent.
- Growing purchasing power of the Indian consumers and hence a regular increase in demand.
- Change in attitude of Government and industries towards foreign investment—creating a liberal atmosphere.
- Sustained pace of economic reforms irrespective of the changes in the political scenario of the country.
- Recent policies such as opening up of the retail industry to single-brand players, permitting FDI in industries like infrastructure and communication and raising the permitted level of foreign ownership in communications also helped India in getting foreign investments.

Prime Minister Manmohan Singh has said that India needs over US $150 billion in infrastructure investment in the next few years. Finance Minister, on his part, has warned that poor infrastructure is cutting economic growth in India by as much as 2 per cent each year. Manufacturing units in the country constantly face power shortages. Logistics operations are impeded by poor roads, and delays at ports. It takes almost 10 times longer to load and unload a ship at an Indian port as compared to best of class ports world-wide. Fixing gaps in infrastructure, including roads, power plants and ports, may help accelerate growth to 10 per cent annually from 8 per cent today. But, this requires a huge investment. This large scale investment cannot be funded by the government alone. Even the private sector in India does not have enough funds to make these investments in near future. Therefore, we have to be dependant on investment by foreign companies, i.e., Foreign Direct Investment (FDI).

The country plans to increase infrastructure spending on roads, ports and telecom by 24 per cent to $22 billion in the current financial year. However, this is still embarrassingly small as compared to the $150 billion China spends on infrastructure annually. Apart from providing money for investment, getting FDI leads to many other advantages like the following:

(a) Foreign investors bring new technologies of manufacturing with them.

(b) Domestic companies get benefitted from the managerial abilities and techniques of foreign partners.

(c) It increases competition in the domestic market and hence improvement in quality and variety of products available to consumers.

(d) As FDI leads to creation of new assets and manufacturing facilities, it helps in reduction of unemployment.

(e) Most of foreign investments is made in export oriented industries which leads to substantial increase in exports.

(f) As FDI is investment for substantially long period, it shows the real strength of the economy.

Though India has been tipped as the hot destination for FDI, the country still has a long way to go to come near to other Asian countries. Some facts about FDI received by other countries will make the picture clear as to where India stands:

1. In 2006-07, as against India's FDI of $5.5 billion, China received $72 billion, Hong Kong $35.9 billion and Singapore $20.1 billion in FDI.

2. India gets only 0.8 per cent of total global FDI flows.

3. Even within developing countries, India gets less than 3 per cent of the total FDI flows to developing countries.

Though, all the macro fundamentals determining FDI flows are going good for India, FDI flows to India have been low as already mentioned. This indicates that India lacks in some of the crucial factors determining FDI flows, mainly infrastructure, labour reforms, and quality of governance. Some major factors of low FDI in flow are mentioned below:

If the issues are addressed by the policy makers, Indian economy will realise its true potential and India will become an economic superpower in real sense. The major problem during 2008-09 has been the slowdown in America and Europe due to which there was a flight of capital from India. The situation will improve when the global economic scenario improves.

O O O

# 6. E-GOVERNANCE IN INDIA

The Indian Government is using Information Technology (IT) to facilitate governance. The IT industry is doing its bit to help as public-private partnerships have become the order of the day. The last two-three years have seen e-governance drop roots in India. IT enables the delivery of Government services as it caters to a large base to people across different segments and geographical locations. The effective use of IT services in Government administration can greatly enhance existing efficiencies, drive down communication costs, and increase transparency in the functioning of various departments. It also provides citizens with easy access to tangible benefits, be it through simple applications such as online form filling, bill sourcing and payments, or complex applications like distance education and tele-medicine. This is why almost every state has an IT policy in place with the aim of evolving itself from being an IT-aware to an IT-enabled Government. State Governments are fast recognising the benefits of an IT-enabled working environment. As of now, e-governance projects are being run only in certain departments. This approach will gradually be extended to all departments, leveraging the power of IT to streamline administrative functions and increase transparency.

It has a vital role to play in all transactions that the Government undertakes. It helps the government cut red-tapism, avoid corruption, and reach citizens directly. Such initiatives help citizens learn about the various policies, processes and helplines that the Government offers. The Governments of Canada, Singapore and Switzerland have implemented such portals, and set the benchmarks in this regard. With the help of IT, the Government can process citizen to government transactions such as the filing of tax returns, death and birth registration, land records, etc.

A strong technology infrastructure can help central and state governments deliver a comprehensive set of services to citizens. Microsoft is working with several state governments to help evolve a long-term technology blueprint for IT infrastructure. It is working with various departments of the central government, and has undertaken several projects and initiatives with state governments as well.

As far as e-governance projects are concerned, the Government is gradually changing its role from an 'implementer' to a 'facilitator and regulator.' It is encouraging private sector participation in e-governance projects, so more projects in e-governance based upon the Public Private Participation (PPP) model should come about in the near future.

Agriculture, power and education are fields where the government makes use of IT to provide services to citizens. The revenue collection department is in the process of using information technology for applications such as income tax. The following are some notable examples:

(i) A Kolkata-based hospital leverages e-governance for tropical medicine. The hospital employs tele-medicine to assist doctors in rural areas as they analyse and treat panchayat residents. This method does away with patients having to travel all the way to Kolkata for treatment. Patients feel better being examined in their own village. Using tele-medicine, the hospital is able to dispense its expertise to far-flung districts. The patient goes for an examination to the local doctor in the panchayat. This doctor is in contact via a voice and data connection with a doctor at the hospital for tropical medicine. Thus, the panchayat resident gets the benefit of being treated by both a local doctor and a hospital specialist.

(ii) The Karnataka Government's 'Bhoomi' project has led to the computerisation of the centuries-old system of handwritten rural land records. Through it, the revenue department has done away with the corruption-ridden system that involved bribing village accountants to procure land records; records of Right, Tenancy and Cultivation Certificates (RTCs). The project is expected to benefit seventy lakh villagers in 30,000 villages.

(iii) In Gujarat, there are web-sites where citizens log on and get access to the concerned government department on issues such as land, water and taxes.

(iv) In Hyderabad, through e-Seva, citizens can view and pay bills for water, electricity and telephones, besides municipal taxes. They can also avail of birth/ death registration certificates, passport applications, permits/licences, transport department services, reservations, Internet and B2C services, among other things.

(v) e-Choupal, ITC's unique web-based initiative, offers farmers the information, products and services they need to enhance productivity, improve farm-gate price realisation, and cut transaction costs. Farmers can access the latest local and global information on weather, scientific farming practices, as well as market prices at the village itself through this web portal—all in Hindi. e-Choupal also facilitates the supply of high quality farm inputs as well as the purchase of commodities at the farm.

## UN E-Government Survey 2008

The United Nations E-Government Survey 2008, released recently, has stated that India has fallen from a rank of 87 in 2005 to 113 in 2008 on e-government readiness.

According to the UN E-Government Survey 2008, India has slipped 26 places in the last three years and been overtaken by countries like Maldives (ranked 95), Sri Lanka (101) and even Iran (108). However, they too, have themselves slipped from their 2005 rankings.

Sweden surpassed the United States as the leader in the overall E-readiness index. With Denmark, Norway coming in second and third respectively, the US slipped to fourth place.

○ ○ ○

# III. INDIA AND THE WORLD

## 1. INDO-US RELATIONS

India-United States military ties have advanced rapidly since September 11, 2001. US charge d'affairs Robert Blake said in August 2004 that new military ties with India was a key plank of its emerging policy in South Asia. The US has sold the much-needed 12 Raytheon AN-TPQ/37 artillery fire (Weapon Locating) radar ($190 million) and Indian Army, Navy and Air Force have conducted exercises with their US counterparts.

### Defence Co-operations

Defence co-operation between the two nations is making measured strides. This includes the American Navy possibly placing a ship repair unit in Kochi, co-operation in military medicine, a regional HIV/AIDS prevention programme and adoption of several US principles and practices in New Indian military establishments. The US Central Command, that covers Pakistan and regions that are of vital interest to India, will open its door to India. India's Net Assessment office (which studies long-term strategic issues and US has one as well), and the Indian National Defence University are receiving inputs from the US Military in doctrinal matters.

The US joint staff continues to sponsor expert visits by officers from India's Joint Defence Staff to various US military installations including their key policy centres and joint training institutions. These visits will help the Indian military gain lessons on jointness which can be incorporated into India's nascent joint staff system. Indian Navy ships Sharada and Sukanya relieved the US Cowpens and escorted US ships in the straits of Malacca and protected them against terrorist attacks and pirates on the high seas. This was also followed by several joint search and rescue exercises as well as the Malabar exercises in the Arabian Sea.

## PM-President Meet

President George Bush and Prime Minister Manmohan Sing set out the roadmap for Indo-US strategic partnership at their September 21, 2004 meeting in New York.

This meeting celebrated the completion of the first NSSP phase. The NSSP is combined with engagement with the private sector through the US-India Economic Dialogue and the High Technology Co-operation Group, which together address a broad array of trade, economic and security issues. The NSSP was announced by George Bush on January 12, 2004, a follow-up to the Bush-Bajpyee November 2001.

Under the first phase, the US agreed to loosen controls over space and dual-use technologies, while India would tighten its regulations on the transfer of sensitive items to third parties. The conclusion of the first phase of the NSSP marks a major milestone in the Indian effort over the last three decades to break out of the isolation from international high-technology commerce after the first nuclear test in May 1974.

The September 21, 2004 joint statement by the Prime Minister, Manmohan Singh and the US President George W. Bush, and the agreement on Phase I of the NSSP which preceded on September 17, were presented by US and Indian officials as the "beginning of a new era of co-operation and trust."

Following are some major achievements of NSSP:

1. Removing the Indian Space Research Organisation (ISRO) headquarters from the Department of Commerce's Entity list;

2. Reducing the licensing requirements for exports to the ISRO subordinates remaining on the Entity list by approximately 80 per cent by removing such requirements for 'EAR 99' and '999' items exported to those facilities; and

3. Applying a "Presumption of approval" for all dual-use items subject to multilateral and unilateral controls, except those controlled by the Nuclear Suppliers' Group, for export to the "balance of plant" portions (non-reactor related end users) of nuclear power facilities which are currently under International Atomic Energy safeguards (Tarapur 1&2 and Rajasthan 1&2).

## High Technology Groups

A meeting of the High-Technology Cooperation Group (HTCG) between India and the US, was held on 11th October 2004 to set the stage for the first meeting of the NSSP Implementation Group. In a move that seeks to raise the bar on the India-US strategic relationship, the two countries have agreed to set up a politico-military dialogue mechanism in the defence technology sector. This was decided at the third meeting of the HTCG held in Washington on November 18, 2004. HTCG is a unique public-private partnership that focuses on what is one of the defining characteristics of Indo-US relations.

## Defence Policy Group

The Indo-US defence cooperation took an upward turn after the 9/11 incident with both countries reviving the apex level Defence Policy Group (DPG) jointly headed by senior civilian officials from both Defence Ministries. The DPG is the highest military level interaction between the two sides and sets the broad policy guidelines for future cooperation and collaboration. Subsequently, three Executive Steering Groups (ESG), one for each service, were formed to implement the broad guidelines laid down by the DPG for further bilateral defence ties. APG meeting was held in New Delhi on 1-3 June, 2004 to discuss the entire gamut of bilateral relations including strategic issues, joint exercises, training and acquisition.

## Missile Defences

India is desperately looking for an effective air defence system against nuclear threats from China and Pakistan. India has been negotiating to acquire US Patriot Air Defence

Systems and is keen to acquire the Arrow-2 anti-missile system from Israel. The United States has offered to sell its Patriotic Missile Defence System to India. The offer was made during the discussions between US and Indian officials on the sidelines of the United Nations General Assembly in September 2004. The US Secretary of Defence Donald Rumsfield, during his December 2004 visit also offered to sell the Patriot Anti-Missile System. The offer came after the assurances provided by India, completing a predetermined "sequence of events" within the framework of the strategic partnership dialogue.

India is interested in the Patriot Advanced Capability-III or PAC-3, the latest version. The Patriot is an air-defence system which can defeat both attack aircraft and tactical ballistic missiles.

## Space Cooperation

For the first time in September 2004, the US dropped its objections to India as an independent space power in February 2004, and acccepted that along with NATO member states and major non-NATO allies like Egypt, Israel, Japan and Jordan, India could join this exclusive club. For the first time, the US was willing to "outsource" research and design in space technology to India.

## Joint Exercises

The Navy has been holding the annual Malabar series of anti-submarine warfare exercise with the US Navy. Besides, the two sides have explosive ordnance, disposal exercises and officer educational exchange programmes. Exercises in Gwalior in February 2004 were a significant stride for the Indian Air Force. The IAF then sent its Jaguar fighters to participate in Cooperation Cope Thunder in Alaska in July 2004. The exercise was hosted by the US and attended by NATO members and some of America's close allies.

## Miscelleneous

With the success of US special forces still at work in Iraq, India has asked the United States to supply arms and equipment worth $150 million through its Foreign Military Sales

Programme, which would allow India to purchase the items under the same terms as the Pentagon, to help expand its elite units. The items include 4,000 waterproof rifles suitable for divers' use, light weight carbines with night sights, silencers and ammunition radio beacons to guide aircraft and helicopters to positions behind enemy lines, portable decompression systems for divers, foldable kayaks for clandestine operations, radio-controlled detonators and watercraft engine silencers.

GE Aircraft Engines will provide 17 F404-GE-IN-20 engine, a variant of the F-404-GE-402, modified to power the single engine LCA with redundant features and a digital control system, as well as logistics support, to the ADA under a $105 million engineering development contact. India has sought United States cooperation in developing optronics, electro-optics, encryption and sensor and jamming technologies. Indian scientists presented their research and development (R&D) requirements on March 4-5, 2004 at a meeting of the sixth Joint Technical Group (JTG) between India and the US. During the meeting the two countries finalised defence research cooperation in the life sciences, human behaviour and nutrition and human conditions in extreme cold climate and high altitudes. With the two countries having signed their first Master Information Exchange Agreement (MIEA) in Washington on February 2004, their defence establishments and laboratories can exchange research information and conduct joint testing and evaluation.

With the signing of the Indo-US Nuclear Deal the relations between these countries have been strengthened further. Together they are likely to script a new tale of development through cooperation.

O O O

## 2. INDO-RUSSIAN DEFENCE COOPERATION

By a rough estimate almost 60 per cent of Indian Army's military hardware, 70 per cent of its Naval hardware and 80 per cent of Air Force hardware is of Soviet/Russian origin.

India's current agenda of force modernisation does not seek to deviate from this trajectory of close cooperation. Indeed, it seeks closer cooperation, albeit with the aims of progressively enhancing Indian self-reliance in the design and production of existing technologies/weapons system and collaborating with Russia in joint design and production of major weapons systems in the future.

During Russian President Vladimir Putin's three-day visit to India way back in 2004, practical steps were taken to raise Russia-India relations to a higher plane. Putin's visit was used to mould further the strategic partnership that was signed with former Prime Minister Atal Bihari Vajpayee in the millennium year. The Indian and Russian leaders met on a yearly basis and Russia-India relations have thus become a continuous process marked by these special events.

Russia has reiterated that the Kashmir issue be resolved in the framework of the Simla Agreement and in continuation with the Lahore Summit and this has featured in every statement between India and Russia and in all Russian documents dealing with the issue, including those after the disintegration of USSR. This has endeared Russia to all parties in India.

Putin made it plain that India's rightful claim for a permanent seat with veto power at the UN Security Council, like the existing permanent members, would get Moscow's support. He fully understood that any arrangement minus veto power, would not satisfy India.

**Countering Terrorism**

A joint statement issued after a meeting of the India-Russia Joint Working Group on Combating International Terrorism has identified the following areas for counter terrorism operations and strengthening bilateral mechanisms:

1. Exchange of information and sharing of experience in their fight against international terrorism;
2. Strengthening cooperation in curbing trafficking in narcotics;

3. Continuing cooperation to address the threat of terrorist financing;

4. Extending support for the effective implementation of the UN Security Council's resolution number 1373 and the work of the Security Council Terrorism Committee; and

5. Continuing consultations on the Comprehensive Convention on Terrorism and the Convention against Acts of Nuclear Terrorism with a view to their finalisation.

The Russian Defence Minister Sergel Ivanov had discussions with Pranab Mukherjee when the former visited India. Both the Defence Ministers agreed to examine upgrading Russian Military hardware, obtaining newer weapons, looking for markets for the jointly-developed supersonic cruise missile, Brahmos, exploring a lease deal on long-range Tupolev-22 bombers, jointly exercising paratroopers and streamline assembly lines for T-90 tanks.

## Global Navigational Satellite System

In addition to upgrading the defence agreements, Russia signed an accord on the joint development and use of the Russian Global Navigational Satellite system for peaceful purposes. Although India has signed a similar agreement with the European Union, the access given by the Russians is at a qualitatively higher level. As its answer to the American Global Positioning System, Russia wants to build the Global Navigational System. At least 18 satellites are needed for the system to cover the globe, and Moscow would like India to contribute with half a dozen.

## Fifth Generation Aircraft

The Russians want to join hands with India to develop a futuristic fighter, technically called fifth generation aircraft. During Ivanov's visit to New Delhi, which preceded Putin's visit, a joint Indo-Russian team of scientists and technicians made a conceptual presentation on the aircraft in the Defence Ministry. An agreement to jointly develop such an aircraft was clinched between Russia and India. Ivanov said his vision of future Indo-Russian military cooperation saw "the two working together along an entire chain, starting from research and development all the way to final production and testing" of fighters. Ivanov said that the present trend in military production is to globalize production and thus Moscow is in talks with not only India but some European countries like France about pooling resources to develop a fifth generation fighter.

During Ivanov's visit, Russia partly conceded India's request for bank guarantees against items ordered from the Russian military industrial complex. The Russian Finance Ministry will give a "comfort letter" to New Delhi in place of bank guarantees.

## Gorshkov Deal

The long-awaited deal for the Admiral Gorshkov aircraft carrier was signed according to which Russia will refurbish the Gorshkov, provide 16 supersonic MIG-29K jets and eight naval helicopters for $.15 billion. The Gorshkov was scheduled for delivery in 2008. In the future, India may consider purchasing 30 more MIG-29K jets and build, with Russia's help, onshore installations to maintain the Gorshkov, for an additional $1.5 billion, since India does not have the docks suitable for the carrier. Evidently, the Russian side hopes to sign more contracts in connection with the upgradation of Gorshkov as plenty of work remains to be done to convert it into a state-of-the-art carrier. The aircraft carrier's flight deck will be extended and a catapult will be installed for short take-offs and landings (STOL). The Russian side has indicated that all these alterations and improvements will take four years or so. Gorshkov was designed to carry a lot of missiles and does not have a full flat-top deck.

The Russian designers will now start working to make it into a true flat-top. The obsolete equipment and weapons have been dismantled and fuel tanks cleaned, fulfilling the pre-contract agreement. Gorshkov, with a sea endurance of 30 days and the capacity to carry more than 2,000 sailors and officers, is perceived as a real force projector for the country.

## Lease of Nuclear Submarine

The two nations have signed the deal for 10-year lease of the submarine of project 971 (Akula-II). The submarine to be leased by India was a project 971 'Nerpa' (Sea Seal) nuclear submarine, which was constructed at the Amur ship building facility, Komsomolskon and was delivered to Indian Navy in 2007. Categorised SSN (Ship Submersible Nuclear), the Akula (shark) does not have the capability to fire ballistic missiles. It has a reported capability to fire the conventional Granat Cruise missiles with a range of upto 3,000 km and is comparable to the US Sea Wolf class. The Akula will buttress the Indian Navy blue water profile, with a reported endurance of 4,500 hours at sea. The package for the lease of two Akula-II along with four TU-22 M 'Backfire' nuclear-capable bombers to India had for long been linked to the Admiral Gorskhov aircraft carrier deal. Under Project 971A, the Indian lease money will partly finance the completion of three to four Akula-II submarines.

## BrahMos Cruise Missile

During Ivanov's visit, Russia and India signed three protocols for fresh investments (estimated at Rs. 250 crores) for the development of the BrahMos supersonic cruise missile. With additional funds from Russia, the influx would help produce nearly 400 missiles that will be fitted on military platforms of both countries.

BRAHMOS-II, the land to land version of the supersonic cruise missile jointly developed by India and Russia, was test-fired for the first time in the Army configuration on 21st December 2004, in a deserted range in Rajasthan. This was the first time that BrahMos was launched from land towards a target on land.

It was the ninth flight of BrahMos and all of them have been successful. It is essentially an anti-ship supersonic missile, which flies at a speed of 2.8 to 3 Mach. Three of the earlier flights were launched from a naval ship towards targets in the sea. India and Russia are to jointly develop the air launched version of BrahMos.

## Stealth Frigates

Russia is learnt to have offered to sell India three more stealth frigates of the Krivak class. Three of these multi-role frigates built under Project 1135.6 have already been inducted into the Indian Navy. Dubbed the Talwar class, these three warships—The Talwar, Trishul and Tabar—form the cutting edge of the 21—ship strong Western Fleet of the Indian Navy. Tabar has earned a reputation of sorts in chasing and sinking pirate ships in international waters. It saved several ships and boats from Somalian pirates in 2008.

## T-90S

A Russian tank builder, Uralvagonzavod handed over last of T-90S main battle tanks to India on April 5, 2004. Under a 2001 agreement, India has bought 310 T-90s for $650 million from Uralvagonzavod. The remaining 210 tanks are being built in India under a technology-transfer deal.

## MIG 29K

India has paid $148 million to Russian Aircraft Building Corporation MiG (RSK. MiG) to buy 16 new MiG 29K aircraft scheduled to be delivered to the Indian Navy by 2007. India not being happy with the pace of the programme was considering withholding instalments until a team from the Navy and HAL visited RSK MiG to assess the production process and finalize contracts with Russian suppliers for spare parts and other equipment for the production of the MIG-29K.

## Russian Engine for the Jet Trainer

The intermediate jet trainer (IJT) being developed as a replacement for the Kirans, will be supplied with an advanced Russian engine with more thrust and superior technology, from the same family as the Su-30 engines. The engine known as the AL-551, has many commonalities with the famous Lyulka-Saturn thrust vectoring engine AL-31 FP, powering the Su-30 MKJ.

# 3. INDO-UK MILITARY TIES

After prolonged negotiations, India and the UK signed an MoU to pave the way for signing of the much-awaited contract for the "Hawk" Advanced Jet Trainees (AJTs). The contracts for the procurement of '24 Hawk-115y' inaugurated in a flyaway condition from British Aerospace and licensed production of 42 more in Bangalore by the Hindustan Aeronautics Limited (HAL) would be worth around £795 million (around Rs. 6,640 crore). The MoU provides for "effective unlimited" product support for 25 years, extendable by another 10 years.

The UK has, under the agreement assured India that it "will not impose any restrictions or prohibitions" during the operational life of the AJTs on the continued supply of aircraft, products, associated equipment, spares and services. The Cabinet Committee on Security had cleared the Rs. 8,000 crore deal some time ago, fulfilling the 20-year old demand of the Indian Air Force (IAF) for the AJTs to train rookie pilots to fly supersonic fighter jets better. The total project cost includes the cost of the AJTs, license fee, training of 75 IAF pilots in UK while the trainers are being manufactured, cost of production by HAL and creation of infrastructure facilities for the IAF. The delivery of the AJTs each costing Rs. 85 crore, will be in 35 months after the contract is signed with British Aerospace. All the 66 AJTs, which can also be used in combat operations, should be made available to the IAF before the end of six years.

Since 1990-91, around 320 Category-I (aircraft totally destroyed) accidents have taken place in the IAF, with 150 pilots having been killed. Many of these crashes have been attributed to "human error" by the pilots. The AJTs will help trainee-pilots make the quantum jump from flying subsonic aircraft like HPT-32 and kiran trainers (take off and landing speed of 140-200 kmph) to fighters like MIG-21s (take off and landing speed of 245 kmph). Most of the accidents take place during the take off and landing phases. An AJT, with a take off and landing speed of around 250 kmph, will fill the existing gap in the training.

## RAF to Train IAF Pilots

As a part of the £795 million contract for Advanced Jet Trainers (AJTs) signed with the British Government and the British Aerospace Systems, manufacturers of Hawk, IAF trainee pilots were sent to the Royal Air Force Galley from July 2004 to be a part of rigours and challenges which the U.K. pilots have been facing for years. The Indian pilots will now learn to fly on the Hawk, world's most produced advanced jet trainer, which also has in impressive safety record. This was the procedure till 2008, when the Hawks were fully integrated into the IAF training. The HawK Interim Indian Flying Training would comprise eight weeks of theory and simulators, 20 weeks (110 hours) of advanced flying training, three weeks (60 hours) of tactical weapons simulations and 14 weeks of live tactical weapons training. There will be four courses a year and each course will have six Indian pilots. This is the largest number of officers and the longest period of training ever done by RAF for a foreign nation. The Indian pilots will be taught air defence, air combat, intercepts, low level evasion, simulated attack and other offensive and defensive manoeuvres besides live firing using three kg bombs and 30-mm cannons at the firing range.

## Defence Consultative Group Meeting

The Indo-UK Defence Consultative Group (DCG), headed by the Defence Secretary, Ajay Prasad and the British Permanent Under Secretary for Defence, Kevin Tebbit, met for two days in New Delhi. The two delegations discussed the holding of joint exercises, continuing with bilateral exchanges of cadets and students at defence and staff colleges, stepping up attendance at training courses and defence equipment cooperation. The eighth DCG meeting took place against the backdrop of India selling 18 years of negotiations for a multi-billion dollar deal to purchase and subsequently manufacture Hawk advanced jet trainers. The DCG, the formal mechanism for maintaining and developing the Indo-British defence relationship, has three sub-groups covering military-to-military contacts, defence equipment and science and technology. The group also discussed greater familiarisation between the Indian and British armed forces by encouraging the provision of increased opportunities for interaction and training, to develop the potential for collaborative defence equipment and research projects with a view to drawing maximum mutual benefit from the respective technological and industrial capabilities and promote cooperation between the defence industries of the two countries.

Deliberations at the DCG included preliminary discussions on the possibility of setting up a joint headquarters either in Hyderabad or Bangalore to meet terrorist threats. The Joint HQ would function a task force and was expected to have a strength of over 100 personnel but would neither have military assets nor troops under its control.

## Drive Against Terrorism

A joint declaration by India and UK to launch a drive against the menace of terrorism together is significant in the sense that both have been the victims of terrorism for a long time. India which first faced the problem in Punjab, has been grappling with terrorism in Jammu & Kashmir since 1989, since Pakistan is using terrorism as an instrument of state policy. The UK, which had been earlier targeted by Northern Ireland terrorists, is now on the hit list of those associated with Al-Qaida. As India and Britain have an extradition treaty signed in 1993, the resolve of the two countries to cooperate with each other in this crucial struggle can bring rich dividends.

## U.K.'s Defence Minister's Visit

Geoffrey Hoon, the British Defence Minister visited India to further strengthen the strategic partnership between the two countries. Mr Hoon pushed his government's case for the next generation Typhoon fighter aircraft, which was manufactured by a European Consortium. India is negotiating with a host of countries on the purchase of the latest fighter aircraft and has dropped enough indications that it is looking beyond the French Mirage 2000-5, an updated version of the Mirage. Hoon's visit was followed by the 10-day visit of the British Chief of General Staff, Lt. Gen. Sir Mike Jackson, to India to hold discussions with Indian defence officials regarding enhancing bilateral defence cooperation to include joint training between the two defence forces, expanding annual bilateral exchanges, training courses and defence deals including joint production. General Sir Mike Jackson visited the Line of Control in Jammu and Kashmir.

After a meeting between Prime Minister Manmohan Singh and his British counterpart at that time, Tony Blair, the Indo-UK joint declaration issued in September 2004 said, the current relationship between the two nations is "the strongest it ever has been."

### Naval Exercises

The British warships HMS Exeter and RFA Grey Rover, took part in the exercises with vessels from the Indian Navy's Eastern Fleet from April 17 to 19, 2004. The exercises were held off the Chennai coast. The exercises named "Konkan" were a prelude to bigger exercises. A 100-member defence industry delegation from the UK visited India subsequently to explore the possibilities of cooperation with India in defence production.

### Pilots Finish Hawk Training

The first batch of six Indian Air Force officers who successfully completed an 11-month training course on the Hawk AJT (Advanced Jet Trainer) on May 24, 2005 in London were complemented by Prince Charles at a special ceremony at the RAF Valley in Hollyhead, North Wales.

The Prince said, "It's a special day. This unique training scheme has been a huge success and Indian pilots should be justly proud."

Training of 75 Indian pilots at the Valley in the next three and half years was part of the deal for 66 Hawks.

# 4. INDIA-AFRICA FORUM SUMMIT

The first-ever India-Africa Forum Summit was held in New Delhi from April 8-9, 2008. It was a meeting of some of the most prominent leaders of Africa with their counterparts from India. No less than six Presidents, two Vice-Presidents and two Prime Ministers congregated, not to mention the several ministers who were also present. Perhaps the foremost of the high-ranking visitors was South African President Thabo Mbeki, a statesman who has visited India in the past and who among the main leaders of his continent is head of one of the most potent African countries.

The Summit was clearly designed as a grand occasion aimed at reaffirming the close bonds that exist between the two sides—India and Africa—and to give a fresh impetus to these historic relations.

## Joint Declaration

At the conclusion of the Summit, it issued a Delhi Declaration and 'Framework for Cooperation' document, which identified the issues of food security, fluctuating oil prices and climate change as the major concerns of the developing world. India and Africa pledged to work together as partners to address the economic and political challenges facing them. The partnership will be based on the fundamental principles of equality, mutual respect and understanding.

Prime Minister Manmohan Singh, who inaugurated the Summit, highlighted the strong relations between India and Africa. The African leaders, on their part, wanted the relationship with India to be on terms of equality. The African countries agreed to back India's candidacy as a permanent member of the UN Security Council.

Both India and Africa emphasised the importance of democratising international institutions and agreed to work closely to re-establish peace and security through the African Union's (AU) policy framework for Post-Conflict Reconstruction and Development.

The Joint Declaration pledged to boost trade and investment and share expertise in agriculture, science and technology, water management and education among others. New Delhi agreed to provide preferential markets to the 32 least developed African countries. It stated that in the next five to six years, India would issue grants for projects in excess of US $ 550 million. Developing infrastructure in Information Technology, telecommunications, power and railways would be the priorities in Africa for the Government of India. The establishment of Departments of African Studies in select universities and the encouragement of greater African news coverage by the Indian media in different regions of the Africa should also be on the agenda.

The Delhi Declaration pledged to develop within a year a joint plan of action at a continental level and an appropriate follow-up mechanism to implement the Framework for Cooperation. It has been resolved to hold the second India-African Forum Summit in Africa in 2011 and there is much than can tangibly happen on the ground before the deadline.

Corporate India can be expected to show growing interest in this venture. Africa is an emerging market and is a continent hugely endowed with rich mineral and other natural resources, including hydrocarbons, coal, uranium, diamonds and much else besides.

While India and African States also explore opportunities for trade markets and prosperity, the globalisation of ideas and practices has been commensurate with the further democratisation of politics in India and Africa since the 1980s. Hithertho marginalised populations and groups on both countries have sought more voice and participation in the affairs of the States.

Further, South South Solidarity, as it has been termed in the Joint Declaration, cannot afford to miss burning contemporary issues in Africa such as those relating to multinational corporations or corporate accountability, or fail to focus on an India-African partnership in specific areas of struggles against poverty, debt relief, aid and policy conditionality, HIV/AIDS, Intellectual Property Rights and World Trade Organisation, privatisation of natural resources, war, conflict and hegemony.

Undoubtedly, there are huge opportunities for cooperation as pointed out by the Chairman of the African Union, Alpha Oumar Konare. The African countries realise that they can benefit considerably from India's growth in various sectors. India, with its experience of the Green Revolution, can also apply a major role in the developments. India's historical relationship with nations like South Africa will make the task easier. India will have to redouble its efforts to increase its presence in the continent where people are ready to welcome it. New Delhi cannot afford to miss the opportunity.

O O O

# 5. SAINT ALPHONSA—FIRST WOMAN SAINT FROM INDIA

Sister Alphonsa (1910-1946), a nun from a remote village from Kerala was declared on 12 October, 2008, the first woman saint from India. This bears testimony to the fact that attacks on Christians in some parts of India during 2007 and 2008 were mere aberrations, and that India offers proper environment for each religion to prosper.

Watched by more than 5,000 Indian Christians who came to the Vatican for the historic ceremony, and lakhs of others, Pope Benedict XVI canonised Sister Alphonsa from Bharananganam village in Kottayam district—who died at the age of 36 in 1946—as a saint. Three others were elevated as saints during the internationally televised ceremony—Maria Bernarda Buelter (1848-1924) from Switzerland, Narcisa de Jesus Martillo Moran (1832-64) from Ecuador and Father Gaetano Errico (1791-1860) from Italy.

The first Indian who attained sainthood hails from a village in Vasai, near Mumbai. St. Gonsalo Garcia was born in 1556 to an Indian mother and a Portuguese father. He did missionary work in Japan before being martyred in 1597. He was declared a saint by the Catholic Church in 1862.

Sister Alphonsa of the Immaculate Conception is the first woman from India to be conferred sainthood and the second Roman Catholic from the country after Gonsalo Garcia. She lived a quiet religious life, helping people around her place in Kerala. She has been hailed for a number of miracles, including two which were officially put up to the Pope. One of the miracles attributed to her is the healing of a young boy's twisted feet after his family members prayed at her tomb at the Alphonsa Chapel at Bharananganam.

The beatification process, the last formal step before sainthood, of Sister Alphonsa began in the year 1996 by Pope John Paul II, who had declared her a 'Blessed Servant of God', when he visited India.

Recalling the life of the new woman saint, who belonged to the Franciscan Clarist order, the Pope said she had been "an exceptional woman saint". She had lived in "extreme physical and spiritual suffering", the Pope added. She "was convinced that her cross was the very means of reaching the heavenly banquet prepared for her by the Father", he said. "May we imitate her in shouldering our own crosses so as to join her one day in Paradise." The Government has decided to issue a commemorative stamp in Saint Alphonsa's honour.

According to her biography released by the Vatican, Saint Alphonsa born on 19 Aug, 1910 to Maria Puthukari in her eighth month of pregnancy as the result of a fright she received when, during sleep, a snake wrapped itself around her waist. Sister Alphonsa had dedicated herself to serving Jesus Christ at the age of seven, calling him "my divine spouse".

Anna Muttathupandathu, also known as Alphonsa Dellimmacolata Concezione, was so determined to enter a convent that she deliberately stepped into a burning fire to disfigure her feet so that her strident aunt would stop her to marry. She was plagued by serious illness for much of her relatively short life, but was known for her compassionate and sympathetic nature. After her death on 28 July, 1946, some miracles were attributed to her. Her burial place has now become a pilgrimage site, especially for those seeking relief from ill-health.

The process of Alphonsa's canonisation, the step-by-step procedure of raising a person to the high pedestal of a saint in the Catholic Church, began as early as in 1953 with the Church setting up a Diocesan tribunal. According to Christian historians, Kerala is the cradle of Indian Christianity with St. Thomas, the apostle, preaching the faith after landing at Crangannore, also known as Kadungallur in 52 A.D. Hundreds of visitors to the sleepy town of Bharananganam in Kerala's Christian heartland offered special prayers ahead of her canonisation.

With canonisation, Feasts can be held and Mass celebrated in the name of St. Alphonsa of Immaculate Conception. Her image can be placed at the altar and her name invoked for prayers by Catholic Church devotees around the world. It is hoped that Saint Alphonsa's dedication to the cause of humanity at large, and Christianity in particular, shall be remembered by people for all time to come and inspire them to do good deeds.

O O O

# 6. INDIA'S FOREIGN POLICY TODAY

The present-day world is full of strained relationships. Tensions are there in Afghanistan and Iraq. The US is bullying Iran. Human rights abuses are happening in Darfur. Tensions are again brewing up between the US and Russia over the proposed Missile defense shield. The challenges are manifold.

Peace and security in India's immediate neighbourhood and for that matter, in the entire region should be our top priority. The struggle against terrorism is the most colossal problem that we are facing. Energy security, creating favourable conditions for sustainable economic development, coping with the chaos prevailing out of the ongoing crisis in Iraq and Middle east, the reform of the Security Council, promoting a more equitable equation between the developed and the developing world in the political, economic and technological realm are some of the challenges facing Indian foreign policy today.

The topmost priority for India is to safeguard its security interests in its neighbourhood. Right now Nepal is on the verge of the collapse again due to the some minor misunderstanding between the Maoists and the Government. In Sri Lanka, the violence is again on the upswing. The porous border between India and our eastern neighbour Bangladesh is creating the problem of insurgency and illegal migration which can be dealt with effectively only in conditions of acceptance of each other's legitimate concerns. The problem of insurgents misusing the territory of Bhutan for launching terrorists operations against India should be resolved within the framework of India's past excellent relations with Bhutan.

There is a rapid growth of understanding between the Afghanistan and Indian Governments. Already we are engaged in numerous infrastructural developments in Afghanistan. We need to expand this understanding into the economic realm as Afghanistan is interested in forging a long-term strategic relationship and this can be built around energy security and transit arrangements. The governing philosophy of India's assistance to Afghan reconstruction has been to respond to Afghan call for help to meet its priority needs. India regards as crucial for regional peace and stability and views her relationship with Afghanistan as direct and bilateral.

The biggest challenge would be the emergence of Pakistan as a moderate Islamic State in the true sense of the term. The rule of military has ended with the holding of elections and the resignation of Musharraf as Pakistan's

President. But the Al Qaeda network and the Lashkar module were built under his nose. Today those very forces have re-emerged in the NWFP and Baluchistan in Pakistan. What was removed by force from Afghanistan has re-emerged legally in adjoining areas but the nerve centre of all this remains in Pakistan.

Our close historical links with Central Asia provide an asset for building important relationships with the republics that emerged in the region following the collapse of the Soviet Union. Today we are exploring new avenues of cooperation, new routes—land, air and sea routes. Statistics suggests that 30 per cent of the medicines consumed in Central Asia are of Indian origin. Indian Information Technology is becoming a part of their system. There is a cultural revival of traditional warmth. We were amongst the first to establish diplomatic missions in all the Central Asian Republics and the area should continue to receive significant focus in the coming years as India seek to forge multifaceted ties to this important region.

Moving eastwards, East Asia has been a natural component of India's foreign policy priorities. India is an Asian country, the second largest both demographically and geographically. Developments in Asia impinge directly on our security and strategic interests. Indian Ocean straddles the most important sea routes that connect the oil producing region of the Gulf with the consumer countries of East Asia. Cooperation between India and these countries is a necessary pre-requisite for the 21st century to become the century of Asia. India's Look East Policy starts from North East Asia and not simply the ASEAN region. Yet, India is excluded from APEC as also ASEM. India has engaged in an effort to craft special trade and investment arrangements through an India-ASEAN Free Trade Area to be brought about in 10 years, a BIMSTEC FTA as also bilateral arrangements such as the India-Thailand FTA and India-Singapore Comprehensive Economic Cooperation Agreement. BIMSTEC and Mekong-Ganga Cooperation are other structural frameworks for India's "Look-East" policy.

Our relations with the United States have entered a phase

of unprecedented improvement with the Indo-US Nuclear deal. India and the United States are, respectively, the world's most populous and the most powerful democracies, having clear commonalities in shaping a new democratic and pluralistic world order. The Prime Minister has described India and the US as natural partners. Our relationship with the US is being transformed. There is an intensive dialogue covering a broad agenda, seeking new possibilities for cooperation. Apart from regular political dialogue, India and US have established over 15 institutional forums that meet regularly. Yet, the challenges remain for better management of relations, given the different geo-strategic and economic contexts, and occasional differences in perspectives.

India's foreign policy has maintained its very close strategic relationship with Russia. The close political contracts that have existed at the highest levels, the regular dialogue through the years, the recent coming together of both countries against the global menace of international terrorism are elements of strength in the relationship. The challenge lies in the field of bilateral trade which has failed to keep pace with the political relationship.

So far as India's relations with China are concerned, they have followed a positive course and a steady effort to overcome past differences and build a growing convergence of interests is being made. The challenge that we face vis-à-vis China is to sustain the steady expansion and strengthening of the relationship in diverse fields even as we attempt to resolve the border issue. The challenge is to balance the legitimate interests of all the others players—Japan, the ASEAN bloc and the US—in a cooperative framework. But the unresolved border issue as also the factors of China's own internal and external policies, the impact of its sensitivity to concerns about proliferation of nuclear and missile technology in the region and the degree to which its economic success would translate into a more democratic, transparent system, should be a subject of intense interest to India as also to the international community as a whole.

Europe is a key trading partner of India and a very important investor of capital. It is important, however, that the bilateral trade between India and Europe be improved which today is far below its potential. Further transformation of the India-EU relationship would require a two-pronged strategy of sustaining traditional links and also exploring new linkages, for instance, in knowledge industries, i.e. information technology, biotechnology, pharmaceutical, etc.

To conclude, it can be said that Indian foreign policy has sought to preserve, with conviction and consistency, the principles that were enunciated by the founding fathers of the republic, both in the development of bilateral relations, and in international forums, where our views have won recognition and respect.

# IV. INDIAN ECONOMY TODAY

## 1. POPULATION CONTROL, ENVIRONMENT AND NGO PARTICIPATION

Poverty and population growth are closely interlinked. Yet promoting family planning amongst the poor is an extremely difficult task. Mr. K.B. Sahay, a Biomedical Engineer, says that a family plagued by want of food, water, fuel, shelter, medical care because of an exploitative social system, can hardly be expected to appreciate the importance of family planning. But unless family planning is popularised amongst the underprivileged classes, known typically for having large families, the country's population control programme cannot succeed because these classes form almost one-third of our total population. It is therefore imperative that the government should avail of the services of the non-government organisations (NGOs) to popularise the family planning programme. Some of the NGOs are quite well known among the poorer classes and have to their credit some achievements in the field of social service. If these NGOs could be persuaded to take up the task of promoting family planning, their credibility and goodwill can go a long way in popularising the idea of family planning.

Philanthropic services undertaken for the limited and narrow goal of self-upliftment (like feeding the beggars occasionally) are no doubt good but it would certainly be far better to take up social service with an aim to eliminate the very cause of human suffering. To do so, the NGOs should concentrate on family planning because our massive population and its rapid growth are the root cause of most of our problems which cannot be solved unless we could control our population.

Although there are a great number of government and non-government organisations working to protect the environment, not one of them has so far highlighted the linkage adequately or stressed to control our growing population and thereby save our ecological balance. Environmentalists in India could, in general, be classified into two groups, one guided by Western models and the other influenced by Gandhian paradigms. The former thinks that ecological problems, though a consequence of over-consumerism and industrialisation can be solved by technological measures irrespective of peoples' lifestyles and levels of consumption, whereas the other group believes that the cause of environmental decay is the consequence of not following the Gandhian model of cottage industries and not encouraging simple living.

The Western model does not bother about the population factor simply because the Western world does not have a problem of overpopulation; and the Gandhian dictum is that the earth has enough for everybody's need but not people's greed and there is no need to control population by contraceptives. Hence neither of the environmentalist groups in India raises the issue of population growth which, in fact, is the main cause of India's ecological problems. It is merely a coincidence that the concern for environment has come before the concern for overpopulation. Or is it because we do not want to take the responsibility for what we are doing to the environment by not controlling our population?

It is important to realise that the impact of population on environment is the function of the number of people it supports at average level of consumption. In other words, low per capita consumption, in a country with high population density as in India, can be dangerous for the global ecology as high per capita consumption and low population levels as in the West. So the excess population in India is as undesirable as the culture of excessive consumerism in the developed countries.

However, realising that India is growing fast in terms of population, we should avail the help of NGOs in popularising family planning in the villages.

O O O

## 2. Amartya Sen's Views on Poverty Round the World

Poverty in India has existed for a very long time. More than a century ago, one of India's greatest minds, Vivekananda talked about it. Half a century later in early 1920s, Mahatma Gandhi described it in great detail. Another half a century later, Amartya Sen wrote the classical essay on "Poverty and Famines" where he analysed the Great Bengal Famine of 1943 in which three to four million people died.

Amartya Sen says that the poor can be divided into three categories, (a) The poor as deprived, (b) The poor as degraded, (c) The poor as exploited. For Sen deprivation is the characteristic of the poor. Ivan Illich identified a more comprehensive concept as a "lack". A poor person lacks consumption, commodities, education, food, health, income, nutrition, etc. This concept accommodates many other realities. Even the very rich in the United States can't afford what all people in the poor countries have personal attention around the deathbed. It also encompasses the issue of inequality that degrades the poor.

However, it may be useful, first to look at people who are recognized as poor, by whatever criteria. The US Bureau of Census estimates, that 13.7 per cent of US population in 1996 were poor. Similarly, the Canadian Council on Social Development estimated that in 1995, 17.8 per cent of Canadian population were poor. If one looks into these poor people, most of the original or native Indians fall in this category in both US and Canada. To make India poor, the British rule managed to cause the death of around 200 million people. Imperialist domination has a lot to do with poverty in India.

Gandhiji fully recognised that poverty follows from exploitation emanating from the reality of an elite-mass contradiction. Gandhi understood such alienation implied in the education pursued by the British colonial administration to produce Macaulayite Indians, "a class of persons Indian in blood and colour but English in opinions, in morals and in intellect." However, Gandhiji believed that one can't be exploited except by one's own cooperation, so that he holds both the exploiter and the exploited responsible for exploitation. Gandhiji followed Vivekananda who argued that it is necessary for the exploited people to stand up, fight and become "men". For the exploiter, Gandhiji proposed the idea of a trusteeship, derived from Gita, placing more faith in the soul part of his identity.

Sen's intellectual output is deeply embedded in the liberal ideology. It makes a major contribution to many of the planks and suffers from its limitations. As liberal thought was being developed in many countries of the world, the Europeans were engaged in colonising people, a process that took hundreds of years of genocidal attacks. As liberal ideology was perfected, imperialism also became the then prevailing order. The liberal ideas were never meant for the colonised and the exploited.

Liberal ideology is based fundamentally on "ontological individualism"—the belief that the truth of our condition is not in our society or in our relation to each other, but in our isolated and inviolate selves.

To Gandhiji, poverty is an exploitative equation between elite and the poor masses. His solution follows logically, development of character among the exploited poor and appeal of trusteeship to the exploiter. Sen considers poverty as an attribute of the poor who need certain "capabilities", defined by education, health and income. His policy recommendation, then, is to offer opportunities for more education, growth and health.

Sen's argument has influenced the measurement of a Human Development Index, based on life expectancy at birth, educational attainment, and real per capita GDP, estimated yearly by the UNDP and published in their annual Human Development Report. The 1998 report provides a ranking of the countries in the world by this measure. Canada tops the list. The bottom 10 list is made up of Niger, Burkina Faso, Mozambique, Zambia, and Siera Leone. No doubt it changes the ranking within but not between the "poor" and the "non-poor" countries. Sen's ideas have also influenced the development of Human Poverty Index—HPI is based on "the most basic dimensions of deprivation". By this measure, poverty level for Trinidad and Tobago is 4.1 per cent, Mexico 10.9 per cent. Thailand 11.9 per cent, as compared with the poverty levels in Canada at 17.8 per cent—judged to be the best country—US 13.7 per cent, and UK 20 per cent. Considering estimates for US, Canada, and UK are well-founded, estimates of HPI raise serious questions about its usefulness.

Sen's policy recommendations are based on the acceptance and adequacy of the existing state and market framework, and appeal to the elite to which he belongs. It is an appeal for compassion. The policy content of Sen's arguments involves a change in the State's expenditures on public health, education and growth, and regulation of parts of the market to avoid gross injustices. This is an easier agenda for change because it is non-threatening and in the interest of the ruling elite, Sen holds.

○ ○ ○

## 3. How To Minimise the Poverty in India

The Indian social system is based on a strong social hierarchy in the form of birth castes. Social class, too, is apparent through money power. The poor and their poverty continue to attract and repel alternatively, politicians, social scientists, religious groups, and others. The poor may be spotted in any caste in any part of India. Though poverty is a universal phenomenon, its nature may be different. The magnitude of poverty is expressed through the poverty line which is different in different nations. In India about 22 million people have been estimated to live below the poverty line.

Poverty is a negative but relative term denoting absence or lack of material wealth to fulfil one's needs. Abraham Maslow presented a hierarchy of human needs as:

(i)   Need for self-actualisation;

(ii)  Esteem need such as need for prestige, success and self-respect;

(iii) Belongingness and love needs such as need for affection, affiliation and identification;

(iv)  Safety need such as need for security, stability and order;

(v)   Physiological needs such as hunger, thirst and sex.

Physiological needs must be satisfied before any of the others can be met: safety needs come before those higher on the list. If one's safety needs are satisfied, one goes on to try to meet one's need for affection, affiliation and identification—feeling a part of society or a segment of it via political parties, school or club. If one meets these needs, one is free to go up in the need hierarchy to one's esteem and self-actualisation needs.

Poverty tends to be characterised by the denial of rights as well as material insufficiency. It may seem paradoxical that many people do not wish to improve their current condition either due to their lack of awareness of societial policies or religious beliefs or prolonged deprivation conditioning or personal reasons. Here is another attempt to define poverty keeping psychological, political, economic and cultural factors in view. Poverty is a state of want of subjective and objective means and opportunities to develop and utilise potential of the individual to minimise the sense of being left behind. Thus, subjective articulation and objective measures are applied onto the persons to be designated as poor. A poor person may belong to either gender, to any age group, to any health condition, to any caste, creed or religion, to any part of the country, may belong to any political affiliation, to any educational background or to any occupation. One thing is, however, universal that poverty divides families, and forces children to work.

The caste system in India has been a traditional drag on society since early times. Some castes seem to suffer from a feeling that all human beings are not equal. This superiority complex among some castes has brought a situation in which the untouchables are the poorest among the poor and suffer as bonded labour, child labour and sex workers.

It was only after independence that the government carried out certain legal reforms to abolish untouchability and to reserve seats in schools and colleges for the scheduled and backward communities. The major part of the benefits has, however, been grabbed by a few privileged Scheduled Castes and Scheduled Tribes. The poorest still remain poor.

In recent past, the question of poverty and development has been discussed both at national and international levels. According to a UNDP-HPI Report, Human Development Index (HDI) measures overall progress in a country in achieving human development and the Human Poverty Index reflects the distribution of progress and measures the backlog of deprivation that still exists. The HPI measures deprivation in the same dimensions of basic human development. The HPI-I measures poverty in developing countries while HPI-2 measures it in industrial countries. A UNDP report shows components and measurements of human development and poverty.

There are numerous causes of poverty which operate in a vicious circle. These could be divided into two groups broadly: chronic or prolonged and acute or critical.

Repeated draughts, floods, or other natural calamities and prolonged war break the backbone of agricultural and industrial economy rendering people in poor health, beggary, prostitution, crime or migrating options. A family may be a victim of chronic poverty on account of the absence of the earning member or chronic/fatal illness of any of its members.

Fire, theft, conflict, loss in business, agriculture or job, steep rise in prices of commodities, and underemployment are some of the critical reasons of poverty. Recently, the suicides by farmers in Andhra Pradesh, Maharashtra and Orissa have been attributed to losses in crops.

The Government of India has been aware and sincere about eradicating poverty. Abolition of Zamindari, stopping privy purses, land consolidation and land ceilings, removal of untouchability, provision of subsidies on agricultural inputs, on cottage industries, and food stuff distributed through fair price shops, reservations for Scheduled Castes, and Schedules Tribes, women, disabled and many other specific poverty elimination programmes are all exemplary actions taken by the government.

However, deprivation, exploitation, denial and refusal by few, neglect and social injustice are still prevalent in our society.

The term minimisation appears better and more practicable than elimination in regard to poverty, because there is no limit to wealth acquisition and it is changeable over a period of time. Two approaches could be thought of poverty minimisation programmes—community-based as well as individual-based.

Using existing indicators, a selected community, slum, village, block or district may be provided with the infrastructure, including roads, transport, water lines, electricity lines, sanitation facilities, fair price shops, schools, basic health centres, and agricultural and cottage industrial consultancy. People should be charged nominally for contribution in these programmes of development. It will instill feelings of participation in construction and maintenance of facilities provided there. Community area specific programme should be made environment-friendly.

If the poverty-invaded area has people of different backgrounds, the needs would be different. Hence, first of all, a needs assessment should be undertaken employing any suitable technique. The needs of everyone should be related to pay loans, to buy instruments, seeds or fertilizers, to buy animals like buffaloes/cows. The entrants to the programme may require monetary help to repair his house damaged by rains or earthquake. He/she may need financial help to send a baby to the school or may have to marry his grown-up son/daughter.

Generally, a few conditions may be enforced before helping such individuals and communities. They should follow the norm of two children per family if they are in the reproductive age. The addicts should be advised to seek the treatment. Some help in getting such treatment should be rendered.

According to World Development Indicators—2007, economic growth in India, China and other South Asian nations will enable the countries to reduce poverty to half the current level by 2015. India and China which account for 38 per cent of the world's population, have largely avoided the financial crisis that shook their South East Asian neighbours. The WDI is published annually by the World Bank. The document says that though the region's gross domestic product (GDP) growth has slowed down from 6.9 per cent in 1996 to 5 per cent in 1998, it had a stabilising influence in Asia.

○ ○ ○

# 4. The Economics of Subsidies

Economics of subsidies is quite simple. Subsidies are usually bad for both microeconomic and macroeconomic reasons. By reducing the prices below the cost of production of subsidised products, one can encourage too much consumption and too little production. By financing them through public expenditure, subsidies tend to raise fiscal deficit and inflation.

But food subsidies are different. A part of such subsidies goes to the producers, paying them, for the amount procured by the Food Corporation of India, prices higher than the cost of production. That neutralises the distinctive effects of subsidies on production. The prices of procurement are generally fixed too high to compensate the marginal, least productive farmers which allows large profits to be reaped by more productive farmers in irrigated and fertile areas. The big farmers' lobby sees to it that the procurement prices, and hence their profits, are not lowered in the name of reducing subsidies. They also make sure that subsidies on fertilizers are not reduced much even though there is ample evidence of excessive use of fertilizers from price distortions.

When food subsidies are reduced by raising the issue prices, they only affect the consumers using the public distribution system. There is very little excessive consumption there, which could be reduced. For the poor, food consumption is practically inelastic. If food prices fall, they have some spare money to spend on other essentials. If they rise they become poorer. Food prices directly affect the level of poverty. And until the poor can be given more income and purchasing power, it will be essential to give them food in affordable prices. The decision of the BJP government to roll back the PDS price rise of food for people below the poverty line was justified. This should, of course, be complimented by policies to improve the delivery system and target the BPL population properly. The poverty line is a statistical concept and the PDS families below that line have to be identified in terms of some visible indicators, such as landholdings or ownership of ancestor's willingness to work for Jawahar Rozgar Yojna and employment assurance schemes at very low wages or on food-for-work programmes.

The entire machinery of local governments and panchayats may have to work for this programme. Even then the targeting may not be complete and some poor above the poverty line may access the supply. This is, however, excusable as these non-poor will also be quite poor by normal standards. The leakage of food from the PDS to undeserving rich is not large and attempts should be made to reduce such leakage.

The argument that subsidies increase fiscal deficit which causes inflation and hits the poor more than others, is also less applicable to the case of food subsidies for PDS.

If other subsidies and anfractuous public expenditures cannot be controlled and fiscal deficit is financed by inflationary money creation, an effective PDS can protect the consumption standards of the poor much better than any other measure. If the PDS covers any other essential items besides foodgrains, constituting the basket of the wage goods, maintaining their prices would help maintaining real wages, and prevent the demand for hiking money wages leading to a further cost-push inflation. Several developing and industrial countries use incomes policy along with monetary policy to curb inflation. Even India has in the past successfully used such policies to bring down the over 20 per cent inflation after the first oil shock of 1973 to less than zero within a year.

There are many ways of controlling inflation just as there are many ways of reducing fiscal deficit. Choosing the reduction of food subsidies first portrays a particular bias—hit the poor who do not have any lobby and who are too scattered to protest. One cannot reduce the procurement prices or fertilizer subsidies as that will upset the rich farmers. If one adds power and water subsidies together with those for other inputs, the profits of these farmers can be very high, and no government has dared to tax agricultural income. One cannot reduce public expenditure or the huge administrative structure using excessive manpower. One cannot reduce the subsidies on loss making public sector enterprises and the wasteful manner of delivering public services, both at the Centre and in the states. Any attempt to raise the tax rates significantly meets with tremendous opposition from vested interests. The administrative effort required to collect more revenues from the same tax rates, by expanding the tax net and disciplining the officials has proved too much for successive governments. The tax-GDP ratio today is only about 60 per cent of what it was in the early 1980s. It is also one of the lowest among all developing countries.

It is important that macro-economic stability is maintained, fiscal deficit is curtailed and inflation is controlled as preconditions for successful reforms leading to sustained growth. Let that growth produce equity, increase the income of the poor, and remove unemployment and underemployment. Until then, let us not hit the poor by rising food prices, as a short-cut to reducing food subsidies.

The poor may not appear to react violently in our country, but they have an uncanny way of casting their votes to teach the government in power an appropriate lesson.

○ ○ ○

# V. EDUCATION IN INDIA

## 1. NEED FOR IMPARTING VALUE EDUCATION IN SCHOOLS IN INDIA

India needs a value education system which will inculcate among the students universal values and enrich their personalities. One frequently hears from the elders that the children of today are going astray because their schools fail to help them build their character. There is a thought in the country which decries the invasion of the visual media while many battle with the questions like: Should sex education be imparted at the school level? Then there are some who worry about the quality of teachers themselves. And a regrettable aspect of life in India is that government-run schools are generally looked upon as poor education factories.

However, there can be no doubt that the country needs a value education system which will inoculate among the students universal values and enrich their personalities— intellectually, physically, emotionally, psychologically and spiritually.

The question of giving a better education system to the country has been engaging the attention of the country almost from the time of independence. A number of high-powered committees and commissions on education were formed. These included the Radhakrishnan Commission (1948-49), Kothari Commission (1964-66), National Policy on Education (1986), Ramamurthi Committee (1990), Central Advisory Board of Education Committee on Policy (1992), Planning Commission Core Group on Value Orientation of Education (1992), and National Steering Committee (2005).

A Parliamentary Committee which reviewed the progress on value-based education found that the efforts of the last 60 years had failed to achieve any concrete results. All the programmes and policies remained on paper, largely because of lack of coordinated efforts by the different implementing agencies.

The student today may be better informed and smarter than his parents but this has come in an environment when the emphasis is on acquiring techniques and not values. It is said that the skills acquired on computers tend to become outdated after a time but values learnt in early days remain forever.

Many are of the view that the present-day education is but an information transmission process. Swami Vivekananda once said, "If education is identical with information, libraries are the greatest sages of the world and encyclopaedias are rishis." The seeds of value education can be implanted first by the mother. But increasingly, school for children starts from a very early age nowadays—at three or four. Therefore, schools can play an important role in imparting value education. These are values which affect both the person and the society—concern for the aged and the handicapped, the deprived sections of society, the dignity of labour, self-dependence and manual labour and so on.

For a country as diverse as India, certain national values should also be imbibed by the school. But the Parliamentary Committee feels that some thought may also have to be given to one's religion and its basic tenets. The suggestions is to make the young impressionable minds aware that the basic concept behind every religion is common belief in God, and the basic principles of one's religion. The need for co-existence has to be stressed and the idea of hatred against any religion should be positively discouraged.

Similarly, for the concept of 'unity in diversity' to be meaningful, a feeling of love for all languages of the country has to be developed at an early age. In fact, the authorities would do well to implement the three-language formula more seriously and across a wide section of the country. Language controversies of Hindi vs English or Urdu or Tamil should be out of question in a value-based education system.

The success of any education system, however, depends a great deal on the teachers. For children of tender age, teacher is a role-model. But inadequacies in the teachers' training programmes do not equip the teacher adequately for this role. The teachers' training programmes need to incorporate value-based education.

The teachers' training programmes need a lot of orientation. The question needs to be settled as to how and when should value education be introduced. Should it be a separate component of the school syllabus? That has to be ruled out since school curriculum is already needlessly heavy. Experts are of the view that value education need not be imparted through a separate class or textbooks. It can be integrated through teaching methods, instructional materials and co-curricular activities. Indeed, teacher of every subject is supposed to be a teacher of fundamental values like democracy, tolerance, co-existence, respect for others' views. Equally important is the role of school environment in spreading the message of value education. It has to be congenial. Full use should be made of the morning assembly and the prayers sung there should strengthen beliefs like secularism and patriotism. Meditation can also play an important role in building character.

Much as some may resent the intrusion of the television at home, they can be used for teaching value education system also—through cartoons, film strips, plays and even plain story-telling. What is needed is that values are projected in a manner that children can relate and should have an earthly quality. The innocent but impressional minds should be able to connect what they see or hear with ordinary human beings they are familiar with. Moreover, great leaders should not be presented in a manner that children feel that it is almost impossible for them to follow their ideals.

The burden of studies seems to virtually hamper activities like NCC, boy scouts and guides. Their revival will promote discipline, cooperation and healthy attitude towards life. An academic activity like increasing reading habits also needs to be encouraged, perhaps in the form of compulsory library period. The Parliamentary Committee has suggested that value-based education should be introduced at tile school level and continued through the college and university levels. But at the advanced stage of education—colleges and universities— values like human rights, co-existence, ethics and comparative study of religion should also be taught. But the committee is not so sure about the stage at which sex education be introduced. All it says is that it should be introduced as a component of curriculum at an "appropriate stage". The Committee, however, realised that in view of wide prevalence of diseases like HIV/AIDS, it has become necessary to expose the young students to sex education—at a level when they have the maturity to grasp the lessons.

○ ○ ○

## 2. Making Elementary Education And Literacy a Fundamental Right

Quoting H.G. Wells, N.D. Shourie says, "Human history becomes more and more race between education and catastrophe." He refers to the lack of achievement of educational ideals in India and says: "It is a matter of real shame that our country has entered the new millennium as the world's largest illiterate nation. Nearly half of our population of more than 100 crore is illiterate. Half of our children including two-thirds of our girls are deprived of schooling even today."

Recent surveys show that 35 million children in the age-group 6 to 10 years do not attend primary school. More than half the children who get enrolled in primary schools drop out before reaching Class V. The literacy rate of girls is well below that of boys. They are in fact marginalised. There is also discrimination within the schooling system along class lines.

Where schools do exist, particularly in the villages, they present a poor picture. Most of them are ramshackle hutments with crumbling walls, leaking roofs, etc. where malnourished children squat on bare earth or on jute mats. There may be a dirty blackboard, but there are no libraries, no furniture worth the name, or teaching aids. The only teaching aid usually used in such schools is a stick to beat the children with. More than half the schools recently surveyed in Bihar, Jharkhand, Madhya Pradesh, Chhattisgarh, Uttar Pradesh, and Rajasthan showed that there was no teaching activity at all. This is despite the plethora of policies and programmes such as Operation Blackboard, the National Mission, the Programme of Non-formal Education, District Institutes of Education and Learning, District Elementary Programme, etc. Unfortunately, most of our data on increasing literacy rates and claims of obtaining district-wise "total literacy" are dubious, as they are based on imparting a minimal capability of writing a word or two in one's own language and to merely put a signature instead of thumb impression.

The framers of the Constitution failed to make compulsory education a Fundamental Right, Directive Principle No. 45 merely prescribed that "The State shall endeavour to provide within a period of ten years from the commencement of the Constitution, free and compulsory education for children until they complete the age of 14 years." In substance, it merely spelled out desirable objective without any compulsion on the State to achieve it and without any enforceability by court, leaving it merely as a declaration in the shape of a duty of the State. If it had clearly been made a fundamental right, the State could not have ignored its duty to ensure the attainment of this objective and would have had to find the means and measures for spreading literacy among all the children to this cause at election time but they have all failed to deliver when in power. The central and state governments have now started saying that improvement of the schools is the duty of the community and that private schools can make up for the inadequacy of government schools.

After more than sixty years of independence we have regressed to spending less than even 4 per cent of our GNP on education and less than half of this amount on elementary education, which is the key to building the future of this nation. Lack of resources cannot be a convincing argument for failing to discharge this national duty. If the government can find the money to implement the Sixth Pay Commission's recommendations which involve additional expenditure to the extent of about 3 per cent of the GNP, surely the requirement of primary education could also be attend to.

Education is a state subject and it is understandable that the central government cannot impose it upon recalcitrant states. Some states and union territories have voluntarily enacted legislation for compulsory elementary education; and that is welcome indeed. Kerala is one state which has shown that it is possible to achieve remarkable results in Indian conditions of reaching nearly 100 per cent literacy. In sharp contrast is the state of Bihar where the literacy rate is below 44 per cent. About 75 per cent of the children who have never gone to school are concentrated in the states of Andhra Pradesh, Bihar, Jharkhand, Madhya Pradesh, Chhattisgarh, Rajasthan, Uttar Pradesh, Orissa and West Bengal.

The matter of primary education has come up before the Supreme Court in a public interest case. The court pronounced as far back as 1993, that the government cannot shirk its responsibility of providing free and compulsory education to all children and that primary education is, in fact, a fundamental right. Thereafter the Government of India drafted the 83rd Constitutional Amendment Bill to place it beyond doubt that it is the responsibility of all states in the country to enact and enforce laws for free and compulsory education. It was introduced in the Rajya Sabha in 1997 but seems to have gone into cold storage.

It has been estimated that nearly 1,20,000 crore of rupees will be required in the next six years to provide for an adequate number of schools of reasonable quality for more than 130 million out-of-school children to take the country close to the semblance of a satisfactory state of literacy by 2010. The constitutional amendment bill proposes an investment of Rs. 40,000 crore—one-third of the estimated in the Eleventh Five-Year Plan. This figure too has apparently scared the concerned authorities and the government does not seem to be prepared to spend even Rs. 8,000 crore per year for providing primary education.

Another matter of serious concern is the non-implementation of the commitments made by the authorities regarding the abolition of child labour. The fact is that children are often prevented from attending schools or are taken out of schools early so that they may become bread-winners. It is indeed heart-rending to see small children carrying loads on their heads at construction sites, wearing rags or striking red hot iron rods to get them into shape in workshops of ironsmiths, or stitching leather articles. In the vicious circle of ignorance, poverty, illiteracy and deprivation, the national objective of total literacy cannot be achieved in a few years time. What is needed is the political will, proper planning and also public pressure.

O O O

## 3. WHAT IS WRONG WITH INDIA'S SCHOOLS

It is often asked in the circles of common people as well as at the gatherings of intellectuals "Is it fair that children of rich and poor families should go to different schools?" Of all the things that make India a nasty place for the majority of its citizens, is that the educational system in India is bifurcated into two streams solely on the basis of income of parents— one for the rich and the other for the poor. First is the government school which is one of the many established on a large scale without care for the quality of standards prescribed by the Central Advisory Board of Education. While the syllabi of these schools are good, their practical implementation is poor. The teachers in government schools, although well paid, always seek extra private income from tuitions to groups of students. These schools have very few extra-curricular activities and their students obtain average marks in board examinations. On the other hand, there are the so-called public schools which are run by private reputed intellectuals or reputed education societies. These schools charge high tuition and other fees from the students but do justice to the provision of teaching and sports facilities. They have strictly intelligent teachers who know their job and can give inspiring lectures to students. Since they charge high fees, they prefer to admit children belonging to the upper strata of life or even upper middle class if the student is intelligent and can pay their high bracket expenses and some donations.

The quality of education in the government schools is so bad that all parents whoever can afford send their children to public schools different from government schools. These schools invest a good lot on equipping their schools with all teaching aids and best quality equipment for their science laboratories. They also make good provision for sports and send their children for sports championships. They try to mould their students into hard intelligent persons who obtain good marks in board and other examinations.

Government schools on the other hand are not well equipped, their buildings are inferior, facilities for libraries poor, and there is an awful atmosphere of all round low standards of education and sports. As the teachers even though paid well nowadays, sometimes prefer to make extra money from tuitions or group coaching of their own students near the examination days. The paucity of funds in writ large on every student's face.

The 1966 Kothari Commission report came out with the concept of so-called neighbourhood schools. In these schools, it was thought that the state would run schools that would be open to all children in a locality and where proper—if not excellent—standards would be maintained. It was thought that over time most parents would be weaned away from public commercial schools.

The reason why such a common educational system did not develop in India was that successive governments never provided the necessary resources to develop it.

Unless the state spends money to improve the infrastructure and quality of its schools, these would never turn into genuine neighbourhood schools where all children could study equably. While decentralisation and community participation would be essential for the proper working of such a system, funding must not be based on the income (i.e. tax paying capacity) of a community or locality, as in the US.

Looking into the future, the PROBE report suggests two scenarios. The first is the scary one—that the two track system may become more widespread and entrenched. The second is that the state takes more initiatives to push for a schooling transition in which quality elementary education is provided to all children. Money is there, what is needed is a political will for educational emancipation of the poor.

O O O

# 4. LITTLE PROSPECT OF ACHIEVING FULL ENROLMENT AT THE PRIMARY STAGE IN THE BEGINNING OF 21ST CENTURY

With the national average of dropouts at 37 per cent, India entered the new millennium as the nation with the largest population of illiterates. Efforts like Operation Blackboard, launched in 1987 to improve both the quality and quantity of primary education, and Non-Formal Programme, launched earlier in 1979, have not achieved the desired results. Yet India continues to have one of the largest primary education systems in the world. According to official figures, 94 per cent of the rural population in the country has schooling facilities within a distance of one km.

This has, however, not enabled the country to attain the objective of universal enrolment of all children. At the end of the Eighth Five Year Plan, majority of the children had been enrolled but yet 6.3 crore of them in the age group of 6-14 years were considered out of the system. The majority of these were girls and children belonging to the scheduled castes and scheduled tribes living in rural areas.

According to the sixth All India Educational Survey in 1993, 11574 rural habitations in the country were without school. It is well known that poverty is a major cause of keeping the children away from school. The National Sample Survey (1986-87) which did a reason-wise survey of school dropouts, found that economic reasons were largely responsible for the high rates of dropouts. But there are some other reasons too that need to be attended to if the situation is to be somewhat improved. These reasons included: (i) lack of interest in education; (ii) domestic chores; (iii) failure in the class; and (iv) male-female discrimination.

A closer look at dropout statistics will show that while the dropout rate goes up after the primary stage, the number of girls discontinuing studies is higher, specially in certain states like Rajasthan and Bihar where it was found to be over 82 per cent in the class one to class VIII levels. While these figures of dropouts are alarming enough, those educationists who examined the question, felt that the method for computing the dropout rate was somewhat ambiguous. The suggestion clearly is that many more students, specially in the rural areas are leaving school at an early stage than the official figures would have us believe. To get a clearer picture of the dropout rate, it may be necessary to adopt a more accurate and truthful method of enrolment. In villages, it is said to be a common practice for the headmaster to show that all school-going children have been enrolled. That many, if not the most, of these children do not really attend school on a regular basis is not taken into consideration. Then there are cases of double enrolment. To check such malpractices, it will perhaps be better to ensure the involvement of village education committees, adhere strictly to the enrolment age in class I and maintain a register to monitor enrolment, retention, and progress of children in a school. The emphasis merely on enrolment should go as it encourages fictitious enrolment which is finally responsible for blurring the actual picture about dropouts in the country.

Although their number may not be large, the children of nomadic tribes and those whose parents are construction workers or even agricultural workers often get no opportunity to get into the school, if they do drop out soon enough. Perhaps, some kind of a residential school be planned for the migratory workers while NGOs may be asked to help motivate the parents for sending their wards to school. Some States are offering incentives to students belonging to the scheduled castes, tribes and other backward classes. This needs to be extended to all children belonging to the weaker sections and also the minorities.

The Operation Blackboard was launched to provide basic infrastructure to all primary schools in the country. That this goal was far from achieved was found some time ago by a Parliamentary Committee which found many of the schools it visited without basic facilities like class rooms, drinking water and toilet. There were also schools where children had to sit on bare floor and the teacher was taking two or three classes in one room.

While the norms for opening schools in the remote hilly and desert areas may have to be relaxed, conditions like these discourage children from attending schools. But more important is the need to introduce a more modern method of imparting education at the primary level with attractive textbooks and modern teaching aids. Since the maximum dropout rate is between the classes I and III, it is necessary to make education for the very young as attractive as possible. A primary school should become a place of not just learning but also joyful experience.

This would also require motivating the teacher who has not looked beyond the traditional and dull methods of teaching.

The ground realities, however, call for some better consideration for the primary school teacher in rural areas where the working environment as well as the load of work cannot be said to be inducive to motivate him or her. Schools without adequate buildings, lack of teaching aids, heavy workload, multigrade teaching responsibilities, are only some of the problems faced by the teacher who also has to manage without proper housing facilities, or travel long distances and perform many other duties which can range from supervising elections, participation in census operations and conducting family planning programmes.

Poor infrastructure, lack of motivation and other factors like dissatisfaction with working and service conditions contribute to a poor progress in the non-formal education. Since a high rate of dropouts is reported in the higher primary classes, particularly classes VII and VIII, it may be a good idea to offer vocational courses related to rural needs after say class VIII.

The Mid-day Meal Scheme, launched on August 15, 1995, was expected to give a big boost to the programme for universalisation of primary education. But controversies seem to surround the otherwise laudable scheme. It has been found that the practice of distributing wheat or rice, without adhering to the stipulated condition of 80 per cent attendance has been abused. On the other hand, there have been many reports of school children falling sick after eating cooked meals. This highlights the need for better monitoring and involvement of parents, teachers and villagers themselves. A pre-requisite for these actions may be the strengthening of the Panchayati Raj institutions.

The examination system at the primary level may also require another look. Is it right to promote a student only if he/she passes an examination? Or the promotion should be on the basis of attendance? It was way back in 1950, the year India became a republic, that the goal of universalisation of elementary education was adopted by the country. The goal was underlined by the National Policy for Education in 1986. It was revised in 1992 to restate that quality education should be provided to all children upto the age of 14 years before the beginning of the 21st Century. The deadline has approached fast but not the attainment of the objective.

O O O

## 5. JOYFUL LEARNING FOR THE YOUNG

Far from the madding crowd of city schools, where the best of education comes to children by rote, a few schools in Madhya Pradesh have devised a unique way of teaching small children by mixing education with environment.

Using articles of utility like cards, newspaper clippings, broken toys, instead of textbooks, children are taught basic concepts. These schools don't have imposing structures like iron gates that could scare a child or a stick-wielding teacher reading monotonously from a textbook.

"School for the children here is a place for fun, enjoyment and opportunity for doing those things which they may not have been able to do otherwise," says Dr. Rajesh Rajoura, Collector of the district. Introduced in primary schools in Amodia, Ajantad, Aagar, Asli, Bodhwada, Chilur, Madad, Nipawali, Salha and Surani—all in Dhar District in Western Madhya Pradesh—the new technique does not use any textbooks and puts emphasis on competency-based assessment of the students who maintain their own attendance and other records in the school.

"This has resulted in bringing the children to the school, increasing the retention rate and providing quality education to the students, many of whom are first generation learners", Mr. N.S. Bhardwaj is an educationist-cum-assistant commissioner of the tribal welfare department, and he is the brain behind the entire plan.

"The aim was to promote creativity, increase the power of expression, eliminate the practice of memorising without understanding and developing curiosity and the spirit of enquiry among them," says Mr. Bhardwaj. "School is not a place for memorising textbook materials by heart and then producing them in the examination. Rather, it should develop the curiosity of the students so that they could ask questions and learn by themselves. Children should not be imposed on the schools. They should come on their own and consider it as a cherished part of their daily routine," says Dr. Rajoura.

"In 1994-95 the Madhya Pradesh government spent Rs. 390 crore on textbooks alone. But I felt a lot of money could be saved if we use articles which we usually dispose of like newspaper clippings, broken toys, cards, etc. Teaching through charts with pictures of animals, flowers, fruits and other things," Bashir Ahmed who teaches in Chilur village says. "The basic purpose of the teacher is to create an image in the child's mind so that whatever he has learnt, is retained in his memory. Spellings can be taught by arranging cards. When I teach them big and small, I ask two students of different heights to stand side by side. I take them to the fields and show them trees of different heights and shapes," he continues.

Children are also provided with raw materials to make their own models, charts, puzzles, which reflect their knowledge and understanding of what they have learnt. Apna konas (special corners) are created inside the classrooms for various activities related to science, Hindi, mathematics and environment studies and models, maps, charts on respective subjects made by teachers and students are displayed in the classroom.

Another teacher in Aali village school says a student cannot fully understand any topic unless he sees its demonstration or visual representation and for this reason, the four corners of the classroom have been converted into literature corner, social science corner, mathematics corner and student's corner.

# 6. SUGGESTIONS FOR UPGRADING HIGHER EDUCATION IN INDIA

The World Conference on higher education held recently in Paris chalked out a comprehensive agenda on the issues for the new millennium. Professor P.N. Srivastava of the Jawaharlal Nehru University (JNU) was among those who attended the conference.

Mr. Srivastava feels India has a great responsibility since we have considerable experience with the largest number of students being trained in democracy and modern political and economic conditions. No one will dispute, he says, that the basic responsibility of the government of any developing country should be to provide good primary and secondary education since good higher education has to be built on this foundation. At the same time, education cannot and should not be divided into watertight compartments.

In the 1980s the World Bank had done a cost-benefit analysis and had indicated a low social rate of return for higher education in developing countries. A suggestion had been made in the document that the responsibility for higher education should be left to the developed countries which were in a better position to support it financially. In other words, developing countries should forever produce woodcutters and drawers of water. A lot of damage has already been done because of such a presumption in developed countries. If followed, it will have a disastrous effect on higher education in India and other developing countries.

## Market Principle

This paper of the World Bank was criticised in many forums including the UNESCO-supported International Association of Universities located in Paris. The document was put in cold storage and the World Bank produced another document, although conceptually not very different, entitled "Higher Education—The Lessons of Experience In The Early Nineties".

This document envisages that "countries prepared to adopt a higher education policy framework that stresses a differential institutional structure and diversified resources base with greater emphasis on private providers and private funding, will continue to receive priority from the World Bank". This appears to be a guided expression of a political vision rather than the result of a comprehensive enquiry or analytical exercise. There is no analysis of the factors behind the relative success of various models in many diverse situations. The document no doubt stresses the role of higher education for economic growth and development in all countries, but at the same time, recommends that their funding through taxes should be minimised.

The development of higher education should follow the market principle, the document suggested. If such a recommendation is accepted, those in the developing countries will suffer. The document also deserves to be challenged and should face the same fate as the earlier one. It is gratifying that the 1994 UNESCO document on capacity building in higher education does not support the World Bank view.

## Fundamental Right

The government cannot afford to compartmentalise education. It has to be emphasised that any country which does not have good university education will never be listened to as an independent country and will never be able to progress. Only countries prepared to tolerate a second rate and subjugated status in the world will neglect higher education. If India has had any position in the comity of nations in the past, it was mainly because it had better higher education than many of the South Asian, mid-Western, African or Latin American countries. This clearly emphasis on higher education, however, does not imply that it should be supported and developed at the cost of primary and secondary education.

At times, statements are made that there are too many students going in for higher education in India. This is farthest from truth. According to the World Development Report published a few years ago, the world has been divided into low income economies which included most of the Asian and African countries, where the number of students going for higher education was 6 to 7 per cent; in middle income economies, the number varied between 25 to 35 per cent; while in the higher income economies of the USA, Canada and Europe the percentage varied from 30 to 60.

In any independent democracy, education is and should be regarded as a fundamental right. Therefore, opportunities have to be provided for all. However, higher education being expensive, a large number of developing countries including India, cannot offer it to all who want it. It will be much worse to provide higher education without adequate facilities. In fact, this is what is actually being done in India in a majority of universities and colleges with the regrettable result that unemployed graduates are being churned out in large numbers. The government, teachers and students are responsible for this situation. There is, perhaps, no other country except India where university degrees can be obtained cheaply both in terms of financial and academic inputs. Those who are not prepared to dedicate themselves to learning and acquiring knowledge, should stay away from higher education.

## Soft Loans

There is no denying the fact that meaningful higher education is expensive and in spite of best intentions, the government will not be able to provide it fully. If it could do it, nothing would be better. However, the real problem with the government is that it feels diffident to admit it. The government should provide for at least 80 per cent of the expenditure and the rest could be raised by the public. The National Policy on Education, 1986, which had been unanimously supported and accepted by all the political parties, has categorically recommended the enhancement that 20 per cent of the recurring expenditure should be met by the increase in tuition fees. Gradually, the contribution of tuition fees has been going down and today it is perhaps less than five per cent. This trend needs to be reversed with the provision that students from poorer sections will not suffer. The provision of scholarships for such students will have to be made. There must also be a provision for soft and long-term loans to be refunded when students start earning.

○ ○ ○

# 7. EDUCATION—INFRASTRUCTURE

The Father of the Nation Mahatma Gandhi once said: "The real education has to draw out the best from the boys and girls to be educated. This can never be done by packing ill-assorted and unwanted information into the heads of the students. It becomes a dead-weight crushing all originality in them and turning them into mere automates."

There is no doubt that education is the most important constituent of good citizenship. It implies cultivation of the mind to make life tolerable and the acquisition of skill for making it possible.

After many decades, one gets the sense that higher education prominently is the nation-building project. At least the UPA Government demonstrates a great degree of attachment to higher education. It knows what ails higher education and has taken quick corrective measures.

The greatest strength of the higher education in the country lies in the fact that there is a large literate population in India. We have inherited a fairly developed, even though it is deficient, education structure. We have more and more people who are keen to take advantage of education. With the current trend and progress, India is expected to emerge as a superpower by the year 2020. The only challenge is to pay more attention to education.

The error that policy-makers have committed was to take research out of the university system and place it in individual centres. Primary research has to start and develop within the university system, not outside it. At present, research performance is very disappointing and returns from scientific investments in the scientific establishments are far from satisfactory.

To create a research and development hub, we must encourage research on an inter-university basis, wherein universities can come together to pool in their resources. Besides the Government and industry can assign special projects to universities that have expertise.

While developed countries spend around 2.5 per cent of their Gross Domestic Product (GDP) on research and development, in India, this figure stands at an abysmally low 0.85 per cent. We are a growing knowledge economy, but we need to learn from our past experiences and more ahead.

In 1951, India's literacy was just 18.3 per cent. Today the rate stands at 64.8 per cent which is quite a big leap for independent India. However, India continues to lag behind several other developing countries in the region.

China's adult literacy rate was 78.3 per cent in 1990 and 85.8 per cent in 2001, when India reported 49.3 per cent and 58.0 per cent respectively. Sri Lanka posted youth literacy rate of 95.1 per cent (1990) and 96.9 per cent (2001) while India's rates were 64.3 per cent and 73.3 per cent respectively.

Census data indicate that the number of literates in india grew by 52 per cent in 1981-91 and 59 per cent in 1991-2001. The absolute number of illiterates increased during 1981-91 but substantially declined during 1991-2001.

The National policy on Education (1986) provides a broad policy framework for eradication of illiteracy and sets a goal of expenditure on education at six per cent of the GDP. As against the goal of six per cent, the total expenditure on education by both central and state governments was only three per cent of GDP in 2002-03.

The 11th Five-Year Plan (2007-12) document proposes an almost 10-fold in outlay for higher and technical education. The planners have set ambitious targets—to attract 15 per-cent students passing out of Class XII (from the current 10 per cent) into higher education by 2012 and 22 per cent by 2017. The way to do this, they say, is to expand and upgrade on an unprecedented scale.

In the new Plan, there is more of everything—30 new Central Universities are to be set up, seven Indian Institutes of Technology (IITs) and Indian Institutes of Management (IIMs), 10 National Institutes of Technology, five research institutes to be called Indian Institute of Science, Education and Research, 20 Indian Institutes of Information Technology (IIITs), two Schools of Architecture and 330 colleges in educationally backward districts. All this is in line with the Prime Minister's announcements in his Aug. 15, 2008 Independence Day speech.

Infrastructure in existing universities and institutions is also in for major upgradation. Among the big beneficiaries of these special grants will be 17, yet-to-be-identified Central universities which will get Rs. 3,298 crore. Besides, 39 engineering institutes will receive a whopping Rs. 6,749 crore, again for revamping up infrastructure. A good dose of funds has also been set aside for upgrading agriculture, management and medical institutions.

But this money comes with a plan. The document envisions wide-ranging reforms in the way higher education is imparted and much of the fund allocation has been tied up to the beneficiary institute carrying out structural changes. Some of these proposals are likely to start a debate and attract controversy. For instance, the document seeks to raise fees for higher education up to 20 per cent of operational costs, which is five per cent at present. Higher education is highly subsidised. The document seeks to reduce this subsidy to improve quality of education. But it has not given the slightest indication that it has a road map for the reform of the public university system. It fails to acknowledge that decades of decline in our Ph.D. programmes have left us with an acute shortage of teachers.

The National Knowledge Commission's (NKC) report on higher education is one in the series that began with the report of the Dr. Radhakrishnan Commission (1948). The valuable reports have met with one common fate—they are often quoted but remain largely unimplemented. It is hoped that such of the recommendations of the NKC as are accepted will be implemented. Most of the recommendations here have already been made in the earlier reports.

Among the recommendations that have been reiterated, one that advocates 1.5 to 2 per cent of the GDP for higher education, assuming a provision of six per cent for education, and the observation that implicit politicisation has made governance of universities exceedingly difficult and much more susceptible to non-academic intervention from outside are worth emphasising.

In order to increase the gross enrolment ratio to 15 per cent, the NKC suggests that India needs as many as 1,500 universities by 2015. It is a modest requirement for a country of India's size and, if implemented it would mean rectifying the major deficiencies.

The number of universities that have been suggested is not too large. Japan with a population of 12.7 crore has 726 universities; Germany with 8.2 crore has 350; the UK with 6.1 crore has 125; and the US with a population of 30.4 crore is reported to have 2,466. China, according to the NKC, has authorised the creation of 1,250 new universities in the next three years.

The National Education Policy has proposed to establish a coordinating body. In the interest of greater coordination of facilities and developing inter-disciplinary research, a national body covering higher education in general, agricultural, medical, technical, legal and other professional fields will be set up.

It is an extremely significant decision. Unfortunately, it has not been implemented. It may be established and designated as the National Board of Higher Education, consisting of the

Chairpersons of the autonomous bodies and the Ministers concerned as members and the Prime Minister as Chairman.

The National Policy has also recommended a coordinating body at the State level, designated as the State Council of Higher Education. If these bodies are established, there would be an elegant structure of regulatory intermediaries representing an academic hierarchy with proper decentralisation and well-defined functions.

In India, higher education suffers mainly due to the tendency to overlook merit and talent, while deciding eligibility for such education. Merit and talent are natural attributes. They may be prevalent widely, but their distribution among the people is not uniform, both in nature and magnitude.

Education has become book-centric or the critical and lack in the practical use of education.

The curriculum today is out of touch with ground realities and little practical import. The curriculum does not provide knowledge that can be utilised to enhance local resources through which employment can be generated in addition to improve the existing conditions. Another major setback is the Government's recent policy on reservation. The reservation policy was conserved to counter India's peculiar socio-economic conceived, in which larger section of the population led a life of humiliation and deprivation. But in recent times, the reservation policy has become a vote bank.

The role of private sector in higher education has been landed by many sections in unambiguous terms. Consequent to the increase in demand and inadequate response on the part of Governments, there has been in recent years a quiet but steady increase in private participation in general and professional education. The world is also witnessing a gradual transformation of higher education from public to private good.

Against the backdrop of this development, the attitude of the political leadership in the country towards private participation appears to be one of disapproval. But the willingness to prevent and inability to regulate, and in general, an indifferent attitude, have led to the pervasive co-existence of the good and the bad.

Private initiative in education is not the answer to every problem. Indeed, it will also create a new set of problems. In this context, the role of the private sector needs to be examined.

Higher education, as an important instrument of change and development, must be depoliticised and modernised if the new education policy is to be an unqualified success.

# VI. POLITICAL PHILOSOPHY

## 1. INDIVIDUAL FREEDOM VIS-A-VIS SOCIAL COMMITMENT

Amartya Sen said in his address at the award ceremony for the Giovanni Agnelli International Prize: "In the circumstances of long-standing disparity and inequity, the underdogs may come to regard their fate as fairly inescapable, to be borne with placidity and calm. They learn to adjust their desires and pleasures accordingly. Since it makes little sense to go on pining for what does not seem feasible, the prospects of which they had typically not had much reason to consider carefully. In the case of the chronically deprived who lack the courage to desire much more than they have and who take whatever joy they can from small mercies, the utilitarian calculus is deeply biased, since their deprivations look less acute in the distorted yardstick of pleasures and desires. The measure of utility may insulate social ethics from appreciating the intensity of the deprivation of the precariously placed hireling, the chronically unemployed, the overworked coolie, or the thoroughly subjugated housewife, who have all learned to keep their desires in check and to make the most of whatever tiny experience of relief that comes their way." In the above one literary paragraph, Amartya Sen has summed up the problems and worries of the poor and the deprived.

Though this issue goes the very roots of the utilitarian calculus, the problem is not just a theoretical one, but has some serious practical consequences. Sen illustrates this by referring to two of the major social features of life in India. One concerning gender inequality—the disparity between men and women. The disadvantages for women are not, of course,

186

unique to India and there is much evidence of extensive gender-based inequality even in the elementary matters of health care and nutrition in many regions across the world (e.g. in most of the countries in the broad belt stretching from West Asia to China). But fairly detailed comparisons of mortality rates, morbidity rates, hospital care, nutritional attention, etc. have been made in India and despite variations between regions within India, they clearly confirm a fairly decisive picture of women being systematically deprived vis-a-vis men in most of the parts, specially rural India.

The diagnosis of significant gender inequality and of the need for change has, however, been forcefully disputed. It has been pointed out that rural Indian women typically do not suffer from the envy of the position of men, do not see their position as one of painful inequality, and do not pine for reform. Even though the politicising of the rural population is altering this picture slowly (a change in which the newly developing women's movements are beginning to play an important part), nevertheless that empirical observation is largely correct as a description of the present situation in rural India. It would be hard to claim that there is, at this moment, widespread dissatisfaction with gender inequality, or a fulminating desire for a radical change among rural Indian women. The real question concerns the interpretation and significance of this observation.

In an objective sense, women in rural India are indeed less free to do various things than men are, and there is nothing in the history of the world to indicate that women will not value more freedom when they actually come to experience it (rather than taking it to be infeasible or unnatural). The absence of the present discontentment cannot wipe out the moral significance of the inequality if individual freedom—including the freedom to assess one's situation and changing it if desired—is accepted as a major value.

It may be useful to compare the approach that Sen has tried to present with some aspects of John Rawls's far-reaching theory of justice which has contributed greatly to a radical regeneration of modern political philosophy and ethics. The Rawlsian theory of justice has, in fact, done much to draw attention to the political and ethical importance to individual to individual freedom. His "principles of justice" safeguard the "priority" of individual liberty similar to liberty for all. His accounting of inequality concentrates not on the distribution of utility but on that of "primary goods". These are the means such as wealth, income, liberty, etc. that help people to pursue their respective objectives freely. Primary goods are means to freedom, but they cannot represent the extent of freedom, given the diversity of human beings in converting primary goods into freedom to pursue their respective objectives. Given the variations in sex, age, inherited characteristics, environmental differences, etc. that may prevail among and within groups, of people, even an equal distribution of primary goods may make people with physical disabilities less free to pursue their own well-being. Furthermore, not only may be disabled people be handicapped in the pursuit of welfare, they may also be disadvantaged—unless they get special facilities—in participating in the choice of common social institutions and in influencing general political decisions (not connected necessarily with their own disabilities).

## 2. Crisis Of Capitalism Is Irreversible—Thought For Tomorrow

The spread, depth, and intensity of the global economic crisis has now occasioned radical critics of capitalism. The End of History sort of triumphalism—after the collapse of rival, socialism—has given way to deep-seated fears that the system is finally unravelling. Slower US growth, recession in Japan, Russia's economic meltdown and above all, the spread of the Asian crises to Latin America have triggered such concerns, stated Chander Mohan in an article recently.

When the likes of Mr. George Soros warn that the "global capitalism was coming undone", matters must really be serious. Elsewhere in South East Asia, Mr. Mahathir Mohammad has been arguing that Asia is now haunted by 'rampant capitalism' blaming speculators for the woes of the region.

What is 'rampant capitalism'? Mr. Mahathir's favourite targets are those like Mr. Soros who move millions across borders, thanks to Infotech. This new breed often erode the sovereignty of nations by controlling exchange rates and short-term movement of capital which are inherently crisis-ridden. And they are different from the old capitalists who were confined to their own countries.

All this is rather similar to Mr. Soros's 'capital threat' which targets not only currency speculators but presumably financials like himself also. He made billions betting against the UK's pound sterling. Since then he has lost heavily with the US stock markets heading southwards and the Russian economy lurching from crisis to crisis. He has now returned to his favourite musings as a philosopher.

The threat of "rampant capitalism" in terms of a world of freer flow of capital has existed in the past as well. Way back in the eighties, its depreciations were witnessed when Latin America sank under the burden of a debt crisis. The late 1990s, however, were quantitatively different as the sheer scale of the havoc dwarfed anything before: Surges of capital out of Asia devastated South Korea, Indonesia, Thailand, and Malaysia dragging down the world economy. The same thing is happening to India in 2008-09.

Till then such economies exemplified the Asian version of state capitalism. Economists saw virtues in whatever these countries did. Their prices were right. Their economic fundamentals were sound. Their policies were outward-oriented. But when investors developed a crisis of confidence and stampeded out with their money, what remained was only a horror story of capitalism.

The Asian boom-bust cycle also signalled a complete retreat from reliance on market forces to a regime of controls. Mr. Mahathir took a radical U-turn from being an ardent votary of capitalism to clamping down exchange rate controls to stem capital flight. To shore up, other economies are also planning to follow suit.

Globalisation is thus attracting fewer starry-eyed advocates than before. The extent to which market driven capitalism is on the retreat is exemplified by the smugness expressed by India's officials. Overall economic growth slowed down to 7.5 per cent but they feel vindicated regarding its one step forwards and two steps backward reform agenda. They argue that India's caution towards full convertibility has saved it from the Asian turmoil.

The constituency for faster reforms and inviting FDI on a substantial scale now has narrowed considerably. Instead of allowing market forces a free rein, officials prefer to retain controls. There is a reluctance to scrap the Foreign Investment Promotion Board. There is an unwillingness to allow foreign players into the insurance sector. There is bold resistance to privitation agenda.

Interestingly, Mr. Soros too considered the spread of market forces as the biggest threat. An important characteristic of the global market economy—in which goods, services, capital and even people move around quite freely—was the dominant belief in the magic of the market place. However, this same market place that brought prosperity earlier went through regular boom-bust cycles, sending ripples of destitution which could trigger a totalitarian backlash in Western democracies.

To Mr. Soros, the problem with *laissez-faire* capitalisation was that its underlying economics had unrealistic assumptions such as the concept of 'equilibrium'. A better approximation was 'reflexivity' in which the perceptions of economic agents determined reality : This was observed in financial markets where buyers and sellers discount a future that depended on their own decisions. As a result, prices fluctuated in boom-bust cycles rather than tend towards 'equilibrium'. Economics minus equilibrium was not a science.

For what made it so dangerous. The uninhabited pursuit of self-interest unleashed only excessive individualism. Too much competition and too little cooperation caused intolerable inequalities and instability. Unless a recognition of common interests took precedence over particular interests "our present system was liable to break down", he argued. A repentant Mr. Soros now believes that the rule of Mammon is complete.

Back to 'rampant capitalism', this rule of Mammon is best exemplified by the US Treasury-Wall Street complex which is aggressively trying to push for an unbridled role for short-term capital to slosh around freely in the world economy. Despite the havoc that it is bringing in its wake, the capitalist interests oppose any form of controls even of the social net IMF variety. Instead of enabling the crisis-ridden economies to cope, these interests push for more openness.

The magic of the markets thus amounts to a brutal social Darwinistic process in which only the fittest survived. As the successful tiger economies fell like dominos, most countries today are less enthusiastic regarding this form of capitalism. The *laissez-faire* doctrine has become a bad word when the Asian contagion is spreading to Latin America and depressing stock markets around the world. Russia's predicament only fuels such fires.

The pendulum is shifting towards unnecessary controls over the economy. Reliance on market forces is less important as the world economy hovers on the brink of a generalised depression. Not surprisingly, observers are drawing parallels with the 1930s when radical critiques of capitalism surfaced till the Keynesian revolution saved the system from breaking down completely.

With no such revolution in the offing, the world economy is passing through its gravest crisis. Each country is left to fashion its own policy response to save itself from the turbulence all around. Maybe a better mix between statism and reliance on market forces may emerge in the process. Maybe technological change can provide renewed impetus for long-term growth. May be a European Union sort of coordinated policy response will find more adherents in the days ahead. Capitalism is under threat as never before.

○ ○ ○

## 3. More Thoughts On 'Passing' Capitalism

Prakash Karat, a member of the CPI (M) politburo, is rejoicing over the downward trend in capitalism, a worldwide glimpse of which was given in the last essay. He has jumped to the conclusion that "there is nothing to be pessimistic about the future of Marxism." Thus far he is right, but not when he says that the "triumph of capitalism is a passing phase." There are reasons to believe "that capitalism may indeed be able to solve the crisis that Marx had thought to be inevitable." But maybe the economists of the world may come out with the needed proposals for creating a mix of socialism and capitalism and save the declining economies of the world.

Marx had pointed out that the pursuit of profit unleashed two opposing forces. On the one hand it led to increased production; on the other hand it led to reduction in the wages. Reduced wages led to a declining demand for the goods whose production had increased. There were too many goods chasing too little demand. Thus "breaks out of an epidemic," he wrote in the Communist Manifesto which, "in all earlier epochs, would have seemed as an absurdity—the epidemic of overproduction."

Never did Marx dream that the labourer would be able to rise within capitalism. He wrote: "The serf, in the period of serfdom, raised himself to membership in the commune, just as the petty bourgeois, under the yoke of feudal absolutism, managed to develop into a bourgeois. The modern labourer on the contrary instead of rising with the progress of industry, sinks deeper and deeper below the conditions of existence of his own class. He becomes a pauper.

Theoretically, Marx is indeed correct. The demand for wages cannot increase in capitalism. But what about the demand from the ruling class itself. Can the ruling class—the capitalists, bureaucracy, labour aristocracy, and stockholders—not provide the demand? The contradiction arose from the inability to digest profits. If profits, instead of being used as reinvestments were to be used for consumption, then where would the problem lie?

In fact, there are reasons to believe that events during Marx's own lifetime pointed in this direction. Engels was to find that such was indeed taking place. Only he and Marx perhaps limited by their historical circumstances, failed to take their argument to its logical conclusion. They could see that the British workers, instead of becoming paupers were raising themselves to share in the profits of capitalism. A year before Marx's death in 1883, Engles wrote to Kautsky, "You ask me what the English workers think about colonial policy. Well exactly the same as they think about politics in general—the same as the bourgeois think. There is no workers' party here, you see, there are only conservatives and liberal radicals, and the workers share the feast of England's monopoly of the world markets and the colonies." The capitalists of England were sharing their profits with their workers. That provided the demand for the goods that were being produced with the work of pauperised workers.

The so-called "crisis of capitalism" stood solved permanently. The capitalists could make profits where the workers were submissive, in this case the colonies, and share those profits with a privileged class, in this case the workers of England, to provide the demands for the goods so produced. These "imperial" workers would provide the demand for the goods produced by their colonial counterparts.

Keynes had perceived this problem. He wrote "Ancient Egypt was doubly fortunate, and doubtless owed to this its fabled wealth, in that it possessed two activities, namely pyramid building as well as the search for precious metals, the fruits of which, since they could not serve the needs of man by being consumed, did not stake with abundance. The middle ages built cathedrals and sang dirges. Two pyramids, two masses for the dead, are twice as good as one, but not so two railways from London to New York." The secret of the Egyptian economy, according to Keynes was that the wealth that could not be profitably invested was used to build pyramids and to mind gold. These works led to the expenditure of profits without generating yet more profits. Such expenditure led to the generation of demand in the economy. A demand-supply equilibrium was attained.

Demand in the Egyptian society was created in the construction of pyramids, in feudal society it was created by the lords, in the colonial society by the consumption by imperial workers. Could then the demand in the 21st century be created by the stockholders?

In an article in *Newsweek*, it has been claimed that the Asian crisis has been largely positive for the United States— serving it with "a good platter of cheap goods and money." It goes on to say that Asian Flight capital has been pumping the US market. The inflow of money from Asia whether by flight capital or dividends from US operations abroad was "pumping the demand by the US economy". The workers of East Asia have been working to supply cheap goods to meet this demand. Just as the feudal lord would employ serfs to produce goods to be used by the nobility; the colonial England employed colonised Indians to produce goods for the workers of Manchester. So US corporations can employ the workers of Thailand to produce goods to be consumed by the US stockholders. The US corporations can invest abroad, use cheap labour to produce goods, repatriate their profits to the US which are distributed among the stockholders. These profits create demand in the US economy; the Asian countries export their cheap goods to fulfil this demand.

The essence of the crisis of capitalism was the contradiction between wages and profits. Marx had correctly said there is little possibility of increase in wages providing the demand for the goods. But what about dividends? The joint stock company has changed the meaning of the 'capitalist'. If the stockholder is the capitalist, then he may well consume rather than invest his dividends.

Of course, this does not mean that the 'workers' will be reduced to paupers, exactly what Marx had predicted. But if the profits get distributed and create demand then the crisis will not occur despite these low wages.

The question that remains is whether capitalism can sustain increased dividend payments along with reduced wages. This is really a social issue. After all, feudal lords will persuade serfs to live a life of frugality amidst their extravagance. And the British did persuade a large number of Indian workers to submit meekly to their trade manipulation.

Given the Information Technology revolution, it is unlikely that the workers of the world will take their misery lying down. But this reduces itself to a contest between wage labourers of Asia and stockholders of America, unaided by the inevitable crisis of capitalism. No longer may such a triumph necessarily be a passing phase, says Mr. Karat.

The crisis of capitalism is not inevitable. Whether capitalism will survive or not, will depend on whether the corporations distribute adequate profits to generate demand or whether the organisations of the workers of Asia can take on the organisations of the stockholders of America.

## 4. DEMOCRACY AND DEVELOPMENT—IDEOLOGY OF DELINKING POLITICS FROM ECONOMY

V.A. Panandikar, a prominent veteran sociologist of India, has stressed the need for delinking of politics from economy, if success in development is desired in a democracy. The Indian State has shown its incapacity to manage its economic institutions as is shown by a haphazard development of the economy in its different spheres. Democracy is essentially a system of governance—not a system of economic management. He says that the people of India will now have to decide about the role of the Indian State. Broad essential state regulation of the economy, yes, state management of the economy, no, he says.

India's success as a democracy is now acknowledged worldwide. India's integrity and unity would not have been assured without the successful functioning of the democratic system. The very success is becoming in some ways an impediment to India's economic development. It is not that there is any inherent contradiction between democracy and economy. But it is the way that relationship between democracy and economy has developed since independence.

Democracy is the best way of governing a diverse, plural and complex Indian polity and society with religious, regional, ideological, caste, sub-caste, language and many other diversities prevalent in India. India has diversity as a strength and has succeeded in democratic governance contrary to Western democratic theory that acute diversities and democracies do no go well together.

The economy on the other hand has its own logic. The way in which India's political institutions have run the economy has been inimical to the interests and even safety of the economy. Political institutions are designed to run the political affairs of a country. They are not designed to manage a complex economy.

The fundamental reason for this problem is the role of the

state in India. Jawaharlal Nehru wanted the country to adopt socialistic pattern of society. He introduced the concept of economic planning along with other aspects of planning in 1954. Indira Gandhi took over the "commanding heights" of the economy in 1969. She even nationalised 14 major commercial banks.

By the late 1950s Nehru found that many state policies were not working well. In July, 1958, he expressed to the chief ministers of various states a sense of frustration and depression viewing the slow progress of Five-Year Plans of development. He wrote: "Democracy and socialism are means to an end, not ends in themselves. If the individual is ignored and sacrificed for the goal of society, there is nothing so wrong." He wrote to chief ministers: "The state should always try to do what it can, provided this is done efficiently and economically." In the early stages of planning, the state played a useful role in the Indian economy. But after the death of Rajiv Gandhi, the Indian economy entered the state of disarray. In actual fact, state finances were in bad shape in the late 1980s. The fiscal deficit of the centre at one stage reached 11 per cent of the Gross National Product. The country's investable resources were eaten away by subsidies, huge electricity board losses, excessive salary bills of the Central and state bureaucracy, and the losses of some of the sick mills in the public sector.

The perilous condition of the economy is well-documented in the economic survey that the Union Finance Minister presented to the Parliament in 1998. And yet the Finance Minister did not adequately address the central issues facing the economy-in the June 1998 budget. There was no debate on the state of the economy in 1998.

Most politicians do not fully realise that our banking system is not in good health. The non-performing assets are very high and threaten the economy. Two reports of the Narsimha Committee are still pending with the government. But the leaders earlier in the UF government and later of the BJP government did not have the courage to take necessary action.

The fundamental question is that politicians in power are less concerned with the economy, and more with patronage because it is this where there are votes and even kickbacks. Most politicians in power and even the bureaucrats are what former Finance Minister says "short-term maximisers". The problem has been greatly compounded by the new emerging elite from among the scheduled castes and backward classes. They do not understand the macro-economic issues.

The lessons are clear. Democracy and the economy, with the commanding heights under state control, do not mix well. More precisely the state should do what it is designed for— manage the politics of the country. The economy should be delinked from the polity. Bad politics under state ownership makes for bad economics. This is the path for slow growth, continuing poverty, an uncompetitive economy, inefficiency and later on economic breakdown. Let the state do whatever it can for the poor and the weak. Let the state also look after the nation's health and concentrate on education.

O O O

# 5. The Concept Of Welfare State As Applied To India

The idea of welfare state was first developed by the social democrats or moderate socialists in Europe. By now it has come to be widely accepted even by non-socialists, although there are differences of opinion about the extent of welfare that the state should provide. There is no conflict between social security and the market mechanism and the two can comfortably co-exist. The real difference of opinion is about the extent of welfare that the state should provide. There is no conflict between social security and the market mechanism and the two can comfortably co-exit. The real difference of opinion is about the desirable size of public sector and the nature and extent of controls that the state should administer in relation to the private sector. People have even started talking of market socialism. More and more people including the less doctrinaire socialists have come round to the view that it is better to allow private sector to function within a reasonably free market system in view of its greater "efficiency", the state retaining such power as is appropriate for availing part of the wealth produced to finance welfare measures. All this assumes that the state is the most suitable instrument for dispensing welfare.

India is a welfare state. It is committed to the welfare and development of its people in general and its vulnerable sections in particular. The Preamble to the Constitution of India, Directive Principles of State Policy, Fundamental Rights and specific sections namely Articles, 38, 39 and 46 in the Constitution stand testimony to the commitment of the State to the provision of welfare to the people in general and the vulnerable sections of society—the poor, scheduled castes and tribes, backward classes, the handicapped and the destitute, in particular.

Welfare is not a matter of charity. Welfare programmes were initially directed to provide a few basic curative and rehabilitative services. Over the years, a developmental orientation in contrast to curative approach to welfare programmes has come into existence. At present these are oriented towards providing preventive, developmental and rehabilitative services to the disabled, aged, addicts, the maladjusted, scheduled castes and scheduled tribes, other backward classes, and weaker sections. With a view to providing an integrated thrust to development of these sections of population, a new Ministry of Welfare was formed by pooling subjects relating to the welfare of the aged, disabled, programmes of social defence, welfare of schedule castes, scheduled tribes and other backward classes, minorities and work relating to wakfs.

## Administrative Set-Up

The population of scheduled castes and tribes was, according to 2001 Census, 16.64 crore and 8.43 crore, respectively constituting 16.20 per cent and 8.20 per cent, respectively of the country's total population of 102 crore. While the Constitution has provided certain protective measures and safeguards for these classes, successive Five-Year Plans have regarded their progress as a major objective of national policy. Besides constitutional safeguards, the State insists on their general rights as citizens with the object of promoting their educational and economic interests and removing social disabilities: (i) abolition of untouchability and forbidding its practice in any form; (ii) promotion of their education and economic interests and their protection from social injustice and all forms of exploitation; (iii) throwing open by law of Hindu religious institutions of public character to all classes and sections of Hindus; (iv) removal of all disability, liability, restriction or conditions with regard to access to shops, public restaurants, hotels or places of public entertainment or use of wells, tanks, bathing ghats, roads and tourist resorts maintained wholly or partially out of state funds or dedicated to the use of general public; (v) curtailment by law in the interests of any scheduled tribes of general rights of all citizens to move freely, settle in and acquire property; (vi) forbidding or any denial of admission to educational institutions maintained by state or receiving grants from state funds; (vii) permitting the state to make reservations for backward classes in public services including schedules castes and tribes in the making of appointments to public services; (viii) special representation in Lok Sabha and State Assemblies for scheduled castes and tribes; (ix) setting up of tribal advisory councils and separate departments in states and appointment of a special officer at the centre to promote their welfare and safeguard their interests; and (x) special provision for administration and control of scheduled castes and tribes and tribal areas.

## National Commission For Scheduled Castes and Tribes

This commission comprises a chairperson, a vice chairperson and five other members appointed by the President. The commission has the following duties: (i) to investigate and monitor all matters relating to the safeguards provided in the constitution; (ii) to enquire into specific complaints with respect to the deprivation of rights and safeguards of the scheduled castes and tribes; (iii) to participate and advise on the planning process of socio-economic development of the scheduled castes and tribes and to evaluate the progress of their development under the Union or any other State, (iv) to present to the President annually and such other items as the commission may decide reports on the working of these safeguards; (v) to make in such reports/recommendations as to measures that be taken by the Union or any State for the protection, welfare and socio-economic development of the scheduled castes and tribes; and (vi) to discharge such other functions in relation to the protection, welfare and development and advancement of scheduled castes and tribes.

The National Commission for scheduled castes and tribes shall, while investigating and monitoring any matter relating to the safeguards provided for scheduled castes and tribes under the Constitution, or any other law for the time being in force or under any order of the government has all powers of a civil court trying a suit and particularly in respect of the following matters: namely (i) summoning and enforcing attendance of any person, from any part of India and examining him on oath; (ii) requiring the discovery or production of any document; (iii) receiving evidence on affidavits; (iv) requisitioning any public record or copy thereof from any court and office; (v) issuing commission for the examination of witnesses and documents; and (vi) any other matter which the President may by any rule determine.

The Union and every State government shall consult the commission on all major policy matters affecting scheduled castes and scheduled tribes. The government had set up three Parliamentary committees, first in 1966, second in 1971, and the third in 1973 to examine the implementation of the constitutional safeguards for welfare of scheduled castes and scheduled tribes. The Committee has since been constituted as a Standing Committee of Parliament on Labour and Welfare.

States and Union Territories have separate departments to look after the welfare of scheduled castes and scheduled tribes and other backward classes. In Bihar, Madhya Pradesh and Orissa, separate ministries have been set up to look after tribal welfare. A number of voluntary organisations also promote welfare of scheduled castes and tribes. Among them important organisations of all-India character are: Harijan Sewak Sangh, Delhi; Indian Red Cross Society, New Delhi; Ramakrishna Mission, Narendrapur; Bhartiya Samaj Sewak Sangh, New Delhi; Ramakrishna Mission, Puri, Silchar, and Purulia, Bharatiya Samaj Unnati Mandal, Bhivandi; and Servants of Society, Pune, Mahashtra. The government also provides grants-in-aid to voluntary organisations of local character working among scheduled castes. During 2008-08, 260 voluntary organisations were given grants-in-aid to the tune of Rs. 50 crore.

There is also a scheme launched by the Centre for the alleviation of poverty among the scheduled castes and tribes through the Ministry of Welfare. Special Central Assistance (SCA) provides 100 per cent grants to States and Union Territories as an additive to their special component plans to give a boost to the development programmes for scheduled castes and tribes with reference to their occupational pattern and the need for increasing the productivity of and income from their limited assets by taking up family oriented schemes for them. The SCA is used to fill the critical gaps and vital missing inputs in family-oriented income generating schemes.

## Coaching and Allied Scheme

Started in the Fourth-Five Year Plan, the scheme imparts

training to scheduled castes and tribes for various competitive examinations held by the UPSC, public sector undertakings, Banking service recruitment boards, etc. Grant is given to the pre-examination centres (PETCs) which are run either by the state/union territories governments or universities or private institutes. Financial assistance is provided to the State/UT governments on a matching basis 50 : 50 over and above their committed liabilities. Some of the coaching centres have made considerable contribution enabling SC/ST candidates getting into IAS and allied services and also in medical, engineering, and banking services.

## Book Bank Scheme

This scheme is intended to provide textbooks for SC/ST students pursuing medical and engineering courses as well as agriculture, veterinary and polytechnic. SC/ST students are also receiving assistance to buy textbooks.

## Pre-Matric Scholarships

Begun in 1977, this scheme is for education development of those who are engaged in the so called unclean occupations, viz. scavenging of dry latrines, tanning, fraying and sweeping with traditional links like scavenging. The scheme as modified from November 1, 1991 provides scholarship of Rs. 25 per month in classes I to V, Rs. 40 per month for classes VI to VIII and Rs. 50 per month in classes IX-X, in respect of day scholars. Rs. 250 per month in classes IX and X is provided. An ad hoc grant of Rs. 500 is granted to day scholars as well as hostellers. The scheme was further modified in February 1994. The income ceiling has been removed. There is no restriction as to the number of children of same parents who would be eligible for scholarship upto class subject, however, subject to the condition that if a third or subsequent child is born after April 1, 1993, a total of only two children in the family would be eligible for scholarship.

## Post-Matric Scholarships for SC/ST Students

This scheme was introduced in 1994-95 for providing

financial assistance to students studying at post-matric stages in different schools and colleges to complete their course. In 1996-97 the number of student scholarships reached 21.48 lakh. The government has also increased the maintenance allowance from October 1995 to the extent of 50 per cent in case of professional and technical courses and 30 per cent in case of non-professional courses. The income ceilings have been revised from Rs. 18,000 and Rs. 24,000 per annum to Rs. 33,400 and Rs. 44,500 per annum.

## Liberation and Rehabilitation of Scavengers

This scheme for Scavengers and their dependents has been formulated with the following components: (i) time-bound survey for identification of scavengers and their dependents with their aptitudes for alternative trades; (ii) training as per trysem norms in identified trades at the local nearest training institution/centres of state governments/central government and semi government and non-government organisations; and (iii) rehabilitation of scavengers in trades and occupations by providing subsidy, margin money loan and bank loan. The scheme provides for funding projects costing up to Rs. 50,000 per beneficiary with 50 per cent of the project cost subsidy with a maximum of Rs. 10,000, 15 per cent margin money loan at a rate of 4 per cent and balance loan from bank.

It may be observed that most of the financial assistance for welfare is distributed among the scheduled castes and scheduled tribes. Even some scholarships for studies abroad are granted to deserving scheduled caste students. Besides the above facilities and amenities by the central and state governments for scheduled caste and tribes, the government has taken initiative to start a few schemes for development of tribal areas, particularly, vocational education in the tribal areas. Besides this, fifteen Tribal Research Institutes (TRIs) have been set by the states of Andhra Pradesh, Assam, Bihar, Gujarat, Kerala, Madhya Pradesh, Chhattisgarh, Maharashtra, Orissa, Rajasthan, Tamil Nadu, West Bengal, Uttar Pradesh,

Manipur and Tripura. Many of these institutes have museums which exhibit tribal articles.

## Welfare of Minorities

A Minorities Commission was set up by the Government of India in January 1978. It was charged with the responsibility of evaluating the working of various safeguards in the Constitution for the protection of religious minorities and to make recommendations to ensure effective implementation of and enforcement of all the safeguards and laws. The Commission reviews the policies of the government of India and the State governments in the matters related to the minorities. The occasional reports of the Minorities Commission are laid on the table of both the houses of Parliament. A 15-point programme for the welfare of minorities was announced by the late Prime Minister Indira Gandhi in May 1983. This programme has the objective of securing the life and property of minorities and for providing special consideration for minorities in public employment and ensuring non-discrimination in development programmes and grant of financial benefits.

## Welfare of the Handicapped

Relief to the disabled is a State subject. In practice, the central government plays a major role in this field. Some of the programmes for welfare of the handicapped are implemented through the non-government organisations and monitored through the state governments. Close liaison is maintained by the Ministry of Welfare with associated Ministries such as the Ministry of Health, Family Planning, Department of Women and Child Development, and Ministry of Labour.

# 6. Re-examining World's Economic Ideology

Amian Dutta, a prominent political philosopher and an economist has come to the conclusion that a new social, political and economic order is likely to be built up in the not-too-distant future not simply to achieve greater social welfare but also to avoid a breakdown of human society. Some political philosophers dismiss this vision of an impending disaster as it is thought by them too pessimistic a view of human affairs. Others consider it as the only realistic side of the situation. They opine that this is the time for rethinking on the fundamental issues concerning human society.

This sets the background for reconsideration of the relationship between ethics, on the one hand, and economics and politics on the other. This is a question on which the ideas of leading thinkers and sociologists are marked by a deep ambiguity since ancient times. There have been swings of attitude from time to time, from one epoch to another but the ambiguity continues.

At the dawn of modern age in Europe, Machiavelli wrote that "a prudent ruler ought not to keep faith when by so doing it would go against his interest". But this was not altogether a new thought. We find anticipations of similar ideas long ago in the writings of Kautilya in ancient India. This is in spite of the fact that neither Machiavelli nor Kautilya was entirely devoid of ideas of morality in his own ways. But their ideas contradicted the teachings of the dominant traditions, particularly religious traditions of their societies. In India, the prescribed four-fold objectives of life comprised the pursuit of wealth and desire-fulfilment within the limits of dharma or right social conduct including truthfulness while the ultimate goal was the attainment of a state of inner peace and freedom. As for Machiavelli, his ideas on the statecraft or the duties of a prince were, to put it mildly, difficult to reconcile with Christian teachings regarding how to behave towards one's neighbours and one's enemies. In a way, statements of people like

Machiavelli were declarations of an intention to emancipate "positive" studies of politics and related social "sciences" from ethics as desired from religion. If this happened to politics, a similar development was only to be expected in the area of political economy. But again, ambiguity persisted all the time. For a number of reasons, the position here is somewhat complex. But we shall try to keep the exposition as simple and straightforward as possible.

Though Adam Smith had some eminent precursors, he is generally regarded as the father of classical political economy. Some of the most influential economists since his time have had strong ethical leanings. Smith himself wrote a tract on the theory of moral sentiments and, along with self-interest, he regarded sympathy as an integral part of human nature. John Stuart Mill, despite his affiliation with classical tradition, was attracted towards a moderate and cooperative form of socialism as a morally and culturally superior economic order. Alfred Marshall, a dominating figure in the Cambridge school of economics at the turn of the 20th century, had unquestionable ethical leanings.

Yet the mainstream of classical and neoclassical political economy was marked by a very different tendency. At least since the time of Bentham (1747-1832), who appeared to subscribe to both psychological and ethical hedonism, economics has fallen under the spell of utilitarianism. The 'economic man' was pictured as rational, self-centred and pleasure-seeking. The development of economics and economic policy was strongly influenced by this idea. The individual in his economic activities and transactions was supposed to aim consistently at maximisation of the sum total of utilities for himself regardless of what happened to others. An interpersonal comparison of utilities was ruled out in the main body of economics.

The main arguments for this exclusion appear to be two-fold. Different people have different tastes, sensibilities and capacities for feeling pleasure or, as many continentals put it "felicity" and, given such differences, it was supposed that there was no basis for a direct comparison. But there was also a more compelling and practical reason for this approach. Utility is derived from consumption. The law of diminishing utility lays down that, beyond a certain point, the extra utility that a person derives from possessing and consuming one more unit of commodity steadily declines. This law of declining marginal utility is apt to have very radical implications for public policy. The presumption is that a given addition to the income of a poor person will add greater utility than the same addition to the income of a rich man who already has a much larger income. If interpersonal comparison of utility is permitted, a radical redistribution of income in favour of the poor would look reasonable on strictly utilitarians ground. The edge of this argument was blunted by the counter-argument that an unequal distribution of income helps savings and investment which promotes growth of wealth.

The advocates of the modern welfare state bypass this dilemma by a reasoning which is partly economic and partly humanitarian or extra-economic. Provision of health care and education up to a certain standard is justified not only on palpable ethical grounds, but it also adds to the productive capacity of the common people and so promotes economic growth. This line of reasoning has the advantage that it avoids a direct conflict with conventional economic theory in the industrially advanced countries while it has also some plausibility for the underdeveloped world.

However, the conventional concept of the "economic man" suffers from some grave deficiencies. It provides a weak basis for explaining and understanding the history of economic development in our time. Deeper reflection suggests that its premises are not even internally consistent. Moreover, it does not provide an adequate basis for constructive thinking on the alternative economic order we need for a safe world and a safe society. This, therefore, is a re-examination of the central tradition of economic thought that has dominated our age.

# 7. THE IMPACT OF WESTERN LIBERALISM ON INDIA

The feature of Indian tradition of peace and tolerance and of Western liberalism is an abiding sentiment of Indian middle class life. It stems from Mahatma Gandhi's rejection of Western ways and strident advocacy of "swadeshi". Gandhi's leadership transformed the nascent Indian nationalist movement into an activist political force and eventually won India freedom from British colonial rule. The key to his success was the support of the great middle class that existed in India at that time. Schooled in the tradition of British liberalism, the Indian middle class spurned its Western ways, at Gandhi's behest and in doing so, provided an impetus to the freedom struggle.

After independence, India embraced socialism under the tutelage of Gandhi's protege, Jawaharlal Nehru, the country's first Prime Minister. In the event, Indian policies expanded the middle class who played big roles in the economy. Thus, for five decades, the country had some development under the Five-Year Plans but the progress was not as phenomenal as could have been. The slow growth could not offset the massive population explosion. A vicious circle of poverty and deprivation established a vice-like grip on the country. In the late 1960s and through the 1970s, middle class youth fled the country to the more salubrious climes of America, Britain and Canada lured by the better prospects for income.

In the 1980s, the socialist profligacy finally caught up with India as deficits widened and the balance of payments turned unfavourable. The denouement came in 1991 when its foreign exchange reserves hit rock bottom, amounting to less than a month of the country's import bill. With bankruptcy staring the country in the face, the leadership moved to reform the massive state-controlled economy.

The economic reforms fuelled unprecedented growth in the size of the middle class. The National Council of Applied Economic Research estimates that the middle class will treble in number to include nearly 30 million households—about 160 million people—by 2010. Apart from the increase in numbers, the middle class is increasingly younger, which is natural in a country where the vast majority of the population is under 40 years of age. This massive and ongoing demographic shift has its effects. With the middle class not only growing but becoming more assertive, Indian politics has turned volatile.

Given the Parliamentary system, where a government can be turned out on a non-confidence vote long before the completion of its five-year term, India has faced frequent political changes. Between 1991 and 1998, five governments ruled in New Delhi. By comparison, between 1947, when India became independent, and 1991, there were just eleven changes in government. Unused to such political instability, Indian commentators widely disparaged the trend as evidence of national decline.

Seizing upon the widespread discontent, the Hindu Nationalist BJP mounted a populist campaign that struck a chord in the burgeoning middle class. An essential plank in the BJP's platform was a diatribe against the foreign influences. In the Hindu Nationalist liturgy, these include the Islamic invasion of India in the medieval age and the advent of Western powers thereafter. Religious bigots who see India's Muslims as foreigners, form the bedrock of the BJP's political support. However, staunch liberal opposition to the anti-Muslim platform restricted the party's appeal to the middle class. To expand its base of support therefore, the BJP broadcast its hate message to include the West and westernised Indians.

In the year 1998, the elections concluded in February itself. The BJP won enough adherents to their communal cause to form a government. It hooked some allies who, on purely opportunistic grounds offered to cast their votes in the Parliament with the BJP. Immediately after assuming office, the Party ordered nuclear tests for which the Department of Nuclear Energy was already prepared. The blasts brought the BJP some publicity and credit. By carrying out the nuclear blast, the BJP hoped to expand its support base, but the euphoria quickly melted when it became evident that BJP had no plan to handle the fallout.

Confronted by a hostile international environment, the government spokesman responded with a fusillade of irresponsible statements that alienated neighbouring Pakistan as well as China. The bankruptcy of BJP's action was exposed when Pakistan too set off a series of nuclear blasts.

Obviously overtaken by events, BJP floundered. In rapid succession, it proceeded to mess up on a large scale. It reneged an agreement with the opposition and installed its own speaker in Lok Sabha. Its various ministers got embroiled in unseemly spats with the bureaucrats such as the Chief Executive of the Prasar Bharti Corporation, the enforcement director, and a secretary in the Urban Affairs. It introduced a regressive budget with irrational levies on gasoline, imports and packaged goods. It made a hash of inter-state relations, seeking to dismiss the Bihar government, but came up against strictures by the President. In the winter session of Parliament, it could not introduce a singly worthy legislation. Its negotiations with the USA on the matter of nuclear proliferation got so confused and opaque, that the US Deputy Secretary of State, Strobe Talbott, had to release a statement outlining the tangled negotiations.

Liberalism has several aspects and influences almost every field of life. Economic liberalism denotes softening of rules and regulations. In political area it envisages rising above party politics and understanding the needs of a given situation and find solutions to problems. America's attempt to bring India into the sphere of nuclear non-proliferation and test-ban through Indo-US Nuclear Deal may be considered an example of political liberalism. In art and culture it may mean mingling of two or more forms or traditions. The combination of Indian and Persian architecture too is a form of liberalism.

Western society is liberal in several ways. They have no taboo on sex and female companionship. However, such liberalism is not acceptable in Indian society. For Indians, sex is not just a game or an act of pleasure. It is a deep, emotional relationship which one should have only with one's life partner. Open defiance of piety of such relationships and nudity, etc. which may be an aspect of western civilisations, but it is adversely impacting Indian society.

O O O

# 8. Gandhi—A Prophet of Modernity

On January 30, every year, the people of India with the exception of those who stand against his ideals, reflect upon the Mahatma's martyrdom. They also utilise the occasion of his death anniversary, to remember his immense contribution to the growth and development of the Indian society. At the same time, they dwell upon the continuing relevance of his theory and practice of the challenges which they face as they look towards the future of India.

According to Ravinder Kumar, a prominent writer, the anniversary of Gandhi's martyrdom had special significance in 1999, as by the end of this year, we had entered a new century, rather a new millennium in human history. India today faces a magnitude of challenges as well as opportunities which lie ahead for the people. By elevating Gandhi as "Father of the Nation", the people of India have already accepted the pre-eminent role which he played in transforming our ancient society into a modern nation. Besides fighting successfully the battle of freedom the moral way, he devised important principles for the uplift of our caste-ridden unequal society to an equalitarian and simple society with ideals of self-sufficiency in every walk of life. His principles of thought and action do hold the promise of guiding us in the future by seeking to carry out social, political and moral experiments of his choice, which alone could create solution to the anguish and dilemmas of the people.

Before we focus our gaze on such issues, it is necessary to say a few words about what the phrase the "Father of the Nation" really signifies. In the long history of the civilization of India, the 20th century stood for the Indian people as a century of freedom, and dramatic and qualitative transformation in a series of social, economic and political domains. The question of political liberty, of freedom from British domination, was simply one aspect of this complex and multi-faceted phenomenon. No less significant were the other integrally associated changes in the social, economic and moral domains.

Equally germane to the issue is the fact that in the course of his societal experimentation, the Mahatma was extremely active in all these theatres. The moral logic and the spatial trajectory of his politics, therefore, have to be understood in relationship with the total transformation which he sought to negotiate within the lifestream of the Indian nation.

At the outset, Gandhi was able to offer to the people of the country no less to the British, as the suppressors of the people, a satisfactory answer to the question of India's identity as a modern nation, and her viability as a liberal and democratic polity. For the British, in the role of Gandhi's political adversaries, questioned the very notion of India as a liberal polity and a viable nation. The subcontinent of India, according to the British, was inhabited by an amorphous civilization constituted, in most of its long history, of factions and warring states at the same time, as the civilization of India was constituted of a profoundly unequal and hierarchical society, highly unsuitable as the base of a liberal polity. But by drawing upon a saintly idiom of militant non-violence, as Gandhi's Satyagraha was, the Mahatma organised one of the most substantial mass movements in world history in the 20th century, to portray the strategic cohesion of Indian society. Further—and this is particularly relevant to the challenges of today and tomorrow—he acknowledged the truly epic plurality of the civilization of India at the same time as he propounded the bold notion that the collective identity of this great mass of humanity was shaped partly by the creative interplay between different moral visions, religious beliefs and social communities; and partly also by the great tradition of non-violence which held the potential to reach out to violence and bitter dissent, and transform them into the great strength of the people of India. Small wonder then that while the common folk of India looked upon the Mahatma as the "Father of the Nation", the world as a whole regarded him as the greatest theorist and practitioner of non-violence in the 20th century.

Gandhi's definition of the collective identity of Indian society as an entity shaped through the creative interplay of different constituents of a uniquely plural social order is something which needs to be highlighted in the context of social turbulence in our times. This is so because of the challenge posed by an alternative definition of an overarching identity of Indian nation, which puts the moral and cultural world of nationalism above that of all the religious systems within India.

There is no doubt that the diverse religious communities of India, to which the people of India are severally tethered, accepted the Gandhian notion of "creative interplay" between different social and moral formations, as the only legitimate base of a democratic order and modern nationhood. Any churlish attempt to displace the Gandhian notion of a truly liberal and composite identity with the disruptive notion of the primacy of one moral order over others would have fractured that multi-communitarian base of the nationalist movement, which alone compelled the British to leave India in 1947.

Any step towards undoing a sacred compact which drew different oral communities into cohesive nationhood could pave the way for the dissolution of the national unity of India, whenever such a step was taken. And such a step eventually brought the partition of the country.

Besides seeking to resolve the vexed question of the collective identity of a society as diverse as Indian society, Gandhi also reflected and experimented upon the matter in which production and distribution of wealth could best be organised within India for the collective good of the people.

Here it would be pertinent to say a word or two about Gandhi's stance towards modern industrial civilization. Contrary to popular belief, he recognised the utility of fashioning instruments of social production which were more efficient than those any unaided human power could have achieved. Gandhi was not against technology—or technological upgradation— per se. After all the Ambar Charkha which he gladly adopted was a technological device. But as a young student at London, he had seen the dreadful impact of untamed industrialization upon the great mass of people. As his texts like *Hind Swarajya* highlighted, Gandhi was deeply concerned about 'satanic' factories, which enslaved humanity at the same time as they generated new wealth. The thrust of his argument has, therefore, to be seen in terms of the contemporary notion of "appropriate" development, or development relevant to the needs, the capacities, and the interests of the common folk in modern society.

What Gandhi talked about was a finely nuanced order of industrial growth, which drew technologies of varying sophistication into an integrated production system which was competitive, at the same time it did not tear apart the fabric of society through generating grotesque disparities between different classes and generating an unholy concentration of power within select sectors of society. Perhaps the upgradation of Indian industry, as we move into an era of competitive production and growing integration into the world economy, can greatly profit from the core argument advanced by Gandhi, as he looked towards system of social production in commodities for humans, which marred material abundance with moral dignity and moral poise.

More than half a century after his death, Mahatma Gandhi remains as always the symbol of individual courage and righteousness, battling the forces of the state. His example inspired Martin Luther King and black Americans the civil rights campaign of the 1960s. At a later date, Nelson Mandela testified to have come under the same influence. Having slid down the moral scale of human values and finding corruption rampant in society around, he said, "We need to pay more heed to the basic principles of Gandhian philosophy if we are to come out of this quagmire."

In many books on Gandhi, his political philosophy comes for discussion from two different angles. In one chapter on the Origins of Non-violence, an attempt has been made to show that some of the ideas espoused by Gandhi were remarkably similar to the teachings of earlier preachers—not only in the East but also in the West. We may recall the role of Cynics, who poured scorn on the material achievements of ancient Greece. Christian monks also abjured the pleasures of the flesh and led hermetic existence. The Quakers and Anabaptists believed in individual communion with God and were of the pacific disposition. Similar stress on non-violence was laid by the Buddhists and Jains. While carrying these ideas to modern times, Tolstoy and Gandhi gave due justification. Green acutely perceives the difference: "It is perhaps misleading to call such religious thinking 'modernist' since it has precedents far back in religious history. But it has an innovative character within each event because it dissolves away the theology that the priests preserve.

Green narrates the lives of Tolstoy and Gandhi side by side in his attempt to bring out the similarities and dissimilarities between them. They were born in two mighty empires and reached manhood under different circumstances. While Tolstoy came from a class that had an important part to play in the construction of the Czarist regime, Gandhi was a product of colonial society. Gandhi and Tolstoy achieved fame in their respective spheres, in literature and the national liberation struggle, but the image that usually comes through is their being in old age. This impression they had succeeded in conveying before they had actually grown very old. It was related to the message they sought to impart.

In Green's words, "Tolstoy and Gandhi rooted in ageing and death, a mode of authority equal but opposite to that authority most of us acknowledge in youth and life. The points at which Tolstoy and Gandhi reacted with each other have been known for long." Tolstoy's book *The Kingdom is God is Within You* made a deep impact on Gandhi when he first read it at the age of 26. Ruskin's *Unto This* and Thoreau's essay on Civil Disobedience were others which sowed the seeds of non-violence in his mind. *Hind Swaraj* was written by Gandhi in 1910 in response to Tolstoy's 'Letter to a Hindu'. He had already, during the earlier years of the 20th century, launched the campaign in South Africa which made him famous. He had conveyed his respect to Tolstoy on his 18th birthday in 1908. The Russian sage had at the same time an opportunity to learn of Gandhi through a reading of *Hind Swaraj* and a biography of the Indian leader by Joseph Doke, published in 1908. Gandhi had sent both books to Tolstoy. In 1910, he had also set up the Tolstoy Farm near Johannesburg as a place of retreat for satyagrahis in South Africa.

Green's books are based on these well known facts. He focuses on opposition to imperialism in the careers of Gandhi and Tolstoy on the moral plane. The religious radicalism that both embodied is to Green the most effective way of combating not only imperialism but any kind of usurpation of power. In Green's opinion "Tolstoy and Gandhi made it their work to rediscover a negative vocabulary. They stood not only against the industrial civilization of the West but also against the youthful exuberance it celebrated and tried to remove themselves beyond history."

Raja Rao, the great India prose writer, wrote about Gandhi that whereas the American, French, Greek or English books on Gandhi are true generally to facts but not so to meaning. Raja Rao invests the character of Gandhi with a new light with memorable aphorisms. He says, "Gandhiji's political activity had a symphonic quality about it." In this orchestration the Boer, the Indian, the British, the Chinaman and Kaffir—indeed even the Hindu, the Muslim, and the Parsi, the Jain, and the Christian—were not at all either adversaries or friends, but modes of a play, as it were, for finally all play "truth's own game".

Nikhlesh Guha, a prominent writer on Gandhi says, "In their own way Green and Raja Rao succeed in showing that Gandhi's significance for the modern man lies in the ideal of life that he embodies more than the day-to-day political struggles in which he was involved in his life time."

O  O  O

## 9. Relevance of Nehru's Foreign Policy

For conducting present-day international relations, Jawaharlal Nehru was the architect of the foreign policy of independent India. Even before independence, in 1946, when Nehru became the Vice-President of the Interim government, he had outlined the policy goals of India's foreign policy. Later on when he became the Prime Minister of the country, he confirmed his views and elaborated some of his ideas and tried to implement them with a fair degree of success. Since then, no Indian Prime Minister developed an entirely new line on foreign policy. Subsequent governments did make adjustments here and there to tide over a crisis or to meet a new international situation. But there was no attempt to take a fresh look at the basic questions in India's foreign policy.

However, with the drastic changes in the international political scene, India finds itself in a dilemma. It was one thing to develop an independent foreign policy and work in close collaboration with one superpower or the other in the bipolar world. But it is another thing to work independently in a multipolar world. There is need for defining India's priorities and discarding some of the shibboleths.

Some time back there was a seminar on foreign policy at the India International Centre, New Delhi. This seminar was conducted in early 1997 in collaboration with the School of International Studies of the JNU to commemorate the Golden Jubilee of India's independence. The seminar was addressed by prominent scholars in the field of foreign policy. The papers read at the seminar were compiled in a book.

The book consists of six papers and two appendices besides a lengthy introduction by the learned editor. The first essay by the then External Affairs Minister I.K. Gujral, outlines the main challenges of formulation of the country's foreign policy in the post cold war period. Gujral correctly reminds that the world view born of India's freedom struggle demanded resistance not only to the British rule in India, but opposition to the worldwide exploitative system. Analyzing Nehruvian tradition theoretically, A.P. Rana, an acknowledged authority on international relations theory shows how it reconciled the natural tension between national security goals and international systemic goals by pursuing both simultaneously. Therein lies the great contribution of Nehru to foreign policy.

According to Rana, the imperative task for India, as state unit today is to properly manage and resolve conflict in its own region. This was also congruent with an urgent concern to the international system. It is possible to build on this congruence through a creative revival of the Nehruvian tradition. The next paper by V.S. Mani, a well known expert on international law is in response to Nehru's expressed interest in the freedom of colonial peoples and equal opportunities for all in theory and practice. He highlights India's contribution to the development of international law and discusses the main problems diluting Indian contributions in recent years.

In the next paper, Tan Chung of China talked about Sino-Indian relations from the perspective of two great civilizations that could make significant contribution to the contemporary world. Without going into the cause and consequences of the border conflict, Tan Chung, reaffirms his conviction that India and China have a lot to learn from each other and could derive mutual benefit from cooperation. S.D. Mani in his controversial paper made a scathing criticism of Nehru's foreign policy. He questioned the basic assumptions of India's foreign policy as propounded by Nehru. He focused on the idiosyncratic aspects of Nehru's foreign policy rather than an objective factors that shaped it. However, most speakers found it difficult to accept Muni's assertion that Nehru had not grasped the reality of power. Some members stated strongly that Nehru not only had a clear understanding of different components of power but also a definite strategy of economic development. It is worth remembering that under his leadership India did quite well. The situation changed for the worse in late 1970s. He was a rare combination of idealism and realism. Admiral Menon who spoke next, based his analysis within current theoretical discourse on multi-ethnicity and weak nation states. In stressing the significance of economic dynamism, he contrasts the experiences of two other larger multi-ethnic states, the erstwhile Soviet Union that failed and the thriving US where visible ethnicity does not jeopardise the economic or political system. Menon's depiction of ethnic strife as a consequence of economic disparities was overtly simplistic.

O O O

# 10. Life And Works Of Professor Amartya Sen —In His Own Words

Sen's earliest memories are connected with Dhaka, and with Shantiniketan. My parents were mostly in Dhaka, so it is really my grandparents that I, quite a lot of the time grew up with. The leading spirit of Bengal, Rabindranath Tagore, had died just at the time when I came to Shantiniketan as a very young boy. I grew up as a child when the riots began and took place there. I must have been seven or eight when I saw a Muslim daily labourer who was trying to deliver some wood in the neighbouring house being knifed by some communal thugs.

### On the Bengal Famine

And then the Bengal famine happened when I was in Shantiniketan. I don't know whether the trauma of the riot deaths was stronger than the trauma of the famine deaths. Both were very traumatic. Once one had understood the complete insanity of communal violence, there was a pattern whereby one knew that there was a human agency involved in a criminal and nasty form. One still had to explain why human beings should behave in such a beastly manner. But at last there was a kind of understanding. In the case of the famine, it wasn't clear what was happening. It was not particularly bad year in respect of food and yet two to three million people died.

I knew of no one among my relatives and friends who had the slightest difficulty in surviving. But then these people were dying in the street. The nature of the class division is the nature of the precarious vulnerability of some groups of people— something which struck me then, but I wasn't able to analyse it. When I went back to studying famine, and then I spent over a decade of life studying famine, some of those thoughts turned out to have been not as childish as I decided they must have been.

## Radicalism and Pluralism

Those were very young, interesting and exciting and happy years. The economics we were taught was of very high standard and might be called neo-classical economics. There was a lot of Marxist thinking which influenced us all among the students and many of us were involved in students' movements of various kinds, but that was a kind of different sphere of life. It wasn't something which belonged to the classes, rather it belonged much more across the street to the coffee house.

The ceaseless dogmatism on that position was very hard for people who were rather more connected to a more pluralist understanding of the nature of reality. I think anything that tries to capture radicalism in one authentic form and denying all other forms, seemed very unattractive to me, both in school as well as in early college in Calcutta, though I was involved in left-wing politics in Calcutta from a broader current.

## The Making of an Economist

As far as Cambridge is concerned, quite a lot of my hard work had been technical, orthodox, quite a lot of it had been informed by concern about people with disadvantage—poor people, you know, a lot of time also with other kinds of disadvantages like gender—and a lot about children. But I have never taken the view that orthodox economics had nothing to offer all these things.

My interest in this area of justice goes back to the time when I was teaching at the Delhi School of Economics. My earliest lectures were on this at that time in Delhi. I have been on one side concerned that the dominant ethical thinking in economic policy making has been the utilitarian one. And on the other side there is a kind of lack of integration of the concerns and criticisms we have in society, of its injustice, with a kind of general view as to what the nature of a just society might be. The utilitarian calculus is really quite the wrong way of thinking about it and I think one has to move in a more objective direction to find as to what is the nature of inequality, exploitation, poverty and so on.

## Home and the World

I have got quite interested in understanding the nature of India's past. This would be one good way for me to have my cake and eat it too. This takes me back in my interest in Sanskrit and Indian classical tradition, and yet to be concerned with some of my more modern concerns like rationality, objectivity and social change and social justice.

One of my grumbles is, we take such a biased view of India's past mainly to distinguish it from the West, to make it look as if it is very different. There is no literature in the world which has as much, aesthetic, materialist, rationalistic writings such as in Sanskrit and Pali together has and have. I think that tradition of heterodoxy, of questioning, is a very important part of India's past and I think when we deny that, in trying to capture India in this limited terms of—you know—of one part of Hindu orthodoxy, I think we made a terrible mistake.

## On Myself

On the whole I have a fairly cheerful temperament and the optimism—yeah I guess there is some optimism one has to be overwhelmed with and there is no escape from that, and yet the fact is there are other people, children, to some extent, friends and the society at large. There is the political issue and there are injustices on which one has views and one hopes to do something to eliminate them. I have always been a rather social person and to some extent a political person too. There are periods when I was very far from being cheerful, but I think something of the social involvement is present in a tendency towards laughter and an ability to take the world as it is.

I have led pretty much my own life, tried to work on subjects which I think are important, and in my judgement for the world too—like I would spend years doing famine or a lot of my time on poverty, equality and so on. But I have not sort of gone out of my way to sacrifice. But people have, people involved in politics, have sacrificed themselves, taking incredible risks.

Involvement with society, with politics and with other people, is a source of both commitment and strength and enjoyment—and if you take on the whole that if there is a problem, particularly the problem with poverty, hunger, undernourishment, inequality, all have solutions which we can get.

○ ○ ○

# 11. ECONOMIC PHILOSOPHY OF AMARTYA SEN

The readers have been told about the important phases of Amartya Sen' life and some of his ideas in the last essay. After being assessed as the most outstanding student in his undergraduate studies, Sen moved on to Cambridge for higher studies in economics. Both as a graduate student and a research fellow, he had the benefit of coming into close contact with some of the most brilliant economists of the time, Picro Sraffa and Joan Robinson. In 1953-54, Cambridge itself was passing through a phase of critical re-examination of some fundamental ideas in economics. With the British Empire no longer there to sing its own praise, the British academics were forced to reflect on state of the debris that the empire had left in different parts of the world.

The study of development economics, specially in relation to the countries with a surfeit of labour, came to be favourably accorded. Sen prepared his Ph.D. thesis on an important aspect of development strategy in these countries—whether to plan for the immediate enhancement of low-productivity employment or to go in for the generation of larger reinvestible surpluses in high productivity occupations. The thesis received wide attention and attracted good reviews. It will be unfair to claim that he solved a knotty problem, but the fuzziness of the problem as it was then discussed was to a large extent dispelled.

The choice of the producer between labour-absorbing and labour-saving technique of production thus ably presented, Sen turned his attention to the wider question of society's choice among a number of alternative policies. Who makes this choice? In a democracy, the choice is assumed to be finalised by the popular will, that is to say by the vote of the majority. So long as the number of alternative policy measures is only two, a clear majority can be ascertained. But as soon as the number of alternatives becomes three (or more) the vote of majority becomes difficult to discern.

Attention to this problem in choices made by majority voting was drawn long before Sen appeared on the scene. But in a series of notes and articles, he succeeded in establishing that the majority decision could be converted into a unanimous decision if certain conditions were fulfilled.

A careful formulation of these conditions led Sen to study problems of economic justice, inequality and poverty. He laid stress on the important fact that man had the capacity to derive happiness not only from his own consumption, but also from the satisfaction of other peoples' wants. It is this trait that offers a way out of the impasse that the economics of welfare had reached by proceeding on too narrow a path. Welfare is not identical with the provision for one's own wants.

The "pleasure principle" had to be replaced by a new definition of economic welfare. With this wider definition, it is possible to agree on measures to reduce social and economic inequality and the eradication of the meanest forms of poverty. Poverty need not be measured by drawing a line, the so called "poverty line", and defining all poor people as those who earn and spend below this line. Inequality among the poor themselves has to be taken into consideration and the interests of the "poorest of the poor" must be given precedence over that of others designated as poor.

However, welfare is not simply a matter of commodity hurdles enjoyed by a person and the next of his kin. The scope of welfare had to be extended much further. A person's right of free speech and free action was as much a constituent of human welfare as the food eaten and the clothes worn. The right to receive education, health care and a guaranteed level of living were precious for their contribution in enhancing human capabilities. They were therefore important ingredients of human welfare. Justice consists in ensuring "entitlements" to every man and woman. Economic welfare is not maximised simply by guaranteeing of minimum of food, clothing and shelter to every citizen as a sort of freedom, as some social reformers are apt to believe.

Years of reflection on problems of social policy formulation brought Sen to a subject that had occupied his mind since a very tender age. The Bengal famine of 1943 had so long been analysed as a problem of overall food shortage. Sen adduced evidence to establish that the situation at that time was not one of terrible shortage of foodgrain. There was sufficient stock to meet the needs of all inhabitants of the then province of Bengal. The famine could occur because the poorest section of the people, mostly landless farm workers, had no purchasing power at their command. In Sen's language, their "entitlement" was short of their needs. In the absence of any mechanism of fair public distribution of food, the poorest section of the people came in towns and cities in search of employment, and died of starvation because of public apathy.

Sen points out that in a free democratic country such mass starvation is not ordinarily allowed to occur, because existence of a free Press guarantees wide publicity for the famine and forces the government to take appropriate action. But the Press is usually unresponsive to the starvation or semi-starvation that goes on undetected in poor countries. The press reports only epidemics of famines and turns a blind eye to "endemic" starvation. Such chronic maladies as the lack of nutrition, poor health services and the lack of educational facilities—all of which comes under the scope of "entitlement"—can be taken care of only by a dependable network of public provisioning.

Even countries with low per capita incomes cannot afford to neglect such basic welfare measures because without health care and education, the latent capabilities of the people cannot be harnessed to the task of national reconstruction. Sen and his associates have also studied the problem of gender inequality inside and outside the family. Both in health care and education, the girl child remains at a disadvantage, especially in poor rural families. The education of a girl child is expected to yield huge social returns, since an educated mother better understands the need for limiting the family size.

Over the years, Sen has written regularly and prolifically on the provisioning of minimum needs. At least on this point he believes there can be unanimity; the problems involved in decision-making by a majority vote need not raise their heads.

Most economists would subscribe to this position in a general way, but the debate will continue on whether public agencies can be devised in all countries to bear the responsibility for a fair set of "entitlements". Someone had said that Sen represents the "conscience of the economic profession," He has rescued welfare economics from "neither here nor there" impasse. But whether the courage of this conscience will be strong enough to overcome the limitations of the often politically-motivated delivery system, remains the question that future generations will have to answer.

# VII. INDIAN POLITY AND ECONOMY

## 1. FOREIGN EXPERTS IN THE PLANNING COMMISSION

Montek Singh Alhluwalia, Deputy Chairman Planning Commission, on September 30, 2004, dissolved the bodies set up to provide inputs for the Tenth Five Year Plan's mid-term review. Rather than succumbing to the Left parties' demands for the ouster of the foreign experts from these consultative groups, Mr. Ahluwalia took an extreme step which means that the Left parties will not be allowed to avail of the institutionalized mechanism to place their views on the Plan process. The Left parties and the Left-leaning economists associated with the groups had threatened to quit if the "foreign experts" representing the World Bank, ADB and Mc Kinsey & Co. were not withdrawn from the Planning Committees.

The Planning Commission became embroiled in a controversy, which at first sight looked like a non-issue, but had substantial media and political fallout. It generated a debate over whether representatives of multinational donor agencies such as the World Bank and employees of private multinational consultancy agencies should be included in Committees constituted by the Planning Commission. The controversy started when it was announced that some Consultative Committees set up by the Planning Commission to provide inputs into the Mid-Term Appraisal would include not only a range of outside experts but also representatives of external donor agencies such as the World Bank and the Asian Development Bank (ADB), along with employees of consultancy companies such as Mc Kinsey and Boston Consulting. It was also evident that such persons had been invited to be on the

227

committees not in their personal capacity but because they belonged to these agencies, specifically in order to ascertain the views of these agencies on programmes and policies in which they have an interest.

In the history of the Planning Commission, this was for the first time that such elements were invited to be part of Committees especially set up by the Planning Commission. The subsequent outcry focused on a number of problems with such inclusion, ranging from the argument that this reflected not only intellectual subservience to the feeling that this suggested a bankruptcy of national talent in this regard. The initial reply provided by the Deputy Chairman did little to rectify matters, as the justification provided was essentially based on the facts that only four of the nineteen Committees that had been constituted, had such members, that these agencies already gave large loans to India, and that Mahatma Gandhi's famous remark about "keeping doors and windows open" could be applied in this case.

## Left Parties' Reactions

The leaders of the Left political parties also made statements against this move, as the controversy continued. However, the Planning Commission remained adamant. In the process, several things became apparent, all of which underlined the complexity of current political economy of the country. Montek has been accused of compromising the country's sovereignty by an outraged Left, which however, has no problems with the presence of Reliance industries and ITC in the panels. A Left leader pointed out that they did not comprise the foreign hand. For the Left, the induction of foreign experts meant formalizing the presence of multilateral agencies in India's plan exercise. Left leaning economists threatened to quit the panel if the experts were not shown the door.

The dissolution of all the 19 consultative groups of the Planning Commission, including those with representatives of the World Bank, the Asian Development Bank (ADB) Mc Kinsey and Boston consultancy settled for the time being the controversy generated by the Left parties' opposition to the formal representation given to foreign agencies in an important government body. The Left parties, who put up a principled resistance to the formal presence of foreign agencies, were not happy with the government's decision to dissolve all the consultative groups. They said that they had only demanded the removal of the representatives of the foreign agencies. Besides, the government did not explain how it would go about the process about the "consulting process."

The Planning Commission argued that since the World Bank and the ADB are already actively involved in financing programmes of the Central and State governments in several areas, this would provide an opportunity for them to share perception on programmes and policies in which they have been involved in an open forum, which would include others who have a different orientation and could express their disagreement. This argument has several problems.

- First, it is difficult to believe that these agencies could provide sound and dispassionate judgement on economic policies on which they have very specific (and remarkably unchanging) views. Indeed, in the Indian context, the often-injudicious policy advice provided by these institutions in the recent past is only too apparent. The former leaders of the State governments of Andhra Pradesh, Karnataka and Madhya Pradesh (to take only three examples) should be able to testify to the adverse role of their advice.

- Second, even these views need to be heard as there is substantial difference between requesting them to provide their opinions formally in a separate context, and providing them with a different degree of legitimacy as "independent" outside experts on par with others who are genuinely independent. This provides these institutions a platform to present their views in a manner that bears the imprimatur of the Planning Commission.

The significance of this should not be underestimated.

There is no question that the Planning Commission must listen to a range of views but this should not involve simple replication of the patterns of the debating societies of the undergraduate colleges that produced some of the current incumbents of this Commission as well as some of its critics. Above all, the Planning Commission is an organ of the Indian State—and within that, an institution with a long and proud history of the nationalist endeavour. And therefore, to represent and be seen to represent the Indian people, it must preserve the essential identity of the Indian State.

To re-examine past policy is a basic mandate of the present Planning Commission. But this cannot be done if the official attitude appears to institutionalize and internalize the status of the same foreign policy advice that needs to be re-examined. Perhaps, the insistence on having such people remain in Committees, despite all the protests, is an unwilling recognition of the changed politico-economic reality, reflecting a feeling of insecurity that without such people being involved, the previous arguments will not be expressed with much force. But that is essential tilting against a political windmill.

The controversy acquired an excessive importance when compared to the many priorities that await the United Progressive Alliance (UPA) government's attention. The new government at the Centre has shown little indication of getting down to addressing the agenda of the National Common Minimum Programme (NCMP). Also, the Left parties expended a considerable amount of energy on the Planning Commission fracas even as other issues cried out for attention. The National Advisory Council has, on the other hand, demonstrated a greater agency than the government is underlying the Planning Commission controversy. Firstly, the new team of members has been given a central role in the formulation and implementation of the UPA government's economic programme. This role goes beyond finding the resources and making allocation for the NCMP. So, clearly, how the Planning Commission goes about its job, will influence its advice and the policies it will draw up. The appraisal process was going to be a test case of the functioning of the new commission. Secondly, in an era when globalization has already whittled away the autonomy of the nation state, should a government go out of its way to institutionalize the involvement of external agencies in decision-making even if, to begin with, this was going to be only in an advisory capacity? When seen in this perspective, the 'foreigner' issue was important, though it did happen to get blown out of proportion.

Foreign economists and experts have been involved in giving advice and have enjoyed close access to decision-making authorities. This dates back to the late 1940's. In fact, a galaxy of international economists were involved in the planning process in the 1950s and 1960s. However, they were involved as individuals—as experts in their areas of specialization—and not as representatives of specific organizations, as in the aborted consultative process.

○ ○ ○

# 2. SECURITIES TRANSACTION TAX (STT) INTRODUCED

The Securities Transaction Tax (STT) was implemented on October 1, 2004 in the Indian financial markets. The market players and analysts who had predicted that the introduction of STT would bring the Indian financial markets to a standstill, have been proved completely wrong.

On the first day of the implementation of the STT, not only the Sensex (India's most popular stock index) witnessed an increase of 91.93 points (highest since the introduction of the STT was announced by the Finance Minister in July 2004) but the Indian authorities also collected over Rs. 50 million in tax revenue. It has been estimated that based on the existing trading volumes in the Indian financial markets, authorities would be collecting sizeable revenue on an annual basis. This is not a small amount in the present times when tax revenues are under severe pressure.

Often termed as "Terminator Tax", the STT was strongly opposed by a lobby of speculators, day traders, abritrageurs, and "noise traders". When the Finance Minister announced the introduction of the STT in the Financial Bill on July 8, 2004, this lobby launched an impromptu agitation against the proposed tax. The Finance Minister had to dilute several key components of his earlier tax proposal, largely under the pressure of this powerful lobby. Under the revised tax regime, investors are liable to pay a 0.15 per cent STT on day delivery-based equity transaction carried out in a recognized stock exchange, to be shared equally between the buyer and the seller. In case of non-delivery transaction, the STT would be levied at 0.015 per cent to be payable by the seller. Going by the trading pattern in the equity markets, it is very clear that the STT had no significant negative effect. Till now, there have been no technical snags in the implementation of the STT as was feared. The tax is collected by the stock exchanges from the brokers and passed on to the exchequer, thereby enabling the authorities to raise revenue in a neat and efficient manner.

In spite of the fact that delivery-based transactions have been taxed under the STT, the trading pattern reveals that the ratio of deliveries to total volumes has improved since its implementation. Another apprehension of the opponents that STT would dry up liquidity in the markets has also proved wrong. On the contrary, there is too much liquidity in the markets and this fact has been admitted by the opponents of the tax. Besides, several loopholes in the existing tax regime have been plugged with the implementation of the STT. For instance, foreign investors who used to take undue advantage of the bilateral tax avoidance treaties, would now be taxed under the STT regime.

The opportunities offered by the STT, if viewed in the context of raising tax revenue, are enormous, provided the Finance Minister withdraws special concessions offered to day traders, speculators and brokers. Despite these concessions and other shortcomings, the STT has the potential to bring stability in the Indian financial markets. However, all problems related to speculation, volatility and instability in the Indian financial markets, would not be resolved by the STT alone. No single instrument by itself, in the present times, can solve all problems plaguing the Indian financial markets. The STT does offer a potent mechanism to deal with multiple problems, if used in conjunction with other policy mechanism, such as banning short selling and insider trading. Indian Government is considering several proposals to further dilute the provisions of the STT. The Government is considering complete exemption from the STT for securities traded in International Financial Centres (IFCs), as part of the Special Economic Zones (SEZs). The IFCs are expected to become offshore financial centres, offering all kinds of financial services including offshore banking, stock trading and commodity trading to both domestic and foreign investors. If transactions are conducted through IFCs, investors would not be subjected to STT and capital gains tax.

There are several justifications for the adoption of the STT in the Indian financial markets. First the underlying logic of the securities transaction tax is to slow down the flow of speculative money as it would be taxed each time a transaction takes place. The STT will be a significant deterrent to speculators and day traders trying to make a quick profit on a huge sum by just trading without taking any deliveries of stocks.

Second, the revenue potential of a 0.15 per cent of the STT provides another justification. On an average, the daily trading in the Indian stock markets is about Rs. 100,000 million. By imposing a 0.15 per cent STT on this volume, the Indian tax authorities can collect Rs. 150 million every day. As the Indian financial markets operate on an average 250 days a year, the STT could generate revenue of Rs. 37,500 million a year.

Third, an additional advantage of the STT is that it could discourage "hot money" flows, which are known for their volatile and destabilizing behaviour.

Fourth, by cutting back financial resources in unproductive speculation, the STT could encourage long-term financial flows. The speculative activity in the financial markets diverts large amount of resources away from productive purposes. As a result, fewer financial resources are available to fund long-term economic development. The STT has the potential to benefit the real economy in the long run.

Fifth, another main benefit of the STT lies in its progressive outlook. As the major players in the financial markets are big speculators, day traders, arbitrageurs, brokers and wealthy individuals whose number in any case is minuscule, the STT would only affect their businesses without directly affecting the majority of Indians.

Sixth, the securities tax is much easier to implement. It is a clean and efficient instrument of collecting taxes from financial markets, as collections will be centralized through the stock exchanges.

Not long ago, taxes on financial transactions have been imposed in several countries including the US, Japan, France and the U.K. Several countries are still implementing different types of financial transactions taxes. The US imposed a financial transaction tax from 1914 to 1966.

Currently, the US has a 0.0034 per cent tax, which is levied on stock transactions. The UK has a financial transaction tax in the form of a stamp duty, which is not levied on transactions per se but on the registration of securities. Presently, the UK levies a 0.5 per cent stamp duty and stamp duty reserve tax on equity and other financial transactions. Belgium is another European country, which has a 0.17 per cent transaction tax on stock and a 0.07 per cent tax on bonds. Transactions in other financial instruments are also taxed under varying rates.

Japan had also imposed a transaction tax till 1999. The tax was imposed on a variety of financial instruments. However, as part of "big bang" liberalization of the financial sector, Japan withdrew this tax in 1999.

France has a transaction tax on equity trading. The tax rate depends on the amount of transactions. The country levies a 0.15 per cent transaction tax on equity trades exceeding one million francs. Among the emerging markets, Malaysia, Singapore and New Zealand have imposed transaction taxes on a variety of financial instruments.

As no single instrument by itself can solve all problems plaguing the Indian financial markets, the STT offers a potent mechanism to deal with multiple problems, if used in conjunction with other policy mechanisms.

○ ○ ○

# 3. FIRST BIMSTEC SUMMIT

The seven member regional grouping has been renamed as the Bay of Bengal Initiative for Multi-Sector Technical and Economic Cooperation (BIMSTEC). It was earlier known as Bangladesh, India, Myanmar, Sri Lanka and Thailand Economic Cooperation. It has been renamed after the inclusion of Nepal and Bhutan as its members. A decision in this regard was announced in the first BIMSTEC Summit held in Bangkok. The new nomenclature may be aimed at preventing Islamabad's entry into the grouping. Also, at the first summit of BIMSTEC, Indian Prime Minister, Manmohan Singh along with leaders from Sri Lanka, Thailand, Bangladesh, Bhutan, Myanmar and Nepal decided to take steps for timely completion of the Free Trade Area negotiations, apart from introducing a special BIMSTEC visa, in a bid to boost trade and investments in the region. The leaders also signed a joint declaration, committing themselves to give a fillip to regional economic cooperation by a slew of measures, including development of infrastructure.

## First Summit

Known now by the acronym BIMST-EC, the regional grouping had started out seven years ago as BIST-EC at Thailand's initiative to foster better trade among three other contiguous countries around the Bay of Bangladesh, India and Sri Lanka. Myanamar, admitted to this grouping in 1997, provided the extra letter to the acronym. Nepal and Bhutan joined the membership early in 2004, but spared the acronym of further upheaval. Yet, this was only the first time that the leaders of the respective governments got together, the earlier engagements being at the working level among trade Ministers and officials of the various countries. The involvement of the top leaders was expected to provide the impetus to regional trade that was missing till now.

## Free Trade

The main aim of the Bay of Bengal Economic Community is to have a free trade zone, on the lines of the European Community by 2017, build superways and optical fibre corridors in the region and boost investments. The first summit of the seven countries hopes to further development by accomplishing the goals set in Bangkok. However, BIMSTEC has a disadvantage: it starts with a low base trade with hardly $700 million among its members. Thus far most of these countries have looked to the West for trade. Not without reason, most countries in this grouping have the same kind of goods to export. For instance, Sri Lanka and India are both large exporters of tea and garments. Bangladesh and India compete in selling jute, seafood and garments overseas.

Essentially, the range of goods is largely competitive rather than complementary, a condition that does not promote natural trade within the community. Indeed, any suggestions or moves towards free trade or trades with low tariffs, have met resistance from domestic industry in each country. The Indo-Sri Lanka free trade agreement that has been in operation for over four years has set off considerable opposition amongst growers of tea and spices in southern India.

With the Indo-Thailand free trade agreement also kicking in right earnest, the automatic industry is nervous at the prospect of competing with imports of automobile components and automobiles in knocked-down condition from Thailand. Ford Motor Company already imports its sports utility vehicle, Endeavour, from Thailand. It is such resistance that the leaders of the region will factor in, as they take the formal steps towards setting a time-table for lowering tariffs on trade within the grouping. Preliminary negotiations indicate that tariffs could be lowered for many items.

The Prime Minister Manmohan Singh found the Summit a "meeting of minds and the focus was on quick, practical and deliverable programmes". He made a number of offers to operationalise BIMSTEC, including sharing ISRO's remote sensing data on agriculture and establishing a weather and climate research centre for the region in New Delhi. As India is one of the global leaders in manufacturing generic drugs, Mr. Singh also offered Indian drugs to BIMSTEC countries. Singh was accompanied by then External Affairs Minister Natwar Singh and National Security Adviser, late J.N. Dixit. The latter's presence raised eyebrows as the summit was on economic cooperation. However, the inimitable Dixit quipped, "National security does not mean only defence. It means security in energy, transport and communication. For economies to grow, there must be good law and order". He interacted with the participants as India has specific security concerns on terrorist and separatist organisations taking shelter in Bhutan, Nepal, Myanmar and Bangladesh, apart from concerns over narcotics and small arms smuggling with Myanmar and Thailand. The summit also agreed to set up a joint working group on terrorism, with India playing the first host.

O O O

# 4. HUMAN DEVELOPMENT REPORT

Commissioned by the United Nations Development Programme (UNDP), the Human Development Report 2007 released in June 2007, has ranked 177 countries based on life expectancy, literacy and income. India ranks 127, the same as the year 2003, but it is considerably worse than it was even three years ago. India was ranked 115th in the 2001 report. India's vibrant multi-cultural ethos, based on a strong and composite policy framework that promotes democracy and diversity has come in for repeated references in the global Human Development Report. The report was jointly launched to the media by the Union Minister of Information, Broadcasting and Culture, S. Jaipal Reddy and the UNDP Resident Representative, Dr. Maxine Oslon.

The Report calls for urgent attention to and national and global action on strengthening multicultural policies in five areas critical for prompting cultural diversity. These include bilingual education, affirmative action, political and legal pluralism including customary and unitary laws and religious practices. In the process, the Report advances the idea that cultural liberty is a vital part of human development because being able to choose one's identity without losing the respect of others or being excluded from other choices, is important in leading a full life. The Report argues, setting diversity in the context of choice rather than tradition, that the people have right to maintain their ethnic, linguistic and religious identities and contends that adoption of policies that recognize and protect these identities is the only sustainable approach to development in diverse societies. The Report says that economic globalisation cannot succeed unless cultural freedoms also respected and protected and underlines that xenophobic resistance to diversity should be addressed and overcome.

**The Report on India**

Like in previous years, the Report assesses progress made by the countries on the Human Development Index (HDI). India continues to make steady progress on the HDI value that has gone up from .579 in the 03's Report to .595 in HDR 2004. On HDI ranking, India is at 127 in 2004 against a total of 177 countries comprising the universe for which data is available for 2004. India's rank on the Human Poverty Index (HPI-I) is 48 in universe of 95 developing countries. On the Gender Development Index (GDI) India's rank is 103 in a universe of 144 countries.

The Report says the ethos of religious and other kind of tolerance in India goes back to the era of Emperor Ashoka in the third century BC. The Report further notes, "His dedicated championing of religious and other kinds of tolerance in India, arguing that the sects of other people all deserve reverence for one reason or another, is certainly among the earliest political defences of tolerances anywhere."

Dr. Oslon, while highlighting the Report's central message to strengthen a strong multi-cultural ethos for progress on human development, said the Report cites the experience of India, Malaysia, South Africa and the United States on the role of affirmative action and strong socio-economic policies in reducing inequalities between groups.

The Report says, "Reserved seats and quotas have been critical to ensuring that the Scheduled Tribes and Scheduled Castes had a voice in India. The allocation of government jobs, admission to higher education and legislative seats to Scheduled Castes and Tribes has helped members of these groups climb out of poverty and join the middle class." The Report notes that at Independence, the Scheduled Castes, Scheduled Tribes and Other Backward Classes could aspire only to a limited degree of upward mobility. The Report, lauding India's policies for ensuring religious freedom, notes that in India, Central Government employees have 17 holidays, 14 of which celebrate the diversity of its religions. The Report, in a similar vein, makes glowing references to India's language policies. The Report says, "India has practised a three-language formula for decades; children are taught in the official language of their State and are also taught in the two official languages of the country—Hindi and English".

For developing approaches to legal pluralism and recognizing the role of the judicial norms and institutions of the communities in different ways, Guatemala, India and South Africa have come in for rich plaudits. The Report says that the rationale for drawing state boundaries in India along linguistic lines is to ensure that each State has one dominant State language, each with its own script, rich vocabulary and literature going back hundreds, if not thousands of years.

Although the Human Development Report has made several laudatory references about India, there are some critical observations especially in the context of Gujarat 2002. Some of them are given below:

Growing distrust and hatred threaten peace, development and human freedom—sectarian violence killed thousands of Muslims and drove thousands more from their homes in Gujarat and elsewhere in India.

Although India is culturally diverse, comparative surveys of long-standing democracies including India show that it has been very cohesive despite its diversity. But modern India is facing a grave challenge to its constitutional commitment to multiple and complementary identities with the rise of groups that seek to impose a singular Hindu identity on the country. These threats undermine the sense of inclusion and violate the rights of minorities in India today. Recent communal violence raises serious concerns for the prospects for social harmony and threatens to undermine the country's earlier achievements.

In South Asia, organized violent attacks on Christian churches and missions have increased. India, despite its long secular tradition, has experienced considerable communal violence, with rising intensity: 40 per cent of casualties due to communal violence since 1954 occurred in 1990-2008. The HDR points out that 36.2% of all casualties in India in communal clashes since 1954 have occurred between 1990 and 2002.

The report emphasizes the need for empowerments of minorities and says that human development is as much about politics as it is about economics. It traces a history of violence and suppression of cultures and identities the world over, including a mention of the sectarian violence in Gujarat. It talks about how we need to recognize and accommodate diverse ethnicities, religions, languages and values—themes that are an inescapable feature of the landscape of politics in the world today.

The HDI rankings are calculated by taking into account a

country's performance in terms of life expectancy, education and per capita GDP. By its relatively poor performance on the education index, India's ranking is adversely affected—a pointer that the renewed thrust on education in the budget was much needed. For some consolation, India has a slightly higher value of HDI than the average for the South Asia region. In the subcontinent, Sri Lanka is ranked the highest at 96 while Bangladesh, Nepal at 138 and 140, respectively, surprisingly outrank Pakistan at 142. Norway tops the list with the HDI value of 0.956, followed by Sweden, Australia, Canada and the Netherlands. Burkina Faso, Niger and Sierra Leone have the worst human development indices.

Indians are among the citizens most proud of their country anywhere in the world—reveals the HDR. What's more surprising is that Indians have greater trust in institutions and democracy than anybody else. Over ninety per cent Indians were either a "great deal" or "quite proud" of being an Indian. That is just a wee bit lower than in the U.S.—not surprisingly the country where national pride is closest to 100%—or in Austria, Canada and Australia, but about thirty five per cent higher than in Germany.

The UNDP report debunks the notion that cultural diversity leads to a clash of civilizations. Instead, it advocates embracing diversity and protecting the rights of minorities as crucial to development. India ranks third after Maldives (84) and Sri Lanka (96) among South Asian Countries. Pakistan with a rank of 142 is the worst performer in the region. In terms of public spending in health (0.9% of GDP), India ranks 171st which is below China (2%), Nepal (15%) and even Bangladesh (1.6%). Only Pakistan (1%) does as badly as India, which leads only four countries—Nigeria, Indonesia, Sudan and Myanmar. However, in private spending on health, India ranks an impressive 18th which is 4.2% of its GDP, ahead of Pakistan (3%), China (3.4%) and other South Asian Countries.

O O O

## 5. BROADBAND POLICY

With a view to providing an impetus to broadband and Internet penetration in the country, the government on October 14, 2004, announced the broadband policy 2004. The policy envisages enhancement in quality of life through various applications in all walks of life and potential of growth in GDP. The prime consideration guiding the policy includes affordability and reliability of Broadband services, incentives for creation of additional infrastructure, employment opportunities, induction of latest technologies, national security and bring in competitive environment so as to reduce regulatory interventions.

Broadband has been defined as an always-on data connection supporting interactive services including Internet access with minimum download speed of 256 kbps per subscriber. The service providers are encouraged to select technologies and equipments offering higher data rate. The new broadband policy aimed to target three million broadband subscribers and six million Internet subscribers with a time frame of December 2005. The policy aims to target 20 million Internet subscribers by the end of year 2010. The new policy encourages creation and growth of infrastructure through various access technologies which can mutually co-exist like optical fibre technologies, digital subscriber lines on copper loop, cable T.V. network, satellite and terrestrial wireless technologies. The choice is left to the service provider. By this policy, the government intends to make available transponder capacity for VSAT services at competitive rates after taking into consideration the security requirements.

In consultation with the concerned ministries, the Department of Telecom will soon propose additional measures with regard to Open Sky Policy for VSAT operators. VSAT operators would be closely associated while determining the transponder usage charges. The service providers shall be permitted to enter into franchise agreement with cable TV network operators. However, the licensee shall be responsible for compliance of the terms and conditions of the licence.

Though belated, the policy is a welcome effort on the part of the Union Government to make the Internet more accessible at a decent speed to many more users who now rely on dial-up connections which are unreliable and slow. A major bottleneck that remains for potential broadband users is the "last mile" problem, since the copper lines which connect phones to the outside world are still controlled by the telecom providers, MTNL and BSNL. The Telecom Regulatory Authority of India's recommendations of unbundling these lines has not been accepted by the government and thus the internet service providers are at the mercy of the telecom giants for getting connectivity to the users.

However, the government has made it mandatory for the telecom operators to provide access to the ISPs, though there will be friction, especially in settling the rates of compensation. For many, however, the delicensing of certain frequencies for W-i F-i points out to a better future, as it would get over the local loop constraints and provide better access. The initiative which will hopefully give a push to the broadband movement in the country has to be commanded. The ISPs must now negotiate contractual arrangements with the dominant telephone companies so that part of some seven million technically feasible lines can be utilized for a franchised version of broadband using the universally popular Digital Subscriber Line (DSL) technology. As TRAI has noted, the experience of several countries indicates that broadband growth could be slow and the service expensive, if dominant telephone networks resisted the unbundling of telephone lines. Always-on Internet access at high bandwidth creates new possibilities to develop multi-media content for information, entertainment and data processing. Broadband growth has outpaced mobile telephony in several countries. The boom is fuelled by software down loads, online gaming and e-commerce.

In the Indian context, affordable high-speed networks can facilitate deployment of Information and Communication Technology for development. Telecommunication experts like Sam Pitroda have forecast a meaningful future for broadband in India, if it can be used widely to add the e-dimension to governance, health, learning and employment.

E-governance is an area that has made unsatisfactory progress because of the difficulty in data exchange with places that have poor telecom links. Today, there is a large base of educational and research institutions in different states that can develop multi-media packages for agriculture extension, vocational training, distance education and basic literacy. Wireless technologies combined with available telephone lines can cater to the requirements. Some encouraging models have emerged—notably West Bengal's telemedicine project which exploits the potential of ordinary copper telephone cables. Convergence of technologies has made it possible to combine the Internet with many other services such as video and telephony. The United States has made universal broadband a policy goal by 2007, as it has been overtaken in recent years by Korea, Japan and China in broadband connectivity.

# 6. Navy's Maritime Doctrine

The Indian Navy's Maritime Doctrine spells out the Navy's role in national security and the concepts it will use to fulfil it. The doctrine calls for building a nuclear ballistic missile submarine and a blue-water fleet able to project power into the Arabian Gulf and beyond. The future mission for the Navy would be to provide conventional and strategic nuclear deterrence against regional states and raise the cost of intervention by extra regional powers and deter them from acting against India's security interests. The doctrine also foresees increasing cooperation with other navies to combat emerging international common concerns like terrorism, transportation, drug trafficking and sea piracy.

The 135 page, unclassified document moves away from the earlier concept of coastal defence and lays stress on:

- Growing concerns to the East.
- Power projection.
- Littoral warfare to support land forces in war.

In addition to the long established threat on the western seaboard (Pakistan), a strategic requirement has emerged to look East as well. This has largely been the outcome of neo-economic powers of the ASEAN region and China aiming to strengthen their naval power. In contrast to earlier, inward-looking strategies, the new doctrine seeks to deal with "conflict with extra-regional power" and protecting persons of Indian origin and Indian interests abroad. The doctrine has three basic constituents—enduring tenets of nature of war, application of these tenets today and predictive element to prepare for the future.

## Nuclear Triad

The doctrine emphasises that nuclear weapons have the potential to deliver a level of damage unacceptable to any regime. It also voiced concern over Pakistan's "hostile posturing" and Chinese plans to configure its naval force to two carrier groups. The doctrine has emphasised that the country needs to develop a nuclear triad with its most effective punch being from under the sea. It also says that it was essential for nation to possess nuclear submarines capable of launching missiles with nuclear warheads, which was essential to the country's nuclear deterrence.

The doctrine says that sea control would be the main strategy that the navy would have to adopt increasingly in future conflicts along with sea denial to the enemy. It also called for exercising sea control in designated areas of the Arabian Sea and the Bay of Bengal safeguarding India's mercantile, marine and sea-borne trade and also providing security to India's coastline, island territories and offshore assets.

## China's Threat

The doctrine takes particular note of China, which has nuclear missile submarines and growing ties with Indian Ocean Rim nations such as Bangladesh, Iran, Thailand, Sri Lanka, Saudi Arabia, Pakistan and Myanmar. The document, elaborating on China says, "The PLA Navy which is the only Asian navy with a Submarine launched Ballistic Missiles Capability, is aspiring to operate much further from its coast than hitherto. The Chinese naval doctrine, as recently articulated, flows out of its overall military doctrine of Active Defence. The PLA Navy's aim of Defence Close to the Coast has been modified to Defence Close to the Ocean". In other words, PLA Navy will move from brown to blue water, that is, transit from being a coastal navy to becoming an ocean. In addition to the existing potent submarine force, the PLA Navy pans to configure its force levels around two carrier groups.

The Chinese have acquired decommissioned aircraft carriers from Australia and Russia to study their construction details and evolve an indigenous design for a carrier by 2015. This is clearly indicative of China's resolve to acquire a formidable naval capability. Besides, the PLA Navy's induction plans include ballistic missiles carrying submarines, nuclear powered attack submarines, conventional submarines (Kilo class and the indigenous Song class), amphibious ships and logistic ships. These inductions would make the PLA Navy capable of projecting power well beyond China's shores. In recent years, there has been an advent of aircraft carrier and submarines in the littorals of Bay of Bengal and adjoining waters.

## Pakistan's Ambitions

The document says that a steady flow of military technology and hardware into Pakistan demands a higher degree of military preparedness. Pakistan purchased three French Agosta 90B submarines incorporating Air Independent Propulsion (AIP) technology and with sub-launched missile firing capability. This would enable Pakistan to carry out attacks on merchant ships, war ships and installations from very long ranges while remaining submerged. Pakistan has also acquired Harpoon missile firing capable P3C Orion Maritime Patrol Aircraft (MPA).

## Maritime Vision

Having voiced the military concerns, the document observes that the Indian maritime vision for the first quarter of the 21st century must look at the arc from the Persian Gulf to the Straits of Malacca as a legitimate area of interest. It is axiomatic that protection of Sea lines of Communications (SLOC) would be an important task of the Navy. For this reason, India and the U.S. Pacific Command have agreed to harmonise engagement objectives to ensure that both work together to preserve the SLOC in the Indian ocean. This will enhance India's regional objectives with US cooperation, and is a key objective of US strategic engagement with India.

## Aircraft Carriers

The document, on the use of an aircraft carrier, says, it would be used for littoral warfare. Great power navies have shifted focus from the concept of control of highways and fighting the great sea battles, and are looking at dominating the littoral. Using sea power to destroy the enemy's land based war waging potential was always the theme of the Soviet Admiral Gorshkov. Now three decades later, it is the focus of US sea power as seen in their operations in Afghanistan and Iraq. If a navy is not in a position to contribute to the outcome of the land battle, it will cease to be of relevance.

## Military Missions

The document has listed a variety of military missions for the Navy, which include:

• To provide conventional and strategic nuclear deterrence against regional states.

- To raise the cost of intervention by extra regional powers, and deter them from acting against our security interests.
- To exercise sea control in designated areas of the Arabian Sea and the Bay of Bengal, and at the entry oblique exit points of the Indian Ocean Region.
- To provide security to India's coastline, island territories, offshore assets and Vulnerable Areas oblique. Vulnerable points from sea-borne threats.
- In case of war, to carry the conflict to the enemy's territory (Pakistan), to stangulate his trade/oil arteries, to destroy his war waging potential and naval assets and to ensure a decisive victory.
- To provide power projection forces, when required to land our Army in an area of interest.
- To rapidly switch forces from the East Coast to West Coast and vice versa to meet emerging threats.
- To counter the Low Intensity Maritime Operations (LIMO) threat.

To provide second strike nuclear capability in the event of a nuclear conflict, the Navy says that with a 'No First Use' nuclear policy, it is better that survivability of India's nuclear deterrent is never in doubt.

To work in conjunction with other two services to preserve, protect and promote India's national interests.

According to the Navy, with infiltration attempts by terrorists being frustrated across the Line of Control, there is the evergrowing possibility of infiltration from seawards forcing the Navy to be involved in LIMO in a greater manner, and for that, a large number of low value patrol ships are required.

## Principles of War

The document gives a list of principles of war such as Security, Offensive, Action, Flexibility, Surprise, Containment, Defence in Depth and Maintenance of Morale, but also says that these principles should be constantly reviewed and applied in carefully-considered combinations. The concepts of maritime over range from surveillance and intelligence, sea control, sea denial to Fleet in Being and 'Guerrede Course'. It would include convoy, blockade, submarine-antisubmarine campaign, amphibious operations and crafts of opportunity, etc. The doctrine also discusses the attributes of maritime forces such as its mobility, versatility, resilience and poise and also the various roles that the Navy can perform, viz. military, diplomatic, constabulary and benign.

## Acquisition Framework

Under the 30-year plan known as Project 75, Indian shipyards will use foreign technology to build about two dozen subs by 2030. The doctrine codifies the strategic framework for nation's existing plan to acquire nuclear-missile submarines. The Navy desires a 198 ship fleet in the future and at present has 140 ships. The Navy's 15 year shipbuilding plan starting 2000 is still pending with the government. According to the submarine plan, the Navy wants 12 submarines to be procured between 2000 to 2013, and hopes to indigenously build 12 more submarines between 2013 and 2030. Eventually, the Navy will have five types of submarines in its inventory; the Russian Kilo and a few leftover Foxtroti, the Amur, the French Scopene and the German HDWs.

After the terrorist attack on Mumbai in November 2008 in which the terrorists entered the city through sea, the role of Indian Navy and Coastguard has assumed greater significance in national security. Perhaps our Maritime Document needs to be updated as per growing threat which is also assuming diabilic proportions.

# 7. Unlawful Activities Prevention Act (UAPA)

The government introduced a Bill to repeal the controversial Prevention of Terrorism Act (POTA) in the Lok Sabha on December 2, 2004. The proposed Legislation provided for the review of all POTA cases pending in courts or which are at various stages of investigation within a one-year time. The then President of India A.PJ. Abdul Kalam promulgated an Ordinance on September 21, 2005 to repeal the Prevention of Terrorism Act (POTA). Simultaneously, the President promulgated another ordinance to amend the Unlawful Activities (Prevention) Act (UAPA) apparently, in order to fill the void created by POTA's repeal in punishing terrorism related offences.

In its National Common Minimum Programme (NCMP), the United Progressive Alliance (UPA) expressed its concern about the manner in which POTA had been misused since its promulgation in 2002 by the Bhartiya Janata Party led National Democratic Alliance (NDA) government. However, the CMP promised to take forward the battle against terrorism.

The Ordinance allows the Review Committee Constituted by the Centre under Section 60 of the repealed Act to review all the cases registered under it in order to ascertain whether a prima facie case existed for proceeding against the accused. The review would be completed within a year from the promulgation of the Ordinance. If no prima facie case was found by the committee, it can be withdrawn. In POTA cases in which the courts have not yet taken cognizance, investigations can be closed. The Ordinance also enables the Centre to constitute, if necessary, more committees to complete the review process within a year. Contrary to the CMP, which only calls for enforcing strictly the existing laws after the repeal of POTA to fight terrorism, the UPA government simultaneously promulgated another Ordinance to  amend the UAPA extensively. The amended UAPA expanded the section on definitions to include terrorist offences, and adds three \new chapters dealing with punishment for terrorist activities, forfeiture of proceeds of terrorism and terrorist organizations. By this amendment, the UPA government has implicitly accepted the NDA's argument that the existing laws are ineffective against terrorist acts.

The UAPA was designed to deal with associations and activities that questioned the territorial integrity of India. When the Bill was debated in the Parliament, leaders, cutting across party affiliation, insisted that its ambit be so limited that the right to association remained unaffected and that political parties were not exposed to intrusion by the Executive. Therefore, the ambit of the Act was strictly limited to meeting the challenge to the territorial integrity of India. The Act was a self-contained code of provisions for declaring secessionist associations as unlawful, adjudication by a tribunal, control of funds and places of work of unlawful associations, penalties for their members, etc. The Act has all along been worked holistically as such and is completely within the purview of the Central List in the 7th Schedule of the Constitution. By Ordinance No 2, the penal provisions concerning terrorism— a subject belonging to the Concurrent List—have been transferred to the UAPA. Because of its peculiar combination, it is bound to lead to confusion in its implementation and when State-specific provisions are sought to be added by the respective legislatures.

The definition of 'unlawful association' has been expanded by Ordinance No 2, to also include any association "which has for its object any activity which is punishable under Section 153A of the Indian Penal code, or which encourages or aids persons to undertake any such activity, or of which the members undertake any such activity". Section 153 A is about promoting enmity among different groups on grounds of religion, race, place of birth, residence, language, etc. By Ordinance No 2, penal provisions of POTA concerning acts of terrorism and terrorist organizations have been transferred to the 1967 Act, but the special enforcement provisions have been dropped.

A special legal framework, substantive as well as procedural, is required to counter-terrorism. Hence, there was POTA and before that TADA, which not only included special penal provisions but also special provisions for enforcement. With the UAPA, only the special penal provisions have been transferred, while the special provisions for enforcement have been dropped. Thus the State apparatus combating terrorism has been debilitated. Among the special provisions dropped are those restricting release on bail and allowing longer periods of police remand for the accused. Now suspected terrorists may roam free under the 'bail a rule, jail an exception' dictum. The police will not get sufficient time to interrogate the accused to investigate the cases which, by their very nature, are complex. In POTA and in TADA earlier, confessions made before a police officer of the rank of Superintendent were admitted as evidence. That proved to be vital in securing conviction of at least some of the terrorists involved in the bid to assassinate M.S. Bitta and in the attack on Parliament. This provision has been dropped. The retrograde step of dropping the important provisions is in stark contrast to the way in which the legal framework has been strengthened in most countries to combat terrorism. The partial transfer of the POTA provisions to the UAPA, is a half-hearted step that will only detract from· the morale and accountability of the State apparatus charged with the task of combating terrorism. What about the arrangement to grant relief to persons who may have been booked for offences of terrorism, either unfairly or without sufficient grounds? That is the concern which has been strongly voiced by the parties that now constitute the UAPA or support it. It is paradoxical that the concern has been ignored in the legislative manoeuvre of September 2. Under Section 60 of POTA, the NDA government had appointed a committee to review cases under investigation, and trial, and state governments could appoint similar committees. By an amendment in late 2003, the findings of these committees were given a binding effect and findings of the Central Committee an overriding effect on those of the State committees. The Central Committee under the chairmanship of Justice A.B. Saharya has painstakingly reviewed a vast number of cases and has provided relief where it was due. That committee though headless since Justice Saharya's resignation was retained for a year. It is a matter of concern that recourse to such a committee was not available for long.

## Criticism of the UAPA

The Unlawful Activities (Prevention) Amendment Ordinance, 2004 has omitted some of POTA's contentious provisions; retained some others and oddly enough, dispensed with certain safeguards in the old law. The bases for claiming that it is not POTA, rests principally on the omission of the provisions in the repeated law that dealt with confessions bail (Section 32 and 49). Section 32 made confessions to a senior police officer, under certain conditions, admissible in evidence. The outrageous provision which does not exist in ordinary criminal law belongs to a police state as it undermines the very notion of a free trial. It encourages the practice of extracting confessions from persons in police custody; which as often as not under South Asian conditions means third degree methods. Under Section 49 (7) of POTA, those accused could seek bail only after a year from the date of detention. This stringent condition was relaxed as a result of the Supreme Court holding that bail could be sought even before the expiry of the one-year period. The amending Ordinance brings the entire issue of bail for terrorist offences within the ambit of ordinary criminal law. Also, the new law does not contain the unduly restrictive provision under which an accused could be kept in detention for up to six months without filing charges.

The amending Ordinance does nothing to change the overly broad definition of what constitutes terrorism, a notorious factor that contributed to the use of POTA against political rivals, grandfathers, children and highly vulnerable tribal folk who would not be cast in the role of terrorists even in a Hollywood pot-boiler. Ironically, a stricter definition of what constituted a terrorist act was contained in POTA's notorious predecessor, the Terrorism and Disruptive Activities (Prevention) Act, 1987. Section 3 (1) of TADA made "intent to overawe the Government" an essential ingredient of a terrorist offence. Disturbingly, the amending Ordinance retains (the POTA provision that made intercepted communication (wire, electronic or oral) admissible in evidence but omits the detailed procedures, in the nature of safeguards against privacy invasion, that were stipulated for tapping telephones or intercepting e-mails. It was the political realization that the only use of POTA could be its misuse that led the major constituents of the APA to make its repeal a major poll plank and later, a commitment in the CMP. By incorporating so many provisions of POTA into another law, the Congress-led government has ensured that anxieties over the direction the war against terrorism has taken in the legal realm will remain. There has been so much clumsiness in drafting that though the provisions of admissibility of evidence collected through the interception of electronic messages have been bodily lifted from POTA, the procedural safeguards put in POTA, are missing. The Supreme Court upheld the legality of telephone tapping but subject to certain safeguards. These safeguards have been omitted

Further, while incorporating a requirement of the order of a competent authority permitting interception to be supplied to the accused before trial, the definition of "competent authority" as given in POTA has been omitted. The result is that this provision is unworkable because no interception can be legally done unless with prior authorization by a competent authority, and as no competent authority has been provided by the Ordinance, any interception will be illegal and inadmissible, the whole purpose of this provision will remain a dead letter. Since the Supreme Court upheld the power of interception subject to safeguards as to comply with the requirement of Article 19 (Right of Privacy), the delition will make all such interceptions unconstitutional and inadmissible.

A very objectionable feature in POTA of permitting the court to keep the identity of witnesses a secret has been retained and incorporated as such in the Amendment Ordinance. Such a provision has been held to be unconstitutional by the Inter-American Human Rights Court and evidence thus obtained is not admissible.

O O O

# 8. NEW WAR DOCTRINE OF INDIAN ARMY

The New War Doctrine of Indian Army is focused on fighting short and intense wars under a nuclear overhang. The much-awaited military doctrine lays emphasis on dealing with regional nuclear threat perceptions and a three-pronged strategy against terrorism. The doctrine is in two parts. The first which will be circulated widely, incorporates the changed operational scenario, the impact of terrorism, organizational and structural changes to meet the challenges of the Revolution in Military affairs and network centric warfare and joint operations. The second part is classified. The first Army doctrine was published by the Army Training Command in August 1998 in response to the Air Force doctrine of October 1995. This is the Army's second doctrine.

"Indian Army Doctrine" predicts that India's next wars will emerge on short notice, will be of short duration and will be fought at high tempo and intensity. Combat zones may be deeper and wider; thanks to better arms and land and spaced-based sensors. Conventional conflict may escalate to nuclear war if a belligerent is determined to avoid defeat, says the document.

After unveiling separate war doctrines, the three armed services are planning to come out with the first ever joint services doctrine. Being drafted by the office of the Combined Integrated Defence Staff (CIDS), the joint doctrine will be ready within a year, according to Admiral, Arun Prakash, the chief of the Indian Naval Staff.

## Highlights of the Doctrine

For the first time, the army has changed the traditional definition of victory. It now states that "success in modern conflict will be defined by an end state—a state of affairs which needs to be achieved at the end of the campaign either to terminate or to resolve the conflict on favourable terms. Victory may not, therefore always be appropriate to be described by the desired outcome of an operation; it may have to be defined in other terms such as reconciliation, stabilization or acceptance of an agreed peace plan. According to the doctrine, "The overall strategic philosophy of India is Strategic Dissuasive Defence, which covers the entire spectrum from deterrence to dissuation to persuasion." The ingredients of army's strategy are: to dissuade and deter; to be effective across the entire spectrum of conflict; to gain and maintain control over physical resources and territory, dominate adversary's forces and deny him freedom of action; and the army may be employed on any of the following tasks—power projection, deterrence, coercion and dissuation, and on a proactive strategy.

The doctrine also calls for creating strategic forces and having airborne and amphibious capabilities. It also talks of big capability in the use of firepower, including a larger role for artillery and smarter ammunition, better nightfighting capabilities and more unmanned aerial vehicles, guided missiles and other high tech equipment. The swiftness of future war requires more special forces to operate behind enemy lines. The doctrine underscores India's need for nuclear weapon delivery systems on land, at sea and in the air. It calls for the Army to be ready to fight amid biological and chemical weapons. Both active and passive defensive measures are being instituted to cater to this requirement. Nuclear, biological and chemical (NBC) protection should be installed on more than 1,500 T-72 tanks and much of India's artillery. The Army's incoming T-90 tanks and four hundred 155mm howitzers will have NBC gear when they arrive. Only 10 per cent of troops have NBC gear and the new doctrine would mean large purchases. The doctrine also proposes to shift from platform-centric to networking warfare, information warfare and the conduct of operations under the glare of the media.

The doctrine identifies 7 forms of information warfare on which India will focus:

- Command and control
- Intelligence-based
- Electronic
- Psychological
- Cyber
- Economic information
- Net work-centric warfare

The doctrine emphasizes combined operations by air, land and sea forces: towards attainment of common objectives, joint operations produce maximum application of the overall combat powers at the decisive point. The doctrine notes that India is emerging as a global power and calls on the military to support this new stance.

**Deception**

"The ability to effect true surprise is progressively reducing and therefore the military planners need to concentrate more on deception, as a good and well-coordinated deception plan would help to achieve surprise," says the doctrine. The doctrine wants deception to be developed as an integral component of peacetime and wartime national security policy.

"Deception is international, purposeful, calculative and deliberate. The target of deception should be the adversary's decision-making system. Often the best and the simplest deception is the presentation of the truth but in such a form that the adversary disbelieves it." The process of deception is interactive and should follow the sequential steps of planning, integration and execution.

"Those charged with planning, approving and executing deception operations must be absolutely adept in all processes that these involve. Training and exercises should integrate the aspect of deception and appropriate resources allotted to develop and refine the art."

Future wars will be swift, intense and short and will be fought in the backdrop of terrorism and nuclear threats. The new doctrine has factored in the changing operational scenario and the impact of terrorism on it. Holding that future wars would have to be fought jointly by the three services, the doctrine laid special emphasis on "structural changes" to ensure the Army met the Challenges of RMA (Revolution in Military Affairs) along with "network centric operations". The new doctrine focuses on 'cold start strategy', which depends on flexible integrated groups with IAF and Navy elements for swift strikes on enemy territory rather than mass mobilization of troops. The limitations of mass mobilization showed up during Operation Parakram which took three weeks for the troops to be marched to their battle position by which time the international community had firmly intervened and the element of surprise was lost. The doctrine emphasizes the need for having self-contained flexible forces comprising all the three services and achieve the military objectives in the shortest possible time. It also stresses on achieving synergy and jointmanship between the Army, Air Force and Navy and exploit their assets for the desired goals, keeping in view the nuclear scenario.

## Operational Strategy

For the first time since Independence, age-old concepts of mobilization of forces and strike concepts of mobilization of forces and strike corps spearheading the attack are being junked. The new doctrine does not believe in dividing the forces into· defensive or attack formations. The aim would be for 'total destruction of objective' but spare enemy's strategic potential to avoid nuclear response. The operations will focus on precision capability and hard impact since massive air, land campaigns would not be possible. In short, no longer will armed forces be mobilized to prepare for war. Global powers in the changed world do not allow it.

The three Strike Corps—Mathura-based I Corps, Ambala-based II Corps and Bhopal-based XXI Corps—will be there only for training purposes. The war will be fought through eight battle groups with integrated elements from the IAF and Navy. The idea is to destroy, not to hold or capture territory.

For nearly five decades after Independence, the Indian Army did not have a written document called army doctrine. But it did have its concepts and procedures about conducting operations and performed creditably. However, a need was always felt to formalize the doctrine of the army, so that everyone became aware of the nuances and actions of units and formations were in consonance with it.

The starting point for formulating a military doctrine is a grand strategy, which lays down the policy framework and conditions under which the military will be asked to wage war or conduct other operations. All three services have produced their own war doctrines without a political directive, detailing the nature of external threats, how they are to be tackled, and what is sought to be achieved militarily, and importantly without catering to a nuclear war, should the nuclear threshold be crossed unwittingly. There is no doubt that a joint doctrine will provide unity of effort and enhance coordination for joint planning, cooperation, mutual trust and implementation, but an army doctrine would still be required.

○ ○ ○

# 9. SATLUJ-YAMUNA LINK (SYL) CANAL

Punjab Assembly unanimously passed a bill on 12th July 2004, terminating all agreements relating to sharing of waters of Ravi and Beas rivers with Haryana and Rajasthan, thus giving a new twist to the SYL issue. The unprecedented move came two days ahead of the Supreme Court deadline to the Centre to hand over construction of the Satluj-Yamuna Link (SYL) canal to the Centre as Punjab had been refusing to complete its part of the canal.

The bill annulled the December 31, 1981 agreement signed by the Chief Ministers of Punjab Haryana and Rajasthan as per which the SYL was to be constructed by Punjab. All other pacts related to Ravi Beas waters also stand terminated. Faced with a raging inter-State row, the Centre referred the controversial measure to the Supreme Court on July 22, 2004 looking for a legal solution through a Presidential reference for a solution of the inter-State imbroglio. The reference made under Article 143 of the Constitution, aims at seeking the apex courts opinion on the Punjab Government's controversial legislation by which it has terminated all accords and obligations to part with SYL water to Haryana and any other state. There has been much confusion, bewilderment and anxiety about Punjab's action in terminating past agreements and accords over river waters.

## Background

In 1955, the then Union Minister of Works and Power helped in securing an agreement on the following allocations of the surplus waters of Ravi and Beas, then estimated as 15.85 million acre feat MAF after excluding the pre-partition use of 3.13 MAP: J&K (0.65 MAF) and Rajasthan (8.0 MAF). The share of Punjab (7.2 MAF with Pepsu merged) had to be divided between Punjab and Haryana after the reorganization of states. This ran into difficulty but in 1976, the government of India settled the dispute by notification under Section 78 of the Punjab Reorganization Act 1966, allocating 3.5 MAF to each state, with the remaining 0.2 MAF going to Delhi. In order to help Haryana to make full use of its allocation, the construction of the Satluj-Yamuna Link Canal was proposed. Punjab was not happy with the decision and filed a suit in the Supreme Court and Haryana too filed a suit to compel Punjab to implement the decision.

In 1981, the then Prime Minister, Indira Gandhi brought about an agreement among the Chief Ministers of Punjab, Haryana and Rajasthan. Under that agreement, the allocations to Punjab and Haryana were 4.22 MAP and 3.5 MAP respectively out of total availability, which had been revised from 15.85 to 17.17 MAP. Punjab and Haryana withdrew their petitions from the Supreme Court. However, the dispute continued and figured in the discussion between the then Prime Minister Rajiv Gandhi and Sant Longowal. The accord between them of July 24, 1985 includes a paragraph regarding the sharing of Ravi-Beas Waters and that was in pursuance of that accord that the Ravi-Beas Tribunal was set up. The tribunal gave its award in 1987 allocating 5.00 MAP to Punjab and 3.83 MAF to Haryana, thus increasing the shares of both states. It was able to do so by taking into account some additional availability of water 'below the rim stations'. At that time, it was found politically difficult to gazette the award because it was unacceptable to Punjab, which was then in a troubled state. Punjab has all along been opposed to the construction of the SYL canal, which would enable Haryana to use its share of the waters and it still remains incomplete. Haryana has been going to court over this. The Supreme Court has been asking the Central government to ensure the expeditious completion of the SYL. It is against this background that we have to view the latest developments.

The Punjab action gives rise to several questions of a legal nature. First, can an agreement to which there are two or more parties be repudiated unilaterally by one party? Agreements and accords are entered into by executive governments; can they be terminated by an act of the legislature? Secondly, it has been argued that Rajasthan and Haryana are not 'basin state', in relation to the Ravi and Beas and have no riparian rights. Ravi and Beas are part of the Indus-system; we have to talk about the Indus basin and not about the Ravi basin or Beas basin. Haryana was earlier a part of Punjab and a state as a whole was surely a 'riparian' in relation to Ravi and Beas. The allocation of waters was made to the state as a whole and not to a part of it. Does a part of the state lose its riparian character because of a division of the State? Assuming hypothetically that Punjab is further divided, will each such division mean that certain portions cease to be riparians? That leads us to the third and very important point, namely that unlike the Cauvery Dispute which is a straightforward upper-riparian/lower riparian dispute, this is really a dispute relating to allocations of river waters made in pursuance of a reorganization of states.

There is a tendency to regard the Ravi-Beas waters as Punjab's own waters, which others are taking away. In fact, there is no ownership or proprietary rights over flowing waters. Thus, neither Karnataka nor Tamil Nadu owns the Cauvery: both have use-rights. Similarly, Punjab has use-rights over Ravi-Beas waters. It does not own them. This has been clearly stated in the report of the Ravi-Beas Tribunal. Punjab has been contending that the availability of water has to reassessed. It says it is less than the 17.17 MAF estimated earlier. If this is true and if allocations to Haryana and Rajasthan remain unaltered, the residue remaining with Punjab might be less than the share allocated to it. Rajasthan is worried about its allocation of eight MAP not fully materialising. Delhi is apprehensive not only about losing its small portion of 0.2 MAF from Ravi-Beas, but even more about the possibility of Haryana responding to Punjab's unilateral action on Ravi-Beas by backing out of the agreement with Delhi on the Yamuna.

We may conclude that such matters should be resolved by agreement, conciliation, meditation or adjudication and not by unilateral action. There might be strong political compulsions behind the Punjab action but these compulsions do not justify actions that are prima facie unlawful or contrary to the spirit of federalism or in defiance of the Supreme Court. The Supreme Court cannot be left to handle all this alone as the Central government has a responsibility to intervene and find an acceptable solution. The crucial question is whether the three states really need the quantities of water that they are asking for. Irrigation in Punjab and Haryana has over the years resulted in a significant incidence of water-logging and salinity. Instead of asking for more water, they should learn to manage water better. One may suggest that they should try and grow whatever they want to grow with less water and maximum productivity per unit of water. As for Rajasthan, we have the extraordinary spectacle of a desert state suffering from waterlogging and salinity problems. Is that not clear evidence of a completely wrong approach? The Rajasthan desert has been an inhabited one with centuries old traditions of good .water-management.

With growing populations, the old traditions of local augmentation of water availability may need to be supplemented by some external water. However, while the desert can and must be made a bit more livable, 'making the desert bloom' is not necessarily a sound idea. Therefore, it must be re-examined whether Punjab, Haryana and Rajasthan require the quantities of water earlier allocated to them or need more water, or can manage with less. The dispute may become more manageable with all-round proper water management. Apart from the governments, a civil society initiative in this regard seems very desirable. The participation of eminent citizens in the concerned state may also help.

O O O

# 10. BASIC EDUCATION—A MUST FOR EMPLOYMENT GENERATION

In the Union Budgets for 2008-09, stress was laid on investing more on the development of human capital but owing to the severe resource crunch faced by the government in recent years, the actual receipts of the departments concerned with the finance ministry have been far less than the lofty commitments made in budgetary statements.

One needs to have a look at what Amartya Sen actually said on nurturing human capital in relation to the conditions prevailing in several states, specially in the countryside. From this remark we can easily draw parallels with the all-India experience.

This would give an idea on whether the claims made on the relevance of investment in human capital were valid enough, without, any proportionate thrust on employment generation and poverty alleviation. According to a Planning Commission's spokesman, the Union Cabinet approved the Ninth Five-Year Plan (1997-2002) incorporating Sen's ideas with a thrust on primary and basic education. The West Bengal government had also announced a plan to launch a drive to primary education in all the districts. This would, according to the government, ensure universal access to primary education to all children in the age group of five to nine years by the year 2002. Besides this, the state government announced the setting up of literacy centres for adults. However, doubts have been expressed even in government circles whether such ideas can be implemented due to paucity of funds, in spite of recent budgetary allocations.

## Elementary Education

The parliament has passed the Constitution 86th Amendment Act, 2002 to make elementary education a Fundamental Right for children in the age-group of 6-14 years. It is proposed to bring in a follow-up legislation with detailed mechanism to implement this act.

## Sarva Shiksha Abhiyan

The Scheme of Sarva Shiksha Abhiyam (SSA) was launched in 2001. The goals of SSA are as follows: (i) All 6-14 age children in school/Education Guarantee Scheme Centre/bridge course by 2003, (ii) All 6-14 age children complete five year primary education by 207; (iii) All 6-14 age children complete eight years of schooling by 2010; (iv) Focus on elementary education of satisfactory quality with emphasis on education for life; (v) Bridge all gender and social category gaps at primary stage by 2007 and at elementary education level by 2010; and (vi) Universal retention by 2010.

The assistance under the programme of SSA was on a 85:15 sharing arrangement during the Ninth Plan, 75:25 sharing arrangement during the Tenth Plan, and 50:50 sharing thereafter between the Central Government and State Government.

The programme covers the entire country with special focus on educational needs of girls, SCs/STs and other children in difficult circumstances. The programme seeks to open new schools in habitations which do not have schooling facilities and strengthen existing school infrastructure through provision of additional class rooms, toilets, drinking water, maintenance grant and school improvement grant. The SSA has a special focus on girls and children of weaker sections. A number of initiatives including free textbooks, target these children under the programme. The SSA also seeks to provide computer education even in rural areas to bridge the digital divide.

During 2004-05, the SSA approved 44,719 new schools, 2,10,431 appointment of new teachers, 29,018 construction of school buildings, 82,538 additional class rooms, construction of 50,044 toilets and provision of Drinking Water for 44,322 schools, free textbook for 6.15 crore children, School Grant for 9,03,191 schools and teacher grant for 32,39,155 teachers against annual district elementary education plan for 598 districts. A sum of Rs. 4,386.47 crore (up to December 2004) was released by Central Government to the States/UTs.

It may be noted that the relevance of basic education has always been linked to the ideal of mass democracy. Universal education, it is argued, would help reduce the disparities in wealth and power by providing young people with skills and competence to make them find a valued place in society. Therefore, the relevance of basic education to social development is a near universal phenomena. Yet there are reasons for arguments in this regard. The Plan document incorporates altered priorities laid down by the government. It includes a provision of Rs. 21,946 crore from the Prime Minister's special action plans (SAPs) in five areas—food, agriculture, physical infrastructure, health, education, housing and drinking water, information technology, and water resources. But the moot question is: How will the proposed expansion and improvement of social infrastructure with huge budgetary support be possible when our government is cash-strapped? The aim is to provide basic and primary education, drinking water, housing, health care and sanitation within five years.

With the non-plan sector dominating the net government expenditure owing to the increase in wages of civil servants, how and from where will the money come to implement these pious wishes of the government? The propagation of basic education is considered an important benchmark for social development. Literate and healthy human beings can cater to the requirement of state-of-the-art technology and can find a ready place in the modern job market. Modem technology cannot march ahead without the supply of educated and skilled workforce. Therefore, investment in education and health is considered a means to an end.

Sen says in this connection that importance has to be attached to the distinct influences that promote or constraint the freedom that individuals have, including their ability to make use of economic opportunities. He emphasises that basic education and health can be important factors for enhancing the level of human capital due to a number of reasons:

(i) Basic education and other features of a good quality life are of importance on their own and not just as human capital geared to commodity production.

(ii) Basic education endows a large number of important personal and social roles which can raise the capacity of human empowerment. There are a number of sociological studies which suggest that in agrarian society like that of India, without much scope for industrial employment, the proficiency arising from basic education is well valued in modern society.

The dismal employment scenario in India, specially in industrial and service sector is a major impediment in implementing a plan of action for spreading basic education for social development. In 1980, when the population of West Bengal was 545.81 lakh, the total employment in public and organised sector was only 26.64 lakh. In 1991, the figure stood at 680.78 1akh and 25.86 lakh, respectively. On the other hand, the level of literacy in 1980 and 1991 was 33.2 per cent and 57.7 per cent of the total population. In 1977, when the population size swelled to well above 750 1akh, the net employment was only 24.79 lakh. Thus, there is little scope for absorbing the neo-literates in gainful employment, other than the agrarian sector, which has already become saturated.

Since the dependence on agriculture sector is steadily increasing in India, the purpose of propagating basic education as a pre-condition to social development stands defeated, apart from the humanitarian aspect of it, for making an individual self-dependent in mind, spirit and temper. At present, the entire third world is induced by the US backed donor agencies to initiate a development strategy of protectionism and industrialisation with a high hope toward "economic growth", "welfare" and "democracy". These schools of thought have tried to address and issue a change only in the realm of social superstructure, mainly through the propagation of basic education and health, keeping the base of society with its economy unaltered. But without restructuring the property relations in favour of the depressed classes, the basic tenet of welfare economics stands debatable for its status-quoist and conservative outlook.

The concept of Sen's thesis joins this bandwagon which is nothing short of a utopia and armchair philosophy. This pejorative assertion gets emboldened when his premise on human capital was examined and X-rayed through the light of reality of our country and also by the fact when Sen failed to name a single country which had emulated his basic tenet of thought into action. Yet the red and the "saffron brigade" had strangely preferred to swear by his name without seriously considering the 'why question' of the malady of economy and society of our country.

## Promotion of Languages

Language being the most important medium of

communication and education, its development occupies an important place in the 'National Policy on Education and Programme of Action. Therefore, the promotion and development of Hindi and other languages listed in the Constitution of India have received due attention.

## Hindi

In order to assist non-Hindi speaking States/UTs to effectively implement the three-language formula, support for provision of facilities for teaching of Hindi in these States/UTs is provided by sanctioning financial assistance for appointment of Hindi teachers in schools under a Centrally-sponsored scheme. Assistance is also given to voluntary organisations for enabling them to hold Hindi-teaching classes. Through the Kendriya Hindi Sansthan, the Government promotes development of improved methodology for teaching Hindi to non-Hindi speaking students. A special course for teaching Hindi to foreigners is being conducted by the Sansthan, on regular basis annually.

The Central Hindi Directorate runs programmes relating to purchase and publication of books and its free distribution to non-Hindi speaking States and to Indian missions. It extends financial support of NGOs engaged in development and promotion of Hindi.

The Commission for Scientific and Technical Terminology, New Delhi, prepares and publishes definitional dictionaries and terminology in various disciplines in Hindi and in other languages,

Financial assistance is given to voluntary organisations and individuals to bring out publications like encyclopedias, dictionaries, books of knowledge, original writing on linguistic, literacy, ideological, social anthropological and cultural themes, critical edition of old manuscripts, etc. for the development of modern Indian languages. States are given special help for the production of University-level books in regional languages. The National Council for Promotion of Urdu Language (NCPUL) has been functioning since April 1996 as an autonomous body for the promotion of Urdu language and also Arabic and Persian languages. One of the outstanding areas of operation of NCPUL has been transfer of information of Urdu speaking population into productive human resource and making them part of the employable technological workforce in the emerging information technological scenario and penetration of computer education to the grass-root level in minority concentration blocks. The Government has set-up National Council for Promotion of Sindhi.

The Govemment also provides facilities for study of all Indian languages. For this the Central Institute of Indian Languages (CIIL), Mysore conducts research in the areas of language analysis, languages, pedagogy, language technology and language use. It runs Regional Language Centres to help in meeting the demand for training of teachers to implement the three-language formula. The Regional Language Centre also provides training for mother tongue teachers in different Indian languages at various levels.

## English and Foreign Languages

The Central Institute of English and Foreign Languages (CIEFL), Hyderbad is Institution of Higher learning deemed to be a University is an autonomous organisation under this Ministry, which undertakes teacher education programme to improve the professional competence of teachers of English at the secondary language. It offers several courses like post graduate certificate and diploma courses in teaching of English and Ph.D. courses in English through the distance mode. It also offers teaching of major foreign languages like Arabic, French, German, Japanese, Russian and Spanish. It has regional centres at Shillong and Lucknow. The CIEFL also implements two Government of India schemes of English Language Teaching Institute (ELTI) and District Centres for English to bring about substantial improvements in the standard of teaching/learning of English in the country for which grants are given by CIEFL to various State Governments.

The National Policy on Education, 1986 (revised in 1992) and its Programme of Action-1992 has laid considerable emphasis on value education by highlighting the need to make education a forceful tool for the cultivation of social and moral values.

To fulfill the objectives of the National Policy on Education, a Central Sector Scheme of Assistance for Strengthening of Culture and Values in Education is being implemented. Under this scheme, financial assistance is given to Governmental and non-Governmental organisations, Panchayati Raj Institutions, etc., to the extent of 100 per cent of grant for the project proposals approved subject to a ceiling of Rs. ten lakh for strengthening cultural and value education from pre-primary education system to higher education including technical and management education.

**Sanskrit Division**

Sanskrit has played a vital role in the development of all Indian Languages and in the preservation of the cultural heritage of India. The Government of India gives 100 per cent financial assistance through State Governments for: a) eminent Sanskrit scholars in Indigent Circumstances; b) modernisation of Sanskrit Pathshalas; c) providing facilities for teaching Sanskrit in High/ Higher Secondary Schools; d) scholarships to students studying Sanskrit in High and Higher Secondary schools; e) various schemes for the promotion of Sanskrit; and f) improving the methodology of teaching Sanskrit in schools, Sanskrit Colleges/Vidyapeeths. Presently the Scheme is under revision.

*Presidential Award* of the Certificate of Honour is conferred on eminent scholars of Sanskrit Pali, Arabic, and Persian in recognition of their lifetime outstanding contribution towards the propagation of these languages, every year on Independence Day. Maharshi Badrayan Vyas Samman has also been introduced for young scholars in the age group of 30-40 years who have made a breakthrough in inter disciplinary studies involving contribution of Sanskrit or ancient

Indian wisdom, to the process of synergy between modernity and tradition,

*The Maharshi Sandipani Rashtriya Veda Vidya Prathisthan, Ujjain* is an autonomous organization, which promotes. a) Preservation, conservation and development of the oral tradition of Vedic studies; b) Study of the Vedas through Pathashalas as well as through other means and institutions; c) Creation and promotion of research facilities; d) Creation of infrastructure and other conditions for the .collection of information and storage of relevant material.

*Rashtriya Sanskrit Sansthan, New Delhi* is an autonomous organisation established by the Government of India in the year 1970. It is the nodal agency for the propagation, promotion and development of Sanskrit Education in the country. It is fully funded by the Government of India in the Ministry of Human Resource Development, Department of Secondary and Higher Education. Rashtriya Sanskrit Sansthan has been granted the status of a Deemed to be University.

*Rashtriya Sanskrit Vidyapeetha, Tirupati,* provides courses of study from Prak Shastri (Intermediate) to Vidya Vardhi (Ph.D.) , The Vidyapeetha has upgraded the Department of Pedagogy to an Institute of Advanced Studies in Education (IASE).

*Shri Lal Bahadur Shastri Rashtriya Sanskrit Vidyapeetha, New Delhi* provides courses of study from Shastri to Vidya Vachaspati (D.Lit.). From 1997-98 the Vidyapeetha started diploma in vedic and refresher courses, two degrees, namely, Vidya Vardhi (Ph.D.) and Manad Upaadhi (Honorary D.Lit.) are also given by Vidyapeetha

## Scholarships

The Ministry of Human Resource Development operates a Centrally Sponsored Plan Scheme, viz. National Merit Scholarship Scheme through States/UTs, under which 100 per cent financial assistance is provided to meritorious students from rural areas studying in classes IX and X. Besides, scholarship is also provided to all the meritorious students on state-wise merit, including students from rural areas, studying from the post-metric to the post-graduate level. The rate of scholarship varies from Rs. 250 to Rs. 750, depending on course of study. Under the Scheme of Scholarship to Students from Non-Hindi Speaking States for Post-Matric Studies in Hindi, the rate of scholarship ranges from Rs. 300 to 1000 per month.

The Government provides scholarships to Indian scholar for Post Graduate/Research/Post Doctoral studies abroad or the basis of officers/received from foreign Government under the various Cultural/Educational Exchange Programme. The details of offers and other conditions are given wide publicity in the leading newspapers while inviting applications for scholarship and are available on Department's website *www.education.nic.in*. The amount and other facilities provided by foreign governments varies from country to country and time to time. 108 scholarships were awarded during the year 2004-2005 under various Cultural Exchange Programmes/ Educational Exchange Programmes.

○ ○ ○

## 11. Life In India's Slums

A sample slum project should act as an inspiration for eradicating the plight of millions of slum dwellers in India. The project may have brought about qualitative changes in the lives of lakhs of slum dwellers, but an estimated 45 million people continue to live in sub-human conditions in thousands of slums across the country. They do not have access to many of the basic necessities of life. This is despite the fact that they live amid an ocean of plenty and prosperity.

This is a major cause of concern as slum dwellers not only form a significant proportion of the total population but also play a significant role in the urban economy. By providing cheap labour for the construction work, selling green vegetables to the urban health-conscious citizen, pulling rickshaws where public transport is not available, and providing cheap domestic help are some of the major economic functions performed by the slum dwellers.

Unfortunately, slum dwellers are looked upon by the rest of society as an appendix causing ills in the urban body. This is misleading. Slum inhabitants are rather like that artery which if blocked would cease the smooth functioning of the whole body. A by-product of industrialisation, and rapid urbanisation slums are areas of low civic amenities with clusters of houses inhabited by low income groups who often work as vendors, flower traders, watchmen, domestic helps, rickshaw drivers, and unskilled labourers working at construction sites.

More appropriately, a slum can be defined as an area of overcrowded and dilapidated usually old housing occupied by people who can afford only the cheap dwellings available in the urban area, generally in or close to the inner city. The term usually implies both a poverty ridden population and unhealthy environment and a district ripe with crime and vice.

The problems of the slum dwellers are manifold. First they live in sub-human conditions. The degraded environment in which they live, take their toll on the physical, mental, and moral health. The slum dwellers mostly live in cramped, overcrowded, and unventilated dwellings. In Mumbai, for example, the slum dwellers and the homeless account for about 50% of the population but they occupy only six per cent of the city's land area. Similarly, Delhi which has the third largest slum population in the country, accommodates an estimated 32 lakh people in about 1,000 slums. According to the 2001 census, some of the slums have a population density of more than 60,000 persons per square km. Given such a mode of living, slum dwellers are exposed to a variety of diseases. Lack of adequate medical facilities further aggravates their plight. There are not enough trained doctors and paramedical staff to look after the patients in the slums.

They are unable to pay the hefty fee charged by the private practitioners and nursing homes.

In a study, it was found that majority of slum dwellers are exposed to water-borne and other infectious diseases. Children and women are more susceptible to such diseases. Added to this is the problem of scarcity due to poverty. Even the basic necessities of the slum dwellers are not met. Contaminated drinking water, lack of sewerage, inadequate schooling facilities for children, no privacy for women and poor supply of electricity are some of the perpetual problems faced by them. All this takes a heavy toll on the health and lives of the slum dwellers.

A large number of slum dwellers in Delhi depend on shallow handpump water which is mostly contaminated. According to an estimate, the entire Delhi population requires about 535 million gallons of water daily (MGD). However, the actual availability is limited to 425 MGD after deducting the operational losses. The shortfall is of 110 MGD which is unequably distributed between the posh colonies who have no shortage even for watering their lawns. The slum dwellers who have to struggle hard for survival do not have even drinking water to their satisfaction. A survey by the Delhi-based National Institute of Communicable Disease found that 50% of water supplied to jhuggi-jhompri is not fit for drinking.

The situation in other metropolitan cities is equally pathetic. In a survey by the Hindu Daily, of the 540 households of Santoshnagar, a slum settlement is considered by Mumbai Municipal Corporation to be well provided in terms of infrastructure. Here it was found that 14% of the households drew drinking water from wells of varying depths. On examination it was found that the water of these wells was contaminated.

Another serious problem facing the slums is increasing crime. Cases of violence for self-preservation, fighting, rape, and stealing are very common. It is a pity that even after over sixty years of independence, the country has not been able to give freedom to a large chunk of our population, who continue to live in bondage of drudgery and deprivation.

## National Slum Development Programme

The National Slum Development Programme (NSDP) was launched in August 1996. Under NSDP, Additional Central Assistance (ACA) is being released to the States/UTs for the development of urban slums. The objective of this programme is upgradation of urban slums by providing physical amenities like water supply, storm water drains, community bath, widening and paving of existing lanes, sewers, community latrines, street lights, etc. Besides, the funds under NSDP can be used for provision of community infrastructure and social amenities like pre-school education, non-formal education, adult education, maternity, child health and primary health care including immunisation, etc. The programme also has a component of shelter upgradation or construction of new houses.

Under the programme, funds in the form of ACA are allocated by the Planning Commission annually on the basis of slum population of the State/UT. While the Ministry of Finance releases the funds to the States under this Programme, the Ministry of Home Affairs releases the funds to Union territories. The States release the funds to the Implementing Agencies as per their requirements. The Ministry of Urban Employment and Poverty Alleviation has been nominated as the Nodal Ministry to monitor the progress of the programme in respect of States.

As reported by the States/UTs, since the inception of the programme and up to 31 March 2005 out of the total funds of Rs. 3089.63 crore released by the Central Government, an amount of Rs. 2130.09 crore has been spent and about 4.12 crore of slum dwellers have benefited from this programme.

## 12. ECONOMIC REFORMS—RECONCILING CONFLICTING AGENDA

According to a prominent economist Arjun Sengupta, designing a programme of economic reforms in a democracy is much more difficult than doing so in a country where the survival of the government does not depend upon elections. For most reform programmes, designing is mainly a technical exercise—whether the different policies are mutually consistent, reinforcing each other, which of them be implemented first and which later, and how much of each policy change would be expected to produce the desired results.

Estimating these relationships is, of course not easy, often dependent on judgements based on experience and understanding. That makes these programmes vulnerable to mistakes and misjudgements. Still the policy makers do not necessarily face the problems acceptable to the majority on whose support the government expects to survive and be reelected.

The perception that the reforms would not in too distant a future yield large benefits to the majority of people is often more important than any actual and immediate benefits from the reforms. Quite often the reform programmes, aimed at stabilization of an overheated economy with high inflation and fiscal deficit, contract income and employment. But the people may be quite willing to accept the hardships if they believe that better days are around the corner.

### Investment Level

If the design of the reform programmes does not generate this perception among the majority, the government, afraid to lose the elections, may slow down the reform process halfway through, reverse some of the policies or worse still adopt populist measures encouraging fiscal profligacy. Fiscal discipline is necessary for the consistency of a reform programme as none of the deregulation and liberalisation measures would work if inflation or fiscal deficit is too high. A politically acceptable programme may thus become even technically unsustainable.

What is more important is that if reforms are seen as unsustainable, with a high possibility of reversal and instability of policies, private investors would be reluctant to increase or even maintain their rate of investment. The recent literature on investment shows that sustainability of policies is often more important than profitability in determining the level investment. This is particularly so in countries where WHO policy environments are changing due to reforms. Invest assessing the risks on the returns of a project are very sensitive to the possibility of a reversal of policies that made investment opportunities more attractive than before. In making any decision in locking funds in irreversible fixed investments, they attach high value to the option of waiting and watching if policies are sustainable.

## Foreign Investors

So if reforms are unsustainable, investments will not increase, but without increasing investments, policy reforms will not work and, cannot be sustained. All reforms by lifting controls and opening up competition, reduce the price distortions and there is almost an immediate gain in output due to improved efficiency. To sustain this gain would require an increase in the rate of investment, so that the static gains in allocation efficiency lead to a higher rate of growth. The increase in investment will require not just a one time rise in output and profitability but reasonable expectation that they will be sustained.

The policy uncertainties would particularly affect foreign investors. In addition to the risks of realising the returns on investment which depends upon the stability of policies regarding relative prices, interest rates, exchange rates and inflation, foreign investors have to worry about repatriation of their profits into foreign exchange, which depends on the stability of exports, import and exchange rate policies.

Even with a moderate probability of these policies being reversed, foreign investors may be reluctant to come in. It would therefore be important to design reform programmes where crucial investments such as infrastructure are not left to be provided only by foreign investors.

If capacities are not created for infrastructure, the potential return on investment in other sectors would fall, discouraging investment in general and lowering the overall growth. Most of the policy changes, however, require a sustained rate of growth for their success. Reduced tax rates, for example, can raise total revenue and avoid increased fiscal deficit, only if there is growth of income and output. Exposing domestic industry to foreign competition that would lead to contraction of inefficient domestic units can lead to increased employment only if there is increased growth in other industries absorbing more labour. Giving up controls and rationing will not raise the prices of essential commodities and inputs very much, if their supplies increase. Improved growth improves the likelihood of success of most policies, and therefore the likelihood of their being sustained. Conversely without growth, policies cannot be sustained, which in turn would lower investment and growth. In addition to promoting growth and investment, designing a reform programme must incorporate special measures providing for education, health, nutrition, social security and rural employment to promote acceptability of the programme to the majority of the people. If a reform programme involves cuts in public expenditure on these counts, it would be seen by the millions as going against their interest.

## Fiscal Deficit

The art of designing such programmes would be to ensure sustenance of social development expenditures within the overall constraint of maintaining a moderate fiscal deficit. Large fiscal deficit makes a reform programme technically unsustainable. A drastic cut in public expenditure on social development will make reforms politically unsustainable.

The ability to reconcile these two conflicting ends will determine the success of the design of reform. Fortunately, effectiveness of a public expenditure programme depends much more on delivery at the grassroots level without wastage, than just on the size of the financial provision. If their implementation can be improved, then with even a moderate rate of growth of the GDP and the same fiscal deficit to GDP ratio, there can be enough provision for basic social services. Public expenditure on social development then would promote sustainability of reform programmes generating expectations of policy stability. That will attract more investment and thereby raise the growth of GDP and generate enough resources to meet the requirement of such social expenditure.

O O O

# 13. CHILD LABOUR IN INDIA

Child labour is often the upshot of poverty, unemployment and illiteracy, when in fact it is the perpetrator of these maladies, says Anandita Chatopadhyay. She counsels that unless the menace of child labour is eradicated the country's progress in the present millenium is bound to be poor.

Human Rights Day comes and goes but this time it was also observed as the 60th anniversary of the Universal Declaration of Human Rights. On this occasion, seminars were held, and pledges taken to eradicate the menace of child labour. But the children of India who languish in slavery in dimly lit, cramped spaces in factories, houses, toiling 16 hours a day, getting little pay and more abuse—life continues as usual.

Slavery was one of the first human rights issue to arouse widespread concern both at national and international levels. Although our civilisation has entered the 21st century, child labour continues as the worst form of slavery in society.

According to the latest census reports, of the 200 million Indian children in the age of 5-14, about 11.3 million are labourers. But NGOs like the South Asian Coalition On Child

Servitude, embarrassingly reveal that there are, in fact, over 60 million child labourers in India working in carpet, bangle, matches, fireworks, brass ware, pottery and brick kiln units and as domestic helpers. The carpet industry has 300,000 children working for it.

A close look at the child labour situation in Delhi shows how grim is the life of children. An NGO estimates that out of about three million children in the age-group of 6-14 years, a million are child labourers, of which 200,000 work as domestic helpers and almost an equal number are bonded labourers. The SACCS alone rescued 45,000 child bonded labourers over a period of 15 years. When the menace thrives to this extent under the nose of the country's lawmakers, the picture elsewhere is anybody's guess.

A labourer in an industrial set-up is one who sells his/her labour to an employer in lieu of wakes under certain work-related conditions such as legal safeguards, work safety, bargaining power, and right to special amenities. But children have no identity as workers. They have just to obey the master and remain at his mercy. There are no minimum wages or working hours for them. Vulnerable to physical and mental exploitation, the children are abused, beaten and sexually exploited and more often than not such abuses go unnoticed.

Despite many laws in India safeguarding the rights of the child, and the UN Declaration of Human Rights, and Convention on the Rights of the Child, aimed at ensuring healthy growth and holistic development of children, child labour in our country has menacing proportions. The main hurdle in the abolition of child labour lies in the laws themselves which are full of loopholes and are anomalous.

In 1986, a law was enacted to prohibit child labour. Certain industries were classified as hazardous. Employment of children, often under the pretext of family work, was banned. This meant that no one should employ children in these hazardous industries not even by declaring them to be relations, sons, daughters, etc. But according to Kailash Satyarthi, Secretary of the SACCS, the factory owners insisted during the raids that child workers were his kith and kin who were learning about the family business. While it is regarded as a lie, the children themselves endorse the statement of the employer.

Often, employers in their effort to circumvent the Indian factory laws, scatter their units in villages, instead of having them under one roof and enslave thousands of child labour under the garb of family trade. One important factor why the employment of child labour continues is that political leadership is generally busy with other matters and do not bother about children. Unless there is a strong political will, the matter is likely to drag on. Many of the state governments have passed some legislation on the style of the Central legislation called Bonded Labour Abolition Act, 1976 and Child Labour (Prohibition and Regulation Act) 1986. Mr. Satyarthi points that there has not been a single case that may have been brought under this subject. "It is not a case of absolute absence of political will that not a single child employer has been brought to book till date though legal instruments mentioned above are quite profound."

It is generally believed that poverty, unemployment, illiteracy and the population explosion are the major reasons allowing child labour to thrive. Our political leaders believe that so long as poverty exists child labour cannot be removed. But the truth is that child servitude is the root cause of the other maladies.

Poverty can never be removed unless child labour is strictly abolished. An Asia Labour Monitor report says "Children in India contribute more than one-fifth to the total GNP of the country". But the 60 million child labour earns less than 10 rupees a day. Thus the total amount is not even one-fifth of what they contribute. If the child labour were not there, the employers will have to pay more than five times they pay to children. But the adults now lose bargaining power as employers have the option of hiring cheap child labour.

○ ○ ○

# 14. Creating Better Films For Home And Export

The pursuit of art is so lonely that only a searing passion of its own vision can sustain it. To venture into unchartered territories of the human condition requires a passion and a sort of madness that is sometimes at the abyss of self-destruction. However, most makers of art films in India seem to think otherwise; after the initial struggle these cineasts want their middle-class existence to be fully secure, says Suresh Jindal.

The state being run by their kind favoured this indulgence. The National Film Development Corporation in its earlier designations as the Film Finance Corporation was intended to give young film makers their first chance to make a film without being polluted by the crassness and vulgarity of mainstream cinema.

Suresh Jindal has rightly said that the real trouble started when the FFC folded up and the all powerful NFDC came into being. Thereafter, bureaucratic roles became dominant. In this process, a massive fraud was played on the public with the connivance of the politicians, new wave film makers, intellectuals and sections of the media. A small group of the people monopolised the scarce resources available, despite the fact that their productions were bankrupting the NFDC. For most of thése films despite the claims to the contrary, never recouped their investments. The only recoveries they made later on were from the government bodies like Doordarshan and the ministry of external affairs.

How many of their films found buyers abroad? We have been brainwashed and deluded into believing that tokenism of the Third World representation at international festivals of this cinema implied an appreciation for it. The Chinese cinema made its international debut much later than ours; its success at both the critical as well as a box-office levels, showed us our own poverty and delusions of grandeur. Those who are regular festival viewers will see the complete indifference it generated among foreign critics.

It is significant that all the purported profits of the NFDC have three sources: (i) the film Gandhi; (ii) the canalising commission that all the mainstream cinema was forced to pay on import of raw stock and export of finished film; and (iii) the monopoly over the import of foreign films along with the Motion Pictures Export Corporation of America. With the commercialisation of Doordarshan, they got the monopoly over telecasting mainstream film-based programmes.

It is an obvious fact that except for a handful of people—-invitees to special screenings, and film societies—nobody has either seen these films, nor are there any chances of their being seen. The impression given in India was that "the 'natives' were not yet involved in the finer sensibilities of international cinema to appreciate these prophetic artists of the future. Hence their works were not expected to set the Ganga and the lacrica on fire." The time has come to ask the question: Have they set the Seine, the Thames, the Potomac or the Danube on fire?

The Volga certainly was put by the non-maligned commercial cinema of Raj Kapoor, Guru Dutt, Mehboob Khan, Amitabh Bachhan and so on. Whether through ignorance or through connivance, through indulgence or conspiracy, a fraud was perpetuated on the public by the selective promotion of some film makers as 'internationally famous' and 'internationally acclaimed'. Nobody cared to ask the 'fundamental 'question of how many awards were won by these producers.

Mainstream cinema gives its surplus to encourage new technology, form and content. Cinema cannot be run from a bureaucratic office by decrees and licensing shops. Cinema is not like other muses—writing, poetry and painting, etc. that can be individually created. Cinema requires the talents and energies of many skills. Cinema is very expensive and must have an audience which can pay for its making. This can only happen with an effective distribution and exhibition network. That requires the talents and energies of another set of people. Such people exist in the mainstream. To condemn them, humiliate them, and act morally superior to them is like committing suicide.

The mainstream cinema, starting with Bhuvan Shome, has always given space-foot for this cinema at the box-office. The success of "Fire", "Bombay Boys", and "Hyderabad Blues", and "Black" shows that there is an audience for it too. Further, since all these films are made without government money, it is clear that there are producers and financiers in the private sector who are keen to support an alternative cinema. The construction of the-state-of-art theatre complexes in Mumbai and Delhi show that there is private initiative to modernise exhibition infrastructure. The government, except for formulating cinema-friendly policy has no business to be in show business.

The sound bytes and glory given to these filmmakers should have been used to seek a vision beyond a narrow self-interest of squandering public funds, foreign travel and unmerited wastage of media space. They should have joined their colleagues in mainstream cinema to change the shortsighted colonial policies of the state. Their very survival depends on critical changes in government policies like exemption from entertainment tax, declaring cinema as an industry, incentives for theatre construction and abolition of the films division tax which was imposed by the British government during World War II to subsidise their propaganda films. They should have rebelled against the government that penalised cinema exports by putting a canalised tax on It.

O O O

## 15. The State Of Tourism In India Today

According to Vijay Thakur, a reputed journalist, India has everything that can attract a tourist—Taj Mahal, many other buildings (historical and industrial), Central Secretariat, Atomic Energy Centres, and Reactors, etc. yet the tourism industry in the country is facing a downward trend as compared to other countries. As a result, India's position in world tourism has been sliding down over the years. Some much more smaller countries are thriving on tourism business doing twice or thrice the Indian quantum of business.

Tourism is the world's third largest industry. Not only it is the source of foreign revenue, but also an important base of economic development. The tourism situation in India has been aggravated by steep currency devaluation in some East Asian countries. The spending of holidays by tourists in those countries has become considerably cheaper compared in India. To some extent cheaper living in the Asian countries is responsible for diversion of tourists from India.

Smaller destinations like Singapore, Malaysia, Hongkong are better placed on the tourist map of the world.

India earns at present only $3 billion from 2.1 million tourists. This is only 0.4 per cent of world's total. The estimated flow of world tourists is over 700 million tourists providing $500 billion revenue. Why does India not enjoy its true share of global tourism? Why don't more visitors flock to India—home to an ancient civilisation with great historical relevance and magnificient people wedded to non-violence taught to them by Mahatma Gandhi, the great hero of India's independence.

It is estimated that in India, tourism has given direct employment to 9.1 million people and indirect employment to about 12.4 million people. The world over a little more than 11 per cent of the world's working population are engaged in tourism related business, according to the World Tourism Organisation.

By the year 2012, tourism will add one new job every second, which means creating in excess of 70 million new direct and indirect opportunities. In short, one in eight people round the world will be working in tourism-related jobs by the year 2012. Another research by the World Travel and Tourism Council shows that the tourism industry is a major contributor to the world's economic growth. It contributes 10.9 per cent of the global gross domestic product and this is further expected to increase to 11.4 per cent in the next five years.

The tourism industry generates, directly and indirectly, an estimated $750 million in exports' world-\vide. This is estimated to grow to $1.4 trillion by the year 2012 (the research was conducted before the Asian crisis, but tourism experts feel no change or little change would take place in the figures). If these figures are taken into consideration, India has not explored even 10 per cent of its tourism potential. If a small country like France can receive 66.8 million tourists almost 27 times more than that of India, there is no reason that India cannot increase the number of tourists it receives 10 times that is from 2.3 million to 23 million, increasing the workforce employed in the tourism industry accordingly.

According to the Ministry of Tourism, the capital and labour ratio is the highest in tourism, for every Rs. 10 lakh of fresh investment creation of jobs is 44.6 in agriculture, 12.6 in manufacturing, 47.5 in tourism and 89 in the tourism sub-sector of hotels and restaurants.

There is a long list of reasons that hamper tourism development in a country:

(i)   non-development of tourism related infrastructure,
(ii)  complexity of taxes,
(iii) shortage of hotel rooms, and
(iv) political instability and lack of will power to improve the system.

In 1980, China ranked 34th while India ranked 19th on world tourism list. But today China has climbed to the ninth rank with judicious investments while India has come down to the 34th position. Development of infrastructure for tourism remains a dream for the country. For instance, smaller destinations like Thailand and Singapore spent in excess of $50 million per year in tourism promotion, which India, which has much more to offer and gain, has planned a budget of only $27 million for the fiscal year 1998-99.

From the consumer point of view, complex tax structures in the hospitality business is another hurdle. As per a rough estimate, taxes in India add to an average of 27 per cent to each dollar spent, with the figure going up to a steep 35 per cent in states like West Bengal. But in other major tourist destinations this percentage is as low as four to eight per cent.

This means a tourist payer pays at least six times higher tax in India as compared to other major tourist destinations in the world. Here a customer has to pay an expenditure tax of 10 per cent on the total amount spent in hotels that offer a room tariff of over $40. In addition to this, there is a service tax, and an excise rate ranging from 3 per cent to 18 per cent (depending on revenue generation). Luxury tax could be as high as 20 per cent.

Sales tax is levied on food and beverage tax ranging from 17 per cent to 20 per cent for soft drinks, and 22 per cent for domestic or imported liquor. The import duty on alcoholic beverage is around 102 per cent on wines and a whopping 262 per cent on spirits imported by hotels and restaurants.

Another big problem for hospital business is the shortage of hotel rooms. The government has announced a target of 10 million tourists for the year 2008 but it hardly took the necessary follow-up actions. To receive such large number of tourists, the tourism industry will require about 95,000 rooms of approved category. Compared to this the country has only 95,000 rooms available just half of the required number. For the additional 1,30,000 rooms, an investment of about Rs. 40,000 crore will be required. Even if this project is spread to five years, about Rs. 10,000 crore investment is required every year.

There is an acute shortage of rooms in the metropolitan cities. According to a report, there would be a growth in demand for hotel rooms in the five metros in the short term, while the supply will grow at a rate of 8.8 per cent. In other related areas, the supply figures are projected at six per cent and nine percent respectively.

With just a pathetic political field, the target of five millions seems an unrealistic figure by the year 2000. Bit if the government makes it in the next five years, it would be a good achievement.

O  O  O

# 16. INDIANS ROUND THE WORLD

In the modern era, distinguished from the ancient civilisational era, the settlement of Indians in foreign countries began 150 years ago when the British recruited them as indentured labour to work on their farmlands and sugarcane plantations in their colonies. In course of time the phenomenon produced "little Indias" in places like Mauritius, Fiji, Guyana, South Africa, Singapore, Uganda, Kuwait, and United Arab Emirates (in West Asia), Kenya, Trinidad, United States, United Kingdom, and Australia.

According to reliable sources, today about 12 to 13 million Indians are scattered in 140 countries of the world.

This is a phenomena, which is not peculiar to India. There are about 11 million Jews, which is about the twice the population of present day Israel, living outside Israel. The number of Chinese living outside China is about 22 million. And 320 million blacks (people of African origin) are living outside Africa.

The British forced migration of Indians as indentured labour to Mauritius, Fiji, West Indies and some of the other colonies from 1830 onwards when slavery was abolished. The Gujarati businessmen have been migrating to South and North Africa since early 19th century as bankers to the slave traders in Africa. After World War II, a large number of Indians have been migrating to the United Kingdom, the United States and Canada. In these countries, there is a considerable presence of Indians today.

According to Prof. Bhiku Parekh, today the presence of Indians is quite significant in 28 countries. No wonder that in

South Africa, Dr. Nelson Mandela's Cabinet has as many as seven ministers of Indian origin. Now the word NRI (Non-Resident Indians) has become very fashionable. There is a certain pride and glamour attached to this word these days and the Government of India is going the whole hog to woo them to invest in India. Although the Indians have been living in many parts of the world for the last 150 years or so, it is only now that they are being recognised and wooed. Why not earlier?

The term NRI was started in 1986-87. Prior to that, none of the Indian governments had evinced any interest in them. The Indian National Congress that spearheaded the movement for freedom did evince enough interest in seeking the help of the overseas Indians in their freedom propagation.

Despite living abroad for 150 years the overseas Indians have not forgotten their country and its religious and cultural traditions. They have constructed some of the most beautiful temples in Europe, Canada, America and Africa. Temples are the centres of their cultural life. Parekh says that Tulsidas's Ramayana, Murari Bapu's katha on Ramayana and Ramdeva's yoga and good health programs are very popular in the USA and UK.

Majority of the overseas Indians are apprehensive of the "lurking ravanas" in their areas (the local goons). So they try to impose restrictions of food and dress on their girls to protect them from being corrupted from the influence of western life style and 'vulgarity' that is shown on television. They have great fears of losing their children under bad influence. The West Indies born overseas' Indian V.S. Naipaul, in his well known book "The Area of Darkness" says that the Indian culture is greater than all the cultures of the rest of the world put together," that is, the degree of attachment the overseas Indians have for India.

○ ○ ○

## 17. The Safety Aspects Of Atomic Power Plants In India

For years it had been known that Tarapur and Rajasthan atomic power plants are not fully safe. In May 1994, following the collapse of the 300-ton concrete dome in Kaiga Atomic Power Project, a complete shutdown of N-power plants in the country for a thorough check up was ordered by Dr. A. Gopalakrishnan, the then Chairman of ABRB. He pressed the bosses of the Department of Atomic Energy (AEA) to attend to safety problems.

The Rajasthan Atomic Power Station (RAPS) in Rawatbhata has a dismal track record. In 25 years it was shut down for more than 250 times due to some fault or the other. Coupled with this are reports that daily wage workers at the plant fall sick occasionally. At Trombay and Tarapur there are tons of radioactive fluids stored in dilapidated tanks and in many cases the welding of the old pipes and containers are in need of urgent replacement. The Bhabha Atomic Research Centre (BARC) in Mumbai has on record more than 25 serious cases of safety problems.

However, in March 1995, when the radioactive spill from the waste immobilisation plant (WIP) at Tarapur leaked into the drain water for a period of one and a half months, the Tarapur Atomic Power Station (TAPS) maintained there was no radioactive release or harmful discharge. Villagers living near the Tarapur nuclear facility panicked that they might have been drinking water contaminated by the radioactive leak for more than a month. While the villagers were not aware of the precise ramifications of consuming contaminated water, even if they had been aware, they had little choice in the matter and continued using it.

Tarapur is 11 km from Boisar station in Palghar Taluka of Thane District, Maharashtra. Several villages are within five km radius, including Akkerpatti (1 km), Ghivali (1.8 km), Pokharan (1 km), Unabat (2.5 km), Uchali (3 km) and Dandi

(4 km). The nuclear plant at Tarapur was constructed as a turnkey project by General Electric Corporation, USA, in four years. It received a special aid dispensation from the United States Agency for International Development, a part of American strategy for seeking the world-wide market for nuclear vendors.

In Tarapur, Akkerpatti and Pokharan are twin villages which share the same sarpanch, Thaksen Patil, a resident of Pokharan who worked for TAPS for seven years as a storekeeper. The two villages have no roads, no primary health centre, and no tap water. The wells were dug 100 years back. Most of the villagers have thatched roofs. A solitary bus comes at 7.45 AM and leaves 10 minutes later. For rest of the day villagers have to walk 2 km to Unabat. The oldest school is Pokharan's primary school which is 112 years old and all the villagers did their schooling there.

Enquiries about the water leakage seeping into the ponds and wells from where they draw drinking water are met with silence by the villagers. After much persuasion Namdeo Achrekar revealed "Bhabha Atomic Research Centre (BARC) officials try to sweep all the evidence under the carpet. They pressurise the villagers not to disclose anything to the stranger on the plea that the entire project falls under Official Secrets Act, 1923." Gopal, another youth quoted from a Marathi magazine published by an anti-nuclear group: "The radioactive spill from the ramshackle tanks seeping into the pond and wells is too slow to show any immediate effect on the villagers residing uneasily near' TAPS. But, in future, radiation could result in severe effects. It might damage chromosomes that in women could lead to abnormal child birth or disabled children." However, the genetic damage does not appear to be seen in first generation but could surface in the future unborn generation. The most frightening aspect of radiation is that its effects though invisible are not reversible. Tarapur has a history of protests—-both mild and violent against such incidents. As early as in 1974, a National Workshop on Sitting and Safety of Nuclear Plants spoke of major accidents at

Tarapur which had two engineers dying instantaneously, while the Chief Engineer died a slow and agonising death over the next three years. Then in 1979, major lack of radioactive water exposed 300 workers to much more than the permissible levels of radiation, which was one milligram per hour per person.

Quite unaware of accidents in TAPS and exposure to radiation hazards, the village elders of Akkerpatti, Ghivali and Pokharan are above any fear. When there are leakages and accidents, officials give out details of safety devices, how the plant has a large number of shells, how the inner core contains concrete and shell and 350-ft chimney that call: do no damage to the villagers as the breeze will take away the radiation.

Every alternate year, men, women and children are picked up for random checking at BARC's clinic of radiation. After the checking they are told they are fine. BARC takes the samples of vegetables, fish, soil and water, but the results of such checking is not announced. "Whenever, there are nuclear leakages, the water of the well heats up like a geyser. But as the water is precious and scarce, caution is thrown to the winds and bathing, drinking and washing takes place as usual."

On being told of the Chernobyl nuclear disaster in 1986, radiation hazards and nuclear effluent leakage, Ashraf Abdul Sheikh of Pokharan-Dandi Machimar Samiti asked, "If there is hazard then why do Nuclear Power Corporation and TAPS officials work and stay in their colony along with their families?" When people ask for roads, the officials say there will be accidents. In this way they justify the nuclear leakage.

The dangers posed by the nuclear power reactors are magnified by the fact that they are also working in nuclear rich USA and Russia. VVER Russian reactors purchased by the Indian government for nuclear power generation are "highly unsafe". However, Russian nuclear industry was facing financial crisis and wanted to sell the VVER reactors to China, Iran and India. Russian Academician Valeri Lvanovich Suboten in his study of the VVER evaluated them as faulty in their safety aspects.

In the wake of the Chernobyl disaster, nine nations signed an agreement to phase out the use of nuclear power by the end of the century, and agreed not to construct any new reactors henceforth. India is among the few major exceptions. With just a few reactors hooked to the national grid, India derives a mere 3 per cent of its electricity. But an ambitious plan to generate 10,000 MW of nuclear electricity is now under implementation. Construction of eight different sites—Kaiga, Rawatbhata, Tarapur and Kudalkunam—are under way.

As for safety, Dr. Raja Ramanna, former Chairman of the Atomic Energy Commission said, "One of the factors to be noticed in the energy establishments is that they are located in green belt areas. Lots of trees are planted and they provide the best cover against radiation. Another practice followed is setting up of exclusion zones. A one-mile radius around the plant is maintained and it is fenced to spill off accidents. We also see that housing sites and other industrial areas do not come up near these plants for a distance of 5 km. We have followed this pattern in Tarapur, Kalpakkarn, Kota, Narora and Kaiga."

Tarapur units are within a range of 100 km off Mumbai. This is alarming since TAPS has continuously displayed serious safety problems. An international nuclear authority has described it as one of "the dirtiest nuclear plants in the world." An accident at Tarapur, in certain types of weather conditions, could make Mumbai city uninhabitable, destroying in the process, the commercial capital of the country which generates about one third of the country's GDP. India's most vital ports, pharmaceutical industries and major industries would have to be shifted off.

Accidents fall into two categories: Power excursion accidents, and coolant accidents. Both types of accidents could cause breach of the reactor vessel and containment structure in which the reactor is housed resulting in release of radioactivity into the atmosphere.

According to a senior official of US Nuclear Regulatory Committee, the most worrisome is the American containment design "GI Mark I" (which we may assume to be the design adopted for Tarapur and other Nuclear Plants). The New Yorker quotes a Nuclear Regulatory Agency (NRCA) study that showed "something like a 90 per cent probability of that containment failing during serious accidents."

What would happen if a similar holocaust like Chernobyl happens in Tarapur? asks Gopal Dongerwar. "Chernobyl disaster was preceded by a series of minor accidents and safety lapses which were not heeded as warning of the catastrophe that was lurking not far away." He added, "over 20,000 inhabitants of the villages near TAPS want to leave." The original demand of the villagers was for relocation but this demand for an alternative piece of land was rejected because as per government rules only those displaced by irrigation projects are entitled for land compensation.

In the absence of any concrete action, Chernobyl and Bhopal seem to be the fate of those living near the Tarapur atomic site.

O O O

# 18. Making The Green Revolution Greener In India

India is today experiencing the new age in cultivation. A growing section of Indian farmers are taking advantage of new technologies and are adopting various methods not just to maximise the yield per hectare but also improving the caloric and nutritional content of the crop. With the introduction of new 'dwarfing genes' in wheat cultivation, the yield has multiplied on an average three-fold. The pests and insects are no longer a problem with Indian farmers who are learning the benefit of biotechnology. Agro-scientists in numerous agro-based institutions in the country are developing new seed varieties which not just improve farm production but also add to the nutritional values of the products.

Agricultural production and marketing in India comprises cash crops and immediate enrichment of the farmer. New techniques like in-vitro fertilization, plant quarantine and cyro-banks are being adopted by the farmers so as to reap the best results from their land.

Pusa Institute of Agriculture, New Delhi, and numerous other institutes recognised for their professional specialisation, are providing ready results of their research. The increase in population in India is at present more than offset by the increase in agricultural production in every field. Thanks to modem techniques developed by the research institutions, farming in India is acquiring an altogether new status. Horticulture and orchid development have become important branches of agriculture as the financial recovery from fruits like grapes, dates and palms, besides mangoes, apples, oranges, pear, raspberry, strawberry, peaches, pineapple, banana and many other varieties. Till some decades ago, the production of many fruits was minimal, but with the help of new techniques of orchid development the fruits are grown in bulk quantities. Most of the dry fruits which were imported in bulk are now sown and reaped in the country—thanks to the new seed varieties, conditions have been created for their widespread yield. Today, they are being cultivated so widely that they not only meet their demand in the country but also are exported on a good scale.

Previously, farmers were reluctant to grow these fruits in India mainly because of the attack by numerous insects. Moreover, their seeds were difficult to be preserved for the next harvest as they would be destroyed by pests. Now the scientists have developed the technique of plant quarantine which protects all fruits from pests and even ants. The quarantine process is based on successive chemical reactions over a period of time which makes the plants totally immune to insects. Scientifically, plant quarantine means prevention pests or pathogens from spreading or multiplying further in case they have already found entry in a field.

Dr. J.L. Kalihaloo of the National Bureau of Plant Genetic Resources (NBPGR) says: "Though plant quarantine may not guarantee permanent protection against pests, the process helps check or delay the introduction of these unwanted organisms in plants. Thus it goes a long way in protecting crops from the ravages of exotic pests and diseases and also from those which are not present in that area but could come in some future time.

It is desirable for the farmers to take the help of experts from any agricultural university which is close to them or attend one of the many workshops being held by these universities from time to time and then apply the controls themselves. Like quarantine, the concept of Cyrobank too is generally gaining popularity among Indian farmers. A Cyrobank preserves seeds in liquid nitrogen under 35 to 40 relative humidity and at four degrees centigrade. Traditionally, farmers had been using crude techniques to preserve seeds. But there are inherent problems with such techniques. One, due to the moisture content in the atmosphere, the yield potential of the seed drops significantly year after year till it finally drops to zero. Secondly, seed are as susceptible to insect attacks as plants and are difficult to preserve. But now farmers can set up their own cyrobanks and preserve seeds in nitrogen solution which not only maximises harvest but also increases the nutritional value of the yield. This technique is widely used in cereal crops like rice, bajra, wheat, gram and pulses.

According to experts at NBPGR, Cyrobanks are becoming very popular in crop-rich states like Punjab, Uttar Pradesh, Haryana, Kerala and Andhra Pradesh. In fact a number of agriculturists are setting up Cyrobanks at home to reduce cost and maximize yield. Another breakthrough which is poised to revolutionise agriculture is the in-vitro conservation and fertilization technique, developed indigenously at NBPGR after several years of painstaking research. The technique helps change the colour, shape, taste, size and caloric value of a particular crop, fruit, or vegetable.

In fact, some of the priority crops in which in-vitro conservation and fertilization has been undertaken are: banana, sweet potato, garlic, ginger, turmeric, pepper and a number of medicinal, aromatic and endangered plants. It is thus possible to grow a banana afft long which could suffice as a meal in terms of its caloric value.

However, despite the advance in techniques and enthusiasm among agro-scientists about these new developments, the results have not started to show at the speed at which they were envisaged. That is because a number of farmers are still resistant to change. Even though students and experts from various agricultural universities often camp in villages, to educate farmers on the economic benefits of introducing these new techniques, it is taking some time before the message is driven home to the farmer.

Says NBPGR's Dr. Karihaloo, "Whenever you introduce something new, specially in the agricultural sector, resistance is bound to arise. But once the farmer is convinced, then there is no looking back."

At the national level, the Delhi-based Pusa Institute has set up a Plant Genetic Resource Centre which has one of the largest collection of crop gene samples in the world. These samples are dried and stored for long periods (10-15 years or more) under strictly controlled environment (around minus 20 degrees centigrade). This reduces the risk of gene changes through frequent regeneration and also prevents the erosion of stored germplasm. "The germplasm diversity available in nature is depleting at such an alarming rate that it has become a global concern to save it for posterity." Conservation strategies seed genebanks and botanical herbal gardens are being set up at the village level which makes the process of conservation fast and simple. These efforts will go a long way in advancing agro-production in India, says Dr. Karihaloo. Agricultural scientists now feel that the actual benefits of the green revolution are just starting to pour in and farmers instead of depending only on nature, can now depend on science for better yields.

O O O

# 19. Government Responsibility For Protecting India's Forests

Forests are a valuable asset of any nation. Some of the countries are reported to have cut out their forests for immediate benefit. They might have needed the wood for making furniture or otherwise used it for some national or individual purpose.

World Commission on Forests and Sustainable Development (WCFSD) has revealed some startling facts about forests in the world. According to the World Commission on Forests, forests have virtually disappeared in 25 countries of the world, 18 countries have lost more than 95 per cent, and another 11 countries have lost about 90 per cent. In the last two decades of the 20th century, the world has been losing 10-15 million hectares of forest annually and causing permanent deforestation.

This warning has significance for India as its record in forest conservation is not very encouraging. According to the "State of the Forest" report for 1997, the total forest cover in India was 633,397 sq km in 1997, compared to 638.879 sq km in 1995. This shows a reduction of the forest cover by 5482 sq km. This much reduction of the forest cover in just two years is a matter of concern as forests perform many functions— ecological, subsistence, and developmental. They help maintain soil and water conditions, contribute to the maintenance of biological and genetic diversity, provide fuel, fodder and other materials to local communities, supply raw materials for industry and provide non-wood forest produce such as tendu leaves, and seeds, and pine resin for local and national economy. Forests also provide livelihood to great majority of tribal people.

The increasing population of India, coupled with lack of integrated planning for forest management is causing a great pressure on forests. Increasing destruction and degradation of forests and trees, specially in the Himalayas and other hilly areas, contribute to erosion of topsoil. Uneven rainfall, and occasional floods are also the result of depleting forests. The biotic pressure further causes degradation of forests.

Since forests are a renewable resource, the Government of India has formulated certain policies to seek the preservation of forests. The Forests. Conservation Act, 1980, banned indiscriminate deforestation of certain areas and the diversion of forest-land for industry or agriculture. Under the provisions of the 1980 Act, prior approval of the Central government is required for diversion of forest land for non-forest purposes. Since the enactment, the rate of diversion of forest land has come down to around 25,000 hectares per annum from 1.43 lakh hectare per annum before 1980. As the permission for diversion of land is difficult to obtain, the rare exceptions carry stipulations for compensatory afforestation and other conditions laid down in the act.

The National Forest Policy of 1988 aims at maintenance of environmental stability through preservation and restoration of ecological balance; conservation of natural heritage; check on soil erosion and denudation of catchment areas of rivers, lakes, and reservoirs; check on extension of sand dunes in desert areas of Rajasthan, and along coastal tracts; finding steps to meet the requirements of fuel wood, fodder, minor forest produce, and timber for rural and tribal populations; increasing productivity of forests to fulfil natural needs, encouraging efficient utilization of forest produce; optimum substitution of fodder and fuel wood; and devising steps to promote peoples' participation in forest preservation.

During the 8th Five-Year Plan, a new programme was initiated which recognised the value of peoples' participation in conservation efforts. Named Association of Scheduled Tribes and Rural Poor in Regeneration of Degraded Forests, the objective of the programme was to improve forests based on bio-mass resource in degraded forests and manage it on sustained basis for domestic needs of the identified communities. By involving scheduled tribes and other rural poor in protection and development of degraded forests, the programme proposed to provide gainful employment and a sustainable base to them.

To operate the NFP-1988, the Government decided to formulate a National Forestry Action Programme (NFAP) and signed a project with UNDP and FAG in 1993. The objectives of the programme were the preparation of the NFAP and long-term, medium term, and short term perspective plans as well as identification and quantification of investment and technical assistance in line with the NFP. Implementation of the NFAP will contribute to sustainable development and the use of forest resources on the one hand and to maintain the ecological balance of the country on the other.

Another feature of the government effort is the establishment of the National Afforestation and Eco Development Board (NAEB) which is responsible for afforestation, tree planting, ecological restoration and eco-development activities all over the country, with special attention to degraded forest areas and lands adjoining forest areas, national parks, sanctuaries and other protected areas, viz. the Western Himalayas, Aravalis, and Western Ghats.

The NAEB implements afforestation schemes under the 20-point programme. It implements the Integrated Aforestation and Eco Development projects scheme under which efforts are on to augment availability of bio-mass, fuel wood and fodder, extend and disseminate proven afforestation and management technologies in the cause of equity and environment conservation with the participation of local communities and generate employment.

A centrally-sponsored scheme "Introduction of Modern Forest Fire Control Methods in India", was launched in 1992-93 to control forest fires with a view to protecting and conserving both natural and man-made forests and to improve productivity of forests by reducing the incidence and extent of forest fires.

Despite efforts of the government and non-government organisations, forests continue to be depleted at an alarming rate. High growth of population and the increasing pressure on limited land is a major reason for this. Lack of vacant landscapes for construction work that is accelerated due to various developmental activities also makes forests an easy target.

There is a lack of awareness among the masses about the urgency of protecting the forests. The efforts of the NGOs too are often at cross purposes contribution to no special conservation. The government should take up urgently to ponder the recommendations of the WSFSD and try to make them a part of its programmes.

The World Commission has already highlighted the need for a systematic approach to adequately support the forest planners and managers. This would require existing academic research, monitoring and policy institutions to come together to establish such a network with financial support from corporations, foundations and governments.

Improved information, analysis, research understanding and training are required to imbue forest policies and practices and increased networking to make that possible in a short time and to effect widespread application. Awareness and education should be imparted to masses in a way that they appreciate the multi-functions of forests and public policies, which governments formulate to ensure the continuation of these functions. A wide range of NGOs and other organisations note that the commission has been playing an increasingly proactive role in promoting sustainable management of forests. The commission feels that the need for attention to the crisis gripping the forests is so urgent that such new and potentially effective mechanisms not limited to governments are necessary to accelerate progress towards solutions.

It is the responsibility of the government to perceive, articulate, defend and secure the public interest. This can be achieved by creating mechanisms by the government for consultations, in which all private interests, the poor and politically weak are represented and through which the public interest also becomes a vested interest.

In a nutshell, the government can play the pivotal role in containing the fast depleting natural resources of forests, which, if ignored, could spell disaster for all of us.

O O O

## 20. VSAT Technology In India

The tremendous strides made by satellite technology during the last few decades has helped expand the frontiers of global communication at a spectacular speed. The launch of the Soviet Sputnik about four decades back which heralded man's leap into space also marked the emergence of innovative satellites capable of changing the style of life on earth.

However, the era of satellite communication was first introduced by the USA who launched the "Early Bird" satellite in early sixties by providing telephone link between USA and Western Europe. Today, the satellite communication is capable of two-way data conversation, beaming TV programmes and broadcasting distress signals for launching search and rescue operations.

As for India, it was as early as 1975 that India carried out an ambitious programme called "SITE" (Satellite Instructional Television Experiment) as part of which developmental programmes were flashed directly to thousands of TV receivers spread across selected villages of six Indian states using the American ATS-6 satellite. A science fiction writer had earlier forecast that "three satellites placed above the earth at a height of 23,000 miles could provide round the clock uninterrrupted communications."

Satellite communications are reliable and inexpensive. These are immune to breakdown in ground-based network and environment hostilities. Further, these do not depend on the distance involved. In the earlier days, ground stations measuring up to 30 feet were required to facilitate two-way communication, but with improvements in satellite technology in course of time together with development of solid state electronics, miniature terminals enabled them to arrive at satellite communications by using rooftop antennas measuring between 1.8 meters to 3.5 meters. The increased power packed in satellites made possible communication using small terminals called VSAT which enabled the setting up of a communication network independent of the existing central communications infrastructure.

In a VSAT system, one does not fall back on repeaters or cables. For a string of powerful spacecraft high up in space is always available as a "celestial repeater". Hence the system is reliable, fast, inexpensive and free from interference from any extraneous source. Further, it does not need any highly qualified personnel to operate it. It is easy to install, operate and shift. Another advantage of VSAT is that it can be straight away connected to equipment like telephone, fax or computer. For the industrial units spread over a large area and situated far away from urban centres, VSAT provides a highly beneficial and productive mode of communication.

A variety of VSAT networks can be operated based on the type of satellites used. In India, VSAT operations are made possible by the extended C-Band facilities available in the second generation Insat Spacecraft. The frequency band is specifically used on the Insat series of satellites and is not pressed into service for other communications traffic. It is less prone to frequency interference and breakdowns. Time Division Multiple Access (TDMA) is the most popular mode of satellite access used in India's VSAT networks. In a TDMA network, the satellite resource is efficiently utilized by dividing a particular frequency into a time slot for transmission.

The Indian VSAT market is today being boosted by the networking requirements of fast moving consumer companies, corporate units and industrial units having multiple points of operations. Industrial units located in remote areas, stock exchanges, corporate houses with country-wide operations, banks and insurance companies are emerging as potential customers of VSAT. In the financial sector, the stock exchanges have taken the lead in adopting VSAT to extend the advantages of screen-based trading facility to the brokers' offices. Thus the introduction of VSAT has brought about a remarkable change in the Indian business environment. The availability of VSAT has helped the companies and corporate units to reduce their operational costs. In recent months, news and wire agencies have taken to VSAT systems to streamline their operations. All VSAT users have discovered that VSAT tariffs are distance insensitive and thus makes for lower operational costs as compared to the line networks.

Essentially, a VSAT ground unit is made up of an outdoor unit and an indoor unit. The outdoor unit comprises an antenna and a Radio Frequency Trans-Receiver (RFT). The RFT receives the down-link signals from the satellites besides transmitting the uplink signal to the satellite after performing the necessary frequency corrections. The indoor unit can be a telephone, fax or a computer which is invariably linked to the outdoor unit.

In India, Wipro BT, RPG satcom, ITI and HCL Communications are among its leading providers of VSAT services and technology. As it is, the market for VSAT service is still in its infancy. According to Simon Omu, Deputy Chief of Wipro BT, the VSAT market is set for a 100 per cent a year growth. Currently, West Europe and North America account for more than 3/4 that of the world-wide installed base.

O O O

# 21. Computers In India

## Software Exports

Despite the prevailing industrial recession and a stunted economic growth, India's resurgent software export industry is looking ahead for a booming growth. Against Rs. 17,200 crore netted in 2005-06 by way of export, the buoyant Indian software export in 2007-08 is poised to earn more than Rs. 11,000 crore.

Sources in National Association of Software and Services Companies (NASSCOM) say that the Indian Software drive remained, insulated from the economic turbulence around and pushed smoothly, its drive for exports. During the year 2007-08, our software exports are expected to increase by 18 per cent. Most of these exports were directed to the USA and Canada. Out of the total exports, Europe accounted for 26 per cent. In recent years, countries in the Asia-Pacific region are looking towards India for their software solutions.

European Community's euro-conversion project could bring to the NASSCOM about $50 million. Besides India, the euro-conversion projects have also been allotted to computer industry in the US, China, Japan and Australia.

The Software Technology Parks of India (STPI) has taken the initiative together with a few Indian IT outfits and the Indo-German Chamber of Commerce to ensure that Indian software and service companies have a fairly good share of the cake. They have created an Indian Special Interest Group and will shortly initiate an accreditation scheme to ensure standard solutions.

At present, exports from STPI account for 38 per cent of the country's exports. As it is, STPIs have been promoted as "complete environment complexes for 100 per cent export units by the department of electronics. Thus STPI serves as one of the largest of network exporting units in India. Meanwhile, a study by NASSCOM shows that there has been a perceptible shift in the last few years from on-site services to offshore services, the latter contributing to about 41 per cent of the export. Today, about 90 per cent of the STPI exports are through offshore development.

According to Raj Naram, Chairman of the NASSCOM for 1999, during the last decade of NASSCOM existence the Indian software industry has grown 30-fold in size to reach an annual turnover of $ 4 billion. He also revealed that NASSCOM has now prepared a growth profile that would make India a software superpower with a turnover of $100 billion by the year 2008. However, the Information Technology (IT) plan outlined on July 14, 1998 by the National Task Force on Information Technology on Software Development has set a target of $50 billion for export of software and related services by the year 2010.

In order to boost the availability of skilled manpower, Department of Electronics has recommended the setting up of national visual institute which will provide for distance education to enhance knowledge of working professionals in the software sector. This institute will seek support from premier engineering outfits and training companies for exposing software professionals in the latest in the industry.

But all said and done, the Indian software industry is miles away from attaining a really global status. For all intents and purposes, India's software exports constitute less than one per cent of the total international market. IT experts are of the view that India is 'still' a marginal player in the software market and its expertise is limited to the provision of on-site services and offshore software development. A study carried out by a team of experts from the Indian Institute of Technology points out that the present industry structure prohibits India from emerging as a major software developer/exporter in the near future.

Similarly, a study by the ICICI (Industrial Credit and Investment Corporation of India) Banking Corporation Limited lists many negative features afflicting the Indian software industry. "New entrants into the Indian IT industry are scared of bureaucratic norms which are stumbling blocks in such ventures."

A New Delhi-based software exporter says, handling IT related issues lack professionalism and vision. On the other hand, Mr. Shyam Kumar, a Bangalore-based software entrepreneur, says that India should start experimenting with new technologies, sites, programmes and plans to emerge as a global IT superpower

## Building Internet Communities in India

World-Tel, a UN sponsored body to spread the telecom revolution around the world, will expand operations in India, particularly southern India, where a network of Internet Community Centres was being set up to bring about an information revolution. "It will bring a revolution beyond any body's imagination," Mr. Sam Pitroda, Chairman World-Tel and a former advisor to former Prime Minister Rajiv Gandhi, says: "In India, we have chosen so far four southern states for building a network of Internet community centres, similar to trunk dialling booths."

"This is because, the four states of Kerala, Tamil Nadu, Karnataka and Andhra are fit for such a networkjng in a speedy manner. Such centres will be different from the America on-line Service where one needs a personal computer at home. Our centres will provide access to all the service and information for their day-to-day needs on open booths. It will bring a revolution beyond anybody's imagination," he went on to say. "All revenue records, licence procedures, payment of electric and telephone bills, school examination results, children's home work, newspapers and hundreds of other things could be made available on Internet in local languages," he continued. He further said, "However, this would happen only if state governments make their database available in the local languages."

Mr. Pitroda went on to say, "We (World-Tel) are ready to provide the structures. The prin ary challenge before India is to change the old mindset." He said the information race was on and it will not wait for any country or person. He said, "Information technology, along with biotechnology, is going to open the floodgates of new life, new values, new methods of working, new ways of thinking and new ways of running the economy." Mr. Pitroda said state controls had kept away non-resident Indians from investing in their native country, "It is difficult to do business in India. There are too many official procedures and people think they need the government support, permission, patronage etc. to do anything worthwhile in India. One has to do a lot of running around and after a while one gets tired of it. There is no clear-cut partnership between the business and the government," he added.

While comparing India with other countries, he said signals of progress from Africa were confusing while those from China were encouraging. But most of all "Latin American countries were very liberal and were making fast progress while making for lesser and lesser controls," he said. "India with its vast reservoir of talent could make a major difference in IT in the 21st century," added Mr. Pitroda.

Explaining the work of World-Tel, Pitroda said, it was the offspring of the UN International Telecom Union with 192 countries as its members and a governing council of 48 countries. "ITU is the oldest institution of the UN. Eight per cent of its members are from developing countries," he said.

"We decided Five years ago at the Telecom Advisory Council of ITU that we should do something for the developing countries. We collected a donation of $500,000 from 30 different companies and hired Mckinsey and Company to study and report on this aspect. The latter itself donated a million dollars. It was after this development that World-Tel was born," he said.

Mr. Pitroda was chosen from three other contenders for the chairmanship of World-Tel. The Council had heads of Telecom from Australia, the USA, and an expert from Kuwait. The World Tel has two projects in hand at present. First, a billion dollar project in Mexico with a World-Tel equity of $100 million and the second in Azerbaijan worth $ 100 million, with World-Tel equity of $ 50 million. He said the World-Tel was also working on projects in Kenya, Tanzania, Zimbabwe, Uganda, Peru, Pakistan, Bangladesh and China. He said, "Our job is to structure a project in one and half years time. We arrange finances, we sit on the board, and become catalysts."

**Better Memory Chips**

As microprocessor speeds continue to increase exponentially, chip manufacturers are scrambling to find a design that will stop memory bottlenecks within a system.

Cashing in on this need is Rambus, a $40 million Silicon Valley-based company in which an American Indian is spearheading the effort to design and market high speed memory interface technology.

Mr. Subodh Toprani, vice president and general manager of Microprocessor's Logic Products Division, says: "Processor speeds will reach speeds of 800 megahertz over the next few years while memory chips are still at 100 mHz." This disparity between a slow memory chip or a dynamic random access memory (DRAM) and a microprocessor could cloud the performance of next generation processors from industry leaders such as Intel, and Advance Micro Devices (AMD).

According to Mr. Toprani, Rambus has the technology to speed up processing by fostering better communication between memory chips and the logic devices that control them such as microprocessors, promising upto six giga bytes per second output soon-to-be-released DRAM design called "RDRAM". A factor likely to spur the adoption of Rambus' technology, Toprani said, is its endorsement by industry leaders such as Intel, NEC and Samsung. Manufacturers of DRAM chips such as NBC, Toshiba and Samsung are already paying Rambus royalties of some 1.5 per cent to adopt the idea.

"Rambus has a chip-to-chip interface, so we have set a standard. If ten companies are using Rambus then the 11th will want to use Rambus because otherwise the chips won't hook up with the other companies' devices," he said.

The new Rambus technology works by packing the three messages that travel between a memory chip and a logic chip on the computer's motherboard for transmission down a single electronic line substantially speeding up the interaction between the memory chip and the processor.

The three messages concerned are the address where the data impulse is to go, the data bits themselves and the instruction that says what should be done with that data. These three messages traditionally run on different paths at different speeds, to be recombined on the memory chip.

According to Toprani, Rambus 'big break' came in 1995 when Japan's Nintendo was looking to leapfrog the popular play station Yideo game made by rival Sony. A new memory was just the trick. Nintendo-64 player game uses Rambus designs with custom made logic chips from NEC to process graphic data at a speed close to that of a supercomputer ferrying the data between memory controller and chips at a speed of 500 million bytes per second. The Nintendo system proved our technology was viable. That set the stage for being seriously considered for PC main memory, Mr. Toprani said.

## DNA Computer Chips

Motorola inc. in the US will collaborate with Packard Instrument Company to· develop a DNA-based computer chip aimed at improving diagnosis of genetically transmitted illness and speeding public health response to epidemics. The two companies will pay 519 million for a five year licence to commercialise a research breakthrough by the Argonne National laboratory and the Eaglehardt Institute of Molecular Biology in Moscow. The agreement marks one of Motorola's first forays in the much hyped and volatile field of biotechnology. The deal was announced at a telephone conference call by officials of the two labs and their new corporate customers.

Fredrico Pena, Secretary of the Energy Department, which overseas Orgonne, gave the venture a dramatic introduction. "This morning we could very well be witnessing the birth of a new multi-billion industry that will allow American and Russian children to live in a substantially healthier world," Pena said.

University researchers who are expected to help identify new uses for the biochips, should begin to receive them in about two years. It will be five years or more before they come into widespread use as a diagnostic tool in doctors' offices," said Richard McKernan, President of Packard Instrument Co. But a University of Chicago scientist familiar with the Argonne-Eaglehardt research noted that the technology is still unproven. And an industry analyst wondered if two companies working with two research labs on opposite sides of the world could muster the focus needed to bring commercially successful biochips to market.

Motorola and Packard will try to capitalise on a discovery by Argonne and Eaglehardt researchers that allows scientists to arrange genetic material "in a gel on a computer chip. Suspending it in a gel gives it three dimensions. When unknown genetic material is introduced to the chip in the presence of fluorescent light, it produces distinctive pattern of light that serves as a kind of signature.

The three dimensionality of this microgel technology should increase the accuracy of identification of genetic material by a factor of at least 10, Packard officials said. Microgel biochips could be used to identify viruses and bacteria in epidemics and identify mutations that cause disease among humans, said McKernan.

Interest in chips is specially high because of the 8-year-old Human Genome Project, a federally funded effort to map, sequence, and decode all the 100,000 or so genes in the human genetic blueprint. The current state-of-the-art in biochips requires using time-consuming, expensive photolithography, making the area ripe for breakthrough. But the micro gel approach has worked only in prototype form, said Robert Hazelkom, a University of Chicago researcher who has worked with· Andrei Mirzabekov, the investor of the technique. "They have still to show that the thing works," said Hazelkom, the Funny L. Pritzker distinguished professor of molecular genetics and cell biology.

So far, the liquid polymer gel has diffused the light passing through it, limiting the effectiveness of identifications, Hazelkorn. In the immensely complex world of biotechnology, the Argonne--Eaglehardt advance has an appealing simplicity, according to McKeeman. But Eddie Hedaya, an analyst for Bio Vest Research Inc. of Hartsdale, New York said that while microgel chips are "very interesting new technology, it is a strongly entrepreneurial activity which needs considerable focus to succeed."

Motorola Vice President Rudyard Istvan said the company would set up a new bioinformatics business unit to make the chips, either at an existing facility at Arizona or Illinois. "We see this as a logical outgrowth of our core competencies," in semiconductors and precision manufacture, Istvan said.

Privately held Packard, a unit of Packaid Bio Science Co., headquartered in Meriden, Conn., will make microrobots to insert genetical material in gel and produce the laser optics for biochip analysis. Both devices will be manufactured at the company's facility in Downers Grove, Illinois.

## Doctor on the Internet

There are neither distress calls to helpline nor letters addressed to any of the numerous agony aunt columns. They are just two of the millions of messages pasted on the bulletin board of an Internet site. Today, Internet medium is providing relief to millions around the globe in the garb of medical help. What is St. John's wort? Can Cycloserine affect the vision of a person? What to do when cornered by a migraine? Just a click of the mouse can answer all these questions now.

Internet has opened new vistas for millions of those who seek a second opinion from a doctor in the other part of the world and the ones who are in dire need of emotional support, says Rodolfo Panteon, a volunteer in a Chile-based, non-profit organisation for AIDS patients, "I don't have any sort of medical or paramedical training but I like to help people. And that is why I go online to help people overcome that phase' in which they feel they haven't got anybody to turn to."

Special cases can be posted on the Internet and help can be asked for. There are a number of doctors and health experts who help online. Many specialists can be consulted who are otherwise inaccessible owing to distance.

The medical data and the sites catering to the needs of a layman are staggering. There is not only the user-friendly Yahoo and also specialised libraries and other government aided sites. Some of the reliable Web sites include those aided by the US government, the healthfinder (www.healthfinder.gov), which has information from federal agencies and non-profit organisations and the Centres for Disease Control and Prevention (www.cdc.gov) which has information like diverse topics like botulism. Hepatitis C, school violence, AIDS research update, family parenting, child care. Then there are special sites for cancer (CancerNet, www.nci.nih.gov), etc.

However, Indian sites for the specific needs of Indian people are yet to make a mark. One of the major ventures on Internet has been taken by the Mumbai-based Health Education Library for People (HELP), which started a site in 1997. Its site (www.healthlibrary.com) is India's first consumer health resource centre. It is the only site on the web which has searchable databases of Indian hospitals, doctors, medical equipment manufacturers, medical libraries and medical colleges. Another site that has a complete list of hospitals in Mumbai and hospitals in other metropolitan cities is www.mahesh.com says Dr Annuradha Malpani, Medical Director of HELP, "Indians are like everyone else—they all need information on their health and medical problems, and the Web is an excellent source! However, there is still very little 'India specific' medical information on the web. For instance, you can find the names and addresses of all doctors in the USA, but you cannot find even "a complete list of hospitals in Mumbai as yet."

So much about the plethora of web sites. All of us know that information technology is the in thing these days; how reliable is this medium? "Can be reliable and unreliable", says Dr. Malpani. "After all the web is a very democratic medium, anyone can publish information on the web, with no quality control measures being implemented." "Just like there are good doctors and bad doctors; there are good web sites and there are bad web sites."

○ ○ ○

## 22. Ram Sethu Controversy

The United Progressive Alliance (UPA) Government's ill-judged affidavit, questioning the historicity of Ram, in response to a Public Interest Litigation (PIL) filed in the Supreme Court against the controversial mega marine project called Sethusamundram Ship Channel Project (SSCP) started a new controversy. It has provided the Bhartiya Janata Party (BJP) once again with a potent electoral slogan and an impetus to revive its Ram Sethu campaign. The project is likely to destroy a 48-km stretch of limestone shoals submerged in the Palk Strait between Dhanushkodi in Tamil Nadu and Thallaimannar in Sri Lanka. Marked on maps as Adam's Bridge, the BJP claims it is one of the most critical sites in the epic story of Lord Ram, the Ram Sethu, the mythical bridge built by the Vanar Sena for Ram so that he could cross over to Lanka in his pursuit of Ravana to rescue his abducted wife Sita, thus giving rise to the belief among the Hindus that claimed that the island is man-made.

However, the protest by the BJP against cutting Ram Sethu on the grounds that any structural change to this would hurt the religious sentiments of the millions of Hindus across the country, is clearly dictated by potential expediency rather than by a desire to preserve the Ram's heritage.

It is believed that proposal for a channel linking the Palk Bay and the Gulf of Mannar goes back to the British period way back in 1860 and since then a number of proposals have been made and six distinct alignments for the passage to go across Ram Sethu have been put forward. It was only in 1998 when the then Prime Minister Atal Behari Vajpayee of the National Democratic Alliance (NDA) Government finally launched the project, which was inaugurated by the Prime Minister Manmohan Singh in 2005.

The project came into limelight when the National Aeronautics and Space Administration (NASA) of the US released some satellite images taken at different times of the chain of sandbars or shoals in the Palk Bay area. These were picked up by various fundamentalists who interpreted them as evidence of the remains of the mythical bridge built by Rama. Some websites also claimed that NASA had concluded that the bridge was man-made as judged from the bridge's unique curvature and composition by age.

On the other hand, Indian Space Research Organisation and two independent scientific agencies—Geological Survey of India and Space Applications Centre, and individual geologists have conducted detailed studies on the geological formations associated with Ram Sethu and all of them have formed same opinion that it is not a man-made structure. Moreover, palaeogeographic studies also revealed that the sea level in the region has oscillated significantly over historical time scales exposing the seabed between India and Sri Lanka periodically. Around six to seven thousand years ago the sea level was 17 metre below the present level, resulting in partial exposure of the seabed. About 10,000 years ago, sea level may have been 60 metre below. Radiocarbon dating suggests that during the last glacial maxima when sea level was at its minimum, the level may have been as below as 118 metres.

The project envisages the dedging of the shallow ocean region the south western Bay of Bengal to create an artificial 167-km long, 300-metre wide, and 12-metre-deep channel-like passage for 10,000-12,000 gross tonnage ships across the island formations called Adam's Bridge or Ram Sethu. It is a discontinuous chain of sandbars dotting a 30-km stretch in the East-West direction between the southern tip of the Remeshwaram island in India and Talaimannar in northwestern Sri Lanka, creating a geographical divide between the Palk Bay and the Gulf of Mannar, which form part of the southern Cauvery basin.

The project which was to become operational by the end of 2008 before it ran into controversies, is expected to reduce the sailing distances of ships plying between Kolkata and Tuticorin by 340 nautical miles. Similarly, the Chennai-Tuticorin route would be reduced by 434 nautical miles. It is anticipated that approximately 3417 ships should use it by 2010 and this would rise to same 7141 ships by 2025.

The revenue earned by way of toll pilotage charges is expected to not only help repay the cost of the project, but also earn profits from the first year of operations itself. Incidentally, India's coastal shipping comprising 530 ships, contributes 10 per cent of sea-borne trade and will handle 110 MT cargo in 2008. This is expected to double in the next five years. Repaying the project capital investment cost at 10 per cent per annum interest over 25 years, would need approximately Rs. 203 crore per year. Considering the annual coal requirement of the 1050 MW Tuticorin Thermal Power Plant, only 215 ships of 30,000 DWT are needed. In addition, another 200 ships would bring petroleum products. The total number of ships annually is not likely to exceed a thousand in any case.

The UPA Government has decided not only to withdraw the counter-affidavit filed by the Archaeological Survey of India in the Supreme Court, but also to redefine the project by choosing another alignment that does not cut through Ram Sethu. It promised to consider all opinions before finalising the Sethusamundram project. The Congress leadership realised that the project may become a political issue with far-reaching electoral implications.

Notwithstanding, the position of the Government and the opposition on the project, no attempt should be made to make political capital out of it. Emotive issues are better abandoned in the larger interest of the country, which has not yet forgotten the traumatic experience it had to undergo as a result of the Ayodhya controversy. It would be better for all the political parties to concentrate on issues like price rise, corruption and law and order on which it can grill the Government.

# 23. NATIONAL RURAL EMPLOYMENT GUARANTEE ACT

Over seventy per cent of India's population lives in rural areas. Providing regular employment to rural people requires serious thought from the Central and State Governments and civil society as key component of actions and initiatives aiming at achievement of the goals of development by 2020. Education and employment are two of the most powerful weapons to fight against rural poverty and achieve sustainable development. In this direction the National Rural Employment Guarantee Act (NREGA) is a revolutionary step. Since independence, it was being demanded that right to work should be included in the list of Fundamental Rights. It was a matter of concern for all Governments that in spite of their best efforts, the problem of unemployment and poverty never came under control. Therefore, the objective of the National Rural Employment Guarantee Scheme is to enhance the livelihood security of people in rural areas by generating wage employment through works that develop the infrastructure base of that area.

The NREGA was brought into force on Feb 2, 2006, initially among 200 most backward district, with the objective of providing 100 days of guaranteed unskilled wage employment to each rural household opting for it. It works a paradigm shift and stands out among the plethora of wage employment programmes, as it confers a legal right and guarantee to the rural population through an act of the Parliament and is not a scheme unlike the other wage employment programmes. The ongoing programmes of Sampoorna Grameen Rozgar Yojana (SGRY) and National Food for Work Programme (NFFWP) have been merged in NREGA.

The NREGA shall cover 200 districts of the country within five years. The focus of the Act is on works relating to water conservation, drought proofing, land development, food control/protection and rural connectivity in terms of all-weather roads. Each district has to prepare perspective plan for five years with a bottom up approach deriving from the needs of the local community. The NREGA envisages strict vigilance and monitoring. Gram Sabha has the power of social audit. Local Vigilance and Monitoring Committees are to be set up to ensure the quality of works. Provisions for due representation in such committees for Schedule Caste (SC)/Schedule Tribe (ST), women has also been made. At least one-third of the beneficiaries are to be women. Key records such as muster rolls, asset registers and employment registers are to be maintained and public access to them ensured. The Act also envisages grievance redressal mechanism and helpline.

There are glaring differences in the levels of the NREGA employment in different States. Some State Governments have clearly decided to own the Act and have seized this opportunity to provide large scale employment to the rural poor at the cost of the Central Government, which foots about 90 per cent of the Act. In other States, the whole programme is yet to take off. Rajasthan was the best performer among all major States in 2006-07 in terms of employment generation per rural household. Indeed, employment guarantee has been a lively political issue in the State of Rajasthan for quite a few years now, and the State also had a high level of preparedness for the NREGA, having organised massive public works programmes almost every year in living memory. It is noticeable that the small State of Tripura in Northeastern India is also doing good, with 87 days of NGERA employment per rural household in 2006-07. In both States, employment generation under NREGA is already quite close to the upper limit of 100 days per rural household.

On the other hand, there are some surprises. Kerala is at the rock bottom, but perhaps this is partly a reflection of the low demand for the NREGA employment in the State, rather than of a failure to provide it. The same interpretation, however, is likely to apply to Maharashtra and West Bengal. The fact that the NREGA is—at present a flop in both States may seem surprising, but it is in line with recent policy priorities. Maharashtra has assiduously sabotaged its own Employment Guarantee Scheme from the early 1990s onwards.

The Ministry of Rural Development has issued specific

guidelines on NREGA which envisage what must be done and what must not be done. The first relates to: (a) verification of eligibility only in terms of local residence and adult status, not economic status; (b) verification to be completed within 15 days of application for registration. The taboos are: (*i*) registering only Below Poverty Line (BPL) families; (*ii*) refusing locally domiciled but migrant families; (*iii*) denying registration on the basis of gender, caste, creed, *etc.,* (*iv*) inordinate delay in verification.

The job card is the basic legal document valid for five years. It enables the registered household to demand guaranteed employment. Minimum wages for State agricultural labourers have to be paid unless the centre notifies a wage rate.

The Act has stated that the share of women in the Act should be one-third. It is encouraging to note that at the all-India level, it is 40 per cent while in Tamil Nadu it has jumped to 81 per cent. In Jammu & Kashmir, Himachal Pradesh and Uttar Pradesh, for example, the participation of women is abysmally low, presumably because the mandate to provide creche facilities at NREGA worksites has been branzenly ignored. Even though the gap urgently needs to be filled through the sharing of experience, there is no denying that the Act is an important tool in social change. If it is effectively implemented, it can reduce the economic dependence of women on men in rural India.

The economic dependence of women on men in rural India plays a major role in the subjugation of women, and in this respect the NREGA is an important tool of social change. However, there are many States which are violanting the Act by failing to ensure that the share of women on NREGA employment is at least one-third. Better arrangements for child care are urgently required to facilitate the participation of women in the NREGA.

Actually, the key to this Act lies in the word 'Guarantee'. There are a number of schemes for the benefit of the poor. In those there are many loopholes like interference from politicians. A guarantee seeks to take this power away from the hands of politicians. It makes it a right, something that people will expect and demand, something they can complain about or in extreme cases, force the Government to provide it. It has the strength to profoundly alter the way bureaucrats treat common people they are suppose to serve.

It would be naive to think that the long history of fraud in public works programmes has come to an end. But recent experience shows that it is possible to remove corruption from NREGA. This calls for strict implementation of the transparency safeguards, as well as firm action whenever corruption is exposed.

The beginning has shown great hope in rebuilding rural society on the solid foundation of employment generation, empowerment of women and the much-needed infrastructure creation. And through meticulous examination of Government expenditure, officials can be held accountable. As awareness spreads, social auditing will hopefully lead to good governance in the rural areas across the country.

○ ○ ○

## 24. IPL–II IN SOUTH AFRICA

IPL–I held in India in 2008 was a grand success. But the second edition of the Indian Premier League had to be shifted to South Africa as the dates clashed with 15th Lok Sabha elections, April and May 2009.

A faction of the Board of Control for Cricket in India (BCCI) had originally planned for England as the replacement venue. However, the Rainbow Nation stood out to be a better choice on multiple levels. It has a readymade Indian-origin audience in cities such as Durban. The small time difference ensures prime-time coverage for Indian audiences. However, the necessity of favourable weather conditions over a period of two months was the crucial factor in finalising the venue.

After the Lahore attack, Home Minister P. Chidambaram had asked for postponement of IPL after elections as providing security to IPL and polls will stretch forces. Later, he agreed to help host IPL but asked for rescheduling of matches that overlap with elections. In response, the IPL officials submitted a revised schedule to Ministry of Home Affairs, keeping a 72-hour long gap between matches and polling dates in each state.

It was rejected by the Ministry on grounds that states were not ready to host IPL. In addition, the Ministry also said that no paramilitary forces would be provided for IPL, and states will have to give their own security.

So, IPL submitted another schedule by dropping Delhi and Jaipur as venues. However, it was only when the governments of Maharashtra and Andhra Pradesh backtracked and said no to IPL that it was decided to take it abroad.

The Indian Premier League on 25 March, 2009 signed a whopping Rs. 8,200 crore Official Broadcast Partner agreement for nine years (up to 2017) with Multi-Screen Media (MSM, formerly Sony) and World Sport Group (WSG). Accordingly, MSM brought the 59 matches live from South Africa on SET Max with the DLF-IPL Season II.

Last year, IPL had signed a contract with WSG-Sony for $ 1.026 billion for 10 years which included a sum of $ 108 million for marketing and promotion.

The fresh IPL agreement witn MSM brought a happy end to a relation between the two that had soured after the BCCI cancelled the 10-year contract stating that MSM had violated the contractual obligations on two counts, mainly quality of broadcast last year and ground sponsor rights.

Durban topped the venue with around 17 matches played followed by Pretoria which hosted 12 matches. Cape Town Johannesburg, Port Elizabeth, East London, Bloemfontein and Kimberley were other venues. All matches were played at IST 4 pm and 8 pm only.

The Schedule is given below :

| April 18 | RR vs RCB | Cape Town (4 pm) |
|----------|-----------|------------------|
|          | MI vs CSK | Cape Town (8 pm) |
| April 19 | KKR vs DC | Cape Town (4 pm) |
|          | DD vs KXIP | Cape Town (8 pm) |
| April 20 | RCB vs CSK | Port Elizabeth (4 pm) |
| April 21 | RR vs MI | Durban (4 pm) |
|          | KKR vs KXIP | Durban (8 pm) |
| April 22 | DD vs CSK | Durban (4 pm) |
|          | RCB vs DC | Cape Town (8 pm) |
| April 23 | KKR vs RR | Port Elizabeth (4 pm) |
| April 24 | KXIP vs RCB | Johannesburg (4 pm) |
| April 25 | KKR vs CSK | Cape Town (4 pm) |
|          | DC vs MI | Durban (8 pm) |
| April 26 | RR vs KXIP | Cape Town (4 pm) |
|          | RCB vs DD | Port Elizabeth (8 pm) |
| April 27 | KKR vs MI | Cape Town (4 pm) |
|          | CSK vs DC | Durban (8 pm) |
| April 28 | DD vs RR | Pretoria (4 pm) |
| April 29 | MI vs KXIP | Durban (4 pm) |
|          | KKR vs RCB | Durban (8 pm) |
| April 30 | DD vs DC | Pretoria (4 pm) |
|          | RR vs CSK | Pretoria (8 pm) |
| May 1 | RCB vs KXIP | East London (4 pm) |
|       | MI vs KKR | Durban (8 pm) |
| May 2 | RR vs DC | Johannesburg (4 pm) |
|       | CSK vs DD | Port Elizabeth (8 pm) |
| May 3 | MI vs RCB | Durban (4 pm) |
|       | KXIP vs KKR | East London (8 pm) |

| May 4  | DC vs CSK       | Port Elizabeth (4 pm)  |
|--------|-----------------|------------------------|
| May 5  | DD vs KKR       | Durban (4 pm)          |
|        | KXIP vs RR      | Durban (8 pm)          |
| May 6  | MI vs DC        | Pretoria (4 pm)        |
| May 7  | KXIP vs CSK     | Pretoria (4 pm)        |
|        | RCB vs RR       | Pretoria (8 pm)        |
| May 8  | DD vs MI        | East London (4 pm)     |
| May 9  | DC vs KXIP      | Bloemfontein (4 pm)    |
|        | CSK vs RR       | Port Elizabeth (8 pm)  |
| May 10 | KKR vs DD       | East London (4 pm)     |
|        | RCB vs MI       | Johannesburg (8 pm)    |
| May 11 | DC vs RR        | Bloemfontein (4 pm)    |
| May 12 | RCB vs KKR      | Pretoria (4 pm)        |
|        | KXIP vs MI      | Pretoria (8 pm)        |
| May 13 | DC vs DD        | Durban (4 pm)          |
| May 14 | MI vs RR        | Durban (4 pm)          |
|        | CSK vs RCB      | Durban (8 pm)          |
| May 15 | KXIP vs DD      | Kimberley (4 pm)       |
| May 16 | CSK vs MI       | Johannesburg (4 pm)    |
|        | DC vs KKR       | Port Elizabeth (8 pm)  |
| May 17 | RR vs DD        | Kimberley (4 pm)       |
|        | KXIP vs DC      | Johannesburg (8 pm)    |
| May 18 | CSK vs KKR      | Pretoria (4 pm)        |
| May 19 | DD vs RCB       | Johannesburg (4 pm)    |
| May 20 | CSK vs KXIP     | Durban (4 pm)          |
|        | RR vs KKR       | Durban (8 pm)          |
| May 21 | DC vs RCB       | Pretoria (4 pm)        |
|        | MI vs DD        | Pretoria (8 pm)        |
| May 22 | 1st Semi-final  | Pretoria               |

| May 23 | 2nd Semi-final | Johannensburg |
| May 24 | Final | Johannesburg |

IPL–II was also a big success. Though the enthusiasm of spectators which can be seen only among the crowds of Indian cities like Mumbai, Bangalore, Delhi, Kolkata, Jaipur and Chennai was missed, yet there was sufficient fanfare, excitement and glamour provided by crowds, players and cheerleaders. Donation of millions of rands for the cause of education in South Africa was a noble gesture. Deccan Chargers (DC) won the tournnament beating Royal Challengers Bangalore (RCB) in the final. Delhi Daredevils (DD) and Chennai Super Kings (CSK) were the other two teams which made it to the semi-final but didn't reach the final.

O O O

## 25. Naxal Terrorism In India

Not a single day passes without the Naxalite violence at one place or the other in the eastern parts of India. The Naxalities are striking at will in Jharkhand, Bihar, Orissa, Chhattisgarh and Andhra Pradesh. They bomb important installations and kill security personnel and innocent people alike. Over 2,200 civilians and 800 security personnel have been killed due to Maoist violence between 2004 and 2008 along with much destruction of public property in several states. The police forces, in their present condition, can hardly be expected to take on the Maoists.

The audacity with which on 22 April, 2009 they hijacked a passenger train in Jharkhand in broad daylight and took 700 passengers hostage speaks volumes about their strength. Luckily, all of them were released unharmed after a six-hour siege, but only after the Naxalites bombed a railway station, torched some oil tankers and caused panic. Targeting infrastructure facilities is a part of their strategy.

With the beginning of the 2009 general elections, the frequency as well as the ferocity of Naxal attacks increased in Orissa, Chhattisgarh, Jharkhand and Bihar though the elections passed of peacefully due to heavy deployment of para-military forces. Of late, the Naxalites have particularly targeted mining areas, not only to make an easy picking, but also to pull down symbols of economic importance. The administrative set-up is weak in these states and the presence of tribal populace provides a base. They have not only been able to scare voters enough to heed their boycott call, but have also been looting explosives with impunity. That is a chilling reminder that they may be able to cause more killings and kidnappings in future.

Even as the circumstances in which 11 Central Industrial Security Force (CISF) personnels were killed in the Nalco siege in Orissa were being confirmed, there came news of Naxal attacks elsewhere: two Central Reserve Police Force (CRPF) men killed on 15 April, 2009, 10 policemen and five election officials the next day. This is 28 officials in four days—more than the entire number of policemen killed in the Mumbai attacks. That is more than what the security forces sustain fighting terrorists and insurgents in Kashmir and the North-east.

In another incident, at least five policemen were killed when Maoists triggered a landmine blast on a vehicle carrying a police patrolling party in Muzaffarpur District of Bihar, when the security personnel were returning from duty an Improvised Explosive Device (IED) blast took place near a bridge. The blast killed everybody except the driver who got seriously injured.

The recent attacks may not be so dastardly as some other Naxalite crimes such as the inhuman slaughter of special police inside their camps in Chhattisgarh or the massacre of Andhra's "greyhounds" sailing on Chilka lake on the way back home after completing a counter-terrorism mission in Orissa, but these too cannot be taken lightly. They underscore that Naxal terrorists can operate with impunity. No matter how clandestinely heinous their crimes, none of them has even been arrested, leave alone being punished. This is so despite the thundering announcements of "massive manhunts" to bring the guilty to justice.

The Naxals were also targeting the candidates as well as the election machinery. They killed a BJP leader and a village head in Dantewada district of Chhattisgarh. Campaigning in most affected areas was confined to urban pockets. Yet, no concerted strategy was evolved to tackle them. Since police drives are launched in a piece-meal fashion, the Maoists quietly disappear from the area of operation and strike somewhere else with impunity.

The latest report of the Comptroller and Auditor-General (CAG) is a severe criticism of the governments of those states affected by Maoist violence for not doing enough to modernise the State Police forces despite funds being available.

In its review of police modernisation in 16 states where there have been several Maoist attacks since 2008, the CAG has found that the State Police forces have been handicapped in their battles with Maoist terrorists. This is largely due to the grave lapses in the proper utilisation of funds, weaponry, communications and training.

The CAG report also did not rule out the misappropriation of funds on the part of some of these state administrations. Thus, it appears that it is not just the Centre that has allowed the Maoists to flourish by following a soft policy towards them, but also the State governments that have been complacent and have not taken appropriate steps to tackle the problem. The result has been today a large area in central India, stretching from the eastern districts of Maharasthra all the way to Jharkhand, has been infested by the Maoists.

In view of the increasing Naxalite attacks, the Central and the State need to rethink their strategies. They must demonstrate the necessary political will and play a leadership role in finding a lasting solution to the crisis. Since the roots of the crisis lie in growing socio-economic inequalities and the lack of basic infrastructure and services, the Centre and the States must address these issues to create an atmosphere of growth and peace.

O O O

# 26. SUICIDE EPIDEMIC AMONG FARMERS

Thousands of farmers have committed suicides across the country in the past decade due to acute poverty and indebtedness reasons. Most of the suicides have occurred in States of Andhra Pradesh, Karnataka, Kerala, Maharashtra and Punjab among many others.

The farmer suicide outbreak is both alarming and tragic, especially when India is enjoying unprecedented economic growth. The crisis in agriculture is undoubtedly a major cause. But an examination of the patterns of suicide suggests that the policy diagnosis is indebtedness, and hence the solution of extending liberal credit may be inadequate.

However, there is clearly more to farmer suicides than indebtedness. In the 1990s India woke up to a spate of farmers' suicides. The first State where suicides were reported was Maharashtra. Soon the reports started coming from Andhra Pradesh. In the beginning major cases were happening among the cotton growers, especially those from Vidarbha alone, but all over Maharashtra showed a significantly high suicide rate. The suicide mortality rates in Andhra Pradesh and Maharashtra are high and growing significantly whereas the rates in Bihar and Uttar Pradesh have been consistently low. There is no obvious reason to believe farmer distress is lower in Bihar and Uttar Pradesh than in Andhra Pradesh and Maharashtra. On an average one Indian farmer committed suicide every 32 minutes between 1997 and 2005. Since 2007, that has become one suicide every 30 minutes. However, the frequency at which farmers take lives in any region smaller than the country—say a single State or group of States—has to be lower because the number of suicides in any such region would be less than the total for the country as a whole in any year.

The suicide rate in the States of Maharashtra, Andhra Pradesh, Karnataka and Madhya Pradesh (including Chhattisgarh) is 'alarming'. Farmer suicides in Maharashtra increased dramatically in 2006, than in any part of the country. The State witnessed 4,453 farmers' suicides that year, over a quarter of all India total of 17,060, according to the National Crime Records Bureau (NCRB) in its report 'Accidental Deaths and Suicides in India, 2006'. That is the worst figure recorded in any year for any State since the first NCRB began logging farmer suicides.

The previous worst—4,147 in 2004—was also in Maharashtra. It has seen 36,428 farmers' suicides since 1995 in official account.

However, as per the Right to Information Act, more than 800 farmers committed suicide in the first six months of 2007. The agrarian crisis forced 607 farmers in Maharashtra, 114 in Andhra Pradesh, 73 in Karnataka and 13 in Kerala to commit suicide.

The suicides in Maharashtra marked an increase of 527 over the 2005 figure. This was four-and-a-half times bigger than that in Andhra Pradesh, the next worst-hit State which registered a rise of 117 farm suicides over 2005. It was also more than twice the increase of 198 in Madhya Pradesh and Chhattisgarh taken together.

Significantly, Maharasntra's upward spike occurred in the year when the relief packages of both the Centre and State Governments—worth Rs. 4,825 crore in all—were being implemented in Vidarbha region, where suicides have been most intense. The NCRB figures show an unrelenting uptrend in what can be termed by the 'SEZ' of (Farmers) 'Special Elimination Zone' States. These states, which account for nearly two-thirds of all farm suicides in the country, include

Maharashtra, Andhra Pradesh, Karnataka and Madhya Pradesh (including Chhattisgarh). As a group, the SEZ States marked an increase of 6.2 per cent in such deaths.

Among them, Maharashtra (4,453), Andhra Pradesh (2,607) and Madhya Pradesh-Chhattisgarh (8,858) show a sharp upward spike.

Karnataka (1,720) reports a decline. Though the all-India numbers for 2006 reflect a very small decline of 61 over 2005 figure of 17,131, the broad trends of the past decade continue. And the trend of rapidly rising farm suicides, particularly post 2001 in the SEZ States, remains unchanged.

So the minuscule decline in the figure for the country as a whole marks no break from the dismal decade-long trend. NCRB data record 1,66,304 farmers' suicides in a decade since 1997. Of these 78,737 occurred between 1997 and 2001. The next five years—from 2002 to 2006—proved worse, witnessing 87,567 farmers take their own lives. This means that on an average, there has been one farmer's suicide every 30 minutes since 2002.

One State outside the Big Four that has seen high numbers of farmers' suicides is Kerala. It saw a total of 11,516 suicides in 1997-2005. Worse, many of these occurred in small districts such as Wayanad. Kerala shows a fluctuating but declined trend over the nine-year period. Kerala's farm suicide rate is very high, and the State remains vulnerable to volatility in the prices of, for instance, coffee, pepper, cardamon and vanilla: A fragility enhanced by the fact that major relief on the debt front requires Central help. Besides, State bureaucracies are extremely hostile to debt relief for farmers. Also, India's Free Trade Agreements (FTAs) with countries and neighbours that produce the same cash crops as Kerala hurts badly. The State's balance on the farm suicides front is thus, very delicate.

The problems of the farmers were quite comprehensive. There was little credit available. What was available was very costly. There was no advice on how best to conduct agriculture operations. Income through farming was not enough to meet even the minimum needs of a farming family. Support systems like free health facilities from the Government were virtually non-existence. Traditionally, support systems in the villages of India had been provided by the Government. However, due to a number of reasons the Government had either withdrawn itself from its supportive role or plain simple misgovernance had allowed facilities in the village to wither away. The other reasons include:

(i)   absence of adequate social support infrastructure at the level of the village and district;

(ii)  uncertainty of agricultural enterprise in India;

(iii) indebtedness of farmers;

(iv)  rising costs of cultivation;

(v)   plummeting prices of farm commodities;

(vi)  lack of credit availability for small farmers;

(vii) relative absence of irrigation facilities; and

(viii) repeated crop failures.

The decision to waive Rs. 60,000 farm loans on an unprecedented scale announced by the then Finance Minister P. Chidambaram in the Union Budget for 2008-09 has attracted widespread appreciation. Almost all the political parties except Bharatiya Janata Party (BJP) have welcomed the move. In fact, most of them were vociferously clamouring for such a measure to relieve the farm sector from the crushing burden of debt. However, the Budget does not spell out the basis of the estimate nor of the institutions, loan categories, and class of borrowers that will be covered by the scheme. By definition, the scheme then applies only to those who have outstanding loans with institutions. Nearly three-fourths of all rural households report that they do not have any outstanding debt.

Andhra Pradesh has decided to take care of those farmers who are not covered under the Union Government's Rs. 60,000 crore loan waiver scheme. It has announced a Rs. 1,690 crore State-level loan waiver, which would cover loans of 43.84 lakh borrowers from Scheduled Castes (SCs), Scheduled Tribes (STs) and Backward Classes and Minorities.

## Farmers's Debt Relief Fund

The UPA Government has set up a Rs. 10,000 crore

Farmers' Debt Relief Fund as the first allocation to its debt waiver scheme. The sum was part of Rs. 43,059 crore cash expenditure of the Government in the third supplementary budget for 2007-08 presented by the Finance Minister.

The farmers who repaid their outstanding agriculture loans in January and February 2008 would be eligible under Rs. 60,000 crore debt relief programme. They will be clubbed with farmers, who have taken loans before March 1, 2007 but were defaulters as December 31, 2007 and continue to remain so.

However, farmers who repaid their outstanding prior to December 31, 2007 would not qualify for any refund or incentive. But sections of bankers have urged the Government to offer incentives to those who have repaid their debts.

The Government's debt waiver scheme is expected to sharply reduce indebtedness of small and marginal farmers, with holdings of less than two hectare. As the scheme has already received massive support in rural India, the UPA Government is now considering extending it to wipe clean bad assets arising from non-farm credit as well.

Alarmed by the persistence of agrarian distress in several parts of the country resulting in those engaged in a life-sustaining profession taking their own lives, the Union Government presented a National Policy for Farmers to the Parliament in November 2007. The document is based on the draft submitted by the National Commission on Farmers in October 2006. This policy, the first of its kind in the history of either colonial or independent India, calls for a paradigm shift from a commodity-centred to a human-centred approach in agricultural planning and programmes.

The objective of the policy is to stimulate attitudes and actions that should result in assessing agricultural progress in terms of improvement in the income of farm families not only to meet their consumption requirements, but also to enhance their capacity to invest in farm-related activities.

○ ○ ○

# VIII. INFRASTRUCTURE OF INDIA'S POLITY AND ECONOMY

## 1. INTRODUCING INDIA—THE PHYSICAL SETTING

India is one of the oldest civilizations in the world, with a kaleidoscopic variety and rich cultural heritage. It has achieved multifaceted socio-economic progress during the years since independence. India has become self-sufficient in food and many other agricultural products and is now the tenth most industralised country in the world and the sixth nation to have gone into outer space to explore nature for the benefit of the people. India covers an area of 3,287,263 sq. km., extending from the snow-capped Himalayan heights to tropical rain forests of the south. As seventh largest country in the world, India is well marked off from the rest of Asia by mountains and the sea, which give the country a distinct geographical entity. Bounded by the Great Himalayas in the north, it stretches southwards and the Tropic of Cancer, tapers off into the Indian Ocean between the Bay of Bengal on the east and the Arabian Sea on the west.

Lying entirely in a northern hemisphere, India's mainland extends between latitudes 8°4' and 37°6' north, longitudes 68°7' and 97°25' east, and measures about 3,214 km from north to south between the extreme latitudes and about 2,933 km from east to west between the extreme longitudes. It has a land frontier to about 15,200 km. The total length of the coastline of the mainland, Lakshadweep Islands and Andaman and Nicobar Islands is 7,516.6 km.

Countries having a common border with India are Afghanistan and Pakistan to north-west, China, Nepal and Bhutan to north, Myanmar to the east, and Bangladesh to east of West Bengal. Sri Lanka is separated from India by a narrow channel of sea formed by the Palk Strait, and the Gulf of Mannar.

India's mainland comprises four regions, namely the great mountain zone, plains of the Ganga and the Indus, the desert region and the southern peninsula.

The Himalayas comprise three almost parallel ranges interspersed with large plateaus and valleys, some of which, the Kashmir and Kullu valleys are fertile, extensive and of great scenic beauty. Some of the highest peaks in the world are found· in these ranges. The high altitudes limit travel only to a few passes, notably the Jelep La and Nathu La on the main Indo-Tibet trade route through the Chumbi Valley, north-east of Darjeeling and Shipki La in the Sutlej Valley, north-east of Kalpa (Kinnaur). The mountain wall extends over a distance of about 2,400 km with a varying depth of 240 to 320 km. In the east, between India and Myanmar, and India and Bangladesh, hill ranges are much lower. Garo, Khasi, Jaintia and Naga hills, running almost, east-wise, join the chain to Mizo and Arakan Hills running north-south.

The plains of the Ganga and the Indus, about 2,400 km long and 240 to 320 km broad, are formed by basins of three distinctive river systems—the Indus, the Ganga, and the Brahmaputra. They are one of the world's greatest stretches of flat alluvium and also one of the most densely populated area of the earth. Between the Yamuna at Delhi and the Bay of Bengal, nearly 2,600 km away, there is a drop of only 200 meters elevation.

The desert region can be divided into two parts—the Great Desert and the Little Desert. The Great Desert extends from the Rann of Kutchch beyond the Luni River northward. The whole of Rajasthan-Sind frontier runs through this. The Little Desert extends from River Luni between Jaisalmer and Jodhpur up to northern wastes. Between the Great and the

Little Deserts lies a zone of absolutely sterile country consisting of rocky land cut-up by limestone ridges.

The Peninsular Plateau is marked off from the plains of the Ganga and the Indus by a mass of mountain and hill ranges varying from 460 to 1,220 meters in height. Prominent among these are the Aravalli, Vindhya, Satpura, Maikala and Ajanta. The peninsula is flanked on one side by the Eastern Ghats where average elevation is about 610 meters and on the other by the Western Ghats where average elevation is about 1,220 meters. rising in places to 2,440 meters. Between the Eastern Ghats and the Arabian Sea lies a narrow coastal strip, while between Eastern Ghats and the Bay of Bengal, there is a broader coastal area. The southern point of plateau is formed by the Nilgiri Hills where the Eastern and Western Ghats meet. The Cardamom Hills lying beyond may be regarded as a continuation of the Western Ghats.

The rivers in India may be classified as: (i) Himalayan rivers, (ii) Peninsular rivers, (iii) Coastal rivers, and (iv) Rivers of the inland drainage basin.

The Himalayan rivers are perennial as they are generally snow-fed and have a reasonable flow throughout the year. During the Monsoon season, the Himalayas receive very heavy rainfall and the rivers discharge the maximum quantity of water in volume. A large number of the streams are non-perennial. The streams of the inland drainage basin of western Rajasthan are few and far between. Most of them are of ephemeral type. They drain towards the individual basins or salt lakes like Sambhar or are lost in the sands having no outlet to the sea. The Luni is the only river of this type that drains into the Rann of Kutchch.

The Ganga sub-basin which is a part of the larger Ganga-Brahmaputra-Meghana basin is the largest in India receiving waters from an area which comprises about one quarter of the total area of the country. Its boundaries are well-defined by the Himalayas in the north and Vindhyas in the south. The Ganga flows through Uttar Pradesh, Bihar and West Bengal and enters Bangladesh thereafter. It has two main headwaters in the Himalayas: the Bhagirathi and the Alaknanda, the former rising from the Gangotri Glacier at Gomukh and the latter from the Glacier short of the Alkapuri Glacier. The Ganga is joined by a number of the Himalayan rivers including the Yamuna— Ghagra, Gandak and Kosi. The western-most river of the Ganga system is the Yamuna which rises from the Yamnotri Glacier and joins the Ganga at Allahabad. Among important rivers flowing north from central India into the Yamuna/Ganga are the Chambal, Betwa and Sone. The Brahmaputra and the Barak flowing from east to west in north-eastern region are international rivers and have immense water resources potential which is still in the initial stages of development.

The Godavari in the southern peninsula has the second largest river basin covering 10% of the area of India. Next to it is the Krishna basin in the region, while the Mahanadi has the third largest basin. The basin of the Narmada in the uplands of Deccan flowing to the Arabian Sea and of the Kaveri in south falling into the Bay of Bengal are each of about the same size, though with different character and shape.

Two other river systems which are small but agriculturally important are those of the Tapti in north and the Pennar in south. These west coast rivers are of great importance as they contain as much as 11 % of the country's water resources while draining about the 10% of the land area.

O O O

## 2. Floristic Resources of India

With a wide range of climatic conditions from the torrid to the arctic, India has a rich and varied vegetation, which few other countries of comparable size possess. India can be divided into eight distinct floristic regions, namely the western Himalayas, the eastern Himalayas, Assam, the Indus Plain, the Ganga Plain, the Deccan, Malabar and the Andamans.

The Western Himalayan region extends from Kashmir to Kumaon. Its temperate zone is rich in forests of chir, pine, conifer and broad-leaved temperate trees. Higher up, forests of deodar, blue pine, spruce and silver fir are found. The alpine zone extends from upper limit of the temperate zone of about 4,750 metres or even higher. The characteristic trees of this zone are high level silver fir, silver birch and juniper. The eastern Himalayan region extends from Sikkim eastwards and embraces Darjeeling, Kurseong and the adjacent tract. The temperate zone has forests of oak, laurels, maples, rhododendrons, alders and birches. Many conifers and junipers and dwarf willows are also found. The Assam region comprises the Brahmaputra and the Surma Valleys with evergreen forests, occasional thick clumps of bamboos and tall grasses. The Indus plain region comprises the plains of Punjab, western Rajasthan and northern Gujarat. It is dry and hot and supports natural vegetation. The Ganga plain region covers the area as alluvial plain and is under cultivation for wheat, sugarcane and rice. Only small areas support forests of widely different types. The Deccan region comprises the entire table land of the Indian peninsula and supports vegetation of various kinds from scrub jungles to mixed desiduous forests. The Malabar region covers the excessively humid belt of mountain country parallel to the west coast of the peninsula. Besides being rich in forest vegetation, this region produces important commercial crops such as coconut, betelnut, pepper, coffee, tea, rubber and cashewnut. The Andaman region abounds in evergreen, mangrove forests. The Himalayan region extending from Kashmir to Arunachal Pradesh through Nepal, Sikkim, Bhutan, Meghalaya arid Nagaland and the Deccan peninsula is rich in endemic flora, with a large number of plants which are not found elsewhere.

India is floristically very rich. It is estimated that there are about 49,000 species of plants including shrubs in the country which represent about 7% of world flora. The vascular flora, which forms the conspicuous vegetation cover comprises 15,000 species. Of these, more than 35% is endemic and has so far not been reported anywhere else in the world. The total plant wealth of the country includes not only the useful large flowered plants including flowering shrubs but also a large number of non-flowering plants like ferns, liverworts, bambo, algae and fungi.

The flora of the country is looked after by the Botanical Survey of India (BSI), Kolkata, along with certain universities and research institutions. The publication of flora of India in the form of fasciles has been started by the Botanical Survey of India. Twenty fasciles have already been published. BSI has brought out facts on the flora of Karnataka (2 volumes), Goa, Daman and Diu (2 volumes), Tamil Nadu (3 volumes), Arunachal Pradesh (3 volumes), Meghalaya (2 volumes), and Tripura (I volume). Publications on state and district flowering and non-flowering flora are also being brought out by the BSI. BSI is also bringing out an inventory of endangered plants in the form of a publication titled 'Red Data Book'. Samples of some of these plants are preserved in botanical gardens and national parks. The dried samples are preserved in the Central National Herbarium, the herbal Herbaria of the BSI and in research and training institutions.

○ ○ ○

# 3. POPULATION PROBLEM—ITS CONTROL IN INDIA

A large population and its continuous, unchecked growth is a major problem for India. All our ailments are related to this problem and quite a disaster awaits the country if this problem is not tackled effectively and urgently.

Poverty is a problem in the country which we keep constantly lamenting about. But, surprisingly and woefully, we fail to understand that the problem of poverty is man-made. The more the population, the more the poverty. We have not been able to educate our poor class that more children are not an asset, they are a liability. For the present the poorer class thinks that every child born to them would in due course, be an earning member—an asset. They fail to understand or we have failed to make them understand that every new child would need more to eat, more to be fed, more space to live. There is an unchecked migration from villages to towns. The town life apparently appears to them so alluring but coming to the towns means living in the most insanitary conditions with no place to rest their heads, so much dearth of space, of drinking water, dearth of basic amenities. Slums grow under most unhygenic surroundings. Jobs are few, job-seekers are more and this leads to their taking to petty crimes to begin with and they turn into 'goons' gradually.

China has a larger population than India. It has a larger land area but still it has controlled their population through stringent measures like 'one child norm'. The only problem with us is that we are a democratic country where every voter has to be kept in good humour. 'Family Planning' and 'Family Welfare' programmes remain a mere euphemistic terminology. No Government policy—whether at the Central or the State level—has come out with a daring and positive pronouncement that families with one or at the most two children shall be given benefits or preferences in jobs or initiatives in business. Then there are difficulties in implementing the family-planning programmes among Muslims. Their socio-religious ethos militates against adopting contraceptives. And none dare touch them on this issue.

There is a National Population Policy in force in India, which is very often referred to. But the will to implement its provisions is not there with the government. The political leaders even with eleven or more children live in a lavish life-style; they have not known the pang of poverty or deprivation; hence they have no incentive or zest to implement the programme. And it is they who have to do it. It is they who, in a democratic set up, have to lead and carry the torch. The masses still remain uncommitted to the concept of a small family. The MLAs and the MPs should be made accountable if the 'family planning' programme is not found catching up in their constituency. U.P., M.P., Rajasthan and Bihar are the sort of states where women remain illiterate and illiteracy of womanhood is a great bane in the proper and effective implementation of this programme. Kerala has shown the way which other states need to emulate.

Let us look into the figures as below and assess for ourselves the growing magnitude of the problem. The population of India as on March 1, 2001 stood more than 1000 million. The second populous country in the world India is the home of 16% of world's total poputation. This is against an area of 2.42% of the total world area.

| Census Year | Population | Decadal Growth Rate |
|---|---|---|
| 1901 | 23,83,96,327 | — |
| 1911 | 25,20,93,390 | +5.75 |
| 1921 | 25,13,21,213 | −0.31 |
| 1931 | 27,89,77,238 | +11.00 |
| 1941 | 31,86,60,580 | +14.22 |
| 1951 | 36,10,88,090 | +13.31 |
| 1961 | 43,92,34,771 | +21.51 |
| 1971 | 54,81,59,652 | +24.80 |
| 1981 | 68,33,29,097 | +24.66 |
| 1991 | 84,64,21,039 | +23.85 |
| 2001 | 101,87,37,436 | +23.60 |

Thus in most states the growth rate declined during the 1911 to 1921 decade. However, Andhra Pradesh, Arunachal Pradesh, Madhya Pradesh, Maharashtra, Nagaland, Tripura, West Bengal, Daman and Diu, Lakshadweep, and Puducherry, which account for one third of the country's population, recorded increase in growth rate. Nagaland registered the highest growth rate of 56.08% while Kerala the lowest 14.32%. Mumbai metropolis continued to be the most populated city of the country with urban population of 12.60 million, Kolkata taking the second place with 11.02 million. Delhi ranked third with the population (urban) of 8.42 million, followed by Chennai 5.42 million.

## Population Density

One of the important indicators of population concentration is the density of population. It is defined as the number of persons per square kilometer. The population density has gone up from 216 in 1981 to 267 persons in 1991. In 1901, it was 77 persons. The 10 heavily populated districts of the country are Kolkata, Delhi, Chennai, Greater Mumbai, Hyderabad, Chandigarh, Mahe, Howrah, Kanpur City and Bengaluru. All of them have a density of 2,000 persons per square kilometre and above, about 6% of the country's population lives in these districts. The average density of these districts is about 7500.

## Sex Ratio

Sex Ratio is defined as the number of females per 1,000 males. In India it has generally been averse to women. The ratio has also declined over the years except in 1981 when it slightly improved to 934 from 926. In 1991, there has been a fall by 8 points to 926 per thousand males. The 2001 Census showed some improvement to 933. Kerala represented a positive spectrum. The state has a higher number of females than males, 1,036 females for a thousand males.

In the Indian context, a sex ratio of 950 can be considered favourable to the females, In some states and union territories, the ratio is as follows: Himachal Pradesh (976), Andhra Pradesh (972), Goa (967), Karnataka (960), Manipur (958) Orissa (971), Tamil Nadu (974), Dadra and Nagar Haveli (952), and Pondicherry (979), Chandigarh (790). Chandigarh had the lowest sex ratio.

## Literacy

For the purpose of Census, a person is deemed to be literate if he or she can read or write any language with understanding. In the 1991 Census, the question on literacy was canvassed only for population aged seven years and above, unlike earlier censuses, which took into account population of five years or above. The final results reveal that there has been an increase in literacy in the country. The rate in 1991 was 52.21 per cent for males and 39.29 for females.

Kerala retained its position by being on top with 89.81 per cent literacy rate in the country. Bihar stood at the bottom with a literacy rate of 38.48 per cent, with Rajasthan being close to it having 38.55 literacy percentage. But literacy among the women was the lowest in Rajasthan with a percentage of 20.44 as compared to 54.99 among the males.

The above figures of population in India highlight the deep concern posed by the rapid multiplication of human numbers in a country like India which is still struggling for self-sufficiency in basic necessities of life. As long as the relationship between the growing population and natural resources remains as hopelessly unfavourable as it is in the developing countries of Asia, as Aldous Huxley puts it, it would be impossible for democracy to take root and develop. To a great extent, the degree of a nation's people's living standards and of increasing national power is determined by the relationship between the growth rate of the economy and the growth rate of population.

It is the problem of the increasing number of mouths to be fed and clothed that alarms people in all parts of the world. Economists are baffled, sociologists are scared, and politicians and administrators are worried. It has created various problems like unemployment, poverty, starvation, malnutrition and illiteracy, besides shelter. And unfortunately those living in the developing countries of Asia, Africa and Latin America, are continuing to get more than their share of problems because of their ever-increasing population.

India, a developing country, comes second to China in the world in the figures of population. Although the world is forty times as large as India in area, the world population is less than seven times as large as India's. One out of every seven persons is an Indian. Obviously, India, like other developing countries, is feeling a great pressure of population.

The population of India has increased from 1028 million in 2001 to 1,100 millions today. More than 6,500 babies are born everyday. To some extent, the main cause in our extraordinary growth is not excessive births, but our victory against death and disease. Our ability to control communicable diseases like malaria, smallpox and cholera and ushering in improving health services has steadily brought down the death rate from 27 per 1,000 in 1951 to just 15 today, while the birth rate has remained about the same. Life expectancy at birth has risen from 32 years in 1950 to 60 today. Thus, our number is multiplying every day. As a result, there are 21 million births a year and about 8 million deaths, giving an annual excess of about 13-14 millions in our already huge population.

The result of our increasing numbers is obvious—much of our effort to raise the standard of living of our people through successive Five-Year plans has been nullified. The growth of population, besides neutralising all developmental efforts, brings distress to the community, to the family and to the individuals. As one of our great economists has said: "To plan when population growth is unchecked is like building a house where the ground is in flood."

What then needs to be done? The remedy is to reduce the number of births. In order to stabilise the relationship between population and the basic necessities of life, we must bring our birth rate down from 41 per thousand to 25 per thousand as quickly as possible. The family planning programme was begun in a modest way in 1951. The importance which the Government of India has attached to birth control is quite evident from the fact that about Rs. 50 crore—half of the outlay on health in each annual plan is set apart for family planning. A Department of Family Planning (now Family Welfare) functions in the Union Ministry of Health. The Government has accorded top priority to the programme of birth control and is making all-out efforts to reduce the birth rate to 25 per 1,000 as early as possible.

Population growth is a stimulant· to economic growth up to a point, but afterwards, as we are witnessing in India, it becomes a serious impediment. Larger population provides abundant labour as well as a big market for consumption. But the alarming rate of increase in population produces an occasional crisis in food situation, necessitating import of foodgrains, involving large amount of foreign exchange which could otherwise be made available for faster economic growth. Although food production has increased to some extent, it is not enough to feed the newly arriving excess population.

High birth rate increases the number of children, making a higher proportion of dependent population unproductive. The number of unproductive consumers is presently put at 400 million. Another consequence of vast growth in population is that it reduces the capacity to save and invest in the national economy. In any developing country, capital formation is crucial to economic growth but in India most of the resources are used up in supporting the unproductive population, so that the problem of poverty gets no solution. Investments for such important projects as highways, rail-roads, communication systems, electrical power and generation, irrigation pumps, etc. are not available to the extent desired. Unless birth rate gets reduced in the country, it is impossible to effect any savings to increase capital formation.

It seems all voluntary methods of birth control have failed to yield any tangible results. What should be taken resort to is for the Government of India taking a decision to officially declare to limit the family size on the principle of one-family one-child norm. This population control policy has greatly succeeded in China. There is no reason why such a policy should not be framed in India without any further delay.

# 4. NATIONAL SYMBOLS OF INDIA

### National Flag

National Flag is a horizontal tricolour of deep saffron (kesari) at the top, white in the middle and dark green at the bottom in equal proportion. Ratio of the width of the flag to its length is two to three. In the centre of the white band is a navy blue wheel which represents the Charkha. Its design is that of the wheel which appears on the abacus of the Sarnath Lion Capital of Ashoka. Its diameter approximates to the width of the white band and it has 24 spokes.

The design of the National Flag was adopted by the Constituent Assembly of India on July 22, 1947. Its use and display are regulated by Flag Code-India.

## State Emblem

State emblem is an adaptation from the Sarnath Lion Capital of Ashoka. In the original there are four lions standing back to back mounted on an abacus with a frieze carrying sculptures in high relief of an elephant, a galloping horse, a bull and a lion separated by intervening wheels over a bell-shaped lotus. Carved out of a single block of polished sandstone, the capital is crowned by the Wheel of the Law (Dharma Chakra).

In the state emblem adopted by the Government of India on 26 January, 1950, only three lions are visible, the fourth being hidden from view. The wheel appears in relief in the centre of the abacus with a bull on right and a horse on left and the outlines of other wheels on extreme right and left. The bell-shaped lotus has been omitted. The words Satyameva Jayate from Mundaka Upanishad, meaning 'Truth Alone Triumphs' are inscribed below the abacus in the Devanagri script.

## National Anthem

The song Jana-gana-mana, composed by Rabindranath Tagore, was adopted by the Constituent Assembly as the national anthem of India on January 24, 1950. It had been first sung on December 27, 1911 at the Calcutta session of the Indian National Congress. The complete song consists of five stanzas. First stanza consists full version of the National Anthem. It reads:

Jana-gana-mana-adhinayaka, jaya he
Bharata-bhagya-vidhata,
Punjab-Sindhu-Gujrata-Maratha  Dravida-Utkala-Banga
Vindhya-Himachal-Yamuna-Ganga
Uchchala-Jaladhi-taninga
Tava shubha name jage,
Tava-shubha asisa mage,
Gahe tava jaya gatha,
Jana-gana-mangala-dayaka jaya he
Bharata-bhagya-vidhata.
Jaya he, jaya he, jaya he,
Jay-jaya jaya, jaya he.

Playing time of the full version of the national anthem is is approximately 52 seconds. A short version consisting of first and last lines of the stanza (playing time is approximately 20 seconds), is also played on certain occasions. The following is Tagore's English rendering of the stanza:

Thou art the ruler of the minds of all people,
dispenser of India's destiny.
Thou name rouses the hearts of Punjab, Sind, Gujarat and Maratha,
of the Dravida, and Orissa and Bengal;
It echoes the hills of the Vindhyas and Himalayas,
mingles in the music of Jamuna and Ganga and is chanted by the waves of the Indian Sea.
They pray for thy blessings and sing thy praise.
The saving of all people waits in thy hand,
thou dispenser of India's destiny.
Victory, Victory, Victory to thee.

## National Song

The song Vande Matram, composed by Bankim Chandra Chatterji was a great source of inspiration to the people in their struggle for freedom. It has an equal status with Jana-gana-mana. The first political occasion when it was sung was the 1896 session of the Indian National Congress. The following is the text of its first stanza:

Vande Matram!
Sujalam, Suphalam, malayaja shitalam,
Shasyashyamalam, Mataram,
Shubhrajyosthana pulakitayaminim,
Phullakusumita drumandala shobhinim,
Suhasinim sumadhura bhashinim,
Sukhadam varadam, Mataram!

English translation of the stanza rendered by Sri Aurobindo Ghosh in prose is:

I bow to thee, mother,
richly watered, richly fruited,
cool with the winds of the south,
dark with the crops of the harvests,
The Mother!
Her nights rejoicing in the glory of the moonlight,
her lands clothed beautifully with her trees in flowering bloom,
sweet of laughter, sweet of speech,
The Mother, giver of boons, giver of bliss.

## National Calendar

National Calendar based on the Saka era with Chaitra as its first month and a normal year of 365 days was adopted from March 22, 1957 along with Georgian calendar for the following official purposes: (i) Gazette of India, (ii) News Broadcasts by All India Radio, (iii) calendars issued by the Government of India, (iv) Government communications addressed to the members of public.

Dates of the national calendar have a permanent correspondence with dates of Georgian calendar: Chaitra I falling on March 22 normally and on March 21 in leap year.

## National Animal

The magnificent tiger, *Panthera tigris* (Linnaeus), the national animal of India, is a rich-coloured well-striped animal with a short coat. The combination of grace, strength, agility enormous power has earned the tiger great respect and high esteem. Out of eight species known, the Indian race, the Royal Bengal Tiger is found throughout the country except the north-western region and also in the neighbouring countries, Nepal, Bhutan and Bangladesh. To check the dwindhng population of tigers in India "Project Tiger" was launched in April 1973. So far, 23 tiger reserves have been established in the country under this project, covering an area of 33,046 sq km.

## National Bird

The Indian Peacock, *Pavo cristatus* (Linnaeus), the national bird of India, is a colourful, swan-sized bird with a fan-shaped crest of feathers on its head, a white patch under the eye and a long slender neck. The male of the species is more colourful than the female with a glistening blue breast and neck and a spectacular bronze-green tail of around 200 elongated feathers. The female is a brownish, slightly smaller than the male and it lacks the tail. The elaborate courtship dance of the male by fanning out the tail and quivering the feathers is a gorgeous sight.

The peacock is widely found in the Indian sub-continent from the south and east of the Indus river, Jammu and Kashmir, east to Assam, south to Mizoram and the whole of the Indian peninsula. The peacock enjoys full protection from the people as it is never molested on religious and sentimental grounds. It is also protected under the Indian Wildlife (Protection) Act, 1972.

○ ○ ○

# 5. MAIN FEATURES OF INDIA'S CONSTITUTION

India is a Union of States and Union Territories. It is a sovereign socialist secular democratic republic, with a parliamentary system of government. The Republic is governed in terms of the constitution, which was adopted by the Constituent

Assembly on November 26, 1949 and came into force on January 26, 1950.

The Constitution which envisages parliamentary form of government is federal in structure with unitary features. President of India is constitutional head of executive of the Union. Article 74(1) of the Constitution provides that there shall be a Council of Ministers with the Prime Minister as head to aid and advise the President who shall in exercise of his functions, act in accordance with such advice. Real executive power thus vests in the Council of Ministers with the Prime Minister as head. Council of Ministers is collectively responsible to the Lok Sabha. Similarly, in states, Governor is head of the executive, but it is the Council of Ministers with Chief Minister as head in whom real executive power vests. Council of Ministers of a state is collectively responsible to the State Legislative Assembly or the Vidhan Sabha.

The Constitution distributes legislative power between the Parliament and state legislatures and provides for resting of residual powers in Parliament. The power to amend the constitution also vests in Parliament. The constitution has provision for independence of judiciary, Comptroller and Auditor General, Public Service Commissions and the Chief Election Commissioner.

## The States And The Union Territories

India comprises 28 States and 7 Union Territories. The names of States are: Andhra Pradesh, Assam, Arunachal Pradesh, Bihar, Chhattisgarh, Goa, Gujarat, Haryana, Himachal Pradesh, Jammu and Kashmir, Jharkhand, Karnataka, Kerala, Madhya Pradesh, Maharashtra, Manipur, Meghalaya, Mizoram, Nagaland, Orissa, Punjab, Rajasthan, Sikkim, Tamil Nadu, Tripura, Uttar Pradesh, Uttarakhand and West Bengal. The Union Territories are: Andaman and Nicobar Islands, Chandigarh, Delhi, Dadra and Nagar Haveli, Daman and Diu, Lakshadweep, and Puducherry.

## Citizenship

The Constitution of India provides for a single and uniform citizenship for whole of India. Every person who was at the commencement of the Constitution (January 26, 1950), domiciled in the territory of India and: (i) who was born in the territory of India or (ii) either of whose parents was born in the territory of India, or (iii) who has been ordinarily resident in the territory of India for not less than five years immediately preceding such commencement, shall be a citizen of India. The Citizenship Act, 1955 provides for acquisition and termination of citizenship after the commencement of constitution.

## Fundamental Rights

The Constitution offers all citizens, individually and collectively some basic freedoms. These are guaranteed in the constitution in the form of broad categories of Fundamental Rights which are justiciable. Article 12 to 35 contained in Part III of the constitution deal with Fundamental Rights. These are: (i) Right to equality before law, prohibition of discrimination on grounds of religion, race, caste, sex, or place of birth and equality of opportunity in matters of employment, (ii) Right of freedom of speech and expression, assembly, association or union, movement, residence and the right to practise any profession or occupation (some of these rights are subject to the security of the state, friendly relations with foreign countries, public order, decency or morality), (iii) Right against exploitation, prohibiting all forms of forced labour, child labour, and traffic in human beings, (iv) Right to freedom of conscience and free profession, practice and propagation of religion, (v) Right of any section of citizens to conserve their culture, language or script and right of minorities to establish and administer educational institutions of their choice, and (vi) Right to constitutional remedies for enforcement of Fundamental Rights.

## Fundamental Duties

By the 42nd Amendment to the Constitution, adopted in

1976, Fundamental Duties of the citizens have also been enumerated. Article 51 'A' contained in Part IV A of the constitution deals with Fundamental Duties. These enjoin upon a citizen, among other things, to abide by the constitution, to cherish and follow noble ideals which inspired our national struggle for freedom, to defend the country and to render national service, when called upon to do so and to promote harmony and spirit of common brotherhood amongst all people of India, transcending religious, linguistic and regional or sectional diversities.

## Directive Principles of State Policy

The Constitution lays down certain Directive Principles of State Policy which though not justiciable are "fundamental in governance of the country" and it is the duty of the state to apply these principles in making laws. These lay down that the state shall strive to promote welfare of people by securing and protecting as effectively as it may, a social order in which justice—social, economic and political—shall inform all institutions of national life. The state shall direct its policy in such a manner as to secure the right of all men and women to, work, education and to public assistance in the event of unemployment, old age, sickness and disablement in other cases of undeserved want. The state shall also endeavour to secure to workers a living wage, humane conditions of work, a decent standard of life and full involvement of workers in the management of industries.

In economic sphere, the state is to direct its policy in such a manner as to secure distribution of ownership and control of material resources of community to subserve the common good and to ensure that operation of economic system does not result in concentration of wealth and means of production to common detriment.

Some of the other important directives relate to provision of opportunities and facilities for children to develop in a ̇nanner.

# 6. FUNCTIONS AND POWERS OF THE PARLIAMENT

Like other parliamentary democracies in the world, the Parliament of India has the cardinal functions of legislation, overseeing of administration, passing of budget, ventilation of public grievances and discussing various subjects like development plans, international relations and national policies. The distribution of powers between the Union and the States, followed as per the Constitution, emphasizes in many ways the general predominance of the Parliament in the legislative field. Apart from a wide range of subjects, even in normal times. Parliament can, under certain circumstances, assume legislative power, falling within the sphere exclusively reserved for the states. Parliament is also vested with powers to impeach the President and the judges of the Supreme Court and High Courts, the Chief Election Commissioner and Comptroller and Auditor General in accordance with procedure laid down in the Constitution.

All legislation requires consent of both the Houses of Parliament. In the case of money bills, however, the will of the Lok Sabha prevails. Delegated legislation is also subject to review and control by Parliament. Besides the power to legislate, the constitution vests in Parliament the power to initiate amendment of the constitution.

The functions of Parliament are not only varied in nature, but considerable in volume. The time at its disposal is limited. It cannot make very detailed scrutiny of all legislative and other matters that come up before it. A good deal of its business is, therefore, transacted in committees.

Both Houses of Parliament have a similar committee structure, with a few exceptions. Their appointment, terms of office, functions and procedure of conducting business, are also more or less, similar and are regulated under rules made by the two Houses under Article 118(1) of the Constitution.

Broadly, parliamentary committees are of two kinds— standing committees and ad hoc committees. The former are elected or appointed every year or periodically and their work goes on, more or less on a continuous basis. The latter are appointed on an ad hoc basis as need arises and they cease to exist as soon as they complete the work assigned to them.

**Standing Committees**: Among standing committees, three financial committees—Committee on Estimates, Public Accounts and Public Undertakings—constitute a distinct group and they keep an unremitting vigil on Government expenditure and performance. While members of the Rajya Sabha are associated with committees on Public Accounts and Public Undertakings, members of the Committee on Estimates are drawn entirely from the Lok Sabha.

The Estimates Committee reports on "what economies, improvements in organisation, efficiency or administrative reform consistent with policy underlying the estimates" may be effected. It also examines whether the money is well laid out within the policy limits implied in the estimates and suggests the form in which estimates shall be presented to the Parliament. The Public Accounts Committee scrutinises appropriation and finance accounts of Government and reports of the Comptroller and Auditor General. It ensures that public money is spent in accordance with Parliament's decision. It calls attention to cases of waste, extravagance, loss or nugatory expenditure. The Committee on Public Undertakings examines the reports of the Comptroller and Auditor General if any. It also examines whether Public Undertakings are being run efficiently and managed in accordance with sound business principles and prudent commercial practices. The control exercised by these committees is of a continuous nature. They gather information through questionnaires, memoranda from representative non-official organisations and knowledgeable individuals, on-the-spot studies of organisations and oral examination of non-official and official witnesses. Between themselves, the financial committees examine and ͟ a fairly large area of multifarious activities of the ͟ent of India.

Leaders of opposition in the Lok Sabha and the Rajya Sabha are accorded statutory recognition. Salaries and other suitable facilities are extended to them through a separate legislation which came into force on November 1, 1977.

Minister for Parliamentary Affairs is responsible for coordinating, planning, and arranging Government business in both Houses of Parliament. In the discharge of this function, his Ministry works under the overall direction of the Cabinet Committee on Parliamentary Affairs. The Minister for Parliamentary Affairs keeps close and constant contact with the Presiding Officers, the leaders as well as the chief whips and whips of various parties and groups. The Minister of Parliamentary Affairs also nominates Members of Parliamentary Committees, Councils, Boards and Commissions, etc. set up by the Government.

O O O

# 7. ADMINISTRATIVE SET-UP AT THE CENTRE TO RUN THE GOVERNMENT OF INDIA

The Government of India (Allocation of Business) Rules, 1961 continue to govern the administration of India. As per these rules, the President of India functions under Article 77 of the constitution of India. The ministries/departments of the Government of India have been created by the President on the advice of the Prime Minister under these rules. The business of the Government of India is transacted in the ministries/departments, secretariats and offices as per the distribution of subjects specified in these rules. Each of the Ministry is assigned to a Minister by the President on the advice of the Prime Minister. Each ministry/department is under the charge of a Secretary who works under the instructions of the Minister, whenever one is there, for his Ministry/Department.

The Cabinet Secretariat is responsible for secretarial assistance to the Cabinet, its committees and ad hoc groups of Ministers, and for maintenance of records of their decisions and proceedings. The Secretariat monitors implementation of the decisions/directions of the Cabinet/Cabinet committees/ groups of Ministers etc. The Secretariat is also responsible for the administration of the Government of India (Transaction of Business) Rules, 1961 and facilitates smooth transaction of business in ministries/departments of the government by ensuring adherence to these rules.

The Cabinet Secretariat ensures that the President, the Vice-President and ministers are kept informed of the major activities of all ministries/departments by means of monthly summary reports. Management of major crisis situations in the country and coordinating activities of various ministries in such a situation is also one of the functions of this Secretariat.

On 15th August, 1947, number of ministries at the Centre was 18. As on July 22, 1997, the Government of India consisted of the following ministries/departments:

1. Ministry of Agriculture—Department of Agricultural Research and Education, Department of Agriculture and Cooperation, and Department of Animal Husbandry and Dairying.

2. Ministry of Chemicals and Fertilizers—Department of Chemicals and Petro-Chemicals, Department of Fertilizers.

3. Ministry of Civil Aviation and Tourism—Department of Civil Aviation, Department of Tourism.

4. Ministry of Coal.

5. Ministry of Commerce, Department of Commerce, Department of Supply.

6. Ministry of Communications—Department of Posts, Department of Telecommunications.

7. Ministry of Defence—Department of Defence, Department of Defence Production, and Supplies, Department of Defence Research and Development.

8. Ministry of Environment and Forests.
9. Ministry of External Affairs.
10. Ministry of Finance—Department of Economic Affairs, Dept. of Expenditure, Dept. of Revenue, Dept. of Company Affairs.
11. Ministry of Food and Consumer Affairs—Dept. of Food and Civil Supplies, Dept. of Consumer Affairs, Dept. of Sugar and Edible Oils.
12. Ministry of Food Processing Industries.
13. Ministry of Health and Family Welfare—Dept. of Health, Dept. of Family Welfare, Dept. of Indian Systems of Medicines and Homeopathy.
14. Ministry of Home Affairs—Dept. of Internal Security, Dept. of States, Dept. of Official Language, Dept. of Home.
15. Ministry of Human Resource Development—Dept. of Education, Dept, of Youth Affairs, Dept. of Culture, Dept. of Women and Child Development.
16. Ministry of Industry—Dept. of Industrial Development, Dept. of Heavy Industry, Dept. of Public Enterprises, Dept. of Small Scale Industries and Agro and Rural Industries, Dept. of Industrial Policy and Promotion.
17. Ministry of Information and Broadcasting.
18. Ministry of Labour.
19. Ministry of Law and Justice—Dept. of Legal Affairs, Legislative Dept., Dept. of Justice.
20. Ministry of Mines.
21. Ministry of Non-Conventional Energy Sources.
22. Ministry of Personnel, Public Grievances and Pensions—Dept. of Personnel and Training, Dept. of Administrative Reforms and Public Grievances, Dept. of Pensions and Pensioners' Welfare.
23. Ministry of Parliamentary Affairs.
24. Ministry of Petroleum and Natural Gas.
25. Ministry of Planning and Programme Implementation Dept. of Planning, Dept. of Statistics, Dept. of Plan Implementation

26. Ministry of Power.
27. Ministry of Railways.
28. Ministry of Rural Areas and Employment—Dept. of Rural Development, Dept. of Wasteland Development, Dept. of Rural Employment and Poverty Alleviation.
29. Ministry of Science and Technology—Dept. of Science and Technology, Dept. of Scientific and Industrial Research, Dept. of Bio-technology.
30. Ministry of Steel.
31. Ministry of Surface Transport.
32. Ministry of Textiles.
33. Ministry of Urban Affairs and Employment—Dept. of Urban Development, Dept. of Urban Employment and Poverty Alleviation.
34. Ministry of Water Resources.
35. Ministry of Welfare.
36. Department of Atomic Energy.
37. Department of Electronics.
38. Department of Jammu and Kashmir Affairs.
39. Department of Ocean Development.
40. Department of Space.
41. Cabinet Secretariat.
42. President's Secretariat.
43. Prime Minister's Office.
44. Planning Commission.

○ ○ ○

# 8. Public Services (All India) In The Country

Before the country's independence, Indian Civil Service (ICS) was the seniormost amongst the Services of the British Crown in India. There was also the Indian Police Service. Although many of the Indian young men avoided to take the selective examination due to fear of involving themselves with the British administration, quite a large number found the ICS competitive examination as a sort of testimony of their extraordinary mental capability and in quite many cases Indians who went to London or Cambridge Universities for studies found it convenient to get themselves selected in the ICS, but later on rejected their appointment as a Deputy Collector to subsequently join the freedom struggle in India.

After independence, the government of free India also felt the need for the All India Service for maintaining the unity, integrity and stability of the nation. Accordingly, a provision was made in Article 312 of the Constitution for creation of one or more of the All India Services common to the Union and the States, Indian Administrative Service and Indian Police Service were, therefore, constituted by the Parliament in terms of Article 312 of the Constitution. After the promulgation of the new Constitution, a new All India Service competitive examination, namely Indian Administrative Service and Allied Services Examination was created to screen the selection of intellectual youth to serve the governmental institutions of the free nation. A common unique feature of the All India Services was that the members of these services were recruited by the Centre and their services were placed under various state cadres and they had the liability to serve both under the State besides under the Centre. This aspect of the All India Services tended to strengthen the unitary character of the Indian Federation.

Today and since then, the Ministry of Personnel, Public Grievances and Pensions is the controlling authority for the Indian Administrative Services. The recruitment to all the three services is made by the Union Public Service Commission (UPSC) through the Civil Services Examination conducted every year. These officers are recruited and trained by the Central Government and then alloted to different State cadres. There are at present 21 state cadres, including three joint cadres, namely (i) Assam and Meghalaya; (ii) Manipur and Tripura; and (iii) Arunachal Pradesh, Goa, Mizoram and the

Union Territories. The authorised cadre strength of Indian Administrative Services as on 1st January 1, 2008 was approx. 1,700 and the actual number of IAS officers in position was close to 13,000.

## Central Secretariat Services

The Central Secretariat has three services: (i) Central Secretariat Service (CSS), (ii) Central Secretariat Stenographers' Service (CSSS), and (iii) Central Secretariat Clerical Service (CSCS). The Section Officers' Grade and Assistants' Grade of CSS, Grade 'D', 'C' and 'A' and 'B' (merged) of CSSS and Grade I and II of CSSS were decentralised. The Grade of Principal Private Secretary of CSSS and selection grade, and Grade I of CSS were centralised. Appointments and promotions in the Centralised grade are made on all secretariat basis. In respect of the decentralised grades, Department of Personnel and Training monitors and assesses the overall requirements of different cadres for fixing zones of promotion against the vacancies in seniority quota and arranges centralised recruitment against direct recruitment. and departmental examination quota vacancies through open competitive and departmental examination.

## Union Public Service Commission

The Constitution provides for an independent body known as Union Public Service Commission (UPSC) for recruitment to Group 'A' and 'B' civil posts under central government and for advice in certain service matters. The Chairman and other members of the Commission are appointed by the President for tenure of six years or till they attain the age of 65 years. To ensure independence, members who were in government at the time of appointment are required to retire from government service on their appointment in the Commission. The Chairman and members are also not eligible for further employment under the government. They cannot be removed except for the reasons and in the manner provided for in the constitution. The annual report of the UPSC lays down details of each competitive examination held and other special appointments made by the UPSC.

### Staff Selection Commission

Staff Selection Commission initially known as the Subordinate Services Commission was set up in July 1976, primarily to make recruitment on zonal basis for non-technical Group 'C' posts under the Central Government except the posts for which recruitment is made by Railway Service Commission and the industrial establishment. The Commission has also been entrusted with making recruitment to Group 'B' services—Assistants' Grade and Stenographer's Grade 'C'. The Commission has a Chairman and two members. This Commission functions from its different regional centres.

Besides the above government recruitments through the UPSC, etc. better employment opportunities exist in the semi-official and non-governmental organisations.

O O O

# 9. THE SYSTEM OF GOVERNMENT IN STATES, UNION TERRITORIES, DISTRICTS AND VILLAGES

The system of government in the states closely resembles that of the Union. The state executive consists of Governor and Council of Ministers with Chief Minister as its head. Governor of a state is appointed by the President for a term of five years and holds office at his pleasure. Only citizens above 35 years of age are eligible for appointment to this office. The executive power is vested in Governor.

Council of Ministers with Chief Minister as head, aids and advises Governor in exercise of his functions or any of them in his discretion. For certain states in the northeast, namely Nagaland, Assam, Meghalaya, Tripura, Mizoram, etc. Governor has the special responsibility to strictly maintain law and order and take special care for their development plans in consultation with the Council of Ministers. This special responsibility is based on the provision of the Sixth Schedule in the Constitution in respect of tribal areas.

All Governors while discharging such constitutional functions as appointment of Chief Minister, or sending a report to the President about failure of constitutional machinery in a state or in respect of matters relating to the assent to a bill passed by the state legislature, exercise their own judgement.

Chief Minister is appointed by the Governor who also appoints other ministers on advice of Chief Ministers. Council of Ministers is collectively responsible to legislative assembly of the state. For every state, there is a legislature which consists of Governor and one or, two Houses as the case may be. In Bihar, Jammu and Kashmir, Karnataka, Maharashtra and Uttar Pradesh, there are two houses—one known as Legislative Assembly—and the other Legislative Council. In remaining states, there is only one House known as Legislative Assembly (Vidhan Sabha).

Legislative Council (Vidhan Parishad) in whichever state it exists, comprises not more than one-third of total number of members in the Legislative Assembly of the state and in no case less than 40 members. About one-third of members of the Council are elected by members of the Legislative Assembly from amongst persons who are not its members, one-third by electorates consisting of members of municipalities, district boards and other local boards in the state, one-twelfth by electorate consisting of persons who have been, at least for three years, engaged in teaching in educational institutions within the state not lower in standard than secondary school and a further one-twelfth by registered graduates of more than three years' standing. The remaining members are nominated by the Governor from among those who have distinguished themselves in literature, science, art, cooperative movement and social service. Legislative Councils are not subject to dissolution, but one third of their members retire every second year.

Legislative Assembly (Vidhan Sabha) of a state comprises not more than 500 and not less than 60 members (with the exception of Sikkim which has 32 members) chosen by direct election from territorial constituencies in the state. Demarcation of territorial constituencies is to be done in such a manner that the ratio of population of each constituency and number of seats allotted to it, as far as practicable, is the same throughout the state. Term of the Assembly is five years unless it is dissolved earlier.

State Legislature has exclusive powers over subjects enumerated in List II of the Seventh Schedule of the Constitution and concurrent powers over those enumerated in List III. Financial powers of the Legislature include authorisation of all expenditure, taxation and borrowing by the state government. Legislative Assembly alone has the power to originate money bills. Legislative Council can only make recommendations in respect of changes it considers necessary within a period of 14 days of the receipt of the money bills from Assembly. The Assembly can accept or reject these recommendations.

Governor of a state may reserve any bill for consideration of President. Bills relating to subjects like compulsory acquisition of property, measures affecting powers and position of High Courts and imposition of taxes on storage, distribution and sale of water or electricity in inter-state river or river valley development projects should necessarily be so reserved. No bills seeking to impose restrictions on inter-state trade can be introduced in a state legislature without prior sanction of President.

State legislatures apart from exercising usual power of financial control, use all normal parliamentary devices like questions, discussions, debates and adjournments and no-confidence motions and resolutions to keep a watch over day-to-day work of the executive. They also have committees on estimates and public accounts to ensure that grants sanctioned by legislature are properly utilized.

## Administration of Union Territories

Union Territories are administrated by President acting to such extent as he thinks fit, through an Administrator appointed by him. Administrator of Andaman and Nicobar Islands and Puducherry are designated as Lieutenant Governors while administrator of Chandigarh is designated as Chief Commissioner. Sometimes, however, the Governor of a neighbouring large state can be concurrently the Administrator of a Union Territory. The Administrator of Dadra and Nagar Haveli can be concurrently the Administrator of Daman and Diu. Union Territory of Puducherry has a legislative assembly which may make laws with respect to matters enumerated in List II or III in the Seventh Schedule of the Constitution. Some bills passed by the Puducherry assembly are required to be reserved, for consideration and assent of the President.

## Local Government

District Governments in India have their Municipalities or Municipal Corporations.

Historically, the former Presidency town of Madras had its Municipal Corporation in 1688 during the British regime. It was followed by Bombay and Calcutta in 1726. The Constitution of free India made detailed provision for ensuring protection of democracy in Parliament and in state legislatures but it did not make the local self-government in urban areas a clear-cut constitutional obligation. There is no specific reference to municipalities except the implicity in entry 5 of the State list, which places the subject of local, self-government as a responsibility of the states.

In order to provide for a common framework for urban bodies and help to strengthen the functioning of the bodies as effective democratic units of self-government, Parliament enacted the Constitution (74th Amendment) Act in 1992, relating to Municipalities. The Government of India notified on June 1, 1993, as the date from which the said act came into force. A new part IX-A relating to the municipalities was incorporated in the Constitution to provide for, among other things, constitution of three types of Municipalities to be called Nagar Panchayats for areas in transition from a rural area to urban area. Municipal Councils for smaller urban areas and Municipal Corporation for larger urban areas, fixed duration of Municipalities, appointment of state election commission, appointment of state finance commission and constitution of metropolitan and district planning committees. All states have set up their finance commissions. For conducting election to urban local bodies, all states and UTs have set up their election commissions. Election to municipal bodies have been completed in all States/UTs except Bihar and Puducherry where this matter is sub-judice.

**Panchayats**

Article 40 of the Constitution which enshrines one of the Directive Principles of State Policy lays down that the state shall take steps to organise village panchayats and endow them with such powers and authority as may be necessary to enable them to function as units of self-government. A new part (IX) relating to the panchayats has been inserted in the Constitution to provide for among other things. Gram Sabha in a village or group of villages. Reservation of seats for Scheduled Castes and Scheduled Tribes has been made in proportion to their population both for membership and chairpersons—holding of elections within six months in the event of supercession of any panchayat.

O O O

# 10. ELECTION COMMISSION—DUTIES AND RESPONSIBILITIES

Election Commission is an independent constitutional authority set up by the Government of India in pursuance of Article 324 (1) of the Constitution. Since its inception in 1950 and till October, 1989, the Commission functioned as a single-member body consisting of the Chief Election Commissioner. On October 16, 1989, the President appointed two more election commissioners on the eve of the general elections to the Lok Sabha held in November-December 1989. However, the said two commissioners ceased to hold office on January 1, 1990 when the posts of two election commissioners were abolished. Again on October 1, 1993, the President appointed two more election commissioners. The new law provided that the Chief Election Commissioner and the two election commissioners will enjoy equal powers and will receive equal salary, allowances, and other perquisites. The law further provided that in case of difference of opinion amongst the Chief Election Commissioner and/or two other election commissioners, the matter will be decided by the commission by a majority. The validity of the new law was challenged in the Supreme Court, where a bench consisting of five judges dismissed the petition and upheld the provisions of the above law by a unanimous judgement on July 14, 1995.

The Election Commission of India is responsible for superintendence, direction and control of preparation of rolls for and the conduct of elections to Parliament and state legislatures, and preparation of rolls for election to the offices of President and Vice-President of India.

Independence of Election Commission and its insulation from executive interference is ensured by a specific provision in Article 324(5) of the Constitution to the effect that the Chief Election Commissioner /shall not be removed from office except in like manner and on like grounds as a judge of the Supreme Court and conditions that Election Commissioners cannot be removed from office except on recommendation by the Chief Election Commissioner.

Plenary powers and superintendence, direction and control, of the preparation of electoral rolls and the conduct of elections vested in the Election Commission under Article 324 of the Constitution supplemented further by Acts of Parliament, namely, Representation of the People Act, 1951, Presidential and Vice Presidential Acts 1952, Government of Union

Territories Act 1963, Government of National Capital Territory Act, 1991 and the Rules and Orders made thereunder.

## Registration of Political Parties

Section 29 A of the Representation of the People's Act 1951 provides for registration of political parties by the Election Commission. A party registered with the Election Commission may be granted recognition of National or State Party on the fulfilment of certain criteria based on its poll performance. If a party fulfils the criteria for recognition under the election symbols (reservation and allotment) order, 1968 in four or more states, it is deemed to be a national party throughout India. In the case of a state party, a symbol is reserved for it in the state or states in which it is so recognised. Such reserved symbols are allotted to the candidates of the parties for which they are so reserved. As on July 1, 1997, 619 political parties were registered with the Election Commission. Out of them eight parties were recognised as National Parties and 38 parties as State Parties.

## Electoral System

The Election law has undergone some important changes with effect from August 1996 by the Representation of the People Act, 1996. Some of the important changes are:

(i)   Disqualification on convictions under the Prevention to insults to National Honour Act, 1971: Any conviction under Section 2 (offence of insulting the Indian National Flag or the Constitution of India) or Section 3 (offence of preventing singing of National Anthem) of the Prevention of Insults to National Honour Act, 1971 shall hereafter entail disqualification for contesting elections to Parliament and state legislatures for a period of six years from the date of such conviction.

(ii)  Increase in security deposits and number of proposers: The amount of security deposit which a candidate for election to the Lok Sabha or a State Legislative Assembly stands enhanced as a measure to check the multiplicity of non-serious candidates. In case of an election to the Lok Sabha or the State Vidhan Sabha, the deposit has been increased from Rs. 500 to Rs. 10,000 for the general candidate and from Rs. 250 to Rs. 5,000 for a candidate who is a member of the Scheduled Castes or Scheduled Tribes. In the case of elections to the State Legislative Assembly, the candidates are required to make a deposit of Rs. 5,000 if they are general candidates and Rs. 2,500 if they belong to a Scheduled Caste or Scheduled Tribe, instead of Rs. 250 and Rs. 125 respectively as was being previously deposited by them. The amended law further provided that the nomination of a candidate in a Parliamentary or Assembly constituency should be subscribed by ten electors of the constituency as proposers, if the candidate has not been set up by a recognised National or State party. In the case of a candidate set up by a recognised party only one proposer would be sufficient. Minimum interval between the last date for withdrawal and date of poll has been reduced to 14 days instead of 20 days.

(iii) There is a restriction on contesting election from more than two constituencies.

The President issued an ordinance on June 5, 1997, called the Presidential and Vice-Presidential Elections (Amendment) Ordinance, 1997, whereby the number of proposers and seconders for contesting election to the office of President of India was increased to 50 each in place of ten number of electors as proposers and seconders, and for contesting Vice-Presidential election, it was increased to 20 each in place of five. The amount of security deposit has also been increased to Rs. 15,000 in place of Rs. 2,500 for contesting election to the offices of President and Vice-President.

## Reservation of Seats

The 57th Amendment Act, 1987 provides for determination of seats reserved for Scheduled Tribes in Arunachal Pradesh,

Meghalaya, Mizoram, and Nagaland by amending Article 332 of the Constitution as follows: Arunachal Pradesh—59 out of 60, Meghalaya 55 out of 60, Mizoram 39 out of 40, Nagaland 55 out of 60.

The Election Commission has arranged for the use of electronic machines in the elections.

## General Elections So Far

The first general election on the basis of adult franchise was held in 1951-52. This was a simultaneous election both for the Lok Sabha and all state Legislative Assemblies (including Part A, B and C states).

Second general election held in 1957, shortly after reorganisation of states, was also a simultaneous election.

In the third general election in 1962, election to state assemblies in Kerala and Orissa became out of step with general election with the result that simultaneous election could not be held in these two states.

Fourth general election to the Lok Sabha was held in 1967, but simultaneous election could not be held in Nagaland and Puducherry.

The fifth general election was held in 1971. After 1967, election to most of the state assemblies were held earlier than normally due with the result that Orissa, Tamil Nadu, and West Bengal had simultaneous election to the Lok Sabha.

The sixth general election was held in 1977. Kerala was the only state where election to Legislative Assembly was held simultaneously with the Lok Sabha election.

When the seventh general election was held in January 1980, elections to constitute new assemblies were held simultaneously only in Manipur, Arunachal Pradesh, Goa, Daman and Diu and Puducherry.

Polling for eighth Lok Sabha elections was held in the last week of December 1984 in 20 States and nine Union Territories, except Assam and Punjab. Elections for assemblies of Tamil Nadu, Manipur, Arunachal Pradesh and Goa, Daman and Diu were also held simultaneously. The term of the eighth

Lok Sabha was due to end on January 14, 1990. But the Lok Sabha had been dissolved earlier.

Hence the election to the ninth Lok Sabha was held in the last week of November 1989. Simultaneous election was held for new assemblies in Andhra Pradesh, Goa, Karnataka, Sikkim and Uttar Pradesh. Election could not be held in Assam as its revision of polls had not been completed. The Ninth Lok Sabha did not serve its full term. The House was dissolved on March 12, 1991.

Elections to 511 seats of tenth Lok Sabha, except for 6 seats in Jammu & Kashmir and 13 seats in Punjab, were held on May 20 and June 6, 8, 12 and 15, 1991.

Elections were also held to the state assemblies of Assam, West Bengal, Uttar Pradesh, Haryana, Kerala, Tamil Nadu and Pondicherry. Bye-election to 15 Lok Sabha seats and 56 Assembly seats in 14 states was held on November 16, 1991. Election to the Lok Sabha and Assembly seats in Punjab was held on February 9. 1992.

Election to 11th Lok Sabha was held in April and May 1996, although the 10th Lok Sabha was due upto July 8, 1996.

Elections to the 13th Lok Sabha were held in 1999 when Atal Behari Vajpayee became the Prime Minister. Dr. Manmohan Singh headed the UPA government after the 2004 elections to the 14th Lok Sabha. The elections for 15th Lok Sabha were held in April and May 2009 in five phases. The UPA formed the government under Dr. Manmohan Singh.

O O O

# 11. India's Defence Preparedness

India's defence policy aims at promoting and sustaining durable peace in the sub-continent and equipping the defence forces adequately to safeguard aggression.

There are four strategic wings of India's defence forces: They are: Army, Navy, Air Force and Coast Guard.

## Army

In the army headquarters in New Delhi, the Chief of the Army Staff is assisted by the Vice Chief of the Army Staff and seven other Principal Staff Officers, namely, the two Deputy Chiefs of the Army Staff, Adjutant General, Quarter-Master General, Master-General of Ordnance, Military Secretary and Engineer-in-Chief.

The Army is organised into five Operational Commands, viz. Southern, Eastern, Western, Central and Northern Commands and one Training Command. Each Command is under a General Officer Commanding-in-Chief who holds the rank of Lieutenant General. General Officer Commanding-in-Chief commanding an operative command is the commander of demarcated geographical area and has both field and static formations under the command. The major field formations are Corps, Division and Brigade commanded by the General Officer of the rank of Lieutenant General, a General Officer Commanding of the rank of Major General and Brigadier, respectively. The major static formations are Area, Independent Sub-Area and Sub-Areas. An Area is commanded by a General Officer Commanding of the rank of Major General and an Independent Sub-Area by a Brigadier.

The Army consists of a number of arms and services. These are Armoured Corps, Regiment of Artillery, Corps of Air Defence Artillery, Army Aviation Corps, Corps of Engineers, Corps of Signals, Mechanised Infantry, Infantry, Army Service Corps, Military Nursing Service, Army Medical Corps, Army Dental Corps, Army Ordnance Corps. Corps of Electrical and Mechanical Engineers, Remount and Veterinary Corps, Military Farms Service, Army Education Corps, Intelligence Corps, Corps of Military Police, Judge Advocate General Department, Army Physical Training Corps, Pioneer Corps, Army Postal Service, Territorial Army, Defence Security Corps. In addition the Army has its own recruiting organisation, Record Offices, Depots, Boys Establishments and Selection Centres and Training Institutions.

## Navy

The Navy is responsible for defence and security of India's maritime interests and assets, both in times of war and peace. The Chief of the Naval Staff at the Naval headquarters, New Delhi, is assisted by four Principal Staff Officers, namely the Vice Chief of Naval Staff, Deputy Chief of Naval Staff, Chief of Personnel and Chief of Material.

The Navy has three commands, i.e. Western, Eastern and Southern with their headquarters located at Mumbai, Vishakhapatnam and Kochi respectively. Each command is headed by Flag Officer Commanding-in-Chief in the rank of Vice Admiral. Western Command and Eastern Command have under them operation fleets, i.e. Western and Eastern fleets comprising warships, submarines, aircraft and other support ships. The southern Naval Command is responsible for all training activities of the Indian Navy.

The Indian Navy is a well-balanced three dimensional force consisting of sophisticated missile-capable warships, aircraft carriers, minesweepers, advanced submarines, and the latest aircraft in its inventory. Many of the warships are of the indigenous design and have been constructed in Indian shipyards. These ships compare well with the ships of similar capability constructed by the advanced countries. The Naval forces are maintained and supported by modern dockyard facilities encompassing state-of-the-art technology. At present it has two major Naval bases at Mumbai and Vishakhapatnam.

## Coast Guard

The Coast Guard was established on February 1, 1977, and was constituted as an independent Armed force of the Union of India with the enactment of CG Act 1978 on August 18, 1978. As the youngest armed force of the Indian Union, the Coast Guard's broad charter of duties includes : (i) safety and protection of offshore installations and artificial islands; (ii) providing protection to fishermen in distress; (iii) protection of maritime environment; (iv) assisting customs in anti-smuggling operations; (v) enforcement of MIZ Act and (vi) safety of life and property at sea.

The general superintendence, direction, and control of the Coast Guard is exercised by the Director General Coast Guard under Ministry of Defence.

The entire coastline of India and the national maritime zones have been divided into three Coast Guard Regions, namely Western, Eastern and Andaman and Nicobar Islands, under the respective commanders of the regions. The Regional Headquarters are located at Mumbai, Chennai and Port Blair. The Coast Guard Regions are divided into eleven Coast Guard Districts based on our maritime states. There are five District Headquarters on the West Coast, namely Porbandar, Mumbai, Goa, New Mangalore and Cochin. Four on the East Coast are: Chennai, Vishakhapatnam, Paradip, and Haldia, and two District Headquarters in Andaman and Nicobar Islands are : Diglipur and Campbell Bay. In addition there are Coast Guard stations and Air Enclaves at various locations.

Beginning with two frigates and five Seaward Defence Boats (SDBs), the Coast Guard Service has made rapid progress during the last 20 years. The service has now developed into a full-fledged maritime organisation with nine Offshore Patrol Vessels (OPVs), one Advanced Offshore Patrol Vessel (AOPV), 21 Fast Patrol Vessels (FPVs), 15 Interceptor Boats (IBs), and ICs, 14 Dornier Aircrafts and 15 Chetak Helicopters. The second Advanced Offshore Vessel and one FPV have also been commissioned.

## Air Force

The Air Force is organised both on functional and geographical basis. There are five operational commands: Western Air Command, South Western Air Command, Central Air Command, Eastern Air Command, and Southern Air Command. In addition, Maintenance Command and Training Command are two functional commands.

At the Air Headquarters in New Delhi, the Chief of the Air Staff is assisted by the Vice Chief of Air Staff, Deputy Chief of Air Staff, Air Officer Incharge Personnel, Air Officer Incharge

Administration, Air Officer Incharge Maintenance, and Inspector General (Flight Safety and Inspection. Each of these Principal Staff Officers is assisted by Assistant Chiefs of the Air Staff.

The Air force has an array of modern aircraft on its inventory besides other high-tech electronic and support equipment. The aircraft fleet consists of fighter bombers, air superiority fighters, interceptors, transport and logistic aircraft and helicopters. The fighter force comprises MiG-21 variants, MiG-23s, MiG-25s, MiG-27s and Jaguars which represent the modern generation strike aircrafts. Older generation aircrafts like the Hunters and Canberras are presently used in training and ancillary transport. MiG-29s and Mirage-2000 are air defence aircraft of the present generation. The transport fleet consists of IL-76s, AN-32s, the indigenously produced HS-748, Dornier-228 which are manufactured under license by HAL and Boeing-737 which are used for VIP duties. While the IL-76s provide the Air Force with heavy lift capabilities, AN-32s and HS-48s are also used in training role besides performing air maintenance and communication duties. The helicopter fleet consists of Chetak, Cheetah, MI-8s, MI-17s and the heavy lift MI-26. All these aircraft are used for high altitude operations and provide logistic support to ground forces. Chetak, Cheetah helicopters manufactured by HAL for the Air Force, are also used for Anti Tank Guided Missile (ATGM) carriers, air borne Forward Air Controller (FAC) and for search and rescue operations. MI-8 helicopters are specially modified to undertake tasks in Antarctica. In addition, the force has been supplemented with MI-25 and MI-35 attack helicopters. HPT-32 and HJT-16 (Kiran) aircraft, both manufactured by HAL are used as basic and applied stage trainers respectively with Kiran being supplemented by Polish Iskara aircraft.

The first batch of women pilots was commissioned on December 17, 1994. Since then women pilots are serving in frontline Air Force transport and helicopter squadrons. Women officers are also serving in Technical, Administrative, Logistic, Education, and Medical branches. The first batch of women Air Traffic Controller and Fighter Controller/DATs was commissioned in May 1996. Thus, all branches of the IAF now have women serving in them.

Commissioned Ranks

Following are the commissioned ranks in the three services. Each rank is shown opposite to its equivalent in the other service:

| Army | Navy | Air Force |
| --- | --- | --- |
| General | Admiral | Air Chief Marshal |
| Lieutenant General | Vice Admiral | Air Marshal |
| Major General | Rear Admiral | Air Vice Marshal |
| Brigadier | Commodore | Air Commodore |
| Colonel | Captain | Group Captain |
| Lieutenant Colonel | Commander | Wing Commander |
| Major | Lieutenant Commander | Squadron Leader |
| Captain | Lieutenant | Flight Lieutenant |
| Lieutenant | Sub-Lieutenant | Flying Officer |
| Second Lieutenant | | Acting Pilot Officer |
| Sub-Lieutenant | | |

The Ordnance Factory Organisation is the largest departmental undertaking engaged primarily in the production of defence hardware for the armed forces and paramilitary/police forces. There are at present 39 Ordnance factories spread all over India. These operate quite a wide range of discipline, technologies and supply critical lethal as well as non-lethal stores for defence forces. The bulk production of 5.56 mm rifle has already been established in an ordnance factory and commenced from 1993-94. The development of light machine gun (LMG) is at its final stage and the bulk production is being planned. A 5.56 rifle with its sight has been developed and production stabilized. A steep rise in production has been achieved, variants, viz. 5.56 mm LMG and 5.56 carbine, are under user trials.

The factories are also producing bombs acquired by Air Force. Besides liquid fuel required for successful trials of Prithvi and Agni missiles, igniters and copper liners for the warheads were also supplied specially for the development of Prithvi Missile.

The production of Ajeya Tank (T-72), Sarath (BMP-11), Infantry combat vehicle is carried out at Heavy Vehicle Factory at Avadi and at Ordnance Factory, Medak, respectively. A sophisticated opto-electronic production unit has been set up at Dehradun to produce the opto-electronic fire control and night vision devices required for Ajeya tank (T-72-MI) and Sarath Vehicle (BMP-11).

Production of Main Battle Tank (MBT) "Arjun" which has now been accepted by the Army for use is also being taken up. To meet the Army's requirement of high calibre ammunition, a new Ordnance Factory is being set up in Bolangir district of Orissa.

As part of diversification efforts, Vehicles Factory, Jabalpur has taken up modification and upgradation of the 'Jonga' to cater to the civilian market.

## Defence Undertakings

There are eight public sector undertakings under the Department of Defence Production and Supplies. These are: Hindustan Aeronautics Limited (HAL), Bharat Electronics Limited (BEL), Bharat Earth Movers Limited (BEML), Mazagaon Dock Limited (MDL), Garden Reach Ship-builders and Engineers Limited (GRSEL), Goa Shipyard Limited (GSL), Bharat Dynamics Limited (BDL) and Mishra Dhatu Nigam Limited. (MIDHANI). The value of the production of the Defence Undertakings was nearly Rs. 15,000 crore in 2006-97.

## Research and Development

Defence Research and Development Organisation (DRDO)

was established in 1958 by amalgamating Defence Science Organisation and some of the Technical Development Establishments. A separate Department of Defence Research and Development was formed in 1980 which operates through network of 50 laboratories/establishments. The Department aims at self-reliance in critical technologies of relevance to national security. It formulates and executes programmes of scientific research, design and development leading to induction of state-of-the-art weapons, platforms and other equipment required by the Armed Forces. It functions under the control of Scientific Advisor to the Defence Minister and also the Secretary, Defence Research and Development.

DRDO has registered significant achievements in its various activities. The notable developmental successes of the Department include surface-to-surface missile Prithvi, the state-of-the-art main battle tank Arjun, flight simulators for aircraft, pilotless target aircraft PTA, balloon barrage system, parallel super computers PACE-PLUS, etc. The weapons and ammunition developed by the organisation and productionised by production agencies include Indian Field Gun, INSAS rifle 5.56 mm, chargeline mine-clearing for safe passage of vehicles in the battle-field, illuminating ammunition for enhancing night field fighting capability, cluster weapon system for FSAPDS-I05 mm and 125 mm FSAPDS ammunition. Multibarrel rocket system PINAKA is undergoing user trials. In the field of electronics and instrumentation, the significant developments are low level tracking radar Indra-I, Indra-II, for army and air force, lightweight Field artillery radar, battle-field surveillance radar, secondary surveillance radar, automatic electronic switch, avalanche victim detector, tidex, EW systems, night vision devices and secured telephone SECTEL. Installation and commissioning of facilities and equipment for fabrication of Galleum Arsenide warfare at Gaetec and artillery cambat command and control systems. Some of the development successes in the area of engineering systems are Bridge Layer Tank KARTIK, military bridging systems, various types of shelters, crash fire tenders, rapid intervention vehicle and state-of-the-art fire detection and suppression system for tanks, naval ships, missile launches and barbette areas.

In the field of naval systems and materials, the Organisation has developed advanced ship sonar system, marine accoustic researchship SAGARDHWANI under water anti-fouling paints, torpedoes, naval simulators, and jackal steels. Submarine sonar and weapon control system 'Panchendriya' is getting ready for harbour/sea trials. The indigenous light combat aircraft (LCA) was rolled out in the presence of Prime Minister on November 17, 1995. LCA got ready for maiden trials in 1997-98. The advanced technology aero engine Kaveri of LCA is undergoing multi test-bed trials. The Kaveri engine has been successfully tested for about 500 starting cycles. Remotely piloted vehicle FACON has successfully undergone 17 developmental flight trials. Integrated-Guided Missile Development programme (IGMDP) comprises four missile systems PRITHVI, surface-to-surface tactical battle field missile; and NAG third generation anti-tank missile. TRISHUL is getting ready for user trials. AKASH and Nag are in advanced stages of development. The programme also included successful development of re-entry technology demonstrator under project AGNI.

LCA and other high quality technological systems are being channelised to make available to common man bio-medical equipment at a fraction of prevailing price of imported systems. A Society of bio-medical technology has been formed for this purpose. Extra light weight floor reaction orthosis (FROs) for polio handicapped persons, cardiac stress analyser, cardiac pacemaker and cytoscan for early detection of cancer cells have been developed and the technology has been transferred to industry.

## 12. RECRUITMENT OF COMMISSIONED OFFICERS IN THE DEFENCE FORCES

Reecruitment to the Defence forces of India is open to all Indian nationals irrespective of caste, creed, community, religion and region. The entry to the officer cadres in the Armed Forces is primarily through the Union Public Service Commission. Only graduates are eligible to join the armed forces through an examination known as the Combined Defence Services Examination (CDSE) conducted by the UPSC twice a year. Candidates who qualify in the examination join the Indian Military Academy (IMA), the Air Force Academy, and the Naval Academy for pre-commission training. Individuals selected for Short Service Commission are trained in the Officers' Training Academy.

The candidates seeking a career in the Armed Forces after completion of 10+2 general education join the National Defence Academy (NDA). The UPSC holds the entrance examination twice a year for entry in the NDA. Candidates who qualify in this examination join the respective Service Academies, viz. the Indian Military Academy for the Army; the Air Force Academy for the Air Force; and the Naval Academy for the Navy, for their pre-commission training.

There is also direct entry of officers through the Service Selection Boards (SSBs) for the Army and the Navy and through the Air Force Selection Board for the Air Force, without any written examination by the UPSC. Candidates in the age group of 26 to 27 years with Engineering degree and post-graduates in specialised subject and age group of 20 to 27 years are eligible for interview by the respective Selection Boards/branches of the Armed Forces.

In July 1992, the Government approved a University Entry Scheme, initially for a period of three years, for induction of engineering students in their final year/pre-final years into the Army. This scheme is already operating in the Air Force and the Navy. Engineering students of various disciplines studying in the final/pre- final years in recognised universities/institutions are eligible for induction into the technical branches/services of the Army as short service commissioned officers with the rank of second lieutenant under this scheme. Their salary is paid in lump-sum on their joining the IMA for training on the successful completion of which they will be granted permanent commission in the army. An intake of 100 officers per year has been planned under this scheme.

With a view to mitigate the shortage of Technical Officers (Engineering) in the Army, the government also approved a Short Service Commission (Tech.) Entry Scheme.

This envisages recruitment of qualified technical graduates through the SSBs and their enrolment in the Officers' Training Academy (OTA), Chennai after medical tests for a 10-month course. At the end of the course, the successful candidates will receive Short Service Commission. Thereafter, they will be governed by the Rules applicable to the short service commissioned officers.

Recruitment of medical officers in the Armed Forces is done through two sources. All MBBS graduates passing out from the Armed Forces Medical College, Pune are granted Permanent Commission. Apart from this, post-graduates/ MBBS degree holders passing out from civilian medical colleges are selected through competitive examinations, on an all-India basis, conducted by the Director General of the Armed Forces Medical College, Pune, partly for grant of Regular Commission and partly for grant of Short Service Commission. The Government recently approved a scheme of induction of NCC 'C' certificate holders to SSC (NT) stream only, through SSB interview without passing UPSC (CDS) examination. This scheme will help in improving the intake in this entry.

A special Commissioned Officers' entry scheme has been inducted in the Army. Under this entry serving JCOs/NCOs/ ORs in the age group of 30-35 years, with an Army Senior School Certificate Pass (Class XI CBSE pattern) qualification, will be eligible for commission after screening/selection through SSB and a Medical Board.

The persons so commissioned will earn promotion up to the rank of Colonel. The officers will be employed in unit as platoon commanders/sub-unit commanders or equivalent appointments, etc. upto the rank of Major. They will retire at the age of 55 years, after serving about 20-25 years as officers. The scheme will not only improve the career prospects of existing JCOs/ NCOs/ORs but also help in making up the deficiencies in the army.

### Recruitment to Other Ranks in Army and Sailors in Navy

There are 12 Zonal Recruiting Offices (ZROs) and 58 Branch Recruiting Offices (BROs) in the country. In addition, there is an Independent Recruiting Office (IRO) at Delhi. In order to inform the potential candidates well in advance of the commencement of recruitment, extensive recruitment publicity is undertaken throughout the country, including in remote areas. Recruitment rules provide for relaxation in respect of educational qualifications and physical standards for the candidates from certain specified backward, remote and tribal regions to give them due representation in the Army. Certain physical standards for certain class/regiment/tribes and other categories have been laid down. Over and above relaxation in physicals are being provided to certain categories of candidates like candidates between 16 to 18 years of age group, national/state level sportsman and one son of a serving soldier, ex-servicemen and of war widows.

### Airmen

Recruitment of Airmen to the Indian Air Force is done through the Central Airmen Selection Board located at the Air Force Station, New Delhi. There are 13 Selection Centres under the Board. A Pilot Project has been undertaken for the direct recruitment of trained manpower from the civil streams in the trades, such as clerks, drivers, and Surveyor Automated Cartography. Besides direct recruitment of technically qualified civilian personnel as JCO (catering) has been introduced.

### Territorial Army

Territorial army is a voluntary part-time civilian force which plays a useful role in the defence of the country. It was raised in 1949 and since its inception, has rendered valuable service, both in times of war and during internal disturbances. The Territorial Army consists of departmental and non-departmental TA units. Departmental TA units are raised from amongst the employees of government departments and public sector undertakings. There are at present 27 departmental and 25 non-departmental TA units. The five ecological battalions are also part of the departmental TA units.

As a result of internal disturbances and terrorist activities in Jammu and Kashmir and other states, and the prevailing conditions along our northern, eastern and western borders, the Territorial Army has of late been called upon to play an active role in assisting the local army formations in these areas. As a result of these demands, all the 25 Infantry Battalions (Territorial Army) have been embodied since 1990-91 for varying periods. The five ecological battalions of TA (called Eco Task forces) have continued their excellent work of environmental upgradation of the degraded areas in Rajasthan, MP, UP, and Jammu & Kashmir. In consultation with Ministry of Environment and Forests, several steps aimed at reducing the cost of these Eco Task Forces, without lowering their output of efficiency, have been taken up. A proposal to reorganise 16 Infantry Battalions (TA) initiated by the TA Directorate, has been approved by the Ministry of Defence.

**National Cadet Corps**

The NCC was established on July 15, 1948. It has now emerged as the single largest structured youth movement in India. It has 1.16 million boys and girls in the senior and junior Divisions in the Army, Navy and Air Force wings. This strength covers 4% of eligible student population in the country. Director General NCC through 16 NCC Directorates spread across the country. There is a Central Advisory Committee for the NCC to provide overall policy guidelines. NCC has the motto: "Unity and Discipline".

○ ○ ○

# 13. MILITARY TRAINING INSTITUTIONS IN INDIA

Sainik Schools were established in the country under a scheme initiated by the Ministry of Defence in 1961. The aim was to prepare boys academically, physically, and mentally for entry into National Defence Academy (NDA). There are at present 18 Sainik Schools in the country, almost one in each state, except in Nagaland, Meghalaya, Tripura, Sikkim, Arunachal Pradesh, Mizoram, Jharkhand, Chhattisgarh, Uttarakhand and Goa. Boys from States and Union Territories which do not have a Sainik School of their own can be accommodated in the schools in the adjoining states. The schools are affiliated to the Central Board of Secondary Education and follow the 10+2 pattern, in science stream.

Admission is made to class VI on the basis of an all-India entrance examination held every year in February in which boys in the age group of 10-11 years are eligible to appear. From 1992-93 academic session lateral admission to class IX has also been started for which the boys have to be 13-14 years of age on July I of that year. Since its inception, over 10,000 boys from these schools have been selected for admission to the National Defence Academy, Naval Academy, Armed Forces Medical College, etc.

## National Defence Academy

The National Defence Academy (NDA), Khadakwasla, near Pune, is a joint services institution which imparts academic as well as service training. The NDA has been brought in step with the national education format of 10+2+3. The syllabus of the Academy was reviewed to meet these requirements and has been approved by the Jawaharlal Nehru University for the grant of B.A./B.Sc. degree at the time of passing out from the Academy. The first course commenced training on revised syllabi in January 1989. After passing out from the NDA, the cadets go to their respective service academies for further training before being commissioned as officers in the Armed forces. The present authorised training strength of the Army, Navy and Air Force cadets at the academy is 1,800. This includes cadets from Bhutan and other friendly countries.

## Indian Military Academy

The Indian Military Academy (IMA), Dehra Dun, caters for training of cadets for admission into the Army. Cadets join the Indian Military Academy as per the following modes of entry: (i) on passing from the NDA; (ii) on graduation from the Army Cadet College which is a wing of the IMA itself; (iii) Direct Entry Graduate cadets who join on qualifying the UPSC examination and the Services Selection Board; and (iv) Technical graduates and University Entry Scheme. The present authorised strength of trainees at the IMA is 1,200 which includes cadets from Bhutan, Sri Lanka, Maldives, Mauritius and Nepal. The authorised training strength of Army Cadet College is 450.

## Officers Training Academy

The Officers Training Academy (OTA), Chennai, imparts pre-commission training for the following type of courses: (i) Short Service Commission Course of 44 weeks for university graduates who qualify in the UPSC examination; (ii) Course of six months for lady cadets (Women's Special Entry Scheme); (iii) Permanent Commission on Special list (PC) (SL) to selected service candidates, who qualify after a training of four weeks; and (iv) Regimental Commission Course for selected Service candidates, who qualify after a training of 13 weeks duration. Authorised training strength of the Academy is 500. So far only 520 lady cadets have been granted Short Service Commission.

Education on public school lines is imparted at the Rashtriya Indian Military College (RIMC), Dehra Dun, principally for the boys who subsequently desire to join the NDA with a view to obtaining a commission in the Armed Forces. The College runs classes from eighth to 10+2 class. Selection for the RIMC is through a written examination-cum-viva conducted through the state governments. Seats for the respective states are reserved based on population. Intake into the RIMC is bi-annual.

## National Defence College

Inaugurated by Jawaharlal Nehru in 1960, the National Defence College is an inter-service organisation functioning under the Ministry of Defence. The NDC is the highest defence training institution in India, imparting instructions on all elements of national security and strategy to officers due to become Major Generals and equivalent and attain similar status in the Civil Services. The head of the college is the Commandant, with six faculty members each (Senior Directing Staff) from the Army, Navy, Air Force, IAS and IFS.

## Army Cadet College

Army Cadet College is a wing of IMA which caters for the training of services cadets selected for Commission. The academic format is similar to the NDA on the lines of 10+2+3 and the syllabus is common. On the completion of the course these cadets also qualify for a BA/BSc degree recognised by the Jawaharlal Nehru University. After passing out from the ACC Wing, cadets join regular course of IMA for training of one year before being commissioned as officers of the Indian Army.

Army School of Physical Training (ASPT) established at Pune in 1947 is the cradle of physical and recreational training in the Army. It a training infrastructure which is second to none in the country to impart systematic and comprehensive instruction on physical training. Selected ranks in the army, students from the police, para military forces and friendly foreign countries attend various courses on physical training and allied subjects at ASPT.

○ ○ ○

# 14. Government's Role In Encouraging And Preserving Indian Culture

Despite numerous onslaughts against the Indian culture through long centuries, its beauty and strength have permeated, survived, and it is continuing to flourish its basic charm in every field. The Indian culture, like any good culture, has assimilated the good points of both Islamic and Christian cultures.

During the British rule, it was the tendency of the British Administrators to try to highlight and encourage the different approaches to culture, instead of discovering and encouraging similarities in the cultures of Hindus and Muslims. Still there is so much common in the two cultures with history having brought together the styles of original Hindu culture to merge with the styles of Islamic culture with passage of time.

Since independence, the Government of India has taken keen interest in preserving, promoting and dissemination of art and culture. There is a separate Department of Culture in the Ministry of Human Resources Development which tries to develop ways and means by which the basic cultural and aesthetic values and perceptions remain active and dynamic among the people. It also undertakes programmes of encouraging and disseminating various cultural values through cultural activities.

To promote and propagate understanding of Indian art, the Government of India established Lalit Kala Akademi (National Academy of Fine Arts) at New Delhi in 1954. To decentralise the activities, the Akademi has opened its regional centres in Lucknow, Kolkata, Chennai, Mumbai and Bhubaneshwar. The name of the regional offices was Rashtriya Lalit Kala Kendra. The Akademi also set up Community Artists Studio Complex with workshop facilities in painting, sculpture, print-making and Ceramics in Garhi Village in New Delhi. Similar workshops and all regional centres were headed by experts capable of giving technical guidance in these disciplines.

Since its inception, the Akademi has organised several national exhibitions of contemporary Indian Art with 10 national awards, each of Rs. 25,000. Three to four special exhibitions every year are organised with some concept involving known and eminent artists of India. Every three years the Akademi organises Triennale India—the most significant exhibition of contemporary art. The Akademi also organises a Rashtriya Kala Mela (National Art Fair) where artists from all over India present their work.

The Akademi honours eminent artists and art historians every year by electing them as fellows of the Akademi. To propagate Indian art outside India, the Akademi participates in the International Biennales and Triennales abroad and also organises exhibitions of works of art from other countries. To foster contacts with artists from outside, it sponsors exchange of artists with other countries under the various Cultural Exchange Programmes and Agreements of the Government of India.

The Lalit Kala Akademi accords recognition to art institutions/associations and extends financial assistance to these bodies as well as state akademis every year. It also gives scholarship to deserving young artists of its regional centres. Under its publication programme, the Akademi brings out monographs on the works of contemporary artists in Hindi and English and books on contemporary, traditional folk and tribal arts authored by eminent writers and art critics. The Akademi also brings out bi-annual art journals, Lalit Kala Contemporary English, Lalit Kala Ancient English and Samakaleen Kala (Hindi). Apart from these, it brings out in large size multicoloured reproductions of contemporary paintings and graphs from time to time.

The Akademi has started a regular programme on research and documentation. Scholars are given financial assistance to undertake projects in contemporary folk, tribal and traditional arts. It has set up an Artists Aid Fund to give financial assistance to ailing artists and other artists who may be in penury.

## Performing Arts

**Music:** The main schools of classical music—Hindustani and Carnatak—continue to survive through oral tradition being passed on by teachers to disciples. This has led to the existence of family traditions called gharanas and sampradayas. The use of classical music as a part of India's culture and used quite often in films is quite popular. It is universally agreed to be the world's best

**Dance:** Dance in India has an unbroken tradition of over 2000 years. Its themes are derived from mythology, legends and classical literature, two main divisions being classical and folk. Classical dance forms are based on ancient dance discipline and have rigid rules of presentation. Important among them are Bharat Natyam, Kathakali, Kathak, Manipuri, Kuchipudi and Odissi. All these forms have become popular enough to be called All-India.

Both classical and folk dances are popular among dance lovers. Their use in pictures produced in Mumbai is somewhat declining. However, the Sangeet Natak Akademi is helping to sustain the classical dance by giving financial assistance to cultural institutions and award fellowships to scholars, performers and teachers so as to promote advanced study and training in different forms of dance and music.

**Theatre:** Theatre in India is as old as her music and dance. Classical theatre survives only in some places. Folk theatre can be seen in its regional variants practically in every region. There are also professional theatres, mainly city-oriented. Besides, India has a rich tradition of puppet theatre, prevalent forms being puppets, glove puppets, rod puppets and leather puppets (shadow theatre). There are several semi-professional and amateur theatre groups involved in theatre plays in Indian languages and English.

**Sangeet Natak Akademi:** Sangeet Natak Academi, the national academy of music, dance and drama, was established in 1953 to promote performing arts in collaboration with states and voluntary organisations. It seeks increased public appreciation of these art forms through sponsorship, research and dissemination. It holds seminars and festivals, presents awards to outstanding performing artists, gives financial assistance for theatre productions, extends financial help to traditional teachers and grants scholarship to students. It operates a scheme of inter-state exchange of troupes to promote national and cultural integration through regional festivals and bringing rare art forms of the region to the fore.

The Akademi has set up a special unit for surveying and documenting various theatrical, musical, and dance forms in the country. Its disk and tape unit has the largest collection of Indian classical, folk and tribal music, dance and theatre items. The Sangeet Natak Akademi runs two zonal institutions for training in dance, Kathak Kendra, New Delhi and Jawaharlal Manipur Dance Academy, Imphal. It took over the Rabindra Rangshala as the third unit in 1993. It gives subsidy for publication of books in various Indian languages and English on music, dance and drama and confers awards and fellowships to distinguished artists and scholars.

**National School of Drama:** The National School of Drama (NSD)—one of the foremost theatre training institutions in the world and the only one of its kind in India was set up by the Sangeet Natak Academi in 1959. Later in 1975, it became an autonomous organisation, financed entirely by the Department of Culture, Ministry of Human Resources Development.

NSD has produced a galaxy of talents—actors, directors, script writers, designers, technicians, educationists who work not only in theatre but in film and television also—winning several awards, national and international. The training in the School is based on a thorough comprehensive, carefully planned syllabus. The systematic study and practical performing experience of Sanskrit drama, modern Indian drama, traditional Indian theatre forms, Asian drama and Western drama give the students a solid ground and a wide perspective in the art of theatre.

Rediscovery of ancient and medieval Indian literature and development of modem literature in major Indian languages and English mark literary activities of present-day India. A large number of literary periodicals and magazines, literary institutions and All India Radio have given impetus to the growth of modem Indian literature.

**Sahitya Akademi:** The Sahitya Akademi was established by the Government of India on March 12, 1954, as a national organisation to work actively for the development of Indian letters and to set high literary standards, to foster and coordinate literary activities in all the Indian languages, to promote through them, the cultural unity of the country. The Akademi has an extensive publication programme policy to carry out its work. With its headquarters at New Delhi, the Akademi has three regional centres at Mumbai, Bangalore and Kolkata and one office at Chennai. Every year since its inception, the Sahitya Akademi has presented awards to the most outstanding book of literary merit published in any of the twenty-two. Indian languages recognised by it. It has also instituted prizes in literary translation.

During 2007-08, Sahitya Akademi awarded Fellowships to many eminent men of letters, the highest honour conferred by the Akademi. During the same period, over 300 titles were published besides ten issues of Indian Literature, seven of Samakaleena Bharatiya Sahitya and two issues of Sanskrit Pratibha.

O O O

# 15. Science And Technology Infrastructure In India

India has had a long and distinguished tradition in science from ancient times. And great achievements have been made during the 20th century. At the time of Independence, India's scientific and technological infrastructure was neither strong nor organised in comparison with that of the developed world. Before

Independence the country was technologically dependent on skills and expertise available in the west. In the last five decades, an infrastructure and capability largely commensurate with meeting national needs has been minimising our dependence on other countries. A large range of industries from small to the most sophisticated have been established covering wide range of utilities, services and goods. There is now a large reservoir of expertise well acquainted with the most modern advances in basic and applied sciences. India is now fully equipped to enable us to make choices between available technologies and provide a framework for future national development.

Scientific and technological activities in India can be classified into the following: (i) Central Government, (ii) State Government, (iii) Higher educational sector, (iv) Public and Private sector, and (v) on-profit institutions/associations. These institutional structures, with their research laboratories, are the main contributors to research and development in the country. These are the Council of Scientific and Industrial Research, Indian Council of Agricultural Research, Indian Council of Medical Research, besides departmental laboratories of various Departments and Ministries, viz. Department of Atomic Energy, Department of Electronics, Department of Space, Department of Ocean Development, Defence Research and Development Organisation, Ministry of environment and Forests, Ministry of Non-Conventional Energy Sources and the Ministry of Science and Technology. In addition, there are about 1,200 in-house research and development units in industrial undertakings supporting research in their respective industries. Agricultural universities with their research stations have been set up under the state governments.

In 1983, the Ministry of Science and Technology drafted Technology Policy Statement with the basic objective of developing indigenous technology and ensuring absorption and adaptation of imported technology appropriate to national priorities and availability of resources. It is aimed at attaining technical competence and self-reliance, reducing vulnerability, particularly in strategic and critical areas and making use of indigenous resources. The TPS also aims at using traditional skills and capabilities making them commercially competitive. Several other measures through technology intervention are envisaged to optimise demand on energy and ensure harmony with the environment. With a view to strengthening the economy, structural reforms have been introduced through adoption of a new industrial policy of delicencing which will have an important bearing on the programmes of development pertaining to science and technology.

Department of Science and Technology set up in 1971, has evolved policy statements and guidelines, provided mechanism of coordination in areas of science and technology in which a number of institutions and departments have interests and capabilities, supported grants-in-aid to scientific research institutions and professional bodies. By the very nature of the activities of the Department, it has to play a catalytic and coordinating role and in this process over the past few years the efforts at promoting science and technology in the states and union territories have also gathered considerable momentum.

The Department of Science and Technology has been playing a critical role in identifying and promoting front-line and priority areas on research and development in various disciplines of science and engineering. This support is provided through Science and Engineering Research Council (SERC), which is an advisory body consisting of eminent scientists and technologists drawn from academic institutions like IITs, universities and national laboratories as well as industry. The Council through its advisory committees, expert committees assists the Department not only in peer reviewing of the proposals but also identifies newer and inter-disciplinary areas of R&D for concerted efforts. The Council with the help of advisory committees, also monitors progress of individual projects sponsored in various disciplines along with monitoring the progress of coordinated and concerted efforts. Every year about 1,000 project proposals are received for consideration in the Department, most of which fall in the category of basic sciences and engineering research.

The Department also supports programmes for setting up of national facility in the form of unit or a core group under the scheme of Intensification of Research in High Priority Areas. Some of the areas include Nonmaterial and Carbon Chemistry, Satellite Research Programme in Plasma Physics, Non-linear Dynamics, Liquid Crystals, Laser Processing of Materials, Mathematical Sciences, Ultrafast Processes, etc. In addition, several national facilities have been set up to cater to the needs of scientific community for undertaking research in advanced areas. These facilities include single crystal X-ray Diffractometer, Geotechnical Centrifuge, High field FINMR, Confocal Scanning fluorescence Microscope, AMS facility. Magneto Telluric facility, etc.

In order to promote R&D activities in the country, the Department also has the responsibility to strengthen the basic infrastructure for research by providing instruments to the scientific community. Regional Sophisticated Instrumentation Centres (RSICs) have been set up to cater to the need of the scientists in that particular region. Besides this, special opportunities are provided to the scientists, such as national and international fellowships, summer and winter schools for training particularly to encourage young scientists for pursuing research career, etc. About 100 scientists are supported every year.

As part of the Technology Development Promotion Programmes, the Department has initiated specific technology missions which develop the product sub-systems/systems such as biology pest control, biofertilizer and aquaculture in the Department of Bio-technology, parallel computing new materials, selected retrofit automation, air navigation system, micro-electronics and phonics in the Department of Electronics; leather and clean coal technologies in the Council of Scientific and Industrial Research. Four initiatives launched by the Department are: advances composites, fly ash disposal and utilization, seismicity and sugar production technologies.

As per the 1983 Technology Statement Implementation Committee's recommendations, the Department has set up an autonomous body, called Technology Information, Forecasting and Assessment Council (TIFAC). The main objectives of Tifac include generation of Technology Forecasting (TF) and Technology Assessment (TA) and Technomarket Survey (TMS) documents and enabling a Technology Information system. These studies have been carried out in a number of areas of human settlement planning/Building Technology and skills, sugar industry, steel, materials technology, automated machinery and production systems, foundary modernisation, energy, high volume industrial gases, prospects for biotechnology products in India by 2000 AD in health and agricultural sectors, fertilizers—a relook and comprehensive picture of Science and Technology status in India. Tifac has taken new initiatives in surface engineering, high performance computational facilities, etc. The major milestones of Tifac's implementation efforts are the technology projects on a Mission Mode approved by the government of India for sugar production technologies, advanced composites and flyash disposal and utilization.

A significant activity being pursued by TIFAC is promotion of specific Home Grown Technologies which are expected to strengthen the linkages between research institutions and industry by commercialisation of technologies developed indigenously. Already about 20 projects are under implementation. These are in the areas of CFC substitute, co-based chemicals, Vitamin-A, 64-bit parallel computer (flosover), high energy rare earth magnets, cobalt recovery, etc.

A recent achievement of Tifac is the generation of Long Term Technology Forecast Reports (also known as Technology Vision 2020). These reports cover sixteen technology areas viz., Agro-Food Processing, Civil Aviation, Electric power, Waterways, Road Transportation, Food and Agriculture, Health Care, Life Sciences and Biotechnology, Advanced censors. Engineering Industries, Materials and Processing,

Services, Strategic industries, Electronics and Communication, Telecommunications. In addition, one report deals with Driving Forces. More than 5,000 specialists from various disciplines participated in this mega exercise.

The Department of Science and Technology also provides support for the National Superconductivity Programme (NSP), a nationally coordinated programme of three government departments/agencies, namely, Department of Atomic Energy, Department of S&T and Council of Scientific and Industrial Research, under the aegis of the National Superconductivity Programme and Technology Board. In the second phase of NSP 55 R&D projects were supported at 36 institutions during the period October 1988 to September 1995.

## Technology Development Board

The Government of India has been collecting a Cess under the Research and Development Cess Act, 1986 at the rate of 5% on all payments made by the industrial concerns towards import of technologies. Out of the Cess collection, the Government was making funds available to the Industrial Development of India for forming a venture Capital fund. In February 1994, the Government decided to credit the Cess into a new fund for Technology Development and Application to be placed at the disposal of the Department of S&T. The Technology Development Board was constituted in September 1996 to provide financial assistance to industrial concerns and other agencies for attempting development and commercial application of indigenously or adapting imported technology to wider domestic application. The government offered Rs. 100 crore into the Technology Fund in 2007-08.

## Nuclear Power Programme

The DAE has been pursuing a 3-stage Nuclear Power Programme. Its first stage comprises setting up of pressurised heavy water reactors (PHWRs) and associated fuel cycle facilities; the second stage envisages setting up of fast breeder reactors (FBRs) backed by reprocessing plants and plutonium-based fuel fabrication plants; the third stage will be based on the thorium-233 cycle. Uranium-233 is obtained by irradiation of thorium.

The Nuclear Power Corporation of India Ltd., (NPCIL), a public sector undertaking of DAE, is responsible for the design, construction and operation of nuclear power reactors. Presently the Company is operating 14 reactors (2 boiling water reactors and 12 pressurised heavy water reactors) with a total capacity of 2770 MWe. TAPP-4 of 540 MWe capacity was commissioned and connected to the grid in June 2005. It is also constructing 5 PHWRs and 2 light water reactors. After the completion of these reactors, the total installed capacity will become 6730 MWe.

The Indira Gandhi Centre for Atomic Research (IGCAR) is engaged in the design and development of liquid sodium cooled fast breeder reactors, has successfully developed the FBR technology and has commenced construction of a 500 MWe Prototype Fast Breeder Reactor (PFBR). For implementation of this project, a new company BHAVINI, that relies on IGCAR for expertise in technology and NPCIL for expertise in project management, has been formed.

For thorium utilisation and demonstrating advanced safety concepts, development of 300 Mwe Advanced Heavy Water Reactor (AHWR) has been going on at BARC Advanced thorium based systems can be set up on commercial scale only after a large capacity, based on fast breeder reactors, is built up.

## Indian IT Industry

Indian Information Technology (IT) and IT enabled services (ITES-BPO) continue to chart remarkable growth. The ITES-BPO sector has become the biggest employment generator amongst young college graduates with the number of jobs almost doubling each year. The number of professionals employed in India by IT and ITES sectors is estimated at over 15 lac. The increased attractiveness of India as an investment destination in IT has led to the reversal of the brain drain-people of Indian origin who went to pursue careers abroad are now attracted to work in India.

## Biotechnology for Societal Development

Demonstration and training programmes on proven and field-tested technologies were continued. The projects implemented could help in increasing skills and income of SC/ST people, rural folk and women trough product and process development and employment generation and improvement of their health status. More than 75,000 people have been benefited through 145 ongoing projects on cultivation of aromatic and medicinal plants, mushroom, biological control of plant pests and diseases, biofuel, plant tissue culture/vanilla, solid waste management, vermicomposting, biofertilizers, aquaculture, seaweed cultivation, floriculture, horticulture, poultry farming, human healthcare, organic farming, sericulture, animal husbandry and preparation of biocrafts. This year 50 new proposals were funded.

## Food Biotechnology

Entrepreneurs meet for technology transfer of high protein biscuits containing 14 per cent protein with high protein digestibility was held and negotiations are in process for getting the technology transferred. Validation of PCR and ELISA assays developed to detect transgenic traits in genetically modified foods is being carried out in five laboratories. Process for production of astaxanthin from green alga *Haematococcus phuvialis* has been perfected. Indivgenous edible mushrooms from triba, forest and Himalayan belts are being explored for their nutraceutical potential. Programmes on assessing the magnitude of zinc deficiency amongst children and management package of diarrhoea have been initiated. Initiatives have ,been taken for development of ready to eat precooked nutritionally fortified food(s) for school going children in consultation with concerned state government departments.

## Microbial and Industrial Biotechnology

Programmes were implemented to develop novel products and processes and to generate R&D leads for utilization by various biotech industries. Gibberellic acid production at a rate of 10mg/l/h has been achieved from a selected Gibberella fukuroi mutant at NCL, Pune in 10 litre fermenter between 48 and 72 h of fermentation time. Work is in progress towards development of process for mass production of targeted delivery of antigens through nanoparticles using sendai virus system at University of Delhi South Campus, New Delhi. The entrapment of ovalbumin in hydrogel nanoparticles made up of cross linked polyvinyl pyrrolidone has been standardized. CFTRI, Mysore is working on production of lip oxygenase and human platelet aggregation inhibitor through fungal fermentation. At JNU, New Delhi, recombinant asparagine has been purified directly from the culture medium using a rapid two-step purification strategy which resulted in a recovery of 70 per cent and a specific activity of 80 per cent of that of the native enzyme. NCL, Pune is working towards assessing effectiveness of cellulase treatment in bio-finishing of desnimat a pilot scale, in collaboration with A TIRA, Ahmedabad. A solvent tolerant strain of *Pseudomonas aeroginosa* isolated at IIT, New Delhi produces extracellular protease and lipase, both exceptionally stable in presence of wide range of organic solvents at high concentrations. The pilot scale reactor for a novel high cell density process for dairy waste water treatment has been designed d fabricated at IIT, New Delhi and installed in the premises of DMS, New Delhi.

# 16. Research And Development In Indian Industry

With the establishment of the Indian Council of Scientific and Industrial Research, which had Research and Development by

Industry (RDI) as one of its first schemes, the Council's undertaking numerous activities in the field of industrial research provided a strong technological infrastructure to industry in the country. The Council's activities covered a chain of national laboratories, specialised centres, various R&D and academic institutions and training centres. A scheme for granting recognition to in-house R&D units in industry operated by the Department of Scientific and Industrial Research was initiated.

The incentives and support measures made available to recognised in-house R&D units in industry were: (i) Income Tax relief on R&D expenditure, (ii) Weighted Tax Deduction for sponsored research, (iii) Customs Duty exemption on goods imported for use in government-funded R&D projects, (iv) Duty Waiver for three years on goods produced on indigenously based developed technologies and duly patented in any of the countries in European Union, USA, Japan, (v) Accelerated Depreciation Allowance on plant and ,machinery based on indigenous technology, (vi) Exemption from price control for bulk drugs produced based on indigenous technology, (vii) Financial support for R&D programmes, (viii) National Awards for outstanding in-house R&D achievements, and other indirect benefits. DSIR is the nodal department for granting recognition to in-house R&D centres.

There were 1786 units having valid recognition on December 31, 2007. Twelve industrial houses received National awards in 2007. Eighteen certificates involving over Rs. 1590 million rupees as cost of plant and machinery based on indigenous technology were issued by the council.

Programme Aimed at Technological Self-Reliance (PATSER) has a scheme which provides on a selective basis partial financial support to Research, Development, Design and Engineering (RODE) projects in the areas of (i) development and demonstration of new or improved product and process technologies, including those for specialised capital goods, for both domestic and export markets, and (ii) absorption and upgradation of imported technology. Under the PATSER programmes, the Department of Scientific and Industrial Research has provided partial financial support to about 80 industrial units.

The Scheme to Enhance the Efficacy of Transfer of Technology (SEETOT) covers the National Register of Foreign Collaborations (NRFC) and Transfer and Trading in Technology (TATT) and Promotion and Support to Consultancy Services (PSCS).

The objective of NRFC scheme is to gainfully facilitate acquisition of technology needed in the country. Major activities include: compilation and analysis of data on approved foreign collaborations; undertaking financial, economic and legal analysis of set of data on foreign collaborations; carrying out technology status studies covering the state-of-the-art technology in use in the country, international trends and other related issues; providing assistance in the effective transfer of technology process.

The TATT scheme aims to promote and support activities towards export of technologies, projects and services. The measures included: support to preparation of reports related to technology export capabilities and experience in select industrial sectors; publicity and dissemination of Indian capabilities through workshops, trade fairs, delegation and video films; and supporting demonstrations of technologies identified for export.

The scheme relating to Promotion and Support to Consultancy Services (PSCS) essentially aims to strengthen consulting capabilities for domestic and export markets. The activities have been mainly towards completing the on-going studies towards documenting consultancy needs and capabilities in important industrial sectors at state levels and providing institutional and programme support to Consultancy Development Centre (CDC). The CDC became a non-profit society, with a view to implementing some of the programmes of DSIR and promote and strengthen the consultancy capabilities in the country. It is not to undertake any commercial activity itself but earn revenues to the extent possible, through specialised programmes and activities. DSIR is providing recurring and non-recurring support to CDC.

O O O

# 17. IRS AND PSLV SYSTEMS IN INDIA

Indian Space Programme was officially started in India in 1972 with the setting up of the Space Commission and the Department of Space (DOS) to promote development and application of space technology, specially in the areas of telecommunication, and television broadcasting, meteorology resources survey and management. Development of satellites, launch vehicles and associated ground systems is integral to the space programme objectives.

The Indian National Satellite System (INSAT) is a multi-purpose satellite system for telecommunications, meteorological observations and data relay, television broadcasting and radio and television programme distribution. It is a joint venture of the Department of Space, Department of Telecommunications, India Meteorological Department, All India Radio, and Doordarshan. Department of Space has direct responsibility for operation and of INSAT space segment.

INSAT system was established in 1983 with the commissioning of INSAT IE. At present the system is served by the last of the first generation INSAT-ID launched in 1991, and four ISRO-built second generation satellites, INSAT-2A, INSAT-2B, INSAT-2C and INSAT-2D launched in July 1992, July 1993, December,1995 and June 1997 respectively. One more satellite in the INSAT-2E series was scheduled for launch in 1998. The successful launch of INSAT-4A, the heaviest and the most powerful satellite built by India so far in December 2005 was a major event.

O O O

# 18. RESEARCH IN OCEAN DEVELOPMENT IN INDIA

India's coastline is more than 7,500 km long and its territory includes 1,256 islands. Its exclusive economic zone covers an area of 2 million sq km and the continental shelf extends up to 350 nautical miles from the. coast. The total domain for the development of oceanic resources and protection of the marine environment extends from the coastal land and islands to the wide Indian Ocean. The Government set up the Department of Ocean Development in 1981 to promote and coordinate the multi-faceted endeavours needed to accomplish the task, and to develop the new emerging area of Antarctic research and deep seabed mining.

Antarctica provides an excellent opportunity for the conduct of scientific research for the benefit of all mankind. It is a pristine laboratory of worldwide significance, which has enabled the researchers to detect and monitor global environment phenomena, such as the depletion of atmospheric ozone, global warming and sea level changes.

Antarctic meteorological research has provided data essential to forecasting in the southern hemisphere. Glaciological research provides important information about the heat exchange budget, and Antarctica's influence on weather and climate.

Geological and geophysical research in Antarctica provides new insights into global geological history and the formation of continents. The earth's geomagnetic field makes Antarctica particularly well-suited to the study of solar terrestrial interactions and cosmic rays which travel from outside our galaxy. The environment of Antarctica provides a unique opportunity to study the specialised adaptations of organisms with their environment and biological research, in providing data essential for decision-making about marine living resources. Human biology and medicine provides information on the physiological adaptation of man to extreme climates and insolation.

The Antarctic Treaty nations are fully committed to scientific research in Antarctica. The signatory parties have recognised the fundamental role that Antarctica plays in understanding global environmental processes and the opportunity it provides for research. The initiation, promotion and coordination of the Indian Antarctic Research, which commenced with the launching of the first expedition during 1981, continues over a very wide range of scientific activities.

The Antarctic research activities have become a regular feature since 1981. Scientific Research expeditions are sent every year. A second permanent station, indigenously designed "Maitri" was established in the ice free area about 70 km away from Dakshin Gangotri, which was selected for the first year round during 1983-84.

The Indian Antarctic Research Programmes have been designed to take advantage of the unique site and environment of Antarctica to understand the key processes that govern our future well-being. The scientific programmes are its essential part and are rooted in these long-term programmes: (i) ice ocean atmospheric system in Antarctica and global environment, (ii) Antarctic lithosphere and Gondwanaland reconstruction, framework for delineating plate tectonic processes and assessment of resource potentials, (iii) Antarctic eco-systems and environmental physiology, (iv) solar terrestrial processes, (v) innovative technologies for support system, (vi) environment impact assessment, and (vii) generating and structuring for database: geological, topographic, thematic mapping and ecosystems changes, environmental parameters, health care, etc.

More than 20 research institutions, universities and government departments are contributing to the success of the Antarctic Research programme. Invaluable logistic support for these activities has been provided by the four services—Army, Navy, Air Force, Coast Guard and by Defence Research and Development Organisation. The Indian Antarctic programmes have provided research and first hand learning opportunities to more than 1,200 persons from different institutions and agencies, including the scientists and the defence services.

It has encouraged development of indigenous technology in specified fields. The annual expeditions to Antarctica have helped to prepare a viable ground for front-ranking research endeavours in basic and environmental science and have won for India a well deserved recognition amongst the Antarctic Treaty Nations. India has a consultative status in the Antarctic Treaty System. It is a member of the Scientific Committee on Antarctic Research and Party to the Convention on the Conservation of Antarctic Marine Living Resources. Fifteen scientific expeditions of Antarctica have been launched in continuation of scientific research programmes on atmospheric science, meteorology, biology, oceanography, earth sciences etc. In addition to these regular expeditions, India also launched an expedition to the Weddel Sea in 1989, a Krill expedition in 1995 and Arctic Sea expedition in 2006.

While using Antarctica as a platform for conducting scientific experiments, India has always recognised the importance of preserving the pristine nature of this remote and unique continent. To uphold this commitment, India, an original votary of the Protocol on Environmental Protection to the Antarctic Treaty, ratified this Protocol way back in April 1996.

India was recognised in 1982 as a pioneer investor in the area of deep seabed exploration with special emphasis on the location and sampling of polymetallic nodules. A mine site of 1.5 lakh sq km in the Central Indian Ocean was allocated by the Preparatory Commission for the International Seabed Authority in August 1987.

India was the first country in the world to register as a pioneer investor in August 1987 on the basis of delineation of a prospective area covering 3 lakh sq km. The survey and exploration efforts till now have been directed mainly to assess the relative concentration and quality characteristics of nodules and broad seabed topography. The sampling grind has been progressively reduced from 100 km to 25 km and later to 12.5 km to get more accurate information on nodules abundance. The survey of mapping and detailed bathymetry of the pioneer area has been subsequently strengthened by the use of multi-beam swath bathymetric system (hydrosweep) on ORV Sagar Kanya. The survey of the entire pioneer area of 1.5 lakh sq km has been completed by using the hydrosweep. Environmental data, baseline oceanographic data on physical, chemical and biological parameters has also been collected. High resolution bathymetric maps of the pioneer area covered during the research cruises have been prepared which give the detailed topography of the area enabling the identification of the sea mounts and sloped which cannot be negotiated by mining equipment.

O  O  O

# 19. ROLE OF THE CENTRAL POLLUTION CONTROL BOARD IN CONTROLLING POLLUTION

The Central Pollution Control Board (CPCB) is the national apex body for assessment, monitoring and control of water and air pollution. This is done by the Board under the Acts for Prevention and Control of Pollution of Water (1974) and Air (1981) and also under the Water Cess Act, 1977. Under the Environment (Protection) Act, 1986, effluent and emission standards in respect of 61 categories of industries have been identified.

Seventeen categories of heavily polluting industries have been notified, namely cement, thermal power plant, distilleries, sugar, fertilizer, integrated iron and steel, oil refineries, pulp and paper, petrochemicals, pesticides, tanneries, basic drugs and pharmaceuticals, dye and dye intermediaries, caustic soda, zinc smelter and aluminium smelter. Out of a total of 1,551 units identified under these 17 categories, 1,259 units have installed adequate facilities for pollution control and 112 units have been closed down. Central Pollution Control Board in consultation with State Pollution Control Boards has identified 22 critically polluted areas in the country which need special attention for control of pollution. These are Vapi (Gujarat), Singrauli (Uttar Pradesh), Karba, Ratlam, Nagda (Madhya Pradesh), Digboi (Assam), Talcher (Orissa), Bhadravati (Karnataka), Howrah and Darjeeling (West Bengal), Dhanbad (Bihar), Pali and Jodhpur (Rajasthan), Manali and North Arcot (Tamil Nadu), Vishakhapatnam and Puducherry (Andhra Pradesh), Chembur (Maharashtra), Najafgarh (Delhi), Govindgarh (Punjab), Udyog Mandai (Kerala), and Parwanoo and Kala Amb (Himachal Pradesh).

An intensive ambient air quality network is proposed to be established in the Delhi State and monitoring of Sulphur, Nitrogen and SPM has been initiated in the cities, towns and villages of Haryana, Uttar Pradesh, Rajasthan and Delhi. Central and State Boards conduct vehicular and noise pollution surveys in different cities of the country.

A customised software package has been prepared by the Board to review the water quality data that is being generated by the 480 water quality monitoring stations. A total of 1,532 grossly polluted industries in 24 States/Union Territories have been identified under the National River Action plan. River Basin documents for the rivers Ulhas, Brahmaputra, Pennar, Indus II, Rishkulya and Chaliyar are under preparation.

The Central Pollution Control Board is the authorised body to check the calibration of the instruments and checking procedures being adopted by the Pollution Checking Centre by the Directorate of Transport for checking vehicular pollution. The Central Board conducts survey for assessment of carbon monoxide emissions from the exhausts of four wheel vehicles with or without catalytic converters. One of the surveys on the status of solid waste generation carried out in 23 metres of the country showed that Mumbai generates maximum solid waste while Vishakhapatnam generates the least.

The Ministry of Environment and Forests is the nodal agency for the management and control of hazardous substances which includes hazardous chemicals, waste and micro-organisms. The Ministry has framed the following restrictions under the Environment (Protection) Act, 1986 : (i) Manufacture, storage and import of hazardous chemicals, 1989, (ii) Hazardous Wastes (Management and Handling) Rules, 1989, (iii) Manufacture, Use, Import, Export and Storage of Hazardous Micro-organisms/Generally Engineered Organisms or Cell, 1989.

A crisis management plan has been worked out to meet chemical emergencies in units handling hazardous chemicals. A central control room has been set up in the Ministry to meet with emergencies caused due to hazardous chemicals and a Crisis Alert System has been established. Guidelines for preparation of crisis management plans have been issued to state governments and financial support is being provided to them to strengthen infrastructure for the purpose. Emergency Response Centres have been set up at Bhopal, Baroda, Manali and Khapali. A Red Book entitled, "Central Crisis Group Alert System" which includes names, addresses and telephone numbers of the Central and State government authorities and experts, to be contacted in an emergency, has been prepared and circulated to all concerned. A Public Liability Insurance Act has been enacted to provide immediate relief to the victims of accidents by hazardous chemical industries.

India is a signatory to the UNEP sponsored Convention on Control of Trans-boundary Movement of Hazardous Wastes from one country to another. This convention was signed by 126 governments of the world in 1989. The convention aims at checking the reported illegal traffic in hazardous wastes from one country to another. The chemicals finding place in international trade have been listed to avoid trade in toxic chemicals.

O O O

# 20. Public Finance In India

The subject of public finance falls in the purview of the Ministry of Finance. Ministry of Finance is responsible for administration of finances of the Government. It is concerned with all economic and financial matters affecting the country as a whole including transfer of resources to the states. Ministry of Finance has four departments, namely (i) Economic Affairs; (ii) Expenditure, (iii) Revenue and (iv) Company Affairs.

The Department of Economic Affairs has eight main divisions, namely (i) Economic, (ii) Banking, (iii) Insurance, (iv) Budget, (v) Investment, (vi) External Finance, (vii) Fund Bank and (viii) Currency and Coinage. The Economic Affairs Department monitors current economic trends and advises Government on all matters of internal and external economic arrangement including working of commercial banks, term-lending institutions, investment regulations, external assistance, etc. Preparation of the Budget of the Union of India as well the state governments and union territory administrations with legislature when under President's rule and their presentation to Parliament is also the responsibility of the Department.

Public Finance Power to raise and disburse public funds has been divided under the Constitution between Union and State governments. Sources of revenue between Union and the states are, by and large, mutually exclusive, if sharable taxes and duties between them are excluded. The Constitution prescribes that (i) no tax can be levied or collected except by an authority of law, (ii) no expenditure can be incurred from public funds except in the manner provided in the Constitution, and (iii) executive authorities must spend public money only in the manner sanctioned by Parliament in case of Union and by the state legislature in the case of a state.

All receipts and disbursements are kept under two separate headings, namely Consolidated Fund of India and Public Account of India. All revenues are received and loans raised and money received in repayment of loans by the Union from the Consolidated Fund. No money can be withdrawn from this fund except under the authority of an Act of Parliament. All other receipts, such as deposits, service funds and remittances go into Pubic Account and disbursements therefrom are not subject to the. vote of Parliament. To meet unforeseen needs not provided in the Annual Appropriation Act, a Contingency Fund of India has been established under Article 267 (1) of the Constitution. The Indian Constitution provides for the establishment of a Consolidated Fund, a Public Account and a Contingency Fund for each state.

The Railways, the largest public undertaking present their budget separately to Parliament. Appropriations and disbursements under the Railway budget are subject to the same form of Parliamentary control as other appropriations and disbursements. However, as the Railways have no separate cash balance of their own, total receipts and disbursements of the Railways are incorporated in the Budget of the Union as part of the General Budget.

## Sources of Revenue

The main sources of the Union tax revenue are customs duties, union excise duties, corporate and income taxes. Non-tax revenues are largely interest receipts, including interest paid by the Railways and Telecommunications, dividend and profits. The main heads of revenue in states are taxes and duties levied by the respective state governments, shares of taxes levied by the Union and grants received from the Union. Property taxes, octroi and terminal taxes are the mainstay of local finance.

## Transfer of Resources

Devolution  of resources from the Union to the states is a salient feature of the system of federal finance in India. Apart from their share of taxes and duties, the state governments receive statutory and other grants as well as loans for various development and non-development purposes.

## Annual Financial Budget

An estimate of all anticipated receipts and expenditure of the Union for the ensuing financial year is laid before the Parliament. This is known as Annual Financial Statement or "Budget" and covers central government's transactions of all kinds, in and outside India, occurring during the preceding year, the year in which the statement is prepared as well for the ensuing year or the 'Budget Year' as it is known.

The presentation of the budget is followed by a general discussion on it in both Houses of Parliament. Estimates of expenditure from the Consolidated Fund of India are placed before the Lok Sabha in the form of "Demands for Grants". All withdrawals of money from the Consolidated Fund are thereafter authorised by an Appropriation Act passed by Parliament every year. Tax proposals of the Budget are embodied in a bill which is passed as a 'Finance Act' of the year. Estimates of receipts and expenditure are similarly presented by state governments in their legislatures before the beginning of the financial year and legislative sanction for expenditure is secured through similar procedure.

## Public Debt

Public debt includes internal debt comprising borrowings inside the country like market loans, compensations and other bonds, treasury bills issued to the Reserve Bank of India, state governments, commercial banks and other parties as well as non-negotiable non-interest bearing rupees securities issued to the international financial institutions, and external debt comprising loans from foreign countries, international financial institutions, etc.

## Finance Commission

Under Article 280 of the Constitution, a Finance Commission is constituted every fifth year or such earlier time as the President considers necessary to receive recommendations on the following subjects:

(i)   The distribution between the Union and the states of the net proceeds of taxes which are to be, or may be, divided between them and the allocation between the states of the respective share of such proceeds;

(ii) The principles which should govern the grants-in-aid of the revenues of the states in need of such assistance out of the Consolidated Fund of India;

(iii) The measures needed to augment the Consolidated Fund of a State to supplement the resources of the panchayats in the State on the basis of the recommendations made by the Finance Commission of the State;

(iv) The measures needed to augment the Consolidated Fund, of the State to supplement the resources of the Municipalities in the State on the basis of recommendations made by the Finance Commission of the States; and

The recommendations of the Commission together with an explanatory memorandum as to the action taken thereon are laid before each House of Parliament. Since the commencement of the Constitution, 12 Finance Commissions have been constituted.

The 10th Finance Commission submitted its report for the period 1995-2000 on 26 November 1994. The Government accepted its recommendations regarding devolution of income tax, Union excise duties, additional duties of excise in lieu of sales tax, grants-in-aid to cover non-plan gap on revenue account, financing of relief expenditure, grants for upgradation, and special problems, grants for local bodies and debt relief.

The report along with an explanatory memorandum on the action taken on the recommendations contained therein was placed on the table of each House of Parliament in March 1995.

The Finance Commission Division of the Union Government implements the recommendations and takes follow-up action on various observations of the Finance Commission.

Pursuant to the recommendations of the Eleventh Finance Commission (EFC) Government of India created a Fiscal

Reforms Facility ( 2000-01 to 2004-05) for incentivising the States to undertake Medium-Term Fiscal Reforms Programme (MTFRP) for fiscal consolidation.

The State Governments were asked to draw up MTFRP envisaging timebound action points on fiscal objectives and reforms, power sector reforms, public sector restructuring and budgetary reforms.

The guidelines issued by the Ministry of Finance on States' Fiscal Reforms Facility envisaged that if the state sector on an average advises five percentage point reduction in revenue deficit as percentage of revenue receipts consistently each year by the FY 2005-06, the sector as whole would come into revenue balance. For monitoring of the fiscal reforms of the states, flexibility in designing toe MTFRI was broadly left to the states. An Incentive Fund was created. Releases from the Incentive Fund were based on a single monitorable fiscal objective, i.e. a minimum improvement of five percentage point in the ratio of revenue deficit as a proportion to their revenue receipt in each year till 2004-05 for the non-special category States. For the Special category States, the eligibility criteria has been revised to two percentage points improvement in this ratio, prospectively from FY 2002-03 onwards. For those States, which were already in revenue surplus, it should be adequate if with improving revenue balance, the State shows a commensurate improvement in their BCR towards the State Plan. The expected improvement is three percentage points each year in BCR as percentage of Non-Plan Revenue Receipts. Monitoring of the facility was a joint exercise conducted on the basis of components of the MTFRP and the improvement in revenue balance captured in a proforma devised for the purpose.

All the twenty-eight States submitted their MTFRPs. Based on the MTFRP as approved by the monitoring committee, all States, except Government of Goa, signed Memorandum of Understanding (MoU)/Letter of Exchange with Government of India.

Based on the recommendations of the Monitoring Committee as on 31 March 2005 incentive grants of Rs. 7216.98 crore have been released to these States under this facility.

Considering the financial position of the State Governments, it was decided that the reforms costs associated with the MTFRP need to be part-funded by the GOI in a blend of grant and loans for funding the VRS cost of the PSUs to be wound up or Department to be down sized. During award period of Eleventh Finance Commission i.e. 2000-01 to 2004-05 (BE), the fiscal improvement of the 28 States in aggregate in the terms of revenue deficit as percentage of revenue receipts is as under:

| | 1999-2000 (Act) | 2000-01 (Act) | 2001-02 (Act) | 2002-03 (Act) | 2003-04 (Act) | 2004-05 (Act) |
|---|---|---|---|---|---|---|
| Revenue Deficit as % of TRR | −27.34 | −23.85 | −24.49 | −21.00 | −22.98 | −14.24 |

**Debt Consoldication and Relief Facility (2005-10):** The Twelfth Finance Commission (TFC) was appointed by President on 1 November 2002 under the Chairmanship of Dr. C. Rangarajan. It submitted its report covering all the aspects of its mandate on 17 December 2004. The TFC report covering the five year period commencing 1 April 2005 together with the Explanatory Memorandum as to the action taken on the recommendations of the Finance Commission was laid on the table of the both Houses of the Parliament on 26 February 2005. Government of India has accepted recommendations of the TFC.

Twelfth Finance Commission has not recommended continuation of Fiscal Reforms Facility recommended by the Eleventh Finance Commission, instead a comprehensive Debt Consolidation and Waiver scheme (2005-10) has been recommended for States, which is also based on their fiscal performance.

This debt relief scheme comprises of consolidation, reschedulement and lowering of interest rate to 7.5 per cent that shall be available to all States with effect from the year they enact the Fiscal Responsibility legislation. Fiscal Responsibility laws would need to have following minimum core provisions:

1. Eliminating revenue deficit by 2008-09.
2. Reducing fiscal deficit to 3% of GSDP.
3. Bringing annual reduction targets to revenue and fiscal deficits.
4. Bringing out annual statement giving prospects for the State's economy and related fiscal strategy.
5. Bringing out special reports along with the budget giving details of number of employees in government, public sector and aided institutions and related salaries.

Twenty-six States have enacted their Fiscal Responsibility Legislation to date and debt consolidation has been completed for 24 states. Based on the quality of fiscal correction and reduction in revenue deficit, Debt write off for 2005-06 has been awarded to 14 of the States to the extent of Rs. 3878.94 crore and 19 States have been awarded debt waiver for 2006-07 to the extent of Rs. 4594.89 crore.

## Share in Central Taxes and Duties and Grants-in-aid

The 12th Finance Commission in its report for the period 2005-10 has recommended a total transfer of Rs. 7,55,752 crore (Share in central taxes and duties of Rs. 6,13,112 crore and Grants-in-aid of Rs. 1,42,640 crore) to States.

The 12th Finance Commission has recommended the continuation of the scheme of calamity relief fund in its present form with contribution from the Centre and the States in the ratio of 75 : 25.

The Commission has also recommended continuation of the scheme of NCCF in its present form with core corpus of Rs. 500 crore. The outgo from the fund may continue to be replenished by way of collection of National Calamity Contingent Duty and levy of special surcharges.

Out of the Centre's share of CRF, a sum of Rs. 2622.94 crore was released in 21005-06, Rs. 3521.06 crore was released in the year 2006-07 and Rs. 999.85 crore was released during the year 2007-08 (upto 31st July, 2007) to the States.

Out of NCCF, central assistance of Rs. 3061.44 was released during the year 2005-06 and Rs. 1962.05 crore during the year 2006-07 and Rs. 13.51 crores released during 2007-08 (upto 31st July 2007), to the States towards calamities of rare severity.

O O O

# 21. Banking In India

Some form of banking, mainly of the money lending type, has been in existence in India from ancient times. It was only a little over a century ago that modern banking was born. The earliest institutions which took banking business under the British regime were agency houses which carried on banking business, in addition to their trade activities. Most of these agency houses were closed down during early 1930s when there was a banking crisis. Even three Presidency banks had to be amalgamated into the Imperial Bank of India.

The first of limited liability bank managed by Indians was Oudh Commercial Bank founded in 1881. Subsequently the Punjab National Bank was established in 1894. The Swadeshi movement which began in 1906 encouraged the formation of a number of commercial banks. Banking crisis in 1913-16 and failure of 588 banks in various states during the decade ending in 1949 underlined the need for regulating and controlling commercial banks. The Banking Companies (Inspection Ordinance) was passed in January, 1946 and the Banking Companies (Restriction of Branches) Act was passed in February, 1949 subsequently read as Banking Regulation Act.

With a view to bringing commercial banks into the mainstream of economic development with definite social objectives, the Government issued an Ordinance on July 19, 1969, acquiring ownership and control of 14 major banks with deposits exceeding Rs. 50 crores each. Six more commercial banks were nationalised on April 15, 1980.

The two decades after nationalization, there was a phenominal expansion in the geographical coverage and financial spread of the banking system in the country. As certain rigidities and weaknesses were found to have developed in the system during the late eighties, the Government of India felt that these have to be addressed to enable the financial system to play its role in ushering in a more efficient and competitive economy. Accordingly, a high level committee was appointed on August 14, 1991 to examine all aspects relating to the structure, organisation, functions and procedures of the financial system. Based on the recommendations of the Committee headed by its Chairman M. Narasimhan, a comprehensive reform of the banking system was introduced in 1992-93. The objective of the reform measures was to ensure that the balance sheets of banks reflected their actual financial health. One of the important measures was relating to income recognition, asset classification and provisioning by banks, on the basis of objective criteria laid down by the Reserve Bank. The introduction of capital adequacy norms in line with international standards was another important measure of the reforms process.

After nationalisation, public sector banks accounted for 91% of the total bank branches and 86% of the total banking business in the country. In the post-nationalisation era, no new private sector banks were allowed to be set up. In recognition of the need for greater competition which could lead to higher productivity and efficiency of the banking system, new private sector banks were allowed to be set up in the Indian banking system. These new banks had to satisfy among other things, the following minimum requirements: (i) It should be registered as a public limited company, (ii) The minimum paid-up capital should be Rs. 100 crore, (iii) The shares should be listed on the stock exchange, (iv) The headquarters of the bank should be preferably located in a centre which, does not have the headquarters of any other bank, and (v) The bank shall be subject to prudential norms in respect of banking operations, accounting and other policies as laid down by the RBI. It will have to achieve capital adequacy of 8% from the very beginning.

## Reserve Bank of India

RBI was established on April 1, 1935 and nationalised on January 1, 1949. This bank was the sole authority for issue of currency in India other than rupee one coins and subsidiary coins and notes. As the agent of the Central Government, Reserve Bank undertook the distribution of one rupee notes and coins, as well as small coins issued by the Government. The bank acts as a banker to the Central Government, state governments, commercial banks, state cooperative banks, and some of the financial institutions. It formulates and administers monetary policy with a view to ensure stability in prices while promoting higher production in the real sector through proper deployment of credit. RBI plays an important role in maintaining the stability in the exchange value of the rupee and acts as an agent of the government in respect of India's membership of International Fund. The RBI also performs a variety of developmental and promotional functions. Most important of all, RBI handles the borrowing programmes of the Government of India.

## Composition of Banking System

Commercial Banking System in India consisted of 218 scheduled commercial banks (including foreign banks) as on 31st March 2006. Of the scheduled commerical banks, 161 are in public sector of which 133 are regional rural banks (RRBs) and these account for about 75.2 per cent of the deposits of all scheduled commerical banks. The regional rural banks were specially set up to increase the flow of credit to small borrowers in the rural areas. The remaining 28 banks, other than RRBs, in the public sector consist of 19 nationalised banks, 8 banks in SBI group and IDBI Ltd. and transact all types of commerical banking business.

Amongst the public sector banks, as on 31st March 2006, the nationalised banks (including IDBI Ltd.) group is the biggest unit with 33,868 offices, deposits aggregating Rs. 10,13,664 crore and advances of Rs. 7,21,066 crore. The State Bank of India group (SBI and its seven Associates) with 13,820 offices, deposit aggregating Rs. 4,90,375 crore and advances Rs. 3,50,961 crore is the second largest. The nationalised banks accounts for 67.3 per cent of aggregate banking business (aggregate of deposits and advances) conducted by the public sector banks (excluding RRBs) and 48.0 per cent of the aggregate business of all scheduled commercial banks. The SBI and its associates as a group accounts for 32.7 per cent of aggregate banking business conducted by the public sector banks (excluding RRBs) and 23.3 per cent of the aggregate business of all scheduled commercial banks (Source: Quarterly Statistics on Deposits and Credit Scheduled Commercial Banks—March 2006).

## Advances to Priority Sectors

Extension of credit to small borrowers in the hitherto neglected sectors of the economy has been one of the key tasks assigned to the public sector banks in the post-nationalisation period. To achieve this objective, banks have drawn up schemes to extend credit to small borrowers in sectors such as agriculture, small scale industry, road and water transport, retail trade and small business which hitherto had very little share in the credit extended by banks. To improve and enhance the flow of credit to the priority sector including agriculture and small-scale industries sectors, the following policy initiatives were taken:

(i)  It was decided to treat investments made by banks in mortgage backed securities (MBS) as direct lending to housing within the priority sector lending subject to certain conditions.

(ii)  Investments made by banks on or after 1 April 205 in the spcial bonds issued by certain specified institutions would not be eligible for classification uner priority sector lending and such investments which have already been made/to be made by banks up to 31st March 2005 would cease to be eligible for classification under priority sector lending in a phased manner.

(iii) Advances granted by banks to farmers, through the produce marketing schemes under priority sector lending, against pledge/hypothecation of agricultural produce including warehouse receipts for a period not exceeding 12 months was increased from Rs. 5 lakh to Rs. 10 lakh.

(iv) Investment limit in plant and machinery for seven items belonging to sports goods, which figure in the list of items reserved for manufacture in the Small-Scale Industries (SSI) Sector, has been enhanced from Rs. 1 crore to Rs. 5 crore for purpose of classification under priority sector advances.

(v) Investments made by banks on or after 1st July 2005 in venture capital shall not be eligible for classification under priority sector lending while such investments already made up to 30th June 2005 would not be eligible for classification under priority sector lending with effect from 1st April 2006.

(vi) Loans to power distribution corporations/companies, emerging out of bifurcation/restructuring of State Electricity Boards (SEBs), for reimbursing the expenditure already incurred by them for providing low tension connection from step-down point to individual farmers for energising their wells, may also be classified as indirect finance to agriculture.

Amount outstanding under priority sector lending by public sector banks during the period June 1969 to March 2006 increased from just Rs. 441 crore to Rs. 4,10,379 crore and accounted for 40.3 per cent of the net bank credit as on the last reporting Friday of March 2006.

With a view to augment credit flow to rural sector, commercial banks were advised by the Reserve Bank to provide at least 10% of their net bank credit of. 25% of their priority sector advances to weaker sections comprising of small and marginal farmers, landless labourers, tenant farmers and share-croppers, artisans, village and cottage industries, Scheme of Urban Micro Enterprises (SUME) and beneficiaries of Differential Rate of Interest (DRI) Scheme. At the end of December 1996, the amount of outstanding advances accounted for 8.7% of their net bank credit and 21.1% of the aggregate priority sector advances.

## Credit Flow to Agriculture

Banks were initially given a target of extending 15 per cent of the total advances as direct finance to the agricultural sector to be achieved by March 1985. This target was subsequently raised to 18 per cent to be achieved by March 1990. In terms of the guidelines issued by Reserve Bank of India in October 1993, both direct and indirect advances for agriculture are taken together for assessing the target of 18 per cent, with the condition that for the purpose of computing their performance in lending to agriculture, lendings for indirect agriculture should not exceed one fourth of the total agriculture lending target of 18 per cent of the net bank credit so as to ensure that the focus of banks on direct lending to agriculture is not diluted. However, all agricultural advances under the categories 'direct' and 'indirect' will be reckoned in computing performance under the overall priority sector target of 40 per cent of the net bank credit. As at the end of March 2006, public sector banks had extended Rs. 1,54,900 crore, constituting 15.22 per cent of the net bank credit, to the agriculture sector. Private sector banks extended Rs. 36,185 crore to agriculture as the end of March 2006 constituting 13.5 per cent of net bank credit.

## Regional Rural Banks

Regional Rural Banks were set up to take banking services to the doorsteps of rural masses especially in remote rural areas with no access to banking services. These banks were orginally intended to provide institutional credit to the weaker sections of the society called 'target groups'. The Regional

Rural Banks (RRBs) are conceived as institutions that combine the local feel and familiarity with rural problems, which the co-operatives possess, and the degree of business organisation as well as the ability to mobilise deposits, which the commercial banks possess. The banks were also intended to mobilise and channelise rural savings for supporting productive activities in the rural areas. However, with effect from April 1997, the cocept of priority sector lending was made applicable to RRBs. The interest rates on term deposits offered and interest rates on loans charged by RRBs have also been freed.

The credit outstanding of all the 196 RRBs was Rs. 32,870 crore as at the end of March 2005 and Rs. 62,143 crore were mobilized as deposits by RRBs till that date. RRBs which comply with certain prescribed conditions are also permitted to open and maintain non-resident accounts in Rupees.

In order to consolidate and strengthen RRBs, the Government of India initiated, in September 2005, the process of amalgamation of RRBs, in a phased manner. Till 31st August 2006, 134 RRBs have been amalgamated to form 42 new RRBs, sponsored by 18 banks in 16 states, bringing down the total number of RRBs to 104 from 196. The amalgamation process is still continuing.

IDBI was established under the same name Act in 1964 as the principal financial institution for providing credit and other facilities assisting the development of industries. IDBI has been providing direct financial assistance to large industrial houses and also helping small and medium industrial concerns through banks and state level institutions. Aggregate assistance sanctioned during 1996-97 amounted to Rs. 17,050 crore. IDBI's outstanding financial assistance in the end of March 1997 was Rs. 43,769 crore.

**Export-Import Bank of India**

The Export Import Bank of India (EXIM Bank) was established for financing, facilitating and promoting foreign trade in India. During the year ended 31st March 2006, EXIM Bank sectioned loans of Rs. 20,489 crore while disbursements amounted to Rs. 15,039 crore. Profit (after tax) of the Bank for the period 2005-06 amounted to Rs. 271 crore.

## Industrial Credit and Investment Corporation of India Limited

ICICI was established in 1955 as a public limited company to encourage and assist industrial units in the country. Its objectives included providing assistance in the creation, expansion and modernisation of industrial enterprises, encouraging and promoting participation of private capital both internal and external, in such enterprises, encouraging and promoting industrial development and helping development of capital markets.

## Small Industries Development Bank of India

SIDBI was established as wholly owned subsidiary of the IDBI under the Small Industries Development Bank of India Act, 1989 as the principal finance institution for promotion, financing and development of industries in the small-scale sector. This bank started its operations from April 1990 and its cumulative disbursements at the end of March 1997 were Rs. 28,780 crore.

## National Bank for Agriculture and Rural Development

National Bank for Agriculture and Rural Development (NABARD) came into existence in 12th July 1982. It was established for providing credit for promotion of agriculture, small-scale industries, cottage and village industries, handicrafts and other allied economic activities in rural areas with a view to promoting integrated rural development and securing prosperity of rural areas. Paid-up capital of NABARD is stood at 2000 crore as on 31st March, 2006. The profit after tax stood at Rs. 857 crore during year 2005-06.

## International Monetary Fund

As part of its mandate for international surveillance under the Article of Agreement, the IMF conducts what is known as Article IV consultations to review the economic status of the member countries, normally, once a year. Article IV consultations are generally held in two phases. During this exercise the IMF mission holds discussions with RBI and various ministries/departments of Central Government. The Article IV consultations are concluded with a meeting of IMF Executive Board at Washington D.C. which discusses the Report. The first phase of 2004 Article IC consultations was held in November 2003. After that another visit was made by the IMF Mission to India in March 2004 for making some interim assessment about the macroeconomic and monetary development situation for the purpose of World Economic Outlook Report.

**Special Data Dissemination Standards (SDDS):** The SDDS indicates norms relating to coverage timeliness and periodicity of data, access to public and integrity and quality of data. The Statistics Department of the IMF linked India's National Summary Data Page to the Dissemination Standard Bulletin Board (DSBB) on 7th July 2003, facilitating international investors and analysts getting information on India.

## Indian Banks Abroad

As on 30th June 2006, eighteen Indian banks—twelve from the public sector and six from the private sector—had operations overseas, which had their presence in 47 countries with a network of 111 branches (including offshore units), 6 joint ventures, 18 subsidiaries and 34 representative offices. Bank of Baroda had highest concentration, with 39 branches, 7 subsidiaries, one joint venture bank and 3 representative offices in 20 countries, followed by State Bank of India with 30 branches, five subsidiaries, three joint venture banks and seven representative offices in 29 countries and Bank of India with 20 branches, one subsidiary, two joint venture banks and three representative offices in 14 countries.

○ ○ ○

# 22. Plans Of Economic Development In India

Planning in India was started with great zeal in 1951 after laying the foundations for varied economic activity and after solving the immediate problems of the partition and rehabilitation.

Planning in India derives its objectives and social premise from the Directive Principles of State Policy. The concept of planning covers both the public and private sectors which are viewed as supplementary to each other. However, when the planning era started in India, the emphasis was more on socialistic pattern of society. Hence, a good deal of public sector undertakings made massive investments in basic and heavy industries and paved the way for a leap-up in the economy.

Although there is presently enough criticism of our continued emphasis on the public sector, it will be nice to remember that Nehru's economic policies which have been given successful implementation by Mrs. Indira Gandhi, Rajiv Gandhi and later Dr. Manmohan Singh that India has achieved some status in world economy. There is no denying the fact that the private sector has also now grown to maturity and thus we find some of the private sector undertakings as showing adequate responsibility in innovating indigenous technology and have otherwise developed manifold with the cooperation of the Department of Science and Technology. Majority of them are regarded now as capable of standing international competition. Moreover, with basic and heavy industries already at the disposal of the industry and the economy, the private sector is now organising itself smoothly in consumer industries.

## First Plan

Keeping in view the large scale imports of foodgrains in 1951 and inflationary pressures on economy, the First Plan (1951-56) accorded the highest priority to agriculture including irrigation and power projects. About 44.6% of the total outlay of Rs. 2,069 crore in the public sector (later raised to Rs. 2,378 crore) was allotted for its development. The plan also aimed at increasing the rate of investment from 5 to 7% of the national income.

## Second Plan

The Second Five-Year Plan (1956-57 to 1960-61) sought to promote the pattern of development which would lead to the establishment of a socialist pattern of society in India. Its main aims were: (i) an increase of 25% in national income, (ii) rapid industrialisation with particular emphasis on the development of basic and heavy industries, (iii) large expansion of employment opportunities, (iv) reduction of inequalities in income and wealth and a more even distribution of economic power, and (v) increasing the rate of investment from 7% of the National income I to 11 % by 1960-61. The plan laid special stress on industrialisation, increased production of iron and steel, heavy chemicals, including nitrogenous fertilizers and development of heavy engineering and machine-building industry.

## Third Plan

The Third Plan (1961-62 to 1965-66) aimed at securing a marked advance towards self-sustaining growth. Its immediate objectives were: (i) an increase in the national income of over five per annum and at the same time to ensure a pattern of investment which could sustain this rate of growth during subsequent plan periods, (ii) to achieve self-sufficiency in foodgrains and increase agricultural production to meet the requirements of industry and exports, (iii) expand basic industries like steel, chemicals, fuel and to establish machine-building capacity so that the requirements of further industrialisation could be met within a period of 10 years or so mainly from the country's own resources, (iv) utilize fully the manpower resources of the country and ensure substantial expansion in employment opportunities, and (v) establish progressively greater equality of opportunity and bring about reduction in disparities of income and wealth and a more even distribution of economic power. The third plan aimed at increasing the national income by about 30 per cent from Rs. 14,500 crore in 1961-61 to about Rs. 19,000 crore by 1965-66 (at 1960-61 prices) and per capita income from 330 to 385 during the same period.

## Annual Plans

The situation created by the Indo-Pakistan conflict in 1965, two successive years of severe drought, devaluation of the currency, general rise in prices and erosion of resources available for Plan purposes delayed finalisation of the Fourth Five-Year Plan.

Instead, between 1966 and 1969, three annual plans were formulated within the framework of the draft outline of the Fourth Plan.

## Fourth Plan

Fourth Plan (1969-74) aimed at accelerating the tempo of development and reducing fluctuations in agricultural production as well as the impact of uncertainties of foreign aid. It sought to raise the standard of living through programmes designed to promote equality and social justice. The Plan laid particular emphasis on improving conditions of less privileged and weaker sections specially through provision of employment and education. Efforts were also directed towards reduction of concentration of wealth and wider diffusion of wealth, income and economic power. The plan aimed at increasing net domestic product (at 1968-69 factor cost) from Rs. 29,071 crore in 1969-70 to Rs. 38,306 crore in 1973-74. Average annual compound growth rate envisaged was 5.7 per cent.

## Fifth Plan

The Fifth Plan (1974-79) was formulated against the backdrop of severe inflationary pressures. Major objectives of the plan were to achieve self-reliance and adopting measures for raising consumption and standard of people living below the poverty line. The plan also gave high priority to bring inflation under control and to achieve stability in the economic situation. It targeted an annual growth rate of 5.5% in national income. Four annual plans pertaining to the fifth plan period were completed. It was subsequently decided to end the fifth plan period with the close of Annual Plan 1978-79 and initiate work for next five years with new priorities and programmes.

## Sixth Plan

Removal of poverty was the foremost objective of the Sixth plan (1980-85). The strategy adopted for the plan consisted essentially in moving simultaneously towards strengthening infrastructure for both agriculture and industry. Stress was laid on dealing with inter-related problems through a system approach rather than in separate compartments, greater management, efficiency and intensive monitoring in all sectors and active involvement of people in formulating specific schemes of development at local level and securing their speedy and effective implementation.

The Sixth Plan's actual expenditure stood at Rs. 1,09,291.7 crore (current prices) as against the envisaged total public sector outlay of 97,500 crore (1970-80 prices) accounting for a 12.5% increase in nominal terms. Average annual growth rate targeted for the plan was 5.2%.

## Seventh Plan

The seventh plan (1985-90) emphasised on policies and programmes which aimed at rapid growth in foodgrains production, increase in employment opportunities, and productivity within the basic tenets of planning, namely, growth, modernisation, self-reliance and social justice. Due to overall favourable weather conditions, implementation of various thrust programmes and with concerted efforts of the government and the farmers, food production during the Seventh Plan grew by 3.23% as compared to a long-term growth rate of 2.68% during 1967-68 to 1988-89 and a growth rate of 2.55% in the 1980s. To reduce unemployment and consequently the incidence of poverty, special programmes like Jawahar Rozgar Yojana were initiated in addition to the already existing programmes. Due recognition was also extended to the role of small-scale industries, food processing industries can play in this regard. The total expenditure during the entire seventh plan stood at Rs. 2,18,729.62 crore (current prices) as against the envisaged total sector outlay of Rs. 1,80,000 crore, resulting in a 21.52% increase in nominal terms. During this plan period, GDP grew at an average 5.6% exceeding the targeted growth rate of 0.6 per cent.

## Annual Plans

The Eighth Five-Year Plan (1990-95) could not take off due to the fast changing political situation at the centre. The new government which assumed power at the Centre by June 1991 decided that the Eighth Five-Year Plan would commence on April 1, 1992 and that 1990-91 and 1991-92 should be treated as separate annual plans, formulated within the framework of earlier Approach to the Eighth Five-Year Plan (1990-95), the basic thrust of these annual plans was maximization of employment and social transformation.

## Eighth Plan

The Eighth Five-Year Plan (1992-97) was launched immediately after the initiation of structural adjustment policies and macro stabilisation policies which were necessitated by worsening of balance of payment position and inflation position during 1990-91.

Various structural adjustment policies were introduced gradually so that the economy could be pushed to higher growth path and to improve its strength to enable it to prevent the balance of payment and inflation crisis in future. The Eighth Plan took note of some of these policy changes which were to come about due to these reforms.

The Eighth Plan aimed at an annual growth rate of 5.6% and an average industrial growth rate of 7.5%. These growth targets were planned to be achieved with relative price stability and substantial improvement in the country's balance of payment.

Some of the salient features of economic performance during the Eighth Plan indicated (i) faster growth of manufacturing sector and agricultural and allied sector, (ii) faster economic growth, (iii) significant growth rates in exports and imports and improvement in trade and current account deficit and significant reduction in the Central Government fiscal deficit. However, shortfall in expenditure in the Central sector due to inadequate mobilization of internal and extra budgetary resources by the Public Sector Undertakings and various departments was witnessed. In the states sector, the reason for shortfall was lack of mobilization of adequate resources due to deterioration in the balance of current revenues, erosion in the contribution state electricity boards and state road transport operations, negative opening balance, mounting non-plan expenditure and shortfalls in the collection of small savings, etc.

## Ninth Plan

The Ninth Plan (1997-2002) was launched in the fiftieth year of India's Independence. The Plan aimed at achieving a targeted GDP growth rate of seven per cent per annum and there was emphasis on the seven identified Basic Minimum Services (BMS) with additional Central Assistance earmarked for these services with a view to obtaining a complete coverage of the population in a time-bound manner. These included provison of safe drinking water, availability of primary health service facilities, universalisation of primary education, public housing assistance to shelterless poor families, nutritional support to children, connectivity of all villages and habitations and streamlining of the public distribution system with a focus on the poor. The Plan also aimed at pursuing a policy of fiscal consolidation, whereby the focus was on sharp reduction in the revenue deficit of the Government, including the Centre, States and PSUs through a combination of improved revenue collections.

The Specific objectives of the Ninth Plan included: (i) priority to agriculture and rural development with a view to generating adequate productive employment and eradication of poverty; (ii) accelerating the growth rate of the economy with stable prices; (iii) ensuring food and nutritional security for all, particularly the vulnerable sections of society; (iv) providing the basic minimum services of safe drinking water, primary health care facilities, universal primary education, shelter, and connectivity to all in a time-bound manner; (v) containing the growth rate of population; (vi) ensuring mobilisation and participation of people at all levels; (vii) empowerment of women and socially disadvantaged groups such as Scheduled Castes, Scheduled Tribes and Other Backward Classes and minorities as agents of socio-economic change and development.

The Ninth Plan envisaged an average target growth rate of 6.5 per cent per annum in GDP as against the growth rate of 7 per cent approved earlier in the Approach Paper. The scaling down of the traget was necessitated by the changes in the national as well as global economic situation in the first two years of the Ninth Plan. Against this, the achievement in the growth-rate on an average was to be 5.5 per cent per annum.

## Tenth Five-Year Plan

The Tenth Five-Year Plan (2002-07) was approved by the National Development Council on 21st December 2002. The Plan further developed the NDC mandated objectives, of doubling the per capita income in ten years and achieving a growth rate of eight per cent of GDP per annum. Since economic growth was not the only objective, the Plan aimed at harnessing the benefits of growth to improve the quality of life of the people by setting the following key targets: Reduction in the poverty ratio from 26 per cent to 21 per cent, by 2007; decadal population growth to reduce from 21.3 per cent in 1991-2001 to 16.2 per cent in 2001-11; growth in gainful employment, at least, to keep pace with addition to the labour force; all children to be in school by 2003 and all children to complete five years of schooling by 2007; reducing gender gaps in literacy and wage rates by 50 per cent; literacy rate to increase from 65 per cent in 1999-2000, to 75 per cent in 2007; providing potable drinking water to all villages; infant mortality rate to be reduced from 72 in 1999-2000, to 45 in 20007; maternal mortality ratio to be reduced from four in 1999-2000, to two in 2007; increase in forest/tree cover from 19 per cent in 1999-2000, to 25 per cent in 2007; and cleaning of major polluted river stretches.

The Tenth Plan had a number of new features, that include, among others, the following:

Firstly, the Plan recognised the rapid growth in the labour force. At current rates of growth and labour intensity in production, India faces the possibility of rising unemployment, which could lead to social unrest. The Tenth Plan therefore aims at creating 50 million job opportunities during the period, by placing special emphasis on employment intensive sectors of agriculture, irrigation, agro-forestry, small and medium enterprises, information and communication technology and other services.

Secondly, the Plan addressed the issue of poverty and the unacceptable low levels of social indicators. Although these have been the objectives in earlier Plans, in the current Plan there are specific monitorable targets, which will need to be attained along with the growth target.

Thirdly, since national targets do not necessarily translate into balanced regional development and the potential and constraints of each State differ vastly, the Tenth Plan has adopted a differential development strategy. For the first time a statewise growth and other monitorable targets have been worked out in consultation with the States to focus better on their own development plans.

Another features of this Plan was the recognition that Governance is perhaps one of the most important factors for ensuring that the Plan is realised, as envisaged. The Plan has laid down a list of reforms in this connection.

## Eleventh Five-Year Plan

The Eleventh Plan which spans 2007-12 envisages a growth target of 8.5 per cent. Besides, growth in agriculture sector has been emphasised because, to achieve the targeted growth of 8.5 per cent, it is necessary to raise the average growth of two per cent of the agriculture sector to four per cent. However, the targeted growths of agriculture sector in Eleventh Plan is 3.9 per cent. This target has necessitated the need for 'Second Green Revolution'. It seeks to promote a strategy of balanced development. The main thrusts are equal distribution and development.

The country made great progress in the field of agriculture as a result of planned growth of economy. It has become self-reliant in the production of food grain. Today, India is the highest producer of milk in the world. Besides, the country also achieved remarkable success in the growth of fruits, vegetables, spices and herbs and medicinal plants. The country has made impressive strides in irrigation development since 1951. The irrigation potential of the country rose from 22.6 m.ha. in 1957 to nearly 150 m.ha. in 2007. The growth in the field of power sector is equally plausible. In this sector, the total installed capacity which was only 2,301 MW in 1950 increased to 1,31,310 MW by the end of March 2007. Under the rural electrification programme, all villages have been electrified.

Education gained brilliant growth during the plan period. The literacy rate has gone up from 18.3 per cent in 1957 to 68 per cent in 2008. The Gross Enrolment Ratio (GER) at primary level has increased from 42.6 per cent in 1950-51 to 97.3 in 2005-06. Similarly, for the upper primary, it has gone up from 12.7 per cent to 70.6 per cent for the corresponding period.

As a result of more than five decades of planned development, per capita income, literacy rate, life expectancy rate rose immensely, while India achieved self-sufficiency in the field of food grains production, and made great strides in the field of science and technology. In short, it made great progress in every sphere of life. But much remains to be done. About one-fourth of its population is still illiterate, about 22 per cent of the total population is still below poverty line. Access to drinking water and health facilities remain a distant dream for a major portion of the population.

Efficient governance is a must for ensuring that targets under the Plan are achieved. Moreover, improved people's participation, involvement of civil society, especially voluntary organisations, civil services reforms for improving transparency, accountability and efficiency, a more equitable system of reward and punishments, awareness campaign, reforms in judicial and revenue system are some of the measures which can help India improve its performance and to make advantages of development accessible to each and all. It is the need of the hour to bridge the gap of socio-economic inequalities so that the benefits of economic achievements reach all sections of our society.

○ ○ ○

# 23. DEVELOPMENT OF INDUSTRIES IN INDIA

Rapid industrial stride has been made in India during the last about six decades of planned development. Industrial production increased at an average growth rate of about 5% per annum during the period 1970-80. The average growth rate increased to 8% in the period 1979-89. The growth has been particularly marked in the newer and more complex industries, such as petroleum products, chemicals and chemical products, metal products, electronics and other electrical machinery, transport equipment and power generation.

The different five year plan periods saw the expansion and diversification of the industrial structure with the establishment of new units in the existing fields as well as the setting up of new enterprises. As a result, the number of industrial units producing iron and steel increased. There are now six major steel plants with a capacity of about 250 lakh tonnes. They produced over 200 lakh tonnes of saleable steel during 2006-07. With the mergers and acquisitions, such as L.N. Mittal's takeover of Arcelor have put into a leading steel maker in the world map. The steel produced by these plants provided the basis for achieving self-sufficiency in a number of engineering goods, from a pin to giant machinery. In the field of new industries, agricultural tractors, electronics and fertilizer industries which practically did not exist in 1951, progressed to such an extent that the import of these products was brought down to the minimum. The drug industry also developed fast. The textiles industry was no longer confined to cotton or jute textiles, but quite a few units produced different types of synthetic fibres. The machine-building industry too made rapid strides. The engineering industry developed enough to supply virtually the entire requirement of power generating equipment, equipment for railways, road transport and communications. Self-sufficiency was reached with regard to sugar and cement machinery, power boilers, material handling equipment and a large number of consumer durables.

The Indian economy has been growing at over 8% annually over the last few years. Industry and manufacturing have played a major role in contributing to this growth. Industry recorded 9.6% growth in 2005-06 while manufacturing grew by 9.1% during the period. The figures reached 10.9% and 12.3%, respectively during 2006-07. There is a global slowdown now and the economy is likely to cool off. But Indian industry is likely to make steady growth during 2008-09 and 2009-10.

## Evolution of Industrial Policy

Independent India's industrial policy was first announced in 1948. This envisaged a mixed economy with an overall responsibility of the government for planned development of industries and their regulation in the national interest. While it reiterated the right of the state to acquire any industrial undertaking in public interest, it reserved an appropriate share for private enterprise. The policy was revised in 1956 following Parliament's acceptance in 1954 of a socialistic pattern of society as the national objective. Under the revised policy, industries specified in Schedule A were to be the exclusive responsibility of the state, while industries specified in Schedule B were to be progressively state-owned, but private enterprise was expected to supplement the efforts of the state in these fields. Future development of industries falling outside the two schedules would, in general, be left to private enterprise. Notwithstanding this demarcation, the policy-makers said, it would always be open to the state to take over any type of industrial production, subject to payment of compensation.

## Industrial Licensing

An important objective of the industrial policy was to prevent the emergence of private monopolies and concentration of economic power in the hands of a small number of individuals. This problem was studied by the Mahalanobis Committee on Distribution of Income and Levels of Living (1960), the Monopolies Enquiry Commission (1964), and the Industrial Licensing Policy Enquiry Committee (ILPIC) (1967). The Administrative Reforms Commission and the Planning Commission also made various recommendations. As a result, the Monopolies and Restrictive Trade Practices (MRTP) Act was passed in 1969 and under the Act the Monopoly and Restrictive Trade Practices Commission was appointed in 1970. The Industrial Licensing was modified in 1970 and again in 1973.

The latest modifications reaffirmed that the Industrial Policy Resolution of 1956 would continue to govern the government's policies in the industrial sphere. All industries of basic and strategic importance, or in the nature of public utility services would continue to be in the public sector. Industries which are essential and would require investment on a scale, which only the state in the present circumstances could provide would also be in the public sector. Some other salient features of the new changes were: A large industrial house for licensing purposes would mean a house having assets, along with assets of inter-connected undertakings (as defined in the MRTP Act, 1969), of not less than Rs. 20 crore as against assets exceeding Rs. 55 crore provided by the ILPIC.

The list of industries which are open for large industrial houses and foreign concerns and subsidiaries and branches of foreign companies along with other applicants, has been consolidated. They cannot, however, participate in the production of any item reserved for the public sector as mentioned in Schedule A or the small scale sector. The Consolidated list covers 19 groups, viz. the following:

1. Metallurgical industries: (i) ferro-alloys, (ii) steel castings and forgings, (iii) special steels, and (iv) non-ferrous metals and their alloys.

2. Boilers and steam generating plants.

3. Prime movers (other than electrical generators) covering (i) industrial turbines, and (ii) internal combustion engines.

4. Electrical equipment: (i) equipment for transmission and distribution of electricity, (ii) electrical motors, (iii) electrical furnaces, (iv) X-ray equipment, (v) electronic components and equipment.

5. Transportation: (i) mechanised sailing vessels up to 1,000 dwt (ii) ship ancillaries, and (iii) commercial vehicles.

6. Industrial.

7. Machine tools.

8. Agricultural machines, tractors and power tillers.

9. Earthmoving machinery.

10. Industrial instruments, indicating, recording and regulation devices for pressure, temperature, rate of flow, weights levels, etc.

11. Scientific instruments.

12. Nitrogenous and phosphatic fertilizers falling under the inorganic type in the First Schedule to the ID&R Act, 1951.

13. Chemicals (other than fertilizers) : (i) inorganic heavy chemicals, (ii) organic heavy chemicals, (iii) fine chemicals, including photographic chemicals, (iv) synthetic resins and plastics, (v) synthetic rubbers,

(vi) man-made fibres, (vii) industrial explosives, (viii) insecticides, fungicides, weedicides and the like, (ix) synthetic detergents, and (x) miscellaneous chemicals (for industrial use only).

14. Drugs and pharmaceuticals.
15. Paper and pulp, including paper products.
16. Automobile tyres and tubes.
17. Plate glass.
18. Ceramic: (i) refractories, and (ii) furnace lining bricks—acidic, basic and neutral.
19. Cement products: (i) portland cement, and (ii) asbestos cement.

The Industrial Policy initiatives undertaken by the government since July 1991 have been designed to build on the past industrial achievements and to accelerate the process of Indian industry internationally competitive. It recognises the strength and maturity of the industry and attempts to provide the competitive stimulus for higher growth. The thrust of these initiatives has been to increase domestic and external competition through extensive application of market mechanism and facilitating forging of dynamic relationships with foreign investors and supplies of technology. The process of reform has been continuous.

## New Industrial Licensing Policy

With the introduction of New Industrial Policy 1991, a substantial programme of deregulation was undertaken. Industrial licensing was abolished for all projects except for a short list of 15 industries relating to security, strategic and environmental concerns. They are: (i) coal and lignite, (ii) petroleum (other than crude) and its distillation products, (iii) distillation and brewing of alcoholic drinks, (iv) sugar, (v) animal fats and oils, (vi) cigars and cigarettes of tobacco and manufactured tobacco substitutes, (vii) asbestos and asbestos-based products, (viii) plywood, veneers of all types and other wood-based products such as particle board; medium-density fibre board and blackboard, (ix) tanned or dressed fur skins, chamois leather, (x) paper and newsprint except bagasse-based units, (xi) electronic aerospace and defence equipment; all types, (xii) Industrial explosives, including detonating fuse, safety fuse, gun powder, nitrocellulose and matches, (xiii) hazardous chemicals, (xiv) drugs and pharmaceuticals (according to drug policy), (xv) entertainment electronics (VCDs, colour TVs, CD players, tape recorders).

The Monopolies and Restrictive Trade Practices Act has been amended to eliminate the need to seek prior governmental approval for expansion of present industrial units and establishment of new industries by large companies. The system of phased manufacturing programme which was designed to enforce progressively greater degrees of local content has been abolished. Industrial location policies have been substantially changed so that industrial location is discouraged only in large cities because of environmental reasons.

A significant number of industries were previously reserved for the public sector. Now no manufacturing sector is reserved except for petroleum and defence equipment. The areas reserved for public sector are: (i) arms, ammunition and allied items of defence equipment; defence aircrafts and warships, (ii) atomic energy, (iii) coal and ignite, (iv) mineral oils, (v) minerals specified in the Schedule to the Atomic Energy (Control of Production and Use) Order 1953, and (vi) railway transport. Even in these areas private sector participation can be invited on a discretionary basis.

Under the new policy, existing units will be permitted to manufacture any new article without additional investment if the article is not subjected to compulsory licensing. This facility will be available without reference to any locational condition. This is an additional facility to existing units. Under the provisions of exemption from licensing for substantial expansion, existing units can in any case manufacture any new article not covered by compulsory licensing or their substantial expansion, the only requirement would be that the industrial undertaking shall file a memorandum in prescribed form to the Secretariat for industrial approval in the Ministry of Industry.

## Common Minimum Programme in Industry

The Government of India decided to maintain 12 % annual growth in the industry, calling it a Common Minimum Programme, as it felt that there was a good scope for public investment as well as private investment. The nation needs and has the capacity to absorb $ 10 billion a year as foreign direct investment. Suitable credit and taxation policies are being devised to ensure that the bulk of new investments, both domestic and foreign, will be channelled into the core and infrastructural sectors. Entry of multinational companies into low priority areas will be discouraged through suitable fiscal and other measures. New incentives and policies will be devised to encourage new industries to be located in the backward districts of the country. An independent Commission will hear and determine tariff disputes as well as recommend appropriate levels of tariffs for different products and different industries keeping in view the larger interests of the country. A Disinvestment Commission has been appointed to direct PSU shares in an orderly and optimum manner. An Expenditure Commission is to be set up to ensure that government money is not wasted on unproductive projects.

The Government has introduced a wide range of policies and programmes to support the development of small scale sector. An extensive institutional support network has been created to encourage small scale industries. These include assistance in marketing through Small Scale Industries Development Corporations at the Union and the State levels, provision of consultancy services, training, common facility services, entrepreneurship training, etc. Apart from the infrastructural support to the small scale sector, Government has invariably pursued a policy of according protection and purchase preference to the small scale sector.

## The Public Sector

Government policy towards public sector has been clarified in the Common Minimum Programme. While the focus of the Economic Policy is growth with social justice, the government has emphasised that the public sector will continue to be an important component of Indian industry. The need for making the public sector strong and competitive has been brought into sharper focus. Sick or potentially sick public sector companies will be rehabilitated through a menu of options. One of the major policy initiatives taken by the government is the establishment of a Disinvestment Commission which will advise the government on steps to be taken in the matter of sick companies. The revenues generated from disinvestment will be utilized in two vital areas, namely health and education, particularly in the poorer and backward districts of the country. A part of such revenue will also be earmarked to create an investment fund to be utilized for strengthening other public sector enterprises. The Disinvestment Commission came into being on August 23, 1996. Sixty sick enterprises have been referred to the Board for Industrial and Financial Reconstruction (BIFR) for formulation of revival/rehabilitation scheme. A master plan has been under implementation for reforming the enterprises under administrative control of the Ministry of Industry. Professionalisation of Board of Directors of Public Enterprises is another thrust area in the Common Minimum Programme. In this context, the Boards of Directors of PSUs have been reconstituted to induct outside experts. In order to reduce governmental interference in the activities of the PSUs, the administrative ministries/departments have been asked to reduce the number of official nominee directors to the barest minimum, limited to a maximum of two.

## 24. PUBLIC SECTOR IN INDIA

Since independence, the public sector in India has been guided by the Industrial Policy Resolution of 1956, which had as its objective the acceleration of the rate of economic growth and speeding up of the industrialisation as means of achieving the socialist pattern of society. The size of the public sector in India is indeed very large. It includes government departments and its companies whether in the Union or state sector, irrigation and power projects, railways, posts and telegraphs, ordnance factories and other departmental undertakings, banking, insurance, financial and other services. The focus here was on the Central public enterprises established as government companies or statutory corporations excluding banking units.

The logic behind public sector undertakings was that private entrepreneurs were always in search of profit and this motive urged them to move in fields where the returns were high and certain. In a developing or in an underdeveloped country, this tendency had many drawbacks. Firstly, as more and more capital was injected in the same type of business, competition increased and with it the costs went up. With increasing costs the prices also increased and markets were hit. Before the introduction of planning in India most businessmen invested their money in traditional industries like jute or cotton or in iron and steel.

One of the arguments in favour of public sector was that government was better capable of controlling the greatest brains by virtue of the stability and status that went with government jobs. The government also had at its disposal the country's resources, men and materials, besides money. It was the government that could stand losses in one direction and cover them from gains in the other. Also, the government could float an undertaking on the principle of minimum profits or on a no-profit-no-loss basis. Such a policy fell beyond the purview of private business and hence government undertakings in industry were desirable or rather necessary in an underdeveloped economy. In other words, the economy of such a country needs to be duly controlled and unless and until capital acquires free movement and diverse channels to cater for higher tastes and better standards of living, a free economy could not work without dissent.

For a successful public sector enterprise, the selection of the manager has to be wisely made. If the manager happens to be a lazy official, or if he is not a patriot, or if he is money-crazy, the public sector enterprise is likely to be a failure. But if the manager is selected from amongst professionals, and can ensure efficient functioning in accordance with the priorities fixed by the higher professionals in authority, a public sector firm has very good chances of achieving success. Without the support of public enterprise system, the development of basic industries in an underdeveloped country is not possible. It is only the government which has the power to raise funds, the like of which can never be achieved even by talented private businessmen, without upsetting the basic economic democracy or without causing undue concentration of wealth. The development of public sector firm is usually carried out in a phased plan of action based on priorities in accordance with the requirements of the economy. The whole economic sphere is brought under control without causing disincentives to the labour force. Economic democracy must accompany political democracy and all development activities in the state coordinated with political ideologies and in accordance of the will of the people.

In any country it is to the advantage of businessmen and groups to achieve monopoly powers and many have attempted to do so. But the public interest lies in competition and the power of the government is sometimes invoked by the common people to bring out the competitive character of the economic system. The private enterprise system would create multiple hazards for those who are dependent on it, such as lesser income from employment, intolerable burden of debt from business failure, old age insecurity, etc. The government steps in to moderate these hazards even in advanced countries by providing unemployment insurance, old age pension, and bankruptcy laws which remove the debt burden.

The private enterprise system also causes severe conflict of interests between groups. Workers and employers face each other in self-bargaining over the terms of employment.

Failure to come to terms in their private disputes can interrupt production and inconvenience. The government intervenes to minimise the strains and stresses.

One of the shortcomings of the private enterprise system is that it does not operate at a steady level. It generates cycles of prosperity and depression in which the people who are fully employed may suddenly slacken or falter in its pace. When workers become unemployed and unproductive, the equipment of a business house stands idle. The uncertainty of steady employment and the hardships which arise when unemployment strikes become a feature of the system which arouses the greatest popular discontent. Government is called upon to minimise their hazards. For these reasons the general public has increasingly demanded the government to intervene in economic affairs.

Even in advanced countries it is becoming common practice to introduce mixed economy which means that a large amount of government economic activity is intermixed with private business activity. The extent of this inter-mixture is indeed quite great in all mixed economies like those of the UK, USA, and India, and it becomes highly artificial to distinguish sharply between "political and economic activity." The existence of a system of private enterprise is supported by a changing state of the popular will, politically expressed (in India by the demand for democratic socialism) and agreed to by the ruling political parties as per its Industrial Policies of 1948 and 1956.

Government intervenes in the economy at many points. It sets the basic social rights, provides a monetary system and uses that system to influence the economy, provides directly those public services which are generally demanded: (i) moderate conflicts among economic groups, (ii) decentralise economic power by necessary legislation, and (iii) take steps to ease the impact of both personal economic hazards and the overall instability of the economic system.

The government invariably plays a leading role in certain sectors like defence production, heavy industries and basic mineral extractions besides the public utilities, roads, railways and communications. In modern times the free private enterprise system can be thought of as a mixed economy, a blend of public and private activity. The public sector has over the years not only grown in size but has also developed enough expertise. In 1991, it employed 22.21 lakh employees with an average salary of Rs. 32,239 per annum. The gross profit of public enterprises touched Rs. 10,246 crore. The R&D expenditure of the public undertakings was Rs. 208 crore in 1990. It has large designing and engineering trained manpower and extended to "high-tech" industries like telecommunications, computers, micro-electronics, ceramics and biotechnology.

The analysis of rate of return in the public sector does not show a bright picture. The total percentage of net profit to capital employed in the public sector is 3.42 and 3.76 in the two years 1989 and 1990, whereas comparatively speaking, it is usually 8.14% in the private sector. But let us not forget the social aspects of the public sector in the country.

After the initial exuberance of public sector entering into new areas of industrial production, providing technical services, trading, financial and services sectors, the public enterprises started facing various problems, some of which were due to historical reasons, while others were related to poor project management, over-staffing, obsolete technology, poor order booking positions, etc. All these put together, the public sector as a whole started showing results far below the desired level of comparison to investments made in them.

The Government announced a new Industrial Policy on July 24, 1991 which envisaged liberalisation and competitive environment. The new policy laid down certain specific areas to be emphasized to make certain public sector undertakings realise their duty to be better performers and more competitive. Under the policy, the Government of India disinvested varying parts of its shareholdings in some PSUs. By the year 1996, the shares of 39 PSUs were disinvested in favour of the financial institutions, mutual funds, banks, foreign institutional investors, and the public. This resulted in disinvestment of 154 crore shares in 39 undertakings realising the sum of Rs. 9,962 crore till 1995-96. In 1996-97, the Government of India disinvested the Videsh Sanchar Nigam Limited (VSNL) through its GDR issue and sold over a lakh of shares with a net realisation of Rs. 379 crore. The shares of these companies were then listed on the stock exchanges. The valuation of the equity of these enterprises on the stock exchanges reflected the perceptions of the public in general and investors in particular, of the performance and expectations of the public from these enterprises. Besides, the Government also offered a part of its equity holdings in some of these enterprises in favour of the employees.

# 25. THE GOVERNMENT POLICY ON FOREIGN CAPITAL

In February 1996, the Government of India set up a Committee under the chairmanship of Ramaswami Mudaliar with the following terms of reference, to examine and report: (i) To what extent import of technical know-how can be dispensed with, (ii) the general conditions under which the indigenous know-how can be capable of commercial exploitation, and (iii) general guidelines regarding the type of cases for allowing foreign collaboration.

The main findings of the Mudaliar Committee were:

1.  Industries where substantial import of capital goods is involved and where the government policy allows foreign capital participation, joint ventures involving foreign equity participation are more beneficial, compared with other forms of collaboration. This has the distinct advantage of ensuring that payment commenses when the overseas collaborator is directly interested in the progress of the Indian venture. The transmission of knowledge is more complete in the

case of joint ventures involving financial participation than in other cases of collaboration.

2. There is need for prior discussion between the Director General of Technical Development and the Council of Scientific and Industrial Research regarding need for foreign collaborations and terms thereof.

3. There is need for the central coordinating unit of the Ministry of Industrial Development and Company Affairs to watch the progress of the disposal of applications for foreign collaboration.

4. A liberal approach would be worthwhile in regard to foreign collaborations in case of substantially export-oriented industries.

5. The Committee does not believe that foreign collaboration has killed indigenous initiative nor does it accept that these agreements have placed us at the mercy of other countries for raw materials and components.

In 1960, the Indian Investment Centre was set up to attract private capital from foreign countries, specially the USA. This Centre had three main objectives:

(i) Collection of basic economic, financial, and legal data of the kind the foreign investor is interested in, and preparation of market surveys concerning investment opportunities in India.

(ii) Functioning as an intermediary between Indian and foreign entrepreneurs and trying to make contacts for the former with the latter and vice versa.

(iii) Provision of guidance to potential foreign investors "through the bureaucratic jingling of New Delhi."

India Investment Centre's help to entrepreneurs took various forms over the years. It identified investment opportunities and provided background information on terms and conditions on which joint ventures were permitted. It was able to attract foreign capital into India as an agency primarily designed to stimulate the flow of foreign private capital and technical know-how within the framework of the Government policies. The guidelines issued by the government on foreign investment specified that: (i) branches of foreign companies will be required to convert themselves into Indian companies, (ii) branches and companies engaged in manufacturing activities which are primarily export-oriented will be allowed to continue on the basis of the existing approvals subject to Indian participation being not less than 26% of the equity of the company, (iii) companies engaged in trading activities will be required to bring down foreign shareholding to the level of 40%. It is obligatory for all branches of foreign companies operating in India and Indian companies with 40% and above foreign holding to obtain the permission of the RBI for continuing their business.

The government is assuming powers of suitably modifying the guidelines on the operation of Foreign Exchange Regulation Act, 1973. Foreign companies operating in a non-beneficial sector may be asked to wind up even if they offer to dilute their foreign holding to 40% as laid down in this act. Further reduction of foreign shareholding to 40% is the only option to these companies. They should alternatively diversify their manufacturing activities with 75% coming under the licensing policy of 1973 or become predominantly export-oriented with a minimum of 60% export of their total production.

The above guidelines were further changed in April 1976 as under:

(i) If a company carries on activities given in the Industrial Licensing Policy 1973 together with activities requiring sophisticated technology and exports account for not less than 75% of total annual turnover, such a company will be allowed to continue its activities subject to the condition that it will increase Indian participation within a specified period, to not less than the 26% of the equity capital of the company.

(ii) If the exports of the above company account for not less than 60% of the total annual turnover, it shall have

Indian participation not less than 49% of the equity of the company.

(iii) If the exports of a company account for more than 40% of the total annual turnover, such a company will be allowed to continue its activities subject to the condition that it will increase within a specified period, the Indian participation to not less than 49% of the equity of the company.

(iv) Cases of companies coming with proposals for substantial exports could be considered on merits for higher level of foreign equity participation, provided such participation is in the overall interest of the economy of the country.

On the question of takeover of the multinational companies, the Hathi Committee recommended in April 1975 that the multinational drug companies should be taken over by the Government and managed by the proposed National Drug Authority.

Hathi was appointed in February 1974 to go into all aspects of the drugs and pharmaceutical industry. The Committee laid emphasis on Indianisation of drug industry and suggested that a more purposeful policy be implemented to blunt the potential of foreign companies to exploit their names and curb the development of Indian sector. The country could never be self-sufficient in drugs because the drug industry is dominated by the foreign units who operate on the principle of free market economics.

When the government withdrew itself from too much interference in industrial activity in the country, and when it started industrial deregulation, it liberalised the provisions of foreign investment. Automatic approval was made available for foreign direct investment up to 51 % foreign equity ownership in a wide range of high priority industries including almost all bulk drugs and formulations.

A high-powered Foreign Investment Promotion Board (FIBP) now provides single window approvals for foreign investment proposals free from any predetermined parameters or procedures. The APB is now a part of the Ministry of Industry and projects up to Rs. 6,000 million are cleared by this Board within a deadline of six weeks. A new Foreign Investment Promotion Council has been created to formulate guidelines for policy and promote investment opportunities in India. Technical agreements receive automatic approval if the proposed royalty payments are within specified parameters. Remittance of dividends and royalties are freely permitted in approved projects and the restrictive conditions of "Dividend Balancing" through proportionate exports now restricted to consumer industries alone.

With a view to injecting the desired level of technological dynamism in Indian industry, Government provides automatic approval for technology agreements related to high priority industries within specified parameters up to: (i) lumpsum payment of up to US $2 million, (ii) five per cent royalty for domestic sale, and (iii) 8 per cent for exports, subject to payment of 8% of sales over a ten-year period from date of agreement or seven years from the commencement of production. Similar facilities are available for other industries as well if such agreements do not require the expenditure of free foreign exchange.

India today enjoys world confidence in the world business community. India is already on the way to becoming a key country in Asia for the flow of foreign direct investment.

O O O

# 26. TELECOMMUNICATION SERVICES IN INDIA

Telecommunication services in India were introduced soon after invention of telegraphy and telephone. First telegraph line between Kolkata and Diamond Harbour was opened for traffic in 1851. By March 1854, telegraph messages could be sent from Agra to Kolkata. By the year 1900, telegraph and telephone had started serving Indian Railways. As in case of telegraph, telephone service was also introduced in Kolkata in 1881-82, barely six years after the invention of telephone. First automatic exchange was commissioned at Shimla in 1913-14 with a capacity of 700 lines.

At the time of independence, Government of India had no rudimentary telecommunication system of world standard. In April 1948, India had only 321 telephone exchanges with 82,000 working connections. Growth of telecommunications service gained momentum after independence and steadily pushed forward in the fifty years of independence. On March 31, 1997, there were 22,212 telephone exchanges with equipped capacity of 177.42 lakh lines and 145.43 lakh direct telephone connections. The exchanges are linked with 30,968 route km of co-axial cable, 54,597 M/w route km of microwave systems. Country's remote areas are linked to the network through 209 satellite earth stations. All the district headquarters are now having Sill facility. The Sill facility has been provided to 13,220 stations. Satellite based Remote Area Business Message Network, a new technology is under operation for exchange of data facsimile, telex messages, etc.

Value added services are enhanced services which add value to the existing basic tele and bearer services. The Department of Telecommunication has decided to franchise value added services to Indian registered companies on a non-exclusive basis. The following services have been identified as Value Added Services: (i) Radio Paging Services, (ii) Cellular Mobile Telephone Service, (iii) Public Mobile Radio Trunking Service (PMRTS), (iv) Electronic Mail, (v) Voice Mail, (vi) Audio-tex Service, (vii) 64 kbps Data using VSAT (using satellite), (viii) Video-tex Service, (ix) Video Conferencing, and (x) Credit Card Authorisation.

The Department of Telecommunications (DOT) has decided to permit the entry of the private operators in Basic Telephone Services. There will be one telephone operator in each Telecom circle, providing Basic Telephone Services. Foreign equity of not more than 49% is permitted for such companies. Already the government has given the licenses for two Telecom circles of Gujarat and Madhya Pradesh.

Telecom Mission, popularly known as "Mission: Better Communications" was launched in April 1986 with the objective of enhancing subscibers, satisfaction level by improving quality of service and increasing accessibility of telecom facilities both in urban and rural areas in a timebound way, to give the nation a continuous improving telecom service in rural, tribal and hilly areas, and a major programme of national digital networks selected, clear-cut objectives and specific targets' were fixed, strategic and operational plans were drawn to achieve the mission's goals.

Wireless Planning and Coordination Wing (WPC) was established in 1952, as the national radio regulatory authority responsible for coordination and regulation of radio spectrum usages in the country. It is the nodal agency for all matters concerning International Telecommunications Union (ITU), a specialised agency of the United Nations for all telecommunication matters and Asia Pacific Telecommunity (APT), an inter-governmental organisation of the Region. WPC assisted by its Monitoring Organisation performs all functions relating to planning, coordination, assignment, regulations, and administration of the uses of the radio frequencies in India, clears site for installation of wireless stations and issues licenses for establishment, maintenance, and working of wireless stations in India, under the Indian Telegraph Act 1885. It is responsible for all matters concerning assignment for all terrestrial, Geo-stationary Satellite (GSO), and non-GSO based satellite networks, including positions in GSO and necessary coordination in this regard both at national and international levels. It also conducts examinations to award certificates of proficiency for aeronautical and maritime mobile services as well as certain value added services on franchise basis, e.g. cellular mobile telephone, radio, VSAT radio trunking has created a large demand on the use of radio spectrum. WPC Wing has undertaken an exercise to revise the National Frequency Allocation Plan (established in 1981) to accommodate the spectrum requirements of these services, besides coordinating the increased demands of various major wireless users in the country.

Telecommunication Engineering Centre is a core technology group under the Telecom Commission, Government of India. It functions in close coordination with all the wings of Telecom Commission and the field units of Department of Telecommunications. Its role and objectives include standardisation and development of generic requirements or technical specifications for telecom euipment services and products; evaluation of equipment services and products, new technologx study, trials and induction, testing and certification of the licensed private telecom service networks.

# IX. RECENT WORLD EVENTS

## 1. 15TH APEC SUMMIT

The 21-member Asia Pacific Economic Cooperation (APEC) was established in 1989 with the purpose of achieving free and open trade in the region by 2010 for rich countries and 2020 for poor nations. This is a major international grouping of countries located around the Pacific Ocean, and its annual summit of Heads of State and Government invariably commands wide attention. The APEC consists of Australia, Brunei, Canada, Chile, China, Hong Kong, Indonesia, Japan, Malaysia, Mexico, New Zealand, Papua New Guinea, The Philippines, Singapore, South Korea, Taiwan, the US, Peru, Russia and Vietnam represent nearly half of the world's trade and 48 per cent of the world's Gross National Product (GNP). Its 2007 Summit was held in Sydney (Australia) in Sept. 2007.

Prime Minister John Howard of the host country Australia described the Sydney Summit as the most important ever staged by his country. Certainly, it drew a galaxy of the world's most important leaders, including the President of the US, Russia and China, the Prime Minister of Japan, and a host of lesser luminaries. As is increasingly the case with such highly visible international gatherings, it also drew a host of protestors vocal and active groups of concerned persons who are critical of what the international community has done, or failed to do, on matters like climate change or trade.

At the culmination of the summit, the leaders issued a Sydney Declaration, which saw real progress in world Trade talks and pledged flexibility and the political will to forge a deal by the end of 2007.

The leaders at the summit called on all nations to give the same commitment to reaching a conclusion to the drawn out Doha round of India talks. The Asia Pacific leaders, whose economics account for more than half of world India, said there was an urgent need to make progress in the World Trade Organisation (WTO) talks.

The leaders expressed a renewed commitment aimed at generating new momentum on the Doha round multilateral trade negotiations. They issued a strong statement insisting on an ambitious, balanced result delivers substantial market access in agriculture, industrial goods and services.

The summit leaders agreed to work toward achieving an aspiration goal of a reduction in energy intensity of at least 25 per cent by 2030. The goal would apply only to the Pacific Rain economics, including non-sovereign territories, under the APEC umbrella. The non-binding commitment to move towards reducing the of emissions of greenhouse gases by 2030 will be reckoned against the levels in 2005.

The important aspect of the Sydney summit, as seen from India's standpoint, was that the APEC leaders emphasised the importance of energy sources entailing 3000 emissions or low-level release of greenhouse gases. This would cover nuclear energy, and the leaders advocated the adoption of suitable technologies too.

The Sydney summit decided against expanding its membership for the time being. The issue will be discussed afresh in 2010. India, seen as a possible candidate for APEC membership, will, therefore, continue to remain outside the premier economic forum. The decision means India will have to wait until at least 2010 when Japan hosts the summit to see if New Delhi can join the elite club of APEC. Besides India, there are 10 other countries looking for the membership of the organisation. They are Colombia, Ecuador, Macau, Mongolia, Pakistan, Sri Lanka, Cambodia, Laos and Myanmar. At the summit, it was also decided that in the year 2008, 2009, 2010, 2011 and 2012, the summit will be held in Peru, Singapore, Japan the US and Russia, respectively.

Until now, India has not been able to do anything more than play the part of a distant onlooker at the events within APEC. The doors have been firmly shut till 2010. More than one effort has been made by India to establish some sort of relationship with the forum, even if immediate membership may not be available. As far as APEC is concerned, it can be expected that when the addition of new members comes up for consideration in 2010, India will be able to make a persuasive case for its entry.

O O O

# 2. RUSSIA-IRAN RELATIONS

The relations between Iran and Russia picked up as a weakened Safavid empire gave way to the Qajarid dynasty in the mid 18th century. The first Persian Ambassador to Russia was Mirza Abulhassan Khan Ilchi Kabir. The Qajarid Government was quickly absorbed with managing domestic turmoil, while rival colonial powers rapidly sought a stable foothold in the region. Plagued with internal politics, the Qajarid Government found itself incapable of rising to the challenge of facing, or even recognising, its northern threat from Russia.

The Russian empire continuously advanced south in the course of two decades of war against Persia. By the end of the 19th century, the Russian empire's dominance became so pronounced that it captured a number of cities, and the Central Government in Tehran was left with no power to even select its own ministers without the approval of the Anglo-Russian consulates.

Russian involvement, continued with the establishment of the short-lived Persion socialist Soviet Republic in 1920, followed by the short-lived Republic of Mahabad, the last effort by the Soviet Russia to establish a communist republic in Iran. In 1941, as the Second World War raged, Soviet Russia and Great Britain launched the Anglo-Soviet invasion of Iran, ignoring Tehran's plea for neutrality.

The end of the Second World War brought the start of American dominance in Iran's political arena, and with an anti-Soviet Cold War brewing, the US quickly moved to convert Iran into an anti-communist bloc, thus ending Russian influence on Iran for years to come.

During the Iran-Iraq war, the erstwhile USSR supplied Baghdad with large amounts of conventional arms. Iran's spiritual leader Ayatollah Khomeini was deemed principally incompatible with the communist ideals of the Soviet Union, leaving the secular Saddam as an ally of Moscow. After the war, especially with the disintegration of the USSR, Russia-Iran relations marked a sudden increase in diplomatic and commercial ties and Tehran even began purchasing weapons from Russia. By the mid 1990s, Russia had agreed to continue work on developing Iran's nuclear programme with plans to finish constructing the nearly 20-year delayed nuclear reaction plant of Bushehr.

In 2005, Russia was the seventh largest trading partner of Iran with 5.33 per cent of all exports to Iran originating from Russia. Trade between the two countries kept on increasing.

The noticeable thing is that Russia and Iran also share a common interest in limiting the political influence of the US in the Central Asia. This common interest has led the Shanghai Cooperation Organisation to extend to Iran observer status in 2005, and full membership in 2006. Iran's relations with the organisation, which is dominated by Russia and China, represent the most extensive diplomatic ties Tehran has shared since the 1979 revolution.

However, the solidity of Russia-Iran relations remains to be seen and tested. Russia is increasingly becoming dependent on its economic ties with the West, and is, gradually becoming vulnerable to western pressures in trying to curb its relations with Tehran.

Unlike previous years in which Iran's air fleet were entirely western made, Iran's Air Force and civilian air fleet are increasingly becoming Russian builts as the US and Europe continue to maintain sanctions on Iran.

Russian President Vladimir Putin and his Iranian counterport Mahmoud Ahmadinejad have signed an agreement on the Bushehr nuclear power station in Iran. The first nuclear power station in Bushehr was scheduled to start operations in Sept. 2007, but the start was been delayed due to a dispute between Russian contractors and Iran over the terms of payment.

The Bushehr plant was expected to become operational in the summer of 2008, producing half its 2,000 MW capacity of electricity.

In Dec. 2007, the Russian company which is building the Bushehr reactor, delivered the first batch of low-enriched uranium-235 under the control of the International Atomic Energy Agency (IAEA). In Jan. 2007, the fourth and fifth shipment of nuclear fuel came from Russia for a power plant being constructed near Tehran.

In April 2008, Iran prepared a package of proposals that covered a nuclear dispute with the West and other issues.

A pioneering visit to Tehran by the President Putin had been seen as a challenging new development with important strategic repercussions. As was widely noted, Putin was the first ruler from Moscow to visit Iran after Josef Stalin in 1943, who went for a famous wartime conference with President Roosevelt and Prime Minister Winston Churchill. Putin's visit took place at a time when Iran's nuclear plans had attracted ominous attention and wide criticism in the West, especially the US. Renewed efforts are on the horizon to push through strengthened sanctions by the UN Security Council against Iran, whose nuclear programme is regarded by the US and its allies as military in purpose.

Putin said that Iran should be permitted to pursue its peaceful nuclear programme. This could imply that the programme is indeed peaceful for all intents and purposes, and certainly did not hold out any threat or warning. His words could give Iran some breathing space and encourage diplomatic activity at a time when there are frequent reiterations of the US determination to stop Iran at all costs.

The US Defence Secretary reiterated that all options are on the table, the then Vice-President Dick Chiney spoke of international action to stop Iran, and the President George W. Bush raised the fear a nuclear-armed Iran could lead to the Third World War.

Viewed against these statements, Russia is indeed on a different level. Moscow evidently has no clear information to corroborate the charge that Iran has a nuclear weapons programme, and after the Weapons of Mass Destruction (WMDs) fiasco in Iraq, few would give automative credence to what the US is stating on the subject. As Iran's leading partner in its civilian nuclear project, Russia may well believe that it has better access to Tehran's thinking and future plans that any other foreign country.

President Putin's visit to Tehran projected a more assertive and capable Russia that was ready to play a bigger role in its own region. It has been a slow revival after the Soviet collapse that forced Moscow to draw in its horns and watch more or less helplessly as its neighbours in central Asia and the Caucasus went outside its orbit.

In recent months however, serious differences between these countries, Russia and Iran have become visible on a number of issues, not Iran alone. The eastward expansion of the North Atlantic Treaty Organisation (NATO) and the US decision to extend its anti-missile defences into countries on the Russian border has revived half-buried fears from Cold War days. The missile treaties that placed restraints on these two major holders of lethal weaponary have been called into question. The visits to Moscow by senior US leaders, including the Secretary of State, have emphasised rather than narrowed the breach. This is not to suggest that any breakdown is in the offing, only to point to the more complex environment of today in which national interests are being pursed.

A resurgent Russia has pushed itself back into the reckowning in the geo-stragetic calculations relating to the Caspian and Central Asia. This is one of the important outcomes of President Putin's visit to Iran.

Besides pressing the question of nuclear developments in Iran, the availability of abundant oil and natural gas in the region will ensure that it remains a focus of constant international attention. India already draws much of its oil requirements from Iran and is bidding hard to obtain natural gas from there and from its neighbour Turkmenistan. It must, therefore, watch these developments closely and be careful about the future trends in the region.

In a balance-of-power world, it is up to Iran to engage Russia in a fruitful partnership and shape it to accept the new situation. How Iran responds to the new challenge and opportunity with fresh ideas and ability to translate them into a consensus for action, will to a great extent determine Moscow and Tehran relations at least for the near future.

O O O

## 3. PHOENIX LANDS ON MARS

The US spacecraft Phoenix landed on Mars on May 25, 2008 to begin its three-month search for water and signs of life. It is in good shape and has successfully sent images of the frozen land. The first images from *Phoenix* also provided a glimpse of the flat valley floor expected to have water-rich permafrost within the reach of the lander's robotic arm. Several image sent by Phoenix, which landed on Mars after a 10-month, 679 million-kilometre journey, revealed a landscape similar to what can be found in Earth's permafrost regions— geometric patterns in the soil likely related to the freezing and thawing of ground ice. The Phoenix mission is led by University of Arizone and managed by the Jet Propulsion Laboratory.

It was the first successful soft landing on Mars since the twin Viking landers touched down in 1976. Rovers Spirit and Opportunity used a combination of parachutes and cushioned air bags to bounce to the surface four years ago. Phoenix avoided the fate of another polar explorer—the Mars Polar Lander—which crashed into the Martian south pole after prematurely shutting off its engines in 1999. Phoenix inherited the hardware of a lander that was cancelled after the Polar Lander disaster and carried similar instruments flown on the ill-fated 1999 mission. Phoenix's descent was nearly flawless. The only unexpected turn was that it opened its parachute seven seconds later than planned, causing the spacecraft to settle slightly downrange from the bull's-eye target. Travelling at 12,600 miles per hour enduring 1,500 °C temperature through the Martian atmosphere, Phoenix first deployed a braking parachute, shook off its protective casing, and then fired 12 small "retro-rockets" that allowed it to land softly.

Phoenix, launched in Aug. 2007, was named for having risen from the ashes of previous mission failures. Only five of the previous 11 international attempts to land probes on Mars have succeeded. Most life search missions follow that water—which is the basis of all life, and it is ice that Phoenix will dig out, with a robotic arm. If it is there, the frozen samples will be examined by on-board instrument which will then transmit the results back. Earlier Mars landings were in the planet's equator, where it was believed there is no water.

There have been 40 attempts to reach Mars out of which 28 have ended in failure, the majority losing contact in route, burning up on entry or being broken to pieces on attempting to land. The Soviet missions Marsnik 1 and Marsnik 2, designed to fly past the planet, fell to Earth shortly after being launched in 1960.

Two years later, the Soviet Sputanik 22 probe exploded, and the first successful fly was not achieved until 1964 when the US Mariner 4 returned pictures of the dusty red landscape.

A Russian mission ended in fiasco when the launch vehicle blew up in 1996. Japan's single attempt to reach Mars failed in 1998 because of problems with its propulsion system. In 1999, NASA lost three missions. In 2003, the European Space Agency's Beagle 2 probe disappeared before landing.

Phoenix planted its three legs in a broad, shallow valley littered with pebble size rocks that should not pose any hazard to the spacecraft. During its prime mission Phoenix will dig through layers of soil to reach the ice, believed to be buried up to 30 centimetres deep. Phoenix will study whether the ice melted during a time in Mar's recent past and will analyse soil samples for traces of organic compounds, which would be a possible indicator of conditions favourable for primitive life. It is not equipped to detect past or present alien life. Phoenix however, is not primarily designed to discover life on Mars but to check for conditions that might be or have been, conducive to it in the past. To this end, the Lander will be directed to deploy a 2.4 metre-long scoop which can dig in up to a metre undergo and to collect samples of soil and ice that its onboard laboratory will then analyse to see if some key chemical ingredients of life such as carbon-based compounds, are preserved in it.

The results will go a long way to help in evaluating whether the environment has ever been favourable for life. Scientists also hope to establish whether the ice ever melts there in response to climate cycles because that, too, would create the conditions for life on Mars.

There are two possible outcomes of this important experiment. The first is that the state-of-the-art instruments, including a wet chemistry laboratory, mass spectrometer and two types of high-resolution microscopes, on Lander's deck will show positive results. The other alternative is that Phoenix will find nothing. This is also a fairly likely outcome since Mars does not fall in the so-called 'Goldilocks's or habitable zone, a region of space in the solar system where conditions are favourable for life.

With Phoenix having landed, the images it returns may prove to be some of the most fantastic in the history of space science. But we should not get excited until we actually see them on our television screens. If Phoenix finds something, it will change the way we think about ourselves.

○ ○ ○

## 4. Slowdown in World Economy

A report published in May 2008 by the Economist Intelligence Unit, of *The Economist,* considers a riskier economic future for the world as a result of the ongoing credit crunch. It foresees 60 per cent chance of a slowdown in growth in 2009, but it now predicts a 30 per cent likelihood that things will get really nasty, with the dollar falling to new lows against the yen and euro and commodity prices plunging as demand slows. America could see Gross Domestic Product (GDP) growth contract by 1.5 per cent, while growth in the big developing economies could slip to the lowest levels in many years. The following graph shows the Real GDP forecast for the year 2009.

It is now quite obvious that the international economy is into a downturn, because it is likely to hit the US, Japan, and the larger European Union countries simultaneously. The IMF reckons that there are 25 per cent chances of the world economy growing by less than three per cent in 2008 and 2009, the equivalent of recession, in its view. The origins of this crisis lie in the biggest asset bubble in history; financial markets have already suffered arguably their biggest shock for 80 years; and America suffering (Britain's housing market, for instance, is showing the same symptoms as America's). But so far there is little evidence that the world economy is falling off a cliff.

US economy was the first to see the slowdown. Evidence is mounting that the economy has slipped into recession and this time consumer weakness is to the fore. The doughty American shopper is being put back by four things: the housing bust, the credit crunch, higher fuel and food costs and, most recently, a weakening labour market. The unemployment rate rose to over 5 per cent in March 2008, while the private sector lost jobs for the fourth month in a row. The IMF had officially predicted an American recession in 2008.

As per the predictions of the US Fed Reserve also, the US economy will grow only 1.3 to two per cent in 2008. In

November 2007, the Fed had forecast that the economy will grow by about 1.8 to 2.2 per cent and unemployment rate will remain at 4.8 per cent. The new forecast is significantly lower than this, including the unemployment rate which is at 5.3 per cent. The consumer spending in the US in decreasing. This is very important considering the fact that it accounts for nearly 70 per cent of the economic activity of the US and more than 20 per cent of global GDP. The housing output has fallen by 24 per cent in the fourth quarter contributing to sharp decline in construction employment.

The rate of job losses in America has been mild compared with previous downturns, and there are many reasons to suppose it will stay that way.

(1) The first is the activism of American policymarkers. Congress started throwing money at the problem early, and after announcing a grand fiscal stimulus package, a second fiscal stimulus is already being discussed alongside a bail-out for the housing market.

(2) The Fed has already lowered interest rates and promised more cuts if the economy stays weak and perhaps most important, sharply reduced the odds of financial-market catastrophe by extending its safety net to investment banks.

(3) Another reason is the changing structure of the world economy. The dynamism and resilience of emerging markets mean that America does not matter as much as it once did. The Indian economy is said to be decoupled from the US economy. The IMF expected global growth to fall from 4.9 per cent in 2007 to 3.7 per cent in 2008 but the Indian GDP growth was maintained above 8 per cent in 2007-08 and is predicted to remain around 8 per cent during 2008-09.

US-European trade constitutes 40 per cent of the world's total and supports 14 million jobs. Therefore, the crisis in the US has repercussions on growth in the Euro zone. The IMF in its recent semi-annual World Economic Outlook report said that Europe will see sluggish growth in coming years because of the recession in the United States, a strong Euro and ongoing turmoil in financial markets. Growth in the Euro area will slow to 1.4 per cent for current year and will fall further to 1.2 per cent in 2009. That compares to a growth rate of 2.6 per cent in 2007. As per the report, the downturn in significant enough that it should trigger a relaxing of monetary policy by the ECB. Consumer prices were forecast to rise 2.8 per cent in the Euro area this year but only 1.6 per cent in 2009.

Germany will face one of the largest slowdowns of any European nation, with GDP growth dropping to 1.4 per cent during 2008 and one per cent in 2009, compared to growth of 2.5 per cent in 2007. Charles Collyns, the IMF's lead economist for Western Europe, said domestic demand in Germany has so far not been able to pick up for the country's heavy dependency on external factors. Outside of the US, Europe has been hardest hit for a financial crisis that has led to more than US $ 200 billion in write downs at investment banks tied to a meltdown in the US subprime mortgage market.

Asian economies though feeling the heat of slowdown in US economy are quite resilient. Though there is slowdown in their GDP growth, it is only a marginal reduction from the high levels. In February, World Bank, revi᠎  d its forecast for China's 2008 GDP growth to 9.6 per cent which is 1.2 per cent lower than the earlier estimate. The bank said that the country is in a strong macroeconomic position to stimulate demand by easing fiscal policy and credit controls, even if the global slowdown will be more pronounced.

As far as India is concerned, consensus GDP growth estimates have been lowered to around eight per cent, against 8.7 per cent in 2007-08. However, manufacturing production rose 8.6 per cent in February 2008 from a year earlier, compared with January's revised 6.3 per cent.

Though curbing the rising inflation is priority of the government of India, it has taken definitive steps to keep the growth going. To encourage employment, the trade policy supplement paid special attention to labour-intensive export industries. For example, it gave a five per cent additional duty credit and carved out separate allocations under existing market-promotion funds for the export of toys and sports goods. Government would set up a joint task force with members from the central and state governments as well as industry to draw up a road map for removing structural hurdles to exports. The task force will study the issues such as reducing waiting periods at ports and airports, developing world-class infrastructure, and setting up global manufacturing hubs for auto parts, drugs, jewellery, handicrafts, textiles, petroleum products and so on.

Economists continue to argue about whether or not emerging economies will follow America into recession. Recent data suggest that decoupling is no myth. Indeed, it may yet save the world economy. Decoupling does not mean that an American recession will have no impact on developing countries. Such countries have become more integrated into the world economy as their exports have increased from just over 25 per cent of their GDP in 1990 to almost 50 per cent today. Sales to America will obviously weaken. The point is that their GDP-growth rates will slow by much less than in previous American downturns.

One of the reason is that while exports to America have stumbled, those to other emerging economies have surged. China's growth in exports to America slowed to only five per cent (in dollar terms) in the year up to January, but exports to Brazil, India and Russia were up by more than 60 per cent. Half of China's exports now go to other emerging economies. Likewise, South Korea's exports to the US tumbled by 20 per cent in the year up to February, but its total exports rose by 20 per cent, due to trade with other developing nations. A second supporting factor is that in many emerging markets domestic consumption and investment quickened during 2007. Their consumer spending rose almost thrice as fast as in the developed world. Investment seems to be holding up even better. According to HSBC, real capital spending rose by a staggering 17 per cent in emerging economies last year, compared with only 1.2 per cent in rich economies. The four biggest emerging economies, which accounted for two-fifths of global GDP growth last year, are the least dependent on the United States: exports to America account for just eight per cent of China's GDP, four per cent of India's, three per cent of Brazil's and one per cent of Russia's. Over 95 per cent of China's growth of 11.2 per cent in the year to the fourth quarter came from domestic demand.

Smaller economies in Asia seem more vulnerable. For example, Malaysia's exports to America amount to 22 per cent of its GDP, and they fell by 18 per cent in the year up to December. Yet its annual GDP growth jumped to 7.3 per cent in the fourth quarter, thanks to consumer spending and a jump in government infrastructure investment.

As the world appears to be heading towards a global recession the need for open trade is as paramount as ever. To stop would be to forego huge benefits; to go backward toward greater protectionism, as some urge, would be to risk falling into the kind to trade wars that deepened the calamity of the Great Depression.

We should remember that given the scale of the financial mess, situation could be a lot worse. On can even argue that after five years of breakneck growth, a more sedate global expansion would be no bad thing: it would dampen inflationary pressures in the emerging world, and weaker domestic demand should shrink America's gaping external deficit— already down from above six per cent of GDP to below five per cent. The recession may not be as severe as many fear, but the recovery could take longer.

## Signs of Revival of Global Economy

Global economic slowdown is showing signs of bottoming, suggesting that revival is not far. Consumer confidence is stabilizing after falling for a year now, providing a glimmer of hope for the deteriorating world economy. Clifford Young of Ipsos Global Public Affairs—the international market research and polling company that carried an online poll in May 2008 said, "It looks like we have hit bottom and so there are glimmers of hope. What we are seeing is that consumers for the most part have been scared, and they have cut expenditures and increased savings. Ipsos polled people in a number of countries like the US, Canada, Mexico, Brazil, Argentina, South Korea, China, Japan, India, Australia, Germany, Russia, Poland, Czech Republic, Hungary, Turkey, Sweden, Italy, England, France, Spain and the Netherlands. Young said that the stabilization is basically happening in the United States, India and China while Europe is still dicy, as are Brazil and Russia. The 23 countries polled make up 75 per cent of world's Gross Domestic Product.

A broad US recovery in 2010 will be followed by a slower global rebound in 2011 or later, according to approximately half of the 300 CEOs surveyed in the newly released fifth annual New York Stock Exchange (NYSE) Euronext CEO Report, entitled "The Road to Recovery" conducted by Opinion Research Corporation (ORC). A large majority of CEOs favour business tax reliefs, low interest rates and liberal lending to boost the economic activity. Many of them also agree on the need to restructure America's financial regulatory system, streamline corporate governance and align the US and international accounting standards. The report reveals how CEOs have been forced to analyse their past habits and "significantly change the way they operate today and plan for tomorrow." However, the US CEOs and their counterparts in other countries have different views on government interventions, though they generally agree on the need to be innovative yet disciplined to successfully emerge from the economic crisis. Duncan Viederaur, CEO, NYSE Euronext stated that global CEOs were responsibly addressing the challenges brought by the financial meltdown and were employing genuine operational discipline and planning for the future. He went on to say that they were focused on maintaining a strong balance sheet and on corporate competitiveness, and were identifying new growth opportunities as well as ways to build value for stakeholders.

In spite of the downturn, most of the CEOs acknowledged that their companies have gained some benefit from the crisis in terms of larger market share, contract renegotiations and hiring of new employee talent. When asked what change they would make to help their companies through future market turmoil, they replied almost in unison that it would be controlling costs and debt and remaining highly liquid. Securing finance topped the list as the internal factor having a greater influence on revenue growth through 2010, with the strength of the management team coming a close second.

Amid reports that retail spending is picking up and the world economy may be stablising, American families say that they are looking beyond the eventual recovery to a more frugal future that is based on saving money as a desirable and permanent financial strategy. The First Command Financial Behaviours Index indicated that the majority of respondents were embracing a more conservative philosophy in their personal finances. About 75 per cent of respondents said that the US was too wasteful before the recession. More than half agree that the economic situation will continue to be bad for some time to come and it will have a long-term effect on their behaviour. They also said that they felt more confident, assured and tension free after developing a disciplined saving mentality. Scott Spiker, CEO of First Command Financial Services Inc. had this to say: "After years of living in a consumption fueled economy, consumers are rediscovering the time-tested values of prudence and self-reliance. This change signals a slower but healthier recovery." "What we don't need," Spiker went on to say, "are encouragements from government or Wall Street to spend more and more. Rather, the time has come for Americans to embrace a new frugality."

This new attitude is emerging at a time when the US outlook on personal finance is improving. About one-third of respondents to the survey indicated that their personal financial situation was stable. Many of them said they were cutting down expenditure though they didn't need to. Only 34 per cent said they were looking forward to the economy bouncing back so that their spending habits could go back to previous ways. Spiker also pointed out that the savings to debt ratio was the most important contributor to financial optimism. Simply speaking, with more savings and less debt, the feelings of financial security increase. Having a reasonable savings-to-debt ratio—as is now being aspired to in America—makes a person feel better about the present and more optimistic about the future. Now Americans continue to cut back expenditure by reducing leisure activities, postponing clothing purchases, shopping at discount stores and increasing their use of coupons. Relatively few consumers who have received tax refund say that they will spend it on non-essential items. The average American according to Spiker has regained fiscal sanity and that is an encouraging sign.

## Business Confidence Rises in India Despite Concerns

According to Confederation of Indian Industry's-bi-annual Business Outlook Survey (CII-BCI), India Inc's business confidence has improved considerably for April-September 2009 period compared to the past six months. "CII-BCI was recorded at 58.7 for April-September 2009-10, reflecting an increase after two consecutive periods of decline. "The rise in the index reflects better expectations for the coming six months and confirms our belief that the worst is likely to be over for the economy," said Director General, CII, Chandrajit Banerjee. However, uncertain global economic outlook and slackening consumer demand still remain major concerns for the business community.

The CII-BCI is constructed as a weighted average of the Current Situation Index (CSI) and the Expectations Index (EI). The CSI that reflects current business conditions has lost 2.5 points for the period April-September 2009-10 as compared with the previous six months. In comparison with the corresponding period last year, the CSI is down 6.9 points, reflecting a decrease in current business sentiments due to the global financial and economic meltdown.

The EI that reflects the expectation of Indian industry with regard to performance of their company, sector and the economy for the period April-September 2009-10 gained 4.9 points as compared to the second half of 2008-09.

The CII survey, which is based on a sample size of 374 companies, revealed that 83 per cent of the respondents expect GDP growth for the year 2009-10 to exceed 5 per cent with the majority expecting it to be between 5 and 6 per cent. On inflation, 86 per cent of the respondents expected inflation to be above 2 per cent in 2009-10, thereby ruling out the possibility of sustained deflation in the economy. Given the ongoing global slowdown, 96 per cent of the respondents feel that it is only in the second half of 2009-10 and beyond, that the Indian economy would witness a turnaround and begin returning to normal growth.

The prospects for investment, capacity utilization, production, employment and exports as elements that build up the business confidence were also looked into by the survey. The survey revealed that 30 per cent of the respondents planned to increase investments during April-September 2009-10. Capacity utilization has improved and 50 per cent of the respondents revealed that capacity utilization for April-September 2009-10 was expected to be in the range of 75-100 per cent compared to 39 per cent of respondents who said that capacity utilisation was in that range. The CII survey revealed that 25 per cent of the respondents expected the inventory levels to increase, lower than the 35 per cent that reported an increase for the past six months.

According to 50 per cent of the respondents, the value of production was expected to increase in the next six months. Further, increase in production was likely because of expected increase in new orders. Over 5 per cent of the respondents expected new orders to increase in the next six months, compared to about 30 per cent of the respondents who revealed that new orders had increased in the second half of 2008-09.

Over 35 per cent of the respondents expressed confidence in expansion of exports for the period April-September 2009-10. Regarding procedural delays, 95 per cent of the respondents felt that the delays had not reduced. This has been a long-standing hurdle for exporters, which raises transactions costs and needs to be addressed urgently.

The CII Business Outlook Survey also asked respondents about their main concerns, such as global economic instability, high interest rate, cost and availability of labour, infrastructure and institutional shortages, currency risks, slackening consumer demand, cost of compliance, surge in imports and risk of deflation.

Although financial markets appear to be coming out of a deep freeze, it is early to say the global slowdown has bottomed, said Standard & Poor's Ratings Services in a report. The report, titled "Fiscal Health of Asian Sovereigns if 'Green Shoots' Wither," is a "what-if" scenario analysis, looking at potential evolutions of selected Asian sovereign fiscal performance over the next few years in two scenarios.

One scenario is Standard & Poor's baseline projections of economic development, in which Asian economies recover sometime in 2010 after steep declines in many of them. "In this scenario, the negative impact on sovereign credit ratings would be minimal, with the possible exceptions of those currently with a negative outlook—Thailand, Vietnam, and India," said Standard & Poor's credit analyst, Kim Eng Tan.

The other scenario is an extended recession, in which most of Asia drags through four consecutive years of contraction. Even in this scenario, which we consider to be remote, our simulation indicates that fiscal pressures are not likely to lead to default although sovereign credit quality in many cases would deteriorate markedly, Tan said.

Meanwhile OPEC in its Monthly Oil Market Report 2009 pointed out that the world economy has seen some positive developments recently with the rally in the stock markets, improved confidence and a more positive sentiment. However, volatility remains high and large uncertainties persist as the world economy struggles to emerge from recession.

In 2009, per capita GDP is expected to fall 2.5% compared to an average drop of 0.4% in previous global recessions of

1975, 1982 and 1991, according to International Monetary Fund (IMF). The result suggest that, unless an investment-grade sovereign makes major policy mistakes, most would remain in that category after an extended-recession scenario, even though their credit ratings could slip by one to four notches. The resilience of these investment-grade sovereigns, with a few exceptions, stems from their relatively strong fiscal positions prior to the crisis. "These governments have years of fiscal consolidation and debt reduction, a sounder banking sector with higher capitalization and better risk management, and stronger external liquidity enhanced by more flexible exchange rate regimes," Tan said. S&P report is a part of a global effort to provide greater transparency and insight to market participants through "what-if" scenario analysis.

Meanwhile Standard and Poor's has come up with a new level of innovation for investors looking to gain exposure to the US and Australian markets while limiting their risk. S&P has launched risk controlled versions of its widely followed S&P 500 and S&P/ASX 200 indices. The S&P 500 Risk Control 10% index and the S&P/ASX 200 Risk Control 15% Index track the return of a strategy which dynamically adjusts the exposure to each underlying index in order to control the level of risk. The S&P 500 Risk Control 10% index targets a volatility level of 10% and the S&P/ASX 200 Risk Control 15% index targets a volatility level of 15%. If the risk level reaches a threshold that is too high, the exposure to the index is decreased in order to maintain the target volatility. If the risk level is too low, then the index will employ leverage to maintain the targeted level of volatility. "At a time of heightened volatility in the world's financial markets, Standard & Poor's new US and Australian based risk control indices will help investors target and control the level of risk in the S&P 500 and S&P/ASX 200 respectively," says Steve Goldin, Vice President of Strategy Indices at Standard & Poor's Index Services. "With risk controlled indices already based upon the S&P BRIC 40 Index, S&P Latin America 40 Index, S&P South East Asia 40 Index, and S&P Global Infrastructure Index, Standard & Poor's is the only index provider to offer indices targeting specific volatility levels," he adds.

Opinions are divided as to when the economic slowdown will come to an end and the world economy will be back on track. But there is a consensus of opinion that some signs of revival are already visible.

O O O

# 5. PAKISTAN AND COMMONWEALTH

The 53-nation group of former British Colonies suspended Pakistan following the then President Parvez Musharraf's declaration of emergency martial law in November, 2007. However, Islamabad called the Commonwealth decision "unreasonable and unjustified". The Foreign Ministry in Islamabad stated that the decision did not take into account the conditions prevailing in Pakistan, and that the emergency was a necessary measure to avert a serious internal crisis.

Whatever the Pakistan's Foreign Ministry had to say, the Commonwealth severely criticized Musharraf's failure to resign as chief of Pakistan's Army, his suspension of the Constitution, and his detention of judges and members of the political opposition. A report of the *The Daily Telegraph,* London reads thus:

Eight Foreign ministers from the former British colonies, including David Miliband, the (British) Foreign Secretary, condemned Gen Musharraf's imposition of emergency rule and suspended Pakistan with immediate effect. "This decision was taken in sorrow, not in anger," said Mr. Miliband, "I'm absolutely clear that democracy and the rule of law are the best allies of stability in Pakistan." The ministers, who met in Kampala, Uganda's capital, on the eve of a full summit of Commonwealth leaders, noted Pakistan's failure to "fulfil its obligations in accordance with Commonwealth principles."

The Commonwealth Ministerial Action Group (CMAG) which supported the decision to suspend Pakistan from Commonwealth stated that the Group stresses the need to foster international peace and security; democracy; liberty of the individual; equal rights for all and opposes all forms of oppression. The Commonwealth's decision was applauded by Human Rights Watch.

The Australian ABC News found the suspension "embrrassing for Pakistan" but stated that it will have "limited practical effect." An analysis in the Guardian said that there was "little the 53-member group can do to hurt Pakistan". It, however, pointed to the fact that the suspension would end the funding of projects designed to encourage economic liberalisation and good governance, and a ban on Pakistan attending meeting of Commonwealth heads of Government. The suspension prevented Pakistan from attending the Uganda Commonwealth Summit held in the last week of November 2007.

It is interesting to note that Pakistan's attitude was in sharp contrast with that of Zimbabwe—suspended from the Commonwealth in 2002. President Robert Mugabe called the group "a mere club" in which "some members are more equal than others." Musharraf, on the other hand was far from being apathetic to the suspension. His deep concern was visible from the fact that he lobbied hard for a delay, making calls to the British Prime Minister, Gordon Brown, asking for a reprieve. Pakistan's then caretaker Prime Minister, Mohammedmian Soomro urged the Commonwealth to send a delegation to Pakistan for a first-hand assessment of the situation. If Pakistan had been worried about suspension, it would not have bothered with such an intense diplomatic effort. Islamabad was well aware of the fact that in the present age of globalisation, no country can revel in an outcast status.

The other nation that currently stands suspended from the Commonwealth is Fiji, ousted after its coup in January 2007 when military chief Bainimarama restored executive powers to President Iloilo and took over the role of interim Prime Minister.

In April 2007, Bainimarama sacked the Great Council of Chiefs and suspended all future meetings after the Chiefs refused to endorse his government and his nomination for Vice President.

Several countries including South Africa, Nigeria and Sierra Leone have been suspended and later readmitted to the Commonwealth. Pakistan had been previously suspended from the group in 1999 when Musharraf seized power in a coup and deposed the democratically elected Prime Minister, Nawaz Sharif. However, it was readmitted in 2004. Pakistan has made democratic progress as elections have been held and Yusaf Raza Gillani—a member of the Pakistan People's Party whose leader Benazir Bhutto was assassinated in December 2007—has been made the Prime Minister. There was a strong opinion worldwide that, putting the regretful episodes behind, Pakistan should be readmitted to Commonwealth. Some people, however, believed that Pakistan must first eliminate terrorism in all its forms and manifestations. It must stop using terrorism and religious extensions as an instrument of policy before it can be taken back to the club of colonial glory and nostalgia, i..e. Commonwealth.

Pakistan was readmitted to the Commonwealth of Nations in May 2008. It was a welcome development as the Commonwealth meetings—which now Pakistan can also attend—will provide opportunities to the leaders of both India and Pakistan to talk on various issues of development of the subcontinent. Pakistan's absence from these meetings due to its suspension as happened in the case of Uganda meeting in November 2007 would have ended these opportunities.

Secondly, although India has made it very clear that it will not accept any third party mediation in the Kashmir dispute, there are several other issues like cross-border terrorism, sharing of Indus water, nuclear proliferation, gas pipeline from Iran to India through Afghanistan and Pakistan, WTO trade regulations, etc. where members of the Commonwealth can use their influence and remove roadblocks. If Pakistan were kept excluded from the group, it is less likely to have remained under the influence of the members.

Thirdly, if Pakistan's suspension meant blockage of funds for its various projects, it would have slowed down growth in the country and adversely impacted trade between India and Pakistan. Promotion of commercial interaction is an important component of India's policy engagement with Pakistan. The financial year 2006-07 witnessed substantial growth of bilateral trade from US$ 320 million during April-August 2005 to US$ 759 million during the same period in 2006. Pakistan expanded its positive list allowing import of Indian goods from 773 to 1075 items which included important food items like onions, tomatoes, potatoes, garlic, sugar, meat and many others. In the present times of global food shortage and rising prices of food items, including in India, import of such items from Pakistan assumes great significance. It is necessary from the global point of view also to help Pakistan grow quickly so that it can contribute towards world food security.

India is host to Commonwealth Games to be held in 2010 at New Delhi. With its readmission, Pakistan will be able to participate in this mega sports events. It will help further India's objective of maintaining cordial relations with its neighbours. Now it is upto Pakistan to maintain law and order in the country and respect human rights and not to repeat the earlier ugly happenings.

O O O

# 6. RETAIL REVOLUTION: A NEW PHENOMENA

A retail revolution is taking its roots in India. Though a new phenomena, yet it is making fast strides and is visible everywhere. In a very short span of two years, it has exploded on the Indian firmament as a huge business opportunity. This vast multicultural country India is transforming from a socialist economy to a consumption led creative economy. Retailing in India is poised for boom time due to unprecedented surge in domestic consumption. Organised modern retail today forms around 9 per cent of total retail in the country.

Changing demographic profiles, increasing income levels, changing lifestyles, urbanisation, technological advancements and liberalisation and globalisation have brought about a dramatic change in consumers aspirations choices, preferences and tastes as well. In this scenario when the population is ageing, that is 50 per cent is less than 50 years old, it encourages production, consumption and innovation, but retailers too have to keep pace with it. As a consequence of the information, communication technologies, the customers in India are demanding international shopping experience. It suggests that future of retailing in India is very bright.

At present, India is one of the top five global destinations for retail investment, which provides employment opportunities to more than 21 million people. It contributes 13 per cent of the nation's GDP. Moving from metro cities to mini-metro cities, the retail sector is penetrating into the smaller towns and cities. Besides consumer durables, footwear, stationary and electronic goods, fashion goods like textiles and jewellery are some of the key thrust areas of retail business. The latest one to enter the list is the food and grocery retail which has suddenly caught the investor's imagination. This is due to the fact that the share of food and grocery currently account for as much as 60 per cent of estimated $ 350 billion Indian retail market. India's food sector is set to expand largely in coming years.

The future of retailing in India is very attractive. It presents great opportunity for international corporate giants like Wal-Mart or Pesco which can carry on business activities with the help of their wide network of retail stores. India's progress in the field of retail sector has been so rapid that it has been ranked for the fourth year in 2008 in the Global Retail Development index (GRDI) as the most attractive market for global retailers to come and start their business.

Retail sector in India is expected to grow at 35 per cent for the next few years because of investments that are pouring into this sector and big corporate giants. It is estimated that the organised retail market will be 20 per cent of the total retailing by 2008.

The growing Indian middle class with its rising consumption is the driving force behind the growth of retail sector in India. The middle class population is around 480 million with monthly household income ranging from $ 150 to $1000. The consumption pattern of this class of society is likely to change in near future as sixty per cent of the population today is below the age of thirty which means that a young working population will not only drive productivity but is also set to cause significant change in consumption and income generation. The average household income in urban areas has grown at a five per cent rate over the last decade. This reflects the growth in purchasing power which in a way has a crucial bearing on the growth of retail business in India.

India's food sector is set to make a boom in an age of retail business. Since India is the world's third largest producer of food with an annual output of 600 million tonnes, world's largest milk producer, second largest in rice, wheat and sugar and third largest in cotton, retail sector has the potentiality to ensure profitability of even small farmers. For bulk supply to retailers, aggregation of production from small holdings will help cut a part of these losses which are caused due to inadequate post-harvest facilities.

Besides, demand for food products continues to rise and mall culture is also flourishing, the future of food sector is very shine. Not only in big cities malls are mushrooming even in smaller cities and towns. Space no longer remains a constraint for the retail business, because real estate business has been flourishing for the last 10 years or so. A couple of years ago, the multi-outlet food and grocery retail chains were confined to only southern parts of the country but today they can be seen everywhere even in smaller towns.

The entry of big corporates giants like Aditya Birla, Tata, Reliance, ITC, Bharti, Godrej into this sector has revolutionised the retail business in India. A large number of retail stores are being opened in different cities. Initial trend in encouraging. Consumers' support and response are satisfactory which is a good sign for this business. Experts hold the view that organised food retail may expand to as much as 10 per cent of the total food.

The performance of the retail sector in India has been attributed to several sectors which include better delivery models, selection of proper location, pricing policy, etc. The size of the organized and modern retailing industry put together is around $29 billion and is predicted to see significant growth in next few years. However, it has to make big efforts to break the dominance of Kirana stores in the neighbourhood.

Government is also formulating policies that may contribute to the growth of retailing in India. Like various sectors of economy, retailing is also being seen as a prospective area for FDI. It is promoting FDI in this sector to facilitate retail growth. Some global giants like WalMart are making tie-up with the Indian corporate players to set their foot here. India displaced Russia to take the first position in 2006 Global Retail Development Index which is a measure of retail investment attractiveness among 30 emerging markets across the globe. This indicates that India is the most favoured destination in terms of investments into the retail sector.

However, there are certain constraints for the growth of retail sector in India. Storage is the biggest challenge. Keeping the size of the country and farm output, warehousing facilities are totally inadequate. Transportation is another major challenge which needs proper attention. In addition, inefficient, inexpensive and specific movement including state-of-the-art equipment for proper handling of the products, cold storages and other such infrastructural facilities are big challenges before the retail sector in India.

In brief, the retail sector in India has immense potentiality which needs to be exploited with efficient strategy, planning and implementation. It has the potential to turn into a win-win situation for all those involved—growers, aggregators, processors, retailers and consumers. But it needs to be carried on with social responsibility.

O O O

## 7. Mergers and Acquisitions

Mergers and acquisitions are most widely prevalent in market-based economies.They are found not only in commodity producing corporate entities but also in financial services providers, including commercial banks and industries. In recent years, there has been a phenomenol growth of M&A in the economy after the reorganisation that the size of a firm is an important matter for business diversification, consolidation, efficiency and introduction of innovations and creative approaches in conducting bussiness.

The phrase mergers and acquisitions (abbreviated M&A) refers to the aspect of corporate strategy, corporate finance and management dealing with the buying, selling and combining of different companies that can aid, finance, or help a growing company in a given industry grow rapidly without having to create another business entity.

Liberalisation, privatisation and globalisation have brought about a radical change in the economic environment of the country and have paved the way for competition within the country as well as abroad.

A merger is a tool used by companies for the purpose of expanding their operations often aiming at an increase of their long term profitability. There are 15 different types of actions that a company can take when deciding to move forward using M&A. Usually, mergers occur by mutual consent setting where executives from the target company help those from the purchaser in a fair process to ensure that the deal is beneficial to both parties. Acquisitions can also happen through a hostile takeover by purchasing the majority of outstanding shares of a company in the open market against the wishes of the target company's board. In the United States, business laws vary from state to state whereby some companies have limited protection against hostile takeovers. One form of protection against a hostile takeover is the shareholder rights plan, otherwise known as the "poison pill".

An acquisition, also known as a takeover, is the buying of one company by another. An acquisition may be friendly or hostile. In the former case, the companies cooperate in negotiations; in the latter case, the takeover target is unwilling to be bought or the target's board has no prior knowledge of the offer. Acquisition usually refers to a purchase of a smaller firm by a larger one. Sometimes, however, a smaller firm will acquire management control of a larger or longer established company and keep its name for the combined entity. This is known as a reverse takeover.

A purchase deal will also be called a merger when both CEOs agree that joining together is in the best interest of both of their companies. But when the deal is unfriendly, i.e. when the target company does not want to be purchased, it is always regarded as an acquisition.

Historically, mergers have often failed (Straub, 2007) to add significantly to the value of the acquiring firm's shares (King, et al., 2004). Corporate mergers may be aimed at reducing market competition, cutting costs (for example, reducing the number of employees, operating at a more technologically efficient scale, etc.), reducing taxes, removing management, "empire building" by the acquiring managers, or other purposes like building a monopoly which may or may not be consistent with public policy or public welfare. Thus, they can be heavily regulated like in the U.S. requiring approval by both the Federal Trade Commission and the State.

Although they are often uttered in the same breath and used as though they were synonymous, the terms merger and acquisition mean slightly different things.

When one company takes over another and clearly establishes itself as the new owner, the purchase is called an acquisition. From a legal point of view, the target company ceases to exist, the buyer gobbles up its entire business and the buyer's stock continues to be traded.

In the pure sense of the term, a merger happens when two firms, often of about the same size, agree to go forward as a single new company rather than remain separately owned and operated. This kind of action is more precisely referred to as a "merger of equals". Both companies' stocks are surrendered and new company stock is issued in its place. For example, both Daimler-Benz and Chrysler ceased to exist when the two firms merged, and a new company, DaimlerChrysler, was created.

In practice, however, actual mergers of equals don't happen very often. Usually, one company will buy another and, as part of the deal's terms, simply allow the acquired firm to proclaim that the action is a merger of equals, even if it is technically an acquisition. Being bought out often carries negative connotations, therefore, by describing the deal as a merger, deal makers and top managers try to make the takeover more palatable.

A purchase deal will also be called a merger when CEOs of both the companies agree that joining together is in the best interest of both of their companies. But when the deal is unfriendly, i.e. when the target company does not want to be purchased, it is always regarded as an acquisition.

Whether a purchase is considered a merger or an acquisition really depends on whether the purchase is friendly or hostile and how it is announced. In other words, the real difference lies in how the purchase is communicated to and received by the target company's board of directors, employees and shareholders. It is quite normal though for M&A deal communications to take place in a so-called 'confidentiality bubble' whereby information flows are restricted due to confidentiality agreements. Accurate business valuation is one of the most important aspects of M&A as valuations like these will have a major impact on the price that a business will be sold for. Most often this information is given in a Letter of Opinion of Value when the business is being valuated for interest's sake. There are other, more detailed ways of expressing the value of a business. These reports generally get more detailed and expensive as the size of a company increases. However, this is not always the case as there are many complicated industries which require more attention to detail, regardless of size.

The dominant rationale used to explain M&A activity is that acquiring firms seek improved financial performance.It is seen that the combined company will reduce duplicate department or operations lowering the costs of the company in relation to the same revenue stream, thus increasing profit.

By absorbing major competitor the company intends to increase its power by capturing increased market share. For example, a bank buying a stock broker could then sell its banking products to the stock broker's customers, while the broker can sign up the bank's customers for brokerage accounts. Or, a manufacturer can acquire and sell complementary products. Furthermore, factors like taxes, overheads and geographical diversifications have also been found other motives behind mergers and acquisitions.

The Great Merger Movement was a predominantly US business phenomenon that happened from 1895 to 1905. During this time, small firms with little market share consolidated with similar firms to form large, powerful institutions that dominated their markets. The methods used were so-called trusts. To truly understand how large this movement was—in 1900, the value of firms acquired in mergers was 20% of GDP. In 1990, the value was only 3% and from 1998–2008, it was around 10% of GDP. However, there were companies that merged during this time such as DuPont, Nabisco, US Steel, and General Electric that have been able to keep their dominance in their respected sectors today due to growing technological advances of their products, patents, and brand recognition by their customers. The companies that merged were consistently mass producers of homogeneous goods that could exploit the efficiencies of large volume production. This rapid increase has taken many M&A firms by surprise because the majority of them never had to consider acquiring the capabilities or skills required to effectively handle such kind of transaction.

The completion of a merger does not ensure the success of the resulting organization. Many mergers (in some industries, the majority) result in a net loss of value due to problems. Correcting problems caused by incompatibility— whether of technology, equipment, or corporate culture— diverts resources away from new investment, and these problems may be exacerbated by inadequate research or by concealment of losses or liabilities by one of the partners.

These problems are similar to those encountered in takeovers. For the merger not to be considered a failure, it must increase shareholder value faster than if the companies were separate, or prevent the deterioration of shareholder value more than if the companies were separate.

Mergers and acquisitions have become fundamental tools to secure business growth. In the past two years, global investors have seen the number of players drop in areas as diverse as the automotive and telecommunication sectors, the pharmaceutical and tobacco industries, finance, insurance and engineering. In each case, the parties involved point to operating synergies, greater market share, cost savings, enhanced service and complementary corporate cultures as the driving forces for, and benefits of, M&A.

Mergers and acquisitions involve greater risks which can be handled with integrated approach and strategic dexterity.

But how can companies such as car manufacturers Daimler Benz and Chrysler, or telecommunications firms Vodafone and Airtouch Communications reap the promised rewards of M&A and avoid the pitfalls of falling revenues? Although success or failure depends on many factors, taking an integrated approach to planning, executing, integrating and evaluating the transaction is a key part of the answer to a successful M&A deal. The use of spectrum risk analysis during the entire M&A cycle further increases the chances of success.

O O O

# 8. SIXTIETH ANNIVERSARY OF NATO

The signing of the North Atlantic Treaty on 4 April, 1949 established the North Atlantic Treaty Organisation. Its headquarters are in Brussels, Belgium. The organisation constitutes a system of collective defence by means of which its member states agree to mutual defence in response to an external attack. The NATO countries are : Belgium, Bulgaria, Canada, Czech Republic, Denmark, Estonia, France, Germany, Greece, Hungary, Ireland, Italy, Latvia, Lithuania, Luxembourg, Netherlands, Norway, Poland, Romania, Portugal, Slovenia, Spain, Turkey, United Kingdom and United States.

An alliance that started as 14 short treaty articles has now evolved into the world's premier security organisation, and contributed to an unprecedented period of peace, freedom and prosperity for all its citizens across the globe.

During the Cold War period, NATO maintained a holding pattern with no actual military engagement as an organisation. In May 1978, NATO countries officially defined two complementary aims of the Alliance to maintain security and pursue detente. This was supposed to mean matching defences at the level rendered necessary by the Warsaw Pact's offensive capabilities without giving a further spur to arms race.

The end of the Cold War and the dissolution of the Warsaw Pact in 1991 removed *de facto*, the main adversary of NATO. This caused a strategic re-evaluation of NATO's purpose, nature and tasks. In practice this ended up entailing a gradual expansion of NATO to Eastern Europe—which is still going on— as well as the extension of its activities to areas that had not formerly been NATO concerns.

The alliance is keeping the peace in Kosovo, it is engaged in both stabilisation tasks and combat operations in Afghanistan, runs an anti-terrorist naval operation in the Mediterranean, assists defence reform in Bosnia and Herzegovina, trains Iraqi security forces, and provides support to the African Union.

NATO has been changing in the Post-Cold War world. With the Soviet warning, NATO set out deliberately to enhance its political dimension. The allies also adopted a new political mission, i.e. the creation of a Europe whole and free. Seventeen years later Europe is, on the whole, unquestionably more democratic and Cold War divisions have receded significantly. New institutions exist, including the Euro-Atlantic Partnership Council, the Partnership for Peace, and the NATO-Russia Council.

France, which left NATO's integrated military command over 40 years ago, has rejoined it. It was a founding member of the alliance in 1949 but it left the military structure in 1966 amid frictions with the United States. France has continued, however, to contribute troops to NATO missions and to participate in NATO's political bodies. In the past, France had preferred to remain outside, but President Nicolas Sarkozy has decided that it would be letter to be inside, rubbing shoulders with the US and other countries.

There was a breakdown of trust between Russia and NATO countries after the Georgian war in summer 2008, when meetings of the NATO–Russian Council were suspended. East-European allies in particular were quick to point to the council's failure during the crisis. By contrast, Germany, France and US apparently believe that Russia and NATO need each other. They argue that trust can be rebuilt through pragmatic cooperation on issues such as Afghanistan, counter-narcotics policy, arms control, counter-terrorism and Iran's and North Korea's nuclear programmes.

The open offer by US Vice President Joe Biden in February 2009 to reset and reorient the relationship was widely welcomed. At the NATO Foreign Minister's meeting in Brussels on 5 March, a decision was reached to resume formal NATO–Russian Council meetings as soon as possible after the April

2009 summit. The success of this move will depend on defining a pragmatic agenda focused on problem-solving rather than high-flying rhetoric.

Though the world has been totally transformed since 1949, NATO still exists because the US is Europe's irreplaceable insurance policy, not only against a resurgent Russia, but against all potential threats. The Europe needs the US to lead simply because the US remains the indispensable power for all seasons.

It appears that NATO has become an indispensable part of the international security environment as of now, though there has been criticism from some countries like India who believe in non-alignment.

O O O

# 9. OPEC AND OIL POLITICS

Most of the luxuries of modern life are dependent on the availability of oil. Almost all transport, including cars, aircraft, trains, buses, is reliant on oil. Food production is dependent on farming machinery and fertilisers, again both requiring oil. Even the necessities of our day-to-day life depend on fossil fuels like petrol, diesel, etc. There is tremendous pressure on the non-renewable sources of energy. In the last 50 years, oil consumption has increased by over 7 times. Worldwide population growth, technological advances, industrial expansion, increased living standards have contributed to its unexpected rise in consumption. Oil production is not going to meet demand in the near future. Over half the world's oil has already been consumed and this was the easier half to acquire. In 2002, the world used three times as much oil as was discovered. Estimations are that the world's oil production will peak sometime before 2020 and oil reserves will be almost depleted by 2040.

The world is in chaos and disorder, too much energy is

needed to supply the booming economies of the Asian countries and other parts of the world. The energy and power need is in quantum leap which was beyond what was predicted.The situation calls for an urgent need to look for some other energy source.

Oil exerts tremendous economic and political influence worldwide, although the line between political and economic influence is not always distinct. The importance of oil to national security is unlike that of any other commodity.

Modern warfare particularly depends on oil, because virtually all weapons systems rely on oil-based fuel-tanks, trucks, armoured vehicles, self-propelled artillery pieces, airplanes, and naval ships. For this reason, the governments and general staffs of powerful nations seek to ensure a steady supply of oil during wartime, to fuel oil-hungry military forces in far-flung operational theatres. Such governments view their companies' global interests as synonymous with the national interest and they readily support their companies' efforts to control new production sources, to overwhelm foreign rivals, and to gain the most favourable pipeline routes and other transportation and distribution channels."

Ex-CIA Director James Woolsey and US Senator Richard Lugar stated that "Energy is vital to a country's security and material well-being. A state unable to provide its people with adequate energy supplies or desiring added leverage over other people often resorts to force. To use his words: "Consider Saddam Hussein's 1990 invasion of Kuwait, driven by his desire to control more of the world's oil reserves, and the international response to this threat. The underlying goal of the UN force, which included 500,000 American troops, was to ensure continued and unfettered access to petroleum."

Five per cent of the world's population, is responsible for 25% of the world's oil consumption while only having 3% of the world's proven oil reserves. As of 2004, the US had 21 billion barrels of proven oil reserves and consume 20.6 million bpd. In 1998, about 40% of the energy consumed by the United States came from Oil.

American dependence on oil imports has grown from 35% in 1973 to 60% by the end of 2006. The Energy Information Administration projects that US oil imports will remain flat and consumption will grow, so net imports will decline to 54% of US oil consumption by 2030. The top five suppliers of crude oil and petroleum products to the United States in 2006 were: Canada, Mexico, Saudi Arabia, Venezuela, and Nigeria.

Critics of the Iraq War contend that US officials and representatives from the private sector were planning just this kind of mutually supportive relationship as early as 2001, when the James Baker III Institute for Public Policy and the Council on Foreign Relations produced "Strategic Energy Policy: Challenges for the 21st Century," a report describing the long-term threat of energy crises like blackouts and rising fuel prices then playing havoc with the state of California. The report recommended a comprehensive review of US military, energy, economic, and political policy toward Iraq "with the aim to lowering anti-Americanism in the Middle East and elsewhere, and set the groundwork to eventually ease Iraqi oil-field investment restrictions." The urgency in report was in contrast to the relatively calm speech Chevron CEO Kenneth T. Derr had given at the Commonwealth Club of California two years earlier where he had said:

> It might surprise you to learn that even though Iraq possesses huge reserves of oil and gas—reserves I'd love Chevron to have access to—I fully agree with the sanctions we have imposed on Iraq.

OPEC was created in 1960. Since then the cartel has been responsible for creating and maintaining policy for member countries regarding oil production as a means of providing a stable world oil market, whilst ensuring sufficient supply to fuel the world's consumption demand.

OPEC Secretary-General Abdullah el al-Badri stated that oil prices are likely to go higher and that the group was ready to raise production if the price pressure was due to a shortage of supply—something he doubted. "In oil prices, there is a common understanding that has nothing to do with supply and demand," al-Badri said on the sidelines of an energy conference in Rome.The OPEC chief said the Organization for Petroleum Exporting Countries will not hesitate to increase production if the group thought the higher prices were due to shortages. But he said more oil will not solve the high prices.Though he agreed that OPEC's production levels were just one of many factors, he said.

The Organisation of the Petroleum Exporting Countries (OPEC), which is normally held responsible for all oil price increases, has repeatedly asserted that oil has crossed the $100-a-barrel mark not because of a shortage of supply but because of financial speculation.

Al-Badri futher stated:

But how much higher it will go, of course it depends on a number of things: the political situation, whether there is a natural catastrophe, whether there are speculations in the market, whether there are strikes in certain producing countries. So there are many other factors other than OPEC production.

The record-high oil prices of early 2008-09 have been propelled by worries about insufficient supply, soaring global demand and a sliding dollar that has made oil cheaper in other countries. A host of supply and demand concerns in the US and abroad, along with the dollar's weakness, have served to support prices, even as record retail gasoline prices in the US appear to be in dampening demand. Oil prices rose to nearly $150 a barrel for the first time in the last week of June as supply concerns mounted and the dollar weakened. Crude Oil is sizzling right now.

Besides,emerging markets are rapidly industrializing, and the world demand for oil is expected to increase 54% over the next 25 years, according to the US Energy Information Agency (EIA),and it is also one of the major factor contributing to the price rice.

Underlying the buoyancy in prices is the closing gap between global petroleum demand and supply at a time when the spare capacity is more or less fully utilised. Much of the increase in demand is coming from China, but that is affecting stockpiles everywhere. This trend, combined with the uncertainty in West Asia resulting from the occupation of Iraq and the standoff in Iran, has created a situation where any destabilising influence—such as political uncertainty and attacks on the oil supply chain triggers a sharp rise in prices.

Prices have more than doubled in the past 12 months. The International Energy Agency (IEA) is revising future price estimates upwards.

Expressing his concern over recent surge in oil prices as the third and worst oil shock to hit the world economy in three decades, the British Prime Minister Gordon Brown said: "This is the third oil shock of the last three decades, and I believe it is the worst oil shock because of the rise in prices and because of the volatility in the market."

Brown told OPEC, the oil cartel, that record oil prices could leave people in oil-consuming countries like Britain facing more years of falling living standards. Certainly, oil prices shooting as high as nearly $150 a barrel were having a severe impact on standards of living. However, the worst affected segment is the section of people living at the lowest strata of society. Since petroleum prices are closely linked to other essensial commodities, they become the greatest sufferers.

OPEC President Chakib Khelil said, "It is impossible to predict. Anything could happen. All I can say is that prices will be high, and will remain high until the end of the year."

In answer to a question, he said he did not think oil would rapidly breach the $200 a barrel mark, adding that prices would continue to perform their habitual yo-yo in relation to factors like geopolitical tensions and the dollar.

King Abdullah of Saudi Arabia, one of the major oil producing countries, called the international summit of world oil ministers in Jeddah to find ways of stabilising the world oil price. And there were high hopes among consumer nations that he would announce a boost in production. But that has not happened, although the Saudis say they are prepared to increase production if the market demands it.

Saudi Arabia ranks as the largest exporter of petroleum, and plays a leading role in OPEC, its decisions to raise or cut production almost immediately impact world oil prices. It is perhaps the best example of a contemporary energy superpower, in terms of having power and influence on the global stage (due to its energy reserves and production of not just oil, but natural gas as well). Saudi Arabia is often referred to as the world's only "oil superpower".

But the OPEC countries do not have concensus over the proposal and they think that the present price rice is not due to demand supply issue, other factors are attributing to this phenomena.

○ ○ ○

# 10. Twenty-Five Years of Indian Troops' Presence on Siachen

Indian troops marked 25 years of their presence on the Siachen glacier on 13 April, 2009 as the army made a pre-emptive move on 13 April, 1984 to secure the glacier from Pakistani aggression under Operation Meghdoot. Since then, the Indian soldiers have endured the extreme tensions at frigid heights of over 21,000 feet. Though the guns have been silent since the 2003 ceasefire with Pakistan, the soldiers' task remains as hazardous as ever.

The Siachen glacier has often been described as the world's highest, coldest and perhaps the most demanding frontline. So far, the army has lost over 700 men, majority to the hostile weather, which poses a formidable challenge. Around 3,000 men defend the 76-km long glacier and more soldiers are lost to avalanches, crevasses and medical complications than hostile fire.

Siachen is a unique battlefield as the oxygen level is about 10 per cent of that available in the plains. Some areas remain cut-off from the rest of the world for six months during winter.

The Siachen glacier acts as a buffer between the Shaksgam valley under Chinese control and Baltistan, which is occupied by Pakistan. Dominating positions on the Saltoro Ridge give India a huge advantage over Pakistani posts located 3,000 feet below. They do not allow the Pakistani army to link up with the Chinese and pose threat to Ladakh.

India has little choice but to remain on Siachen. If the glacier is vacated, Pakistani troops would take over the glacier and recapturing it would be virtually impossible.

Since 1984, the army and the Indian Air Force (IAF) have mounted a huge logistical exercise to maintain troops at forward posts and to evacuate casualties. The pilots take their Cheetah helicopters, based on a design of 1960s vintage and meant to fly only at altitudes of up to about 15,000 feet, to posts located as high as 21,000 feet.

The pilots have just 20-30 seconds to drop supplies to the soldiers before the Pakistani guns open up. The IAF's Mi-17s and army Cheetah helicopters remain the lifeline for the troops. Sometimes all a helicopter carries is a jerrycan of kerosene.

The origin of the Siachen dispute lies in a cartographic controversy. The Line of Control (LoC) begins north of Jammu and ends abruptly at a mountain height called NJ 9842. Beyond that lies the glacier in no man's land as per the Indo-Pak 1949 Karachi and 1972 Suchetgarh agreements. But since the 1970s, several international maps had begun to depict the Siachen glacier as part of Pakistan. This included the National Geographic Society's Atlas of the World, University of Chicago's A Historical Atlas of South Asia and the Times Atlas of the World, published in London. All of these showed the Ceasefire Line (now the LoC) clearly extending from NJ 9842 in a north-easterly direction right up to the Karakoram Pass and onto the Chinese border. Until then, the glacier was not even in Pakistani maps.

Apparently, the source of this cartographic confusion seemed to be some maps initially produced by the US Defence

Mapping Agency, depicting the LoC running from the vicinity of NJ 9842 north-east to the Karakoram Pass, in the 1970s and 1980s. The best explanation for this error by America's mapmakers appears to lie in the possible "translation" of Air Defence Information Zone (ADIZ) markings, which provides zoning boundaries for air controllers in civil/military aviation. This showed the extension of the LoC from NJ 9842 to the Karakoram Pass, and thus became an article of faith for the Pakistanis. However, several ADIZs could pass through one country, and these need not identify a boundary line. But the publication of such maps by many of the world's leading Altases further encouraged the Pakistani army to contest the LoC sanctity.

Conditions of Siachen are among the toughest on the earth. The temperature can drop to −60°C. The soldiers have to trek for many days to reach the farthest post.

Establishing India's hold on Siachen is a measure of Indian soldiers' strength, determination and endurance.

O O O

# 11. Alternative Energy Source: Biofuel

Our society is currently dependent on carbon fuels or its energy needs. However, carbon fuels, in particular oil, are becoming increasingly scarce, and are often cited as aggravating conflicts if produced in a politically unstable country. The combustion of carbon fuels also produces pollution, and are the most likely culprit for global warming. The search is on for viable alternative energies.

Non-renewable energy sources like solar energy, tidal energy, hydroelectricity, biomass, hydrogen, geothermal power are vastly more abundant than non-renewable sources. Unfortunately, these sources are much more difficult to exploit. Hydroelectricity, tidal, and geothermal sources in particular require building expensive facilities to harvest the energy.

These facilities are efficient and clean, besides being exhaustive. Hence, they are reliable sources to energy crisis.

The solar energy raining down on the Earth from the Sun has tremendous potential to provide for the energy needs of the entire planet. We just don't have the technology to tap that efficiently. Even fossil fuels are essentially solar energy gathered by long dead plants and locked up from the past. Solar energy is the safest, most available energy source. Ideally, it could replace other sources in feeding the global energy grid.

Biofuels such as bioethanol and biodiesel can make a big difference in improving our environment, helping our economy, and reducing our dependence on non-renewable energy sources. It presents one of the most viable and effective solution to the current energy crisis. Small changes in crude oil prices or supplies can have an enormous impact on our economy—increasing trade deficits, decreasing in industrial investment, and lowering employment levels. Developing a strong industry for biomass fuels, power, and products will have tremendous economic benefits including trade deficit reduction, job creation, and the strengthening of agricultural markets.

The International Energy Agency's World Energy Outlook 2006 concludes that rising oil demand, if left unchecked, would accentuate the consuming countries' vulnerability to a severe supply disruption and resulting price shock. The report suggested that biofuels may one day offer a viable alternative, but also that "the implications of the use of biofuels for global security as well as for economic, environmental, and public health need to be further evaluated".

The combustion of fossil fuels such as coal, oil, and natural gas has increased the concentration of carbon dioxide in the earth's atmosphere. The carbon dioxide and other so-called greenhouse gases allow solar energy to enter the Earth's atmosphere, but reduce the amount of energy that can re-radiate back into space, trapping energy and causing global warming.

One environmental benefit of replacing fossil fuels with biomass-based fuels is that the energy obtained from biomass does not add to global warming. All fuel combustion, including fuels produced from biomass, releases carbon dioxide into the atmosphere. But, because plants use carbon dioxide from the atmosphere to grow, the carbon dioxide formed during combustion is balanced by that absorbed during the annual growth of the plants used as the biomass feedstock—unlike burning fossil fuels which releases carbon dioxide captured billions of years ago, but the result is still substantially reduced net greenhouse gas emissions. Modern, high-yield corn production is relatively energy intense, but the net greenhouse gas emission reduction from making ethanol from corn grain is still about 20%. Making biodiesel from soybeans reduces net emissions nearly 80%. Producing ethanol from cellulosic material also involves generating electricity by combusting the non-fermentable lignin. The combination of reducing both gasoline use and fossil electrical production can mean a greater than 100% net greenhouse gas emission reduction. In the case of ethanol from corn stover, the reduction has been calculated to 113%.

Both bioethanol and biodiesel are used as fuel oxygenates to improve combustion characteristics. Adding oxygen results in more complete combustion, which reduces carbon monoxide emissions. This is another environmental benefit of replacing petroleum fuels with biofuels. Petroleum, diesel and gasoline consist of blends of hundreds of different hydrocarbon chains. Many of these are toxic, volatile compounds such as benzene, toluene, and xylenes, which are responsible for the health hazards and pollution associated with combustion of petroleum-based fuels. Carbon monoxide, nitrogen oxides, sulphur oxides and particulates, are other specific emissions of concern. A key environmental benefit of using biofuels as an additive to petroleum-based transportation fuels is a reduction in these harmful emissions.

## Energy Security and Inclusive Growth

India has made rapid strides during the last two decades

in various fields of socio-economic development. But, inclusive growth has somehow eluded India so far as large masses of the country still live in poverty and destitution. There have been several reasons for this incomplete growth, but the major among these has been lack of energy security. Petroleum products which are the backbone of industry are so scarce that we have to import them regularly. Heavy import bill takes away large chunks of our exchequer, as a result of which capital required for various projects of development falls short— slowing down economic growth and depriving people of the necessary benefits which may have brought a perceptible change in their lives.

The price of petrol has a tendency to remain high these days. It increases transport cost of various types of goods supplied to people. The prices of such goods, in turn, remain high. This affects poor people the most because they get less quantity of goods for the limited income they have. Agriculture which is the mainstay of our economy requires modernisation by the increased use of implements like tractors, threshers, and pumps to draw water to irrigate the fields. These implements need diesel. If the cost of diesel remains high, efforts to modernise agriculture suffer a blow. Most of our farmers are poor. They cannot afford to buy fuel at high price. If their farming methods remain primitive, the crop yield does not improve, and the farmers are not able to lift themselves out of poverty. Thus, poverty alleviation requires regular supply of fuel at cheap rate. Fossil fuels like coal and petroleum are not going to last very long. Alternative sources of energy are indispensable to build energy security.

When India entered into the nuclear deal with America, the main objective was to build energy security by harnessing nuclear energy for peaceful purposes. Countries like France meet their energy demands from nuclear energy. India also has to do the same sooner or later. After the Indo-US nuclear deal, India has also received waiver from Nuclear Suppliers Group (NSG) to get the supply of nuclear fuel. But, it will take another decade or so before nuclear energy is used to make an impact on India's growth. Before that, new nuclear plants will have to be set up with latest technology from countries like America and France. A nuclear plant takes about five years to start and become operational. There is also one year's testing time for its smooth functioning.

Till such time the nuclear energy is harnessed in sufficient quantities, we must develop alternative sources of energy like solar energy, wind power, tidal power. Jatropha plants are being sown in large tracks of lands, but such a move has not been found suitable in a country like India where maintaining food security for the large population is another major problem. Many countries which are struggling to provide foodgrains to their people have already given up the idea of Jatropha plants to get oil to lessen their dependence on petrol. Poor masses in India need foodgrain as well as regular energy sources. Under these circumstances we should maintain a balance and save our resources.

O O O

## 12. EXECUTION OF SADDAM HUSSEIN

The execution of Saddam Hussein took place on December 30, 2006. Saddam was sentenced to hanging after being convicted of crimes against humanity by the Iraqi Special Tribunal following his trial for the 1982 murder of 148 Iraqi Shi'ites in the town of Dujail in retaliation for an assassination attempt against him.

Saddam was President of Iraq from July 16, 1979, until April 9, 2003, when he was deposed during the 2003 invasion of Iraq by U.S.-led forces. After his capture in ad-Dawr near his hometown of Tikrit, Saddam was held in United States custody at Camp Cropper to face trial by the Iraqi Special Tribunal for war crimes, crimes against humanity, and genocide. On November 5, 2006, he was sentenced to death by hanging.

On December 30, 2006, Saddam was taken to Camp Justice to be executed. The Iraqi government released an official video of the execution, including Saddam being led to the gallows and stopping after the noose was placed around his neck. Controversy arose due to the surfacing of a mobile phone recording of the hanging that included audio, and showed Saddam falling through the trap door in the gallows. The audio, which was not in the official video, revealed taunts between Saddam and the executioners, which drew criticism over the environment of his execution.

On December 31, 2006, Saddam's body was flown to his birthplace of Al-Awja near Tikrit and was buried in a palace near his family's resting place.

The death sentences handed down against Saddam Hussein and three other prominent figures in his regime are the outcome of show trial concocted for political purposes. Amid unspeakable atrocities being committed against the people of of the Republican Party in Iraq every day by the US occupation forces, a hand-picked court had condemned the former Iraqi dictator to die. The timing chosen for the sentence was an attempt to reap maximum electoral fortunes by energising its right-wing base with the prospect of a high profile legal lynching.

The execution of former Iraqi president Saddam Hussein served not justice, but the political purposes of the Bush administration and its Iraqi stooges. The manner in which the execution was carried out—hurriedly, secretively, in the dark of night, was a mockery of any semblance of legal process—only underscores the lawless and reactionary character of the entire American enterprise in Iraq.

The most fundamental political motive of the Bush administration was its desire to kill a major opponent, openly, before the eyes of the world, simply to demonstrate its ability and will to do so. In the view of the White House, Saddam was an object lesson to any future opponent of American imperialism: defy the will of Washington, and his bloody fate could be yours.

In a statement, Iraq's Prime Minister, Nouri Maliki, said the execution had closed a dark chapter in Iraq's history.

But in the Sunni-dominated city of Tikrit, once a power base of Saddam, people lamented his death.

"The president, the leader Saddam Hussein is a martyr and God will put him along with other martyrs. Do not be sad nor complain because he has died the death of a holy warrior," said Sheik Yahya al-Attawi, a cleric at the Saddam Big Mosque.

The Iraqi president was born in a village just outside Takrit in April 1937. In his teenage years, he immersed himself in the anti-British and anti-Western atmosphere of the day. At college in Baghdad he joined the Baath party.

After the overthrow of the monarchy in 1958, Saddam connived in a plot to kill the Prime Minister, Abdel-Karim Qassem. But the conspiracy was discovered, and Saddam fled the country.

In 1963, with the Baath party in control in Baghdad, Saddam Hussein returned home and began jostling for a position of influence. During this period, he married his cousin Sajida. They later had two sons and three daughters.

But within months, the Baath party had been overthrown and he was jailed, remaining there until the party returned to power in a coup in July 1968. Showing ruthless determination that was to become hallmark of his leadership, Saddam Hussein gained a position on the ruling Revolutionary Command Council.

For years he was the power behind the ailing figure of the President, Ahmed Hassan Bakr. In 1979, he achieved his ambition of becoming head of state. The new president started as he intended to go on—putting to death dozens of his rivals.

Within hours of his death, bombings killed at least 68 people in Iraq, including one planted on a minibus that exploded in a fish market in a mostly Shiite town south of Baghdad.

A couple hundred people also protested the execution just

outside the Anbar capital of Ramadi, and more than 2,000 people demonstrated in Adwar, the village south of Tikrit where Saddam was captured by US troops hiding in an underground bunker.

In a statement, Saddam's lawyers said that in the aftermath of his death, "the world will know that Saddam Hussein lived honestly, died honestly, and maintained his principles."

"He did not lie when he declared his trial null," they said.

Saddam Hussein, President of Iraq for the past two decades, had the dubious distinction of being the world's best known and most hated Arab leader.

And in a region where despotic rule was the norm, he was more feared by his own people than any other head of state. A former Iraqi diplomat living in exile summed up Saddam's rule in one sentence: "Saddam is a dictator who is ready to sacrifice his country, just so long as he can remain on his throne in Baghdad." Few Iraqis would disagree with this. Although none living in Iraq would dare to say so publicly.

The Iraqi people are forced to consume a daily diet of triumphalist slogans, fattened by fawning praise of the president. Saddam was forced to flee Iraq in 1959 and spent four years in exile in Cairo.

Back in Iraq, he rose through the party ranks. When it finally seized power from Abdul Rahman Mohammed Aref in 1968, Saddam Hussein emerged as the number two figure behind Gen Ahmad Hassan al-Bakr.

Now the power behind the throne, he took over when Bakr was quietly shunted aside in July 1979 and began the reign of terror that was to keep him in power for so long.

Saddam Hussein took the posts of Prime Minister, Chairman of the Revolution Command Council and Commander-in-chief of Armed Forces.

Within a year, he launched Iraq into a massive and risky adventure. As Richard Dicker, international justice director of

Human Rights Watch, explained in a column Friday in the *Guardian*, the legal procedure was a travesty.

"The trial judgment," he wrote, "was not finished when the verdict and sentence were announced on November 5. The record only became available to defense lawyers on November 22. According to the tribunal's statute, the defense attorneys had to file their appeals on December 5, which gave them less than two weeks to respond to the 300-page trial decision. The appeals chamber never held a hearing to consider the legal arguments presented as allowed by Iraqi law. It defies belief that the appeals chamber could fairly review a 300-page decision together with written submissions by the defense and consider all the relevant issues in less than three weeks."

Rather than a tribunal modeled on Nuremberg, where the surviving Nazi leaders received far more extensive due process rights than were accorded Hussein, the proceedings in Baghdad resembled a Stalinist or Nazi show trial, with a puppet judge, a predetermined verdict and a sentence carried out in the dead of night.

The Iraqi leader was not, however, tried and sentenced under the auspices of a working class tribunal. He was the subject of a kangaroo court established by an occupation regime after the invasion and conquest of Iraq by the United States. In other words, his crimes were judged and the penalty imposed by those guilty of even greater crimes than his own.

An editorial in the *Washington Post* perfectly captures the hypocrisy with which the Bush administration, the congressional Democrats and Republicans, and the American media approached the case against Saddam Hussein. The Post sententiously declared its general opposition to the death penalty, before declaring that if it was appropriate for anyone it should be applied to "Saddam Hussein—a man who, with the possible exception of Kim Jong II, has more blood on his hands than anyone else alive."

It was a grim end for the 69-year-old leader who had vexed three US presidents. Despite his ouster, Washington, its allies and the new Iraqi leaders remain mired in a fight to quell a stubborn insurgency by Saddam loyalists and a vicious sectarian conflict.

The execution took place during the year's deadliest month for US troops, with the toll reaching 109. At least 2,998 members of the US military have been killed since the Iraq war began in March 2003, according to an Associated Press count.

President Bush said in a statement issued from his ranch in Texas that bringing Saddam to justice "is an important milestone on Iraq's course to becoming a democracy that can govern, sustain and defend itself, and be an ally in the war on terror."

He said that the execution marks the "end of a difficult year for the Iraqi people and for our troops" and cautioned that Saddam's death will not halt the violence in Iraq.

O O O

# 13. RISING TERRORIST ACTIVITIES

Terrorism is the cruellest form of crime. It is one of the serious problems that society faces today. It's an issue of global concern. The presence of terrorism can be felt all across the globe. It is one of the serious challenges that the countries of the world face—developing or developed. However it is not a new phenomenon. Its presence can be traced back to ancient society. But over the years the incidence of terrorism has increased unexpectedly and its face has become more horrific. Despite strategies and policies of governments of the countries of the world, the activities of terrorists are rising manifold.

Terrorism has its presence everywhere ranging from Indonesia, Malaysia to Sudan, Somalia, Egypt and Nigeria and Peru, Chile, America to Ireland.These countries are directly or indirectly facing the threat of terrorism. It has sprung up everywhere. Terrorists are the geatest enemies of society because they undermine the stability of society by creating chaotic conditions leading to mass killing, damage and destruction. Generally, public places like airports railway stations, hotels etc. are their targets, but sometimes they shift their focus to some soft targets, like schools, hospitals, trains and buses where security is lax and security forces are not always very vigilant.

A terrorist sees himself as engaged in an unofficial war with political objectives and identifies his cause with the fight for human rights. To the terrorist himself, of course the means he adopts are justified. Terrorism is the product of our socio-economic and political situations and wrong policies of the government that make them stray from the mainstream of society. It is also harboured by countries like Pakistan against India since the former cannot match the latter's military might to wage a direct war.

Terrorism has been a persistent and worsening problem for Israel during 2008, with an increase in mass-killing attacks and a significant increase in rocket attacks from the Gaza Strip, according to a new report released in Israel. The latest in the spate of incidences of terrorism have been the tube blast in London, foiled attempt to blow off the flight between London and America, Madrid blasts and blasts in Jaipur, Varanasi, Bangalore, Ahmedabad, Delhi and terrorist attack on Mumbai. These incidences claimed hundreds of innocent lives and caused mass damage to property. The latest target to terrorism have been the former Prime Minister of Pakistan, Benazir Bhutto and a cabinet rank minister of Sri Lanka. Today, the Al Qaeda is dominating the world of terrorism. The increase in "mass-killing" attacks is due to the improved operational capabilities and higher motivation among various terrorist organizations.

In India, home to the world's second largest Muslim population, terrorist incidents have increased in number and intensity. Official counter-terrorism operations have also become more indiscriminate. These are based on the US model of understanding "Islamic terrorism" and fighting it by solely military means. This has produced human rights violations and widespread discontent among Muslim youth

The Middle-East is the globe's most volatile region. Now it is seething with enormous anger, and more violence and conflict than it did before the Sep. 11, 2001 terrorist attacks on New York and Washington. And South Asia, the political birthplace of the Taliban and al-Qaeda, and home to two nuclear rivals engaged in a half-century-long hot-cold war, remains a cauldron of discontent.

Five years after US President George W. Bush launched his "global war on terrorism", the world has become more unsafe, more divided, more strife-prone, more paranoid, and ironically, more vulnerable to terrorism.

"The greatest political setback for the US is that the global war on terrorism is now widely seen as a figleaf for America's imperial project," says Achin Vanaik, political scientist and author of several papers on terrorism. "American neo-conservatives thought they could use the global war on terrorism to establish total and lasting US global hegemony, a sort of modern-day Roman Empire which would allow no rival to emerge for decades. Today, they are looking for an exit strategy."

The "global war on terrorism", waged by a primarily US-British coalition, has deeply hurt and antagonised millions of Muslims the world over. It has created rifts within the Western bloc and alienated the United States' own allies.

Worst of all, the global war on terrorism's greatest manifestation, in Iraq, is regarded by a majority of the US population as a mistake. A recent poll finds that a third of the US respondents think the terrorists are winning the war on terrorism. In an earlier survey, 70 per cent backed it.

Iraq is a bloody mess, fast resembling Vietnam in the late 1960s. The deaths of over 100,000 Iraqi civilians, a number estimated by the medical journal *The Lancet*, have produced deep resentments against the occupation, as have the excesses and human rights violations in Fallujah and Abu Ghraib. Iraq may even be "disintegrating" as US military cables say. It has certainly become unmanageable.

The influence of terrorism can be felt in the constant threat to the security, routine life and damage done to the mental health of the people who survive the tragedy, apart from the loss of life and property.

## Global Response

Rising terrorist activities and their spread to hitherto unaffected areas have made the governments of all the countries realise that the dimensions of this menace have become so huge that it needs concerted efforts to put an end to terrorism. Severely affected countries like India and America have prepared general strategies including beefing up intelligence, joint naval operations, etc. to fight this menace, but Mumbai terrorist attack of September 2008 proved that these measures and strategies were not enough. It was felt that the countries like Pakistan which have been harbouring terrorism should be forced to cooperate to maintain a terrorism-free world order. Immediately after becoming Amercia's President, Barack Obama gave a clear message to Pakistan that if it did not help fight terrorism, the financial aid given to it will be withdrawn. Pakistan promised to do so. America was then able to send its troop to fight against the Talibans who had been resorting to a lot of bloodshed in the border areas of Pakistan and Afghanistan.

Irked by Pakistan's help to America, the Talibans increased their activities and effected a number of explosions in various cities of Pakistan through suicide bombers. Troubled by some hardliners, Pakistan was initially unable to take any action, but as the terrorist activities become a daily affair and a threat to Pakistan's very existence was perceived, it started taking military action against the Talibans openly with the aid and support of the United States of America. By mid-2009, a large number of Talibans had been killed and its fear had been removed from the people's hearts. But still much needs to be done to ensure that peace prevails in West Asia.

While this may be taken as a welcome development, there is another aspect of Pakistan's diplomacy. It has taken no action against those who perpetrated the beastly attack on Taj, Heritage and other places in Mumbai, despite the fact that complete evidence of this crime had been provided to Pakistan. It has not only said that the evidence given by India was not sufficient but also released the mastermind of the attack saying that this involvement has not been proved in the court. Such a stand makes a mockery of international efforts to fight terrorism. Kasav, the terrorist who was caught alive on the eve of terrorist attack on Mumbai in September 2008 has revealed how the plan was hatched by Jamat-ud-Dawa in Pakistan. He has disclosed the ugly fact of Pakistan harbouring terrorist attacks against India. But despite immense pressure from India, Pakistan has not brought the perpetrators of this heinous crime to justice. India has shown exceptional restraint so far although many people had asked the government to go for some surgical operation to destroy terrorist camps in Pakistan. The result of terrorist activities has been that the process of dialogue between India and Pakistan to find a peaceful solution to bilateral issues including Kashmir problem has been suspended indefinitely. India has made it clear tha unless Pakistan shows some credible evidence of taking some concrete action against terrorist outfits, there can be no talks with it on any issue. As things stand today, Pakistan seems either adamant or under the grip of hardliners and its military chief, General Kiyani, which does not augur well for the cause of peace and security in the region.

Killing of LTTE chief Prabhakaran and ultimately putting an end to Tiger Elam's fight, the Sri Lankan government has won a long battle. It may usher in a new era of peace in the region. India has the challenge of violence by Maoists and Naxals. Our eastern region is afflicted by bomb attacks or mine blasts. The government should look into the socio-economic problems of the people who resort to such violence. As for Maoists, India should seek China's help to maintain peace and security in the eastern region. Both India and China should reach a consensus on their stand with regard to Tibet, Nepal, Myanmar and Bangladesh. Once the terrorist outfits operating in that region get the message that both these countries are together, they will have to stop their operations.

Terrorism anywhere is a threat to civil society. All the nations should join hands to fight it and abolish it completely.

O O O

## 14. BEIJING OLYMPICS

The 2008 Summer Olympics were held in Beijing, China from August 9-24, 2008. Mainland China fielded the most athletes. As with the 2008 Summer Olympics, equestrian events were held in Hong Kong and sailing events in Qingdao. On June 26, 2005, The Beijing Olympic Committee announced that the slogan for the 2008 Olympics will be "One World, One Dream".

The Olympic Games is an international multi-sport event subdivided into summer and winter sporting events. The Summer and Winter games are each held every four years (an Olympiad). Until 1992, they were both held in the same year. Since then, they have been separated by a two year gap.

Every four years the finest athletes in the world gather in one location to compete against each other and to determine who best exemplifies the Olympic motto—Citius, Altius, Fortius—meaning "faster, higher, stronger." This gathering, known as the Olympic Games, is the most celebrated sporting festival in the world. The games attract athletes from over 200 nations and strive for a record in this mega event.

From the 241 participants from 14 nations in 1896, the Games grew to nearly 11,100 competitors from 202 countries at the 2004 Summer Olympics in Athens. The number of competitors at the Winter Olympics is much smaller than at the Summer Games; at the 2006 Winter Olympics in Turin Italy, 2,633 athletes from 80 countries competed in 84 events. But 203 countries participated in the Beijing Olympics. This is a noticeably higher number than the number of countries belonging to the United Nations, which is 193.

The Olympics are one of the largest media events. In Sydney in 2000 there were over 16,000 broadcasters and journalists, and an estimated 3.8 billion viewers watched the games on television. The growth of the Olympics is one of the largest problems the Olympics face today. Although allowing professional athletes and attracting sponsorships from major international companies solved financial problems in the 1980s, the large number of athletes, media and spectators makes it difficult and expensive for host cities to organize the Olympics. For example the 2012 Olympics, which will be held in London, is based on an updated budget of over £9 billion which is one of the biggest budgets for an Olympics to date. Even if sponsorships do lighten the load in terms of the debt that these countries make, undoubtedly they make additional load on the exchequer of the host country.

Despite the Olympics usually being associated with one host city, most of the Olympics have had events held in other cities, especially the football and sailing events. The 2008 Beijing Olympics marked the third time that Olympic events were held in the territories of two different NOC's: at the 2008 Olympics, equestrian events were held in Hong Kong ,which competes separately from mainland China.

In ancient times Olympic Games were a series of athletic competitions held between various city-states of ancient Greece. The prizes were olive wreaths, palm branches and woollen ribbons. But the things have undergone a sea change. Now it is associated with prestige, pelf and pride.The winners become stars; prizes showered on them.

Athletic festival originated in ancient Greece. It was revived in the late 19th century. Before the 1970s the Games were officially limited to competitors with amateur status, but in the 1980s many events were opened to professional athletes. Currently the Games are open to all, even the top professional athletes in basketball and football (soccer). The ancient Olympic Games included several of the sports that are now part of the Summer Games program, which at times has included events in as many as 32 different sports. In 1924 the Winter Games were sanctioned for winter sports. The Olympic Games have come to be regarded as the world's foremost sports competition.

Olympics had special potential for the promotion of peace among their often warring city-states. This potential was especially important to Pierre, baron de Coubertin, and his predecessors who played a key role in the revival of modern Olympic. They made great contribution in advancing international understanding and the cause of world peace through Olympics. The Olympics have proved this with a marked success.

During the ancient times normally only young men could participate. Upon winning the games, the victor would have not only the prestige of being in first place but would also be presented with a crown of olive leaves. The olive branch is a sign of hope and peace.

Even though the bearing of a torch formed an integral aspect of Greek ceremonies, the ancient Olympic Games did not include it, nor was there a symbol formed by interconnecting rings. These Olympic symbols were introduced as part of the modern Olympic games.

The five Olympic rings were designed in 1913, adopted in 1914 and debuted at the Games at Antwerp, 1920.

The Olympic motto of Citius, Altius, Fortius, motto was proposed by Pierre de Coubertin on the creation of the International Olympic Committee in 1894. De Coubertin borrowed it from his friend Henri Didon, a Dominican priest who, amongst other things, was an athletics enthusiast. The motto was introduced in 1924 at the Olympic Games in Paris.

The Beijing Olympic Games 2008 were special for India on more than one account. It had sent the largest contingent ever for the country with a hope to win some medals. The nation became delirious with joy when Abhinav Bindra struck gold in 10 m air rifle. Notwithstanding Hockey's eight golds—

the last won 28 years ago, this was the first individual gold for India. The icing on the cake was provided by Sushil Kumar who won a bronze medal in wrestling, and Vijender Kumar who won a bronze medal in boxing. China emerged as the leading sports country with 51 golds while Michael Phelps proved his might with a record 8 golds in swimming.

O O O

# 15. CHANDRAYAAN-1 — INDIA'S MOON MISSION

India became the sixth country to launch Moon mission when Chandrayaan-1, a cuboid spacecraft built by the Indian Space Research Organisation (ISRO) was propelled into space on top of an improved Polar Satellite Launch Vehicle (PSLV-C11) from the Satish Dhawan Space Centre at Sriharikota spaceport in Andhra Pradesh in October, 2008.

The take-off and flight of the Moon rocket was a magical moment that Indians—particularly our space scientists—had been eagerly and anxiously waiting for. Within minutes, the lift-off elevated India's position in the world. As dawn broke over Sriharikota, the mighty brown and white 44.4 metre tall four-stage PSLV-C11 rose from the launch pad to carry the 1,400 kg spacecraft 3,84,000 km away to the Moon in the first leg of its mission. Chandrayaan-1 was scheduled to reach its orbit 100 km from the Moon Catchup on November 8 and drop the Moon impact with an Indian tricolour painted on it.

After its perfect launch, the spacecraft was guided by ISRO Telemetry Tracking and Command Network (ISTRAC) looked at Peenya which is the local point of all the operational activities of Chandrayaan-1. The Indian Deep Space Network (IDSN) at Byalalu is a key communication point for Chandrayaan-1, with its 32-metre dish antenna dedicated to the mission. The Indian Space Science Data Centre (ISSDC), also located at Byalalu, receives data from IDSN and the other external stations and processes, retrieves and distributes to the user agencies including those that have placed payloads in the mooncraft.

## Aims of the Lunar Mission

The main aims of the lunar mission are summerised below:

1. Chandrayaan-1 will prepare a three-dimensional atlas of both the near and far side of the Moon for a deeper understanding.

2. It will conduct chemical and mineralogical mapping of the entire lunar surface to ascertain the distribution of natural resources on the lunar surface.

3. It will search for helium-3, considered among the cleanest fuels known. It is sparsely available on Earth. Scientists believe that if helium can be harnessed in nuclear reactors, it will go a long way in solving Earth's power problems. While Earth may have only 15 tonnes of helium-3, Moon is thought to contain up to 5 million tonnes, enough to produce energy for 8,000 years.

4. It will search for water ice and study lunar rocks. The hunt for water is significant as ISRO has not ruled out the possibility of a manned lunar landing in the 2020s. Although none has been definitely detected, recent evidence suggests that there is water on the moon.

## Characteristics of Moon

It is pertinent to note the major characteristics of moon which are as follows:

1. Moon is the nearest celestial body to Earth and lies at a distance of about 3,84,000 km.

2. Moon is the only natural satellite of Earth. It travels round the Earth once in 27.3 days and takes the same time to spin around its own axis. Thus, one hemisphere of the Moon (the 'far-side') is not visible to us.

3. Moon's diameter is one-fourth the size of Earth and its mass is 1/81 of Earth.

4. Gravity on the surface of the Moon is only one-sixth of that on Earth.

5. Like Earth, the Moon too is a world with mountains, plateaus, plains, lowlands and, of course, craters.

6. Unlike Earth, the Moon does not have an atmosphere. Liquid water cannot exist on the Moon. But information from recent missions has raised the possibility of presence of water as ice in its polar regions.

7. Formation and evolution of our Moon is important in understanding the history of our solar system.

## Studying the Moon and the Solar System

Chandrayaan-1's blasting off towards the Moon has been indicated as the hotting up of what is being described by many as the lunar gold rush. The presence of Helium-3, believed to be a clean and excellent fuel of the future, is just one of the reasons why countries want to literally reach for the Moon. One of India's aims is to harvest helium-3, a nuclear fusion material. The Moon is thought to contain up to 5 million tonnes of helium-3. The other possibility is that the Moon is considered as an important link in understanding the formation and evolution of the solar system. Since it has no atmosphere, it is a place believed to be fossilized in time. It means that rocks which were created when the Moon was formed, still exist there—in a preserved state since no geological activity takes place there, unlike the Earth.

One of the key objectives of Chandrayaan-1 is chemical, mineral and topographic mapping using a set of cameras in different wave-lengths. Since this spacecraft will move around the lunar orbit for two years, it is expected to yield valuable information, including the possible presence of water and helium-3. This makes an orbital mission like Chandrayaan much more valuable than earlier Lander missions, which were limited to just a few regions.

Through the Antrix Corporation, with headquarters at Bangalore, ISRO offers a plethora of services related to space. ISRO has considerable experience in the design, manufacture, launch and operation of both communication and remote-sensing satellites. Through the highly successful INSAT and GSAT programmes, Antrix has standardized three flight-proven satellite platforms in the weight class of 1,000 to 3,500 kg. Antrix also offers sub-systems designed for effective integration, including spacecraft, thermal mechanisms, power systems, communication systems and attitude orbit control systems. Antrix also claims a huge customer base of companies like the Israel Aircraft Industries, EADS, Mitsubishi Electric, Immarsat and Eutelsat. It has been selling its high-qualified imagery through the Space Imaging Corporation of the US for the past ten years or so.

Now India is looking at designing a capsule that can carry two humans on board our GSLV rocket. It is a major technological challenge to develop this technology, select and train astronauts and upgrade the launch vehicle. The project report for the same has been cleared by the Space Commission and India hopes to have its first manned mission to Moon by 2015.

O O O

# 16. DEEP SEA EXPLORATION

Two-thirds of the earth's surface is covered with water. There lies a storehouse of innumerable resources beneath the ocean's depths. Throughout history, scientists have relied on a number of specialised tools to measure, map and view the ocean's depths. One of the first instruments used to investigate the sea bottom was the sounding weight. Viking sailors took measurements of ocean depth and sampled seafloor sediments with it. This device consisted of a lead weight with a hollow bottom attached to a line. When the weight reached the ocean bottom and collected a sample of the seabed, the line was hauled back on board ship and measured in the distance between a sailor's outstretched arms—a 1.83 metre unit called a fathom. This term is still used for nautical depth. Dutch inventor, Cornelius Van Drebel is accredited for building the first submarine. Drebel tested the submarine in the Thames river in Britain during 1620 to 1624. King James I is said to have taken a short ride in the submarine. From 1872 to 1876, a landmark ocean study was undertaken by the British scientists abroad HMS Challenger, a sailing vessel that was redesigned into a laboratory ship.

The Challenger expedition covered 127,653 kilometres and is given credit for providing the first real view of major sea floor features such as the deep ocean basins. It discovered more than 4,700 new species of marine life, including deep-sea organisms. Deep sea exploration advanced dramatically in the 1900s with a series of inventions, ranging from sonar— a system for detecting the presence of objects under water through the use of sound—of manned deep diving submersibles such as Alvin. Alvin can carry a crew of three people to depths of over 4,000 metres and is equipped with lights, computers, cameras and highly manoeuvrable arms for collecting samples in the darkness of the ocean's depths. Now, deep sea technology has become a frontier technology for harnessing non-living resources lying on the seabed. One of the important non-living resources to be harnessed are the nodules termed as Polymetallic Nodules which are available at depths greater than 4000 metres in the deep sea. These nodules contain Manganese (27 to 30%), Copper (1-2%), Nickel (1-2%), Cobalt (0.2-0.3%), besides traces of other minerals. Copper and Nickel available from terrestrial resources in the Indian subcontinent.

Deep sea mining is a highly challenging field, with the depth of water and weather conditions being the major constraints. The mining system has to collect nodules efficiently from the ocean floor having soil of low bearing strength and traverse through the sea floor of varied topography. Further, the nodules are required to be transported to the mining ship from a depth of 5000 metres, discharge tailings from the ship with minimum environmental disturbances and the ship has to have extensive on board handling facilities. At such depths, the pressure is very high and the sea bed is soft like thick grease.

India is now among the list of developed countries in the area of deep sea technology, by unveiling devices for deep sea exploration recently. These are: Underwater Crawlen, In-Situ Soil Property Measurement System and Remotely Operable Vehicle (ROV). Since India is a pioneer investor in polymetallic nodules exploration, a site of 1,50,000 sq. km has been allotted to India in the Central Indian Ocean Basin by the International Sea Bed Authority (ISBA) of the United Nations. This mining site is located about 2000 km down south of Kanya Kumari. India is the only country having a mining site in the Central Indian Ocean Basin, the others being in the Pacific Ocean.

The Ministry of Earth Sciences through National Institute of Ocean Technology, Chennai, has for the first time developed a world class remotely operated vehicle, a deep sea mining machine and deep sea *in situ* soil testing machine which work in most extreme conditions. It comprises a crawler based machine which can travel on the seafloor, collect nodules to make slurry and pump the same to the ship. The underwater crawler system has been successfully tested at a depth of over 450 metres where pressure is 45 times the atmospheric pressure. It is an underwater robotic vehicle.

The seabed is very soft at greater depths. It is therefore essential that the seabed property is measured *in situ* first to provide undisturbed underwater realities. To achieve this objective, a soil testing machine has been developed by NIOT to measure the soil property *in situ* at a depth of 6000 metres. The system has been developed keeping in view the weight and contact area in the soft seabed to measure soil property without disturbing the original elements of the seabed.

It is virtually impossible for humans to undertake repairs, change tools, etc. at greater depths. Therefore, a Remotely Operated Vehicle is required to undertake such jobs. NIOT has developed ROV which is electrically operated and is equipped with two manipulators and can carry 150 kg of load for mounting scientific and mission oriented tools. This objective has been successfully tested at a depth of 250 metres. Further tries with greater depths are under way.

O O O

# 17. G–20 London Summit—April 2009

The London G-20 Summit was held on 2 April, 2009. In it, the world leaders announced US$ 1 trillion deal to help the world economy battling one of the worst downturns in history. The amount will be given to International Monetary Fund (IMF) and other institutions to facilitate world trade.

This amount will include $250 billion of special IMF currency called Special Drawing Rights (SDRs). In addition, the IMF will see its own resources tripled, with up to $500 billion in new funds. The G-20 has also agreed to trade a package worth 250 billion over two years to support global trade. This will help the fund support countries in financial distress and revive trade flows which will largely be in the form of guarantees.

Together with the $1.1 trillion boost, world leaders have also agreed that the age of bank secrecy is over and have pledged to work for greater transparency. The booster dose, together with measures by individual governments across the world, would total to a fiscal stimulus package of a whopping $ 5 trillion by the end of the year 2010. This is expected to help the global economy return to its normal growth path much earlier than has been predicted so far.

These measures will restore confidence in the economy, ensure growth and create jobs. It will repair the global financial system and rejuvenate lending. It will also strengthen financial regulation as demanded by most developed nations.

The G-20 leaders also agreed to take action against non-cooperative jurisdictions, including tax havens like Jersey, Monaco and Cayman Islands, among others, which allow people to hold numbered accounts that protect their identities and frighten financial rules to bring hedge funds and credit rating agencies under closer supervision. "We are undertaking an unprecedented and concerted fiscal expansion, which will save or create millions of jobs that would otherwise have been destroyed. It will, by the end of next year, amount to $ 5 trillion, raise output by 4 per cent and accelerate the transition to a green economy", said UK Prime Minister Gordon Brown, the Chairman of London Summit 2009.

Though the London Summit was a follow-up to the G-20 meet in Washington held in 2008, this meeting assumed far greater importance in the light of collapse of the global financial system over the past few months. The overall agenda of this meeting was to find ways and means to overcome the global recession and impose stricter regulations over the global banking sector. The Summit has been called "a turning point in world financial regulation.

Scores of diplomatic delegations including India's, had hectic meetings before the start of the Summit. Prime Minister Manmohan Singh became one of the first world leaders to have a one-on-one meeting—his first with US President Barack Obama in London in global diplomatic circles where things matter. The meeting between the two leaders was warm and cordial and the two discussed developments in South Asia as well as global issues like energy security and climate change. President Obama described Manmohan Singh as a "wise and marvellous" man and hailed India's "high stature" because it had "unleashed economic forces" and said a lot of it had to do with "the wisdom of Dr. Singh".

Dr. Manmohan Singh joined a select group including Russian President Dmitry Medvedev, Chinese President Hu

Jintao, Saudi Arabia's King Abdullah and South Korean Lee Myung-bak for the honour, alongwith Queen Elizabeth II. Dr. Singh and President Obama discussed bilateral, global and regional issues and took forward the US-India enhanced relationship.

Given that India has maintained its position in the world economic map despite of the recent downturn, the G-20 was an opportunity to cement the country's position firmly at the top of table, though the overriding sentiment in the Indian camp ahead of the general elections seemed to be a cautious wait-and-watch attitude. China was undoubtedly the major player at the Summit, as the world eyes its lucrative surplus to bail the world economy out of the downturn. It has emerged as a key player in international efforts to revive the global proceedings.

Apart from an opportunity to reinforce India's image as an emerging global player, it is also a platform to push world leaders for a realignment of the international balance of power. It is the first forum where the countries like India are on board for important decisions—unlike the G-8, where India, China, Brazil and South Africa are invited as mere observers.

As G-20 drew to a close, Dr. Singh said "the fact that India is accepted as a major player on the world economic stage is itself an achievement. Besides, the $ 1.1 trillion injected into the global economy would stimulate trade and output, which would certainly be to India's advantage, since it was basically the external environment that had hit India's growth trajectory."

Manmohan Singh advised leaders of the industrialised nations on how to handle the difficult political job of taking tips from developing countries and allay anti-globalisation and protectionist fears of their disgruntled populace. He said "leaders of developing countries have struggled to overcome doubts and fears of our public to persuade them of the merits of integrating with the global economy". He went on to say, "As we deal with immediate problems, we must also be careful not to sacrifice the gains of openness of trade, direct investment and immigration". "We must ensure that countries hurt by the massive withdrawal of private capital that has taken place, which is unlikely to be reversed in 2010, are able to rely upon an increased flow of resources from the international financial institutions. Risks lie in doing too little rather than too much, and we are not doing enough to ensure recovery in 2010. If we cannot agree to do more, we should at least send a clear message that we will watch developments carefully in 2009 and act speedily to do more, if necessary". Dr. Singh added further.

A day before the start of the G-20 summit, protestors clashed with riot police in downturn London breaking into the heavily guarded Royal Bank of Scotland and smashed its windows. Earlier, they tried to storm the Bank of England and pelted police with eggs and fruits. At least 4,000 anarchists, anti-capitalists, environmentalists and others jammed into London's financial district for what they called "Financial Fool's Day".

India is open to the idea of contributing a total of around $ 20 billion—roughly Rs. 100,000 crore—towards increasing the capital base of the IMF, the World Bank and the Asian Development Bank (ADB) as part of the global effort to enable these institutions to lend more. The contribution, which is likely to be spread out over the next two years, will be in proportion to the quotas or shareholding that India has in these multilateral bodies.

The London G-20 Summit was a milestone in many ways. The decision to inject US$1.1 trillion in the world economy was an unprecedented move. It showed the solidarity of world leaders to fight the contagion. The abnegation of protectionism was another welcome gesture to ensure that global trade was not ignored on the pretext of local trade. The most important decision perhaps was to bring strict financial regulation to ensure that such severe recessions do not occur in future.

# 18. UNITED NATIONS CLIMATE CHANGE CONFERENCE

The 12-day United Nations Climate Change Conference ended in Bali (Indonesia) on December 14, 2007. It was attended by over 11,000 delegates from 188 countries and the global media. The conference concluded much as expected in a fog of self-protection by the principal polluters. The US kept to its anti-Kyoto Treaty stance by blocking mention of fixed targets of carbon reduction of 25-40 per cent by 2020 as proposed by Europe in the main language of the Bali Framework Agreement. As the framework accord is itself only a statement of intent, to be used as a guide to produce, or successor to the Kyoto pact by the end of 2009, the hard bargaining that is to come is painfully evident.

The Bali Conference brought to the fore noteworthy, but not entirely independent, developments in matters relating to Global Warming. Firstly, countries are stating and agreeing to one thing, and doing another. Secondly, help to developing countries has hitherto not received due attention but a start may have been made. Finally, the unglamorous task of monitoring and verification of emissions needs to develop credible and ascertainable methodologies to impart confidence in the veracity of estimates.

The Conference has sought to finalise an agenda on the basis of which countries are committed to negotiating a new agreement to be concluded by 2009. It took place against the backdrop of the Fourth Assessment Report of the Intergovernmental Panel on Climate Change, which emphasised that greenhouse gases should peak by 2015 and that emission cuts by 2020 of 25-40 per cent by rich countries are needed to prevent the possibility of a four degree centigrade rise in global temperatures. The Kyoto Protocol, which has been ratified by Australia recently, binds signatories to reducing emission of GHGs by at least five per cent below 1990 levels over the period 2008-12.

In fact, it is helpful to assess the progress at the Bali

Conference in terms of meeting long, medium and short-term challenges of Global Warming. It is also opposite to gauge evolution in this subject area in the light of recent occurrences that are symptomatic of the type and insincerity of National Governments. Starting with the long-term objective of cutting emissions in consonance with FAR-IPCC, the Bali Conference failed to agree on specific targets because the US was forced to drop its demand that emission targets for the developing countries should be part of the road map, as also its opposition to the developing countries' demand for technological and financial help.

India and China had raised last-minute objections to the accord, which would for the first time have required developing countries to accept emissions reduction commitments. India wanted countries to set their own targets, allowing it to limit the impact of the regulations on its economy. China was seeking new consultations outside of the plenary session.

The controversy centred on whether the developing countries' emission-reduction measures should be called "action" or "contributions". The developing countries had come under strong pressure and even faced threats of trade sanctions to also accept mandatory emission reduction commitments that is "unfair and unjust".

Developing countries are not required to accept emission reduction commitments under the Kyoto Protocol, and they state that any such commitments would cramp economic growth. In this context, the Group of Seventy-Seven (G-77) has been resisting concerted efforts from some developed countries to press for a comprehensive new agreement.

The Bali Conference reached a deal to tackle greenhouse gas emissions from deforestation, hailed as a sign of developing countries commitments to fight Global Warming. The breakthrough might eventually allow poor but forested nations to turn conservation into a tradeable commodity, with the potential to earn billions of dollars selling carbon credits.

But one of the scheme's key architects warned that, if

successful, it would create such large emissions reductions that carbon markets could collapse unless rich countries take on more stringent reduction targets.

The destruction of forests produces about 20 per cent of man-made carbon dioxide emissions. So their conservation is vital to limiting rise in global temperatures.

The "Bali Action Plan" that has emerged from the Bali Conference is not only a roadmap for the diplomatic journey for over two years, but also a clear indication of things to come; the pushing and shoving has already begun. And this is after a breakthrough was hailed at the end of the conference.

One notable initiative at the conference came from Europe which is high in the ranks of polluters but comes to Bali with a number of specific ideas for cuts in emissions by major industrialised countries. Already Europe is committed to reducing its own emissions by 20 per cent by the year 2020 and it did what it could do to pin down others to similar cuts. But it could not persuade the US and Canada, which have always held out against such targets, nor could Japan, another major polluter agree, being already in difficulty with meeting the targets it had accepted at the Kyoto in 1997.

○ ○ ○

# 19. World Food Crisis

A major food crisis may hit the world as global food stocks have fallen to their lowest levels for decades. The warning has come from no less an authority than the UN. There is a similar warning from the World Bank and the International Monetary Fund (IMF). Stating that millions of people are at risk of starvation as a result of decreasing food stocks, the UN Secretary-General Ban Ki-Moon has warned that shortages of food are devastating consequences for the world's most vulnerable communities.

A recent World Bank report on Millennium Development Goals pointed out that since 2005 the prices of essential food items hit 20-year high level at $ 500 per tonne, price of wheat increased to 28-year high mark. Wheat prices worldwide have jumped 120 per cent in 2007, and 181 per cent in the last 36 months, according to the World Bank. On April 25, the annual inflation rate of Japan hit a decade-high of 1.2 per cent, which was driven by rising commodity costs.

There are several factors contributing to this global food crisis. Firstly, the rate of population growth has outstripped the rate of growth in food production in some developing regions, especially in sub-Saharan Africa and South Asia. Secondly, less rice is being planted in some countries as land becomes exhausted or otherwise unsuitable for cultivation or is converted to other uses such as subdivisions, malls and resorts. Thirdly, water shortage poses a problem as rice yield depends critically on water. A study by the International Water Management Institute (IWMI) suggests that by 2020, one-third of Asia's population could face acute water shortage.

Fourthly, droughts, pest infestation, the spread of plant, diseases and other creeping disasters drastically reduce rice production.

Fifthly, rising consumption in emerging nations has created increased demand on the global cereal supply.

Sixthly, the expanding biofuels industry has caused the conversion of ricelands to corn and other crops that are sources of biofuels.

Last but not the least, the growth of the middle class in China and India has increased the demand for meat which requires the consumption of more feedstock.

Besides, droughts in Australia have been one of the major causes of food crisis. Six long years of drought have taken a heavy toll, reducing Australia's rice production. It is one of the several factors contributing to a doubling of rice prices in the last three months—increases that have led the world's largest exporters to restrict exports.

However, the then US President George W. Bush in May 2008 drew fire from parties cutting across the country's political spectrum for his latest statement blaming, among other factors, the rising prosperity in India resulting in people's "better nutrition" for the prevailing international food crisis and spiralling world food crisis.

There are over 300 million people in India who belong to the middle class. That is bigger than America's entire population. And when you start getting wealth, you start demanding better nutrition and better food, and so demand becomes high, and that causes the prices to go up, the US President said.

Bush's remarks came close on the heels of his Secretary of State Condoleezza Rice's statement that "apparent improvement" in the diets of people in India and China and consequent food exports caps are the reasons for the present world food crisis. Bush's unwarranted remarks have been slammed by almost all political parties regardless of their differing views on the reasons for the rising inflation in India.

The sharp rise in prices of all basic commodities have raised the possibilities of food riots in a number of poor countries. Recently, a mob in Bangladesh set many shops and vehicles afire and looted shops to protest against the rising prices.

In some countries, the higher prices are leading to riots, political instability and growing worries about feeding the poorest people. Food riots contributed to the dismissal of Haiti's Prime Minister and leaders in some other countries are nervously trying to calm anxious consumers. Keeping this in mind, the Finance Ministers and Central Banks of the Group of Eight (G-8) countries called for urgent action to deal with the price spikes, and several of them demanded a reconsideration of biofuel policies adopted recently in the

West. The most acute effects have been seen in Egypt, where thousands of people have resorted to violence due to shortages of basic food commodities and rising food prices. At least 10 people have been killed in recent riots that occurred at Government-subsidised bakeries.

Surge in global food prices could reverse all gains made in cutting poverty since 1998. Poor people in Yemen are now spending more than a quarter of their incomes, just on bread, before they pay for other essential food for their children, let alone basic health care or shelter.

The World Food Programme (WFP) cut off rice deliveries to 1,344 Cambodian schools in March 2008 after prices doubled and suppliers defaulted on contracts. China, Vietnam, India and Egypt have curbed overseas scales to safeguard domestic supplies and cool inflation. Soaring prices may put basic foods beyond the reach of the poorest people, raising the risk of a 'silent famine' in Asia. Thailand, which ships one-third of the world's exports, may follow its Asian neighbours in limiting sales. Food shortages have triggered riots and protests in Uzbekistan and Ivory Coast. In Feb. 2008, riots over food prices increase in Cameroon left 40 people dead. Even in North America the crisis has triggered violence. In the Philippines, people are lining up under the scorching sun to buy up three kilos of rice which is about 40-50 per cent cheaper than the commercial variety.

The WFP has made an urgent appeal for an additional US $ 755 million to fill the missing gap so it can carry out its humanitarian work. The UN agency is facing a 40 per cent increase in the cost of food since it prepared its $ 3.1 billion budget for 2008. WFP usually helps between 80 and 90 million people a year and it is entirely funded by voluntary contributions.

**US Aid:** The former US President George W. Bush ordered the release of $ 200 million (Rs. 800 crore) in emerging aid to help countries where surging food prices have brought worst hunger and sparked violent protests. Bush directed Agriculture

Secretary Ed Schafer to draw down the amount from a food reserve known as the Bill Emerson Humanitarian Trust.

The move would help deal with the impact of rising commodity prices on US emergency food aid programmes and help meet unanticipated food needs of countries in Africa and elsewhere. Over the long run, the source problems will need to be identified, the source where the food is, so that there is a long-term plan in place that helps take care of a world's poor and hungry. The US is already the largest provider of food aid in the world. It delivered more than $ 2.1 billion (Rs 8,400 crore) of food aid to 78 developing nations in 2007. The estimate for 2008 is $ 2.5 billion over Rs. 10,000 crore.

**ADB Loans:** Asian Development Bank (ADB) has promised financial help for nations fighting the world food crisis and attacked plans for a rice cartel. Loans will help countries subsidise the price of food staples for the poor. The multinational lender will also provide two billion dollars (1.3 billion euros) in loans in 2008 and 209 to finance agriculture infrastructure projects such as rural roads and irrigation system to help boost for output.

**ASEAN Cooperation:** Trade Ministers of the 10-member South East Asian Nations (ASEAN), who met in Jakarta on May 4, agreed to cooperate in security food price stability in the region. The Ministers acknowledged that the sky-rocketing world food prices, caused among others by global growing demand, higher cost and bad weather, have become a threat to South Asia's economic stability.

To meet the threat, ASEAN countries have to increase food production and maintain the agricultural business and regulations, the Ministers said in their joint announcement.

Two factors aggravating the world food crisis can be neutralised only through global cooperation. The switch from food crops to biofuels in the US and the European Union, often by subsidising their farmers, is one of them. The pernicious influences of climate change on food production are well-documented and they can be countered only with the active participation of the developed countries. The latter should also be persuaded to rethink their biofuel policies.

○ ○ ○

## 20. President Obama : A New Era In American History

Barack Hussein Obama took over as America's 44th President on 20 January, 2009. Forty-seven year old Democrat had defeated Republican John McCain to make history as the first black to be elected US President.

The dawn of the new Democratic era—with Obama allies in charge of both houses of Congress—ended eight years of Republican control of the White House by George W. Bush, who left Washington as one of the nation's most unpopular presidents, the architect of two unfinished wars and the man in charge at a time of economic calamity that took away many American's jobs, savings and homes. With Obama taking oath as America's President, the United States turned a page and closed a chapter.

The Americans have wisely elected not just their own leader but a new leader of world because of the universal demand for change for the better that springs from Obama's election. He represents the hopes and aspirations of all minorities and the dispossessed everywhere—people and nations—who together constitute a majority of the world.

The dream of the great black American, Martin Luther King Jr. nearly 50 years ago came true with Obama's oath-taking. The US demonstrated why it is still the greatest country in the world when Americans of all colour, class, creed reaffirmed the vision of Abraham Lincoln, considered to be their greatest-ever President. America is a land of greater equality, opportunity, tolerance and democratic values than any other nation of the world.

Obama is wiser than his youthful age. He has run the most efficient election campaign in the US history. He has been unruffled by slights and slurs. If, as the new president of the USA for the next four years, he demonstrates the same vision and sensibility that has been displayed during the election campaign, he can win a second term and turn the US and the world around.

Throughout the US elections season, Obama campaigned consistently as the candidate for change. In a sense, however, by giving a landslide victory to its first ever African-American president, the US already is a different country. Before the election, there were some doubts if Americans would be able to break the radical barrier. A few decades ago, it was unthinkable for a black person to occupy a high office, let alone the presidency. Obama's victory has reflected America's diversity as much as it acknowledges his ability to appeal to voters across race, class and age.

The most important challenge facing the US President is to maintain the US' premier standing in the eyes of the world. As the new President, he must re-establish the US as a country that listens, that engages with others, and that has, in the famous phrase from the American Declaration of Independence in 1776, "a decent respect to the opinions of mankind".

George W. Bush, who left behind two unfinished wars and an economy in turmoil, said goodbye to the American people on 16 January, 2009, declaring in his final address to the nation that while he had some setbacks during his turbulent eight years in office, "I have followed by my conscience and done what I thought was right".

On his way out, Bush defended his decisions on the Iraq war. There have been over 4,000 US deaths since the invasion in Iraq and toppling of Saddam Hussein in 2003. He said that "not finding weapons of mass destruction was a significant disappointment". The accusation that Saddam had and was pursuing weapons of mass destruction was Bush's main justification for going to war against Iraq.

Bush admitted another miscalculation. Eager to report

quick progress after US troops ousted Saddam Hussein, Bush made a victory speech in front of a "Mission Accomplished" banner, a sign that turned out to be wildly optimistic. "Clearly putting 'Mission Accomplished' on an aircraft carrier was a mistake", he said.

Defending his eight-year presidency, Bush said that all his decisions were in the "best interests" of the country and listed the "new historic and strategic partnership" with India as one of his foreign policy successes. "We have opened a new historic and strategic partnership with India with the successful culmination of a historic Indo-American nuclear deal", Bush said. He also cautioned that another terrorist attack remained the "gravest threat" for the US.

The Bush era came to a close with more than 150,000 US troops fighting in two war zones and the world's largest economy reeling under the worst financial turmoil after the Great Depression of 1930s.

The US is presently facing many crises including its worst financial downturn. The election of Obama signifies a rejection of eight years of Republican policies which have contributed to creating the recent turmoil.

The US image is more tarnished in some ways by the failure of financial icons than that of its political leadership. Americans have rarely put their best men at the top of the political hierarchy. The corporate world, in principle, lifts the most meritorious to the top and gives them astronomical compensation in recognition of their professional worth. The Bush administration has made mistakes in globalised world that the US dominates militarily but not US investment banks and insurance giants like AIG as that drains out credibility for the US global campaign for good governance, its best practices, transparency, prudential norms and market discipline. The collapse of these banks has shaken the faith of the votaries of the market economy and the American model of corporate governance. Lack of financial control has proved to be the bane of American economy in recent years.

In his initial months, the gloomy economy consumed much of the new president's energies and he has so far shown signs of clear thinking on how to get the nation up to its feet again. He has already bought a second stimulus package besides sector-specific plans, bailouts and taken some important monetary measures to revive the economy.

The major tasks before Obama are enumerated below :

1. After George W. Bush's abject failure at Annapolis to leave a lasting legacy by securing peace in West Asia, Obama has the onerous task of starting it all over.

2. The global financial meltdown is Obama's immediate challenge.

3. Ties with Russia have strained over NATO expansion and its invasion of Georgia. They need to be improved.

4. US soldiers in Iraq are hoping Obama will keep his promise of a 16-month timetable for withdrawal.

5. The Obama team will have to keep up the pace of high-level visits to South Asia to prevent the potential for military conflict between India and Pakistan.

6. US dependence on foreign oil is seen as both a security and economic threat. Obama would have to boost energy efficiency, and develop non-conventional sources of energy.

7. The Obama team has already established that it will give greater attention and provide resources on stabilising and securing Afghanistan. It should coordinate closely with the Indian leadership as it reviews the strategies for Afghanistan.

8. Iran's nuclear ambitions and manoeuvering in the Persian Gulf region pose a threat to long-time American ally Israel. This needs to be addressed.

9. The lawless tribal region of Pakistan is a sanctuary for the Taliban and Al-Qaeda. Obama has promised to go after Al-Qaeda. He has to fulfil this promise.

10. Establishing India's strategic role in Asia, it will be

important for Obama to signal that his administration is committed to building the strategic relationship between the US and India.

11. Obama should somehow demonstrate that he takes the US relationship with India seriously and recognises the important role India can play in promoting peace and stability in the Asian region.

12. Bush strained ties with Europe after unilaterally deciding to attack Iraq. The responsibility of bringing multilateralism into decision-making on issues with a global impact rests with Obama.

13. Europe wants the US to agree to a binding international agreement on cutting carbon emissions. Obama has to consider this favourably.

14. China's improved international clout would make it more difficult for Obama to seek better human rights standards from Beijing. The growing trade imbalance also puts US on the back foot.

India believes that Obama is a pragmatic leader who understands that American industry needs to be competitive not just in the US but in Third World countries as well. His victory has been hailed in India amidst hopes that new administration's policies would bring about a turnaround in the world's largest economy from the piling rubble of global financial turmoil. This would mean two things: (i) sound demand generated for world products and services from a robust US economy, and (ii) an absence of protectionism to ensure that domestic growth does not come in the way of overseas interests.

The revival of the US economy is critical for India and for the world at large. India exported goods worth nearly $60 billion to the US in 2007-08, which is about one-third of its total exports. It is expected that this trajectory of growth—which began with the March 2000 visit of President Clinton to India—will continue into an Obama administration due to sheer commonality of democratic values and interests between these two countries.

With India, the US has one of its most important relationships in this present uncertain time. Both countries, are working to protect their people and values from the 21st century threats while at the same time respecting and maintaining the rule of law and cultural pluralism.

The world's oldest democracy and the world's largest democracy are natural partners, sharing important interests and fundamental democratic values. Both have been victims of catastrophic terrorist attacks and have a shared interest in succeeding in the fight against Al-Qaeda and its operational and ideological affiliates.

Indo-US ties have been on an upswing over the last decade, which got further strengthened with the signing of the Indo-US civilian nuclear agreement. This deal will bring the two countries closer than ever before. There is a growing convergence between the two democracies. Hopefully, a rejuvenated US leadership can work to India's advantage. Obama and the Democrat establishment are eight years behind the curve on US-India relations. India's best bet in the Obama camp may be vice-president Joe Biden, who is an old friend of India.

Obama has identified working with India and Pakistan to try to resolve the Kashmir issue in a "serious way" and listed it as a critical task for his administration. Pakistanis are full of expectations while India has been opposed to the internationalising of the Kashmir issue and Obama's high interest in this complicated discord. Obama has identified resolving the matter as a key to tempering Islamabad and concentrating its energy on the war on terror that is consuming Pakistan.

So far Obama has shown the signs of turning out to be one of America's most successful Presidents. He has shown the ability to grasp the seriousness of major problems afflicting the world today, i.e. financial downturn, terrorism, human rights violations and political conflicts, among others. His determination to fight these problems can be seen from his actions.

○ ○ ○

# 21. World Economic Forum Meeting — Davos, Switzerland

The annual meeting of the World Economic Forum (WEF) was held from 28 Jan to 1 Feb 2009 in Davos, Switzerland. There were about 2500 participants from 96 countries, including politicians, industrialists, academics, financiers, economists and representatives of well-known Non-Governmental Organization (NGOs).

Political leaders arrived depressed and left almost despondent with fear after exchanging horror stories of just how savage and sudden the downturn had been in the past months. Montek Singh Ahluwalia summed up the 2009 gathering of the World Economic Forum in the following words: "Confidence grows and falls at the rate a coconut falls."

It was supposed to be the year the United States came in from the cold at the annual gathering of world leaders. But instead of receiving a warm response, American policies were rebuked again and again in rhetoric that recalled the anger of the Bush years—mainly aimed at what the world views as the new threat of protectionism by the US.

There was, however, a deep reservoir of goodwill for President Obama and the change in direction he represents. But despite the pledges to encourage international trade and economic cooperation that accompanied the closing sessions of the gathering on Feb. 1, there were clear signs that deep divisions between the US and the rest of the world remained.

The criticism came from the usual sources, such as Prime Minister Vladimir V. Putin of Russia and Premier Wen Jiabao of China, who both criticised a long pattern of excessive consumption, risky borrowing and inadequate regulation in the US. But more significant, fierce criticism also came from economic and political leaders of European allies like France and Germany.

Whether the issue was the recent bailout for the American auto industry or proposals favouring American steel producers in the stimulus package, foreign officials warned that any move towards protectionism would have serious consequences for Washington and the rest of the world. As word of the "Buy American" provision in the stimulus package to help the US steel industry spread through Davos, the tone against protectionism, became sharper.

Washington sent a relatively low-profile contingent which did not address the issue of protectionism directly, but preferred to stick with the big picture.

Officials of several countries were also concerned about how the US Government will pay for Mr. Obama's stimulus package, which could ultimately cost more than $ 1 trillion. A binge of new borrowing by Washington could effectively crowd out other borrowers by pushing interest rates higher over the long term, and would be especially painful for developing countries that rely on foreign capital. It could also stoke inflation as soon as the global economy eventually begins to recover.

But no other economic power—Japan, China or a European nation—seemed ready to step up and fill the role traditionally played by the US. It was the irony of the situation, that everyone was still looking to the US for leadership to fix things or at least make things better.

There was much soul-searching in Davos as to why consumers appeared to have a deep loathing of some leading corporations. Thus, the whole sessions were devoted to the need to rebuild trust. This was a recognition that widening inequality, corporate greed and a lack of suitable regulation helped to create the problem.

Barack Obama, a significant absentee had put his finger on the problem when he gave Wall Street a dressing down for paying $18.5 billion in bonuses last year and simultaneously set up a task force to find ways of bringing help to American working families.

What the new president identified was that the economic system of the past 30 years has been skewed towards those at the top. In the US workers were able to improve their living standards only by sending spouses out to work, working longer hours and double (sometimes tripple) jobbing. When even that was not enough, they borrowed more.

Kris Gopalakrishnan of Infosys, said at the summit "Trust will get rebuilt only if we go back to fundamental values of integrity, leadership and fairness". Stephen Green, the Chairman of HSBC, said that some of the practices in the financial sector had not contributed to human welfare.

There was plenty of finger-pointing, but the word "sorry" was conspicuous by its absence. Unless the public is given proof that those who made such monumental policy errors are paying a price, it is hard to see how trust will ever be rebuilt. Interestingly, there were some who thought that putting financiers in the dock might be the only way to convince the public that the guilty were being punished.

Politicians now have to make a choice where they can have a stable economic system and avoid protectionism. They have to act and act fast. The public may trust Government more than it does business. The countries have to join together to fight difficult conditions created by economic downturn.

O O O

## 22. Russia—A Resurgent Power

Russia, the largest country in the world in area, stretches across the continents of Asia and Europe. It extends for over 9600 km from the Baltic Sea to the Pacific Ocean and for 4,800 km from North to South.

Russia, an independent country since December 1991, is 75 per cent of the total area of the erstwhile Soviet Union and has 50 per cent of its total population. About 70 per cent of the USSR's total industrial and agricultural output came from Russia.

Russia has now taken the place of the former Soviet Union in international fora. Russia adopted the name 'Russian Federation'. The collapse of the erstwhile Soviet Union also heralded the degradation of Russia's status as a major power monger in what was called the Cold War era of yore. The Western bloc, spearheaded by the US, continued without any competition thereafter and has generally secured for itself the title of the world's sole superpower in current international relations.

The US has effected military intervention in Afghanistan, Iraq and kept a vigil on the Asia Pacific region with impunity and is presently busy trying to browbeat Iran. All this has been possible because there is nobody to present an effective opposition front to America's dominance of most global sensitive spots.

Russia's problems were further exacerbated through two successive ineffectual Presidents. First was Mikhail Gorbachov whose 'glasnost' and 'perestroika' made any difference either to his country's standing or to the Western bloc's attitude towards it. Next came Boris Yeltsin who took refuge in vodka whenever he found things were getting too complicated for him to handle. His performance during the Balkan crisis was deplorable. Consequently, Russia became somewhat of a loose ball without any direction and remained so till Vladimir Putin became the country's President.

Putin, a dynamic person, has firmly set his eye on two aspects of Russia's resurgence—first of all, to positively address its faltering economy and second to regain its place as an appreciable power centre. He appears to be on the right course for both his objectives. While the economy is taking its own path to betterment, President Putin is now trying to uplift Russia in global politics with the intention of relocating itself in a position from where Moscow can take a hegemonic control in international relations again. His initial pronouncement in this context was strongly objecting to the North Atlantic Treaty Organisation's (NATO) expansion eastwards to within reach of Russia's European border.

However, the Western block, with the European Union playing a leading part, paid little heed to his objections and is at present locked in a fresh controversy over a missile defence system that this bloc wants to set up in Eastern Europe. Although the bloc's leader to wit, Washington furnishes vague replies when queried by Moscow as to against which enemy is this system being established, it is apparent that the bloc is pursuing a policy of sanitising its territorial entity from any visualised Russia threat, be it real or imaginary.

Another factor that bothers Russia is the increasing membership of the European Union wherein former Russian States are being wooed to join. Hungry, Poland and Czech Republic set the stage for this entry and these States are now cocking a snooks at their previous partner.

At present, Russia has virtually no influence in West Asia as all the Arab countries directly or indirectly enjoy a good equation with the US. Making matters worse are periodic reports that Russia's insurgency problem with the Chechen rebels is being fuelled by Wahabi ideology from West Asian countries, egged on by the US.

Russia has recovered to considerable height from the crippling aftermath of the break-up of the Soviet Union and is now in a position to reassert its national pride, mainly regaining its earlier place and influence in the international arena. It is truly concerned about its security environment, especially about the enlargement of American military process close to its borders, a sort of re-run of the old encirclement policy by displaying, deploying and developing its military clout, Russia is only resuming what the West on its part never stopped doing.

The Putin leadership wants to convince Russians that the era of want and weakness is past and they are, military and otherwise, second to none again, thereby creating the right ambience for Putin's successor in the Kremlin to stay the course.

O O O

## 23. CONFLICT IN TIBET

Tibet is in the midst of a mass democratic uprising against Han Chinese communist rule. Some of the more fanciful news, stories, images, and opinion pieces on the 'democratic' potential of this uprising have been put out by leading western newspapers and television networks. The reality is that the riot that broke out in Lhasa on March 14, 2008 and claimed a confirmed toll of 22 lives involved violent, ransacking mobs, including 300 militant monks from the Drepung Monastery, who marched in tandem with a foiled 'March to Tibet' by groups of monks across the border in India.

In Lhasa, the rioters committed murder, arson, and other acts of cruelty against innocent civilians and caused huge damage to public and private property. The atrocities included dousing one man with petrol and setting him alight, beating a patrol policeman and caring out a fist-size piece of his flesh, and torching a school with 800 terrorised pupils covering inside. Visual images and independent eyewitness accounts attest to this ugly reality, which even compelled the Dalai Lama to threaten to resign.

There was violence also in Tibetan ethnic areas in the adjacent provinces of Gansu and Sichuan, which, according to official estimates, took an injury toll of more than 700. Western analyses have linked these incidents to the March 10 anniversary of the failed 1959 Tibetan uprising, non-progress in the talks between the Dalai Lama's emissaries and Beijing, China's human rights record, and the Beijing Olympic Games, which were though be held as scheduled from August 8 to 24.

Dalai Lama has been criticised by the Chinese as an anti-

motherland conspirational politician, a wolf in monk's robes'
while many Tibetan exiles are exasperated with the failure of
his middle way. His strategy has been one that is neither anti-
China nor anti-Chinese. He seeks to make a moral appeal to
the conscience of the Chinese people and Government.

The real problem arises from two demands pressed by the
Dalai Lama. The first is his concept of 'high-level' or 'maximum'
autonomy in line with the 'one country', two systems' principle.
The Chinese Government points out that this is applicable only
to Hong Kong, Macao, and Taiwan, and that the kind of
autonomy that the Dalai Lama demanded in Nov. 2005 cannot
possibly be accommodated within the Chinese Constitution.
Secondly, the 2.6 million Tibetans in the Tibet Autonomous
Region (TAR), which constitutes one-eighth of China's territory,
from only 40 per cent of the total population of Tibetans in
China. The Chinese Government makes the perfectly
reasonable point that acceptance of the demand for 'Greater
Tibet' or 'one-administrative entity' for all 6.5 million ethnic
Tibetans means breaking up Qinghai, Gansu, Sichuan, and
Yunnan provinces, doing ethnic re-engineering, if not 'cleansing',
and causing enormous disruption and damage to China's
society and political system.

There is little the world can do to force China to change
its tactics and plans to suppress the uprising. The reality of
the Middle Kingdom, with its economic might, far outstrips the
needs of Tibet and Tibetans vying for independence or
autonomy. For China, it is as much a show of resolve as it is
a matter of face—both of which cannot be given away in a year
when Beijing is preparing to showcase the Olympics, that
grand coming out event for which the country has been
preparing for years.

So intertwined are everybody's interests with the world's
biggest factory and the world's biggest commodity guzzler that
none—including India—can wag a finger and accuse China of
something China doesn't want to be accused of. From the
Pacific Islands to Africa and from Australia to South Africa,
China has the world in its economic grip. Chinese money builds

stadiums, railways, oil pipelines and presidential palaces. Australians apparently can't dig fast enough to satisfy China's needs for metals.

In India, where the Dalai Lama and thousands of Tibetan refugees live, Indians buy a number of Chinese-made goods. Besides bilateral trade, India also has the political and diplomatic compulsions that could impact our relations with our giant neighbour. India gave up Tibet's cause long while ago and it probably makes little sense to revive it in a manner that would surely upset China now.

The Dalai Lama's frustration is visible in his threats of resignation. A believer in non-violence, he gave up his dream of an independent Tibet long ago and agreed to settle for Tibetan autonomy within China. His representatives have held on-and-off secret talks with the Chinese government in the past several years. Since 1959, when the Dalai Lama escaped to India as the Red Army walked into Lhasa, the Chinese government has poured billions of dollars into Tibet and connected the once far-flung region by rail to the government's seat in Beijing. Over the years, tens of thousands of ethnic Han Chinese have poured into the once inaccessible region in search of employment and business, skewing the population balance and making Tibetans unhappy. The migrants are there to make money as much as global companies that have set up shop in China, the world cannot complain.

Tibet is evidently central to China's India strategy, as making Tibet an integral part would give China more elbow room to claim Indian territories. In other words, China could try to settle the Sino-Indian border dispute with the help of Tibetan documents.

Nevertheless, the humiliating deference undermines India's national interests as a rising Asian power and mars its credentials as a liberal democracy. India must find ways to resolve this without getting tangled in a war of diplomacy against China over Tibet. At the very least, India can be more supportive of the Dalai Lama's call for Tibetan autonomy within China's borders. After all, even the Chinese secretly admit that any decision on the political future of Tibet will have to acknowledge the Dalai Lama's absolute leadership of Tibetans— spiritually as well as politically.

O O O

## 24. Democracy in Bhutan

Bhutan is no more a kingdom, following its first parliamentary elections held in March 2008. These elections marked a new direction in Bhutan's over 100 years transition to a democratic, constitutional monarchy. People's Democratic Party (PDP) and Druk Pnuensum Tshogpa (DPT) were the only parties fighting the polls held on a bi-party system. PDP was led by former Prime Minister and King Kheshar's uncle Sangay Ngedup. The DTP, which roughly means Bhutan United Party, was also headed by a former Prime Minister, Jigmey Thinley. These two parties vied with each other in proving to be more loyal than the King. Not surprisingly, the runaway winner in the contest, DPT, emerged as the party perceived as the more royalist of the two. With 44 of the 47 seats, DPT sees the vote as a mandate for continuity. The new Government, under Jigme Thinley, would do no more than continue the policies laid down by the 'Dragon Kings' over the years. The Himalayan Kingdom has done equally well in raising per capita income and preserving its natural environment. The King will continue to hold wide influence, although not supreme power.

The country will have a bicameral legislature. The 25-member upper house is called the National Council. Twenty of its members are elected and five are to be appointed by the King. The lower house, called the National Assembly, has a strength of 47 members, elected for five years on the basis of universal adult suffrage. A total of 318,465 citizens, i.e. nearly 60 per cent of the Bhutanese population, have registered as voters for the National Assembly elections. The royal family and religions leaders do not exercise their franchise as they are to remain above politics.

Democracy in Bhutan is indeed a vision of the monarch. The fourth King Jigme Singye Wangchuk, initiated the democratic process more than 25 years ago with the phased devolution of powers from the centre to the district and block levels and subsequently in 1998 from the throne to the elected Cabinet Ministers. In 2005, he announced a draft democratic Constitution focused on parliamentary government with the King as the titular head. The Constitution provides for removal of the monarch under certain exigencies through impeachment which requires three-fourths majority in the Parliament. The Constitutional monarch has to retire at the age of 65. The king abdicated the throne in December 2006 in favour of his eldest son, Keshar Namgyal Wangchuck.

It is an encouraging sign that the democratic experiment in Bhutan has been launched at a time of peace and prosperity, in sharp contrast to its neighbours—Nepal, Pakistan, Bangladesh and Myanmar—which are witnessing bloody struggle for democracy. In fact, the decline and ignominious fall of the monarch in Nepal must have influenced, in some indirect way, both the monarchy and the people of Bhutan. King Jigme Wangchuk did not want anyone in his line to become a prisoner of circumstance.

Evidently, many Bhutanese have more faith in their king than in the accountability of their untried political parties. However, it is to the credit of the monarchy in Bhutan which has ensured smooth transition to democracy without any palpable pressure from force inside or outside their country. In this unique transition, democratic education preceded the elections. This is rare not only in the region, but also elsewhere. The national TV channel, Bhutan Broadcasting Service and three national newspapers carried extensive campaigns meant to educate the people about the dangers of coercion or corruption. The Election Commission of Bhutan, in particular ensured free, fair and accountable polls.

A viable solution of the Bhutanese refugee problem is in extricably linked to India's regional foreign policy. During the past 15 years, echoing Bhutan, India has insisted that the refugee problem was and remains a purely bilateral issue between Nepal and Bhutan. Other powers, conscious of India's geo-strategic clout in the two Himalayan kingdoms, are not overly inclined to intervene on the refugee issue. India has compelling security reasons to consider a "change of tack". It is time India put pressure on Bhutan to allow refugees to return home in safety and with dignity and end discrimination against its ethnic Nepali citizens.

Thus, the transition to democracy in Bhutan is a victory for their remarkable kings, the State, private institutions, and not importantly the Bhutanese people.

○ ○ ○

## 25. Terrorist Attack on Mumbai

November 26 and 27, 2008 proved to be fateful days for Mumbai as eight places of India's financial capital were attacked by terrorists. Taj Gateway, Oberoi, CST Terminus, Santa Cruz Airport, Colaba and 2 hospitals were the places which bore the brunt of cowardly and inhuman acts by Pakistani terrorists which were linked to Jamat-ud-Dava—a terrorist outfit supported by Lashkar-e-Tayyeba (LeT). As many as 183 innocent people lost their lives and over 300 were injured in the dastardly act. Nine terrorists were eventually gunned down in the joint operation by Indian Army, NSG commandoes and Mumbai Police. One terrorist named Ajmal Kasav was captured alive.

The attack was well planned. A gang of 10 terrorists left Karachi in a mid-sized vessel. Midway they switched to two rafts and berthed at Badhwar Park. They reached Mumbai through sea route and met two locals at Cuffe Parade. They hid for about five hours and then headed out in three groups. Two fidayeen reached CST, aiming to take hostages but could not. Instead, they started firing indiscriminately, killing many people and scooted to nearby Cama Hospital to take hostages. When this plan failed, they again sprayed bullets on people. Additional Commissioner of Mumbai Police, Ashok Kamte was gunned down outside Metro. ATS Chief Hemant Karkare reached Cama Hospital. He thought that terrorists had run away and removed his bullet proof vest. He was immediately hit in the chest and was killed. The other two groups of terrorists managed to enter Hotel Taj and Nariman House, killed people and took hostage some foreign nationals including Americans and Israelis.

While the whole nation was in shock and anger at this tragedy, the brave policemen led by NSG commandoes were deployed to thwart the terrorists' evil design of killing innocent people and blowing up the Taj. As the terrorists had huge ammunition with them, including grenades, the operation took two days to complete before all the terrorists hidden there were killed.

The attack appeared to be aimed at getting international attention. It was also believed that the attack was intended to hurt the economic prosperity of India by creating a fear in the minds of foreigners to venture into India through various types of businesses. It aimed at reducing the number of European visitors to India, damaging the country's travel and tourism. Since hotel Taj is a symbol of India's heritage, terrorists' attack on it had the dubious objective of destroying it. Since Mumbai is India's financial capital, the city was specifically targeted to make a dent on the country's economy. The captured terrorist Kasav confessed the evil design of blowing up the Taj.

As Mumbai struggled through its darkest night of 26th November, 2008, it was daytime in the US. TV channels across America followed all the action all day long—even as the country headed into Thanksgiving. Terrorist attacks normally tend not to discriminate among the likely victims, but in this case there was a conscious plan to focus on American, British and Israeli nationals. Both Taj and Oberoi have a sizeable concentration of high-value tourists from the US and the UK. Perhaps India's strengthening relations with these countries which are helping the country march towards economic prosperity have made Pakistan—who is harbouring terrorism against India—green with envy to indulge in such cowardly and reproachful acts.

Pakistani link to the terrorist attack has been clearly established. The confessional statements of Kasav, the belongings of terrorists seized from their bodies, the mobile phone of one terrorist that fell from the window of hotel Taj while he was hurling a hand grenade—all proved beyond doubt that all the 10 terrorists belonged to Pakistan

The mood of the general public in India irrespective of caste, creed or community was angry and understandably so. There were marches and protests in various parts of the country urging the government to take concrete action against Pakistan which has been the source of all terrorist activities in several Indian cities which include New Delhi, Jaipur, Hyderabad, Bengaluru, Varanasi, Malegaon, besides Mumbai. Pakistan, following its old style, continued to deny having any hand in the terrorist attack. It even refused to accept that the terrorists involved were Pakistani nationals. It asked India to provide concrete proofs regarding the identity of terrorists. The Indian Government issued strict warnings to Pakistan. It asked Pakistan to hand over the notorious terrorists which were involved in earlier attacks. Pakistan did the eyewash of arresting a few of them only to let them go after some days. Shedding crocodile tears, Pakistan expressed sadness on the tragic incident and assured to cooperate with Indian authorities. Pakistan also said that it itself has been a victim of terrorism for so many years now. But all this becomes meaningless in the wake of the fact that several terrorist organizations are based in Pakistan and its successive governments—including that of Pervez Musharraf and of newly elected Asif Zardari— have done nothing to stop these organizations.

The 26/11 Mumbai terrorist attack has brought forth several questions, some of which are: What should India do to stop being on the receiving end of terrorism harboured by Pakistan? How should it beef up its security on sea, air and land? What stance should it keep towards Pakistan? Should it fight a war with Pakistan or at least go for direct surgical operation to destroy terrorist bases in Pakistan? These questions are not easy to answer. But clearly the intelligent minds and powers that be are now more than ever set to the task of finding solution to the problem of terrorism. India is a great country. Its people are strong. The acts of terrorism unite them instead of dividing them. When the Taj and Trident re-opened on 21st December, 2008, the world got the message that nothing can defeat us.

○ ○ ○

## 26. NEW LEADERSHIP IN CHINA

President of China Hu Jintao emerged as the man in total control of the Communist Party of China at the end of the 17th Congress of the CPC, a landmark political event, in Beijing in October 2007. He skilfully ensured the removal of his formidable rival, the 68-year-old Vice-President Zeng Quinghong, from the powerful Central Committee of the party. The other two key leaders who have also lost their coveted positions are security Chief Luo Gan and Anti-Corruption Beureau head Wu Guenzheng. But the primary target of Hu was Zeng, known for his skill for political manoeuvring. Hu faced little difficulty in ousting the three Central Committee member because of the acceptance of the idea promoted by him that those nearing 70 years or having crossed this age limit should be made to quit.

Hu has succeeded not only in getting rid of the man who could have posed a serious challenge to his authority as the top leader of the CPC but also ensuring the acceptance of his favourite programme of promcing a scientific outlook on development. This reflects China's worries relating to the excessive use of the available resources, environmental degradation and yawning rich-poor divide as the country marches forward with double-digit economic growth.

President Hu Jintao has been re-elected as the General Secretary of the ruling CPC for the second term till 2012, signalling political stability and continuity in the world's most populous nation. Hu won the fresh mandate from the newly-elected CPC's 17th Central Committees after its first plenium. In this way China's leadership has been determined till 2012.

Belying the expectations of Hu's camp, the Central Committee apparently denied Hu the free hand to name his protege Li Keqing as his potential successor at the next party Congress in 2012. But in an apparent compromise, the party had elevated Hu to the status of pantheon of leaders like Chairman Mao Zedong, Deng Xiaoping and Jiang by enshrining in the CPC Constitution his pet vision of "scientific outlook on development" to ensure a balanced and sustainable development and mitigate the sufferings of millions of poor Chinese peasants.

Hu was also re-appointed Chairman of the powerful Central military Commission of the CPC, the top military organ of the party. He succeeded Jiang Zemin as party leader at the 16th CPC National Congress in November 2002. He was elected a member of the Politburo Standing Committee of the CPC Central Committee in 1997.

In the pecking order of the CPC, the 54-year-old Xi Jinping, the Communist Party boss in Shanghai was ranked ahead of Li, who is considered Hu's choice. The 52-year old Xi seen as a candidate of Jiang, also based in China's commercial capital Shanghai.

The oldest was Jia Qinglin, 67, head of the top advisory body to Parliament and composed mainly of non-communists. Liu Yandong, 61, minister of the party's United Front Work Department which is responsible for winning over non-Communists, became China's most powerful woman following the retirement of "Iron Lady" Wu Fi from the party's decision-making body.

The 17th National Congress of the CPC adopted a resolution to amend the CPS Constitution, enshrining "scientific outlook and development" and other strategic thoughts as enunciated by Party leaders since 2002. The amendment was immediately effective.

The concept of "scientific outlook on development" is described as a continuation of the important thoughts on development expounded by the three generations of the Party's Central Collective leadership and a concentrated expression of the Marxist outlook on the world. It is a scientific theory that is in the same line as Marxism-Leninism. The Constitution now defines the basic objective of the Party as turning China into a prosperous, strong, democratic, culturally-advanced and harmonious modern-socialist country. The new elaboration on harmony is aimed at addressing some deep-seated issues on China's reforms and opening up.

China has registered big economic gains since the reform and opening drive launched three decades ago, but the country side lags, causing concerns that the urban and rural gap might undermine social harmony. However, no significant change in foreign policy was outlined though a concern for projecting Chinese soft power did some articulation. China does not see itself in isolation but, given its size, is engaged with the world, preferably through a democratic international order. With the successful holding of Beijing Olympic in which China also proved to be the leading sports nation in the world with gold medals, the country has projected communist China's strong face to the world. Now at the heart of all the pledges is dedication to all-round, coordinated, and sustainable development oriented at public welfare, the fulfilment of which calls for sophisticated balancing all the time. For the high hopes the country pins on them, the new leaders of the Party should work hard so as not to let the people down.

O O O

# 27. POLITICAL WAR IN THAILAND

Thai Prime Minister Abhisit Vejjajiva on 24 April, 2009 lifted the state of emergency he had imposed 12 days earlier on Bangkok and surrounding provinces to quell anti-Government protests. He called for constitutional reforms in a bid to heal the deep political rifts behind the recent violent protests.

Bangkok has been relatively calm since troops and local residents fought running street battles with red-shirted supporters of exiled former Prime Minister Thaksin Shinawatra seeking to topple Abhisit and force new elections on the state. But Thailand's four-year old political crisis, which has eroded confidence in the tourism and export-driven economy, is far from over. The pro-Thaksin political opposition has accused Abhisit of using harsh methods to stop the protesters, who forced the embarrassing cancellation of ASEAN Summit.

Abhisit rejected the charge but agreed to an independent inquiry into the clashes, which killed two people and injured more than 100 others. He said lifting the decree showed he was serious about reconciliation. A court granted bail to three leaders of United Front for Democracy against Dictatorship (UDD) detained since 14 April, 2009.

Issue-based protests during international meetings are nothing new and have come to be accepted as part of democracy. But what happened at the beach resort of Pattaya on 11 April was a special interest protest that put the hosts to shame. A mob of supporters of former Prime Minister and business tycoon Thaksin Shinawatra stormed the venue of an Association of South East Asian Nations (ASEAN) Summit. Prime Minister Abhisit Vejjajiva was forced to cancel the summit, declare an emergency in Pattaya, and airlift the visiting heads of state of Government to safety. The next day, the 'Red shirts, further aroused by the strong man who fled the country after being deposed and convicted, took officials of the Interior Ministry hostage. With the embattled Government imposing an emergency in Bangkok, the protestors responded by blocking highways leading to the capital. The Government and the defence forces finally cracked down on the protestors, and also on opposition leaders.

This was the second time the Thailand Summit of ASEAN had to be put off because of uncontrolled political protests. In Dec. 2008, the month in which the Annual Summit is normally held, turmoil created by 'Yellow Shirt' protestors, compelled postponement of the meet.

Thailand's military has once again demonstrated its centrality in the democratic politics of a key Southeast Asian country. A show of military force, not its actual use, in the final stages of the latest wave of anti-Government protest proved to be a success.

The Thai Army was at pains to emphasise that its crackdown in April 2009 was carried out through the use of only non-lethal force. Military spokesmen asserted that 'paper bullets' or 'practice blanks', not live ammunition, were used. There was "no civilian death" at the hands of the army in its execution of an emergency decree.

Though, the pro-Thakisn protesters seem to have lost the battle, the current political war in Thailand is far from over. The story of Thailand's experiment with democracy in the context of military primacy in politics is still continuing.

Before Thaksin became a duly elected Prime Minister at the turn of this century, the country was struggling for a "Thai-style democracy". Exuding charisma in reaching the top, the business tycoon who donned the mantle of a pro-poor leader, first won acceptance like no one before him had. But, by the time the military moved against him, his political life was dotted with high ratings and low controversies. However, his image as a pro-poor leader still remained largely unsullied, especially among the Thai-Buddhist majority.

The Muslim minority in southern Thailand did feel more alienated than before, because of his 'militarist' response to 'separatism' in that region. So, his 'cavalier' attitude to rights violations in his 'wars' against rebels and drug barons gave the Thai elite a chance to bring him down from power. And, they did this, emboldened further by his perceived disregard for the 'conflict of interest' in matters concerning the state and his own businesses.

Mr. Thaksin is now a fugitive, following his conviction, in absentia, in a 'conflict of interest' case. But, he has been galvanising his political base at home through video-addresses and phone-in speeches to his supporters at public rallies.

Encouraged by this, he gave a call for "people's revolution" on the eve of a series of regional summits Thailand was to host at Pattaya.

A societal polarisation has now become the critical aspect of the ongoing crisis in Thailand. The divide is defined by the alienation between the civil-military elite, on one side, and the disaffected poor masses, on the other. The key question is : Will electoral politics, help bridge the gap? It appears that for now, Mr. Abhisit is fighting shy of reforming the military-crafted Constitution and seeking a mandate in his own right as a leader. Only time will tell whether he succeeds in his objectives or not.

O O O

# 28. West Asia on a New Roadmap

The Palestinian State has now become the universal standard for all solutions to the long Palestinian-Israeli conflict. The international community applauds the concept. Former US President George W. Bush proudly declared it as his 'vision'. The Israelis have come to it belatedly, after a gap of so many years of steadfast refusal and rejection.

At present, Israeli Prime Minister Ehud Olmert not only supports the idea but proclaims it as in existential Israeli interest. Without it, Israel is fated to disappear under dire assault from the ever-expanding Arab population in both Israel and the occupied territories. This apparent human tide may yet bring disaster to the Jewish State, by demanding equal civil rights to those of Jews themselves.

Ending an eight-day trip through West Asia in which the US President lavished praise on the Egyptian President Hosni Mubarak, emphasising the country's role in regional security and the Israeli-Palestinian peace process on a new roadmap while publicly avoiding mention of the Government's actions in jailing or exiling opposition leaders and its severe restrictions on opposition political activities. He highlighted democratic reforms as the foundation for peace and security throughout the region, Bush, however, avoided any direct criticism of

Mubarak, an autocratic leader in power since 1981. In the past, Bush had criticised Egypt for its arrest of political dissidents.

President Bush called for stopping of Israel's military occupation of land the Palestinians' claim for a State and an end to the terrorist threat over the Jewish homeland, spelling out the US bottom line for ending the long and bloody Middle-East conflict, but came away with no breakthrough or apparent concessions from separate talks with Israeli Prime Minister in Jerusalem and with Palestinian President Mahmoud Abbas in the Palestinian West Bank. There was no joint meeting of the three leaders, but Olmert and Abbas assured Bush they were serious about reaching an agreement. The points for peace negotiations outlined include:

- There should be an end to the occupation that began in 1967.

- The agreement should establish Palestine as a homeland for the Palestinian people, just as Israel is a homeland for the Jewish people.

- These negotiations should ensure that Israel has secure, recognised and defensible borders.

- They must ensure that the State of Palestine is viable, contiguous, sovereign and independent.

The notion of a State was an offshoot of the Palestinian struggle and not its nodal point. However, there was a period from the mid-1970s onwards when the State could have represented the point where Palestinian national aspirations met the boundaries of what is possible.

Now this concept is less attractive than ever. Olmert demands that Palestinians must give up their history. The then President Bush decided for them what their borders and rights must be. The British Prime Minister Gordon Brown points a finger and tells Palestinians that they would not get a State at all unless it meets high standards of governance. Arab League has put forward a plan that offers Israel an opportunity for integrating into the region if it tenders justice to the Palestinians. The US is also supposed to be working together with the European Union, Russia and the UN. Many leading Arab States are wary of Iran's growing influence in the region. Saudi officials are of the view that the unresolved issue of Palestine is further bolstering Iran's image in the region. Iran is a strong supporter of the Palestinian cause. Iran and Syria are among the strongest supporters of Hezbollah, which inflicted an improbable unlikely defeat on the Israeli military in 2006. Both the countries are also supporters of Hamas, which controls Gaza and is democratically elected voice of the Palestinian people.

Prior to the US-hosted Annapolis Summit on West Asia, held on November 27, 2007, the Israeli Knesser had approved a bill barring any agreement to divide Jerusalem. Israel has been insisting that its obligations under the roadmap suggested by US will only be implemented after the Palestinian Authority suppresses all anti-Israel violence, including fighting terrorism and dismantling terrorist networks.

The other important demand, which the Israeli Government has been making is that the Palestinian Authority recognise Israel as a Jewish State.

A process of talks between Palestine and Israel has been initiated which leads to a new roadmap. The hope has been expressed that the outlines of a full peace deal may be shaped by the end of 2008, by the time President Bush's term comes to an end.

O  O  O

## 29. Kosova Declares Independence

Kosova became independent from Serbia on February 17, 2008 and ended a long chapter in the bloody break-up of former Yugoslavia. The proclamation was made by leaders of Kosovo's 90 per cent ethnic Albanian majority, including former guerillas who fought for independence in a 1998-99 war which claimed about 10,000 civilian lives. All 109 deputies present at the session in the capital Pristine voted in favour with a show of hands. Eleven deputies from ethnic minorities, including Serbs, were absent.

The autonomous province of Kosovo has proclaimed political independence, something that was expected a long time ago. To recall, ethnic violence erupted in Kosovo in the late 1990s when the Slobodan Milosevic regime in Belgrade removed Kosovo's status as a special province. This was followed by a wave of repression that forced the Albanian majority to live in fear as second-class citizens. Under President Ibrahim Rugova—who adopted Mahatma Gandhi's tactics of passive resistance—the Albanians fought the oppression, creating their own schools, Parliament and infrastructure. In the subsequent wave of ethnic cleansing unleashed by Belgrade, tens of thousands of people were killed, leading to the creation of the Kosovo Liberation Army. The bloodbath stopped only after the US-led North Atlantic Treaty Organisation (NATO) forces drove the Serbs out, and Kosovo became a UN protectorate under the UN Security Council Resolution 1244 of 1999.

Kosovo's unilateral declaration of independence has thrown the fragile Balkan peace into question and caused much disquiet in the world. Former US President George W. Bush said that the people of Kosovo are independent though he stopped short of formal recognition of independence. However, it was sufficient for Serbia, the State of which Kosovo is a province, to withdraw its Amabassador from Washington—which has since recognised Kosovo. Russia, for its part, declared that it will resist Kosovers' accession to the UN. The European Union, the world's most powerful trading bloc and a rather ineffectual player in international affairs, has decided to leave the issue of recognition to individual member States, through a 2000-strong EU mission of police, judges and administrators is to replace the UN presence in Kosovo. *De facto*, the UN is not performing its function in Kosovo and real power will go to the Mission of the EU. The EU insists on its right to institute such a body, referring to this resolution. But then again, its legitimacy is highly doubtful. Germany, Italy, France, and the UK have recognised the seceder, with others due to follow suit, while many of the smaller EU states oppose recognition.

India's Ministry of External Affairs issued a statement correctly noting that as Kosovo does not meet all three conditions for recognition, namely "a defined territory, a duly constituted Government in charge which is accepted by the people, and which has effective control over an area of governance", India is not offering recognition and would prefer the issue to be "resolved through peaceful means and through consultation and dialogue." Even in the Kosovo's assembly, the 11 Kosovers, Serbs and other ethnic-minority members boycotted the vote, and, if Prime Minister Hashim Thaci's promise of strong protection of ethnic minorities is not fully honoured, it is likely that the ancient ethnic and other hatreds will again cause ethnic cleansing, war or even worse.

In practical terms, Kosovo will be a new type of international protectorate, and local authorities will be quite limited in their actions. Potentially, Kosovo may enter into a conflict with its Western Partners. If Belgrade exerts economic pressure on Kosovo, the situation in Kosovo may become even worse. In the long-term, Kosovo's economy will fully depend on the EU, and international financial institutions will hardly be able to render assistance to a province with such vague status. Second, it is impossible to exclude the possibility of armed clashes.

There are enough radicals capable of provocations among both the Kosovers and the Serbs. More than half the Serb population lives south of Mitrovica, scattered in small enclaves, some of which could be just as big a headache for the Kosovan Government and its backers. In the Lipjan area, near the centre of Kosovo, 10000 Serbs live uneasily alongside a similar number of Albanians. The municipality is, in theory, the sort of multi-ethnic paradigm the new country is meant to be, led by an Albanian Mayor and a Serb Deputy.

The Kosovo conundrum will have unpleasant repercussions in unstable countries like Bosnia, Georgia, Macedonia, Moldova and Azerbaijan. The minorities in these countries will take it as a direct precedent. In the mid 1990s, when the State of Bosnia and Herzegovina was set up in line with the Dayton Accords, its ethnic Communities, the Serbs, the Croats and the Muslims were denied self-determination. The international patrons of Bosnian sovereignty compelled these three communities to unite into a single state. The new state was built on the non-ethnic principle. Kosovo's independence rests on the ethnic principle that allows the Bosnian Serbs to demand self-determination and accession to Serbia. Bosnia's redivision is fraught with gigantic problems for all Europe. Macedonia is a country with a tangible Albanian minority that is rapidly growing. The Albanians have a higher birth rate than the Slaves. Although the idea of Greater Albania is more in the nature of a political venture, the Albanians may view themselves as a divided ethnic community. The Kosovo case is likely to influence developments in other parts of the world. The implications for various multi-ethnic countries will be serious. A successful and internationally supported Kosovo's Unilateral Declaration of Independence (UDI) will be seen as a precedent by secessionist and separatist watched by various governments, including in India, Sri Lanka and Pakistan.

The UN mission, has obviously failed to encourage integration between Serbian and Albanian communities that even use different currencies and telephone networks. And it is doubtful if the European Union task force, which is reportedly standing by to replace the UN mission, can do any better. In the event, there could possibly be an exodus of Serbs from the some areas to the Serb-dominated north, or even an attempt by the north to secede from Kosovo and join Serbia.

There is a general problem that is linked not only with Kosovo. International institutions are growing weaker and stepping back from resolving urgent issues. The inability of the great powers to come to terms with the rules of conduct results in the degradation of almost all global organisations.

International law is increasingly turning from the foundation of decision-making into an instrument for legalising what has already been taken care of.

O O O

## 30. IMF Reforms

In the biggest reforms since its inception, the International Monetary Fund (IMF) overwhelmingly approved a plan to boost the voting shares of China and three other emerging economic giants to better reflect their clout in the world economy.

The resolution on giving more to the four countries got an overwhelming 90.6 per cent of votes, while only India, Brazil and 21 other developing nations in the 184 member IMF cast a ballot against the proposal. Only 85 per cent of the total votes were required for adopting the resolution.

After the reform, India's voting rights in IMF gets diminished to 1.91 per cent as against 1.95 previously while that of China has increased from 2.98 per cent to 3.72, Mexico from 1.21 to 1.45, South Korea from 0.77 to 1.35 and Turkey from 0.45 as against 0.55 per cent earlier.

Consequent upon the increase in powers of these four members, even developed countries had to forego some of their voting rights, with United States now having 17.1 per cent as compared to 17.4 previously.

Japan too is left with 6.13 as against 6.24 per cent earlier. Germany will have 5.99 against 6.09 earlier, France and Britain 4.94 as against 5.03 and Italy 3.25 as against 3.31.

Earlier, India had joined forces with Argentina, Brazil and Egypt to lead a campaign against the latest IMF reform plan suggesting a simple and transparent formula that truly reflected and the economic standing of all countries. But India will have to wait for 2008 when the second stage of broader reforms will follow. Well, India's failure at the meetings is seen as failure, not just in the sense of being ignored by the governing body, but also because its recent economic accomplishments went unrecognised. But to understand India's predicament, first we have to understand the reform measure in the backdrop of what has existed.

The powers, technically described as quotas, determine a country's voting rights and access to funds in IMF. It was calculated in 1944. Also important to remember is that the number of quotas overall is fixed. A quota increase for some members may come at the cost of some others.

The problem arises essentially because reallocation of quotas is done sporadically. The original, horrendously complicated formula for fixing quotas was drawn up on the basis of three things: (i) the size of a member-country's economy, (ii) the quantum of its foreign exchange reserves, and (iii) the economy's propensity to volatility. It made sense in 40's that China's quota was less than that of the Netherlands or Belgium. But does it make sense in 2006? China's economy is now twice the size of the Belgian and Dutch economies combined. But both Belgium and the Netherlands still have larger IMF quotas than China.

Europe as a whole commands around one-third of IMF quotas, though it roughly has the same share in world economy. But in case of America, its share of the world economy is also about one-third but it's share of the IMF quotas is about 17. Though it roughly have the same share in world economy. However it's enough to block any special business (that requires 85 per cent approval of the body).

But there is another view. India's claim for a larger say in the IMF's affairs comes at a time when the organisation itself is fast losing its relevance. Its surveillance and assistance role are no longer keenly sought by many countries, including India. Its publications and database are of course, among the best, but they alone do not help the IMF to retain its original stature. Today, India's economy is much stronger than what was absent 60 years back.

So, in a larger context, India's failure to secure larger quotas in line with its status may not be a major setback at all.

O O O

# 31. Iran's Nuclear Issue

The Iranian nuclear issue has once again been brought to the fore with the key European Countries' proposal meant to enlist the support of Russia and China for the possible UN Security Council sanctions against Iran, should Iran refuse to abandon uranium enmeshment. The compromise which would drop the automatic threat of military action of Iran remains defiant—is part of a proposed basket of incentives meant to entice Iran to give up enrichment, a possible way to nuclear arms. It also spelt out the penalties if it does not. It is worth pointing out that Russia and China have opposed calls by the US, the UK and France for a resolution threatening sanctions and enforceable by military action. If Iran remains defiant, the proposal calls for a Security Council resolution imposing sanctions under Chapter VII, Article 41 of the UN Charter. But it avoids any reference to Article 42—which is the trigger for possible military action to enforce any such resolution.

## The Purpose

Iran's attachment to nuclear development is rooted in its own tumultuous history. The Islamic Republic is trying to use its nuclear programme as a bargaining chip to end the varying degrees of international isolation it has been forced to endure since the Islamic revolution in 1979. Unquestionably, most Iranians want to find a way to end economic sanctions so that the country could use its vast oil wealth—an estimated US $10 billion surplus this year—to fix the country's infrastructure among other ills.

Iran views its uranium enrichment programme in conformity

with the nuclear Non-Proliferation Treaty (NPT) to which it is a signatory. Article IV of the NPT provides any signatory "an inalienable right to develop, research, produce and use nuclear energy for peaceful purposes" and to acquire technology for this purpose from other signatories.

In June 2006, the major world powers struck what officially called "substantial agreement" on a package of incentives for Iran to halt sensitive nuclear fuel work as well as penalties if it did not. But, despite its hardline credentials, the new administration in Iran under President Mahmoud Ahmadinejad, appears is open to negotiations. Recently, he sent a letter to the US President, George W. Bush proposing new solutions to international problems and the current fragile situation of the world. Ahmadinejad's recent announcement of Iran's success in enriching uranium to reactor grade level is part of that strategy: a signal that "Iran has achieved what it can, and is now prepared for talk", albeit from a position of strength.

The present situation presents an excellent opportunity to negotiate a nuclear restraint agreement with Iran, under which it stays within the NPT framework, and performs pilot scale enrichment under strict International supervision, and within the constraints of intrusive Additional Protocol of the International Atomic Energy Agency (IAEA).

O O O

# 32. UNREST AMONG INDIANS IN MALAYSIA

The unrest among people of Indian origin in Malaysia, because of active State discrimination and biased attitude against them, takes us back two hundred years. At that point, Indians in South Africa—not to mention Fiji, British, Guyana, Kenya and other British colonies—suffered from the racial biases of the State. In September, 1906 at the Empire Theatre in Johannesburg, Indian delegates from all across the

Transvaal, led by one man, Mahatma Gandhi, took a vow to peacefully resist all forms of discrimination. That man was later to dominate the socio-political life of Indians and become the Father of the Nation. Today, it is instructive to note what Gandhiji did a hundred years ago.

Indians in Malaysia have finally placed their issue of marginalisation on the country's mainstream political agenda and in the wider focus of the international community. They have done so by choosing the occasion—the ongoing celebration of the country's 50th year of independence from the British and the recently concluded 53-nation Commonwealth Summit—and the target, post-imperial Britain.

The multi-racial Government of Malaysia was quick to rebut the charges from the sizeable section of the country's population. Numbering nearly two-million, Malaysian Indians constitute roughly eight per cent of the diverse population which has a core Malay majority, and form the third largest section after Malays and ethnic Chinese.

The trouble began when the Malaysian lawyers of Indian origin led by Waytha Moorthy Ponnusamy filed a class action at the Royal Court of Justice in London. The lawsuit was filed to sue the British Government for US $4 trillion (US $1 million for every Indian in Malaysia) because it held the British responsible for 150 years exploitation of Indians who were brought to Malaysia as indentured labour to work in rubber plantations. The lawsuit also held the British Government responsible for not taking any action to protect the rights of the Indian majority—in the Constitution when Independence was granted to the country. As the Indians, who are largely of Tamil origin, are economically the weakest ethnic group, they could not afford the legal fees. Subsequently, a petition was circulated with 1,00,000 signatures to be presented to Queen Elizabeth of the UK to appoint a Queen's counsel to argue the case.

To submit the petition at the British High Commission, the Hindu Rights Action Force (HINDRAF) organised a rally on

November 25, 2007. Because of the alleged discrimination against Malaysian Hindus, more than 30 Hindu organisations formed an umbrella. The HINDRAF has charged the Government for its so-called unofficial policy of Hindu temple cleansing in Malaysia after eight places of worship were torn down or given demolition notices in three months. It is also demanding the repeal of Article 121(1A) of the Constitution that was amended in 1988 to State that the Civil Court had no jurisdiction on matters under the purview of the *sharia*.

The rally was not granted permission by the police, but nearly twenty thousand people gathered near the Petronas Twin Towers in the capital of Malaysia—Kuala Lumpur—carrying life-size portraits of Queen Elizabeth and Gandhiji to indicate the non-violent nature of their protest. But HINDRAF failed to submit the petition after the police crackdown on the protesters. However, HINDRAF leaders have claimed that the petition was faxed to the High Commission.

Five leaders of the Malaysian Indian activist group HINDRAF were arrested under controversial security laws that allow for detention without trial. HINDRAF enraged the Government by mounting a mass rally which was dominated by Muslim Malays. The five arrested leaders were P. Uthayakumar, M. Manoharan, R. Kenghadharan, V. Ganabatirau and T. Vasanthakumar.

As far as Malaysian Indians are concerned as compared to Indian diaspora in Fiji and in the West Indies, they are rather dynamic. Although the bulk is still working class, largely engaged in rubber and palm oil estates, a few have moved up the social ladder finding white collar jobs in industries. Ananda Krishnan, who figures among the wealthiest Malaysians, is a Tamil of Sri Lankan origin. Besides a few examples, Indians are economically and politically the weakest section of the society and their conditions are further deteriorating. According to HINDRAF, the percentage of Indians in the Civil Services fell from 40 per cent in 1957 to under two per cent in 2005. Half the 523 Tamil schools are not funded by the Government.

Indians constitute only five per cent of the total university intake of 45,000 in 15 public universities. The Indians are also demanding repeal of Article 153 of the Malaysian Constitution, which provides special statistics states that nearly 40 per cent of convicted criminals are Indians, but this only indicates the economic status of the minority community.

Prime Minister of Malaysia, Abdullah Ahmad Badavi has taken the line that the Government will continue to the ethnic Indian community through the Malaysian Indian Congress (MIC), a long-time constituent of the ruling coalition. HINDRAF's demand for a "fair deal" covers not only educational and job opportunities but also protection to Hindu temples.

The Government has also launched a major plan to protect the Hindu temples in the country in a move to assuage the feelings of the ethnic Indians, who protested against alleged demolition of their places of worship in the Muslim-majority nation. No temples, either legal or illegal, will be demolished without a thorough check and discussions with the MIC.

India's Minister for Overseas Affairs was requested to make an official visit to Malaysia to hear the grievances of the Indian community. If ever we needed a Ministry as this, it is now. The visit, it was said, would be more purposeful for Indians than merely organising the Pravasi Bharatiya Divas.

If we find that there is discrimination and if the Malaysian Government continues to deny this, then India must do whatever it can to prevent such racial discrimination. We must respond with non-cooperation with Malaysia, as a country.

# 33. Fifteenth SAARC Summit

South Asian Association for Regional Cooperation (SAARC) was established in Dec. 1985 in Dhaka, the capital of Bangladesh. The concept of SAARC was originally mooted by the then Bangladesh President Zia-ur-Rahman. SAARC has eight member states—Bangladesh, Bhutan, India, Maldives, Nepal, Pakistan, Sri Lanka and Afghanistan.

SAARC is committed to improve the quality of life in the region by accelerating economic growth, social progress and cultural development, promoting self-reliance, encouraging mutual assistance, and increasing cooperation with other regional and international organisations. The SAARC Charter stipulates that decisions should be made unanimously and that bilateral and contentious issues should not be discussed.

One major objective of SAARC is the eradication of poverty in the region. In 1993, SAARC endorsed an Agenda of Action (AoA) to help achieve this programme. A framework for exchanging information on poverty eradication has been established, which will submit its report to the Council of Minister. It is supported by ad hoc programming committees consisting of senior officials, who meet the examine the budget of the Secretariat, confirm the calendar of activities and resolve matters assigned to it by the Standing Committee.

South Asian Free Trade Area (SAFTA) Framework Treaty was signed by the Foreign Ministers of the member countries. The treaty seeks to remove trade barriers and bring about phased elimination of tariffs and establishment of a ministerial level mechanism for administering the treaty and disputes settlement among member countries.

As per the treaty, the developing countries of SAARC will reduce their tariffs to between zero and five per cent for Least Developed Countries (LDCs). It also envisages that member States shall give 'special regard' to the situation of LDCs when considering the application of anti-dumping and consternating measures that members may adopt, including the removal of barriers to intra-SAARC investment, harmonisation of custom facilities, transit facilities for efficient intra-SAARC trade and simplification of procedures for business.

The SAARC Secretariat was established in 1989 to coordinate and oversee the activities of SAARC. It consists of the Secretary-General and a Director from each member-State. The Secretary-General is appointed by the Council of Ministers, after being nominated by a member-country. In 1998, it resolved to formulate a SAARC Social Charter, which was to incorporate agreed objectives in areas such as poverty eradication, promotion of health and nutrition, and the protection of children. It is determined to reinvigorate regional poverty reduction in the context of the UN General Assembly's Millennium Development Goal (MDG) of halving extreme poverty by 2015.

The SAARC Standing Committee comprises the secretaries of foreign affairs of the member-countries. Its overall responsibility is to monitor and coordinate the programmes and financing. It determines priorities, mobilises resources and identifies areas of cooperation. The Committee usually meets twice a year. It was extended from two to three years at the Ninth SAARC Summit, held in Male (Maldives) in 1997.

The Director of SAARC is nominated by member countries and is appointed by the Secretary-General for a term of three years. There is a SAARC Council of Ministers which consists of the ministers of foreign affairs of member-states, who meet twice a year. It may also meet in extraordinary session at the request of the member countries. Its responsibilities include formation of policies, assessing progress and confirming new areas of cooperation.

The integrated Programme of Action of SAARC is implemented by eight Technical Committees. They include Agriculture and Rural Development; Energy and Environment; Meteorology and Forestry; Human Resource Development; Science and Technology; Social Development; and Transport and Communications. Each committee is headed by a representative of a member. All the committees meet once a year.

The Charter of SAARC provides for annual meetings of the Heads of the States or Government. It also hosts six monthly meetings of Council of Ministers—its highest policy-making body. As far as chairmanship of SAARC is concerned, it is not fixed; it remains with the country which had hosted the last summit and it is transferred to the new host at the time of next summit.

SAARC is committed to improve the quality of life in the region by accelerating economic growth, social progress and cultural development, promoting self-reliance, encouraging mutual assistance and increasing cooperation with other regional and international organisations.

The 15th SAARC Summit was held in Colombo on 2–3 Aug., 2008. The two day summit was attended by Presidents Hamid Karzai of Afghanistan, Mahinda Rajapakse of Sri Lanka and Moumoon Abdul Gayoom of Maldives, Prime Ministers Manmohan Singh of India, G.P. Koirala of Nepal, Jigmey Thinley of Bhutan and Yusuf Raza Gilani of Pakistan as well as Fakruddin Ahmed, Chief Advisor of the caretaker Bangladesh Government.

The leaders of the Summit issued Colombo Declaration, titled "Partnership for Growth of our People". The leaders expressed deep concern over the serious threat posed by terrorism to peace, stability and security of the region and emphasised the need for the strongest possible cooperation in fighting terror and transnational organised crime, especially in the area of information exchange.

The Colombo Summit was held in an atmosphere vitiated by terrorists. As expected, the recent terrorist attacks at the Indian Embassy in Kabul and the incidents of bomb blasts in Ahmedabad, Bangalore and Jaipur overshadowed the annual gathering. In a declaration, the summit called for the "strongest possible cooperation" to meet this "serious threat". Terrorism remains the "single biggest threat to our stability", as emphasised by Prime Minister Manmohan Singh. There is need for the SAARC members to launch a joint drive to tame the monster to prevent it from destablising the entire region.

The Summit also adopted the Convention for Mutual Legal Assistance in Criminal Matters which can help in identifying and punishing those involved in terrorist violence. Pakistan obviously has to contribute to the fight against terrorism as most of the dreaded outfits involved in such crime have been operating from its territories. First of all, Pakistan has to rein in its intelligence agency, the ISI, which found veiled reference in the speech delivered by Afghanistan President Hamid Karzai for sponsoring terrorism.

Any collective effort for economic advancement of the South Asian region can bear fruit only when the terrorist problem is handled successfully. It has strained the India-Pakistan peace process. The South Asian Free Trade Agreement (SAFTA) will not be easy to implement in such an atmosphere. SAARC leaders will have to launch a concerted drive to eliminate terrorism so that they can concentrate on development projects. There is no dearth of natural resources and talent in the region to transform South Asia into a powerful engine for global economic growth.

The declaration observed that an effective and economic regional telecommunication regime is an essential requirement of connectivity, encouraging the growth of people-centric partnerships. It also called for a uniformly applicable low tariff for international direct dial calls within South Asia. The SAARC leaders expressed satisfaction over the signing of the charter of the SAARC Development Fund (SDF) and welcomed its early operationalisation from available funds. The SAARC leaders also granted observers status to Australia and Myanmar. The identified projects relate to women empowerment, maternal and child health and teachers' training. Maintaining that an effective and economical regional telecommunication regime was an essential requirement of connectivity, they stressed the need for the member-states to endeavour to move towards a uniformly applicable low tariff.

The summit approved the SAARC Convention on Mutual Legal Assistance Treaty (MLAT). The treaty is considered pathbreaking as it brings greater cooperation among security forces of SAARC member-states to track, arrest and hand over criminals and terrorists.

The treaty's objective is to strengthen two SAARC conventions on Terrorism and Drug Trafficking. However, there was no consensus on two major provisions of the proposed treaty. These were on participation by the requesting parties' security officers in taking evidence, and incorporation of the word 'terrorism' with respect to tracking funds meant for financing acts of terrorism.

The SAARC Journalists Summit adopted the Colombo Declaration with a call for taking concrete remedial measures to remove hindrances in the way of greater connectivity, partnerships, people to people contact, and free movement of information, goods and services across borders. The declaration, adopted after consultation among attending journalists, urged the member-states of SAARC to take short- and long-term comprehensive measures to eradicate extremism and violent practices by both the state and non-state players against civilians and journalists.

The declaration stated that media is inseparable from the fundamental human and civil rights guaranteed by the constitutions and enforceable through an independent judiciary in a democratic system where both the state and society respect freedom, show tolerance to dissent and practice pluralism. It urged the SAARC countries to investigate into all acts of violence and intimidation against media professionals in their territory, and bring persons or outfits who have allegedly committed such crimes to justice and give proper compensation to the victims.

The declaration urged the multilateral and bilateral institutes to gave cooperation and provide financial assistance to any country based on the indicators which would project the degree of its respect for freedom of expression and effective protection of press freedom. It called for complying with the commitment of the UNESCO Resolution No. 29 to promote legislation with the intention of investigating and prosecuting the killers of journalists and combat impunity.

The declaration emphasized on adopting SAFMA's Protocol on Freedom of Information and implement SAFMA's Protocol on free flow of information and movement of journalists across borders.

The declaration called for taking resolute action against all expressions of intolerance towards freedom of expression and for the safety of journalists in risky situations to ensure respect for their professional independence. It urged to sensitise news organizations, editors and managers about the dangers surrounding their colleagues, when covering or investigating stories, particularly at locals levels.

Further, the declaration called for promoting actions that secure safety of journalists. The actions include training for journalists, safety codes, health care, life insurance and equal access to social protection for the freelance journalists like full-time staff. The declaration also urged mass communication departments to include the impact of crimes against journalists in their curricula.

## 34. Swine Flu Spread

After bird flu in 2007 and 2008, swine flu affected people in several countries in 2009. World Health Organisation (WHO) confirmed 1000 cases of influenza and infections with 26 deaths from 20 countries, in May 2009.

India, on 27 April, issued a swine flu—rechristened as A(H1N1) infection by the World Health Organisation—advisory and asked travellers to India coming from the affected countries such as Mexico, US, Canada, New Zealand, Spain, France and UK to report symptoms of cough, cold and fever to airport health authorities. The Government, however placed no restrictions on eating pork or testing pigs for the virus.

Swine flu was confirmed in three more countries on 30 April, prompting the World Health Organisation to raise its flu alert level to five, a warning that the world is on the brink of an epidemic.

WHO officials raised a global alert to an unprecedented level as swine flu was blamed for more deaths in Mexico and the epidemic spread to some other countries, with the first cases confirmed in West Asia and the Asia-Pacific regions.

Swine flu spread to several countries and appeared to be jumping borders via airplane flights. In New Zealand, a group of students and teachers were confirmed with the virus after a recent trip to Mexico, where the virus was suspected to have infected nearly 2,000 people and caused more than 150 deaths. Another case was confirmed in Israel.

The pandemic alert raised to Phase 5 was a warning that the new swine flu virus was demonstrating a level of infectivity in humans that could take it rapidly to every country across the globe. WHO's Phase 5 is just one step short of a full pandemic alert.

The change to a higher alert is a signal to governments, ministries of health and other ministries, the pharmaceutical industry and the business community that certain actions should now be undertaken with increased urgency and at an accelerated pace.

Phases 5 and 6 "represent periods of time when the virus is beginning to spread from country to country" and becoming established. It can be interpreted to mean that we are already in that process. Phase 6 can be interpreted to mean that the virus is establishing itself in more regions and more countries.

Pigs have long been feared as a mixing pot for flu viruses. Apart from harbouring porcine flu viruses, pigs can also be infected by both human and bird flu strains. The genetic material of the flu virus is in eight segments. So if two or more strains of flu infect a cell, their progeny can receive a mix of those genetic segments.

The result, as in the case of the new H1N1 strain of swine flu, can be a potent virus that humans have not encountered before and against which their immune systems are almost defenceless. Analysing the genetic make-up of the new swine flu, scientists have found it to be a mix of genetic material from pig, human and bird flu viruses.

The WHO officials emphasised, however, that with the new swine flu showing robust human-to-human transmission, the risk of catching the disease did not come from pigs or pork consumption. Rather the virus was spreading through people who had become infected.

Health authorities across Asia are scrambling to limit the spread of swine flu as two confirmed cases were reported in one of the world's most densely populated regions. South Korea reported that a 51-year old woman, who recently visited Mexico, tested positive for swine flu, while Hong Kong's first confirmed case was a 25-year old Mexican who arrived in the city from Mexico via Shanghai.

Though Government said that no case of A(H1N1) flu had been reported in the country, a 25-year old man, who returned from Texas in the US, was admitted to the Ram Manohar Lohia Hospital, New Delhi on 2 May, 2009 with suspected symptoms. The man reportedly turned up at the hospital due to media coverage. He was kept under observation in the isolation ward but did not show any symptoms of A(H1N1) flu.

The Health Ministry has decentralised its stockpile of Oseltamivir, the drug that is most effective against the virus.

Mock drills—random sample collection at all international airports of the country to be sent to labs for testing—were started to identify critical gaps in its existing sample collection and transportation mechanism.

In its preparation for a pandemic or an outbreak of a deadly influenza virus, possibly the H1N1 flu, State governments were asked to collect samples from passengers showing any sort of ill health, not necessarily influenza symptoms, and send them to the National Institute of Communicable Diseases (Delhi) and National Institute of Virology (Pune) for testing.

India has four bio-safety level III labs—NICD, NIV, National Institute of Cholera and Enteric Diseases (Kolkata), and Regional Medical Research Centre (Dibrugarh) that have the capability of handling dangerous pathogens like the H1N1 virus. Samples were picked up from India's 22 international airports irrespective of whether they get one international flight a day or one flight a week.

Mexico, which was said to be the starting point of swine flu, moved past the peak of an H1N1 flu epidemic in May 2009 and was in the "phase of descent", the Government said, although world health officials still felt that the unpredictable virus could become a pandemic.

Mexico's Health Minister Jose Angel Cordova said the outbreak appeared to have peaked in Mexico between 23 and 28 April and fewer people had admitted themselves to hospitals with serious flu symptoms after that.

However, new cases of the virus, which mixes swine, avian and human flu strains, were still being tracked across the world. Colombia became the latest country to report a confirmed case of the disease.

The other countries which have reported laboratory confirmed cases but with no deaths were : Austria, Canada, Denmark, France, Germany, Hong Kong, Israel, Netherlands, New Zealand, Republic of Korea, Spain, Switzerland and the United Kingdom.

In a latest research, a virus believed to have originated from pigs was found to be jumping from humans to swines. Canada reported the globe's first reverse transmission of H1N1 from humans to pigs. The country's health officials believe the infection that was found in 220 hogs—about 10 per cent of the farm's pig population—spread from a farm worker who became ill during a trip to Mexico. Another worker on the farm was being tested for symptoms.

Interestingly, the same H1N1 strain that was infecting humans was found to have caused the infection in pigs. The global health body, WHO, however, was quick to reiterate that at present there was no recommendation to cull pigs.

Some countries, including Mexico, where the disease caused maximum damage, started to believe that the worst was over with the outbreak having peaked between 23 and 28

April, 2009. But what most nations and WHO were most worried about was what they called "the second wave of the H1N1 Pandemic".

Behavioural studies conducted on earlier pandemics have shown that they came in two phases—the first wave usually being mild followed by a more devastating wave, in autumn and winter months.

All four of the well-known pandemics have come in waves. It was what happened during the deadly 1918 Spanish flu outbreak that killed over 50 million people.

There was a concern about the infection travelling to the Southern Hemisphere, as that part of the world was heading into the winter months, when influenza viruses become active.

The only way to fight such pandemics is to strengthen the system of early detection of infection, isolating infected people from public at large in medical centres, giving them proper medical attention, and last but at least, making people aware how to save themselves from being infected.

O O O

## 35. G-8 SUMMIT

The three-day Summit of the Group of Eight (G-8)—the US, the UK, France, Italy, Japan, Canada, Germany and Russia—concluded in the Japanese city of Hokkaido on July 9, 2008. Apart from G-8 countries, eight other nations also attended the summit that include India, China, Brazil, South Africa, Mexico, Australia, South Korea and Indonesia. The leaders of the G-8 patched together a deal to fight climate change, but failed to convince big emerging economies that rich countries were doing enough. Climate change was the most contentious topic at this year's G-8 summit in Japan, which also tackled geopolitical problems from the crisis in Zimbabwe to worsening security in Afghanistan as well as soaring food and oil prices and poverty in Africa.

The G-8 Summit endorsed a plan for cutting greenhouse gas emissions to combat climate change. But, as the saying goes, the more things change, the more they remain the same. The plan is to cut emissions by half by 2050. Good only, not so good at all. The fine print is that no base year has been set. Ideally it should have been 1990, the recognised baseline in all climate change negotiations from Rio through Kyoto to now. Second, and even more important, the 'commitment', is non-binding—meaning as in Bali last year and several meetings before that—this is a pious resolution.

The outcome is obviously a trade-off between the European Union (EU) and the US. The EU, to its credit, has over the years shown an admirable commitment to reducing emissions without riders, but the US has steadfastly refused to take the matter seriously. So this is a compromise to show the world that something has transpired while keeping the issue in limbo. And that is where the issue of India, China and other developing and emerging economies come in. At the behest of the US, all commitments still come with the rider that India and China must also undertake to cut emissions but that is a less than fair demand. G-5 countries—India, China, Brazil, Mexico and South Africa have iterated that, at least to begin with, developed countries, not just G-8, must show the way by undertaking unilateral emissions cuts, because in the process of developing they have been responsible for sending up by far the largest part of greenhouse gases that are now causing climate change. Therefore, as environmental groups are saving, developing countries must not only take on unilateral, binding cuts but also bigger cuts say 50 per cent over 1990 by 2020 and between 80 and 90 per cent by 2050. According to the World Wildlife Fund (WWF), the G-8 countries alone account for over 60 per cent of the carbon dioxide accumulation in the Earth's atmosphere. Despite this, the G-8 statement barely endorses what leaders of nearly 200 countries had signed up to in the original UN Climate Change

Convention during the 1992 Earth Summit. The outreach Five countries have been urging G-8 to cut greenhouse gas emissions by more than 80 per cent by 2050. Amongst other new initiatives, the G-8 launched an energy forum to deal with rising oil prices and other challenges flowing from the crisis of energy security. To enhance energy security, the leaders at the Summit proposed holding an energy forum to focus on energy efficiency and new technologies, which could also contribute to dialogue between producers and consumers.

The Indian position was articulated by Prime Minister Manmohan Singh when he said that while India would not accept targeted reductions in emissions, he could ensure that per capita carbon emissions, which at present were 1.2 tonnes against 20 tonnes in the US, would be no higher than the average of the developed world. However, the PM said that India was ready to commit that its per capita emissions would never exceed that of the developed countries.

Deeply concerned about the soaring food prices, the G-8 also called on nations with sufficient food stocks to release some of their reserves to countries in need to help cope up with the situation. Huddled in talks amid tight security in this spa resort, the G-8 leaders said they were "deeply concerned" about soaring food prices and supply shortages in some developing countries. They also called for countries with sufficient food stocks to make available a part of their surplus for countries in need, in times of significantly increasing prices and in a way not to distort trade.

According to World Bank estimates, rising food prices have pushed 100 million people Below the Poverty Line (BPL) across the world.

The Summit backed Prime Minister Manmohan Singh's proposal for a forum to set up a dialogue between producers and consumers to stabilise soaring oil prices which posed a "serious challenge" to world economic growth. As the threat from spiralling inflation became the top economic concern for the G-8, their leaders voiced "strong concern" over sizzling oil prices and an increase in crude production and refining capacity to dampen the crude market.

The leaders expressed stong concern about elevated commodity prices, especially of oil and food, since they pose a serious challenge to stable growth world-wide, have serious implications for the most vulnerable, and increase global inflationary pressure. As a way to enhance energy security, the leaders proposed an energy forum focused on energy efficiency and new technology to help a dialogue between producers and consumers.

Some of the G-8 leaders also blamed speculation behind the doubling of oil prices to $145 a barrel, a point flagged by India at the recent emergency meeting of Oil Ministers in Jeddah.

The G-8 pledged to ensure biofuel policies were compatible with food security and asked countries with enough food stocks to release reserves to cope with rising costs. It failed to focus on subsidies on grain and oilseed biofuels which have tempted farmers to grow ethanol and palm oil plants and convert food into fuel. The EU President Jose Barroso proposed a one billion—euro fund to alleviate poverty in developing countries but details are unclear.

The G-8 Summit also reiterated its earlier commitment to raise annual aid levels by $50 billion by 2010, of which $25 billion is intended for Africa. However, there has been widespread criticism of the G-8 for not having been able to meet commitments made at Gleneagles in 2005. According to a June 2008 report of the African Progress Panel, set up to monitor Gleneagles commitments, under existing plans of the G-8, spending falls short by $40 billion of its promised $50 billion.

The Hokkaido Summit was particularly important for India as it provided Prime Minister Manmohan Singh an opportunity to convince the world's richest nations about India's needs for alternative sources of energy to meet its burgeoning power requirements. Many of them are members of the Nuclear

Suppliers' Group (NSG) with which India will have to deal once it completes negotiations on a nuclear safeguards agreement with the International Atomic Energy Agency (IAEA). This all is a part of the UPA Government's decision to operationalise the 123 Agreement it signed with the Bush Administration three years ago. In the end, the G-8 nations adopted a more robust approach to civil nuclear cooperation with India to help meet its growing energy needs. In other words, India's position on the nuclear issue has found ready acceptance among the seven countries with the largest economies. This marks a turn-around from the time India's nuclear ambitions raised eyebrows among the developed nations. Realisation would have dawned on them that India has an exemplary record as nonproliferation concerned.

The Hokkaido Summit leads to the conclusion that the rate of progress on critical issues between successive summits is questionable. The leadership of the richest countries in the worlds needs to reflect their responsibility to the global community at large and the expectations that are aroused, which call for bolder measures and major changes in the interests of protecting the planet and all species living on it.

O O O

## 36. AFGHANISTAN BOILING

For the past few months, terrorist attacks inside Afghanistan have been on the rise and the country is boiling. The recent terror attacks targeted Indian Embassy. A suicide bomber carrying explosives killed at least 41 people and injured 141. Four embassy personnel were killed, including India's defence attaché, R.B. Mehta, and a senior diplomat, B.V. Rao.

There have been several attacks in Kabul in 2008. In January, six people were killed in a Taliban attack on Serena Hotel. Two months later, six people died in a car bomb attack on a military convoy. In April, there was an assassination attempt on Afghan President Hamid Karzai. The incident is one of the deadliest in Kabul in recent times. That the Indian embassy was the target is not surprising considering that New Delhi has close ties with Kabul and is actively involved in aid and reconstruction work in Afghanistan.

Kabul is now within the striking range of the Taliban like any other part of the troubled country. The US-led international coalition against terrorism has clearly failed to control the worrying situation. President Karzai's hold has further weakened. Sadly, the Taliban, which ruled Afghanistan for nearly five years till its Government was overthrown in the wake of 9/11, continues to function with impunity as a violent extremist morvement. And no one seems to have an answer.

The emerging scenario is as much disturbing for India as for the countries directly involved in the fight against the Taliban. Many Indians, including engineers, working for the reconstruction of Afghanistan, have lost their lives in Taliban attacks. India has deployed units of the Indo-Tibetan Border Police (ITBP) in Afghanistan but the situation is such that it cannot provide foolproof security to the Indians working on various projects, including the Zalanj-Delaram highway project, which has often been targeted by the Taliban.

There is no escaping the reality that a Civil War is on in Afghanistan. Its Taliban insurgency has established itself in the country's southern and eastern districts and has demonstrated the capability of launching terror strikes in Kabul itself. And it will target anybody who assists the Afghan government. Islamist militants have effective rear bases in Pakistan's tribal areas bordering Afghanistan. Islamabad sees terror camps on its territory as somebody else's problem, and the international community has not yet been able to persuade it to take a tough line on the camps. US involvement in Iraq has compounded the problem.

Yet this is not surprising, as President Karzai has been openly accusing Pakistan of promoting Taliban-linked terrorism in Afghanistan. The Taliban has been successful in carrying on its destabilizing activities mainly because the militant outfit gets logistical training and other kinds of support from the Pakistani side of the Durand Line.

New Delhi is apparently finding it difficult to stomach the denial by Pakistan as well as the Taliban. The extremist movement, which has its umbilical chord in Pakistan, is known for not owning up the responsibility for any of its destructive activities if most of those dead are ordinary civilians.

Reverting to the consulates in Afghanistan, Pakistan has consistently taken objection to those in Kandahar and Jalalabad, alleging that these are being used by the Research & Analysis Wing (RAW) to foment trouble in Pakistan's minority provinces of Baluchistan, where a virtual revolt has been on for years, and Sindh.

This brings to the pertinent point that to understand the present horrifying state of affairs in Afghanistan—to reverse it would be an extremely uphill tasks—it is necessary to go to its roots in 2001, immediately after 9/11. The Americans committed the "original sin" at the very start of their commendable campaign to oust the Taliban and Al-Qaeda from their bases in Afghanistan, with the help of the Northern Alliance. They were in a position to arrest or kill Osama bin Laden and leaders of the Taliban, headed by Mullah Omar. But they let them escape through the mountains of Tora Bora, together with many Pakistani collaborators of the two outfits.

The 2007 United Nation as Assistance Mission in Afghanistan report on suicide attacks in Afghanistan indicated that Taliban suicide bombers are often inept. In many instances they have killed only themselves and not their intended targets. Also most of them are uneducated and come from the poorest segments of the population. It seems highly unlikely that they could have improved in the short period of less than a year. In addition, in all of the latest terrorist attacks in Afghanistan, the Afghan police seem to have assisted the terrorists. The infiltration of Afghan security forces is out of reach and beyond the capability of the Taliban. Only Al-Qaeda has the capacity to recruit security officials and organize highly sophisticated attacks in the heart of well protected cities such as Kabul and Kandahar.

Since political turmoil started in Pakistan at least over a year ago, all military pressure has shifted away from the tribal area in Pakistan, where Al-Qaeda and the Taliban have established their safe houses and training camps. The recent peace agreement between the newly elected civilian government of Pakistan and the Taliban has given the latter an implicit approval to intensify their attacks inside Afghanistan. Indeed, Al-Qaeda has benefited from the chaos in Pakistan and has had ample time to regroup and step up its terrorist attacks. The offer of talks to the so-called moderate Taliban factions by President Karzai has made them feel that the international coalition against terrorism has developed symptoms of weariness. Pakistan's policy of "peace" deals with the Taliban has also emboidened its activists. The extremists on both sides of the Khyber Pass have a destructive agenda. Deals of the kind offered by Islamabad cannot make them leave the path of violence as the recent killings near Islamabad's Lal Masjid and the bomb blasts in Karachi prove it. While Pakistan needs to abandon its kid-glove approach, the US-led efforts against terrorism calls for an urgent review. The Taliban and other terrorist outfits must be tamed in the interest of peace and progress in the region and elsewhere.

# X. SCIENCE & TECHNOLOGY

## 1. LINEAR COLLIDER TECHNOLOGY DEVELOPMENT

With the choice of technology to build a high-energy linear collider, the world community of particle physicists has moved a step ahead in the efforts to answer some of the fascinating questions about the nature of the universe.

The International Committee for Future Accelerators (ICFA), took the first step way back in 2004 in setting the stage for the world community of particle physicists to embark upon an international collaboration of unprecedented nature and scale towards realising the goal of understanding the fundamental nature of matter, energy, space and time. The ICFA announced its decision on the choice of technology to be adopted to build the future gigantic particle accelerator—the liner collider—which physicists expect will enable them to unravel the mysteries of nature at the sub-atomic level.

### Accelerator Configuration

Accelerators impart energy to sub-atomic particles with magnetic fields and radio frequency (RF) fields and accelerate them so that they travel at high speeds in evacuated chambers as collimated and focused beams.

They are essentially of two kinds. In one kind, they move in circular enclosures and the machines are variously called cyclotrons, synchrotrons or storage rings, depending on the energies achieved and the particles that are accelerated. In the other kind, particles are accelerated in linear structures called linear accelerators (LINACs). Two opposing LINACs make up a linear collider (L.C.) The proposed L.C. will bring intense high-energy beams of electrons (e-) to collide head-on with positrons (e +, the antimatter counterpart of electrons) travelling with equal energy in the opposite direction. The envisaged total energy that would be available for particle production through electron-positron annihilation is 500 billion or giga electron volt (Ge V) in the first phase to over 1000 Ge V or one tera electron volt (Te V) in the second phase. Acceleration up to these energies will be achieved in 30-40 km long LINACs housed in tunnels.

One Te V is about the energy motion of a flying mosquito. What makes this energy so extraordinary is that, in an accelerator, it is squeezed into a space about a million times smaller than a mosquito). However, it would be too costly ($ 7-8 billion) for a single nation to undertake such a huge project, especially after the experience of the cancellation by the Clinton Administration of the super conducting super collider (SSC) project midway in 1993. Therefore, the L.C. has been mooted as a global venture and will be called the International Linear Collider (ILC).

**Technology**

From two mature technologies, developed over the last nearly 12 by two different high-energy-physics groups--a Japanese-U.S. collaboration that promoted the "warm" technology and a European collaboration that promoted the cold technology—the ICFA made the difficult but necessary choice to enable the international effort to take off. It has picked the "cold" technology, in which the basic accelerating structure will use super conducting niobium cavities where the electric field due to L-band RF field of 1.3 gigahertz will give energy kicks to electron bunches. This technology has been perfected at the German accelerator Laboratory DESY in Hamburg as a collaborative venture (called TESLA) of 55 institutes in 12 countries. On the other hand, the "warm" technology, which the committee has rejected, uses copper accelerating cavities at room temperature operating at a higher (X-band) RF of 11.4 Ghz.

This has been perfected at the Japanese eccelarator laboratory KEK in Tsukuba in collaboration with the Stanford

Linear Accelerator Centre (SLAC). An order of magnitude lower energy (50 Ge V) electron—positron linear collider has been running at the SLAC since 1989.

## India's Efforts

India is one of the few developing countries that have, in recent years, made a reasonable mark in high-energy physics, particularly in international collaborative experiments. At the CERN the European Centre for Panicle Physics in Geneva, Fermilab and Brookhhaven, U.S., India has made significant contributions in software as will as hardware, particularly particle detectors. In fact, the Department of Atomic Energy (DAE) has set up an accelerator technology development group, which has a major cooperation agreement with the CERN for collaborating on the LHC. The India-CERN cooperation agreement was first signed in 1991 with a view to participating in CERN's technical projects. This was followed by signing a protocol in 1996 for specific participation in the LHC under which nearly 20 projects have been assigned to Indian groups. The major ones among these are the setting up of two of the detectors in the LHC, namely the Compact Muon Solenoid (CMS) and A Large Ion Collider Experiment (ALICE).

Indin scientists have been contributing in a big way in LHC-related soft are as well. In recognition of the contribution to the CERN's activities, India was granted an observer status in the council of the CERN in December 2002. With growing worldwide interest in the line collider, Indian scientists have been carrying out studies under the Liner Collider Working Group (ILCWG). The ILCWG is a multi-institutional forum that includes scientists from the DAE and non-DAE institutions as well as universities. It has been contributing to the deliberations of the ACFA as well as to the technical sub committees of the ILCSE. The DAE organised an India-ACFA Meeting at the Centre for Advanced Technology (CAT), Indore. An India-U.S. Interaction Meeting on Linear collider, organised by the Department of Science and Technology, was held in Delhi in November 2003.

These culminated in India hosting the sixth ACFA workshop on Physics and Detectors for Linear collider in December 2003 at the Tata Institute of Fundamental Research (TIFR), Mumbai. Indeed, some Indian research contributions to L.C. physics have formed a significant component of the international effort in setting benchmarks for the collider, which have served as important inputs for the technology choice.

This Indian participation in this global venture appears to be very much on cards. A representative had been sent for the meeting on collider funding held at the CERN. "While Indian scientists (mainly phenomeno logists) have been involved in LC-related activities right from inception, it is necessary to develop a strategy quickly for involvement as a nation in a formal, institutionalised manner", points out Rohini Godbole, a professor at the Indian Institute of Science (HSC) Bangalore.

India has developed sole expertise in fabricating super conducting cavities, albeit, of low current carrying capacity for ion accelerators at the Nuclear Science Centre (NSC), Delhi, and TIFR. This could be an area where India can possibly contribute if R&D in the area is initiated and the expertise consolidated upon. However, if India is to ontribute meaningfully in the LC technology development, first it should have an independent management structure, with appropriate funding, and identify key leaders as part of it.

О О О

# 2. INDIAN BIOTECHNOLOGY

The Indian biotechnology industry is gaining momentum. With revenues of over $ 985 million in 2007-08, the fledgling industry, in spite of all hurdles, is well on its way to cross the psychological barrier of $ 1 billion in the current year. It is poised to leverage its scientific skills and technical expertise to make a global impact from a strong innovation led platform.

## Natural Resources

There are 42 National Research Laboratories in the country employing 18,000 scientists. There are more than 350 college level educational and training institutes offering degrees and diplomas in biotechnology, bio-informatics and the biological sciences producing nearly five lakh students annually. There are over 120 medical colleges churning out 20,000 medical practioners a year. Given this skilled source pool, India is in a good position to create a sustainable biotechnology business. Both in terms of infrastructure and markets, the sector is gradually building critical mass.

## Biotechnology

Biotechnology is a set of rapidly emerging and far-reaching new technologies with great promise in areas of sustainable food production, nutrition security, health care and environmental sustainability. Biotechnology is globally recognized as a rapidly emerging, complex and far reaching new technology. Biotechnology can, over the next two decades, deliver the next wave of technological change that can be as radical and pervasive as that brought about by IT. The recent and continuing advances in life sciences clearly unfold a scenario energized and driven by the new tools of biotechnology. The convergence of advances in biology-genomics, proteomics, bioinformatics and information technologies is driving the emergence of new bioeconomy. During the last five years, biotechnology industry has been growing at a rate of 40% and in 2005-06 exceeded US $ 1.5 billion in turnover.

A number of new initiatives have been taken up during the year to achieve this goal, which include increased number of Ph.D. post-docs including overseas fellowships, rapid grants for young investigators, innovation fellowships etc. A major success has been the launch of public/private partnership scheme-Small Business Innovation Research Initiative (SBIRI), which promotes highly innovative early stage, pre proof-of-concept and late stage development research emphasizing on important national needs. During the year, the Autonomous

Institutes have concentrated on technology and product development besides basic science. New International Collaborations have been forged with Denmark, Netherlands, US, Finland, UK, etc. Several of these are dedicated to tailored agricultural and vaccine and diagnostics technologies for regional/local needs.

## Medicinal and Aromatic Plants

Four gene banks have been further strengthened with respect to collection conservation and characterization of more number of germplasm accessions. A rapid and highly reproducible protocol for *in vitro* propagation of *Picrorhiza scrophulariflora* has been developed. High yielding lines of *Nothapodytes nimmoniana* with more than 1% camplothecin were identified from Western Ghats. Evaluation of the performance of elite tissue culture plantlets vis-a-vis stem cuttings of vanilla (*Vanilla planifolia*) in farmers' field over an area of 20 ha in Tripura state has been initiated. Cell-cultures of *Commiphora wightii* were grown in 2 litre stirred tank and 6-litre airlift bioreactor for guggulsterone production. A network project on development of standardized herbal product for bovine mastitis has been initiated.

## Plant Biotechnology

Support continued during 2007 for research and development projects on forestry, horticulture and plantation crops. The thrust of the activities was on plant tissue culture for mass multiplication of desired planting material, use of molecular markets for characterization of genetic diversity and superior accessions with reference to identified desirable traits, molecular biology tools for production of improved varieties through transgenic and molecular breeding approaches. The population genetic structure and diversity in Himalayan pines is also being analysed. Molecular tools were also used for genome evaluation and characterization. Projects in the area of horticulture crops focused mainly on production of disease free quality planting material, improvement of crops, with specific reference to extended shelf-life and genetic characterization studies. A brainstorming session was organized on improvement of forest based resources including both timber and non-timber through biotechnological interventions.

## Animal Biotechnology

Efforts are underway for the improvement of animal productivity, development of newer animal vaccines and diagnostics, molecular characterization of indigenous breeds of livestock and development of animal by-products. New programmes were initiated in the area of animal nutrition and development of newer animal vaccines. Standards were developed for estimation of mycotoxins in animal feed and distributed to various laboratories for routine analysis. A novel and potent anthrax vaccine which includes mutants of legal factor and edema factor was developed which provides better efficacy *in vivo.* Vaccines for Rabies, *Clostridium,* Hemorrhagic septicaemia, Foot and Mouth disease. Bovine brucellosis, Bovine tuberculosis etc. are in various stages of development. Phage display technique was used as an alternative to hybridoma to produce mono specific antibodies against recombinant gag antigen of Bovine Immunodeficiency Virus.

## Aquaculture and Marine Biotechnology

Programme on biosurfactants, exploration of marine enzymes, bioactive molecules, reproductive biology and cell cycling, plasmid immune response, neuro-peptide synthesis, bioreactors, vaccine development for fish, bacteriophage therapy in improvement of shrimp larvae, oligonucleotide probe for monitoring vibrio counts in hatcheries, genetic characterization of marine organisms, organ development, cell lines from seabass, shrimp genomics and fish nutrition are being implemented. Biosurfactants were screened using marine *Acinetobacter genospecies*. A prototype for raceway based shrimp production technology was utilized for nursery rearing of shrimp. Studies on occurrence of human pathogenic viruses in coastal marine waters were carried out. Marine cyanobacteria and chlorella species were studied for over expression of superoxide dismutase enzyme useful for bioremediation and salt tolerance. Bioactive molecules were explored for antibacterial, antiviral and anitcancer agents. Role of bacterial plasmid gene was studied in pathogenesis of Epizootic, Ulcerative Syndrome and its virulence.

## Competitive Advantages

Given the human biodiversity that exists in India, its efforts to attain a leadership position in biotechnology look achieveable. This offers unique human gene pools as powerful as those of Iceland, for exclusive genomic and pharmaco-genomic studies. Indian companies have a golden opportunity to unravel high value IPR by way of disease-linked genes and the diagnostic and therapeutic products emanating thereof. For example, thalassemia is a genetic disease prevalent in many inbred Indian societies. Given the proper approach, India can convert the disadvantage of a diseased population into a strong research advantage, which can translate into therapies and cures for thousands in India and other parts of the world.

India's plant and microbial biodiversities also provide a treasure trove for drug discovery. Many of the international pharma majors have collaborative HTS (high-thoroughput screening) programmes with universities worldwide and are now entering into similar prospecting partnerships with several Indian companies. Added to this is India's inherent knowledge base of ayurvedic and unani medicine, which offer a unique mining opportunity for new drug molecules.

India's vast and diverse disease and patient population also provides an enormous clinical development opportunity. The cost of drug development is largely attributed to the cost of conducting clinical trials.

Indian CROs (Clinical Research Organisations) have an opportunity to access the $ 10 billion global market for clinical trials. The presence of a large talent pool of medical and paramedical professionals is conducive to building a strong Clinical development infrastructure.

International CROs have already recognised this opportunity and have set up operations in anticipation of policy changes that will enable clinical trials to be carried out in India on equivalent lines of those conducted elsewhere.

Thus, there exists an exciting opportunity for biotech companies in the US and Europe to forward integrate their drug development programmes at lower cost and shorter time lines in India which would provide them with a lower cost validation option over trials conducted in the more expensive research environs of the West. Alternatively, the monetary risk could be shared with an Indian partner who is keenly seeking to backward integrate into research and discovery. The biotechnology sector is already showcasing India's potential to attaining leadership in vaccine production, genetically modified crops and clinical development.

O O O

## 3. Organic Farming

Organic farming is being touted as the panacea for a whole range of maladies afflicting Third World rural society. These range from low agricultural output to wasteful dumping of massive doses of farm chemical on cultivated lands as to reach toxic levels. It is cited as being the viable relief from the fatigue of the Green Revolution besides heralding holistic solutions to rural poverty alleviation providing employment opportunities to rural women. It includes claims that organic foods are healthier for human and animal consumption. Stated succinctly, any method of cultivation that does use any manufactured chemical such as urea, pesticides, fungicides, etc. for raising a crop or during its transit through harvest, storage, processing into foods and distribution is regarded as "organic".

This is how ancient man's foray into agriculture began centuries ago. The soil abounded in naturally occurring minerals which supported raising healthy crops that gave a plentiful harvest. Disease and pest pressure was minimal or non-existent and human need for the farm produce was limited owing to the small size of the community and the sparce animal population.

As demand for food production increased, over a period of time, with the increasing population, new methods and techniques to increase farm productivity became necessary. The advent of chemistry coupled with a better understanding of crop production improvement techniques via chemical fertilizers to replenish depleted minerals in the cultivated lands. Strides in other disciplines helped arming the farmer with pesticides and fungicides to combat pestilent microbes and insects that devoured grain and crops. Modern organic farming is much the same as our forefathers practised but in a significantly different era with its attendant pressures brought about by efflux of time.

The soil today is nowhere as rich in native minerals as witnessed centuries ago because of constant depletion brought about by farming and other physical phenomena, some natural others inflicted by human development. Similarly, the biotic stresses on plant have increased manifold because microbes and insects that live on them are constantly evolving to resist their annihilation wrought by human intervention via chemical warfare and from their own zest to survive and succeed.

This brings us to the question of the unique primacy of organic farming. Undoubtedly, Organic farming reduces built-up of residual chemical (insecticides, pesticides, fungicides, etc.) on the surface of plant leaf, it and grain which, when not adequately washed, enters human and animal gut which can be injurious to health. Yet, equally, abstinence from the use of such chemicals has led to build up of deadly mycotoxins in foods that are every bit as dangerous to human and animal life—fumonisins by Fubarium afflicting maze and aflotoxins by Aspergillus damaging chilly, groundnut, cashew, etc. Likewise it is a well-established fact that organic farming gives low yield and therefore jacks up the price of farm produce. Besides, claims of organic produce tasting better are nothing short of pandering to the whims of the rich who can afford to pay twice as much for the same rice or cucumber as raised by traditional farming.

The biochemical pathways of the plant in absorbing the minerals from the soil, photosynthesis or grain filling do not differentiate between the different sources of macro- and micro-nutrients made available to it, be it from a bag of manufactured compound fertilizers or from a bale of farm yard manure underpinning the lack of superiority of any mineral derived from living beings (plant, animal or microbe) compared to the one manufactured in a chemical plant. This is so because plants and animals absorb chemicals and process them in their elemental form and not the compound or complex form that we frequently encounter them as.

Thus, the elemental form of nitrogen is what is absorbed from urea, ammonium nitrate, DAP, farm-yard manure or processed organic waste available to the plant before it is converted into a host of other molecules that go to form carbohydrates, proteins and fats in living tissues. Likewise, the rice we eat is a complex carbohydrate which is broken down to its elemental form of carbon, hydrogen and oxygen before being further processed and is not absorbed in the compound form. From a different perspective, a drop of cobra venom or ricin from castor bean, both genuinely organic substances, would prove to be just as lethal as hydrogen cyanide manufactured in a chemist's lab regardlers of the former being devoid of any 'inorganic contamination'—two random examples merely to underpin the fact that there is nothing sacrosanct about organic.

As to the other claims that organic farming provides employment to women labourers in weeding operations (because organic farming does promote excessing growth of weeds in the absence of chemical control for weeds or cleaning of harvested grain (damaged by insect) and fungal attacks in the absence of chemicals to control this damage), it is waxing eloquent on employment opportunities of the back-breaking and unremunerating kind. This is perpetuation of low yields at the farm, recurrent attacks of weed, microbes and pests, so rural farmers can continue to produce less and stagnate in perpetual poverty, their womenfolk can be yoked to uneconomic employment while the affordable rich can take their pick at a fabulous premium for no intrinsic worth in return! Instead of making a false pitch for organic foods on fictitious premises, it is best left to the choice of the producer and the consumer to make his pick based on truthful, science-based knowledge. While equally sharing the truth about organic foods, we owe it to them to allay any unfounded fears of new technologies.

## 4. INDIA AND THE INTERNET

On October 20, 1997, Department of Telecommunications (DOT) and Jalan Committee announced concrete measures for the enhanced usage of Internet. One such measure was to allow the entry of private sector Internet Service Providers (ISPs) in India. This is a healthy step for the development of Telecom and Communication industry in particular and for the national economy in general.

This bold step (and many more steps likely to be taken in future) would open the new vistas for the latest technology for new millennium in this country. Internet is an intricate web of satellite and optical cable network. These networks connect millions of computers worldwide. Information is shared in the form of (text) data, pictures, graphic and voice between the computer system through this latest technology. Internet is the information super highway which would be used by people from all walks of life. Its applications would include surfing, database access, information about cities and their vital services, education, business communication and entertainment.

In India, 43,000 computers have been linked to Internet so far. This includes dial-up and leased connection. At present, there are three types of Internet accounts for which the price varies from Rs. 10,000 to Rs. 550 for 550 hours. The license fee of the ISPs has been waived for a five year period. However, the ISPs have to give a bank guarantee which is equivalent to the license fee for one year.

Videsh Sanchar Nigam Ltd. (VSNL) is the sole provider of Internet services in India. The revenue structure does not favour the Indian businessman, students and scholars. The Internet Services Providers ISPs would be able to rationalize the fee structure. A private ISP could provide Internet connection at one tenth of the cost of VSNL. It is worth noting that rate for Internet connection in the West is only US $15-20 per month.

Most of the hardware vendors are modifying their computer configurations for making them more Internet-friendly. In 1996 alone, the market was flooded with many web servers. Most popular uses of Internet in India include web browsing. E-mail and File Transmission Protoco (FTP). Roughly 125 establishments in India have either set up or are in the process of setting up internet accounts. By the turn of this century, we would have 12,000 establishments utilizing Internet. The credit for this would highly be attributed to a growth in the number of PCs, networking (LAN and WAN) and electronic commerce. Table I shows the trends of Internet connections in India.

| S.No. | Year | Internet Connections (millions) |
|-------|------|---------------------------------|
| 1 | 1997 | 0.2 |
| 2 | 1998 | 0.45 |
| 3 | 1999 | 0.8 |
| 4 | 2000 | 1.5 |
| 5 | 2001 | 3.5 |
| 6 | 2002 | 8.0 |
| 7 | 2005 | 12.0 |
| 8 | 2007 | 16.0 |
| 9. | 2008 | 22.0 |

The Internet revolution has taken the Indian business and Industry by storm. Internet browsing and its constituent www, have been beneficial for the Indian Industry for marketing its products and services. Electronic mail is the single biggest advantage of such a facility.

Further, Indian businessmen have been able to generate brand awareness of their products and are able to seek partners (financial and technical) in short time span.

With the liberalization of the economy and the emerging business and economic opportunities, the government has been considering the creation of a national information backbone which would be used for national information infrastructure and for the promotion of Internet services.

DOT and VSNL may not like to give away the Internet business to the ISPs on a platter. The DOT officials claim that they are providing excellent services and that private operators may not be able to deliver quality services at low cost. However, some state and private sector players in communication business feel that DOT is a hardcore monopoly and that privatization of the Internet services is an imminent reality.

India must get out of the agricultural age and must jump on to information technology bandwagon. The possibilities on the Internet are numerous. For example, it would be possible to have voice transmission via the Internet in near future. All the major nation streams—defence, industry, software development and exports, international trading, bilateral agreements, information exchange and information needs for daily usage—would benefit from this latest technological marvel.

Today, there is a lack of a good data transmission network in India. DOT would have to increase the capacity in intra-state transmission network. Private operators are likely to provide good quality networks as quality would decide their competence and hence, their market niches.

According to a survey, there is a demand for 7,00,000

Internet connections in the four metropolitan cities. The problem is of the supply and not of the demand. High operating cost could be another factor which is deterring some of the prospective customers from booking on to Internet. It is just possible that they are waiting for an opportune moment of reduced Internet costs.

In a population of I billion, there are only 43,000 Internet connections. We have tremendous software export capabilities. We have the second largest English speaking manpower in the world. Yet, the Internet users are very few. On the other hand, there are 40 million Internet connections worldwide and eighty per cent of the business is being carried out through Internet.

Our software exporters would witness more growth which would demand Internet services. Our International trading would also depend upon Internet connectivity. The micro-computer costs are falling everyday. India must take this opportunity in the right stride and must use this new gift of information technology for the benefit of her citizens.

Currently, the most serious application of Internet is in the area of E-mail. The E-mail services are very cheap and are used by businessmen and individuals world-wide for information transfer. The next major usage is in the area of electronic Commerce (e-Com). This service involves the speedy transfer of a business and accounting information worldwide. Other services provided by Internet include cinema, latest happenings around the world, city guides, data base browsing an entertainment.

Unfortunately, there are some thorns attached to this technology. Operating costs are still high as modem connection is required (which would transfer info nation through STD connection). Further, information available on most of the web sites is garbage. Finally, children or youngsters use Internet for obscene information access and for cheap entertainment. The usage of Internet for business and for data transfer is not being done in India. However, it is being hoped that India would be fully Internet-linked within three years and would utilize its potential for making her mark in this wonderful age of information technology.

### News on Internet

AIR news is also available on the Internet. The official website of NSD www.newsonair.com is being accessed by wider audience.

A major initiative to bring Real Radio on the Internet has been achieved by making available audio of the news bulletans on the website. The five-minute hourly bulletins are now available on the website. The major news bulletins at 0800 hrs., 0815 hrs., 2045 hrs., and 2100 hrs. are available with audio on the website.

The NSD website carries audio dispatches from AIR Correspondents along with the scripts of top news items on the home page. The Current Affairs interactive programme 'Spotlight' can also be heard on the website. The NSD has provided the scripts of Hindi news bulletins in Devnagari on the website for the Internet users. Hindi news headlines are also available on the website.

Regional language bulletins with audio are available on NSD's website. Internet users can listen Marathi, Kannada, Gujarati, Tamil, Telugu, Bengali, Punjabi and North Eastern bulletins in English using Internet. These bulletins are of special interest to non-resident Indians who can now keep abreast of listen to even the local happenings of their States while being in the US, Europe, Africa or any part of the world.

# 5. Is Computerization Necessary?

Computers have been dominating the world technological scenario since 1970s. The wonderful machine has not only won over the hearts of billions but also, it has entered all walks of life. The latest trends in computerization include Internet, Pentium based systems and Artificial Intelligence. The computer could not be defeated by man in a game of chess. And the irony is that the computer is a product of human brain itself.

Indian economy has grown at a sluggish pace for the past five decades. The GNP and exports figures are not very rosy vis.-a-vis. our Asian neighbours, for example, Taiwan, Indonesia, Malaysia and Singapore have come up with "Swift Economies" which have catapulted them into international business platforms. And let us not forget "the land of rising sun" which has risen from the ashes of the Second World War to become the number one economic superpower of the globe.

And precisely, how was that possible? The plain answer is—computers are a part of these economies and control the productivity and commercial functions in close unison with the international economic powers. And therefore, they prosper at very fast rates.

Computers are the electronic devices which make us efficient. They help us do more creative work by doing the repetitive tasks themselves. They help us create, design, programme, communicate and above all, help us earn. In India, millions of homes are thriving because their members are dedicated to this fascinating profession.

We cannot imagine any area where computerization has not been done—business, banking, electronic publishing, engineering design, international communication through e-mail, creative designing, fashion designing, etc.—the list is endless.

One must raise a valid question—will computerization make people redundant? The answer is no. And the reason is simple—the man who was doing the job of a clerk would now execute more productive assignments. So, he would contribute more to his company, society or nation. And in this effort, he would always be accompanied by his friend—the computer. Computerization is creating more jobs for DTP specialists, programmers and hardware professionals. It is a sound business proposal for the new entrepreneurs, a sea of knowledge for the ever inquisitive student and a child's delight as he can play all types of games on it. In sum, it is a natural necessity and would improve knowledge levels, productivity, earnings and living standards of all the classes of society.

Japan, the USA, the UK, Germany and France have used computers extensively for automobiles, factories, business transactions, health management, education and communication. These are the economic and military superpowers of the world. If India wants to emulate them on economic, technological and defence fronts, complete computerization and linking of Indian economy and industry with international information superhighway is a must. This is possible only with the help of computers and Internet networks.

Computers save our time. They make us more efficient and complete the repetitive tasks in a small time interval. Computer programmer from India are the best known programmers in the world. Computer programming has vital applications in Internet website design, telecommunications, engineering design and Computer Integrated Manufacturing (CIM). If routine jobs are handled by computers, executives and operatives are able to concentrate on more productive and result-oriented tasks. Creativity and thinking are beyond the limits of computers although major breakthrough has been achieved in the field of Artificial Intelligence.

Computerization is essential in Indian context as tele-communication and satellite imagery are computer-based. The life in urban cities cannot be imagined without telephone, E-mail, fax, Internet connectivity and cellular phones. Most of these services warrant the usage of computer for operation and maintenance. Therefore, computerization is necessary in urban areas.

In rural areas as well, computerization can play a vital role in crop development, seed research, crop disease management, rural employment, software development for rural sector industries and rural education. Rural telecommunication scenario has been revolutionized by computers. Now, we can make an ISD and SID call from all remote corners of India, thanks to telecommunication revolution which is essentially coupled with computer operations.

Education is a vital sector in which computers could play a vital role. The state governments and the central government have put special emphasis on computerized education and Internet. Internet operations would be opened for the private Internet services providers (ISPs). Further, all accounting, commercial, technical and classified information is stored and managed by computers. Hence, computers are indispensable tools in the modern era.

In sum, we can state that India must computerize her economy, business, scientific, weather, educational and other operations for glorious passage into the new millennium. The world is a global village now and India can hook onto the world through computerization only. This technology would benefit her on economic, technological and social fronts. The new millennium would truly belong to computers !!

○ ○ ○

# 6. Superlasers And Nuclear Weapon Technology

Nuclear weapons, nuclear explosions and the latest concepts in nuclear technology are being discussed in great detail now-a-days. The reason could be attributed to the nuclear explosions conducted by India and Pakistan during May, 1998. The nuclear scenario in South Asia is hot.

In the meanwhile, nuclear scientists are busy in discovering the new technologies in nuclear science. Let us discuss a few latest concepts.

It is quite amazing to imagine that the sizes of nuclear bombs of the future could be equal to the size of a tea cup. They could weigh, at the most, one kg. They could be very cheap. They could be carried to the desired site with the help of small missiles and artillery systems. Therefore, we have now arrived at a new concept in nuclear bomb technology which claims that small is beautiful. These are the fourth generation nuclear weapons with a yield equivalent to 1-10 tonnes of TNT. They are lethal but are not restricted under the CTBT.

The CTBT does not allow any nuclear explosions. However, it allows the micro-explosions with a yield of up to 10 tonnes. The Fourth Generation Nuclear (FGN) weapons could be used as weapons but not for mass destruction. Note that a conventional nuclear device is 10,00,000 times more powerful than the conventional weapon. The FGN is only 1,000 times more powerful than the conventional weapon system. Dr. Andre Gsponer, a nuclear physicist at the Independent Science Centre in Geneva, Switzerland has been actively involved in FGN weapons projects. Mr. Gsponer states that FGN weapons would be able to fill the gaps between the conventional and nuclear weapons.

The five masters of the universe—The USA, China, Germany, the UK and France—have a decisive edge in the FGN weapon technology. But Mr. Gsponer feels that more nations could join for the development of FGN weapons as they are cheap, manageable and do not attract any CTBT provisions for complete ban. The other area of nuclear expansion is the thermonuclear device.

A thermonuclear device is different from the other conventional nuclear weapons. A conventional nuclear device is based on the concept of nuclear fission in which a heavy isotope (Uranium-235) breaks up into two smaller isotopes of comparable atomic masses when the mother isotope is bombarded by high speed rays of extremely high energy levels. The fission or the breaking up of the heavy nucleus into two lighter nuclei releases energy. The bombs dropped at Hiroshima and Nagasaki (named 'Little Boy' and 'Fatman') were fission devices. A thermonuclear device is one in which two lighter nuclei combine (under severe conditions of high temperature and pressure) to form a heavy nucleus.

For example, in the sun, the atoms of hydrogen are combining to form one molecule of helium.

The process takes energy in the form of heat and pressure in the initial stages. However, when the fusion process takes place, there is a release of tremendous amount of heat energy, light and radioactive rays. That is the sole reason why the sun has been generating energy on its own for several billion years and would continue to do so in future as well.

The "keen and progressive" nations of the world are working on the FGN weapons as well as on' the thermonuclear devices. It must be pointed out that India has already acquired the thermonuclear technology.

The FGN weapons could use either the fusion fuel or the fission fuel. The yield generation mode in the fission process is the sub-critical mode which is not forbidden under the CTBT. Sub-critical bums are not suitable for making high-yield weapons but are ideal for a yield of 1-100 tonnes.

For this type of explosive, the suitable technique is the usage of magnetic compression for increasing the density of the fissile material and a very small amount of anti-matter to initiate the critical bum. While the anti-matter and lasers would be used as igniters, the main charge could be deuterium-tritium pallets of 0.5 cm size and these would be compressed by a factor of 1,000. Japanese scientists have been able to achieve the maximum compression of these pallets by increasing the density to 600 times that of the original density.

Further, the other vital player in this technology is the laser. Some nations have developed superlasers by increasing their intensities. The minimum cost of the superlaser is US $ I million.

The world has not been able to define what constitutes a nuclear explosion. However, the CTBT allows the micro-explosions with a yield of 10 tonnes. According to the CTBT draft, these are not nuclear explosions in technical parlance.

Table 1 shows the list of superlaser laboratories around the world which carry out the research and development of FGN weapons.

## Table I: Superlaser Laboratories Around the World

| S.No. | Laser Type | Location | Country |
|-------|-----------|----------|---------|
| 1. | Petawatt | (1) Lawrence Livermore Institute<br>(2) UM, Ann Arbor | USA |
| 2. | Trident | (1) LANL<br>(2) UC, San Diego | USA |
| 3. | LABS II | (1) LANL<br>(2) UI, Chicago<br>(3) UM, Ann Arbor<br>(4) WSA, Pullman<br>(5) Stanford University | USA |
| 4. | Vulcan | Rutherford Appleton Lab | UK |
| 5. | Titania | Rutherford Appleton Lab | UK |
| 6. | Sprite | Rutherford Appleton Lab | UK |
| 7. | Petawatt | CESTA, Bordeaux | France |
| 8. | P-102 | (1) CEL-V, Limell<br>(2) LOA, Palaiseau | France |
| 9. | ELIA | University of Bordeaux | France |
| 10. | Atlas | (1) Max Born Institute, Berlin<br>(2) MPQ, Garching | Germany |
| 11. | Petawatt | Institute for Laser Energetics | Japan |
| 12. | Petawatt | APRC, Riken | Japan |
| 13. | BM | Not known | China |
| 14. | Not known | St. Petersburg | Russia |

The former vice chairman of the Joint Chiefs of Staff, Admiral David Jeremiah stated at a conference on Molecular Nano technology (1995)—"The battlefield of the future will be dominated by smart weapons that will allow us to reduce wholesale destruction and the tremendous expenditure of ordnance. The goal is finer precision, more selectivity, less need for mass." He further stated that "big-nukes" are of lesser importance. Therefore, he emphasized upon the slimming of the nuclear technology and the resultant derivation of the FGN weapons. Admiral Jeremiah also stated that these slim weapons had "greater potential to radically change the balance of power."

CTBT is just an instrument for legitimizing the possession and perfection of nuclear weapons by the nuclear States. But we really do not know what is going on in the laboratories around the world. FGN weapons could be utilized against the enemy whereas a nation would think at least for ten times before she uses a "major nuclear option" against any country. The development and usage of full-fledged nuclear weapons is costly, morally agonizing and technically difficult. The usage of slim nuclear devices like the FGN weapons is cheaper and morally acceptable. However, it is technically out of reach for most of the nations. Experts state that this technology could be acquired by many non-weapon states in the times to come.

The FGN weapons and the superlaser laboratories have added a new dimension to the nuclear weapon scenario; the small and slim nuclear missiles which pose another 'real' threat to the only living planet in our part of the universe. We pray that good sense may prevail and this deadly technology may be diverted towards peaceful applications of nuclear energy.

○ ○ ○

# 7. WHAT TO IMPORT: TECHNOLOGY OR PRODUCTS?

India is a growing nation of 90 crore people. Her requirements for survival and growth are typical. We followed a very selective and conservative economic policy during the formative years of Indian economy. However, since the beginning of the nineties, free market forces have been allowed to play for ensuring all round development in the industrial and economic fronts.

Indian economy is in a nascent stage. It is not as mature as Japanese, European or the US economies. Hence, we need technology imports more often than other developed nations do. We also import products which are basically raw materials, finished and semi-finished components, spare parts, chemicals, accessories and electronic goods in Complete Knocked Down (CKD) or Semi Knocked Down (SKD) conditions.

For growth on a long term basis, technology import is essential. For growth on a short term basis, products have to be imported. Products raise the living standards as well. As Indian economy and industry are developing, new products and technologies need to be imported. For example, India is a major importer of petroleum products, electronic goods and parts, gold, vital chemicals, fertilizers capital equipment, computer parts, processing machinery and medical equipments. Similarly, India is also importing technologies for power generation, rail and road construction, civil aviation, mining, nuclear power generation and utilization and for other infrastructure related projects. The question now arises—what should we import? Technology or products?

If we import only the products, we would be the biggest consumers of foreign goods on account of our burgeoning population, We would produce more (in terms of agricultural, industrial and service related outputs) in order to import these products, Our living standards would improve. Imports would increase, Gross Domestic Product (GDP) would also increase as imports would necessitate the generation of additional resources. So, economy would certainly grow. For example, petroleum products are imported by us and we import them only after we generate enough of resources so that we could pay in US dollars. That would automatically mean that our exports would also grow.

However, there would be no investment in infrastructure development. Construction of roads, rails, steel, coal, power and fertilizers would be ignored. New technologies for generation of better products or services in these core areas would not be developed. There would be no generation of additional jobs which is an essential ingredient of our economy. The rising population must be absorbed in productive operations. There must be jobs for our masses—from workers to managers. But if we import products only, we would not be able to achieve the low unemployment level. This could lead to large scale industrial unrest. The product consumers would work hard to earn extra money (so that they could buy those products). However, the basic engines of economy would not generate opportunities for jobs, business or entrepreneurship. Hence, in the long run, they would not be able to buy imported goods.

Product import would lead to decline in service import. The import of services includes industrial and management consultancy. As this is not related to product import, nobody would buy these vital services from abroad, As a result, we would be deprived of the latest developments in computers, Internet, electronics, management consultancy, human re-engineering, telecommunications, farming, plant breeding, agriculture and other vital fields. India would lag behind other developing nations. Our services sectors would also suffer because services are always supported by latest technologies which are imported.

Now let us take a look at the other side of the picture as well. If we import only the technologies, we would develop the basic infrastructure to arrive at the self-reliance stage. We would be able to develop new and indigenous technologies on our own once we have imported latest technologies for power generation, defence, mining, shipping, metal extraction, chemical plants, fertilizers and telecommunications. Indians can adopt all types of imported technologies for their local needs. The example of PARAM can be cited. the first full operational supercomputer built by Centre for Development of Advance Computing (CDAC). We can create records in economic development, industrial production, software development and exports, manufacturing and allied areas provided that we are fully conversant with the latest technologies from the West. Another example can be cited of the Indian software brain power. The computer was developed in the USA and was adopted by Indians. Now Indians comprise the largest technical manpower pool in the USA for on-shore and off-shore software development jobs. This proves our versatile capabilities and abilities to adopt to new technologies.

Import of new techniques would lead to more production. This would, in turn, lead to more jobs and a rise in the GDP. Hence, there would be a rise in the productivity of core sectors, secondary industrial sectors and services sectors. There would be a boom in Indian economy. Exports would grow which would make up for increased imports (for import of technologies).

But there are some strings attached to the import of technologies. We have to spend first and the payoffs would come later. In case of product import, the import would automatically trigger off a chain reaction in the economy. But industrial infrastructure would take years to develop. The import of technologies would not have a visible impact on the economy. True, it would pay us later. But the Indian populace needs products as well. Living standards would have to be raised. Vital life saving drugs must be imported. Computers and vital electronic components must be purchased within specific timeframes. Product imports cannot be stopped as Indian economy would not start producing these products within a short time span. True, our indigenous manufacturing would lead to the development of industry and economy. But our industry would not be able to produce good quality products (which are at par with imported ones) immediately.

The solution has to be sought in terms of a balance between the two imports. The two basic guidelines in this context are:

(A) We have to import those products which cannot be produced at home (For example, petroleum, vital electronic components, etc.) The national exchequer has to bear the burden of these imports. These products do not require technology import but understanding and adoption of technology is free of cost or cheap by all standards.

(B) We must try to indigenize the production of all other products which could be manufactured at home. (For example, steel, vital medicines, computers, telecom equipments, agricultural equipments, etc.). These products could be manufactured in India. In order to produce the best quality, we can import latest technologies from abroad. The basic infrastructures would have to be built or upgraded. Technology import would also be a burden on our national exchequer. However, we would learn the art of making good products with gradual exposure to latest technologies.

Therefore, the action plan could be summarized as follows:

(1) Import those products which cannot be produced or which cannot be manufactured economically in India.

(2) Manufacture those products and technology which are vital for:

    (a) infrastructure development; and

    (b) for raising the living standards of the masses.

Both these categories have to be given a certain ratio. Let us give it a ratio of 40 : 60 (products : technologies). We should import lower quantity of products because products do not improve our productivity and technological upgradation at all. They raise our living standards. The technology imports are investments for the future. They build our nation so that she becomes more independent and self-reliant. Our main objective should be a growing and self-sustaining economy without foreign aids and assistance. This ratio would be ideal for the achievement of our national objectives and for the attainment of a healthy rate of economic development.

The main issue of economic development must never be ignored at any cost while importing products and technologies. The State as well as the importers must ensure that the imports being effected by them are for the benefit of their industry, region and nation. The foreign cash reserves are limited and the world-wide secession has triggered off industrial slowdown and a reduction in exports. Hence, imports of any kind must be resorted to after careful discussions and predictions about the future of international trading in the times to come.

# 8. The Electrical Power Scenario

Electrical power is the most vital energy input for the industry, the household and the national economy. India with a bursting populace of 110 million power hungry individuals is the leading nation among the developing countries concentrating on cost-effective power generation, transmission and distribution for her ever growing needs.

The history of electrical power in India is more than a century old. The British rule brought the electrical power generating stations in the late nineteenth century in Maharashtra. The first Prime Minister of India, the late Jawaharlal Nehru inaugurated the Bhakra Nangal dam in the late 1950s and thus laid the foundation of a power-rich country. The railway routes between New Delhi-Bombay (Mumbai) and New Delhi-Chennai were electrified during the sixties and remain operational till date. The Amritsar-New Delhi route is being electrified and would take only a few years before it commences full-fledged operations.

The post-independence era brought power generation, transmission and distribution in the hands of the state. The states were granted permission for promoting their own electricity boards.

India has 28 States and 7 Union Territories, each one having power stations located within its state capital. The vital arms of the states are the major power producers in the country. The key power players include National Hydroelectric Power Corporation Ltd. (NHPC), Nuclear Power Corporation Ltd. (NPCL), National Thermal Power Corporation Ltd. (NTPC) and Gas Authority of India Ltd. (GAIL).

During the beginning of the 1990s, the Indian economy surged towards a free market, a multinational culture and an efficiency-oriented global village. The electrical power needs became more prominent due to rapid industrialization and bustling population pressures. The chronic power shortages forced the state, the entrepreneur and the household to look for alternative sources of power. This resulted in power generation efforts ranging from 4 KW (in the form of a portable generating set) to 10,000 MW (in the form of a nuclear power station).

During the 1990s, when the free market winds blew stronger, the corporate sector was allowed to have its own captive power plants. The foreign companies like Enron, GEC, Westinghouse, etc. were invited to invest in private power generation and deliver electricity at a price India could afford. The major entrants on the scene had to face severe teething troubles, mainly due to the lack of infrastructure and due to the modus-operandi of the state. The plans are afoot for generating power through corporate resources and distributing the same through private agencies under the supervision of the state.

By all international norms, India has been declared a "power shortage country" and the one severely handicapped for future growth on account of shortage of electrical energy.

Table below (given on next page) compares India with the other South East Asian countries in terms of annual power generation and capacity (installed and proposed addition).

The countries, which have not yet developed "power generation infrastructure," are trying to develop the same. At the same time, the nations of the world—irrespective of their status of developing or developed nations—are trying to exploit the alternative sources of energy. The chief alternative sources for the generation of electric power are:

(a) Wind Power (using the wind mills for generating AC or DC, drawing water from the earth for irrigation purposes).

(b) Solar Power (using photoelectric cells for generating current and subsequently, charging the batteries for usage at a later stage).

(c) Tidal Power for generating (taming the tides electricity using the ocean thermal energy conversion (OTEC) process and using the electrical power so obtained for simple industrial applications).

## Table I: Power Generation and Capacity of South East Asian Countries

| Country | 1995 Estimated | | Future Projection Capacity Addition (MW) | | |
|---|---|---|---|---|---|
| | Annual Generation (GWH) | Installed Generation (MW) | 1995-2000 Capacity | 2000-05 | 2005-10 |
| India | 3,51,020 | 80,880 | 56,000 | 90,000 | 90,000 |
| Thailand | 78,880 | 13,427 | 9,409 | 8,930 | 9,852 |
| Indonesia | 61,964 | 26,063 | 10,968 | 14,122 | — |
| Pakistan | 53,425 | 12,721 | 7,000 | 3,000 | 8,000 |
| Malaysia | 38,821 | 11,525 | 4,032 | 4,000 | — |
| Philippines | 33,073 | 10,017 | 4,438 | 8,389 | 13,573 |
| Singapore | 20,676 | 4,513 | 1,770 | 1,200 | 2,400 |
| Vietnam | 17,400 | 4,280 | — | 4,020 | — |
| Bangladesh | 10,805 | 2,908 | 1,033 | 2,042 | — |
| Sri Lanka | 4,783 | 1,387 | 640 | 432 | 613 |
| Myanmar | 3,500 | 793 | 635 | — | — |
| Bhutan | 1,620 | 360 | 45 | 91 | 1,000 |
| Nepal | 1,117 | 296 | 116 | 286 | 455 |
| Cambodia | 172 | 39 | 96 | 100 | 500 |
| Laos | 112 | 260 | 360 | 681 | 1,500 |

(d) Hydel Power (controlling the flow of the rivers and reservoirs and using their hydro-potentials for generating base load for the industry and the household).

The next seven years would witness an investment of Rs. 3,00,000 crores and would allow 200 power plants to operate on the Indian soil. The installed capacity which was 75,000 MW in 1996 is likely to be doubled to 1,50,000 MW by the year 2003 AD.

The power-hungry world is concentrating on projects with generation capacity of 1000 MW and above. Table II shows this in a lucid manner and also pinpoints the Indian projects which rustle shoulders with the other giant projects in the world.

## Table II: The Biggest Global Power Projects of Capacity 1,000 MW and Above

| Name | Country | Capacity (MW) | Fuel Type | Company/ Promoter | Status |
|---|---|---|---|---|---|
| Tucurui II | Brazil | 2,450 | — | CVRD, Billiton Aloca | Agreed |
| Dabhol closure | India | 2,450 | Gas/Naptha | Dabhol Power Company | Implemented requires fresh fresh financial |
| Shajjo C | China | 1,980 | Coal | Consolidated Electric | Implemented; operation in Power Asia 196 |
| Teeside | Britain | 1,875 | Gas | Teesside Power | Implemented |
| Litze | Taiwan | 1,500 | Orimulsion fired | Chang-Hung Power | Agreed; likely to be operational in 2000 |
| Ita | Brazil | 1,450 | Hydro | AAI | Agreed |
| Farmosa | Taiwan | 1,340 | Coal | Mailiao Cogeneration | Agreed, operation by 2001 |
| Keti Bandar | Pakistan | 1,320 | Coal | Consolidated Electric Power Asia | Agreed; likely to be operational 2000 |
| Tanjung Jati | Indonesia | 1,320 | Coal | Consolidated Electric | Agreed, requires frest PPA; Power Asia operation in 2000 |
| Taichung | Taiwan | 1,320 | Coal | Hoping Power | Agreed; likely to be operational in 2002 |
| Lumut | Malaysia | 1,303 | Gas | Sikap Power | Implemented, financed in 1995; operation by 1996 |

| Name | Country | Capacity (MW) | Fuel Type | Company/ Promoter | Status |
|---|---|---|---|---|---|
| Hub River | Pakistan | 1,292 | Oil fired | Hub Power Co. | Implemented financial closure in 1995 |
| Paiton I | Indonesia | 1,230 | Coal | Paiton Power Co. | Implemented; financial closure in May 1995; operation in 1999 |
| Paiton II | Indonesia | 1,200 | Coal | Jawa Power | Implemented; PPA in April 1995; financial closure in March 1996; operation in 2000 |
| Tanjung Jati-B | Indonesia | 1,200 | Coal | Bakrie Consortium | Agreed; PPA under negotiation; operation in 2003 |
| Sual | Philippines | 1,200 | Coal | Panganasinam Electric Co. | Implemented; financed in 1995; opeation in 1999 |
| Visakhapatnam | India | 1,040 | Coal | Hinduja National | Agreed Power Ltd. |
| Hoping | Taiwan | 1,000 | Coal | Hua Tung Power | Agreed |
| Ho-Lung | Taiwan | 1,000 | Oil fired | Miaoli Power | Agreed |
| Mangalore | India | 1,000 | Coal | Mangalore Power Co. | Agreed; received most clearances. |

N.B.: (a)  **Implemented** means the projects had finance and are commissioned under construction or are certain to go ahead.

(b)  **Agreed** means those projects which have all the necessary agreements needed to postert but avert financing.

**Courtesy:** *Powerline* Magazine.

The nuclear explosions conducted by Indian scientists on May 11, and May 13, 1998 sidelined a very crucial issue-nuclear power generation. India would utilize her nuclear engineering abilities for peaceful purposes only and the most prominent application would be nuclear power plants spread throughout the nation. India has fully operational atomic power plants in Tarapur (400 MW), Kota (400 MW), Kalpakkarn (200 MW), Narore (200 MW) and Kakrapar. No doubt, our nuclear power generation ability would rise with increased expertise in nuclear engineering in the years to come. Coal and gas- based power plants are likely to take a backseat. Naphtha-based power plants are also likely to be in vogue in future. Hydro power plants do have a great potential but these projects entail heavy initial costs. Thermal power plants could be supplied coal for at least 150 years to come. These plants, coupled with hydro-power plants, could supply the base load for the national grid. The peak loads could be met by naphtha-based plants, nuclear power plants, and oil-fired or gas-fired power plants.

Table II compares the global power projects, whereas Table III throws light on the subsidies offered in India to the major economic heads.

### Table III: Subsidy Offered to Economic Heads
(Rs in crore)

| S.No. | Electricity Sale to Economic Head | 1996-97 | 1997-78 Revised Estimates | 1998-99 Annual Projectile |
|-------|-----------------------------------|---------|---------------------------|---------------------------|
| 1. | Agriculture | 15,628 | 18,296 | 20,432 |
| 2. | Domestic | 4,234 | 4,714 | 5,340 |
| 3. | Inter-state Sales | 285 | 235 | 331 |
| | Total | 20,147 | 23,245 | 26,103 |

The economic survey (2006-07) demonstrates that the subsidy for agriculture and domestic sectors would be around Rs. 50,000 crores by the end of 2007-08 period. Further, the survey points out that the total commercial losses of the State

Electricity Boards (SEBs) are likely to go upto Rs. 15,000 crores in 2007-08. The reason is attributed to low plant load factor and heavy transmission and distribution losses. The total power generation during 2006-07 was 577.6 billion KW which shows a rise of about 6 per cent over the corresponding period last year. The average plant load factor of thermal plants has improved to 64.4. Further, the addition of capacity generation during April-December period was 1,636 MW whereas the target was of 1,998 MW.

The demand of power far outstrips the supply in India. We need power conservation measures (at home and in domestic sector), power generation attempts (at state and national levels) and power transmission and distribution management (through better international technologies available at global levels). Power is the lifeline of a nation. We must generate enough power for survival and overall technological and economic growth.

O O O

# 9. THE INFORMATION TECHNOLOGY REVOLUTION

The new millennium has seen a complete revolution in the history of mankind—the information technology revolution. Although information technology has already entered the homes, offices and hearts of our global citizens, yet some new feats are likely to be performed by our information technology experts within a period of a few years.

We know that information technology is the fastest growing field in the world. India has a major stake in this field and our software experts, hardware firms and information technology specialists have been contributing a great deal towards this ever-growing field. For example, the annual revenues of Indian software industry would touch the US$ 30 billion mark by the year 2010. During 2006-07, the Indian software exports were

21.6 per cent in the global customized software market which is a great achievement keeping in mind that there was an overall recession in most of the major economies of the world. Therefore, our interest in information technology is natural as Indians have already made their presence felt in this vital field.

Let us now discuss what lies ahead. We are already aware of mobile phones, pagers, LAN/WAN networks, high speed and thrilling games, Internet and finally, very high quality software for various engineering, scientific and business applications. The information technology experts are aiming even further. Let us have a look at the future.

The first major area of Information Technology (IT) in the next few years to come would be Electronic Mail (briefly termed as e-mail). This is a high speed communication mode through Internet. An e-mail costs less than one Rupee per page and can be sent to or received from any corner of the world. This unique facility is already operational in the West. In India, it is catching up fast. It is cheap, economical and efficient. All we need is a computer (a pentium computer with 32 MB RAM and 266 MHz CPU speed would be good enough), an e-mail connection, a telephone with STD facilities and a modem card. E-mail would be the medium of communication for the future. It would eliminate the need of postage, courier and telephonic conversation. Data, text, picture, tables and all types of special information can be transferred via the e-mail.

Second most vital area of development would be Electronic Commerce (also called e-com). E-com has already been initiated in Europe and the U.S.A. The concept is simple; we would send an e-mail to the nearest grocery shop for our daily grocery needs. The information would be sent to the grocery shop through Internet and the grocery would be delivered at our door step. The concept of e-com goes even beyond this. Corporate firms would float their tenders and projects through Internet. The vendors, management consultants, engineering consultants and other business associates would discuss the project online through Internet. The costing, calculations, engineering details and prices would be shared online. The orders would be placed online and the executions would also be through Internet. The information transfer would involve engineering information and all types of text, graphics, tables and figures. The concept of e-com is picking up in the Indian industry as well.

Information technology would make its presence felt in consumer electronics as well. In fact, it has already created new concepts at home and in the office. Examples could be cited of mobile phone trunking systems, computer monitors with facilities of television, digital monitors, high memory Magneto Optic Drives (MO drives), Digital Video Disks (DVDs) for video applications, STD calls at the rate of Rs. 3 per minute, high definition stereo systems and a host of facilities for the telephone users. These services have not been provided in India with complete efficiency or in all parts of the country. However, it is hoped that within two years, these new gadgets of information technology would storm the markets of urban and rural India.

Another significant development envisaged in the field of information technology is the advent of Internet shops in all the parts of urban India. Internet surfers would be delighted to send e-mail, receive e-mail, surf through various sites of Internet and collect information required by them. Internet is also full of fun. All the magazines, newspapers, city guides, fashion news, movies and other entertainment shows are available on-line on Internet. So, we should not be surprised if the STD booth in our area would have Internet connectivity. Earlier, people were crazy about video games. In the years to come, people would surf through Internet for education, information, business and leisure.

Further, the new millennium would find people communicating with great ease. The mobile communication modes would become very cheap. The price of the mobile phone has already come down. Further, a new technology has been developed which would enable our telephone to be used as a mobile phone. A base set would be connected to the telephone line at our home or in our office. We would carry an instrument like the mobile phone with us. We can communicate with our office or home in which the base set has been installed and there would be no charges payable. The base set would also be able to communicate with the mobile set. Further, if we want to make a call (while we are on the move), we would be able to do so through our telephone (or base set). But the range of this mobile phone would be limited to 25-30 kms.

Further, another extension to the technology of mobile communication described earlier would be quite thrilling. This is a combination of radio mobile trunking system and mobile phone. We would have a base set installed at our office or our residence where we have been allotted the telephone connection. We can have any number of mobile sets which would always be linked to the base set. The mobile sets would be able to communicate with the base set at nil cost. Further, the base set would also be able to communicate with them. And what is more, the mobile sets would also be able to talk to each other. They would be able to use a single phone connection (connected to their base set) for making mobile phone calls. The entire system would be efficient—but would remain limited to a distance of 15-25 kms only. Their range is likely to be increased as the researches in the field yield more concrete results.

Satellite phones would be another feather in the cap of IT professionals in the new millennium. We would have satellite phones for talking to any person, across the globe or for sending fax or E-mail to him. Satellite phones are not popular in India. But going by the current trends in IT, we could soon witness major growth in India. Cost is the basic inhibiting factor; when the costs would come down, the satellite phones would be sold like hot cakes.

Information technology would usher the modern man in the era of paperless office. All the offices and homes would be connected through LAN/WAN networks and Internets. The Internet connectivity would also be common by the beginning of new century. Information would be collected, analyzed, tabulated, presented and transferred electronically and through cordless modes. The real emphasis would then be on performance and not on paperwork.

Other vital growth areas of IT would include multimedia, animation Internet, website development, Computer Aided Engineering, Computer Aided Design, Computer Integrated Manufacturing; Artificial Intelligence, Factory Automation and new facilities in telecommunications. The trends are healthy and are likely to spread through the Indian subcontinent. However, resource shortage, industrial recession, policies of the government and above all, global IT trends could adversely affect the growth of the IT products and services in India. Let us hope that the healthy trends spill over into the new millennium.

○ ○ ○

# 10. Science and Technology Infrastructure In India

Scientific research in India is carried on under three major sectors, viz. the Central Government, the State Governments and the various inhouse research and development units of industrial undertakings, both under the public and the private sectors. The bulk of the research effort in the country is financed by major scientific agencies such as the departments of Science and Technology, Atomic Energy, Space, Scientific and Industrial Research, Electronics, Non-Conventional Energy Sources, Environment Cleanliness and Development, Biotechnology, Indian Council of Medical Research, etc. There are about 260 research laboratories within the purview of these major scientific agencies carrying out research in different areas. Besides, there is a large number of scientific institutions under the Central ministries/departments which carry out research programmes of practical relevance to their areas of responsibility. The States supplement the efforts of the Central Government in areas like agriculture animal husbandry, fisheries, public health, etc. The institutions of higher education carry out sizable work in the field of science and technology and are supported by the University Grants Commission (UGC) and the Central and State governments. They also carry out sponsored research projects financed by different agencies.

A number of incentives are being provided by the Government to industrial establishments in the private and public sectors to encourage them to undertake research and development activities. Consequently, scientific research is gaining momentum in many of the industrial establishments. As on today, there are over 3,000 in-house research and development units in the public and private sectors which were recognised by the Department of Scientific and Industrial Research.

The science policy of the government of India based on the Scientific Policy Resolution adopted by the Parliament on March 4, 1958 lays stress on the Government's responsibility to secure for the people the benefits from the acquisition of scientific knowledge and practical application' of research. It is also the Government's policy to encourage individual initiative for dissemination of knowledge and to foster programmes to train scientific personnel to fulfil the nation's needs in the fields of science, education, agriculture, industry and defence. In the national priorities, science and technology has been recognised as major instrument for achieving national goals of self-reliance through economic and multifaceted socio-cultural development. New Departments of Environment, Ocean Development, Non-Conventional Energy Sources, Scientific and Industrial Research and Biotechnology have been set up to deal with nationally important and newly emerging areas that call for significant science and technology inputs. Significant achievements have been recorded as a result of the policy. The technology policy statement announced in January 1983, was in response to the need for guidelines to cover a wide-ranging and complex set of related areas, keeping in mind the capital-scarce character of a development economy. It aims at ensuring that country's multifarious problems are tackled so as to be able to safeguard its independence and unity. Among its objectives are attainment of technological competence and self-reliance, provision of gainful employment, making traditional skills commercially competitive, ensuring maximum development with minimum capital, modernisation of equipment and technology, conservation of energy, ensuring harmony with environment, etc.

To evolve instruments for implementation of the technology policy, the Government set up in June, 1983, a Technology Policy Implementation Committee. On completion of its tenure in mid 1987, it has given way to a new autonomous body designated as Technology Information Forecasting and Assessment council (TIFAC). It has been constituted for strengthening the national capabilities in the areas of technology forecasting and assessment and to provide the Government with independent policy options and advice. Working under the Department of Science and Technology, the council monitors Technological developments in India and abroad.

The Department of Science and Technology (DST) which was set up in 1971, has been assigned the responsibility of formulating policy statements and guidelines on science and technology; promoting new areas to science and technology; undertaking or financially sponsoring scientific and technological surveys, research design and development, supporting national research institutions and scientific bodies. It also coordinates all activities relating to international science and technology. It also provides support to the Science Advisory Council to the Prime Minister, the National Science Advisory Council to the Prime Minister, the National Science and Technology Entrepreneurship Development Board, the National Council for Science and Technology Communication and the Technology Information Forecasting and Assessment Council.

Over the years, the Department has made sustained efforts to promote and accelerate the development of science and technology in the areas relevant to social application, coordination of inter-disciplinary multi-institution programmes and providing support to academic and other research institutions for carrying out basic and applied research. The Department has been catalytic and instrumental in identifying, formulating and implementing a large number of programmes with the help of the expertise available within the country and abroad, in frontline emerging areas such as biotechnology, materials, plasma physics, etc. These programmes are ultimately expected to yield results of direct relevance to national development.

The two existing promotion schemes, viz. General Research Scheme and Science and Engineering Research Council have been integrated into one, i.e. R&D funding mechanism. The broad objectives of this scheme are: (i) to promote research in newly emerging and front-line areas of science and engineering including multi-disciplinary fields, and (ii) to selectively promote general research capabilities in relevant areas of science and engineering, taking into account, existing research capabilities of most of the institutions.

As a part of promotional programme, emphasis has also been given to encourage participation of younger scientists in science and technology activities by providing them support for creative research through project support, and for participation in international conferences. Besides, they are provided opportunities to interact with eminent scientists through contact programmes. As a part of this scheme, a new programme has also been initiated to support young research workers who have extra spark of originality and motivation.

The Department has specific programmes to promote science and technology and its application to benefit specific disadvantaged groups. These are : (1) Scheme for Young Scientists; (2) Science and Technology Application for Rural Development; (3) Science and Technology for Women; (4) Science and Technology for Weaker Section; and (5) Utilisation of Scientific Expertise of retired Scientists, in chosen areas of science and technology was initiated in 1986 for building national capability in selected frontline areas through training of talented youth under the guidance of pioneering experts at reputed international centres and utilising their talent to further expand the expertise base of our institutions.

The specially designed programmes on this objective relate to: (i) assistance to professional bodies, learned societies and science academics; (ii) support for participation of Indian scientists in major international scientific conferences; (iv) setting up of regional scientific instrumentation centres; (v) long-term support to scientific research institutions; and (vi) assistance to states and union territories to established councils for science and technology.

Long-term institutional infrastructural requirements for science and technology are met through the creation of autonomous and independent structures under the overall umbrella of the Department. The states are also encouraged to set up secretariats and councils for science and technology which act as focal points for planning, coordinating and promoting science and technology activities. The councils for science and technology or departments of science and technology have been set up in nearly all the states and union territories.

The engineering and technology schemes cover research and development activities related to industrial, social, regional and consumer requirements in addition to research in frontline areas. The applied research is sponsored in close cooperation with industry and user agencies to build up competence in various sectors and to achieve self-reliance. Major activities under the scheme are: (i) Thrust area programmes—research and development projects are being encouraged and supported in the areas of : (a) member separation processes, (b) irrigation and water management, and (c) robotics, (ii) Newer, fibres and composites initiated in 1975. This programme has centred around development of specific fibres and resin systems along with development of equipment and setting up of regional test laboratories and is now directed towards introducing polymers and their composites into industry through design, development and manufacture of specific products. The projects cover areas of: (a) polymer alloys, (b) applications as bio-materials, (c) wider application for international aids, (d) scale-up of impregnating pitch, (e) specific application in two wheelers, four-wheelers, automobiles, marine vessels and aircrafts, and (f) commercialisation of terephthalamide fibre, (iii) cryogenics and ceramics—work on design, fabrication and testing of liquid nitrogen plant of 10 litres per hour is continuning till the technology gets commercialised in 1991. An integrated programme of design, development and fabrication of a liquid helium plant to meet indigenous conditions and requirements will be supported until it is commercialised in 1994, and (iv) National Coordination of Testing and Calibration Facilities—this programme had been formulated essentially to ensure an improved quality of industrial products, provide consumer protection and promote export of industrial goods. The objectives of the scheme are: establishment of accreditation/recognition by the Central Government of testing facilities in various sectors; setting up hierarchy of calibration facilities suited to the national needs. About 200 laboratories are exposed to be accredited soon.

The National "Science and Technology Entrepreneurship development Board, established in 1982, has been devoting attention to provide increasing opportunities of gainful self-employment for science and technology persons since its inception. Some of the major prograrmmes initiated are: (a) organisation of entrepreneurship development programmes; (b) creation of entrepreneurial awareness through camps; (c) setting up of science and technology entrepreneur parks; (d) establishment of entrepreneurship development cells in academic institutions; (e) setting up of task forces in selected backward districts for identifying resources, skill and need-based entrepreneurial opportunities for S&T persons; (f) training teachers from colleges and universities in the development of entrepreneurship skills; (g) introduction of entrepreneurship in course curricula of engineering degree, diploma and science courses; (h) encouraging group employment schemes, and (i) bringing our publications, videos and related materials.

The main focus of the activities of the Board has been on promotion of entrepreneurship in small-scale sector by S&T persons. About 456 new units have been set up through these measures. It has also been consistently promoting close interaction between academic institutions and industries to bring about up gradation in products, processes and equipments and also for commercialisation of indigenous technologies. In addition, about 2,600 jobs have been created on a sustained basis.

O O O

# 11. POWER RESOURCES OF INDIA

The country's coal resources are placed at about 112 billion tonnes. But these are unevenly distributed, mostly occurring in the eastern and central parts of the country. The present rate of coal raising which is about 1400 million tonnes per annum is required to go up to about 1700 million tonnes by the year 2010. Assuming 50 per cent recovery of the reserves in the ground, the depletion time will only be about 120 years.

Moreover, the ash in Indian coal is highly abrasive and poses serious problems to power plant equipments. Coal prices over the last 15 years have been rising at a faster rate than general inflation and this trend is likely to continue in future. Coming to the environmental aspects of burning coal for power generation, it is now recognised worldwide that acid rain is a major environmental hazard.

In view of these factors, energy planners are agreed that a gradual shift from coal to other energy sources is essential from the long-term point of view. So far as hydel power is concerned, there are increasing difficulties of valuable forest areas and problems posed by rehabilitation of relatively large populations. It is also not clear, if the present level of production of oil and gas (on-shore and off shore) which is about two third of the present consumption, could be maintained during the next 15 to 20 years. Electricity generation based on gas which is now being considered on a limited scale due to temporary availability of gas is not a long-term solution.

Alternative sources of energy such as solar, wind, and bio-gas are diffused and can only have limited applicability.

Thus, when one looks at the energy situation on a total basis in a long-term perspective, it is evident that some new forms of energy such as nuclear which could make a large addition to the energy resources has to be developed in a big way. The currently known uranium reserves in the country can support a pressurised Heavy Water Reactor Programme of about 10,000 MW. However, with continuing efforts being made on exploration, it is likely that additional uranium deposits may be identified as has been the experience in the case of oil and natural gas.

The long range potential of nuclear energy in India also depends on fast breeder reactors. Even with the existing proven reserved of 70,000 tonnes of uranium, it is possible to attain an ultimate capacity of about 3,50,000 MW by the latter half of 21st century using heavy water reactors followed by fast breeders.

The question of safety of nuclear reactors and consequences of their normal and off-normal operations have been receiving the most intensive attention for over 40 years, right from the time work was undertaken on the design and construction of the very early reactors. In fact, the subject of reactor safety, which in earlier days was called "Reactor Hazards Evaluation", has received greater attention than even the question of design itself. More people have been involved in the analysis of safety of reactor systems than in the design of the systems themselves. Some of the Indian engineers and scientists have been trained formally in reactor safety and hazards evaluation as part of their initial orientation of reactor design work. So far as the performance of Indian reactors is concerned, their safety record has been good. There are six units in operation and from the point of view of plant personnel, general public or the environment, no serious problem has arisen in them.

Simultaneously, with the commencement of the design effort on a reactor project, a Design Safety Committee has been set up for that project consisting of people now engaged on the design of the reactor unit. The Department of Atomic Energy Safety Review Committee (DAESRC), consisting of experts in different disciplines and not involved in the actual designing, building or running of the plant carries out a second level review and audit.

There is yet another review by the Atomic Energy Regulatory Board (AERB). In the construction and operational phases also, reviews are carried out at these levels. Thus, there is a well-organised system of reviews and these result in a fool-proof system of evaluation of designs and operating practices. The different safety committees are also empowered to call for either a reduction of power level or even closure of an operating unit if in their opinion, running of the unit constitutes danger either to the plant or plant personnel or to the general public.

There is a system of keeping track of all 'unusual occurrence'. What is called an 'unusual occurrence' in the jargon of nuclear reactor technology is really not so unusual in normal life. For example, when a pump or diesel generator is started by pressing its push button and if it does not start, the event is called an 'unusual occurrence' even though it might not have any implications so far as the safety of reactor is concerned.

In the case of nuclear reactors, all these unusual occurrences, no matter how insignificant, are systematically documented, reviewed and analysed to find out the cause of the incident and for taking corrective actions by way of design modification, revision of operating procedure or replacement of a component with one having much higher reliability. A single 'unusual occurrence' cannot give rise to any concern about the safety of the plant operators or the general public. The design of the reactor installation foresees that malfunctioning of components or systems can take place and this should not result in a compromise to the safety of the installation. This approach of analysing all unusual occurrences is unique to the nuclear industry and has contributed in a great measure towards making nuclear power production, a safe activity.

In a nuclear reactor, the basic process of production of heat is by the splitting or fissioning of uranium nuclei. In this process, the heat which is liberated is carried away by a coolant. In the reactors at Rajasthan, Chennai and the ones coming up at Narora and Kakrapar, the reactor coolant is heavy water. The heat produced in the reactors is transferred from this heavy water to ordinary water flowing in the steam generator. The steam drives the turbine generator to produce fission electricity. When the uranium nuclei splits, it produces fission products which are radioactive. Special measures are taken to ensure that this radioactivity is safely contained under all circumstances. There are many barriers which ensure that the radioactivity is contained. First, there is the cladding of the fuel which is an alloy of zirconium. The fuel bundles are placed inside the closed heat transport system which consists of high pressure components made from special steel or zirconium alloys. The entire reactor system is surrounded by a massive containment building. (In the case of Kalpakkam and subsequent reactors, the containment buildings housing the nuclear reactor have a special feature—the double containment).

In order to ensure that the spread of radioactivity is prevented under all circumstances, the design of these barriers, the quality control measures taken in the manufacture of the components, building and structures and the surveillance of quality in service, are all maintained at an extremely high level.

One of the most important questions concerning the safety of nuclear reactors is to ensure that adequate cooling is provided for the nuclear fuel at all time including periods when the reactor is in a shutdown condition. Normally, the cooling of the nuclear fuel is done by the heavy water of the primary heat transport system. When the reactor has been shut down for some time, the quantum of heat decay is such that it is more appropriate to provide cooling through another system which is called "shutdown cooling" and one system is adequate for safe cooling of the reactor. The "main cooling" through the steam generated by the process of natural convection, that is, without the intervention of any pumps, is also adequate to carry away the decay heat.

Special provisions are made in the design to ensure that adequate cooling of the fuel takes place even when there is a rupture in primary heat transport system, leading to large escape of heavy water from the reactor system. In such a condition, continued cooling of the nuclear fuel is maintained through an emergency core cooling system which provides cold water from three different resources. As a further backup, the cold heavy water moderator in the reactor vessel, which surrounds the fuel channels, can serve as an important heat sink in some postulated severe accident sequences involving loss of normal coolant simultaneous with failure of emergency core cooling. This practice can be called "defence in depth" concept where there are many lines of defence, one backing another. Even in the case of no external power supply to the reactor installation, on-site power through emergency diesel generators and batteries is provided to ensure effective cooling of the nuclear fuel.

○ ○ ○

# 12. Satellite Communications Of India Compared With Those Of The West

Before going into India's efforts in satellite communications field, it would be worthwhile to review the international scene-growth and status of technology and applications. In 1945,

Arthur Clarks predicted that the geosynchronous orbit at an altitude of about 36,000 kms will be the most suitable orbit for communications. A satellite in this Orbit "views" about one third of the surface of earth, and hence three such satellites could provide global communications. Thus, while SPUTNIK heralded the space age in 1957, SYNCOM-I, a geo-synchronous satellite; later renamed Early-Bird ushered in the era of operational satellite communication in 1964.

The extensive use of satellites for global communications started with the formation of INTELSAT in April, 1965. Since then the membership of INTELSAT has undergone considerable changes, the basic objective of the international organisation namely providing international communications to the member states on a commercial basis at economical rates has remained. As of now, INTELSAT has launched five generations of satellites and more are under development. INTELSAT has also played a leading role in the development of requisite technology.

With the vast expanse of the Soviet Union, spanning eleven time zones, it was natural for erstwhile USSR to go in for satellite for domestic communication. Use of 12-hour orbit proved to be ideal for covering the higher latitudes (70 degree North) of USSR. Thus, MOLNIYA Satellite in conjunction with the ORBITA ground system provided domestic satellite communications for quite sometime till the emphasis gradually shifted to geosynchronous satellite, which could cover most of the populated regions and regions of population growth. At present, USSR operates many geostationary satellite systems (such as Stationar, Raduge, Gorizont, etc.) to provide a variety of communication services including communications to remote and isolated communities, medical guidance and education through such links, etc. With its Anik-C and Anik-D series, Canada has also started Direct Broadcasting of TV programmes from satellites as an interim measure.

The real explosion of satellite communication system in the developed world can really be attributed to the far-reaching decisions taken in the USA regarding irregulation of communications environment in the late seventies. This led to commercialisation and diversification of the market and also demand for new services that could best be provided with satellites. The increased competition also led the new entrants to the choice of satellite medium for conventional telecommunication where it proved to be economical. Further, the regulations on receive-only terminals was done away with. This almost "opensky" approach led to the establishment of several satellite systems, some of them exclusively for special applications such as business and data communications. However, most of the capacity built-up is being used primarily for TV programme distribution.

The Western Europe, which has had a fairly good terrestrial communication system was also late in going for a satellite-based communication system, though certain experimental programmes had been underway for quite a while. However, the establishment of European Space Agency and EUTELSAT hastened the process and presently, several systems, some covering Western Europe as a whole and some meant only for particular countries (e.g., France and Italy) are being established. Japan has also established domestic satellite communication systems and has indeed been the first country to experiment with a 20-30 GHz satellite. Australia is also establishing a satellite system for domestic communications and broadcasting.

Indonesia was the first amongst the developing countries to establish an operational communications satellite system called PALAPA in 1976. Satellite system is ideally suited to provide the vital communications infrastucture in a fairly large country consisting of more than 13,000 islands spread over a large ocean areas (extending from E-950-140E longitude). The capacity of PALAPA system (consisting of at present two satellites) is also leased to neighbouring countries like Malaysia and Thailand. Several other developing countries like Brazil, Argentina, etc. also have initiated the process for setting up satellite systems. Twenty-two Arab countries have joined together to establish a regional satellite system called ARABSAT.

The first ARABSAT satellite is expected to be launched in 2015. China which has a strong and fairly advanced space programme launched its own experimental geostationary communications satellite in 1984 with a Chinese launch vehicle. China has also leased INTELSAT capacity for domestic communications and has announced plans for establishing a TV broadcast satellite system. In fact, it is expected that by the end of this decade more than 50 countries will lease about 90 transponders from INTELSAT for domestic use.

The rapid growth of communication satellites can be judged by the fact that there is a large number of satellites that occupy the geostationary orbit in the Indian ocean region. This has also led to the crowding of orbit and the frequency spectrum both of which are reusable natural resources. Though the resources of orbit-spectrum are not depletable, when one country is using a particular portion, no one else could use the same. This constraint has given rise to the apprehension on the part of many countries that have no need to establish a geostationary satellite communication system immediately (but may want to do so at a later time), that the early starters may pre-empt the resources. A World Radio Administrative Conference under the aegis of the International Telecommunication Union took place in two sessions in 1985 and 1988 to come to the grips of the issue of equitable use of the orbit-spectrum.

India has taken a path of planned self-reliance in the field of satellite communication in the spirit of international co-operation. India has done reasonably well in this field, thanks to the vision and efforts of the founders of space programme. It is, thus, that while the first training centre was established with the assistance of United Nations Development Programme, the Satellite Instructional Television Experiment (SITE) was conducted with the active collaboration of the USA.

The ATS-6 satellite, with a design life of two years and costing about Rs. 200 crores, was made available to India for conducting one-year experiment.

SITE is still the largest experiment in human communication for national development. It was conducted in 2,330 villages dispersed over 20 districts in six economically backward states for a period of one year. SITE was a leap forward in the use of satellite technology of direct broadcasting for educational and developmental purposes.

SITE was an innovative venture as for the first time, both technical (hardware) and social (software) aspects of the experiment were carefully studied for evolving a future satellite-based television broadcasting system in India. Both in production and engineering, several innovations have been made to meet the challenge. In case of social evaluation, more or less field experimental design has been followed to measure the effect on the rural TV viewers largely unexposed to any mass media prior to commencement of the experiment.

TV viewing directly triggered the process of change in which illiterate women and men gained knowledge of health innovations and family planning at least as much as literate men and women. It also led to adoption of some of the agricultural practices which were not dependent upon external and specialised information and least dependent upon agricultural developmental agencies and their infrastructure.

Significant gain in empathy, educational and occupational aspiration for male children was found. In the area of political socialisation, the illiterate rather than literate male viewers showed greater gain. In overall modernity, both attitudinal as well as in behavioural information, significant gain was observed.

SITE has been hailed as the largest communication experiment conducted anywhere, and the success achieved is due to the end approach adopted. SITE was preceded by study of national developmental needs, the possible approaches and the technical and economic aspects. While SITE concentrated on satellite TV broadcasting to community receivers, it was followed by experiments in telecommunications (telephony, data communications, etc.) using the Franco-German satellite SYMPHONE and APPLE.

Through a series of experiments has been gained very valuable experience in hardware, software and management of satellite based system which is relevant for operational systems.

INSAT System will introduce three special series on a semi-operational basis. There are Disaster Warning System, News Dissemination Service and Time Dissemination Service. In all these cases, simple and inexpensive receivers will be located in the user premises and these will receive the information broadcast from one or more central locations. The Disaster Warning System will have an added feature in that the Cyclone Warning Centre could selectively address through the Satellite, a group of receivers located in a zone that is likely to be hit by a cyclone. The News Dissemination Service will offer a combination of facsimile transmission and several channels of teleprinter messages so that the user can select the type of news or information that is of his/her interest. All the stations of All India Radio (over 100) will be networked for National Programmes of news through four channels using INSAT. A simple scheme has been evolved for this purpose. One channel is also available for regional programme distribution and for programme exchange between regional centres on a time-shared basis.

INSAT also carries a Data Relay Transponder which is used to collect meteorological data from about 110 remote and unattended Data Collection Platforms. Similarly, the VHRR imageries transmitted by INSAT are being disseminated to twenty meteorological offices through a combination of satellite and terrestrial media.

The TV broadcasting relies on INSAT to a great extent. Except for 9 locations which are connected through a terrestrial microwave link, all other stations of Doordarshan are networked though the satellite using TV Receive Only terminals (TVRO). The massive expansion of TV coverage in the country by deployment of about 200 Low Power Transmitters (LPT) in conjunction with TVROs is a major step in meeting a long felt need. However, the most important feature of INSAT communication applications and technology and plans is that it is the first satellite with S-band Community TV broadcast capability. INSAT-I has two high-powered transponders for TV broadcasting and Direct Community TV Receivers with 3.6 metre mesh antenna are being batch -produced in the country.

The global scenario in Satellite Communications is changing fast. Though, for Fixed Satellite Service (primarily telecommunication, TV distribution, data communications, etc. between fixed locations) the 4 and 6 GHz band is still widely in use, there is an increasing trend to utilise the higher frequency bands.

The Eighties was the decade of information revolution in India. The satellite broadcasting, telecommunications and remote sensing which were mere buzz words in foreign journals and magazines became a reality.

The age of satellite technology dawned with the launch of first of the INS AT-I series-INSAT-IA in 1982. The plan was for launching two satellites in the air, recalls U.R. Rao, Chairman of the Space Commission, "one providing the benefits, the other, an on-orbit spare." But the bird in the sky, was a disaster. In the spring of 1982, the much publicised mulipurpose satellite, expected to revolutionise broadcasting, telecommunications and meteorology jammed its solar sail. An INTELSAT satellite had to be leased to fulfil the needs of the country.

As India waited for INSAT-IB's launch the following year, "television was born," says O.P. Khushu, Doordarshan's Chief Engineer. The year 1982 saw the launch of the national network linking seven programme producing centres, switching from black and white to colour, and hosting the Asian Games. It was in this year that Doordarshan earned more money than ever before—Rs. 1000 crores.

It took another year for the sister satellite INSAT-IB to be launched. And the benefits were immediately visible. The government decided to expand coverage to 70 per cent of the population. It was not possible if India continued with high power transmitters. So, Doordarshan switched to low power transmitters, and the isogstics changed. Khushu recalls how it happened. "Normally", he says, "the low power transmitters need civil and infrastructural support. The three or four rooms in a vantage location. The power constraint was eliminated as well. The LPT consumes one kilowatt of power—what one consumed in a household, as against the HPT consumption of 100 KW. The LPT can be produced like a consumer product—with indigenous know-how." But hardware was not all. The blueprint that emerged from the Asian Games came in handy in handling the NAM and CHOGM conferences, several festivals abroad and the Cricket World Series.

With giant strides in Doordarshan's hardware and a boost to its software capabilities, India began to feel the real impact of broadcasting. The morning and afternoon shows also entered the Doordarshan arena. Doordarshan also started sponsoring its own programmes—documentaries, telefilms, serials, and feature films.

Latest development in the satellite technology have been useful in other areas as well. R.P. Sirkar, the director of the meteorological department says: "In November 1977, in Orissa cyclone, about 10,000 people perished. During a similar cyclone in 2003, the death toll was less than one thousand, because of timely warning by the satellites". In another sphere, IRS-IA which was launched from Baikanaur cohesmodrome in Russia, helped India join the pantheon of SPOT and Landsat remote-sensing from Europe and the US. This satellite has a number of successes to its credit. It has monitored recent floods in Brahmaputra. It has also helped in delineating agro-climatic zones for significant inputs in agriculture planning, mapping forestry and wasteland, locating ground water, geological mapping and in integrated drought management.

The satellite technology has really made revolutionary changes in the field of long distance communications. It has made the world one by linking cities of the world with each other. Almost 65 per cent telecommunications in India is through INSAT. Rao says that within a period of three years the entire cost of the satellite Rs. 675 million was recovered, the bulk from leasing telecom services. The satellites have also helped India truly reach out to the masses. "The specialised field of the expert has become the province man in the street."

O O O

# 13. SPACE RESEARCH IN INDIA

The Indian Space Research Organisation (ISRO) is responsible for the planning, execution and management of space research activities and space application programmes of this Department. It is engaged in the development and fabrication of various categories of rockets and satellites for different application programmes. Along with it, facilities for launching rockets and test and evaluation of allied sub systems are being established. On the space application site, development of various instrumentations and systems either have been accomplished or are in hand in the fields of satellite telecommunication. TV broadcasting and reception via a satellite, remote-sensing of natural resources and of meteorological parameters from a satellite, etc. It conducts training courses in the satellite communication technology which are attended 'by trainees from many developing countries.

ISRO operates and maintains the Thumba Equatorial Rocket Launching Station (TERLS) and encourages international collaboration in space research experiments using rockets. It is the sponsoring agency for the Indian scientist to participate in the space research programmes supported by foreign space agencies.

The Thumba Equatorial Rocket Launching Station (TERLS), the first establishment in India for space research using rockets, became operational with the launching of a sounding rocket, on 21st November, 1963, for the investigation of the upper atmosphere. Thumba is located about eight kilometers north of Thiruvananthapuram and the magnetic equator passed very close to it. Due to the presence of the magnetic equator, the study of the upper atmosphere and ionosphere of this region has great scientific importance and this is the reason for establishing the rocket launching range at Thumba. Besides, there is no other rocket launching range on the magnetic equator anywhere in the world. So, the Thumba range has fulfilled the long felt need of the international scientific community for studying the equatorial ionosphere with the help of sounding rockets. The United Nations has recognised this range as an international facility. Since its establishment, scientists from different countries—the USA, erstwhile USSR, the UK. France, West Germany, Japan have conducted many scientific experiments from TERLS using rockets in close collaboration with the Indian scientists. The areas of investigation include meteorology, neutral upper atmosphere, ionosphere and X-Ray astronomy. So far, about 350 rockets have been launched from Thumba for scientific experiments and many of these rockets have been supplied by those countries whose scientists have participated in collaborative experiments from this range. Since December, 1965, TERLS has been functioning as a UN sponsored facility.

Actions were initiated in 1965 to set up an experimental satellite communications earth station (ESCES) at Ahmedabad for providing first hand experience and training the Indian engineers in this new field. The station became operational in 1967 and has since been conducting training courses which are being attended not only by the Indian engineers but also engineers from many developing countries in Asia, Africa and East Europe. Thus, ESCES is functioning as an international training centre in satellite communications technology.

At present the major establishments under ISRO/ Department of Space are the following:

(a) The Vikram Sarabhai Space Centre (VSSC) at Thumba near Trivandrum; and its advanced laboratory in Bangalore (Bengaluru) for building the satellites, the Indian Scientific Satellite Project (ISSP);

(b) The Space Applications Centre (SAC) at Ahmedabad;

(c) The SHAR Centre on the Sriharikota Island in Andhra Pradesh.

The Vikram Sarabhai Space Centre (VSSC) is primarily devoted to activities oriented towards space technology, with the objective of achieving self-reliance in these fields. From its inception, the VSSC has created the necessary infrastructure in diversified fields for this purpose. Specific achievements of this centre can be traced to the areas of rocket experiments from the Thumba range and technology development projects.

VSSC has developed Menaka series of rockets specifically meant for meteorological purposes. The regular weekly launchings of the Soviet M-l00 rockets since December, 1970, under collaboration with the Hydro Meteorological Services of the USSR have provided meteorological data in atmospheric temperatures and wind conditions, for synthesis of statistical models for weather prediction. Feasibility studies are being made for suppression of hailstorms, experienced in the northern parts of the country through launching of rockets for releasing hail suppression materials over hail formations.

Extensive rocket experiments have also been carried out for measurement of parameters of the ionosphere and the equatorial electro jet. These have thrown light on the processes involved in the ionosphere and the cyclic changes that occur in the ionospheric medium throughout the year and at specific periods of intense solar activity and magnetic storms.

In addition, propagation characteristics of the ionospheric regions have been determined through ground-based experiments and also experiments using international ionsopheric sounding satellites.

Fabrication process, involving fiberglass winding and helical welding of steel strips for production of rocket chambers, have been developed, which would be useful to industries. requiring lightweight structures. Already, know-how developed for production of fibre glass components have found application in electrical industries and the telecommunications industry. Typical spin-off products include switching levers, whip aerials and parabolic reflectors using fiberglass material.

The Rocket Propellant plant set up as early as 1969 has been producing various types of propellant grains with diameters ranging from 75 mm to 1000'ntnl and weighing 10 kg to 3,000 kg. Even though initially the ingredients were to be imported, very good progress has been made to use mostly indigenous materials at present.

Control components have been developed for high performance and high accuracy requirements which find applications in the aerospace industry. These include rate gyroscopes, hydraulic and pneumatic components and a range of electromechanical and optical transducers. In this process, precision fabrication technology has been developed to a remarkable degree. A pressure transducer unit has been set up at Bengaluru which will supply pressure transducers against the requirements of European space programme.

In the field of electronics, significant contributions have been made which are in the nature of augmenting national capability in this sophisticated field. Miniaturisation has been affected in the product design. Radio frequency transmitters, receivers, signal conditioners and encoders, etc. have been developed and tested to withstand the rigour of rocket flights. Miniature onboard data processors are also being designed for specific applications. These have found wide utility in aircraft industries, meteorological research and ultimately in communication satellites of our own when we decide to go for them. Peripheral equipments including those required for electronic data processing systems have been developed indigenously and the know-how for some of the products has been transferred to Kerala State Electronic Development Corporation. These include X- Y plotters and digital incremental plotters. A range of ground support facilities have been indigenously developed to augment the capabilities of the rocket launching range which find potential application in other industries as well. Ground stations for receiving data from rocket payloads and satellites have been developed and these will find application III data collection and remote control.

A surveillance radar has been developed and installed in the rocket launching range. Such equipment would find use in surveillance at sea coasts and airports. A medium range tracking radar has been designed and developed indigenously which will find application in tracking aircrafts, meteorological balloons, rockets arid missiles. The significant feature of this project is the pooling of expertise from various agencies like TIFR, BARC and ECIL for development of sophisticated subsystems.

In the field of education, lasting contributions have been made by this centre through design of curricula for courses in Space Technology as well as space sciences. Management and co-ordination of the efforts of about 3,000 scientists and technicians of varied disciplines to realise major space projects will be a trend-setter for the management of large scale and complex projects in the country.

The first Indian satellite, Aryabhatta, was launched from a Soviet Cosmodrome on 19th April, 1975, into a 600 km near -circular earth orbit. The primary objective of this programme was to establish in India, capability in satellite technology more explicitly, to design and fabricate indigenously, a space-worthy system and evaluate its performance in orbit, evolve the methodology of conducting a series of complex operations on the tracking system besides the establishment of the relevant infrastructure for the fabrication of such sophisticated spacecraft systems.

The operation of Aryabhatta can be broadly evaluated under four major headings-satellite technological systems, technological experiments of relevance to our future programme, scientific experiments and performance of ground stations.

The successful launching of the satellite and its performance in orbit have shown that the satellite structure is round and space-worthy. The primary sources of power, namely 18,000 blue-violet silicon solar cells mounted on the body of the satellite and the chemical batteries are functioning properly. The primary power source energises 14 different regulated power lines which provide specially conditioned power to the various equipments on the satellite. Out of these, only one power line, which is connected to the scientific experiments package, showed some malfunction. Due to this, the scientific experiments had to be switched off after the first four days of operations.

The temperature of the outer skin of the satellites varies from about +1000°C to –600°C during each orbit as the satellite goes from the sunlit to the dark hemisphere. For proper functioning, the temperature inside the satellite where all the equipments are mounted, should be controlled. The passive temperature control method adopted for this purpose is working extremely well and is maintaining the inside temperature within the design limits of 0.0°C and 400°C.

In order to dynamically stabilise the satellite in orbit, it was spun at 50 revolutions per minute (rpm) on the fourth day after launch by releasing compressed dry air from one of the six spherical titanium bottles. Due to the electromagnetic force, in space, the spin rate decreases with time thus requiring the satellite to be re-spun periodically. Since, during the first three months, the spin rate has decreased from 50 to only 28 rpm, the available gas onboard the satellite should be sufficient for 600 days as against the earlier estimate of 180 days. In other words, the satellite performance has far exceeded earlier expectations, primarily due to the care taken in its fabrication in ensuring its magnetic cleanliness.

The data from the satellite which is transmitted to the ground in a coded form are regularly being received at ground stations located at Sriharikota (SHAR), Bangalore (Bengaluru) and Bears Lake (near Moscow). To enhance the data coverage, tape recorders are installed in the satellite which can transmit the data stored for 40 minutes in 4 minutes. Telemetry down-link from the satellite has been functioning so well that strong signals are being received at the ground stations even when the satellite is just over the horizon. Likewise, the performance of the telecommand system has been very satisfactory—all the commands sent to the satellite have been executed faithfully.

A number of· technical experiments, having relevance to future ISRO programme, have been successfully conducted with the satellite. Several tones were sent to the satellite from the ground and through this tone-ranging technique, the distance to the satellite from the earth, as it passes over the ground station, has been measured to correct 1 km. One is familiar with the apparent change in the pitch of a railway engine whistle as it approaches or recedes from a platform. This is called the Doppler Principle. Using the same principle, the speed of the satellite has been measured correct to 20 metres per second (satellite speed is about 8 km per second).

Likewise, using the interferometric technique, the direction coordinates of the satellite have been obtained. With the successful completion ·of the tracking experiments, the first tracking network in India has now been established.

A communication experiment with the satellite has been successfully conducted by transmitting live voice messages from SHAR to Bangalore via the satellite. This has given valuable inputs which will be of use in the future communication satellite programme of ISRO.

Inspite of Aryabhatta being our first satellite, it is highly sophisticated. It has about 12,000 electronic components in addition to 18,000 solar cells and other mechanical parts. There are 25,000 interconnections within the satellite and the total amount of wire used, if stretched· across, exceeds 7 km in length.

India has become the first country in Asia to broadcast specially designed programmes for rural India with electricity generated from atomic power.

The programmes televised from SITE contain information on agriculture, animal husbandry, health and hygiene and other developmental areas such as special programmes for teachers' training and children's education, in addition to entertainment, in local idiom. The special programmes for school audiences are telecast every morning.

A direct broadcast satellite system of the magnitude involved in SITE, with the necessary infrastructure for maintenance, feedback and evaluation, has never been in operation before. For the first time in the country, a TV system has been designed and set up primarily for educational purposes by a team of people from fields as diverse as the social sciences education, programme production, physics and engineering. A variety of new managerial skills and techniques have been developed to harmonise this complex of expertise.

The earth station of AST is the prime earth station sending up programmes to the satellite and receiving and monitoring the signals from the satellite. This station is equipped with a solid 14-metre diameter parabolic antenna and is capable of tracking the satellite. A separate 7 metre diameter antenna has been installed to receive the SITE programme sent up from Delhi to the satellite. These are relayed to the Pij (in Kheda district of Gujarat) transmitter using a cable and microwave link. The back-up earth station at Delhi has a l0-metre diameter antenna and is used to transmit news and other national programmes from Delhi. It also receives programmes emanating from Ahmedabad and is connected to the terrestrial TV station of AIR via cable. The earth station at Amritsar is connected to the TV transmitter in that city. A beacon station set up in Nagpur helps the satellite to keep pointing towards the centre of India.

The other field of major activity at SAC is to develop expertise in remote sensing technology for its diverse applications. Remote sensing is the derivation of information about terrestrial features and phenomena from a distance using visible and invisible electromagnetic radiations emitted or scattered by features and phenomena at or near the earth's surface. It is also capable of monitoring pollution on a global basis. The really new thing is the use of light, invisible to the human eye.

The ambitious Satellite Instructional Television Experiment (SITE) was launched in 1975. It covered in a single simultaneous sweep, 2400 villages in six states, having four different languages. The experiment covered about 1,500 hours of television programmes, the bulk of which were produced by Doordarshan. Various evaluation studies commended the experiment for contributing substantially to' a gain in knowledge and a positive change in the attitude of viewers. India launched the INSAT for the expansion of television in the country. INSAT-IA had to be abandoned in 1982 because of certain technical snags, but INSAT-IB has been fully operational since October, 1983. The satellite is being utilised for radio and television, telecommunications and meteorological purposes. In the case of television, it serves to carry programme to rural and tribal' areas in the remote parts of the country.

Instructional in nature, the INSAT programmes can be broadly calssified as: area-specific items like rural programmes and educational programmes for primary school children. The area-specific programmes have their thrust on agriculture, animal husbandry, health and hygiene, family welfare, adult education, social awareness, national integration, weather forecast and ·topical hints to farmers. The bulk: of these programmes are required to be prepared in field areas. The programme planning is being done by Doordarshan producers, in consultation with various allied departments in the Central and State Governments.

O O O

# 14. WONDERS OF MODERN SCIENCE

Science is all-inclusive and very comprehensive and touches the life of everyone in more ways than we can imagine. It has taken huge strides during the last 4-5 decades. Its achievements, discoveries and inventions have been really fantastic and wonderful. It has been pushing forward with a terrific speed in every walk of our lives. Life without science and its various boons is unthinkable. In the field of energy, agriculture, entertainment, medicine, armament, space, computer application, communication, transportation, to name just a few areas, science has revolutionised our life. It has helped man conquer diseases, distance, space and the forces of nature. Nations have come much closer now to one another and the interdependence, cooperation and interaction among them have tremendously increased. The whole world has now turned into a global village.

Man's thirst for knowledge, discovery, inventions and self-expansion are limitless. He is an ambitious and highly intelligent being always engaged in pushing farther and farther the limits of his knowledge and enlightenment. Science is the name of the process by which man satisfies these urges and aspirations. Science has helped in understanding and solving the mysteries of nature. And it is just a beginning because the knowledge is very vast, deep, limitless and wonderful. The beginning has been marvellous and augurs well for the humanity. Man is now on board in excellent ship of science in the vast and uncharted oceans of knowledge. So, he is ready to face any challenge, brave any storm, however violent and strong. The search, the quest for the truth goes on, on and on.

Science has made life easy, convenient, comfortable, better and more meaningful. Science has made many dreams come true. It has helped him to reach the moon and other planets and soon he may go beyond the solar system in a very big way.

Satellite communication has ushered in an unprecedented revolution in information technology. Fax, E-mail, video-conferencing, roaming mobile phones, etc. are now very common things. Information technology has entered into the era of internet, worldwide web, highway and super highway. The discovery of atomic energy and its increasing use has been one of the greatest achievements of modern science. It has been as significant as the discovery of the wheel and fire in the primitive stage of human progress and evolution. It has opened new floodgates of progress, development and achievements, despite the tragedies like Chernobyl where a nuclear reactor exploded on April 28, 1986, which sent a huge cloud of radiation over Sweden, Finland, Norway and Denmark besides Russia itself.

Science is knowledge, and knowledge is power. Now, we must know how to use this power to our advantage and not to our destruction and ruin. Science in itself is neither good nor evil and neither, blessing nor a curse. It is its use which makes it good or bad. That is why it is rightly said that science is a good servant but a bad master. Science is a means and not an end in itself and should be used as a servant, as a means, an implement to improve the quality of life. The misuse and abuse of science and its inventions are bound to make life horrible, a nightmare and trauma. That is certain and man must set his priorities, programmes and policies in the light of this bare fact.

In the fields of medicine, hygiene, .nutrition and surgery, the achievements of science have been equally excellent. Heart-transplantations and that of other organs are now very common. Many fatal diseases have been eradicated or are on the way of eradication. And yet diseases like HIV/AIDS, malaria, cancer, etc. are to be conquered and eradicated. Necessity is the mother of invention. It is these challenges which inspire scientists to move on forward to new and better discoveries, achievements and inventions. Today, man feels more safe, secure and healthy in comparison to his forefathers. Man's longevity and life expectancy have now considerably increased and child and infant mortality decreased. Science has completely changed our outlook on life and things and many superstitions and blind beliefs are now things of the past. Remote satellite sensing helps us in forewarning of floods, earthquakes, droughts and other such natural calamities. Epidemics, famines, etc. are now no more there on such scales and frequencies as they used to be a half century ago.

In the field of entertainment, the boom in cinema, television, video, recorded music and cable network has brought entertainment to our door-steps and into our pockets. The technological and scientific wonders in the fields of biotechnology, genetic engineering, computer application, superconductivity, etc. have been really superb. Now, hybridisation of genes is possible under which a piece of DNA of one organism can be grafted on the DNA of another organism. Thus, 'cloning' has opened up vast opportunities and limitless possibilities in the field.

Similarly, a new generation of robots has taken the world by storm. A time was there when robots existed in science fiction only. Today, there are thousands of industrial robots. The first ever robot was produced in America in 1960. Since then, robotics has come a very long way of progress and phenomenal success. For example, Japanese scientists recently exhibited the humanoid robot or P-2, a remarkable man-machine which could walk, wander, detect and avoid obstacles. These new generation robots are wonder machines which can think and possess sense and even feel. These are remarkable advancements in the field of artificial and mechanical intelligence which make man really proud. The landing of American Sojourner Rover on Mars and its amazing exploratory work on the frozen Martian surface is another big achievement of modern science. The victory of the Deep Blue over the legendary Garry Kasparov is another example of scientific strides in the recent days. The IBM super computer Deep Blue created a chess history by defeating the reigning world champion in a classical match of the chess. But, it should not be taken as victory of the machine over man.

It is ultimately man who won because Deep Blue is only a machine and product of human intelligence. It has no brain of its own and no emotions, feelings and imagination at all. In the words of Dr. Feng Hsu, the research scientist connected with this super computer, "Deep Blue is less intelligent than the stupidest man on the Earth."

The fear that artificial and mechanical intelligence may enslave mankind and super computers have control on man are baseless and a figment of imagination. Such conceptions have no scientific foundations. No super computer or robot, however intelligent, sophisticated and advanced, can ever be self-determining as man. They cannot have the mind, creativity, feelings, imagination, hopes, and inspirations of a man. Man is the crown of creation and wisdom, and can never be overtaken by a machine. A machine cannot start by itself. It will always need human help to get going. It is basically wrong to think in terms of man v.s. machine. Machines are for man and not vice versa. Machines are simply tools and implements. They are programmed and set in motion by their maker, the man.

○ ○ ○

## 15. Ecotoxicology, Warfare and Ecology

Ecotoxicology is concerned with the toxic effects of chemical agents on living organisms, particularly on population and communities within a defined ecosystem. It includes the transfer chain reactions of those toxic elements and their close relationships with the given environment. Ecotoxicology is different from classical toxicology in that it is a four-pronged subject. Any assessment of the ultimate impact of a pollutant on the ecosystem must consider each of the four distinct processes, viz.:

(i) The chemical and physical form of the pollutant released into the environment and the medium into which it is released. The quantities, forms, types and sites of releases must be ascertained.

(ii) Changes effected in the pollutant by biotic and abiotic processes during the transit time, i.e. from the source of release to the receptor. The pollutants are transported geographically into different biotic phenomena and chemically transformed creating compounds with quite different toxic properties and environmental effects. The exact nature of these processes is not known for most of the pollutants and thus needs to be studied scientifically.

(iii) Quantitative metabolism of the transported pollutant and the receptor organism. This enables the calculation of accumulation of toxic agents in the available food chains and doses thereof to receptors. The identification of the nature of the target organism and the type of exposure to the transported pollutant is extremely important.

(iv) The effect of these doses or receptor individuals, populations and communities and the response of individual organism, population and community to specific pollutants over a given time scale has to be studied.

## History of Ecotoxicology

Environment contamination is not a new menace. The international efforts to initiate remedial measures probably originated from the widespread apprehensions caused by the atmospheric testing of nuclear weapons in the 1950s and 1960s. The United Nations created the Scientific Committee on the Effects of Atomic Radiation in 1955. Its aim was to assess the magnitude of environmental radiation and its hazards to human population. Later, individual environmentalists and some organisations studied and publicised the possible risks of large scale contamination by industrial chemicals either released intentionally in the form of pesticides, etc. or unintentionally during production processes.

In 1968, the United Nations decided to hold an International Conference on Environment at Swedish capital, later called the Stockholm Conference. Addressing the Conference, India's former Prime Minister stressed inter alia the need for adopting environment friendly ways and provide enough economic opportunities to tribals who live around forests so that they do not indulge in wanton deforestation. The idea was to preserve the natural purification system of the atmosphere and keep the toxic effects to the minimum. Most of the present day international environmental activities are organised in the light of Stockholm Conference.

## Scope

In the year 1969, the International Council of Scientific Unions (ICSU) formed the Scientific Committee on Problems of the Environment (SCOPE) to study the influence of human race on environment as well as the effects of environmental changes on human health and welfare. The Committee seeks to synthesise environmental information on following aspects:

(i)   Biochemical cycles,
(ii)  Evolution of ecosystems and other dynamic changes,
(iii) Human settlements and environment,
(iv)  Simulation modelling of environmental systems,
(v)   Ecotoxicology,
(vi)  Environment monitoring,
(vii) Communication of environmental and societal assessment and the response therefore.

Ecotoxicology is essentially a study of the effects of released pollutants on the environment and on the biota that inhabit it. Human beings are the most important of biotic atmosphere. They not only alter the environment but also produce the pollutants and release them into the environment. Hence, the growing importance of ecosophy, i.e. concern for environmental and ecological matters. The history, scope and significance of ecotoxicology were also reviewed by Trupant in 1975.

## Intake and Update of Pollutants

The entry of substance into the lungs, gastro-intestinal tract or subcutaneous regions of animals constitute intake. The fate of the taken material will be governed by the process of absorption. Uptake, on the other hand, is the absorption of the substance into extracellular fluid for systematic circulation. In this case, the fate of the taken material will be governed by the metabolic processes in the host.

In humans, the radio-nuclides are believed to be absorbed through skin. In an experiment, radioactive iodide applied to human skin, appeared in the thyroid gland. Oshorne, an eminent scientist showed in 1996 that in 'workmen', two-thirds of the total absorption of tritiated water vapour took place through lungs and one third by way of skin.

When a substance is inhaled by a person, it may be deposited in the nasopharyngeal regions, tracheo-bronchia or alveoli in the lungs. In all these regions, the substance is either absorbed into the extracellular fluids or transported to the pharynx from where it is swallowed into the digestive system. The most important site of absorption are the alveoli. Materials taken up from them either go to the blood stream or lymph.

## Results of Experiments

The results of some experiments conducted to study the toxic effects on animals are given below:

Dichlorobiophenyl is rapidly absorbed from the upper gastrointestinal tract and is taken to liver for metabolism and excretion through intestines. Thus, liver and intestines are prone to infection.

Dieldrin is absorbed the same way. However, the metabolic conversion is much slower; only a part of the substance is metabolised and excreted while the remaining amount is redistributed into the storage depot of adipose tissue for a repetition of the process. This results in weakening of the digestive system of the organism.

Methylmercury is absorbed by the aquatic animals like fish through their gills. The respiratory uptake depends on the rate of metabolism. Fish with higher metabolic rate have higher uptake and are more prone to be affected.

The knowledge of retention of a pollutant in the animal's body is useful to determine toxic effects. It is obtained either by estimation or the measurement of total amount excreted per unit time. Values have been fixed for tritiated water, lead, cobalt, etc. in humans and methylmercury in plants. The retention sometimes varies with the body weight. In experiments, specific values have been obtained for tritiated water, lead, cobalt and strontium for human beings and for methylmercury in aquatic plants like *Elodea* and *Utricularia*. Variations in retention time of caesium have been found in mammals depending upon their body weight. The organ or tissue of the body which is most affected by the uptake of a toxicant is called the critical organ. Sometimes, the concentration of heavy metals in hair is measured to calculate the concentration in the body. For instance, the concentration of methyl mercury in the hair is 300 times more than in blood.

## Absorption of Toxicants by Plants

Plants absorb toxicants either from soil or water through roots, or directly from the atmosphere. The usual pathway of absorpiton of gaseous pollutants is through the leaves. Other chemicals present in the atmosphere as particulate forms may be impacted into leaf surface but rarely reach the stomata. Such toxicants include: zinc, cadmium, lead, copper and nickel. Lead is known to gather on plants and trees that grow alongside highways in proportion to the flow and density of traffic. Sedimentation from atmosphere also contaminates soil and vegetation. Lead in the topsoil along roadside may be as high as 30 times that in the non-roadside soil. The introduction of lead-free petrol and CNG is therefore a welcome step for the health of greenery.

## Warfare and Ecology

Humanity got its first taste of destruction by an atomic weapon when America dropped atom bombs on Hiroshima and Nagasaki in August 1945. War in Europe was scientific enough with pilotless planes and rockets but the devastation caused in the Japanese cities was unheard of. A single bomb had killed as many, wounded as many, as a mass said of 279 huge aircrafts laden to capacity with bombs striking at a city ten times as populous.

The effects on those who were remove from immediate injury were also large. Many of them contracted wasting diseases where the corpuscles of the blood diminished. Surface wounds, grazes, abrasions and scratches closed and for no reason reopened. The red blood count and white blood count lost proportion.

Incalculable damage was done to environment and nature strived for years to re-establish her equilibrium.

## Gulf War I and II

During Gulf War I, heavy atmospheric clouds were formed over the skies of Arabian pennisula making US military operations difficult even during day time. The dense fog covering the entire area was in fact emission of oil soot that had wafted from over six hundred environmentally destructive oil well fires throughout Kuwait and drifted through the air for upto a radius of 1000 miles. The fires skewed million tons of carbon in the air resulting in the largest oil spill in history. It took fire crews nine months to put out the blazes. The intake and uptake of such large quantities of toxins by human, animals and vegetation was consequently huge and manifested themselves in various diseases, endangering and even extinction of certain prone species.

The United Nations Environment Programme (UNEP) and ecological experts have agreed that the ecological disaster brought by hi-tech Gulf War II will be even more astonishing.

## Immediate Effects

(i)   The Iraq and Arabian peninsula will witness change of surface and desert species affecting Iraqi tribes which are solely dependent on them. Hundreds of birds and sea species have already been killed by layers of thick, black oil spills.

(ii)  An extensive damage has been caused to Mesopotanian marshes, an area of connected lakes and floodplains along the Tigers and Euphrates.

(iii) About six million to eight million barrels of oil dumped into Indian Ocean created catastrohic oil slicks for sea animals. The oil also coated the shoreline and destroyed natural habitats for several species of reptiles.

(iv) Iraq is a major transit spot for migrant birds between European and African continents. Large groups of birds migrate to this place over land and sky every spring and autumn. The vast expanse of wetland and marshes in the south of Iraq are natural sanctuaries for tens of thousands of water birds. The modern weapons like depleted uranium, high-energy microwave and clustered bombs used by the US and allied armed forces are doing incalculable harm to these natural habitats and the species.

According to experts, nearly 40 species of rare water birds, crustaceans and mammals exterpated from the land of Iraq during Gulf War I. It is apprehended that current war may take a toll of over 70 types and sub-types due to toxic effects, surface contamination and destruction of natural habitats due to heavy bombardment, tank movement, landmines and other military operations.

Experts are of the opinion that the Gulf War Syndrome was caused mainly by the leakage of chemical and biological preparations and environmental pollution due to flagrant oil well burning and depleted uranium bombs dropped by US army.

## Long-Term Ecological Damage

The research data indicate that the micro granules produced after the explosion of the depleted U-bombs will cause a long term damage to the ecological environment. There will be an obvious increase in the number of patients suffering from carcinoma, cardio-vascular and neurological disorders, cataract, hematopoietic problems and decrease in fertility.

The French experts who conducted a study of Gulf Wars I and II for comparative analysis said that the frequent use of the depleted U-bombs by the US armed forces in 1991 and the recent use of research type of chemicals and explosives is sure to cause new disasters in the Middle East.

It is apprehended that in the recent Gulf War II, the Arabian peninsula is likely to witness a climate change. The desert temperature has already increased by 2°C. The war is also threatening Iraq's agriculture and river in a major way since Saddam Hussain's troops had used ferryng of missiles and other war equipments through the river systems that attracted US attacks leading to massive dumping of missiles and explosives into river waters.

The large scale use of mines in river and sea waters by Saddam's forces have also led to water pollution and destabilisation.

The recent study by the United Nations Environment Programme (UNEP) suggests that Iraq, Kuwait, Jordan and the Arabian peninsula will witness massive new human health hazards unknown to medical experts.

The natural course for civilised minds which we think we would have been to decry all war and any of its manifestations particularly those which are instrumental in the devastation of environment.

O O O

# 16. 4G Technology

4G (also known as Beyond 3G), an abbreviation for Fourth-Generation, is a term used to describe the next complete evolution in wireless communications. A 4G system will be able to provide a comprehensive IP solution where voice, data and streamed multimedia can be given to users on an "anytime-anywhere" basis, and at higher data rates than previous generations.

Just as the second generation was a total replacement of the first generation networks and handsets; and the third generation was a total replacement of second generation networks and handsets; so too the fourth generation cannot be just an incremental evolution of current 3G technologies, but rather the total replacement of the current 3G networks and handsets. The international telecommunications regulatory and standardisation bodies are working for commercial deployment of 4G networks roughly in the 2012-2015 time scale. At that point it is predicted that even with current evolutions of third generation 3G networks, these will tend to be congested.

Though there is no formal definition of what 4G is, yet there are certain objectives that are projected for 4G. These objectives which include 4G will be a fully IP-based integrated system. It will be capable of providing between 100 Mbit/s and 1 Gbit/s speeds both indoors and outdoors, with premium quality and high security.

Many companies have taken self-serving definitions and distortions about 4G to suggest they have 4G already in existence today, such as several early trials and launches of WiMax, which is part of the formal ITU standard for 3G. Other companies have made prototype systems, calling those 4G. While it is possible that some currently demonstrated technologies may become part of 4G, until the 4G standard or standards have been defined, it is impossible for any company currently to provide with any certainty, wireless solutions that could be called 4G cellular networks that would conform to the eventual international standards for 4G. These confusing statements around "existing" 4G have confused investors and analysts about the wireless industry.

4G is being developed to accommodate the Quality of Service (QoS) and rate requirements set by forthcoming applications like Wireless Broadband Access, Multimedia Messaging Service (MMS), Video Chat, Mobile TV, HDTV content, Digital Video Broadcasting (DVB), minimal service like voice and data, and other streaming services for "anytime-anywhere". The 4G working group has defined the following as objectives of the 4G wireless communication standard:

1.  A spectrally efficient system (in bits/s/Hz and bits/s/Hz site);

2.  High network capacity; more simultaneous users per cell;

3.  A nominal data rate of 100 Mbit/s while the client physically moves at high speeds relative to the station, and 1 Gbit/s while client and station are in relatively fixed positions as defined by the ITU-R;

4.  A data rate of at least 100 Mbit/s between any two points in the world;

5.  Smooth handoff across heterogeneous networks;

6.  Seamless connectivity and global roaming across multiple networks;

7.  High quality of service for next generation multimedia support; (real time audio, high speed data, HDTV video content, mobile TV, etc.)

8.  Interoperability with existing wireless standards; and

9.  An all IP, packet switched network.

In short, the 4G system should dynamically share and utilise network resources to meet the minimal requirements of all the 4G enabled users.

Almost all of the systems from this generation were analog systems where voice was considered to be the main traffic. These systems could often be listened to by third parties. Some of the standards are NMT, AMPS, Hicap, CDPD, Mobitex, DataTac, TACS and ETACS.

All the standards belonging to this generation are commercial-centric and they are digital in form. Around 60 per cent of the current market is dominated by European standards. The second generation standards are: GSM, iDEN, D-AMPS, IS-95, PDC, CSD, PHS, GPRS, HSCSD and WiDEN.

To meet the growing demands in network capacity, rates required for high speed data transfer and multimedia applications, 3G standards started evolving. The systems in this standard are essentially a linear enhancement of 2G systems. They are based on two parallel backbone infrastructures, one consisting of circuit switched nodes, and one of packet-oriented nodes. The ITU defines a specific set of air interface technologies as third generation, as part of the IMT-2000 initiative. Currently, transition is happening from 2G to 3G systems. As a part of this transition, numerous technologies are being standardised.

As per the 4G working groups, the infrastructure and the terminals of 4G will have almost all the standards from 2G to 4G implemented. Although legacy systems are in place to adopt existing users, the infrastructure for 4G will be only packet-based (all-IP). Some proposals suggest having an open platform where the new innovations and evolutions can fit. The technologies which are being considered as pre-4G are the following: WiMax, WiBro, iBurst, 3GPP Long Term Evolution and 3GPP2 Ultra Mobile Broadband.

Technologies employed by 4G may include Software-defined ratio (SDR) receivers, Orthogonal Frequency Division Multiplexing (OFDMA), Multiple Input/Multiple Output (MIMO) technologies, UMTS and TD-SCDMA. All these delivery methods are typified by high rates of data transmission and packet-switched transmission protocols. 3G technologies, by contrast, are a mix of packet and circuit-switched networks.

When fully implemented, 4G is expected to enable pervasive computing, in which simultaneous connections to multiple high-speed networks provide seamless handoffs throughout a geographical area. Network operators may employ technologies such as cognitive ratio and wireless mesh networks to ensure connectivity and efficiently distribute both network traffic and spectrum.

The high speeds offered by 4G will create new markets and opportunities for both traditional and start-up telecommunications companies. 4G networks, when coupled with cellular phones equipped with higher quality digital cameras and even HD capabilities, will enable blogs to go mobile, as has already occurred with text-based moblogs. New models for collaborative citizen journalism are also likely to emerge in areas with 4G connectivity.

A Japanese company, NTT DoCoMo, is testing 4G communication at 100 Mbps for mobile users and up to 1 Gbps while stationary. NTT DoCoMo plans to release their first commercial network in 2010.

4G technologies are sometimes referred to by the acronym "MAGIC", which stands for Mobile multimedia, Anythime-Anywhere, Global mobility support, Integrated wireless and Customized personal service. It aptly explains the salient features of these technologies.

O O O

# 17. RISAT–2 : INDIA'S SURVEILLANCE SATELLITE

The Polar Satellite Launch Vehicle (PSLV–C12) put in orbit Radar Imaging Satellite (RISAT–2), a surveillance satellite on 2 April, 2009, which could keep a watch on the country's borders.

This was the first time the Indian Space Research Organisation (ISRO) put in orbit a RISAT in the microwave band. It can take images of the earth day and night, see through clouds and identify objects on the ground. The 300 kg RISAT–2 has been procured from Israel.

Another satellite, ANUSAT, built by Anna University, Chennai, was also put in orbit by the PSLV–C12, which is an experimental communication satellite meant for storing and relaying information.

The RISAT–2 could precisely look at water bodies and vegetation. Its images would have wide ramifications in managing disasters such as cyclones, floods and landslips. It would also be "a powerful tool" in estimating the paddy acreage. Additionally, it can also be used for surveillance purposes and its images can be used for identifying arms caches and bunkers.

Both the RISAT–2 and ANUSAT were injected into orbit 550 km above the earth at an inclination of 41 degrees, 19 minutes after lift-off from the Satish Dhawan Space Centre at Sriharikota.

RISAT–2 was developed by ISRO in collaboration with the state-run Israel Aerospace Industries. It can see through clouds, darkness, fog and even a few inches deep into the soil to check how wet it is.

The advanced capabilities are on account of its Synthetic Aperture Radar (SAR) that uses microwave radiation to 'see'. Only few other space leaders such as Canada, the European Union and US use this technology. Though, RISAT–2 will enhance ISRO's capability for earth observation and surveillance across the border, ISRO chairman G. Madhavan Nair, denied the satellite was a spy in the space.

RISAT–2 can see features on ground like buildings, water bodies and roads. Its coarse resolution is 10 metres and its finest is 1 metre, enough to spot a small car. But it is not good enough to see human movements or track terrorists.

India's launch of the military spy satellite RISAT–2 is not just about the Synthetic Aperture Radar (SAR), but about taking a quantum leap in its defence surveillance capabilities, specially as India strengthens its defences in the post–26/11 world. It gives India an eye on its restive borders with Pakistan, China and Bangladesh.

The launch means terrorist movement on the LoC will now have a greater chance of being picked up by Indian forces. The importance of acquiring pre-emptive capabilities can hardly be overstated. India's earth observation programmes have thus far been related to agriculture, monsoon and education. RISAT puts India squarely in the limited league of nations with military use of satellites. The capacity building will help India leverage its space capabilities better in terms of its defence requirements.

RISAT–2 and RISAT–1 (to be launched in early 2010) satellites will generate a huge amount of data in the form of real-time high resolution imagery, which would need to be analysed and acted upon quickly. ISRO has not spelt out the names of agencies that will use RISAT data or the infrastructure it plans for coordination with other national agencies.

It is not known whether the National Technical Research Office, has established the facilities to convert satellite data into usable intelligence inputs. To this end, the country will need a new crop of professionals well versed in remote sensing as well as security issues. Otherwise ISRO's efforts in generating valuable data may meet the fate that the earlier satellites like Edusat met, where the lack of adequate ground linkages led to their sub-optimal use.

The launching has not only enhanced India's surveillance capabilities but also firmly established it as one of the most successful space-faring nations.